THE MIRACLE OF ANALOGY

THE MIRACLE OF ANALOGY

or

The History of Photography, Part 1

KAJA SILVERMAN

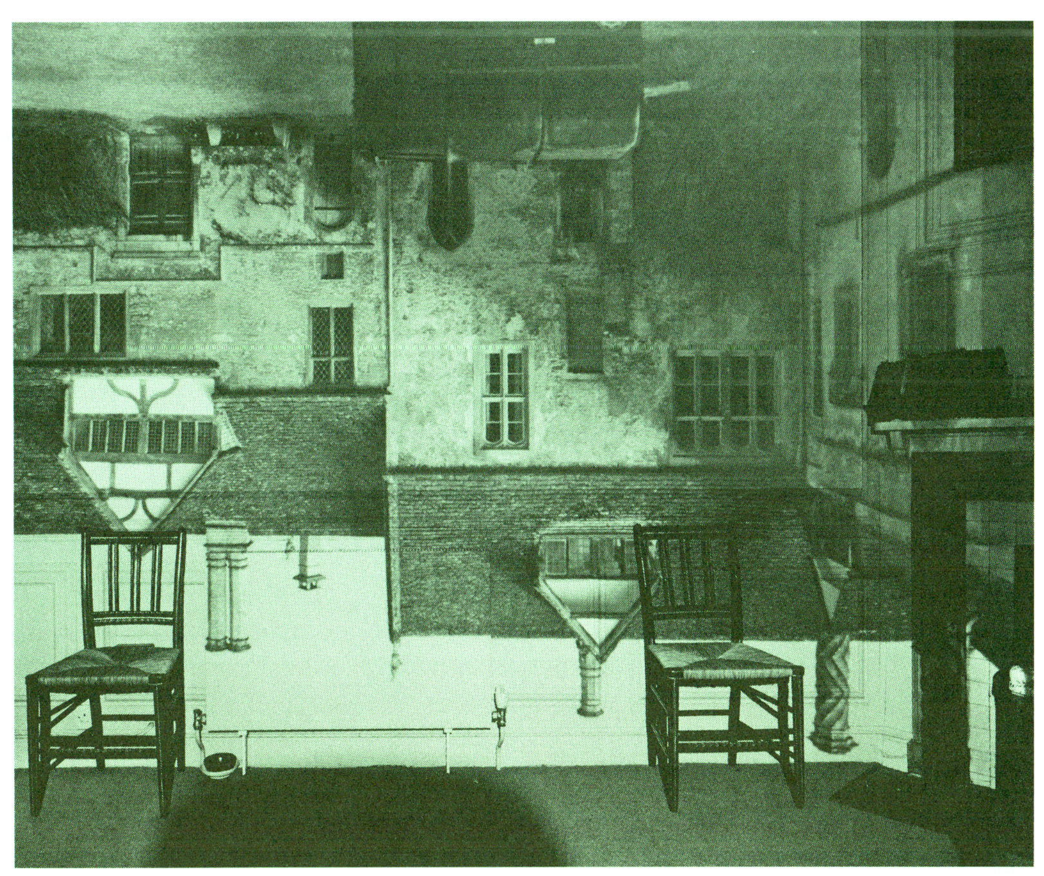

STANFORD UNIVERSITY PRESS   STANFORD CALIFORNIA

Stanford University Press
Stanford, California

©2015 by the Board of Trustees of the Leland Stanford Junior University. All rights reserved.

Frontispiece: Abelardo Morell, *Camera Obscura: Courtyard Building, Lacock Abbey, England*, 2003. Silver-gelatin print. Image © Abelardo Morell, courtesy of Edwynn Houk Gallery, New York.

No part of this book may be reproduced or transmitted in any form or by any means, electronic or mechanical, including photocopying and recording, or in any information storage or retrieval system without the prior written permission of Stanford University Press.

Printed in the United States of America on acid-free, archival-quality paper

Library of Congress Cataloging-in-Publication Data

Silverman, Kaja, author.
 The miracle of analogy, or, The history of photography / Kaja Silverman.
    volumes cm
 Complete in two volumes.
 Includes bibliographical references and index.
  ISBN 978-0-8047-9327-8 (v. 1 : cloth : alk. paper) --
  ISBN 978-0-8047-9399-5 (v. 1 : pbk. : alk. paper)
 1. Photography--History. I. Title. II. Title: Miracle of analogy. III. Title: History of photography.
 TR15.S49 2015
 770--dc23
                                    2014036175
 ISBN 978-0-8047-9400-8 (electronic)

Designed by Bruce Lundquist
Typeset at Stanford University Press in 10/15 Adobe Caslon Pro

For those I love.

TABLE OF CONTENTS

ACKNOWLEDGMENTS

Since I embarked on this book while teaching at Berkeley, I want to thank those who formed my community there, and with whom I shared so much, both personally and professionally: Wendy Brown, Judith Butler, T. J. Clark, Samera Esmeir, Ramona Naddaff, and Anne Wagner. Because I wrote most of the book since arriving at Penn, I also want to thank my colleagues and students in the History of Art for welcoming me so warmly, and making me so glad to be here. Warm thanks are due as well to Aaron Levy at the Slought Foundation and the curators at the Institute of Contemporary Art for our rich and energizing collaborations.

I discussed many of the ideas in this book with Leo Bersani, David Eng, Homay King, Erica Levin, Danny Marcus, and Rob Miotke, all old friends and trusted interlocutors. The manuscript benefited enormously from the written feedback of an exceptional group of readers: George Baker, Brooke Belisle, Natalia Brizuela, Todd Cronan, Jacques Khalip, and Andrew Moisey. I am especially indebted to André Dombrowski, who not only patiently listened to me rehearse every version of every idea in the book, but also pored over a late draft and provided me with an invaluable commentary.

I wouldn't even be at Penn if it were not for the generosity of Keith L. and Katherine Sachs, dear friends and art collectors extraordinaire. My life has been enriched beyond compare by the gift of a Mellon Distinguished Achievement Award, which—among many other things—covered the expenses related to this book.

Thanks are also due to George Conn, who worked tirelessly on the permissions for this book; Kaelin Jewell, who formatted the manuscript; George, Kaelin, and Amy Gillette, who checked all of the citations; and Jan McInroy, who graciously agreed to serve once again as my copyeditor.

Finally, I want to thank Emily-Jane Cohen, my editor at Stanford University Press, for her ongoing and unfailingly intelligent support of my work.

THE MIRACLE OF ANALOGY

INTRODUCTION

WE HAVE GROWN accustomed to thinking of the camera as an aggressive device: an instrument for shooting, capturing, and representing the world. Since most cameras require an operator, and it is usually a human hand that picks up the apparatus, points it in a particular direction, makes the necessary technical adjustments, and clicks the camera button, we often transfer this power to our look. The standardization of this account of photography marked the beginning of a new chapter in the history of modern metaphysics—the history that began with the *cogito*, which seeks to establish man as the "relational center" of all that is, and whose "fundamental event" is "the conquest of the world as a picture."[1] It did so by fixing a problem that had emerged in the previous chapter: the problem posed by human perception. In order to replace the sky and earth with his mental representations, Descartes had to "call away all of [his] senses" and "efface even from [his] thoughts all of the images of corporeal things."[2] His camera-wielding successor could picture the world—or so he claimed—without closing his eyes.

When we challenge this account of photography, it is usually by appealing to the medium's indexicality. Since an analogue photograph is the luminous trace of what was in front of the camera at the moment the photograph was made, we argue, it attests to its referent's reality, just as a footprint attests to the reality of the foot that formed it. The philosopher from whom the concept of indexicality derives—Charles Sanders Peirce—uses it to describe both signs that are linked to an unfolding situation or event and those that are linked to a prior situation or event. "I see a man with a rolling gait. This is a probable indication that he is a sailor . . . ," he writes in "What Is a Sign?" "A weathercock *indicates* the direction of the wind. A sun-dial or a clock *indicates* the time of day . . . [and] a tremendous thunderbolt indicates that *something* considerable happened, though we may not know precisely what the event was."[3]

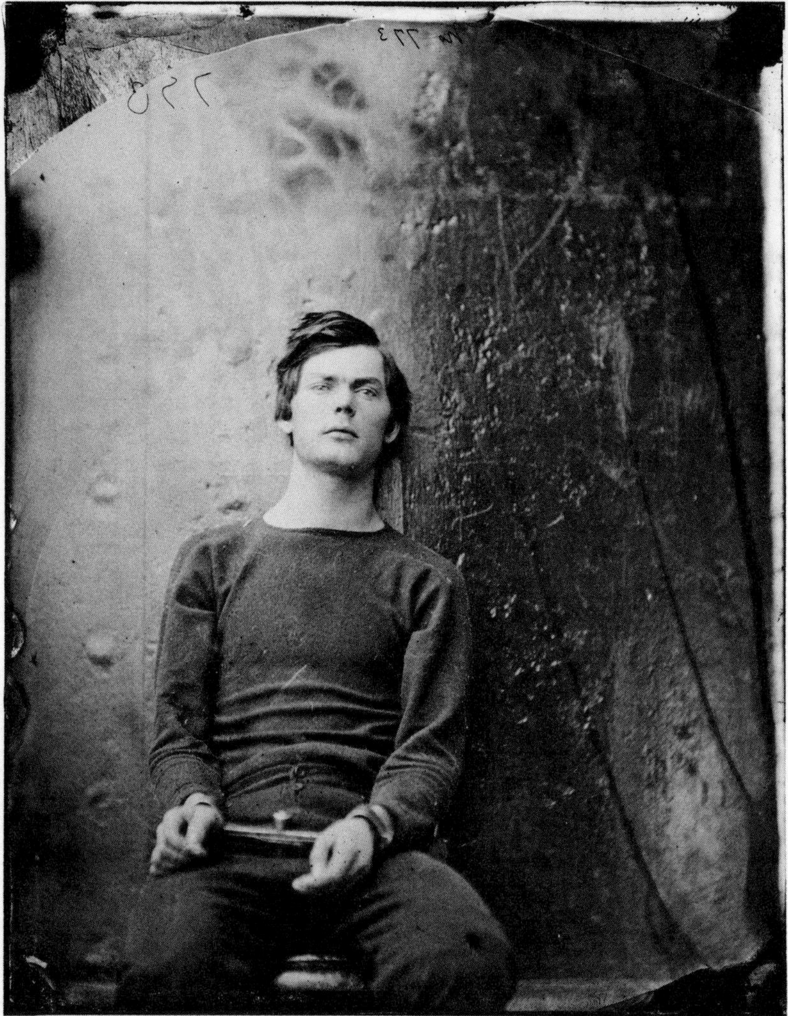

Figure 1. Alexander Gardner, *Washington Navy Yard, D.C. Lewis Payne, in sweater, seated and manacled, 1865*. Albumen print from collodion wet-plate negative. Courtesy of the Library of Congress.

Discussions of photographic indexicality, though, always focus on the past; an analogue photograph is presumed to stand in for an *absent* referent—one that is no longer *there*.[4] A photograph is "in no way a *presence*," Roland Barthes writes in "Rhetoric of the Image," an influential and widely read essay from the mid-sixties. "Its reality is that of the having-been-there."[5] Although Barthes associates the photographic image more with the future perfect than the past in *Camera Lucida*, he does not temper the image's finality. Looking at Alexander Gardner's 1865 photograph of Thomas Payne, one of four conspirators hung for the attempted assassination of members of Abraham Lincoln's cabinet, he writes: "I observe with horror an anterior future of which death is the stake. By giving me the absolute past of the pose (aorist), the photograph tells me death in the future . . . I shudder . . . *over a catastrophe which has already occurred*." Barthes then extends this bleak claim to all photographs. "Whether or not the subject is already dead," he concludes, "every photograph is this catastrophe."[6]

Many leftist artists and writers have gravitated to this account of the photographic image. For some, like Walter Benjamin and the young Hans Haacke,[7] it seems to give photography an evidentiary power—the power to expose what might otherwise escape justice. "It has justly been said that [Atget] photographed [the empty streets of Paris] like scenes of crime," Benjamin writes in section 7 of "The Work of Art in the Age of Its Technological Reproducibility." "A crime scene, too, is deserted."[8] Others attribute a memorial value to the photographic image, engaging with its "pastness" in ways more melancholy than accusatory. For Ana Mendieta, who photographed the ephemeral traces left on the landscape by her absent body, and W. G. Sebald and Eduardo Cadava, whose work never fails to move me, an analogue photograph is the

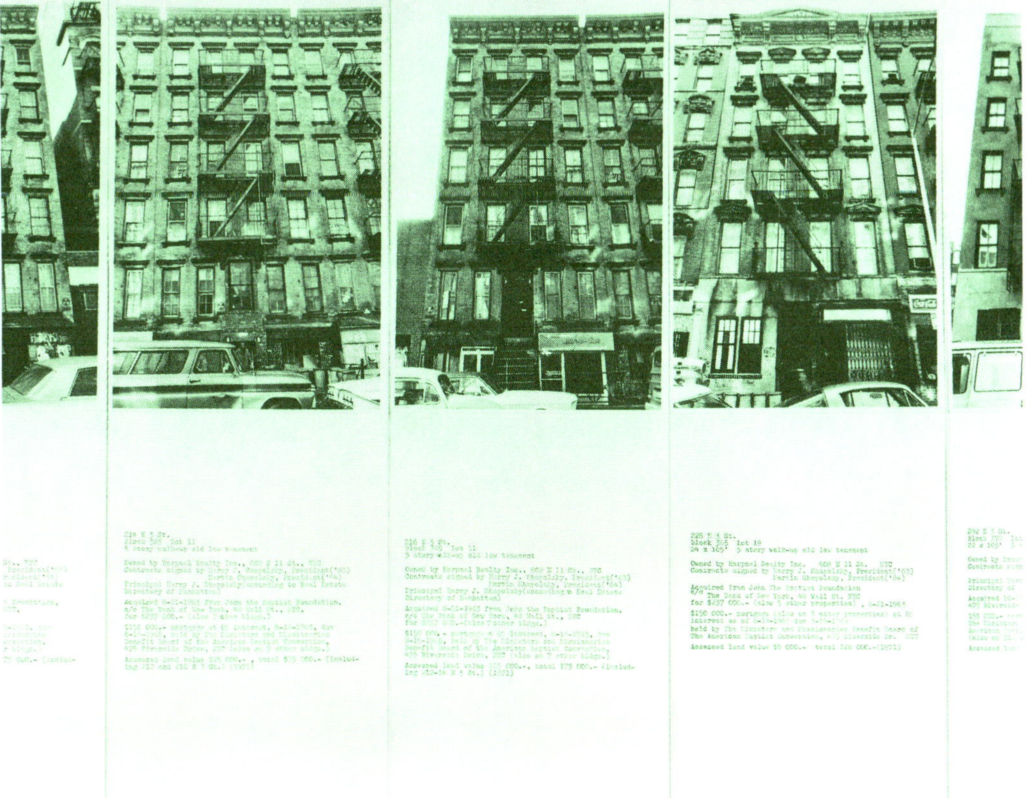

Figure 2. Hans Haacke, *Shapolsky et al. Manhattan Real Estate Holdings, A Real Time Social System, as of May 1, 1971.* Photographic installation. Reprinted with permission of the artist. © Hans Haacke/Artists Rights Society (ARS).

umbilical cord connecting us to what we have loved and lost, to what is gone because we failed to save it, or to what might have been, but now will never be.[9]

But although there have been pitched battles between those who champion the evidentiary value of the photographic image and those who emphasize its constructedness, the former is only another way of overcoming doubt. If a photograph can prove "what was," then it is the royal road to certainty—the means through which we know and judge the world. And if what we see when we look at a photographic image is unalterable, then there is only one thing we can do: take "what is dead" or "going to die" into our "arms."[10] Barthes's mobilization of the future perfect in this and other passages in *Camera Lucida* renders the future as unchanging as the past. This account of the photographic image consequently both expresses and contributes to the political despair that afflicts so many of us today: our sense that the future is "all used up."

In 1931, Benjamin wrote an essay about this malaise, which he calls "left-wing melancholy." It is "the attitude," he writes, "to which there is no longer, in general, any corresponding political action." It affects those who are "remote from the process of production."[11] Although Benjamin is merciless in his condemnation of those who have succumbed to left-wing melancholy, he was on the verge

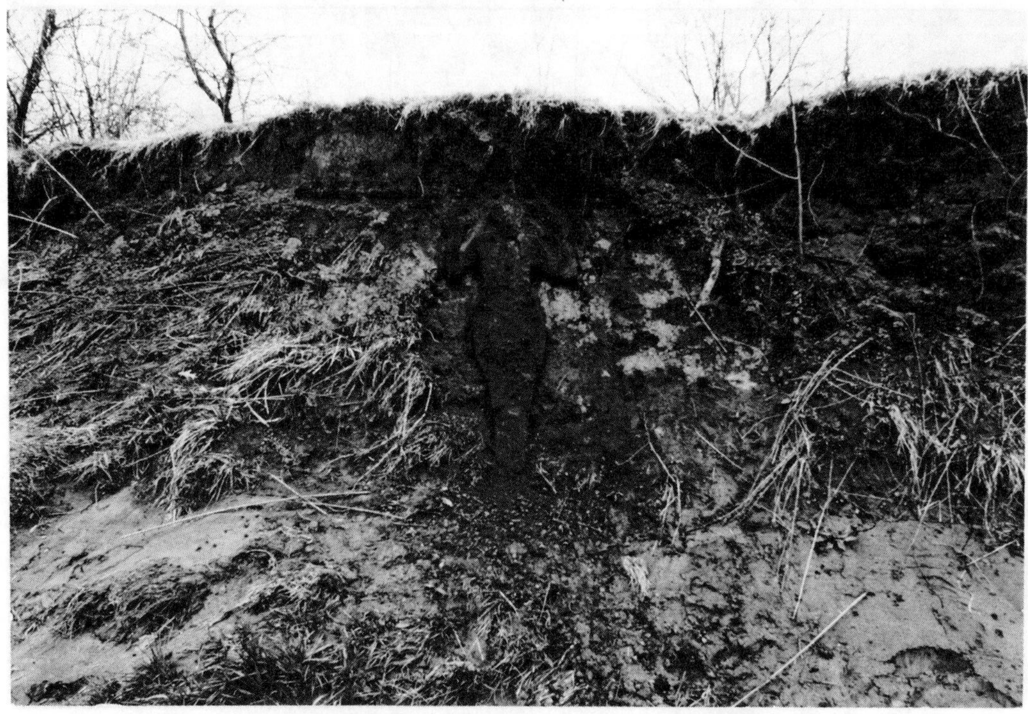

Figure 3. Ana Mendieta, *Untitled (from the Silueta series)*, 1980. Silver-gelatin print. © The Estate of Ana Mendieta Collection, L.L.C. Courtesy of Galerie Lelong, New York.

of capitulating to it himself. Not only was he an unemployed Jewish intellectual living in a country that he would soon be forced to flee, but he, too, was "remote from the process of production," since he was a member of the bourgeoisie.

As I show in *The Promise of Social Happiness*, the companion volume to this book, Benjamin had been searching for years for a way of defining himself as a left-wing intellectual, but he could not get past Marx's dictum that "revolutionary ideas" can come only from the "revolutionary class," i.e., the proletariat.[12] The events that followed—the fall of the Weimar Republic, Hitler's rise to power, the implementation of the "Final Solution," the signing of the Hitler-Stalin Pact, and the increasing Stalinization of the Soviet Union—rendered his personal situation more and more desperate. They also showed that a proletarian revolution does not automatically lead to a classless society, and that communism as Marx defines it is not a reliable bulwark against fascism. Unable to answer the question "What is to be done?" Benjamin had no protection against the "fatalism" he had earlier excoriated, so in 1935 and 1936[13] he tried to find a "cure"—to imagine an action that would be capable of defeating fascism and fulfilling Marx's agenda, and to which he himself could also contribute. He turned for this purpose to photography, and the result is an even more melancholic account of the medium.

Since photography is able to replicate a work of art "many times over," Benjamin argues in "The Work of Art," it permits everyone to own a copy of something that was previously available only to an elite institution or a privileged individual.[14] Photography and film can also "captur[e] assemblies of hundreds of thousands," allowing multitudes of people to see themselves as a collectivity.[15] They thus replace a "unique existence" with a mass existence, and proletarianize our perceptions.[16] And this is only the beginning of what these technological images can do for us. With their help, we can "liquidate" the "cultural heritage" from which fascism derives its power, resurrect it in a new form, and renew humanity. We can also seize the "totality of the instruments and forces of production," and usher in a classless society, whose members will "develop" all of their "capacities."[17]

But far from undermining the cult of the fascist leader, industrial photography and film helped to establish it. Hitler descends godlike from the clouds in Leni Riefenstahl's *Triumph of the Will*, and National Socialism used film and photography to promote many of its other goals. And in the case of neither National Socialism nor capitalism did exhibition value "drive back" cult value. It was through the ubiquitous display of his photographic image that Hitler assumed cult value, and it is through a similar display that the commodity assumes its otherworldly luster. Finally, instead of helping capitalism to destroy itself, industrial film and photography have prolonged its life. They are the shop windows in which most commodities gleam, and they operate according to the same logic.

A successful capitalist transaction begins with the illusion that a commodity is uniquely wonderful, and ends with the "discovery" that it is identical to millions of others.[18] Ideally, the consumer moves with lightning speed from the first stage to the second, so as to be ready for the next iteration of this two-stage process, but each disillusionment weakens his capacity to believe in the next commodity's uniqueness, and eventually he may lose it altogether. This can be a salutary loss—one that prompts him to look for another way of relating to the world around him. However, the disillusioned consumer can also hunker down in commodity fetishism's depressive position. His goal will then be to show that everything is the "same." He may claim to be working on behalf of the masses, but this equalization has nothing to do with democracy. The Great Leveler proves that everything is identical the way commodification has taught him to do: through a de-idealizing appropriation. This is a destructive act, and disillusionment is its motor force.

"Aura" means many different things in "The Work of Art." One of them, although Benjamin would dispute this, is the glow with which objects shine in the first stage of commodity fetishism, a glow created through exhibition value. When he calls for the destruction of the aura, it is also in the terms dictated by commodity fetishism. "*The present day masses [want] to 'get closer' to things . . . ,*" Benjamin proclaims. "Every day the urge grows stronger to get hold of an object at close range in an image or, better, in a facsimile, a reproduction . . . The stripping of the veil from the object, the destruction of the aura, is the signature of a perception whose 'sense for sameness in the world' has so increased that, by means of reproduction, it extracts sameness even from what is unique."[19]

When Benjamin writes that the "cult of the movie star" preserves "the magic of the personality which has long been no more than the putrid magic of its commodity character,"[20] he shows that the logic of commodification had already invaded the sphere of human relations, saturating them with the same disillusionment. It's difficult to embrace seriality when it takes the form of a million copies of the same fanzine, or a film sequence with a *mise-en-abyme* of identically dressed women sitting at identical grand pianos, like those in Busby Berkeley's *Gold Diggers of 1935*. It becomes even more difficult when we think of the aggression behind these reiterations.

This account of photography is also as shadowed by absence as the other two. The medium allows us to view works of art in absentia and to create copies that have no original, Benjamin argues in "The Work of Art."[21] It performs activities that were previously performed only by human beings, thereby rendering the latter superfluous.[22] It also "sucks" the aura "out of reality" by "purging" images of their aesthetic value,[23] and it "detaches" the film actor's image from his "person," thereby dispensing with the need for his presence.[24] Benjamin buttresses this last claim with a passage from Luigi Pirandello's *The Turn*. "The film actor feels as if exiled," this passage reads, "exiled not only from the stage but from his own person. With a vague unease, he senses an inexplicable void, stemming from the fact that his body has lost its substance, that he has been volatilized, stripped of his reality, his life, his voice, the noises he makes when moving about, and has been turned into a mute image that flickers for a moment on the screen, then vanishes into silence."[25]

Benjamin's attempt to turn this passage into another paean to technological reproducibility falls miserably short, and his follow-up remarks in the next section ring even more hollow. "*The representation of human beings by means of an apparatus has made possible a highly productive use of the human being's self-alienation,*" he enthuses in the first sentence.[26] If the reader pursues this train of thought to the end of the section, as I have often done in the past, although I am now incredulous at my own credulity, he will arrive at a chilling description of the spectatorial economy to which this separation leads. "When [the screen actor] stands before the apparatus," Benjamin writes, "he knows that in the end he is confronting the masses. It is they who will control him. Those who are not visible, not present while he executes his performance, are precisely the ones who will control it. This invisibility heightens the authority of their control." It would be hard to imagine a more compelling argument for presence than this celebration of absence, with its one-way windows and unopposable power.

As I will demonstrate in the last chapter of this book, Benjamin offers a very different account of photography in "Little History of Photography." In the first half of this 1931 essay, he privileges pre-industrial instead of industrial photography, and associates it with a disclosive rather than an evidentiary truth. He also attributes it to the world, instead of to technology, treats it as an analogy, instead of an index or a copy, and associates it with development, instead of fixity. Even more astonishingly, Benjamin suggests that the photographic image is propelled by a mysterious kind of intentionality toward a particular look—one that has the capacity to recognize it, and thereby to redeem it. It travels through time and space to reach this look, and when it arrives, something extraordinary happens. The present discovers itself within the past, and the past is realized within the present.[27]

All these concepts resurface in Benjamin's later account of messianic history. "The past carries with it a secret index by which it is referred to redemption," he writes in "On the Concept of History." "There is a secret agreement between past generations and the present one . . . our coming was expected on earth . . . like every generation that preceded us, we have been endowed with a *weak* messianic power, a power on which the past has a claim."[28] The power described in this passage is the capacity to perceive the similarities between our generation and a previous generation. It is "messianic" because recognition precludes repetition—because if we see that we are on the verge of reenacting an earlier generation's mistake, we will adopt a different course of action. This messianism is "weak" because there are no final solutions, because every generation "must strive anew to wrest tradition away from the conformism that is working to overpower it."[29]

At moments of danger, Benjamin argues, earlier generations alert us to the mistake that we are on the verge of making through an image that bursts out of the continuum of time and travels toward us. They do so because we are in a position to "change the character" of *their* "day."[30] If we recognize the present in this image from the past, and also understand that it is "intended" for us,[31] we will redeem both the past and the present. At the moment in which this redemption occurs, which Benjamin calls "*Jetztzeit*" or "now-time," "what is" becomes co-present with "what was," just as it does in "Little History." "It's not that what is past casts its light on what is present," he observes in *The Arcades Project*, or that "what is present casts its light on what is past; rather . . . what has been comes together in a flash with the now to form a constellation."[32] If, however, we ignore a previous generation's warning, we doom it, as well as ourselves. It is because of the reversibility and reciprocity of this relationship that the past has a "claim" on our weak messianic power.

Not only does the image described here "behave" like the photograph described in "Little History," but it also resembles a photograph in several other ways. Benjamin repeatedly associates it with a "flash," and at a key moment in *The Arcades Project* he quotes the following passage from André Monglond: "The past has left images of itself in literary texts, images comparable to those which are imprinted by light on a photosensitive page. The future alone possesses developers strong enough to reveal the image in all its details."[33] Strangely, though, photography is not the vehicle through which the past addresses the present in "On the Concept of History" and *The Arcades Project*; that role is reserved for language, with its "non-sensuous similarities."[34]

Benjamin turns to language because he has stripped the photographic image of its redemptive properties. If it is one of a potentially infinite number of identical and industrially generated copies, it cannot be the bearer of a mysterious intentionality, nor can it help us see the similarities between pre-

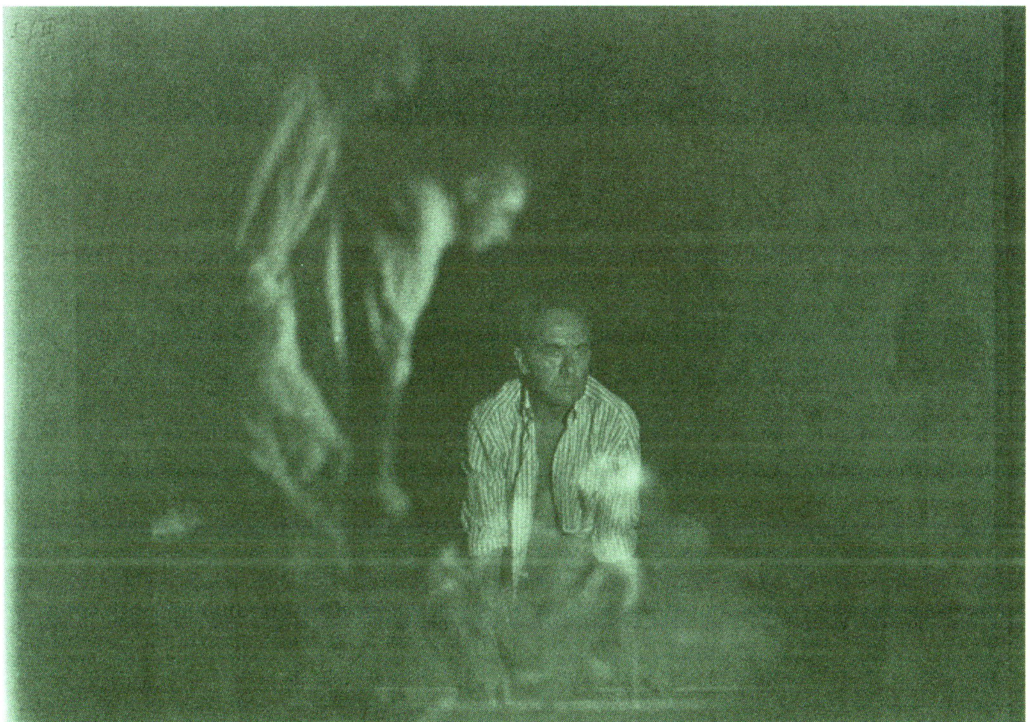

Figure 4. Gerhard Richter, *Six Photos. May 2–7, 1989 (c / 4 May 1989)*, 1991. Silver-gelatin print on resin-coated paper. Courtesy of the artist.

vious generations and our own; it promotes repetition, not recognition. And although language also houses similarities, they are nonsensuous,[35] and nonsensuous similarities are "only a faint residue of the magical correspondences and analogies that were familiar to ancient people."[36] They also "flash up fleetingly out of the stream of things only in order to sink down once more."[37] Finally, nonsensuous similarities seem to originate within us—to be a mental construct, rather than a call from the world or a historical summons. They consequently can't do for us what the concentration camp photographs that landed on Gerhard Richter's "doormat" in the mid-sixties did for him: persist as "unfinished business" until he was able to respond to them.[38]

THE IDEA THAT PHOTOGRAPHY MEANS "CAMERA," and that the camera is an instrument for mastering the world, emerged early in the history of the so-called medium. In a chilling passage in his 1859 essay "The Stereoscope and the Stereograph," Oliver Wendell Holmes not only characterizes the world as a picture, whose essence inheres in its photographic representability, but suggests that once this essence has been extracted, the world itself can be thrown away. "Form is henceforth divorced from matter," this passage reads. "In fact matter as a visible object is of no great use any longer . . . Give us a few negatives of a thing worth seeing, taken from different points of view, and that is all we want of it. Pull it down or burn it up, if you please."[39]

The notion that a photograph is a trace of its referent—and therefore both evidentiary and memorial—is every bit as old. In 1857, Lady Eastlake declared the medium's "unerring records in the service of mechanics, engineering, geology, and natural history" to be "facts of the most sterling and stubborn kind," and therefore "the sworn witness of everything presented to [its] view."[40] And since "every form that is traced by light is the impress of one moment, or one hour" in the "great passage of time," she writes in another passage in the same essay, photography also "give[s]" us our child's "shoes" or his "inseparable toy" with a "strength of identity that art does not even seek."[41]

However, Holmes's and Eastlake's essays contain many passages that anticipate Benjamin's first account of photography—that foreground the limits of human vision, that attribute the photographic image to the world, and that suggest that photography's truth is disclosive, rather than evidentiary. Both authors also call it a "gift," and identify us as the recipients of this gift. Lady Eastlake repeatedly characterizes the photographic image as an emerging image: one that approaches us from the future, and that arrives in the present. Finally, both Eastlake and Holmes suggest that photography may have important ramifications for human relationality. She maintains that those involved with photography form "a kind of republic," and he makes similar claims when talking about the stereoscopic image.[42]

Many of these ideas figure prominently in other early descriptions of the photographic image as well, particularly in those provided by William Henry Fox Talbot. "It is not the artist who makes the picture, but the picture which makes *itself*," Talbot observes in an 1839 letter to the editor of the *Literary Gazette; and Journal of the Belles Lettres, Arts, Sciences, etc.* "All that the artist does is to dispose the apparatus before the image he requires . . . At the end of the [allotted] time he returns, takes out his picture, and finds it finished."[43] They also appear in seventeenth- and eighteenth-century descriptions of the camera obscura, and when they vanish from photography, they resurface elsewhere: in painting, sculpture, literature, philosophy, psychoanalysis, cinema, and time-based work. They invite us to think anew about photography.

This book is a response to that invitation. As I hope to show, photography isn't a medium that was invented by three or four men[44] in the 1820s and 1830s, that was improved in numerous ways over the following century, and that has now been replaced by computational images. It is, rather, the world's primary way of revealing itself to us—of demonstrating that it exists, and that it will forever exceed us. Photography is also an ontological calling card: it helps us to see that each of us is a node in a vast constellation of analogies. When I say "analogy," I do not mean sameness, symbolic equivalence, logical adequation, or even a rhetorical relationship—like a metaphor or a simile—in which one term functions as the provisional placeholder for another. I am talking about the authorless and untranscendable similarities that structure Being, or what I will be calling "the world," and that give everything the same ontological weight.

These similarities are authorless and untranscendable because there is no metaphysical agency to which they could be imputed, and no other domain to which we might retreat, in order to be alone. As Walt Whitman writes in an inexhaustibly rich passage, "A vast similitude interlocks all / All spheres, grown, ungrown, small, large, suns, moons, planets, . . . / All distances of place however wide, / all distances of time, [and] all inanimate forms." It also includes "all souls, all bodies though they be ever so different, or in different worlds, / All gaseous, watery, vegetable, mineral processes, the fishes, the brutes, / All nations, colors, barbarisms, civilizations, languages, / All identities that have existed or may exist on this globe, or any globe, / All lives and deaths, all of the past, present, future."[45] It is also only through this interlocking that we ourselves exist. Two is the smallest unit of Being.

Most of us are willing to acknowledge some of these similarities, but extremely reluctant to acknowledge others, particularly those that call our autonomy, agency, unity, and primacy into question. Photography is the vehicle through which these profoundly enabling but unwelcome relationships are revealed to us, and through which we learn to think analogically. It is able to disclose the world, show us that it is structured by analogy, and help us assume our place within it because it, too, is analogical. A negative analogizes its referent, the positive prints that are generated from it, and all of its digital offspring, and it moves through time, in search of other "kin." As I discovered over and over again while writing this book, photography also analogizes the analogies that reside at the heart of human perception: those through which we see and are seen. Since it almost always does so in a visual way, it gives them a second power; it holds open the perceptual "open,"[46] helping us recognize what we might otherwise foreclose.

Every analogy contains both similarity and difference. Similarity is the connector, what holds two things together, and difference is what prevents them from being collapsed into one. In some analogies these qualities are balanced, but in others similarity far outweighs difference, or difference, similarity. One of the most miraculous features of an analogy is its ability to operate in the face of these imbalances: to maintain the "two-in-one" principle even when there is only a narrow margin of difference, or a sliver of similarity. In the last chapter of *Flesh of My Flesh*, I suggested that there is something inherently photographic about analogies in which there is only a little difference.[47] The analogies that link one print of a negative to all of the other prints of the same negative turn on variations so slight that we have a hard time seeing them, and we sometimes find it difficult to distinguish a photograph from its referent, even though we know very well that they belong to different registers.

I explore this kind of analogy here as well, and explain why some photographs—like the famous "Winter Garden" portrait of Barthes's mother in *Camera Lucida*—seem ontologically connected to their referents. But I also address analogies in which there is an overwhelming amount of difference, which is bridged through reversible reversals, or what Maurice Merleau-Ponty calls "chiasmus." This, too, is a quintessentially photographic kind of analogy. Photography models it for us through the inversion and lateral reversal of the camera obscura's image stream, the positive print's reversal of the reversal through which its negative was made, the two-way street leading from the space of the viewer to that of the stereoscopic image, cinema's shot/reverse shot formation, and the cross-temporal practices of some contemporary artists. I say "model" because we, too, are bound to each other through reversible reversals, and because it is there, and only there, that the promise of social happiness can still be glimpsed.

Not only is the photographic image an analogy, rather than a representation or an index, but analogy is also the fluid in which it develops. This process does not begin when we decide that it should, or end when we command it to. Photography develops, rather, *with us*, and *in response to us*. It assumes historically legible forms, and when we divest them of their saving power, generally by imputing them to ourselves, it goes elsewhere. The earliest of these forms was the pinhole camera, which was more "found" than invented. It morphed into the optical camera obscura, was reborn as chemical photography, migrated into literature and painting, and lives on in a digital form. It will not end until we do.

THE SECOND COMING

IT IS AS IMPOSSIBLE to know when photography began as it is to know when our first ancestors opened their eyes, but if we were able to locate one of these events, we would not have to search long for the other. The two photographic processes that were unveiled in 1839 by Louis-Jacques-Mandé Daguerre and William Henry Fox Talbot built on a number of earlier chemical experiments and discoveries, even the most cursory survey of which would include Angelo Sala's 1614 discovery that a nitrate of silver darkens when exposed to sun, Heinrich Schulze's 1724 realization that this darkening can be used to make an image, Thomas Wedgwood's late-eighteenth-century attempts to do just that, and John Herschel's 1819 discovery that hyposulphites can dissolve the unreduced salts of silver, which led to the invention of "hypo," a photographic fixer. Pride of place, though, would be given to Joseph Nicéphore Niépce, whose chemical experiments resulted in the first photographic image.[1]

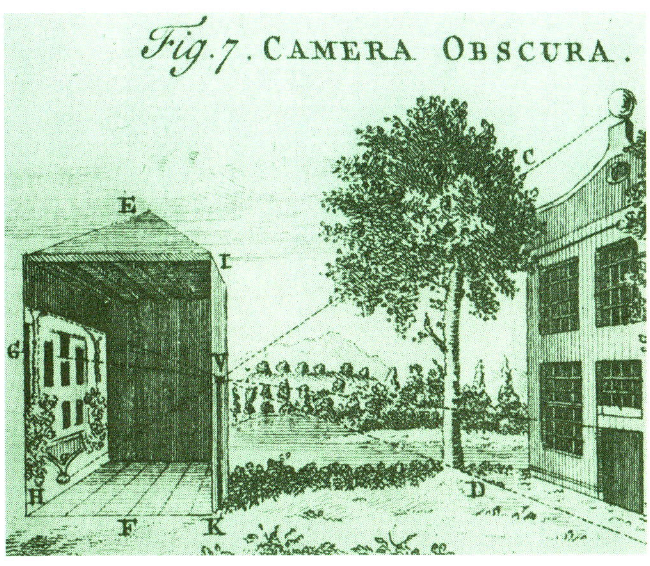

Figure 5. Thomas Jeffreys, Illustration from *A New and Complete Dictionary of the Arts and Sciences*, 1754.

Daguerre and Talbot also relied on a much older optical device: the camera obscura.[2] The classical camera obscura—the one that was the norm from the thirteenth to the seventeenth centuries—was a darkened chamber with a small aperture through which light entered, bearing a reversed and inverted stream of images that both originated in the external world and analogized it. This continuous flow of mobile and evanescent images existed only in the "now" in which it appeared, and since the viewer had to enter the camera obscura in order to see it, the two were spatially as well as temporally *co-present*.

This device formalized optical principles that had been accidentally discovered centuries earlier and that are as old as light itself. In the fifth century B.C., the Chinese philosopher Mo Ti noted the "image-making properties" of a small aperture.[3] A century later, Aristotle was struck by the many crescent-shaped images of the sun that appeared on the ground beneath a tree during an eclipse of the sun, and attributed them to the small spaces between the leaves.[4] In the eleventh century, the Arab scholar Alhazen discovered the same principles while investigating the formation of images in a darkened room, and he viewed the sun during an eclipse from a similar place. He described the latter experience in the following way: "If the image of the sun at the time of an eclipse—provided it is not a total one—passes through a small round hole onto a plane surface, opposite, it will be crescent-shaped . . . If the hole is very large, the crescent shape of the image disappears altogether and the light [on the wall] becomes round if the hole is round . . . with any shaped opening you like, the image always takes the same shape . . . provided the hole is large and the receiving surface parallel to it."[5]

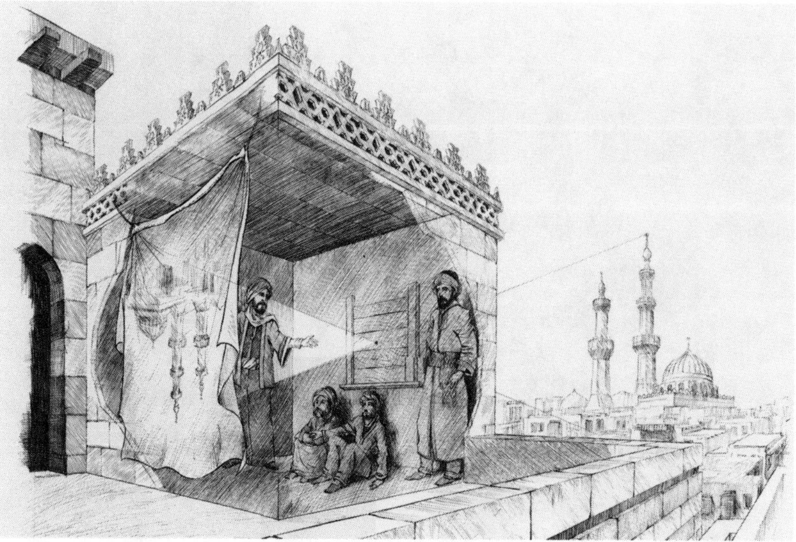

Figure 6. Alhazan and his camera obscura in Cairo, Egypt, in the eleventh century. Courtesy of Ali Amro. © Muslim Heritage, Ltd.

"Receiving surface" sounds odd to a contemporary ear, since it suggests that the optical device that figured so prominently in the early years of chemical photography was *receptive*, rather than *productive*, but Alhazen is not the only early commentator who speaks in these terms; receptivity is a recurrent trope in pre-1700 accounts of the camera obscura. "When at the time of an eclipse of the sun, its rays are *received* in a dark place," John Peckham observes in *Perspectiva communis* (1279), "through a hole of any shape, it is possible to see the crescent-shape getting smaller as the moon covers the sun."[6] "When the images of illuminated objects pass through a small round hole into a very dark room [and] you *receive* them on a piece of white paper placed vertically in the room at some distance from the aperture," Leonardo da Vinci writes in Manuscript D, "you will see all those objects in their natural shapes and colors."[7] "If you have a piece of white paper or other material upon which [the images] of everything passing through the aperture may be *received*, you will see everything on the earth and in the sky with their colors and forms," Cesare Cesariano remarks in a note in his 1521 translation of Vitruvius's *Treatise on Architecture*.[8] "The visible radiations [of] all [of] the objects without are intromitted, falling upon a paper, which is accommodated to *receive* them," Sir Henry Wotton writes in his famous 1620 letter to Francis Bacon about Johannes Kepler's tent camera obscura.[9]

Since the viewer had to enter the classical camera obscura in order to see its images, he was also a receiver.[10] This would have been hard to ignore, because the device had no focusing mechanism. The only way the viewer could render its often hard-to-see images more legible was to move around the sheet of paper on which they were received until he found the point at which they came into focus—i.e., to participate in the reception process. Daniele Barbaro describes this practice in his 1568 book, *La Pratica della perspettiva*. "If you take a sheet of paper and place it in front of the lens," he writes there, "you will see clearly on the paper all that goes on outside the house. This you will see most distinctly at a certain distance, which you will find by moving the paper nearer to or farther away from the lens, until you have found the proper position."[11]

For centuries, the camera obscura was primarily used to watch solar eclipses, and it was put to this purpose because the human eye cannot tolerate the amount of light that floods into it when it looks directly at the sun.[12] It consequently testified to the external source not only of the images that appeared on the screen, but also of those perceived by the human eye. So long as Christianity and Platonism were the dominant forces within Western thought, the notion that light enters the human eye from outside was unproblematic; illumination was, after all, a privileged signifier for both God and the demiurge.

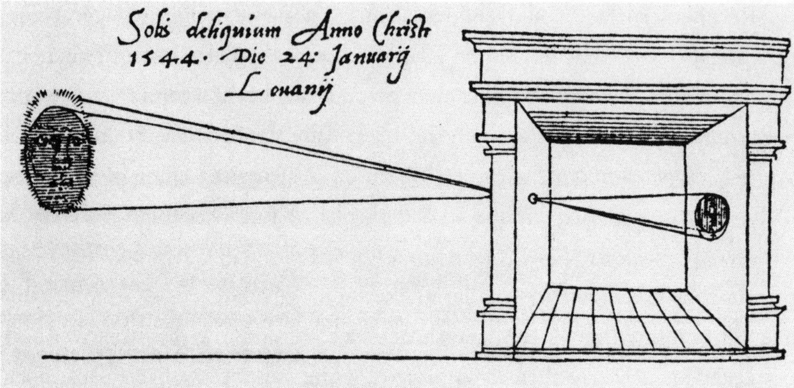

Figure 7. Illustration from Gemma Frisius, *De radio astronomico et geometrico liber*, 1554. Courtesy of the National Media Museum/SSPL.

Since both systems of thought emphasize how blinding this divine light can be, the fact that a solar eclipse could be safely viewed only from the refuge of a camera obscura was also neither noteworthy nor particularly disturbing. And since the images that appeared within the device issued from a higher agency, they could be presumed to be a reliable source of information about what was happening in the external world.

However, in 1490 Leonardo noted that the human eye also resembles a camera obscura—that rays of light enter its dark "chamber" through a "small aperture," just as they do in the latter device, and that they also bear an inverted and laterally reversed stream of images.[13] Because he was a largely secular thinker, he realized that both image streams originate in and refer back to a terrestrial source.[14] He was also alive to their aesthetic properties. Leonardo likened the camera obscura's images to "paintings,"[15] and searched for other unauthored art works in the external world. "Cast your glance on any walls dirty with such stains or walls made up of rock formations of different types," he advises his fellow artists in *Ashburnham I*, "If you have to invent some scenes, you will be able to discover them there in diverse forms, in diverse landscapes, adorned with mountains, rivers, rocks, trees, extensive plains, valleys, and hills."[16]

I say "unauthored works of art" because Leonardo did not view image making as a strictly human activity. He believed that there is an aesthetic capacity in all worldly things that allows them to generate images of themselves. "Every body fills the surrounding air with infinite images of itself," Leonardo writes in one notebook entry. "All bodies together, and each by itself, give off to the surrounding air an infinite number of images . . . each conveying the nature, color and form of the body which produces it," he observes in another.[17] This activity is self-presentational, and our look is its "lodestone." Bodies give themselves to be seen by us by sending us analogies or "portraits" of themselves. Leonardo was also interested in a different kind of human art making—one that would begin with the acceptance of this gift. "The mind of the painter must resemble a mirror, which always takes on the color of the object it reflects and is completely occupied by the images of as many objects as there are in front of it," he observes elsewhere in *Ashburnham I*.[18]

Ancient scholars had two conflicting theories of vision. For some, as James S. Ackerman explains, "the eye was passive and simply received emanations from the outer world," but for others it was "active and cast out rays or a spirit to touch the seen object."[19] When Leonardo urges painters to let their minds be "filled by as many images as there are objects before it," he might seem to be drawing on the first of these theories. In fact, though, he is only describing the initial stage in a complex process—one that is as much about giving as receiving. This process begins when the world conveys a visual analogy of itself to the human eye. The viewer receives this gift by relating it to similar things within his own memory reserve. Leonardo's artist goes one step further: he generates an external analogy for the one created through the "marriage" of the world's visual analogy with the viewer's mental analogy. This opens the analogical network to other viewers.

Paul Valéry provides an excellent description of this process in "Introduction to the Method of Leonardo." "At first the process [of receiving something] is undergone passively, almost unconsciously," he writes, "as a vessel lets itself be filled: there is a feeling of slow and pleasurable circulation. Later ... one assigns new values to things that had seemed closed and irreducible, one adds to them, takes more pleasure in particular features, finds expression for these; and what happens is like the restitution of an energy that our senses had received. Soon the energy will alter the environment in its turn, employing to this end the conscious thought of a person."[20] Daniel Arasse also talks about the unusual dynamism and reciprocity of Leonardo's analogies, and says that the result is an "unfinished universality"—one oriented to the future.[21]

Leonardo isn't the only early-modern viewer of the camera obscura who compares it to the human eye. Johannes Kepler also likens the inverted and laterally reversed images that enter this organ to those that enter the camera obscura, and he pushes the comparison a step further: he characterizes the retina as the ocular equivalent of the camera obscura's "receiving screen." "Vision ... occurs through a picture of the visible object at the white of the retina and the concave wall," he writes in his 1604 book, *Ad Vitellionem paralipomena*, "and those things that are on the right outside, are depicted on the left side of the wall, the left at the right, the top at the bottom, the bottom at the top."[22]

Kepler calls this reversed and inverted "picture" the "retinal image," and refuses to posit a higher visual faculty that would rectify its "deformations." "Vision occurs when the image of the whole hemisphere of the world that is before the eye . . . is set up at the white wall, tinged with red, of the concave surface of the retina," he declares in another passage in *Ad Vitellionem paralipomena*. "How this image or picture is joined together with the visual spirits that reside in the retina and the nerve, and whether it is arraigned within by the spirits . . . to the tribunal of the soul or of the visual faculty . . . I leave to the natural philosophers. For the arsenal of the optical writers does not extend beyond this opaque wall."[23] Kepler thus refuses to argue that the blindness of the seeing eye can be overcome through the clarity of mental representation.

Like Leonardo, Kepler is also obsessed with analogies, or what he calls "correspondences," and he sees the camera obscura as the agency of their disclosure. His analogies, though, are divinely authored, and they operate synchronically rather than diachronically—as elements within a vast and already fully articulated system—a finished rather than an unfinished universality.[24] He also gives his retinal discovery a stabilizing name; it is an "image," rather than a "flow of images." Finally, he conducted his cosmological observations with a camera obscura whose inversions and reversals were "corrected" through two convex lenses.[25]

René Descartes seemingly picks up where Kepler leaves off in Discourse 5 of the *Optics*. He urges those who do not believe that the inverted and reversed images of the external world appear on the surface of the retina to peel away the back layers of the eye of a dead person or animal, insert it into the aperture of a camera obscura, facing outward, enter the camera obscura, and look at the retina from the other side. They will then perceive images just like those that appear on the camera obscura's receiving surface.[26] But as we can see from the accompanying diagram, the experiment described by Descartes is calculated to *disprove* rather than to *prove* Kepler's claim. By placing a lifeless eye in the aperture of the camera obscura, Descartes renders the retinal image both visible and mechanical, and by positioning the viewer in front of this image, he transforms the latter from a blind receiver of external images into a knowledgeable observer of what he sees. A few pages earlier, he flatly declares that "it is the mind which senses, not the body."[27] As Maurice Merleau-Ponty observes in "Eye and Mind," Descartes's *Optics* is "the breviary of a thought that wants no longer to abide in the visible and so decides to construct the visible according to a model-in-thought."[28]

This is hardly surprising. Certainty was the defining attribute of the subject Descartes aspired to be, and there was only one foundation on which he was willing to base his beliefs: himself. The retinal image discredited this "self," since it showed that the images that our eyes receive do not correlate in a one-to-one way with the objects from which they derive. There is also a disconnect between the retinal image and what we "see," which means that there must be an agency within us that reverses its reversal and inverts its inversion before we perceive it. Shutting one's eyes and closing one's ears might block out the external world, but it offers no protection against this internal "other."

Descartes is clearly haunted by this thought, because he spends as much time in the *Meditations* and *The Discourse on Method* worrying about whether he is deceiving himself as he does worrying about whether others are deceiving him. He tries to banish it by transforming the device that Kepler compares to the human eye into a signifier for a new kind of interiority—one befitting a sovereign subject. The heated room to which he retreats in

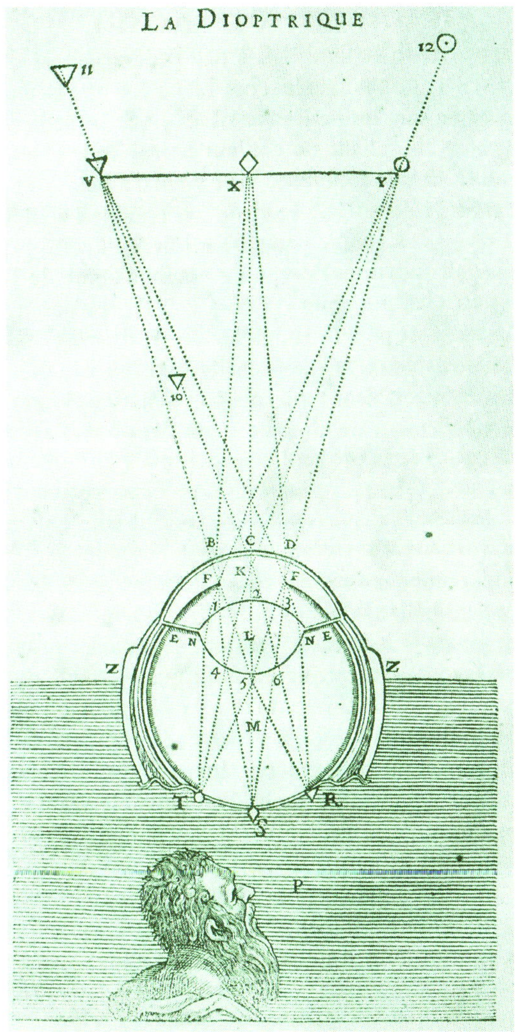

Figure 8. Illustration from René Descartes, *Discours de la Méthode*, 1637. Courtesy of the Fisher Rare Books Library, University of Toronto.

his search for truth is like the isolated space of a camera obscura, the darkness into which he is plunged when he closes his eyes like the darkness of that enclosure, and the mental representations that he places before his inner eye like the images that pass before the eyes of its viewer. Unlike the images in the physical camera obscura, or the mind described by Leonardo, though, those that appear within Descartes's mental camera obscura are stable, and he is both their producer and their viewer.

John Locke also invokes the camera obscura when describing *his* version of the modern subject. Since he believed that "external and internal sensations" were the "only windows" through which the light of understanding could enter into the "dark room" of the mind, he could not simply dispense with the outer eye, as Descartes had done, so he transformed the analogy between the physical device and its mental counterpart into a contrasting set. Like the camera obscura, the mind is a chamber into which images come, Locke argues, but what happens thereafter is very different. In the former, images enter and leave in a disorderly fashion, because perception reigns supreme. In the latter, though, what arrives is conceptually organized, and remains where it has been put, because understanding governs perception. "The *understanding* is not much unlike a closet wholly shut from light, with only some little opening left ... to let in external visible resemblances, or ideas of things without," Locke writes in *An Essay Concerning Human Understanding*, "would the pictures coming into such a dark room but stay there, and lie so orderly as to be found upon occasion, it would very much resemble the understanding of a man."[29] The "orderliness" described by Locke could be secured only by immobilizing the external world, and suspending the associative faculty through which we respond to its images.

Gottfried Leibnitz quotes this last passage in chapter 11 of *New Essays on Human Understanding*, but he disputes every one of its assumptions.[30] Kepler's discovery cannot be neutralized by privileging the mind over vision, he argues in the following paragraph, because they are both part of the same system. The defining attribute of this system is also the one that Kepler dramatizes through the retinal image: receptivity. But the "brain," as he calls it, isn't an empty vessel into which images of the world flow; it is "diversified by folds representing items of innate knowledge and ... this screen or membrane, being under tension, has a kind of elasticity or active force." It consequently "acts (or reacts) both to past folds and to new ones coming from impressions of the species." These actions and reactions consist of "vibrations or oscillations," like those we see when a cord is "plucked," and produce "something of a musical sound."[31] Leibnitz's account of perceptual reception is thus as dynamic, reciprocal, and analogical as the one Valéry presents in his reading of Leonardo.

LEONARDO also isn't the only early-modern commentator who talks about the aesthetic properties of the camera obscura's images. Barbaro notes the "gradations, colors" and "shadows" of these images, and encourages his readers to trace their outlines on a sheet of paper, so that they will have "the entire perspective."[32] G. Battista della Porta recommends the same thing, and explains how to achieve this goal in the first edition of his popular book *Magiae naturalis*. His instructions, though, are very different from the ones Leonardo offers to his fellow painters. Instead of encouraging his readers to make paintings that correspond with the images that appear inside the camera obscura, della Porta urges them to outline those images with a pencil, so that all that they have to do is "lay on the colors."[33]

Since the epistemological crisis that was precipitated by the discovery of the blind spots at the heart of human vision was partially resolved by adapting the camera obscura to the psychic exigencies and representational demands of the modern subject, it was increasingly relegated to the category of a "tool." In the sixteenth century, lenses were placed in the aperture of the camera obscura, making its images larger, clearer, and brighter. In the seventeenth century, mirrors were used to render them upright.[34] They could then be "reflected downwards onto a drawing-board with paper," and traced, permitting even those who were not skilled to produce a satisfactory drawing.[35]

The camera obscura also became portable,[36] and later in the century it was transformed from a receptacle that contained the viewer into a much smaller box, whose images were available to an external eye, through either an aperture or an arrangement of the sort described above. It

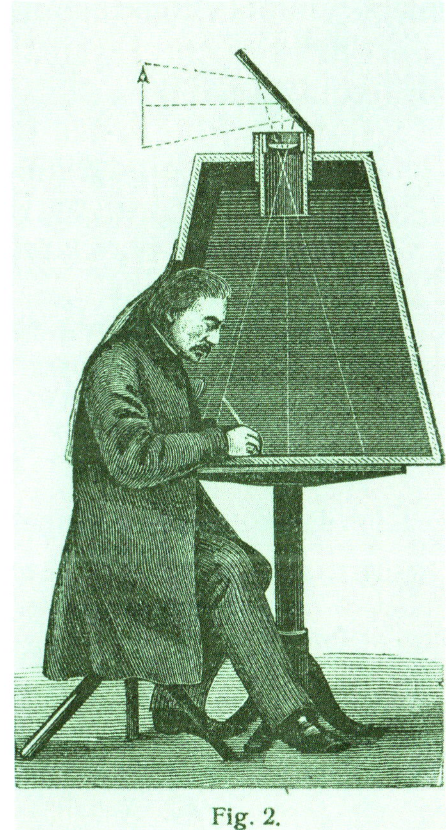

Figure 9. Illustration from Otto Lueger, *Lexikon der Gesamten Technik*, 1926.

was equipped with better lenses that enlarged its images, and in 1685, Johann Zahn designed a camera obscura that could be manually focused by moving the lens, instead of relocating the screen.[37] In the eighteenth century, the device was incorporated into tables and desks, where one could sit and draw, and added to sedan-chairs and carriages, so that it could be enjoyed in transit. It was also used as a sketchpad by scientists and travellers, as well as artists.[38]

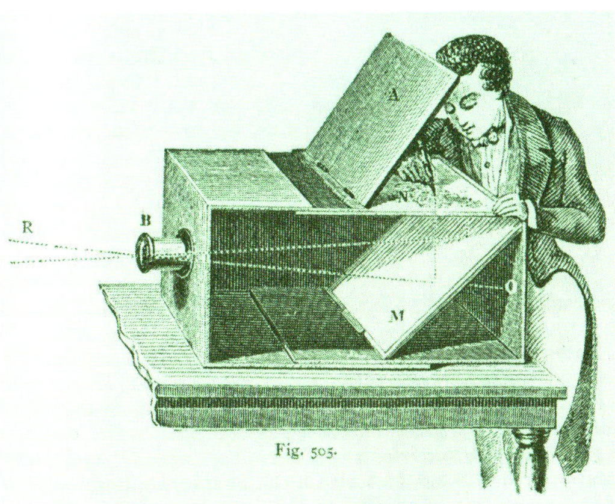

Figure 10. Illustration from Adolphe Ganot, *An Elementary Treatise on Physics*, 1882.

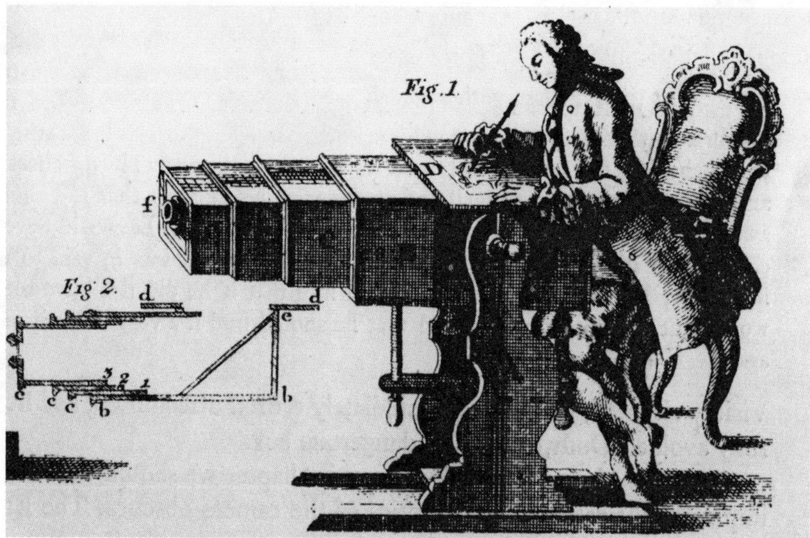

Figure 11. Illustration from G. F. Brander, *Wissenschaftliche Instrumente aus seiner Werkstatt*, 1769 (detail).

People began thinking of the camera obscura as a mechanism for "taking likenesses," instead of receiving them. In 1694, Robert Hooke presented a paper about a camera obscura of his own design to the Royal Society in London. In this paper, which he called "An instrument of use to take the Draught or Picture of anything," he told his listeners that "any Person shall be able to give us the true Draught of whatever he sees before him," by "nimbly running over, with his Pen, the Boundaries or Outlines" of the image that emerges within its darkened chamber.[39] In a 1773 letter to his partner, Josiah Wedgwood offered to travel to London with a camera obscura, in order to "take a 100 views upon the road."[40] And in a 1777 letter to the Reverend William Mason, Horace Walpole not only substituted the verb "to take" for the verb "to receive"; he also described a camera obscura that dispensed with, and improved upon nature, permitting the artist to produce rapid, strong, and precise drawings.[41] This apparatus "no longer depends on the sun, and serves for taking portraits with a force and exactness incredible," he wrote. "This instrument will enable engravers to copy pictures with the utmost precision."[42] The original now exists only so that a copy can be made. The picture is "ready drawn for [man]," as Hooke put it, so that instead of laboriously drawing from nature, he can quickly trace its outlines. The copy also amplifies upon the "beauty" of the original.[43]

Like Descartes's "clear and distinct ideas," the drawings produced by tracing the outlines of the camera obscura's images transformed a mobile, ephemeral, and untotalizable flow into a single, stable, circumscribed representation. They also promoted the fantasy of a sovereign subject. "What [was] in its entirety," as Heidegger would say, was "now taken in such a way that it first is in its being and only is in being to the extent that it is set up by man, who represents and sets forth."[44] There was no room within this account for the aesthetic qualities of the camera obscura's image stream.

Fascinatingly, though, a counter-discourse emerged in the seventeenth century that foregrounded the pictorial properties of the camera obscura's images, and attributed them to the world. Athanasius Kircher characterized nature as a "painter" in his 1646 book, *Great Art of Light and Shadows*,[45] and in 1662, Constantijn Huygens wrote that "all painting is dead by comparison [with the camera obscura's images], for here is life itself, or something more noble . . . Figure, contour, and movement come together naturally therein, in a way that is altogether pleasing."[46]

This account of the camera obscura resurfaced in the eighteenth century. In 1704, John Harris wrote that if the sun is shining brightly on the objects outside the camera, "you will have the colors of all things there in their natural paint, and such an admirable proportion of light and shadow, as is impossible to be imitated by art; and yet I never saw anything of this kind that comes near this natural landscape."[47] In 1712, Joseph Addison observed that "the prettiest landscape" he ever saw was "one drawn on the walls" of a camera obscura.[48] In 1740 Benjamin Martin maintained that the camera obscura's images are "infinitely superior" to "the finest performance of the pencil."[49] And in 1764 Count Francesco Algarotti declared that "nothing is more delightful to behold" than nature's pictures.[50]

Alexander Pope not only echoed this praise, he also claimed that worldly things draw their *own* pictures with the "pencils" of light that emanate from them, and he located this action in a continuous present tense. Pope converted a grotto on his property into a camera obscura, and in 1725 he told a friend that "when you shut the doors of this grotto, it becomes on the instant, from a luminous room, a camera obscura, on the walls of which all of the objects of the river, hills, wood, and boats, *are forming* a moving picture in their visible radiations."[51] As we can see from this last sentence of this passage, "nature" had a broad meaning for Pope—one closer to what I am calling "the world" than to what we think of as nature.

It also had an expansive meaning for some of the other writers I have just mentioned, particularly for Algarotti, who equates it with "exterior objects" in an important passage in *An essay on painting*. He returns in this passage to Kepler's notion of the retinal screen, and uses it to underscore the receptivity of the human eye. "Nature is continually forming . . . pictures in our eyes," this passage reads. "The rays of light coming from exterior objects, after entering the pupil . . . proceed to the retina, which lies at the bottom of the eye, and stamp upon it, by their union, the image of the object, towards which the pupil is directed."[52] Because the camera obscura functions in an analogous way, Algarotti observes, it is able to reveal this "grand operation" to us—an operation about which we might otherwise know nothing.

But the camera obscura is much more for this eighteenth-century writer than an instrument of self-knowledge; it is the agency through which we learn to see the world differently. "We cannot look directly at any object that is not surrounded by many others, all darting their rays together into our eyes, that it is impossible we should distinguish all the different modulations of its light and colors," Algarotti writes. "At least we can only see them in so full and confused a manner, as not to be able to determine any things precisely about them."[53] In the camera obscura, on the other hand, "the visual faculty is wholly brought to bear upon the object before it." This is due in part to the surrounding darkness—to the fact that the "light of every other object is, as it were, perfectly extinguished." But the camera obscura also inducts us into a new way of seeing through the "force and brightness" of its images.[54] In the passage that follows, Algarotti suggests that this "force and brightness" are the result of an aesthetic intensification; he praises the "justness" of these pictures' "contours," the "exactness" of their "perspective and of the chiaroscuro," the "vivacity and richness" of their colors, and the "infinite variety" of their "tints."[55]

This description of the camera obscura's images sounds like an early draft of Heidegger's "The Question Concerning Technology." We have exalted ourselves to "the posture of the lord of the earth," he writes there, and relegated everything else to the status of "standing reserve"—raw material for us to do with as we wish. We do not see that nothing can escape this instrumental logic, and that we are "at the point" where we ourselves "will have to be taken as standing-reserve."[56] But the essence of technology is nothing technological; it is, rather, "*poiēsis*" or "revelation." There are two kinds of *poiēsis*. The first is the product of human labor; it results from "the skills and activities of the craftsman," the "arts of the mind," and the "fine arts." The second kind of *poiēsis* has a very different source; it occurs through the "arising of something from out of itself." Heidegger compares it to "the bursting of a blossom into bloom," and calls it "*poiēsis* in the highest sense,"[57] because it houses a "saving power."[58] It has the power to save us because it resists our attempts to establish ourselves as its source—because it is so manifestly a "self-showing" and a "self-giving" on the part of the world. It is by "coming to presence into the beautiful" that something gives itself to be seen, Heidegger writes near the end of the essay, and he repeatedly associates beauty with illumination: with "light," "radiance," and a "shining forth."[59]

THE DRAWINGS that the modern subject produced with the help of the optical camera obscura satisfied his desire for a stable representation, but they did not halt the stream of images inside the device, or alter them in any other way. The experimentation that led to the heliograph and the daguerreotype was clearly driven by the desire for a more decisive victory—one that would allow man to "harness" the world's power, and force its drawings to obey his commands. Niépce described heliography as a "technique" for "taking views," "fixing" them "with the action of light," and "reproducing them by printing."[60] When extolling the brevity of his exposure times, Daguerre also reached for the verb through which some viewers described their relationship to the camera obscura after lenses and mirrors had been added to it, and that would soon become ubiquitous in photographic circles: the verb "to take." "By this process," he writes, "without any idea of drawing, without any knowledge of chemistry and physics, it will be possible to *take* in a few minutes the most detailed views" (my emphasis).[61]

Later in the same essay, Daguerre goes one step further: he installs himself

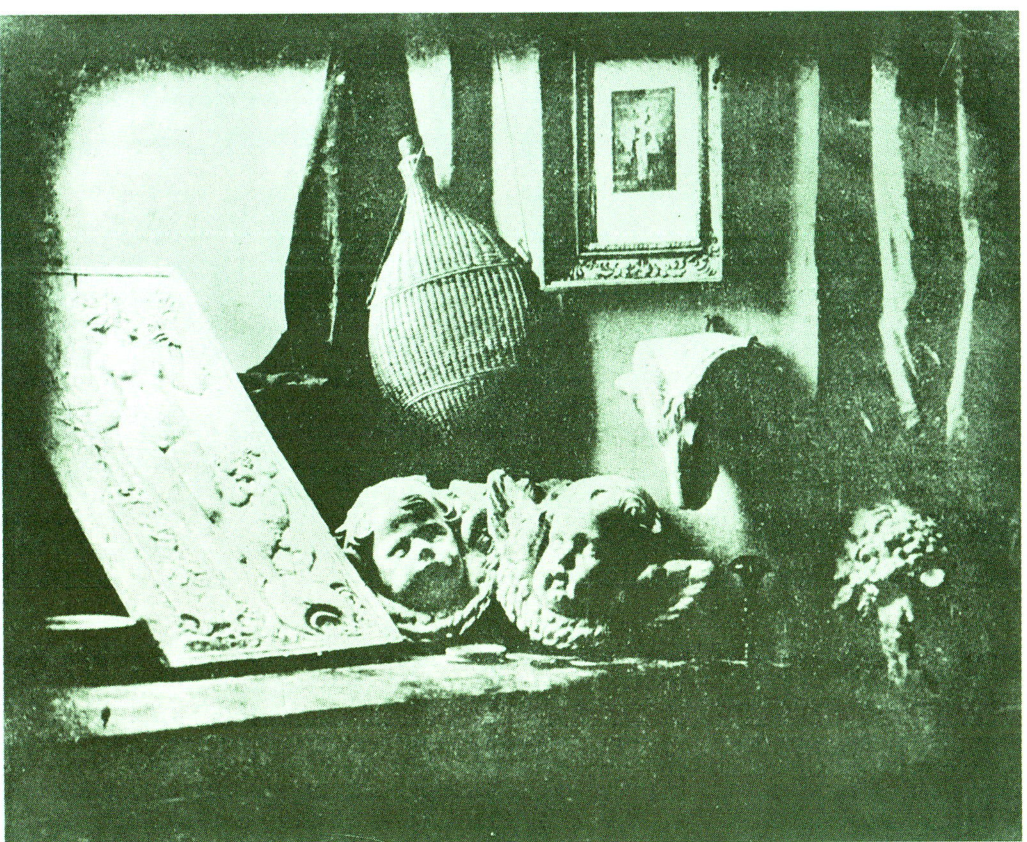

Figure 12. Louis-Jacques-Mandé Daguerre, *Intérieur d'un cabinet de curiosités*, 1837. Daguerreotype. Courtesy of the Société Française de Photographie, Paris.

in the position of the giver, and relegates nature to that of the receiver. "The DAGUERREOTYPE is not merely an instrument which serves to draw Nature . . . ," he boasts, "it is a chemical and physical process which gives her the power to reproduce herself."[62] Some early viewers not only repeated these claims but amplified them. In a lengthy 1839 review of the daguerreotype, Jules Janin compared Daguerre to God: "We have a fine passage in the Bible, God said, 'Let there be light' and light there was. You can say to the towers of Notre Dame, 'Place yourself there;' the towers obey. Thus have they obeyed Daguerre, who one bright day transported them to his home from the gigantic foundation-stone upon which they are built."[63] It is impossible "to command more imperiously," he declares a few paragraphs later. Another commentator maintained that "even a shadow, the emblem of all that is most fleeting in this world, [was] fettered by the spell of [Talbot's] invention."[64]

However, the verb "to receive" figures much more prominently than the verb "to take" in early accounts of photography. Daguerre uses it when talking about the part played by the camera obscura in the production of his photographs, and Edgar Allen Poe suggests that it is the defining attribute of the daguerreotype. Although the photographic plate "does not at first appear to have *received* a definite impression," he wrote in 1840, it later assumes "a miraculous beauty."[65] David Brewster also uses the verb many times in his 1843 account of the existing photographic processes,[66] and it is ubiquitous in both Talbot's writings and Lady Eastlake's 1857 article.

A number of the other tropes that eighteenth-century writers associated with the camera obscura also resurfaced in the first two decades of chemical photography.[67] Niépce called the images that emerged from his experiments "heliographs,"[68] and Holmes titled an 1863 essay about the medium "Doings of the Sunbeam."[69] Talbot wrote that "it is not the artist who makes the picture, but the picture which makes *itself*. All that the artist does is to dispose the apparatus before the image he requires. . . . At the end of the [allotted] time he returns, takes out his picture, and finds it finished."[70]

Many writers also conceptualized the source of the photographic image as a hand, rather than an eye. Talbot imputed the images that were generated through his technique to the "pencil of nature,"[71] and characterized the negatives that emerged from his cameras as "photogenic drawings;"[72] Daguerre described the daguerreotype as "the imprint of nature,"[73] and a contemporaneous reviewer attributed the photographic image to the "rectilineal pencils of light."[74] At one point in her 1857 essay, Lady Eastlake metaphorizes the light that generates the photographic image as an eye, but this eye is not human, and it behaves more like a stylus than an organ of vision. With a "wink," it traces

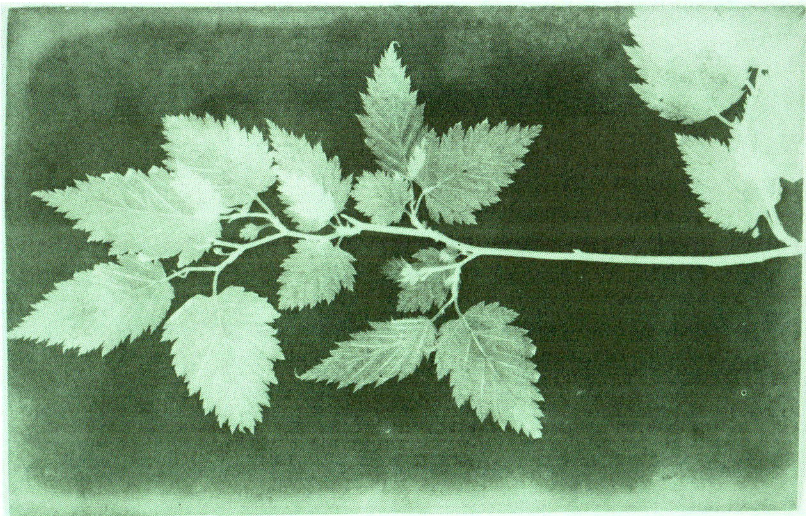

Figure 13. William Henry Fox Talbot, *Leaves on a stem*, 1842. Salted paper print. Courtesy of the National Media Museum/SSPL.

"the glory of the heavens, the wonders of the deep," and "the most fleeting smile of the babe."[75] In another passage from the same essay, Lady Eastlake calls it a "solar pencil."[76]

Talbot and his contemporaries were also amazed by the detail and precision of the photographic image, which revealed things they could not see. "The perfection and fidelity of the pictures are such, that, on examining them by microscopic power, details are discovered which are not perceivable to the naked eye in the original objects," Sir John Robison wrote in 1839.[77] "In a view up the street, a distant sign would be perceived, and the eye could just discern that there were lines of letters on it," Samuel Morse remarked the same year, "but so minute as not to be read with the naked eye." In the daguerreotype, by contrast, "every letter was clearly and distinctly legible, and so also were the minutest breaks and lines in the walls of the buildings and the pavements of the street."[78] "The perfection [of the photographic image] exceeds the accuracy of the eye as its judge," noted another commentator.[79]

Surprisingly, these early viewers and practitioners did not rush to resolve the discrepancies between what they saw and what the camera showed by establishing one as the truth and the other as an illusion. Neither did they conclude that sensory perception is duplicitous, or take epistemological shelter within the domain of mental representations. They understood that their look and the photographic image opened onto the same world—*their* world. I say "world" because the numerous references to nature in this literature once again show that it signified something much larger for its authors than it does for us.

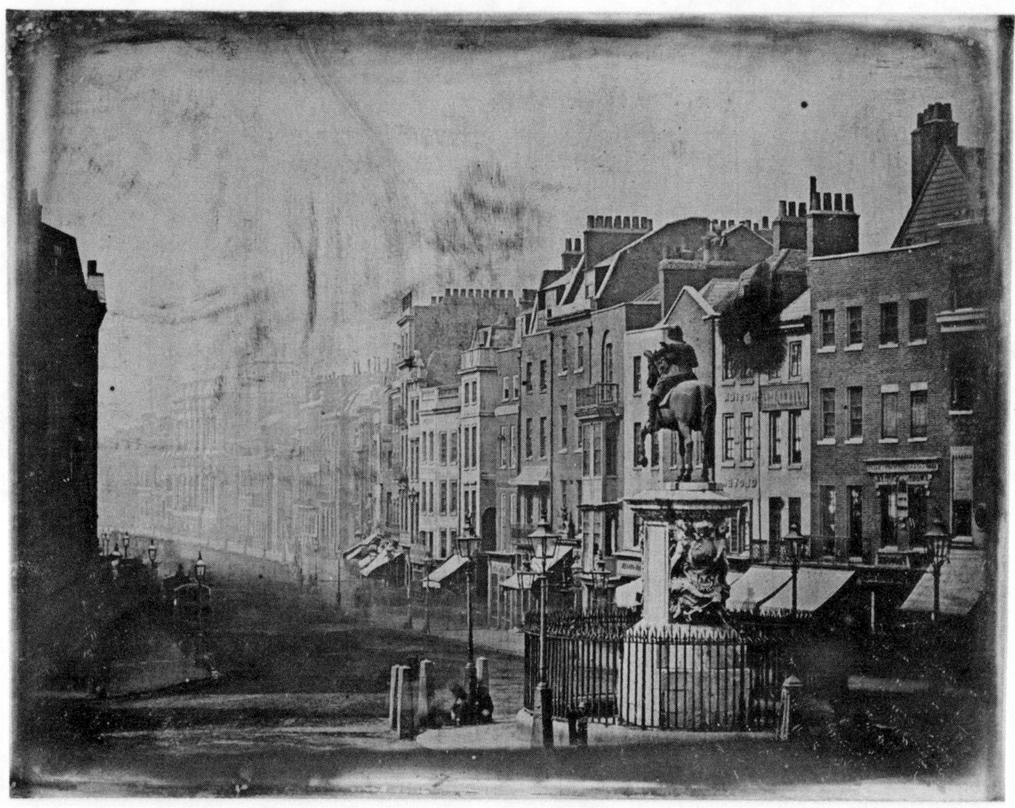

Figure 14. "M. de Sainte-Croix," *Parliament Street from Trafalgar Square*, 1839. Daguerreotype. © Victoria and Albert Museum, London.

As can be seen from the constant references to drawing, painting, and engraving in the passages I have just quoted, many early viewers of the photographic image were also struck by its aesthetic qualities, and a number of them saw it as a superior kind of art making. Talbot tried to "take sketches" with the aid of Sir William Hyde Wollaston's camera lucida while traveling in Italy. He found them wonderful when viewing them through the prism of this device, but when he looked at the drawings directly, he found the marks left by his "faithless pencil . . . melancholy to behold." Talbot repeated the experiment with a camera obscura, but he was neither patient nor skillful enough "to trace all of the minute details visible on the paper." He abandoned his quest to become a better draughtsman, and began searching for a way of preserving these "fairy pictures."[80]

Commentators expressed similar sentiments after looking at the first daguerreotypes and "photogenic drawings."[81] An anonymous reviewer in an 1839 issue of the *United States Democratic Review* described the daguerreotype as a "master-piece" designed "by Nature herself."[82] The editor of an 1839 issue of *Belles Lettres* urged his readers to improve their draughtsmanship by making her their "drawing-mistress,"[83] and another reviewer declared the medium to be "as great a step in the fine arts, as the steam-engine was in the mechanical arts."[84] Talbot extolled the "inimitable beauty of the pictures of Nature's drawing which the glass lens of the Camera throws upon the paper in its focus."[85]

Some commentators also linked photography to a specific *kind* of picture: the self-portrait.[86] One reviewer wrote that henceforth "every fixed object" would be able to paint itself with the "pencils of light," and transfer its "mimic image to the silver tablet."[87] Since many of Talbot's photographs were made by placing an object directly on a sensitized sheet of paper, and this object prevented the area beneath it from darkening when the paper was exposed to light, this object could be literally said to draw its own portrait, but commentators did not limit their claims to this kind of photograph. An anonymous reviewer wrote that "*all* nature, animate and inanimate, shall henceforth be its own painter," and also the "engraver, printer and publisher" of the resulting portrait, so that each of us can have our own "copy" (my emphasis). He also suggested that photography is the world's way of revealing itself to us, and of showing us how it wants to be seen—i.e., of awakening us from our Cartesian dream and reasserting

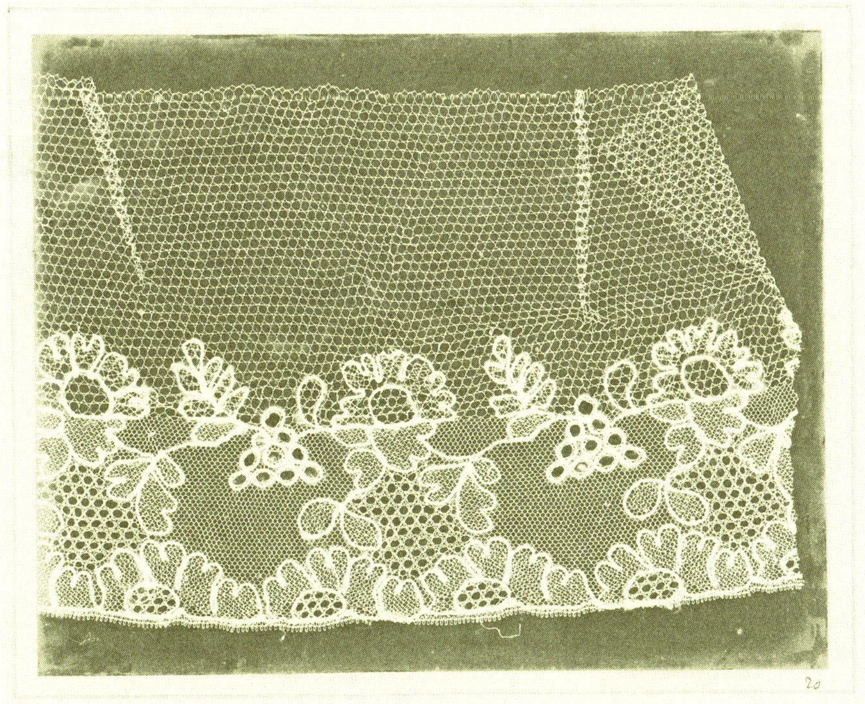

Figure 15. Henry Fox Talbot, *Lace*, 1842. Salted paper print. Courtesy of the Metropolitan Museum of Art, New York.

its primacy. "Ye artists of all denominations that have so vilified nature as her journeymen, see how she rises up against you, and takes the staff into her own hands," this extraordinary passage reads. "Your mistress now, with a vengeance, she will show you what she really is . . . Every church will show itself to the world without your help. It will make its wants visible and known on paper."[88]

IN A STRIKING PASSAGE in her 1857 essay, Lady Eastlake compares the appearance of the photographic image to the creation of the world, just as Janin does in his 1839 review, but she uses the verb "to reveal" twice in this passage, suggesting that the photographic image may actually have more to do with the *disclosure* of the world than with its *creation*. "The prepared paper or plate which we put into the camera may be compared to a chaos, without form and void, on which the merest glance of the sun's rays calls up image after image, till the fair creation stands revealed," it reads, "yet not revealed in the order in which it met the solar eye. For while some colors have hastened to greet [the sun's] coming, others have been found slumbering at their posts, and have been left with darkness in their lamps."[89]

Lady Eastlake also invokes a second biblical story in this passage: the parable of ten virgins who fall asleep while waiting for a bridegroom, and whose lamps go out while they are sleeping.[90] Five are able to relight their lamps when the bridegroom returns, because they have brought extra oil, but the others are unprepared. The bridegroom takes the "ready" virgins to the wedding banquet, but shuts the door on the others. In its scriptural context, this story is an allegory for the Second Coming. The wedding banquet stands for the Rapture, the bridegroom for Christ, the virgins with bright lamps for those who will ascend to heaven, and the others for those who will be left behind.

Since it is difficult to think of any nineteenth-century British context in which this parable would not have been viewed as embarrassingly anachronistic, Lady Eastlake's reliance on it is odd, to say the least. However, she wasn't the only prominent figure in the world of British photography who gravitated to the story. Julia Margaret Cameron based two 1864 photographs on it: *The Five Wise Virgins* and *The Five Foolish Virgins*. In each of these photographs, five women dressed in vaguely historical garb impersonate the virgins mentioned in the title. Although there are no references in either photograph to a bridegroom, a number of the story's other elements have been retained.

The figures in *The Five Wise Virgins* hold lamps, and because they are so tightly framed, particularly at the top of the photograph, they also seem to be ascending—an impression that is strengthened by the blur at the base of the image. The middle figure is distinguished from her companions through her clothing

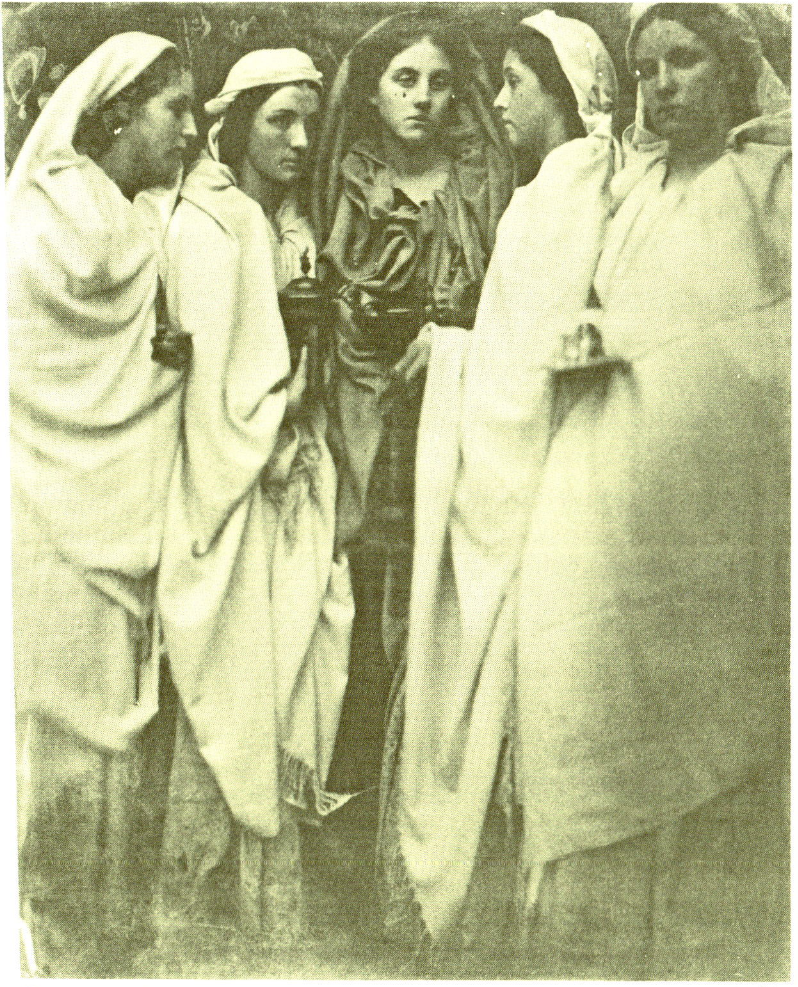

Figure 16. Julia Margaret Cameron, *The Five Wise Virgins*, 1864. Albumen print from collodion wet-plate negative. © Victoria and Albert Museum, London.

and demeanor, which centers the photograph both morally and compositionally, and three of the other figures turn toward her, as in a medieval triptych.

The figures in *The Five Foolish Virgins* also fill the frame horizontally—so much so that the figure on the left seems on the verge of being squeezed out of the picture. However, there is so much space above their heads that we can see part of the ceiling and a backdrop attached to the wall behind them. Their feet are cropped off by the lower frame of the image, but we know that they are standing on terra firma, because the backdrop tells us that they are in a photographic studio. *The Five Foolish Virgins* also has no moral or compositional center; all of the figures are dressed in a similar way, and their heads form a level band across the upper portion of the picture.

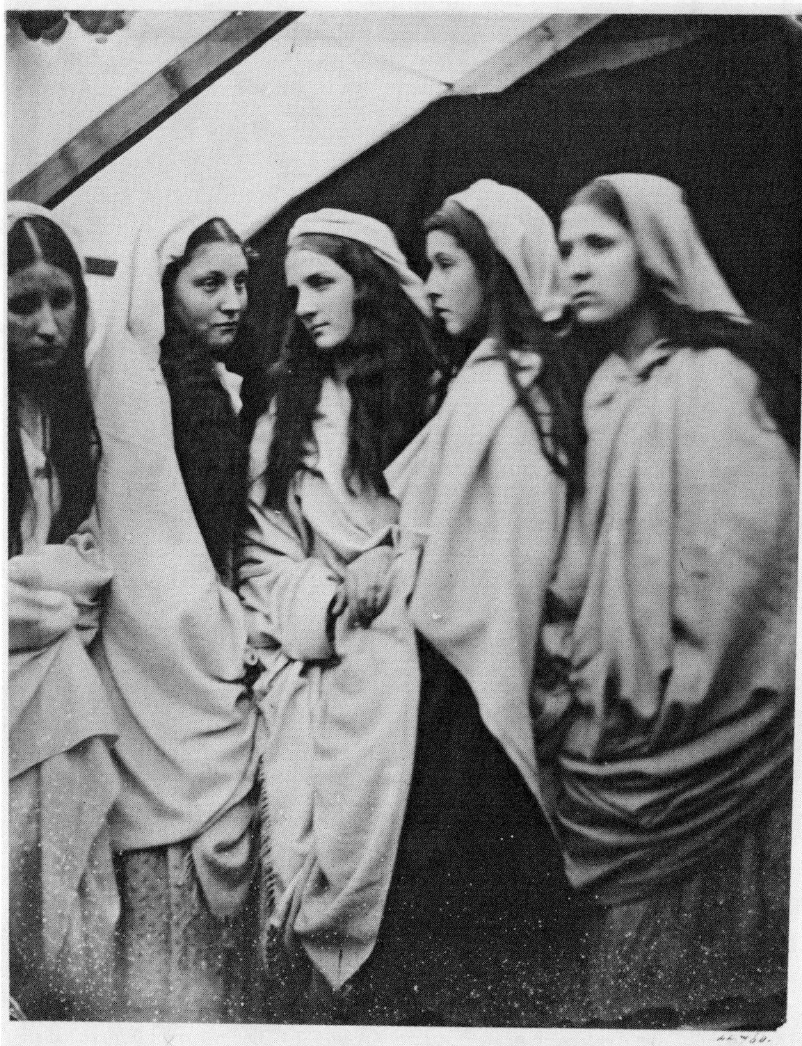

Figure 17. Julia Margaret Cameron, *The Five Foolish Virgins*, 1864. Albumen print from collodion wet-plate negative. © Victoria and Albert Museum, London.

But although the distinction between those who ascend to heaven and those who are left behind is clearly marked, it is also undermined in a number of ways. To begin with, the central figure in the first photograph looks more like a Madonna than a "wise virgin," which scrambles the interpretive wires in all kinds of ways, and disables the story's marriage premise. The poses of the figures who turn toward her are also misaligned, and their looks do not meet. Finally, the figure on the far right doesn't seem to be a member of this group. She turns away from the others, thereby preventing the photograph from actually becoming a triptych, and foregrounding its horizontal over its vertical axis. She also gazes directly out at us, both welcoming and returning our look.

Although this figure is compositionally marginal, she is the real center of the photograph.

On closer inspection, some remnants of a triptych can also be glimpsed in *The Five Foolish Virgins*. Although there is no "eyeline match," three of the five figures turn toward each other, and appear to be looking at each other. The figure on the left looks down, which pushes her even further out of the picture, but the one on the right is emphatically there, and utterly riveting. Unlike all of the other figures in this photograph, who are sharply delineated, she has Cameron's signature "blur," and she gazes intensely out-of-frame, at an unseen object. With the forward tilt of her body, she both signals its appearance, and anticipates its arrival. She thus occupies an analogous position to the one occupied by the figure who gazes out at us in *The Five Wise Virgins*, both conceptually and compositionally, and like the latter, she steals the show.

Lady Eastlake's apparent reason for invoking the parable of the wise and foolish virgins is unrelated to Cameron's photographs. She uses it to expand on the distinction between "laggard colors," like red and yellow, and "impatient" ones, like blue and violet, i.e., colors that are slow to inscribe their traces on the recipient plate and those that do so quickly.[91] However, the biblical story has nothing to do with slowness or quickness, and the distance between the colors described in this passage and the bridesmaids in the biblical parable is so vast as to be unbridgeable. The real reason why Lady Eastlake turns to this parable is because it is the pivot through which she shifts from her first account of photography to her second—from the notion that photography *creates* the world to the notion that photography *reveals* it. Although this might seem a trifling distinction, it is in fact profound. The world did not disappear when Descartes replaced his sensory perceptions with mental representations; it was still there, but it was no longer *present*. The heliograph, daguerreotype, and calotype were the means through which it attempted to rectify this situation—to "come forward," or "presence."

Lady Eastlake uses the story about the wise and foolish virgins to effect this shift because photography *is* a second coming, and the only one we are ever likely to experience: the second coming of the world. The parable also analogizes the other part of the photographic event: the part that has to do with us. Like the bridegroom, the photographic image arrives from elsewhere, hoping that we will see it. Unfortunately, though, this does not often happen, because there are two kinds of viewers: those who "hasten to greet it" and those who miss the encounter for which they should have been waiting. I will end this chapter with an artist who is as ready for that encounter as the figures on the right side of Cameron's diptych, but who requires no theological alibi: the Cuban American photographer Abelardo Morell.

IN 1991, Morell covered the windows of the living room in his Quincy, Massachusetts, house with black plastic and cut a small opening in the plastic. Light entered the room through this opening, just as it did in the first pinhole camera, carrying a reversed and inverted stream of images, but instead of landing on a screen in a space that was set apart for that purpose, or whose normal functioning was temporarily suspended, it spilled onto the walls, ceiling, and contents of what was still recognizably a domestic space. Morell then focused his camera on this visual palimpsest and exposed the negative.[92]

The exposure lasted eight hours—almost as long as the one that produced the earliest extant photograph—but Morell did not call the resulting photograph "View from a Living Room," or even "View of the Houses across the Street." Instead, he called it *"Camera Obscura Image of Houses Across the Street in Our Livingroom,"*[93] a title he later changed to *Houses Across the Street in Our Living Room, Quincy, Massachusetts."*[94] The first version of the title attributes the inverted image to the camera obscura, rather than Morell's camera or his look. The amended title links it to a specific place—Quincy, Massachusetts.

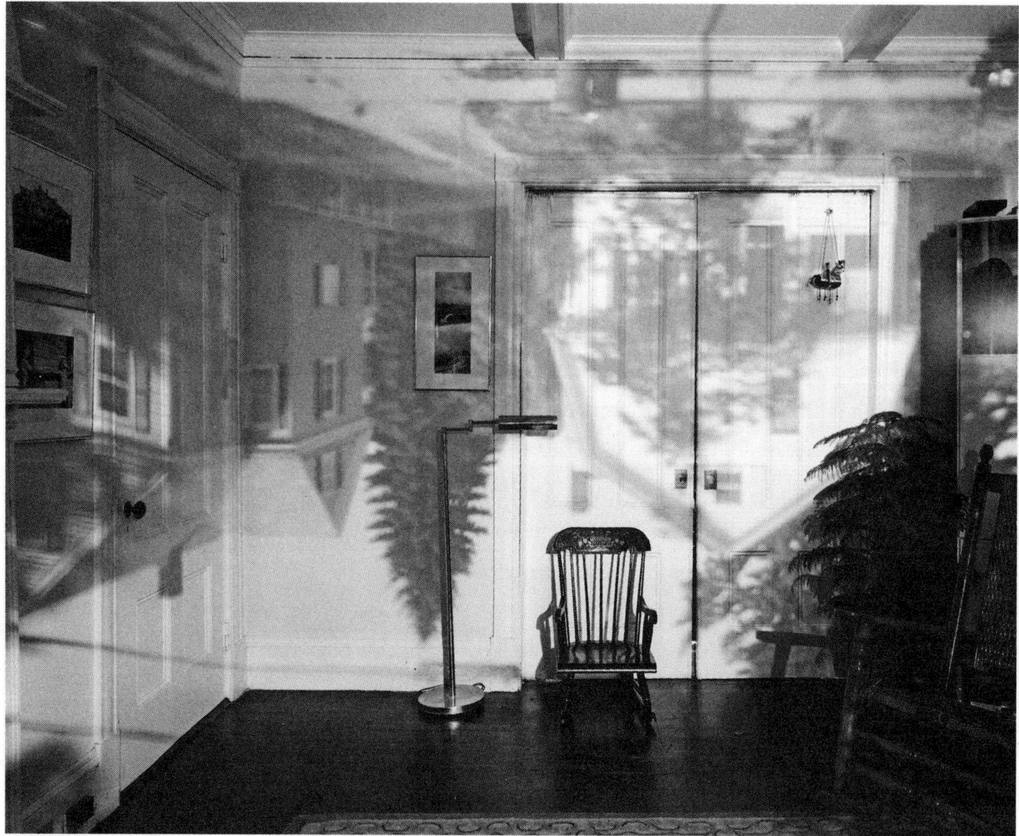

Figure 18. Abelardo Morell, *Camera Obscura Image of Houses Across the Street in Our Livingroom*, 1991. Silver-gelatin print. Image © Abelardo Morell, courtesy of Edwynn Houk Gallery, New York.

It also suggests that although the camera obscura played an enabling role in the creation of the photograph, the upside-down part of the image actually originated in the houses themselves.[95] They entered Morell's living room through what might be called an "ontological extrusion," and during the eight hours it took to make this photograph the living room and the houses were co-present, both temporally, and spatially.

The intimacy of this relationship is even more marked in a closely related photograph, whose name underwent a similar transformation. In this photograph, which was initially called *Camera Obscura Image of Houses Across the Street in Our Bedroom*,[96] and later *Houses Across the Street in Our Bedroom, Quincy, Massachusetts*,[97] the upside-down image extends from the wall behind a bed down to the pillows and coverlet below. The bed invites us to think about the people who sleep in it, and—through an almost inevitable extrapolation—those who sleep in similar beds on the other side of the street.

The photograph consequently functions as a receiving room for Morell's neighbors, as well as their houses. In the years since he made these two photo-

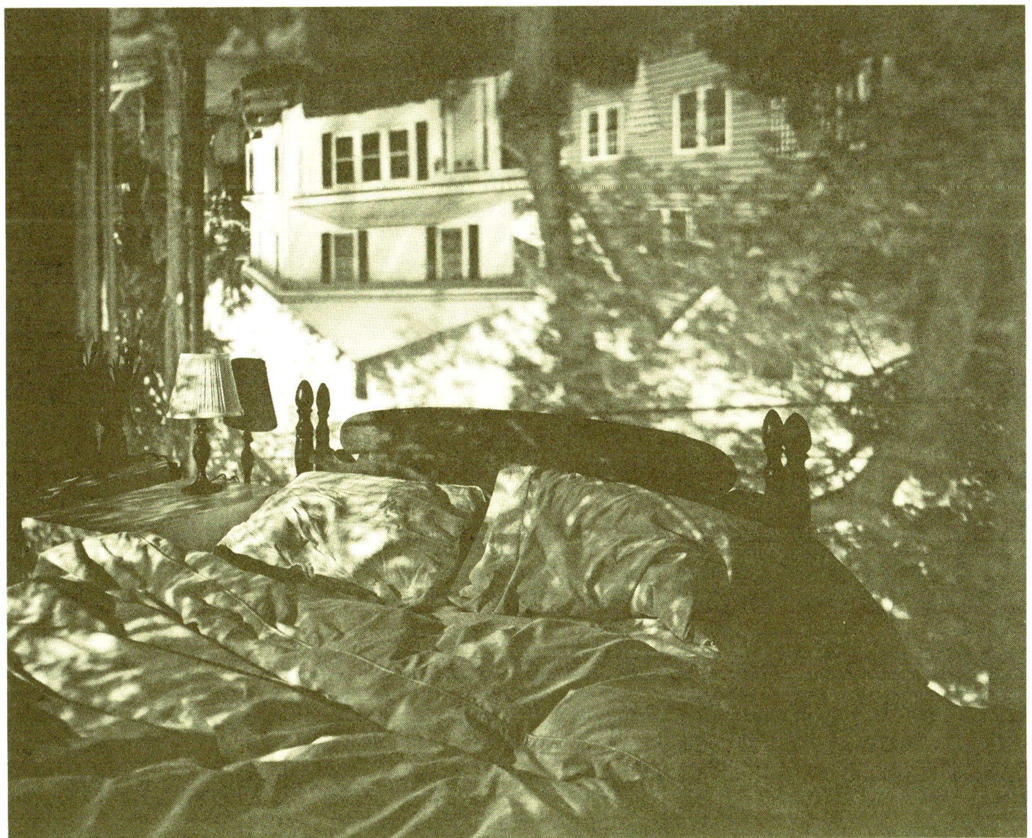

Figure 19. Abelardo Morell, *Houses Across the Street in Our Bedroom, Quincy, MA*, 1994. Silver-gelatin print. Image © Abelardo Morell, courtesy of Edwynn Houk Gallery, New York.

graphs, the artist has facilitated similar encounters in many other places. These venues are often bedrooms, but even when this is not the case, Morell thinks of the encounters as "couplings." "One of the satisfactions I get from making this imagery," he writes, "comes from my seeing the weird and yet natural marriage of the inside and outside."[98]

In 2005, Morell began making color camera obscura photographs. The first of these photographs welcomes an inverted and reversed image of the exterior of the Philadelphia Museum of Art into one of the museum's own galleries, and pairs it with a painting that performs the same action in reverse: Giorgio de Chirico's *The Soothsayer's Recompense* (1913). Part of the upside-down image of the museum's exterior also enters the de Chirico painting, establishing it as a co-creation. The same is true of the photograph in which the transformed painting appears. The interior and exterior meet, as Elizabeth Siegel puts it, "to form a new image."[99]

Around the same time that Morell turned to color, he began using lenses and prisms to sharpen the focus of the camera obscura's images and reverse its reversals.[100] He also started working with a digital camera. Since the images that

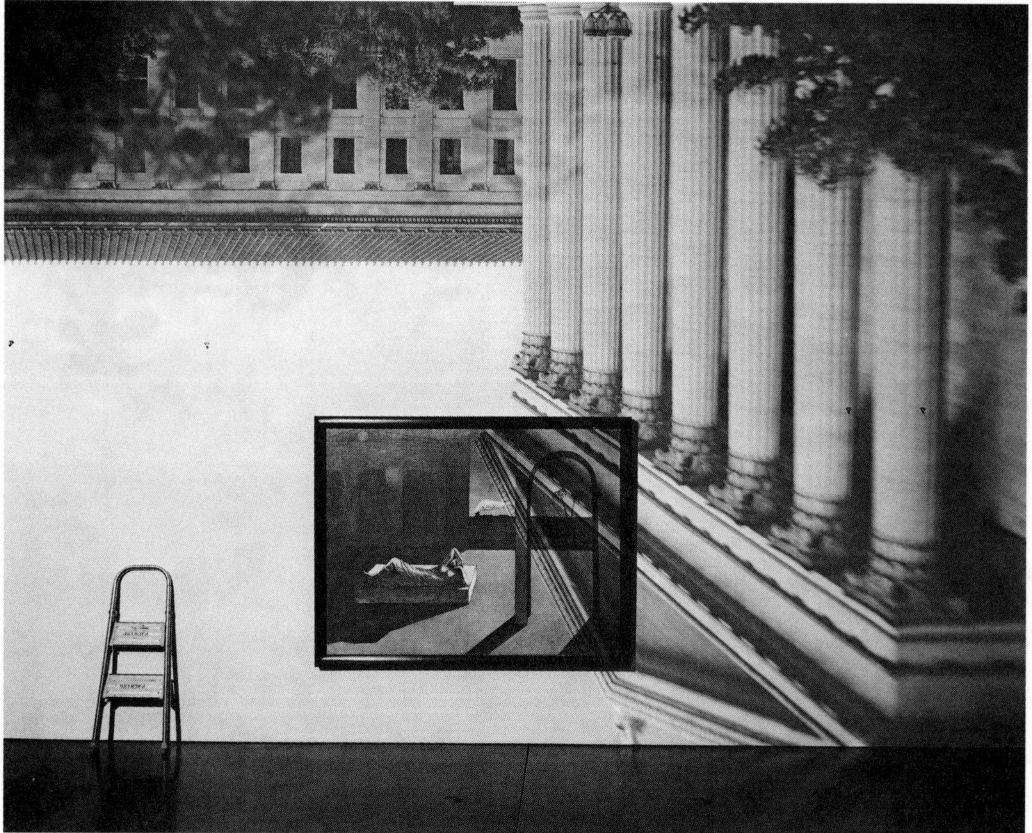

Figure 20/Colorplate 1. Abelardo Morell, *Camera Obscura: The Philadelphia Museum of Art East Entrance in Gallery #171 with a de Chirico Painting*, 2005. Inkjet print. Image © Abelardo Morell, courtesy of Edwynn Houk Gallery, New York.

enter the camera obscura are many-hued, Morell's shift from black-and-white to color photography can be seen as a logical extension of his original project, and although his lenses and prisms "upped" the technological "ante," they too have a historical precedent. Digital images, on the other hand, are generally assumed to be non-referential and non-indexical, and therefore discontinuous with the camera obscura and chemical photography. Morell, however, believes that digital photographs also have a disclosive potential, and that they may even have the capacity to render "the universe next door" *more* present than its antecedents could. "I have . . . been able to shorten my exposures considerably thanks to digital technology," he confides in a short essay on his website, "which in turn makes it possible to capture more momentary light. I love the increased sense of reality that the outdoor has in these new works—the marriage of the outside and the inside is now made up of more equal partners."[101]

It is perhaps for this reason that Pope's beautiful description of his grotto camera obscura always makes me think of one of Morell's more recent works, *Camera Obscura: View of Central Park Looking North—Fall* (2008). This work

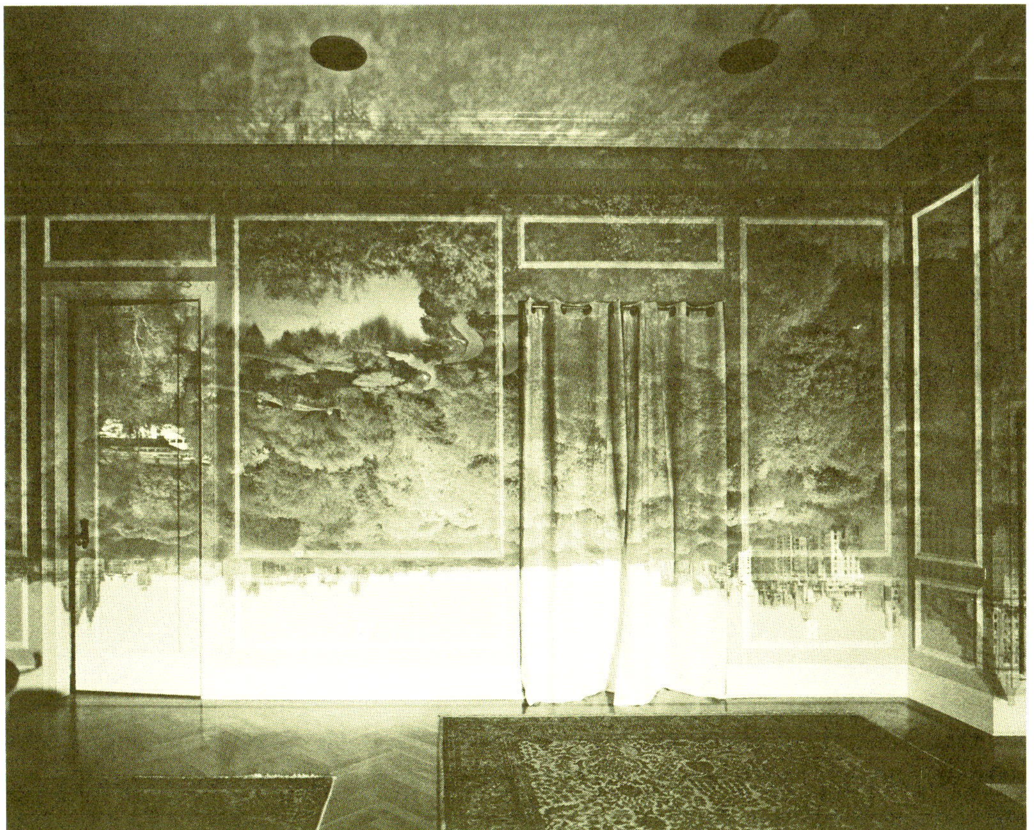

Figure 21/Colorplate 2. Abelardo Morell, *Camera Obscura: View of Central Park Looking North—Fall*, 2008. Inkjet print. Image © Abelardo Morell, courtesy of Edwynn Houk Gallery, New York.

is part of a series of photographs that were produced at different times of year in a New York City hotel, using one of its rooms as a camera obscura. Unlike the names that Morell gave his earlier camera obscura photographs, the name that he assigned to this one contains the word through which the photographic image was subordinated to the human look: "view." The photograph itself, however, completely redefines this word.

As Morell shows us by positioning his camera in front of a wall, instead of a window, the view to which the title alludes was not carved out of the world by the photographer's look, and then "captured" by his camera. It was drawn, rather, on the wainscoted wall of a darkened hotel room through the "visible radiations" of external objects: trees, lakes, and buildings. It was also a "moving" rather than a fixed "picture," and although this picture has now been incorporated into a photograph, it still is. Central Park's autumnal self-portrait retains this power because Morell waited for it to arrive, and embraced it when it did. Although he did not make it, he knew that it was good.

Chapter 2

UNSTOPPABLE DEVELOPMENT

THE TROPES that Alexander Pope and Count Francesco Algarotti associated with the camera obscura resurfaced in the 1830s and 1840s because chemical photography picked up where the camera obscura left off, both technically and ontologically. This might seem a puzzling claim, since unlike the images that appear inside the camera obscura, which are mobile and ephemeral, the defining attributes of analogue photography are immobility and permanence. The photographic image was, however, neither immobile nor permanent in the first decades of its history. It emerged slowly, through the gradual accretion of the traces inscribed on a "recipient-plate" by the light emitted by the external world, and it often disappeared shortly after it arrived.[1] And even when this image did not blacken or fade, there was an instability at its core.

Niépce began experimenting with chemical photography in 1814,[2] significantly earlier than either Daguerre or Talbot. He was drawn to it not for aesthetic reasons, but rather because he saw it as a potentially reproductive medium, like lithography—a vehicle for generating multiple copies of already existing images.[3] Niépce repeatedly tried to actualize this potential by waxing or oiling an engraving, placing it on a surface coated with a light-sensitive varnish, and exposing it to the sun. In 1822 he succeeded in making a permanent contact negative of an engraving of Pope Pius VII. Others followed, some of which he had acid-etched, in order to render them more reproducible, and from which he managed to extract a few faint paper contact positives.[4]

In 1816, Niépce also began trying to "obtain" a printable "view" of nature with the help of a camera obscura.[5] As we saw in the previous chapter, many seventeenth- and eighteenth-century users of this device also described their activities in this way, and for them, too, "taking" a "view" of nature meant arresting the camera obscura's image stream, and forcing the resulting image "to remain on the table."[6] They sought to become "takers" rather than "receivers" of these luminous images by tracing their outlines on a sheet of paper. In most of the devices that were designed for this purpose, the screen was a tabletop, on which the user placed his tracing paper. He gazed down at the image stream, which was projected onto the screen from above or below. The "views" that he "took" with this device were thus manifestly derivative—copies of a preexisting model that issued from an external source. This was not a psychically sustainable arrangement for the modern subject, whose defining feature was "originality."

The optical camera obscura that Robert Hooke described to the Royal Society in 1694 made it much easier for the user to attribute what he saw to his own look.[7] This cone-shaped device fit over his head, moved when he did, and allowed him to "point" at whatever he wanted to "see." The screen functioned simultaneously as a viewfinder and a drawing surface, and its snug position within the camera obscura concealed the fact that the image stream entered the device from the other end. The user seemed to be looking *through* the camera obscura, at the world outside, and recording what he saw (see chapter 3, figure 40).

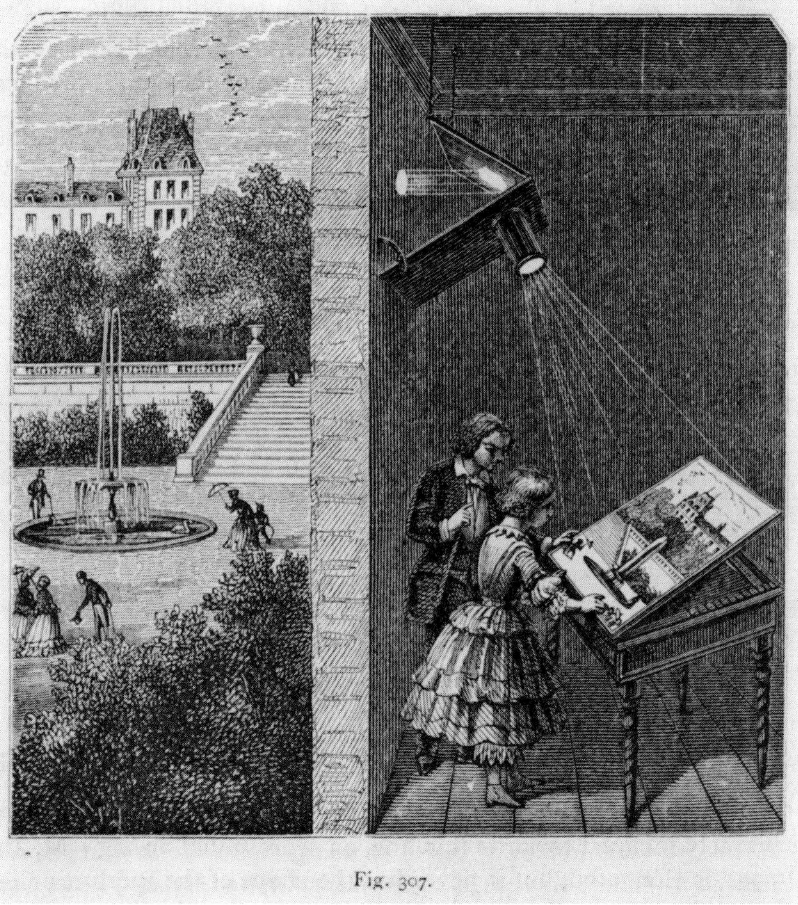

Figure 22. Illustration from Adolphe Ganot, *Natural Philosophy*, 1872.

Niépce pushed this project further. Instead of tracing the camera obscura's images on a sheet of paper, he tried to make the camera obscura draw what *he* saw. The "view" that he wanted the camera obscura to "take" had his signature all over it; it was the one that met his eyes when he looked out of the window of his attic workroom. Niépce installed a camera obscura in this window many times in 1816, and his letters to Claude, his brother and sometime collaborator, are full of references to the courtyard, and of laborious attempts to align his photographs with it. "I have made the experiment *in accordance with the procedure known to you*," he wrote in May of that year, ". . . and I saw on the white paper all of the bird house which one can see from the window, also a faint image of the casement which was less illuminated than the outside objects."[8] "The white mass, which shows only dimly at the right of the bird house . . . is the pear tree . . . and the black spot above the tree top is an opening between the branches," he wrote three weeks later.[9]

Niépce also referred to the photographs that he hoped to extract from the camera obscura as "view-points" ("*points de vue*").[10] This phrase recalls both the vanishing point in a perspectival painting and the fixed position from which such a painting becomes intelligible—a position that affords the person who steps into it a powerful sense of mastery.[11] It also anticipates Hollywood cinema's imputation of what the viewer sees to a fictional look, through the shot/reverse shot. And the way in which Niépce talks about the camera obscura indicates that he did indeed regard it as his ocular representative; he mentions the lens far more often than the screen or the darkened chamber, and he describes it as an "artificial eye."[12] A striking passage in one of Claude's letters shows that this was a shared assumption. "I have read and re-read the interesting details you kindly transmitted to me . . . ," he wrote Nicéphore in 1822, "attentive and following with your eyes the admirable work of light; and *I thought I myself saw a 'point de vue' which I had great pleasure in remembering*."[13]

Niépce's 1816 experiments with the camera obscura produced several negatives of the buildings onto which his studio window opened, but they vanished shortly after he removed them from the apparatus. He called these short-lived photographs "retinas" ("*rétines*"), presumably because they resembled an afterimage.[14] This formulation also recalls the retinal image, the concept through which Kepler theorized the opacity of human vision.[15] Sometime in the summer of 1826 or 1827,[16] Niépce coated a polished pewter plate with a mixture of bitumen of Judea and lavender oil, put the plate in a camera obscura, and once again installed the device in his workroom window. When he removed it eight hours later, the plate was blank, but after he washed it with lavender and white petroleum, a direct positive image of the adjacent structures and buildings appeared on its shiny surface, and the bitumen hardened into an enduring image.[17] It was with this image, Georges Potonniée and the Gernsheims declare, that photography began.[18]

But *View from the Window at Le Gras* wasn't the result for which Niépce had been waiting, either. Because of the length of the exposure, sunlight illuminates the buildings from both sides, and the photograph also shows us the traces inscribed on the pewter plate during the intervening period. It is the precipitate of eight hours of continuous change, and this process occurred in tandem with, and as a consequence of, another metamorphosis—one transpiring in the external world. *View from the Window* thus not only loudly proclaims itself to be a "photogenic drawing," but also recalls Leonardo's dynamic analogies.[19]

Since Niépce didn't know what light had inscribed on the pewter plate until he took the plate out of the camera obscura and washed it with lavender and

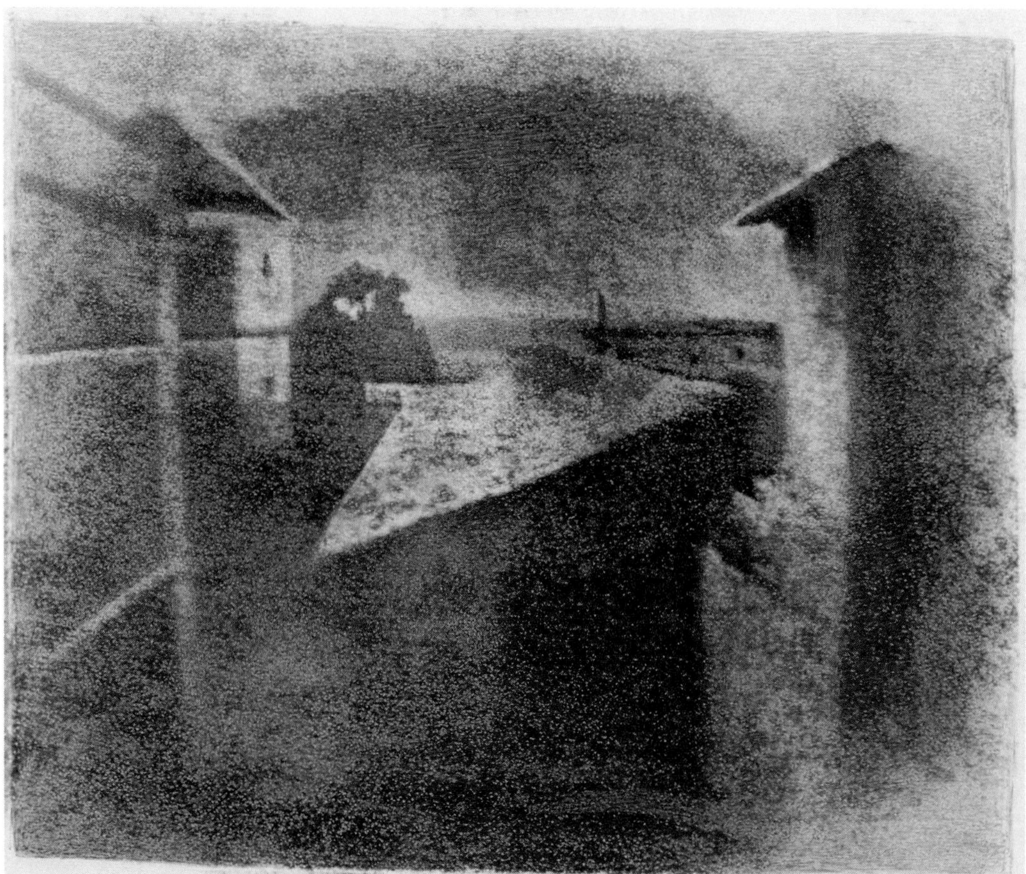

Figure 23. Nicéphore Niépce, *View from the Window at Le Gras*, ca. 1826, as enhanced by Helmut Gernsheim, 1952. Silver-gelatin print and watercolor from original heliograph on pewter. Courtesy of the Harry Ransom Center at the University of Texas at Austin.

white petroleum, his decision to remove it after eight hours was completely arbitrary. It would also have been arbitrary if he had been able to witness what was happening, since the "view" that traced its picture on the shiny surface never assumed a final shape. Niépce must have realized at some point that his difficulties had less to do with chemistry than with the sky and buildings, because he reordered his priorities. His first goal was no longer to make a re-producible image, he announced in an 1828 letter. It was, rather, to replicate a different prototype: the *world*. Only then could he resume his earlier quest. "My sole object [is] to copy nature with the greatest fidelity, [and it is] to that which I attach myself exclusively," he told the engraver Lemaître, "for only when I have succeeded in this can I seriously begin to tackle the various fields of ap-plication of which my discovery is capable."[20] But Niépce still didn't understand the basis of his difficulties; he thought that all he needed was a better lens.[21]

Daguerre joined forces with Niépce in 1828, and continued experiment-ing with photography after the latter's death. He encouraged his partner to focus his reproductive efforts on nature, rather than preexisting images,[22] and he also practiced what he preached; the daguerreotype offers a "faithful" but unreproducible image of its referent. But Daguerre was not really interested in collaborating either with Niépce or with nature.[23] He wanted to establish himself as the source of the photographic image, and he believed that the best way to do this was "to arrive at such rapidity that the impression could be pro-duced in a few minutes, so that the shadows in nature should not have time to alter their position,"[24] and so much detail that the viewer would believe himself to be looking at solid and recognizable forms. "In order to obtain a perfect image of nature only three to thirty minutes at the most are necessary . . . ," he writes. "By this process, without any idea of drawing, without any knowledge of chemistry and physics, it will be possible to take in a few minutes the most detailed views, the most picturesque scenery."[25]

This account of the daguerreotype clearly tapped into the unconscious desires of some of his reviewers, because they not only repeated his claims but hyper-bolized them. "M. Daguerre shows you the plain plate of copper," Hippolyte Gaucheraud enthused. "He places it, in your presence, in his apparatus, and, in three minutes, if there is a bright summer sun, and a few more, if autumn or winter weaken the power of its beams, he takes out the metal and shows it to you, covered with a charming design representing the object towards which the apparatus was turned. Nothing remains but a short mechanical operation—of washing, I believe—and the design, which has been obtained in so few mo-ments, remains unalterably fixed, so that the hottest sun cannot destroy it."[26] And Sir John Robison declared, "The new art has been discovered to fix these wonderful images, which have hitherto passed away volatile—evanescent as a dream—to stop them at our will, on a substance finely sensible to the immediate action of light, and render them permanent before our eyes, in traces represented by tints in perfect harmony on each point, with different degrees of intensity."[27]

As another reviewer makes painfully evident, this fantasy of "immediate action" and "absolute fixation" was yet another iteration of the Cartesian dream. But the dream had a new narrative—one that acknowledged the challenges posed by photography. Yes, there is indeed a world, this narrative goes, and it has an "eye," called the sun, that is the "all-powerful agent of a new art." However, this seemingly omnipotent force is our "willing and obedient slave"; it performs all of the physical labor, while deferring to our aesthetic judgment. If we wish a monument to "appear in relief, free from any surrounding effect that may lessen its noble effect," it will make the monument stand forth, "isolated as the column in the Place Vendôme." We can also "obtain" all of the other "effects" that we desire to create through the "same admirable process," from "the earliest dawn" to "twilight's close."[28]

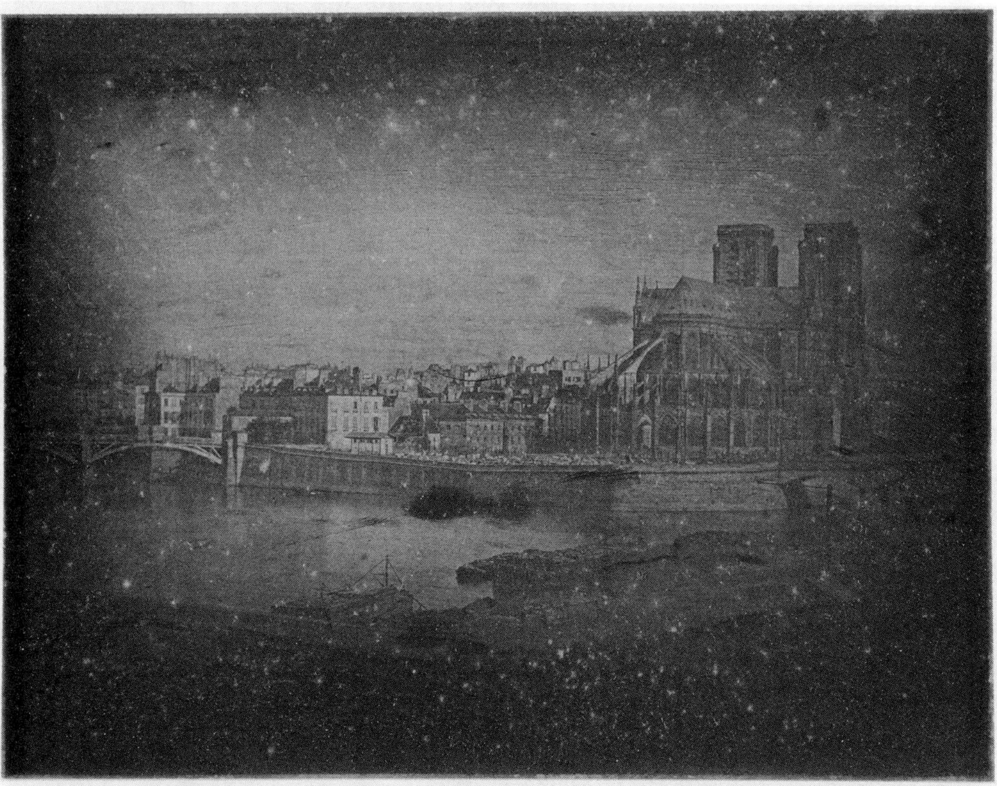

Figure 24. Louis Daguerre, *Notre-Dame and the Ile de la Cité*, ca. 1838. Daguerreotype. Courtesy of the Harry Ransom Center at the University of Texas at Austin.

But Daguerre did not succeed in preserving any of his photographs until 1837, and those that survive are far from "fixed." The daguerreotype has to be angled to be seen, and it shifts in certain positions from a positive to a negative image. It is also extremely fragile, as was already apparent to Daguerre's contemporaries.[29] Since it is produced through the impress of light on a silver-plated surface, rather than the copper beneath this plating, it can be easily rubbed away, and it must be framed behind sealed glass to keep the silver from oxidizing.[30] An odd complaint also surfaces in some of the reviews. "Motion," as one commentator puts it, "escapes [Daguerre], or leaves only vague and uncertain traces."[31] Three of the reviewers who level this complaint attach it to a particular set of photographs—those devoted to the Boulevard du Temple.

In 1839,[32] Daguerre attempted—perhaps consciously, but in all likelihood unconsciously—to remake *View from the Window*, with different protocols. Like Niépce, he installed a camera obscura in the upper-story window of his workroom, in order to "take" the "view" that he saw when he looked out of it. Like his predecessor's experiment, his also began in the early morning and ended in the late afternoon. But rather than pointing his camera obscura at a cluster of buildings on a country estate, Daguerre pointed it at the Boulevard du Temple, one of the busiest streets in Paris, and instead of producing one photograph, he produced three.[33] He also made each of them at a different time of day—the first in the early morning, the second at noon, and the third in the late afternoon. Although his exposures were long by today's standards, they were infinitesimal by comparison with Niépce's; according to one reviewer, they lasted only thirty seconds.[34] Each daguerreotype is consequently the precipitate of a very small part of the period that they collectively represent. Finally, this period is more symbolic than real; two of the photographs were made on one day, and the third on another day.

Daguerre repeated this experiment with two other locations the following year: the Place de la Concorde and the Tuileries Palace.[35] Neither series has survived, but we have two contemporaneous descriptions of the first. "In one of these designs, you may almost tell the hour of the day," the first reviewer writes. "Three views of the [Luxor Obelisk] are taken; one in the morning, one at noon, and the other in the evening; and nobody will mistake the effect of the morning for that of the evening."[36] The Luxor Obelisk was immediately recognizable in all three "views" of the Place de la Concorde, the other claims, and "the effect of the morning light [was] distinctly discernible from that of the evening, though the sun's altitude, and consequently the length of the shadows, [were] the same in both."[37] We can see from these descriptions what Daguerre was hoping to accomplish with the Boulevard du Temple series. By replacing a

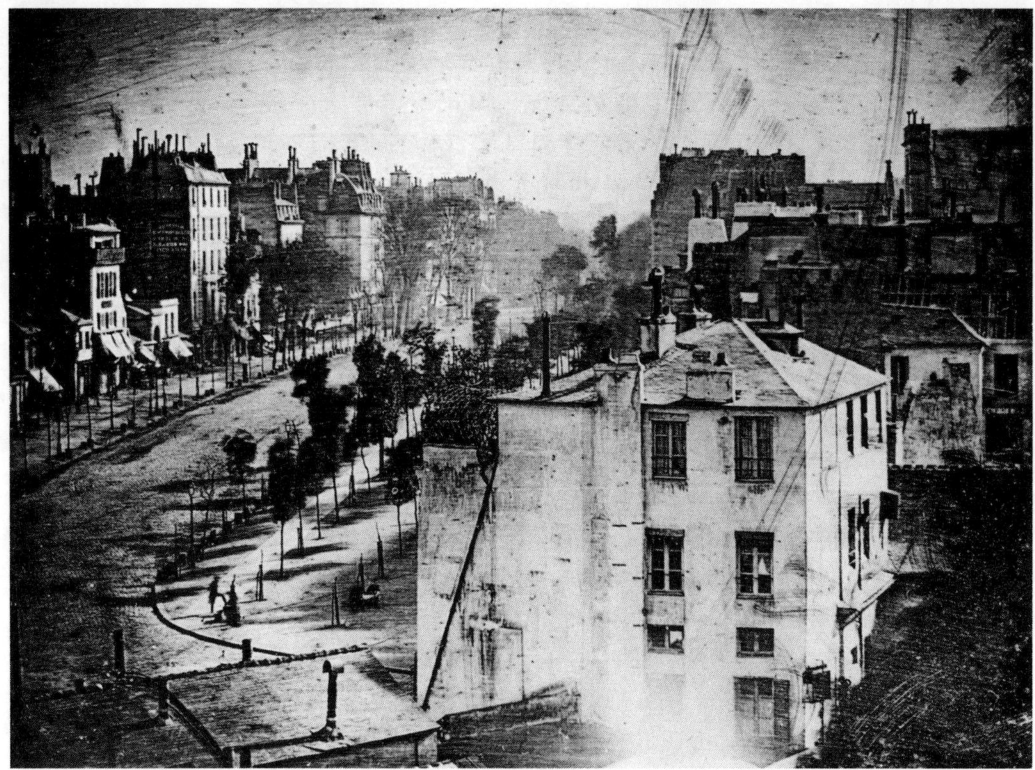

Figure 25. Louis Daguerre, *The Boulevard du Temple*. 1838. Daguerreotype. Courtesy of the Bayerisches Nationalmuseum (inventory no. R 6312.1-8).

photograph created through eight hours of uninterrupted exposure with three photographs representing the beginning, middle, and end of a hypothetical day, he was trying to rationalize time, and solidify form.

Daguerre seemed to have achieved these goals in the Place de la Concorde series, at least in the minds of his reviewers. No one, though, could determine the time of day from the Boulevard du Temple photographs, nor did they correspond to what Daguerre's contemporaries were used to seeing when they ventured into his neighborhood. Samuel Morse visited Daguerre's studio shortly after he made the daguerreotypes, and described the first of them in a letter to his brother. He talks about the mysterious absence of vehicles and crowds in a location that was normally overflowing with both, and the equally mysterious presence of part of a human figure in the lower left frame. "The Boulevard, so constantly filled with a moving throng of pedestrians and carriages, was perfectly solitary, except an individual who was having his boots brushed," he writes. "His feet were compelled, of course, to be stationary for some time, one being on the box of the boot-black, and the other on the ground. Consequently his boots and legs are well defined, but he is without body or head, because these were in motion." Morse concludes that "objects moving are not impressed."[38]

Gaucheraud provides a similar reading of the last photograph in the series, which was also devoid of vehicles and crowds, and which apparently contained two horses, one of whom—like the human figure in the first photograph—was only partially present. (I say "apparently" because this photograph is lost.) "Nature in motion is not represented or at least not without great difficulty . . . ," he writes. "In one of the views of the Boulevards . . . all that was walking or moving does not appear in the design; of two horses in a hackney coach on the stand, one unluckily moved its head during the short operation; the animal is without a head in the design." Since photographers need their subjects to remain stationary for an extended period of time, Gaucheraud concludes, they should focus on things that are inherently motionless, like inanimate nature and architecture.[39]

Morse's preoccupation with the tiny human figure—or, as has been more recently argued, two tiny human figures[40]—in the left frame of a photograph in which so many other things are happening is odd. It is even stranger to find Gaucheraud attributing immobility to architecture when discussing this series, since the most prominent thing in the two surviving photographs is the building in the foreground, and it is far from still. Not only does it occupy a slightly different position in each photograph, but it also moves in multiple directions within them. In the first daguerreotype, the building both emerges from and retreats back into the mist in the background and at its base, and in the second it simultaneously rises out of the darkness that engulfs its lower half and sinks back into it. This is a striking instantiation of the kind of movement I discussed in chapter 1: of the "coming forward" or "presencing" of the world through self-presentation. It also reminds us that every disclosure is a partial concealment—that nothing ever stands fully exposed before us.

Although the building in the foreground of the Boulevard du Temple series is manifestly the same "body" in both daguerreotypes, it also looks very different in the second daguerreotype than it does in the first; it is squatter, its windows are larger, and its façade has three levels instead of two. I take the word "body" from Henri Bergson, who uses it to emphasize the "evolutionary" nature of all phenomena. Everything "changes at every moment," he writes in *Creative Evolution*. It also does so "*without ceasing*" (my emphasis). There is, consequently, no such thing as a form; there is only *formation*. These infinitesimal metamorphoses are, however, imperceptible to the human eye. When "successive images" differ slightly, we consider them all as "the waxing and waning of a single *mean* image," and when a body alters enough to

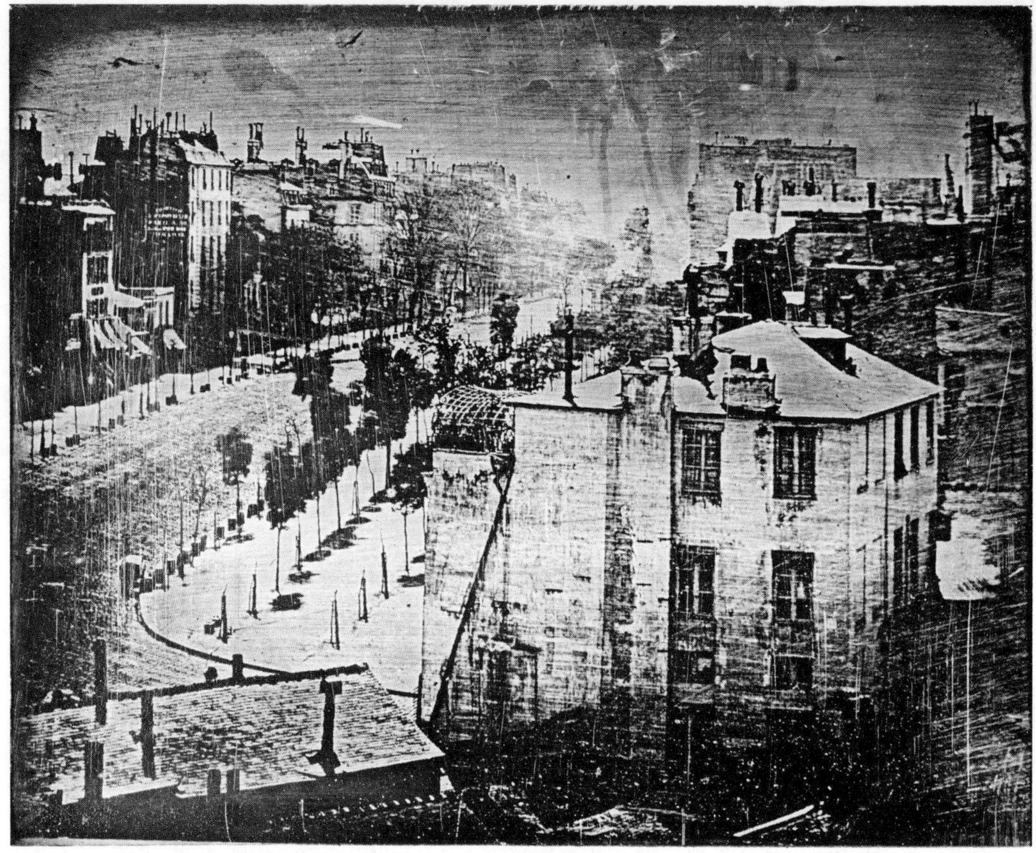

Figure 26. Louis Daguerre, *The Boulevard du Temple*. 1838. Daguerreotype. Courtesy of the Bayerisches Nationalmuseum (inventory no. R 6312.1-8).

"overcome the inertia of our perception," we say that it has "changed form."[41] We also have a vested interest in not perceiving them, since they are epistemologically unmooring. But the movement that escapes *us* is highly visible in the Boulevard du Temple photographs—and not just through the building in the foreground. Through their partial appearance, the man and the horse help us to see that they, too, are less beings than "becomings," and one cannot look at the daguerreotypes for very long without feeling the ground shifting beneath one's feet. This part of Paris was unrecognizable after Baron Haussmann finished "renovating" the city.

There is also another kind of movement in the Boulevard du Temple daguerreotypes, and that is the one through which they emerged. The industrialization of photography has made this movement almost impossible to see, but it was hard to miss in the late 1830s and early 1840s, since exposures were not only long but manifestly developmental. Some pictorial elements appeared earlier than others, and continued evolving until the photograph was chemically stabilized. The photographer consequently had to decide whether to under-expose the "slow" colors so that the "speedy" ones would not be overexposed, or to overexpose the latter so that the former would not be underexposed. Although Gaucheraud does not recognize this movement *as movement*, he describes it brilliantly. "Trees are very well represented [in the Boulevard du Temple daguerreotypes]," he writes "[but] their color . . . hinders the solar rays from producing their image as quickly as that of houses, and other objects of a different color." And this "causes a difficulty for [the] landscape, because there is a certain fixed point of perfection for trees, and another for all objects the colors of which are not green. The consequence is, that when the houses are finished, the trees are not, and when the trees are finished, the houses are too much so."[42]

Robison provides both the most detailed and the most perceptive account of the Boulevard du Temple photographs. Like Morse, he notes the absent crowds and the partial appearance of the man who is having his shoes shined, and explains both through the length of the exposure, but instead of conclud-ing that "objects moving are not impressed," he writes that "vacillating ob-jects make indistinct pictures."[43] This formulation makes room for the ceaseless metamorphosis of the building and the man, and the simultaneity within the photograph of presence and absence, and appearance and disappearance.

Robison also addresses all of the developmental aspects of the series: the gradual emergence of the buildings at dawn, the slow appearance of the image on the photographic plate, and the modulation of light over the course of the day. "A set of three pictures of the same group of houses, one taken soon after sunrise, one at noon, and one in the evening; in these the change of aspect produced by the variations in the distribution of light, was exemplified in a way which art could never attain to," he observes. "One specimen was remark-able from its showing the progress made by light in producing the picture. A plate having been exposed during thirty seconds to the action of the light and then removed, the appearance of the view was that of the earliest dawn of day; there was a grey sky, and a few corners of buildings and other objects beginning to be visible through the deep black in which all the rest of the picture was involved."[44] This passage restores the temporal continuum that Daguerre works so hard to interrupt, and de-substantializes the Boulevard du Temple.

IN 1834 AND 1835, Talbot produced a number of negative photographs by sensi-tizing numerous pieces of paper with sodium chloride and silver nitrate, insert-ing them in tiny camerae obscurae, and exposing the devices to the sun for half an hour.[45] Like Niépce's first successful camera photograph, Talbot's features a window in his house: the oriel window in the south gallery of Lacock Abbey.

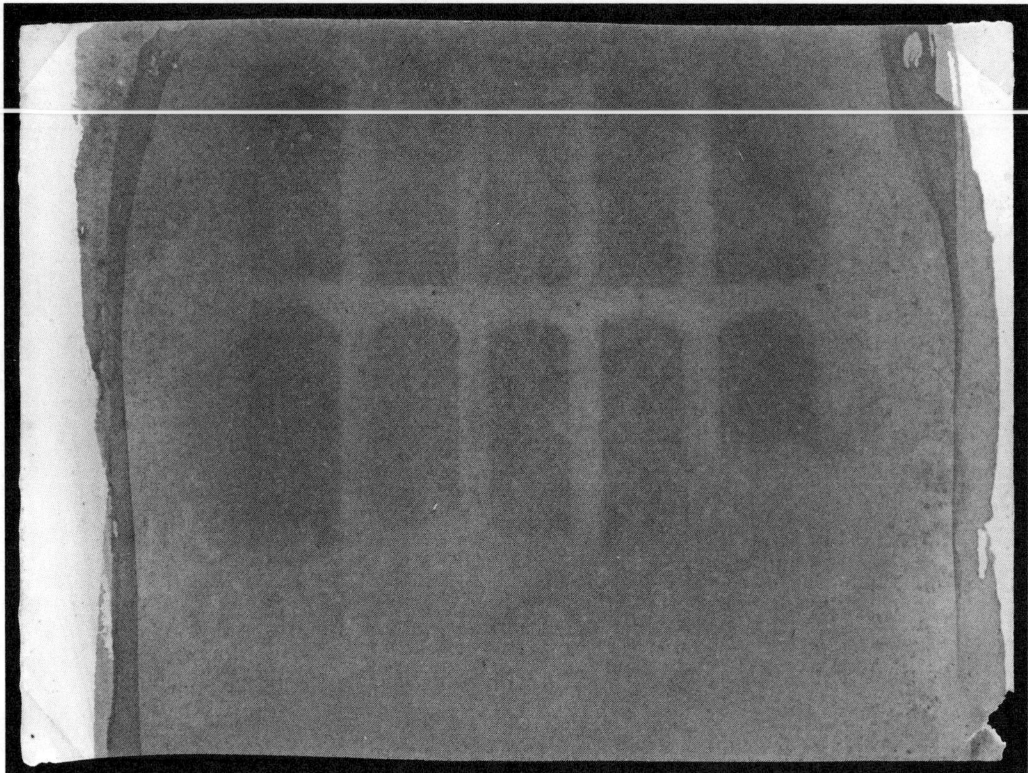

Figure 27. Henry Fox Talbot, *The Oriel Window, South Gallery, Lacock Abbey*, ca. 1835. Photogenic drawing negative.

However, rather than offering a view *from* this window, it offers a view *of* it. It also differs from Niépce's first photograph in another significant way: it can't be attributed to Talbot. The camera obscura within which the photographic plate was exposed to light sat on the mantelpiece across from this window, a position from which only the fireplace could have "looked."[46]

In 1840, Talbot discovered that an image had appeared on a piece of paper that had been in the camera obscura for only a short time, and this discovery helped him develop a new process. By sensitizing his paper with silver nitrate and potassium iodide, moistening it with a solution of acetic acid, silver nitrate, and gallic acid shortly before using it, removing it from the camera obscura when there was only a latent image, and then bathing it in a gallic silver nitrate solution, he dramatically reduced his exposure times—sometimes to as little as thirty seconds. He called the images that resulted from this new and improved process "calotypes."

But Talbot found it almost impossible to retain the images that emerged from his photographic experiments. His early photographs blackened or faded when exposed to light,[47] and although he had better luck with his calotypes, most of which he "fixed" with "hypo," there were still numerous casualties. The images on many of the plates in *The Pencil of Nature* vanished, and a reviewer of the 1862 International Exhibition wrote that some of the calotypes that were exhibited there had "fad[ed] before the eyes of the nations assembled."[48]

Talbot's surviving photographs are also labile in another sense, one that re-calls both *View from a Window*, and the Boulevard du Temple daguerreotypes. They seem—as Gail Buckland puts it—to be "in a state of evolution, of slowly being created by dancing rays of light."[49] And although Talbot was alarmed by the blackening and fading of his photographs, he loved watching the latent image slowly emerge on a sheet of sensitized paper after he removed it from the camera obscura. "I know of few things in the range of science more surprising than the gradual appearance of the picture on the blank sheet," he confided in a February 19, 1841, letter to the editor of the *Literary Gazette*.[50] Talbot also saw this process as a continuation of what happened inside the camera obscura, and attributed it to the same agency. His photographs were not only drawn with the pencil of nature, they were also "self-developing." "One day last September,

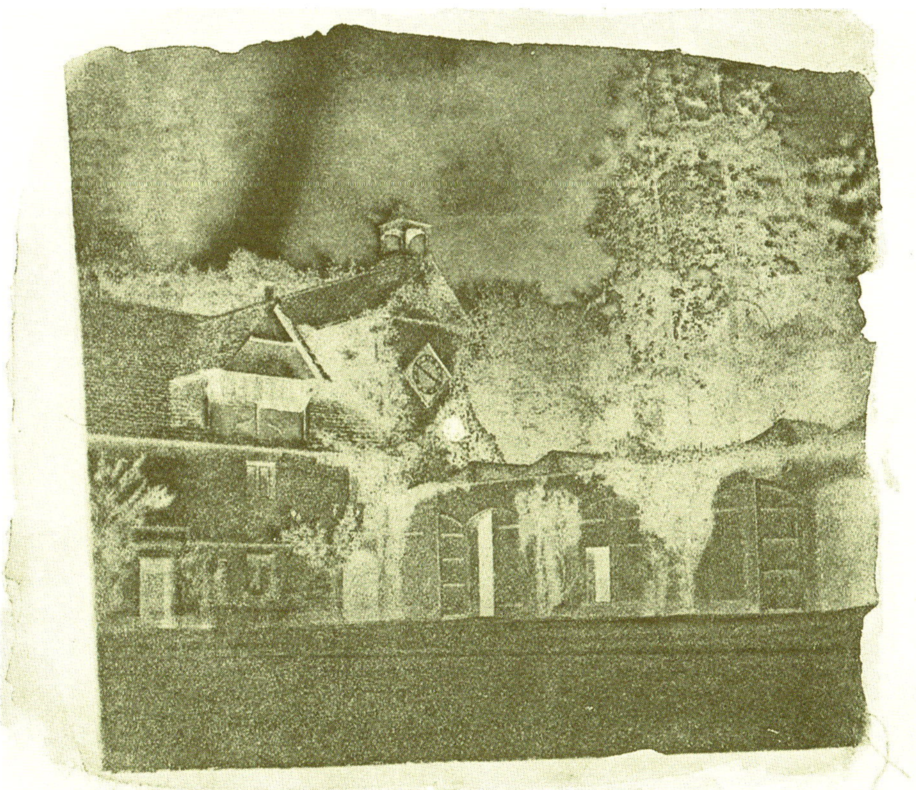

Figure 28/Colorplate 3. Henry Fox Talbot, *The Stable Court, Lacock Abbey*, ca. 1841. Calotype negative. Courtesy of the National Media Museum/SSPL.

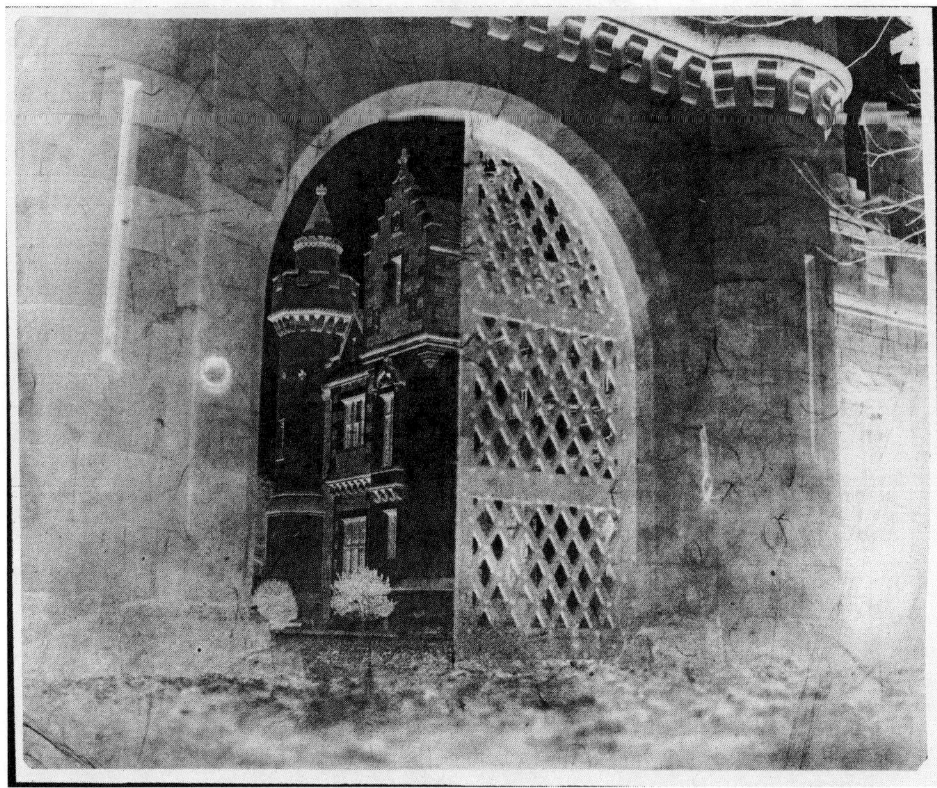

Figure 29/Colorplate 4. Henry Fox Talbot, *Entrance Gate, Abbotsford*, 1845. Calotype negative. Courtesy of the National Media Museum/SSPL.

I had been trying pieces of sensitized paper . . . in the camera obscura, allowing them to remain there for only a short time," he recounts in the same letter. "One of these papers was taken out and examined by candlelight. There was little or nothing to be seen upon it and I left it lying on a table in a dark room. Returning sometime after, I took up the paper and was very much surprised to see upon it a distinct picture . . . the only conclusion that could be drawn was that the picture unexpectedly *developed itself* by a spontaneous action."

Sir David Brewster provides a similar account of Daguerre's procedure in "Photogenic Drawing, or Drawing by the Agency of Light." He characterizes the transformation of a latent daguerreotype into an actual one as a reflexive process, and identifies the people, places, and things that are disclosed through it as the agents of this auto-development. "After remaining a number of minutes, depending on the intensity of the light, the plate is taken out of the camera," he observes, "and placed in what is called a mercury box. There it is exposed to the vapor of mercury. . . . and, after a certain time, the operator, looking through a little window in front of the box, observes the landscape, or figures, gradually *developing themselves* on the surface of the plate."[51] This description, which applies with uncanny precision to the Boulevard du Temple series, locates the daguerreotype's self-development in an ongoing "now" that is more akin to the temporality of the camera obscura's images than to the one we usually attribute to the photographic image.

In an important passage in *The Pencil of Nature*, Talbot confesses that he is constantly seeing new things in his surviving calotypes, suggesting that they went on developing after they were chemically stabilized. "It frequently happens ... that the operator himself discovers on examination, perhaps long afterwards, that he has depicted many things that he had no notion of at the time," he writes. "Sometimes inscriptions and dates are found upon the buildings, or printed placards, most irrelevant, are discovered upon their walls: sometimes a distant dial-plate is seen, and upon it—unconsciously recorded—the hour of the day at which the view was taken."[52] He also makes another astonishing claim: that faded photographs can be "revived" by re-exposing them to the chemicals through which they were developed, and that when they reappear, they often contain new things.[53]

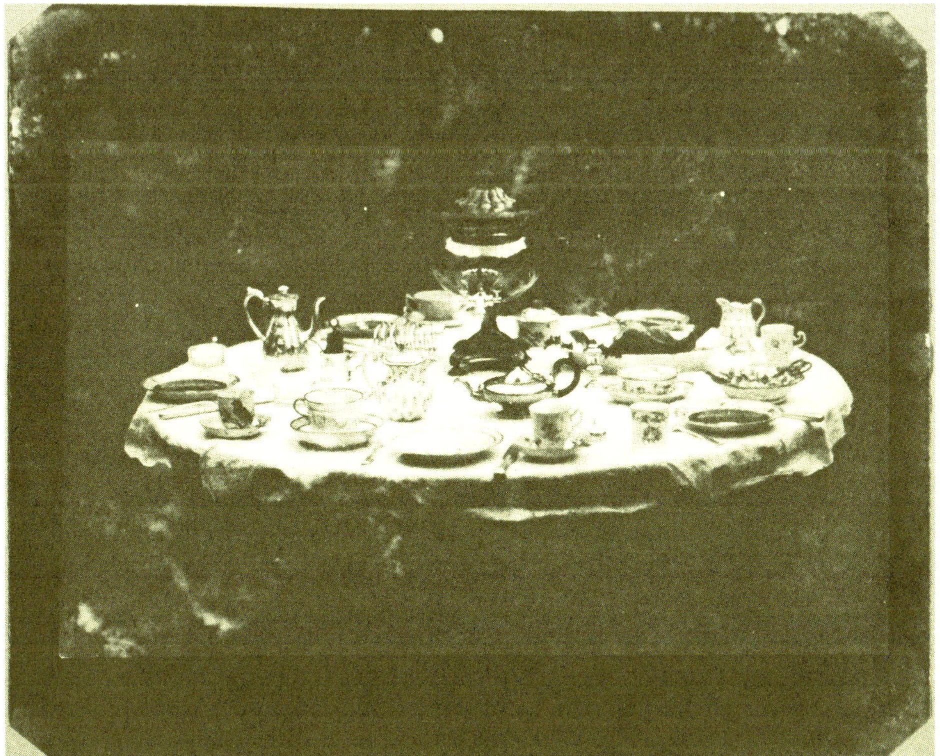

Figure 30. Henry Fox Talbot, *Table set for tea*, ca. 1843. Salted paper print. Courtesy of the National Media Museum/SSPL.

Once again the vehicle of this continuing development is analogy, but of a kind that I have not yet described. Like the analogies through which *View from a Window* and the Boulevard du Temple series were created, those through which Talbot's photographs first emerged were forged in the here and now, and the image evolved in tandem with the world. The analogies through which his photographs continued to develop after they had been chemically stabilized were trans-temporal; they connected an image from one moment in time with an image from another. As Talbot suggests, some of these analogies were psychic. "A casual gleam of sunshine, or a shadow, thrown across [the viewer's] path, a time-withered oak, or a moss covered stone may awaken a train of thought and feelings, and picturesque imaginings," he writes in another passage from *The Pencil of Nature*.[54] Others took a material form, and it was usually during the reproductive process that this material self-development began.

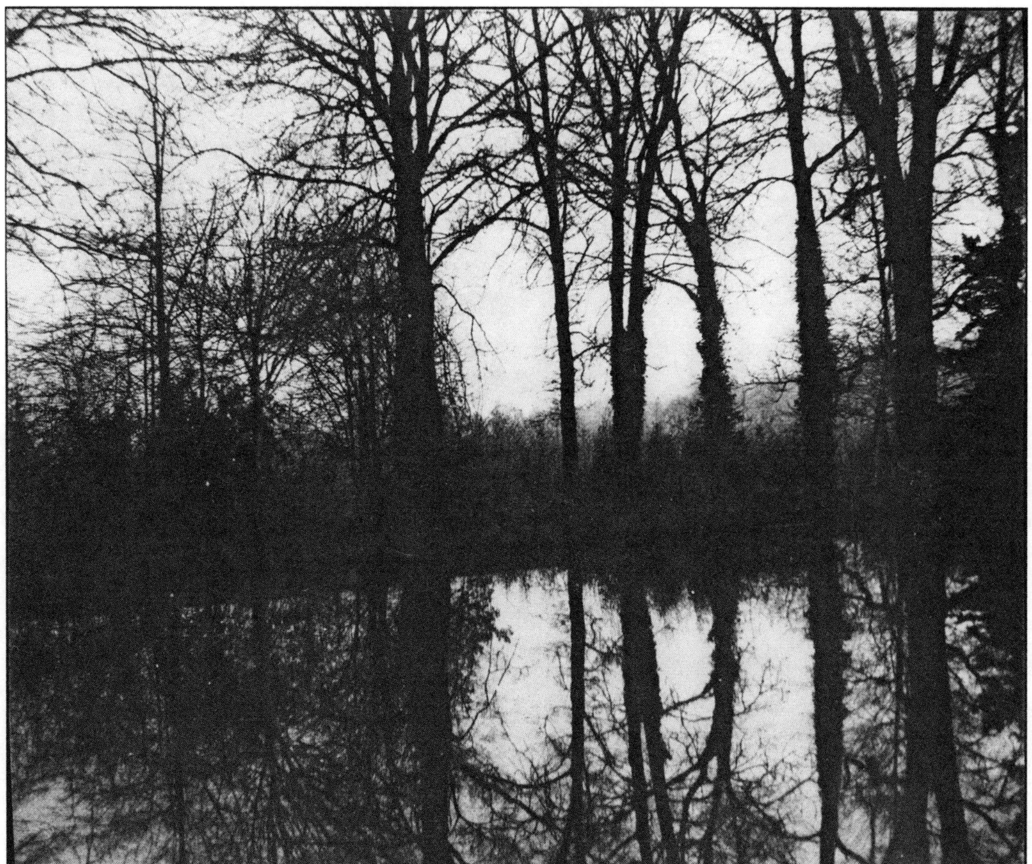

Figure 31. Henry Fox Talbot, *Winter Trees, Reflected in a Pond*, ca. 1841. Salted paper print. Courtesy of the National Media Museum/SSPL.

AS WE HAVE ALREADY SEEN, Daguerre was not interested in reproduction; his photographs were "one of a kind." Although Talbot invented the process that allowed multiple positive prints to be made from a negative, that was not what drew him to photography either. He was slow to deploy it, and when he finally began to "reverse" his "reversed" images, as he called them, he did so by placing a sheet of sensitized paper directly on the negative, then exposing it to light. Since this procedure had to be repeated every time he wanted a positive print, and nothing about it was standardized, the resulting images are far from identical and he defends their differences in *The Pencil of Nature*.[55]

The only one of the three figures I have discussed in this chapter who thought of photography as a primarily reproductive medium was Niépce. He tried to use it to copy engravings, to "take" what he saw when he looked out of his study window, and—finally—to make prints of *View from a Window*. The first of these attempts led to a few recognizable images, the second to one that is barely legible, and the third to nothing at all. Niépce attributed his inability to reproduce *View from a Window* to the "metallic reflection" of the pewter plate, and thought that he would be able to "obtain a vigorous picture" from a glass plate,[56] but history suggests otherwise. In the years since Niépce removed the photograph from the camera obscura and washed it with lavender and white petroleum, there have been numerous attempts to reproduce it, none of which has succeeded.

In 1827, Niépce went to England to visit Claude, who was gravely ill, and he took *View from a Window* with him. While he was there, he met Francis Bauer, a well-known botanical draughtsman, who encouraged him to write a memoir about his discovery for presentation to the Royal Society. Niépce wrote the memoir, but he was so secretive about his process that nothing came of it.[57] He left *View from a Window* with Bauer when he returned to France, and after Bauer's death it passed through several other hands. It was publicly exhibited in 1885 and 1898, and then passed into obscurity.[58]

Helmut and Alison Gernsheim spent six years trying to track down *View from a Window*, and in 1952 they finally found what they were looking for, in a large trunk in England. When he first saw the photograph, Helmut Gernsheim recounts in his most comprehensive account of this discovery,[59] he thought that he was looking at a mirror in an Empire frame. He went to the window, and angled the plate in various directions, and eventually the image came into view. Astonishingly, given that Gernsheim wrote this essay more than half a century after the industrialization of photography, he attributes its appearance to the courtyard, rather than to Niépce's action, or his own intervention. He also suggests that this self-disclosure happened gradually; the "entire courtyard scene *unfolded itself* in front of my eyes," he observes (my emphasis).[60]

Gernsheim persuaded the owner of the heliograph to donate it to his extensive photography collection, and immediately tried to photograph it, but all that appeared in the resulting images was his camera. He then asked Scotland Yard to help him reproduce it, reasoning that since photographers there were "so expert in detecting invisible spots, scratches, hair, and fingerprints where the eye can see nothing at all," making a copy of a "clearly recognizable image" should be "easy game." When Britain's famous detective agency declined to put its public services to private uses, he turned first to the *Times*, where the project was deemed to be "impossible," and then to the National Gallery, whose highly skilled photographers tried, but failed, to reproduce *View from a Window*. Finally, thinking that the "giants of the photographic industry" would feel "in honor bound to produce a result," Gernsheim approached the Research Laboratory of the Eastman Kodak Company in Harrow, and the director agreed to try. But although the Eastman Kodak technicians worked on the project for three weeks, Gernsheim found the resulting photograph a "gross distortion of the original," and prohibited its publication until 1977.[61]

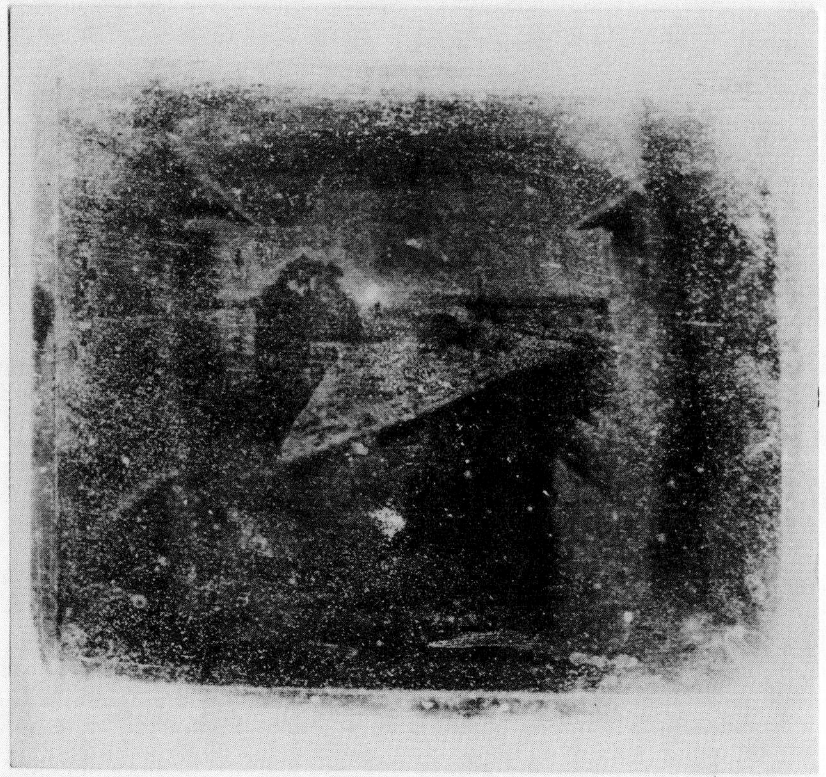

Figure 32. *View from the Window at Le Gras* as reproduced by the Kodak Research Laboratory (Harrow, UK), 1952. Silver-gelatin print from original heliograph on pewter. Courtesy of the Harry Ransom Center at the University of Texas at Austin.

As we can see from the first institution to which he turned for help—Scotland Yard—Gernsheim imputed an evidentiary value to the photographic image. He believed that a photograph of *View from a Window* would preserve this "important document," and he approached the heliograph itself in the same way. "Though Niépce's estate, Gras, was altered to some extent by later owners, the tower (pigeon house) on the left of the photograph still stands, and is in fact *on the left* when looking out of the window of Niépce's attic workroom," he writes in *The History of Photography*, "a proof that a prism was used when taking the photograph. These two facts make it quite certain that the view cannot have been taken before 1826."[62] This passage recalls those in which Niépce tried to align his photographs with what he saw when he looked out of his workroom window.

In 1963, Gernsheim gave *View from a Window* to the Harry Ransom Center at the University of Texas, Austin, and in June 2002, the center sent it to the Getty Conservation Institute to be examined and reproduced. The institute's technicians adopted an even more forensic approach to the

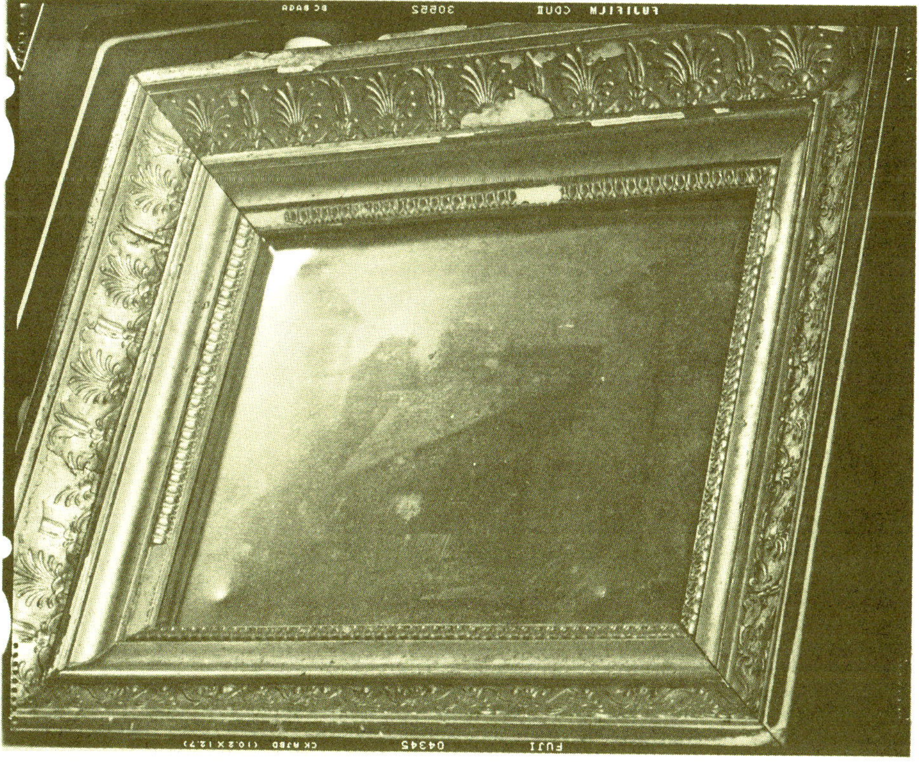

Figure 33/Colorplate 5. *View from the Window at Le Gras* in its original frame. Courtesy of the Harry Ransom Center at the University of Texas at Austin.

photograph. They spent "a day and a half with the original heliograph in their photographic studios in order to record photographically and digitally all aspects of the plate." They also documented it "under all manner of scientific lights, including ultraviolet spectra," and "produced new color film and digital/electronic copies of the plate, in an attempt to reveal more of the unretouched image while still providing a sense of the complex physical state of the photograph."[63] But the digital images that are displayed on the Harry Ransom Center website are no more revealing of the "unretouched image" than the Kodak photograph is.

Gernsheim and the Getty technicians attribute the heliograph's unreproducibility to Niépce's underexposure of the original plate. This explanation, however, is unnecessary, because there is no blame to apportion. The Kodak photograph and all of the images that have appeared on the Harry Ransom Center website are not "bad copies," or even "representations of representations";[64] rather, they are some of the analogies through which the heliograph has continued to self-develop. This creative evolution began with a nonphotographic image, and gained momentum through another unholy alliance: a "manipulated" photograph of an over-painted photograph.

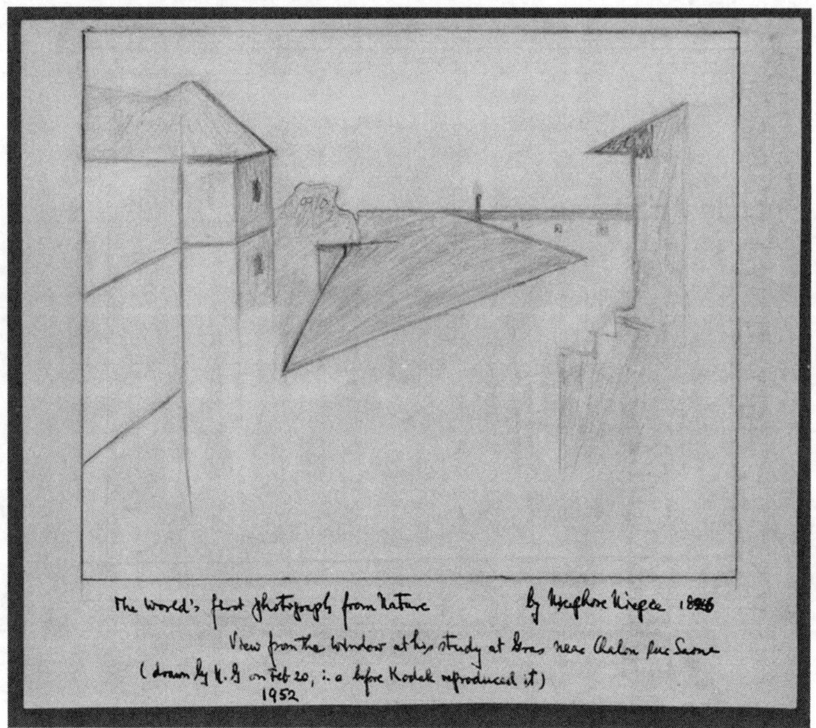

Figure 34. Helmut Gernsheim, drawing of *View from the Window at Le Gras*, 1952. Pencil on paper. Courtesy of the Harry Ransom Center at the University of Texas at Austin.

When Gernsheim realized that he would have to surrender the heliograph to a "research laboratory" in order to have it reproduced, he decided to make a drawing of it on the same scale, so that he would have a record of the "crucial document" if something happened to it. We do not usually attribute evidentiary value to a drawing, and this one warrants no exception. Instead of an elusive image hidden in the illusionistic depths of a shiny pewter plate, it is a legible sketch on a flat sheet of non-reflective paper. It also privileges line over mass, and reverses the photograph's tonal values. But this does not mean that the heliograph and the drawing are two separate images. The shapes in the drawing echo those in the heliograph, and the heliograph also resembles the drawing in some surprising ways. *View from a Window* would be as useless in a court of law as the drawing; it corresponded *with* the ceaselessly changing scene outside Niépce's window on the day it was made, rather than *to* it. It was also drawn with a "pencil": the pencil of light. These are aspects of the photograph that we would not see without Gernsheim's drawing. *View from a Window* reasserts itself as heliograph—a gift from the world to us—in an astonishing way: through an image drawn with a human hand.

When the Kodak technicians failed to produce a satisfactory copy of *View from a Window*, Gernsheim had nowhere else to go, so he and his wife spent nearly two days applying pointillist watercolor dots to one of their prints, so as to make it more representative of the heliograph. When he photographed this over-painted photograph, he "held back the sky, the roof of the barn, and a few other features that were bright in the original, not black." Gernsheim was keenly aware of the differences between the heliograph and this image. His photograph of the over-painted photograph is "a more uniform and clearly defined image" than the Kodak print, he writes in "The 150th Anniversary of Photography," but its "pointillistic effect" is "completely alien" to Niépce's "medium," which is "as smooth as a mirror."[65] However, he nevertheless called it the "rare original" in his 1952 account of his study, and mandated that it be the heliograph's primary representative for twenty-five years.

Much later, after this "ruse" was discovered, Gernsheim responded to his critics in the following way: "Because it became known that I had touched up Kodak's reproduction some people ignorant of the original plate, misconstrued my intention, believing I had been trying to improve on Niépce, whereas I had merely been trying to improve upon Kodak, to restore Niépce."[66] The word "intention" figures prominently here; it is, indeed, the pivot on which his defense turns. Gernsheim's detractors imputed the wrong intention to him, he argued, and he was sure that when they realized that he was merely trying to reassert Niépce's intention, they would exonerate him.

But not only can we never fully know what anyone else intends, we can never fully know what *we* intend. Gernsheim was also contending with another intentionality, one that militated against a return to the "original": the photograph's own impulsion toward a further self-development. This impulsion was the driving force behind the many transformations to which Gernsheim subjected *View from a Window*. I say "many" because the drawing and the over-painted photograph weren't the only analogies generated by Gernsheim. The entire process began with a mental image or group of images, and when Gernsheim touched up the photograph, he analogized this analogy. The over-painted photograph is—as Barbara Brown discreetly puts it—"his approximation of how he felt the original should appear in reproduction."[67]

Even now, it is to this image that most of us turn when we want to look at *View from a Window*, and for good reason. Like the heliograph, it evolved slowly, through the gradual accumulation of marks. In the former case, as in the latter case, there was no necessary end point to this evolution. Finally, although the heliograph's "image layer" was long assumed to consist of a solid coat of bitumen, the Getty's "XRF analysis" showed that it is actually a random pattern of bitumen "microdots."[68] Since Gernsheim died long before the Getty analyzed the heliograph, he never knew about these microdots, but they surfaced through his dots of watercolor paint, like an image in a developing bath.

In spring 2013, an "interactive" version of *View from a Window* appeared on the Harry Ransom Center's website. It is a digital composite of two other images: Gernsheim's drawing, and the most frequently exhibited of the center's "high-tech" photographs of the heliograph. The former is superimposed on the latter, and used to divide it into identifiable segments. If one clicks on a segment, as one is invited to do, its outlines light up with an orange glow, and the pertinent information appears to the left of the image (e.g., "bake house roof, no longer standing"). This is a continuation of the forensic project begun by Niépce and renewed by Gernsheim and the Getty technicians. But once again another intentionality also makes itself felt. Although the two composited images echo each other, they do not merge. Some of the lines of the superimposed diagram extend beyond or cut into the shadowy shapes of the underlying buildings. These discrepancies prevent the image that they both inhabit from forming a seamless whole. The "interactive" version of *View from a Window* is consequently manifestly analogical, and it links chemical photography to digital photography, as well as to drawing.

A 2005 work by Joan Fontcuberta—*Googlegram: Niépce*—is another installment in this ongoing story, and the one with which I will conclude my own narrative.[69] From a distance, *Googlegram: Niépce* looks like a blown-up, slightly

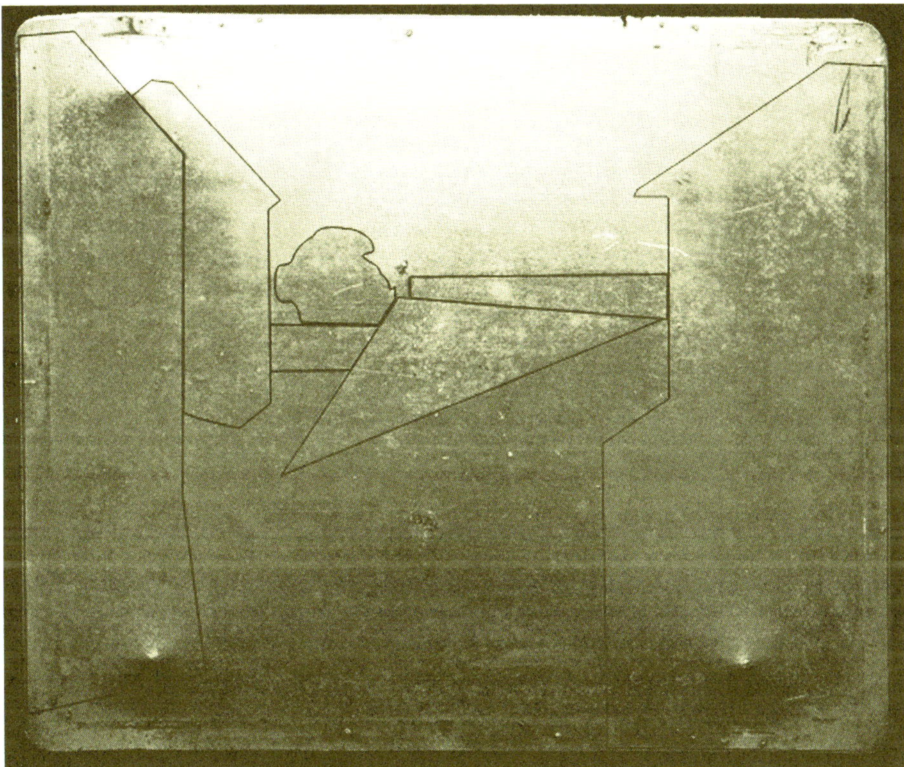

Figure 35/Colorplate 5. *View from the Window at Le Gras* with Gernsheim's pencil drawing superimposed. Courtesy of the Harry Ransom Center at the University of Texas at Austin.

colorized version of Gernsheim's over-painted photograph. As one approaches the work, though, it begins to morph. First the image becomes less resolute, then it turns into an abstract picture, and eventually it dissolves into a vast mosaic of tiny jpegs. There are far more images here than our eyes could ever see, even if we were to spend the rest of our lives looking at them, making *Google-gram: Niépce* a powerful reminder of the limits of human vision, and the inexhaustibility of the perceptual world. The work also challenges our sovereignty in another important way: by exposing us to a multitude of other intentionalities.

Two of these intentionalities are computational. Fontcuberta begins a Googlegram by locating an image that is "an icon of our time," and that is linked to one or more words. He then conducts a Google image search with this word or set of words, and reconstitutes the iconic image with the jpegs to which this search leads through a freeware photomosaic program.[70] The search part of this process ignores both the visual qualities of the images it finds and their affinities to each other; it is relentlessly linguistic. But it also treats words as classificatory units, rather than as sources of meaning or one of the "houses" of Being. It is thus as impervious to the complexity of the *words* with which

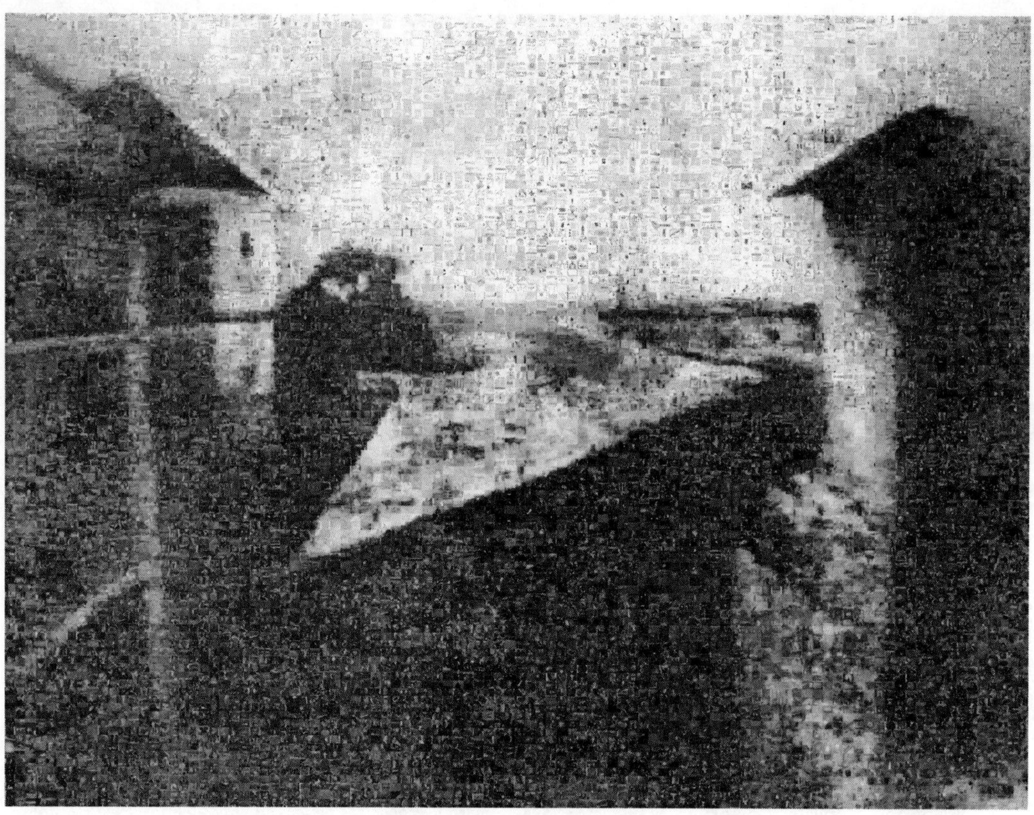

Figure 36/Colorplate 6. Juan Fontcuberta, *Googlegram: Niépce*, 2005. Chromogenic print. Courtesy of the artist.

it searches as it is to the *images* it finds, and this leads to all kinds of errors, or what Fontcuberta calls "archive noise."[71] Although the photomosaic program is also relentlessly single-minded and indifferent to the images with which it works, its "logic" is visual, instead of verbal. It arranges the jpegs strictly according to their "chromatic value and density."[72]

The iconic image that Fontcuberta refashions in *Googlegram: Niépce* is of course Gernsheim's over-painted photograph, and he searched for its 10,000 jpegs with the words "photo" and "foto." Since *View from a Window* is often called "the first photograph," on the Internet, as in the classroom, there is an unusually tight connection between it and the search words, but since every image on the Internet is a digital photograph, the search also encompassed all of them. The photomosaic program forged similar links between the over-painted photograph and these digital photographs. *Googlegram: Niépce* is a photograph constructed out of 10,000 smaller photographs, found by searching with the words "photo" and "foto" and assembled by a photomosaic program. There seems to be no room here for anything but these two meaningless and highly reiterative intentionalities, both of which scream "photography."

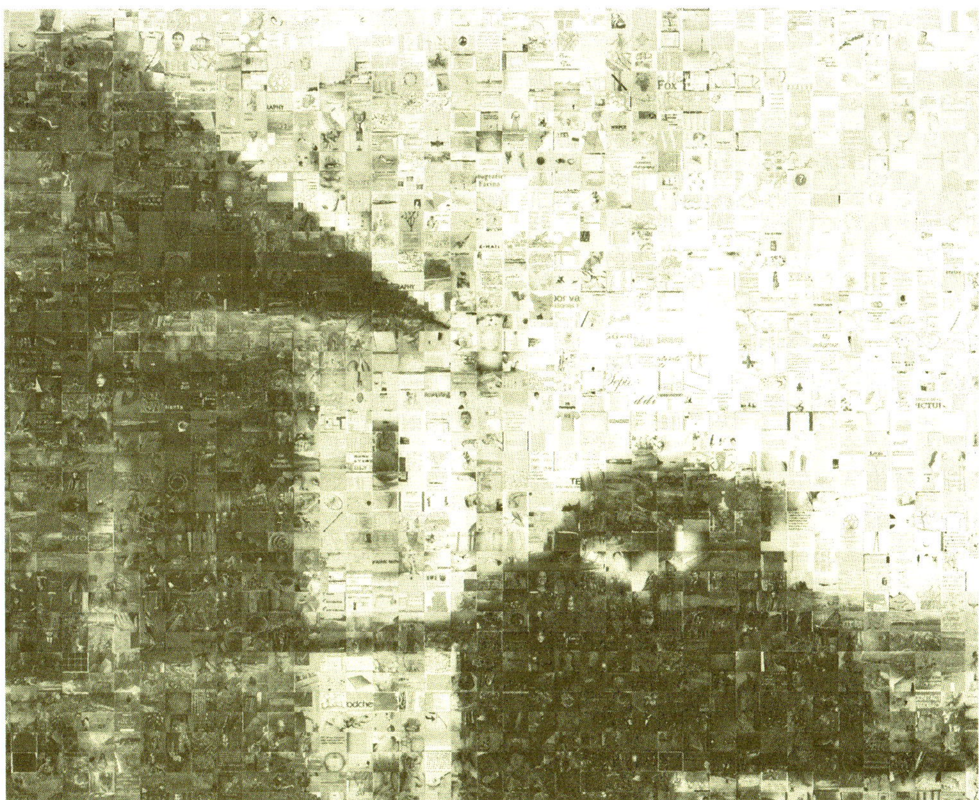

Figure 37/Colorplate 7. Juan Fontcuberta, *Googlegram: Niépce* (detail). Courtesy of the artist.

But although a photomosaic promotes totality from a distance, it works against it up close, as do all mosaics, and Fontcuberta is interested in this double optic. He also believes that the "structure of mosaic"—which dates back to 3000 B.C.—can be found in all photography. Chemical photography is "an irregular mosaic of silver halogen molecules," he writes, a printed image is a "mosaic of dots that inform the photomechanical frame," and a digital photograph is "produced by the grey tint of pixels."[73] As we have already seen, the Getty technicians also found a mosaic when they analyzed *View from a Window*, and Gernsheim brought this mosaic to the surface with his pointillist dots. And not only is *Googlegram: Niépce* itself a mosaic, but its 10,000 jpegs also render both the bitumen dots in Niépce's photograph and the watercolor dots in Gernsheim's over-painted photograph *hyper-visible*.

The photomosaic program also adds something to the mosaic tradition, something that makes room for another kind of intentionality. In a conventional mosaic, Fontcuberta writes, each component is "a pure spot of color without meaning," but in a photomosaic it is a photograph, which "still [has] a meaning by [itself]." This meaning isn't the kind we mobilize by identifying

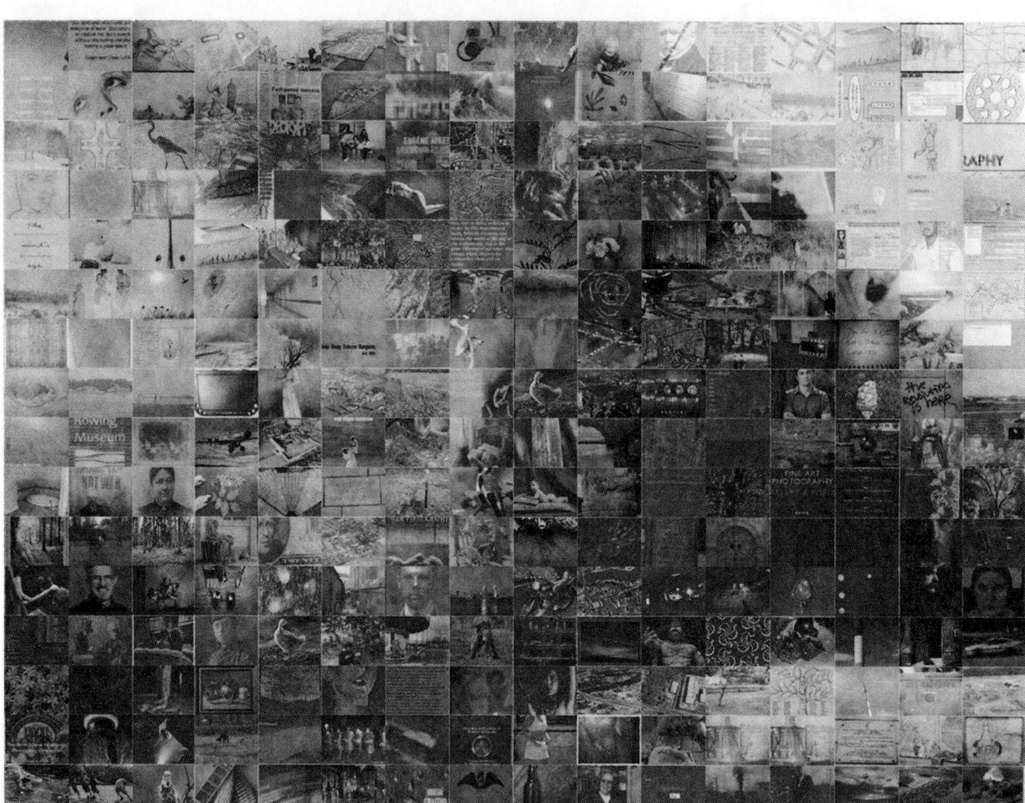

Figure 38/Colorplate 7. Juan Fontcuberta, *Googlegram: Niépce* (detail). Courtesy of the artist.

what is "in" a photograph; it is, rather, the inexhaustible significance that every being should always have for us, and that the photographic image helps us to experience. The first time I came close enough to see the sea of faces in *Googlegram: Niépce*, I had this experience. I felt that they "expected" my arrival, and that there was a "secret agreement" between them and me. I also knew—with the kind of knowledge that bypasses all reason—that this agreement gave them a "claim" on me.[74]

Although Fontcuberta does not say so, the 10,000 jpegs that make up *Googlegram: Niépce* also have yet another kind of intentionality. When we conduct a Google image search, the search engine looks for the images that have been most frequently linked to our search word. These links, however, have been forged by other Internet users, and reflect their predilections, antipathies, rivalries, and desires, instead of our own. That is why we are so often frustrated by what the search finds. By running his Google image search through a photomosaic program that arranged the results according to chromatic value and intensity, Fontcuberta prevented himself from selecting the jpegs that he liked and eliminating those that he found alien or irritating. He opened the door of his work to images that were tagged and uploaded by thousands of other users, and in which their affects were still lodged. He did so, I believe, because the human psyche is another of the places where the photographic image develops.

WATER IN THE CAMERA

IN 1989, Jeff Wall published a short essay called "Photography and Liquid Intelligence." Like most of the other writings that we return to again and again, it is full of seemingly unresolvable contradictions. These contradictions radiate out from the notion of "liquid intelligence," which links terms that are hard to think together and whose locus keeps shifting. Sometimes Wall attributes this intelligence to liquids, sometimes he situates it within chemical photography, and sometimes he imputes it to nature, the world, or even the cosmos. He distinguishes it at every point in his argument from another kind of intelligence: "optical" or "technological" intelligence. But this concept is also unstable, and he adopts a different attitude toward it in the second half of the essay than he does in the first.[1]

Wall begins "Photography and Liquid Intelligence" with one of his own works, *Milk* (1984). In the lower right corner of the light box, an apparently indigent man sits on the pavement in front of a red brick wall. The wall fills most of the right side of the picture, and part of the left. There is an inexplicable gap between it and the next building, where weeds are collecting. This building is a hodgepodge of materials and architectural signifiers, all of which feel strangely truncated, and none of which has any discernible function or meaning. It combines a narrow strip of fake bricks with a large window framed in black metal, and a patch of stucco wall. The window connotes "shop," but what its glass reveals of the interior—a small door opening onto a staircase—suggests that it is a residential building. This is form at its most arbitrary.

The man's left hand is clenched, and his left arm—whose angularity rhymes with the horizontal pattern of the brick—is rigid with anger. He looks to the right, and his left knee is also turned in this direction, but his right knee points in the other direction. He holds a milk carton in a brown paper bag in his right hand, out of which milk erupts. Since this is one of Wall's most "psychological" works, one is sorely tempted to read the liquid symptomatically—to interpret it as a signifier of the man's rage against the social order from which he is excluded,

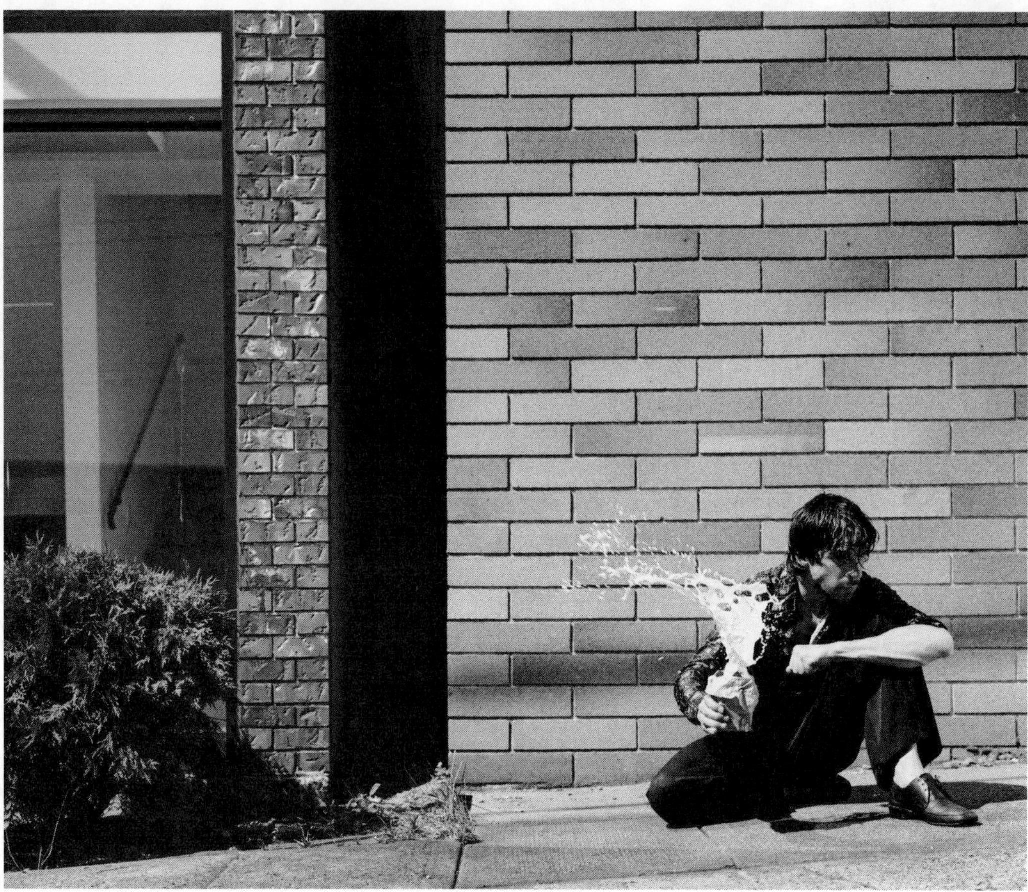

Figure 39/Colorplate 8. Jeff Wall, *Milk*, 1984. Transparency in light box. Courtesy of the artist.

and his body's double directionality as the manifestation of an internal division. The light box, though, is named after the milk, not the man, and Wall also focuses on the milk in his 1989 essay. He associates it with lability and incalculability, and he opposes it to "form," rather than to society or a psychic entity.

"In *Milk*, as in some of my other pictures, an important part is played by complicated natural forms," Wall writes. "The explosion of the milk from its container takes a shape which is not really describable or characterizable, but which provokes many associations. A natural form, with its unpredictable contours, is an expression of infinitesimal metamorphoses of quality."[2] This is the first instantiation of the concept invoked in the title, and Wall invites us to interpret it both literally and metaphorically: as a quality that liquids have and also as the fluidity of what we imagine to be solid forms. Photography is based on a dramatically different kind of movement, he declares: the mechanical opening and closing of the shutter. This movement gives it a "substratum of instantaneity."[3]

The passage I have just summarized could have been lifted directly out of Bergson's *Creative Evolution*, and it seems the perfect segue to one of the philosopher's primary claims: the claim that since photography brings everything to a halt, it is incapable of registering these metamorphoses.[4] Wall, however, heads off in another direction. He argues that the camera's instantaneity permits it to "see" much more quickly than we do—almost as fast as liquids metamorphose. This makes it the ideal medium for representing this movement. The fact that it does so in such a "dry" and "glassed-in" way is also an advantage rather than a disadvantage, since it shows us that photography is an "institution," remote from nature.[5] By immobilizing the movement whose properties it renders visible, photography demonstrates that its intelligence is "ocular," not "liquid." And the glass needs to be there, because you "certainly don't want any water in your camera."[6]

Later in the same paragraph, Wall reshuffles the deck. Chemical photography relies on water and other fluids, he now argues, and these fluids connect it to "very ancient production-processes" from "the origins of techne"—processes like washing, bleaching, and dissolving, that have not emerged "from the mineral and vegetable worlds."[7] They also give it a liquid as well as an ocular intelligence. Photography's liquid intelligence makes it unpredictable and uncontrollable, and hence hard to "rationalize." Computation liberates the dry part of the medium from this unhappy alliance by eliminating liquids "from the immediate production-process."[8]

There are echoes of Heidegger in this argument,[9] and they become more pronounced as Wall proceeds. Technology may be the vehicle through which we purge photography of liquidity, he argues, but the intelligence behind this evacuation is human. The goal of the exercise is also dispiritingly familiar: separation from and conquest of the world. "Th[e] expansion of the dry part of photography I see metaphorically as a kind of hubris of the orthodox technological intelligence which, secured behind a barrier of perfectly engineered glass, surveys natural forms in its famous cool manner," Wall writes. And this look may not be as "cool" as it appears to be. Human vision becomes "ballistic" when it is "augmented by glass."[10] It is now the world that needs protection, not the camera.

At first glance, this argument meshes perfectly with the narrative I have been recounting. In the first chapter of its history, photography's intelligence was entirely liquid. A continuous stream of evanescent images entered the darkened space of the camera obscura from outside, dynamically analogizing its equally labile source, and encouraging the viewer to "energize" the world by corresponding with it both psychically and aesthetically. This liquidity washed away all of the distinctions on which modern subjectivity depends, and rendered certain knowledge impossible, so seventeenth-century man attempted to "ocularize" the camera obscura by substituting mental representations for the perceptual world, and transforming the camera obscura into a device for arresting its image stream.

Most of the latter devices were incorporated into tables and desks, at which the viewer sat, and on which he drew. Although they encouraged him to see himself as the source of the resulting image, they did not attribute the stream of images on which he based his drawing to his look. The camera obscura also mediated his encounter with the world. He was consequently still at the mercy of the device's liquid intelligence. But in 1694, Robert Hooke designed an optical camera obscura that fit over the head of its user and moved when he did, as if it were a part of his body. The figure in the illustrative etching of this device draws on the screen "through" which he surveys the world, in a seemingly unmediated way. The "ballistic" and "projectile" qualities that Wall associates with the "glassed-in" look are communicated through its shape, and its user towers over the landscape in which he stands, his head in the celestial light. "I see, I draw, I conquer" is the etching's implied caption.

And what was only a dream in 1694 is now a reality. "Woolgathering Freudians" may worry about "the allusions to firearms and warfare that permeate the terminology of photography," as Todd Gustavson remarks in his history of the camera,[11] but the rest of us happily "load" our camera, "aim" at what we want to "capture," and "shoot." And since our cameras are digital, and we process them on our computers, everything is calculable. Soon there will be no more darkrooms or developing labs, and photography will be completely dry.[12] However, it wasn't until the 1880s that the verb "to take" decisively replaced the verb "to receive" and "shoot" became a synonym for "take." It was also only through the industrialization of chemical photography that this shift occurred. Most of the terms through which we conceptualize the medium were manufactured for us, just like our equipment and material.

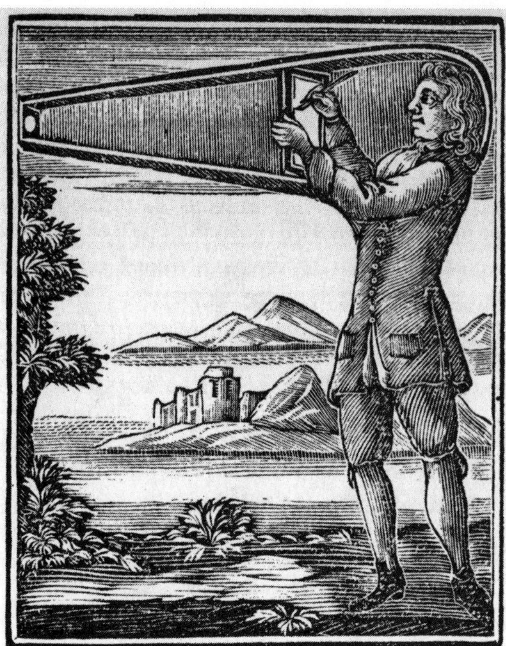

Figure 40. Engraving from Robert Hooke, *Philosophical Experiments and Observations*, 1727.

THE OCULARIZATION of chemical photography began—as one would expect—with the camera. Daguerre designed the apparatus for which his process
called, and signed a contract with his brother-in-law Alphonse Giroux to man-
ufacture and sell it. The device, which was similar to the one he himself used,
was a fixed-bed, double-box camera, which the operator focused by sliding the
rear box into the slightly larger front box. Twenty-five percent of the profits
from this enterprise went to him, and his name was used to market the camera
and undercut competitors. Giroux attached a plaque to the device that read:
"No apparatus is guaranteed if it does not bear the signature of M. Daguerre
and the seal of M. Giroux."[13]

To make the camera more attractive, Giroux sold it with a kit containing
everything else that an operator would need to make a daguerreotype: polished
plate, spirit lamp, mercury box, box for iodizing, chemicals, and buff stick. He also
equipped it with a landscape-type lens, presumably so that he could patent it as
a new design, and others followed suit. In 1841, N. P. Lerebours added a simple
shutter to a camera of similar design, in 1843 Charles Chevalier hinged the sides
of the boxes, allowing the camera to be folded up, in 1845 another French manufacturer created a camera with a three-box focusing system, and in 1851 W. &
W. H. Lewis designed a camera with an internal bellows that was transportable
and that permitted the operator to change the focus and alter the perspective.[14]

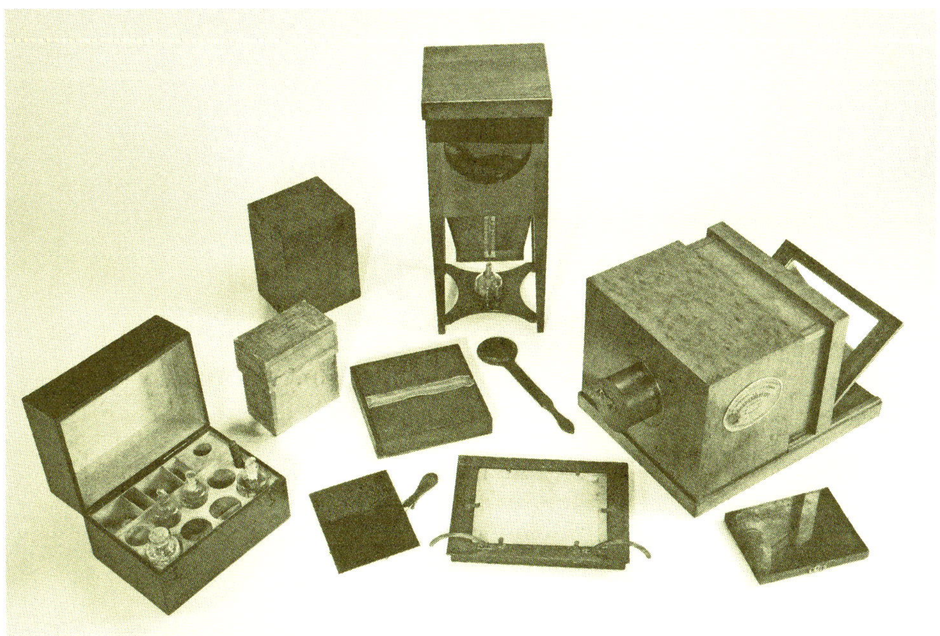

Figure 41. Giroux daguerreotype camera, 1839. Courtesy of the George Eastman House, International Museum
of Photography and Film.

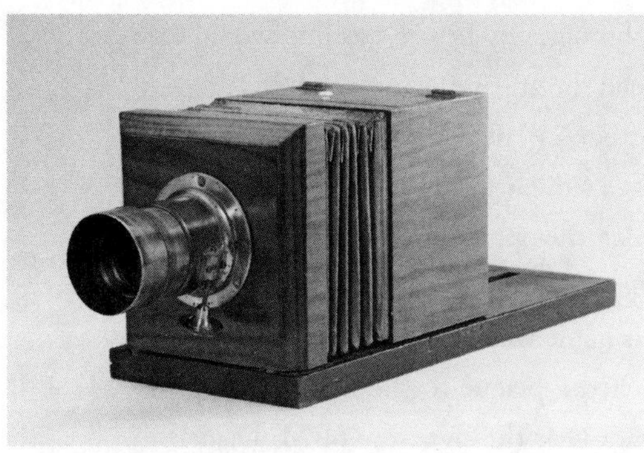

Figure 42. Lewis daguerreotype camera (quarter plate), ca. 1851. Courtesy of the George Eastman House, International Museum of Photography and Film.

These innovations made the camera easier to use, but they did nothing to conceal the distance between the operator's look and the camera lens. Not only were the lens and the viewfinder at opposite ends of the device, but focusing the lens and exposing the photographic plate were manifestly separate events. The photographer also had only limited control over the first, and none over the second. In order to bring the image that would later emerge into conformity with the one he wanted to "obtain," or even to have some sense of the one that he was likely to receive, he was obliged to open the camera shutter, slide a ground-glass plate into the frame designed for the photographic plate, look at the image that appeared on it, and adjust the lens until it came into focus. Because of the amount of light in the camera, this image was faint, so focusing it required a lot of guesswork. In order to expose the photographic plate, the photographer had to remove the ground glass, close the shutter, slide the plate into the frame, and reopen the shutter long enough for the image to be received. And once the photographic plate was in place, he was unable to see what was happening inside the camera.

Between 1858 and 1862, three cameras were created that should have made it easier for the operator to believe that he was "in control." In 1861 Thomas Sutton designed and patented a single-lens reflex plate camera, which narrowed the gap between focusing and exposure.[15] A mirror was positioned between the lens and the photographic plate, which reflected the luminous image stream entering the camera to the viewfinder, obviating the need to replace the ground glass with the photographic plate prior to exposure, and giving the operator a much better sense of what the camera would be "seeing." After focusing the lens, he raised the mirror with a manual lever so that the photographic exposure could occur.

In 1858, Thomas Skaife created a small camera with a lens so fast that it could register slow-moving objects. He modeled it on a gun, and named it the "Pistolgraph." People also perceived it as a weapon; Skaife was "nearly arrested" when he directed it at Queen Victoria—and cameras were by then a familiar part of the cultural landscape.[16] The Pistolgraph couldn't be "fired from the hip," since it required a tripod, but in 1862 the French company A. Briois began manufacturing

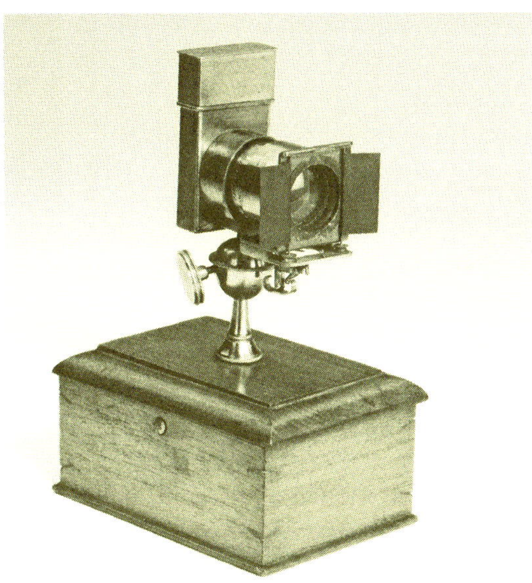

Figure 43. Pistolgraph by Thomas Skaife, London, ca. 1859. Courtesy of the George Eastman House, International Museum of Photography and Film.

a gun-shaped camera that was designed to be handheld: Thompson's Revolver Camera.[17] Like the Colt revolver,[18] on which it was modeled, Thompson's Revolver Camera had a rotating cylinder that allowed its user to "shoot" multiple times before "reloading."

Surprisingly, though, Sutton's single-lens reflex camera never went into production, and there is a dearth of information about it, suggesting that it didn't appeal to the popular imagination.[19] There was also little interest in the gun-shaped cameras; the Pistolgraph wasn't reproduced, and only one hundred issues of Thompson's Revolver Camera were manufactured.[20] These devices didn't catch on, I believe, because the other aspects of chemical photography were still so "wet"—literally as well as metaphorically. The medium's practitioners experimented with a dizzying number of chemicals and foods in their attempt to find substances sensitive enough to receive the photographic image "expeditiously." The season, the weather, and the time of day all complicated this search, because what

worked in one set of conditions often failed to work in another, and often for reasons that were difficult to understand. "When'er the wind is in the East, / Use twice the seconds at the least," wrote a midcentury wit. "And if the East incline to the North, / Take not the wretched sitter forth. / Come cloud electric, or of hail, / Then every picture's sure to fail, / But with light zephyrs from the West, / In scarce five seconds 'tis imprest" / And if the West incline to South, / In three you have eyes, nose and mouth."[21]

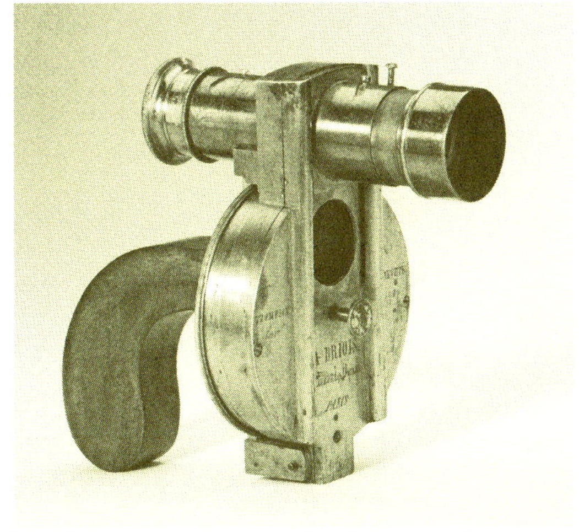

Figure 44. Thompson's Revolver Camera, ca. 1862. Courtesy of the George Eastman House, International Museum of Photography and Film.

There are several similar passages in Lady Eastlake's 1857 essay, in one of which she observes that photography is "too profoundly interlocked with the deep things of Nature to be entirely unlocked by any given method," and in another of which she concludes that the "subtle agenc[y]" on which the photographer depends will "never be taught implicitly to obey."[22]

Photography's practitioners also searched long and hard for a substance potent enough to retain the images that appeared on their recipient plates. After so many of the calotypes in *The Pencil of Nature* vanished, photographers started using albumen paper, but these prints were also unreliable. In 1855 the Royal Photographic Society of London created a Fading Committee to address the problem.[23] And since the daguerreotype was one of a kind, and Talbot's positive prints so varied, photographers were no closer to reaching the third and most important of Niépce's goals: reproduction.

In 1851, Frederick Scott Archer introduced the collodion wet plate, which required only a few seconds of exposure and which produced a sharply delineated negative on a glass plate, from which many nearly identical positive prints could be made. It was a complicated process, though, with many steps, all of which had to be performed within ten minutes, before the chemicals dried. After polishing the plate, the photographer coated it with a solution of collodion, ether, alcohol, potassium iodine, and nitrated cellulose, making sure that it was evenly distributed. He then sensitized the plate by dipping it in a bath of silver nitrate, and placed it in the camera. The silver nitrate solution often dripped, resulting in stains and chemical buildup on his equipment, and the

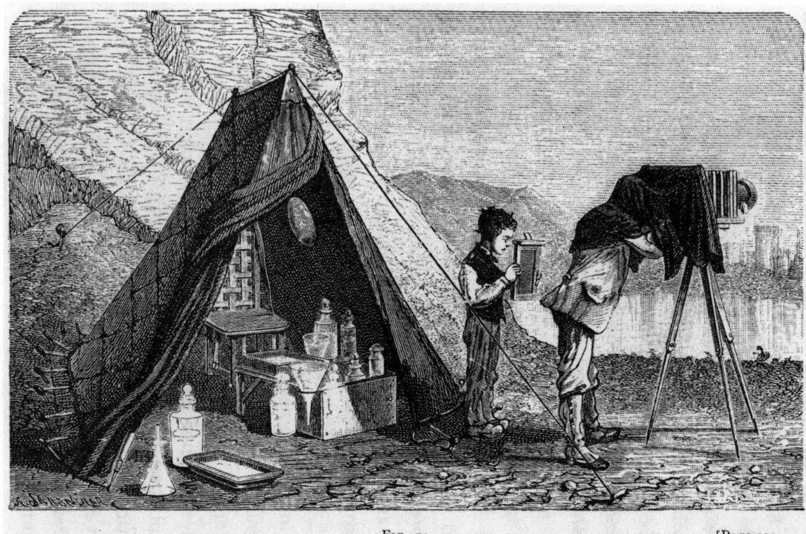

Figure 45. Illustration from Gaston Tissandier, *A History and Handbook of Photography*, 1877.

chemicals with which he coated the plate eventually clogged the silver nitrate solution, causing the process to fail. If he wanted to work outside a studio, he had to travel with a darkroom and bottled chemicals.[24]

And this was only the beginning of the photographer's travails and tribulations. Oliver Wendell Holmes provides a detailed account of every stage of the wet-plate process in "Doings of the Sunbeam," and it shows that the development of the negative was as suspenseful in 1863 as it was in 1840. "We open [the camera] and find our milky-surfaced glass plate looking exactly as it did when we placed it in the shield," Holmes writes. ". . . We pour on the solution. There is no change at first . . . What if there were no picture there? Stop! What is that change of color beginning at the edge . . . ? It is a border, like that round the picture and then dawns the outline of a head."[25] The rest of the image slowly emerges, but then begins to disappear. Not until it has been washed in water, re-treated several times with the developing solution, rewashed, "plunged" into a "bath" of hyposulphite of soda, washed yet again, dried, and varnished is the negative fully there. Making positive prints from this negative was—as Holmes demonstrates—every bit as messy, laborious, and unpredictable.[26]

The liquid intelligence of photography also expressed itself in another way in the 1850s and 1860s: one that encroached on human vision. In the early 1830s, Charles Wheatstone and Sir David Brewster, who had already written extensively about the afterimage and other optical "illusions," began investigating the physiological bases of another retinal peculiarity: binocular disparity. Those of us who have two eyes see something slightly different with each of them, in two dimensions. Our brain ascribes these differences to depth, and fuses the two images together. Consequently, instead of perceiving two flat images, we generally perceive one three-dimensional image.[27]

Binocular disparity serves a crucial spatial function: it allows us to experience the "thickness" of the world. However, its discovery compounded the challenges that Kepler's notion of the retinal image had posed to earlier thinkers.[28] Not only is this image inverted and laterally reversed, but there are *two* of them, and they are not identical. And not merely are we unable to see these images in the guise in which they are received, but we do not see them *at all*, because an internal agency combines them, over which we have no control.

In 1838, Wheatstone created an optical device that exploited this blind spot: the stereoscope. He used mirrors to deliver reflections of slightly different images to each of the viewer's eyes, demonstrating that we also read difference as depth when the perceptual objects are flat.[29] This had even more dramatic implications for human vision, as Laura Burd Schiavo notes in an excellent 2003 essay.[30] By "creating a situation in which we 'see' that which is not really there, the stereoscope insinuated an arbitrary relationship between stimulus and sensation," she writes. It also denaturalized the system of perspective, which is predicated on a "single, ideal eye" and which assumes there to be "a direct correlation between the object and the retinal image."[31]

In 1849, Brewster invented the first lens-based stereoscope, in 1851 Jules Duboscq began making stereographic daguerreotypes, and in 1854, George Swan Nottage founded the London Stereoscopic Company for the production and sale of stereoscopes. Within two years, the Gernsheims report, "the stereoscope was in use in all parts of the world, and it was estimated that this firm alone, which then offered 10,000 stereoscopic slides, had already sold half a million instruments." By 1858, the number of available slides had increased to 100,000. The London Stereoscopic Company's motto was "No home without a stereoscope."[32] It might seem odd that a device that was used to demonstrate the unreliability of human vision should have become so popular, but most midcentury commentators saw it as an "instrument"—a tool "for furnishing visual truths,"[33] or for facilitating visual pleasure. "Nothing better displays the beauties and marvels of Photographic Art," an American commentator wrote in 1858.[34]

For some midcentury commentators, the stereoscope was also photography's "employer." "In every part of the globe" photographers are busily "taking binocular pictures for the instrument," Brewster enthused in *The Stereoscope*.[35] Others believed that the stereoscope answered to man, just as photography answered to it. "If in the order of things the cheap popular toy which the stereoscope now represents was necessary for the use of man," Lady Eastlake declared, "the photograph was first necessary for the service of the stereoscope."[36] Promoters of stereoscopes and stereo cards took this last argument

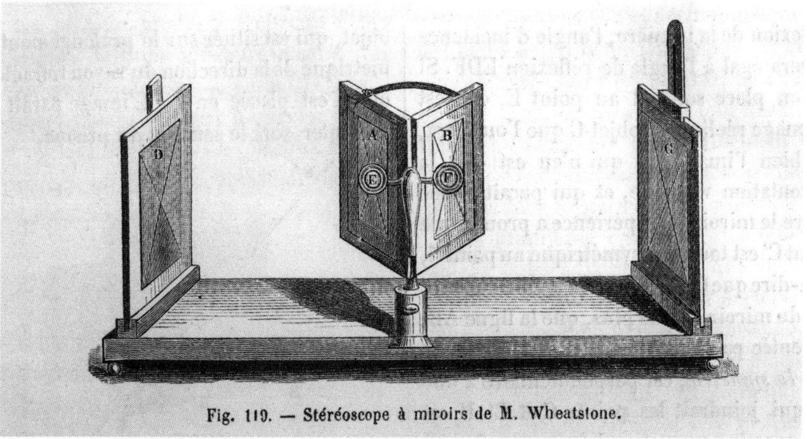

Figure 46. Illustration from Louis Figuier, *Les Merveilles de la Science*, 1869. Courtesy of the Max Planck Institute for the History of Science, Berlin.

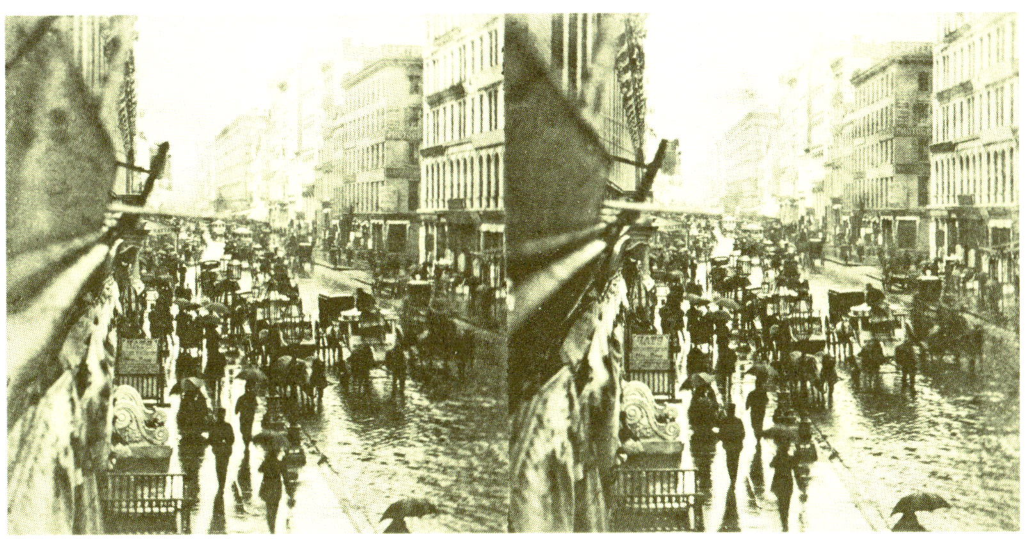

Figure 47. Unknown photographer, *Stereoscopic view of Broadway, New York City*, ca. 1860. Albumen print stereocard. Courtesy of the National Media Museum/SSPL.

one step further. Not only does the stereoscope serve man, and photography the stereoscope, they declared, but the photographer also serves the viewer. Cameramen traverse "lands and seas," cross "rivers and valleys," and ascend "rocks and mountains with their heavy and cumbrous photographic baggage" for "our gratification and instruction"—so that we may "have the advantage" of examining stereoscopic images by our fireplace, without being exposed to "the fatigue, the privation, and risks" of these "daring and enterprising artists," Antoine Claudet wrote in 1860.[37]

However, not everyone subordinated photography to the stereoscope, and the stereoscope to the human look. For John Ellis, photography and stereography were a couple, and one in which there was—surprisingly—no power differential; in 1856, he wrote that they were "indissolubly joined for their mutual advantage" or "dignification."[38] Holmes also emphasized the closeness of this relationship. In 1861 he designed a simple, handheld stereoscope for photographic stereo cards that was widely adopted,

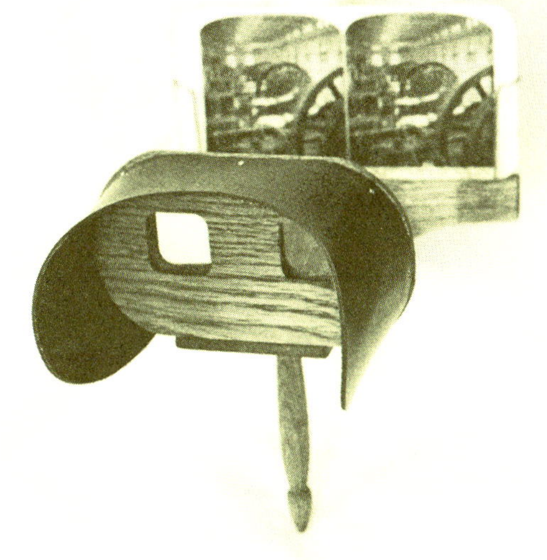

Figure 48. Holmes stereocard viewer. Courtesy Wikimedia Commons.

and that did nothing to conceal the fact that they contain two non-identical images. He also wrote three essays about the stereoscope, which are full of information about and reflections on photography. In the first—"The Stereoscope and the Stereograph" (1859)—he provides an extended account of the differences between a negative and a positive print. In the second—"Sun-Painting and Sun-Sculpture" (1861)—he takes us on a "stereoscopic trip across the Atlantic" through a series of detailed descriptions of photographically-based stereoscopic images. And in the third—"Doings of the Sunbeam" (1863)—he provides the extended account of the collodion wet plate from which I quoted earlier.

In "The Stereoscope and the Stereograph," Holmes also mobilizes all of the tropes that Talbot and other early writers associate with the calotype and daguerreotype, and reaffirms their saving power. We "owe" the "creations of our new art" to the "sun itself," he writes, who is "a master of chiaroscuro," and "the first of colorists."[39] Its illumination permits man to "paint his miniature" simply by "looking at a blank tablet," and "a multitudinous wilderness of forest foliage" to stamp itself "so faithfully and minutely" on that surface that every leaf is "perfect."[40] Unlike man-made pictures, which show only what the artist has seen, a "perfect photograph" is "absolutely inexhaustible." There are "as many beauties lurking [in it], unobserved, as there are flowers that blush unseen in forests and meadows."[41]

Photographs also teach us to see analogically. "[A] point which must have struck everybody who has studied photographic portraits is the family likeness that shows itself through a wide connection," Holmes writes in "Doings of the Sunbeam." "We notice it more readily than in life . . . There is something in the face that corresponds to *tone* in the voice . . . and this kind of resemblance . . . we may observe, though the features are unlike."[42] Finally, photographs challenge our belief in stable forms. "Flitting moods which have escaped one pencil of sunbeams are caught by another," Holmes observes in "Sun-Painting and Sun-Sculpture." "Each new picture gives us a new aspect of our friend; we find he had not one face, but many."[43]

Photography should consequently fill us with "inconceivable wonder," as it did its first viewers, Holmes argues, but it has become "such an everyday matter" that "we forget its miraculous nature."[44] Stereography shows us that photography is a "divine gift"[45] in two ways—through the stereo card, which I will discuss here, and through the stereoscopic image, which I will discuss in the next chapter. Holmes refers to the two side-by-side photographs on a stereo card as "twin pictures," and attributes a disclosive power to them: the power to reveal the similarities that structure our world. "Among the accidents of life, as delineated in the stereograph, there is one that rarely fails," he writes in "The Stereoscope and the Stereograph, ". . . wherever man lives, you will find the *clothes-line* . . . How it brings the people who sleep under that house before us to see their sheets drying on that fence!"[46]

The slight differences that distinguish one photograph on a stereo card from the other also show us that beings are as mobile and evanescent as the camera obscura's image stream. "It is common to find an object in one of the twin pictures which we miss in the other . . . ," Holmes observes in "The Stereoscope and the Stereograph." "In the lovely glass stereograph of the Lake of Brienz, on the left-hand side, a vaguely hinted female figure stands by the margin of the fair water: on the other side of the picture she is not seen. This is life; we seem to see her come and go . . . Here is the Fountain of the Ogre, at Berne. In the right picture two women are chatting, with arms akimbo, over its basin . . . on the left side there is but one woman, and you may see the blur where the other is melting into thin air as she fades forever from your eyes."[47]

All of the stereo cards that Holmes mentions feature water—a pool, a basin, a fountain, a lake—and most of them also include women. The women stand by the water or lean over it, and eventually they become as fluid as it is, and course through his thoughts, in a striking instantiation of liquid intelligence. "All the longings, passions, experiences, possibilities of womanhood animate that gliding shadow which has flitted through our consciousness," he writes, "nameless,

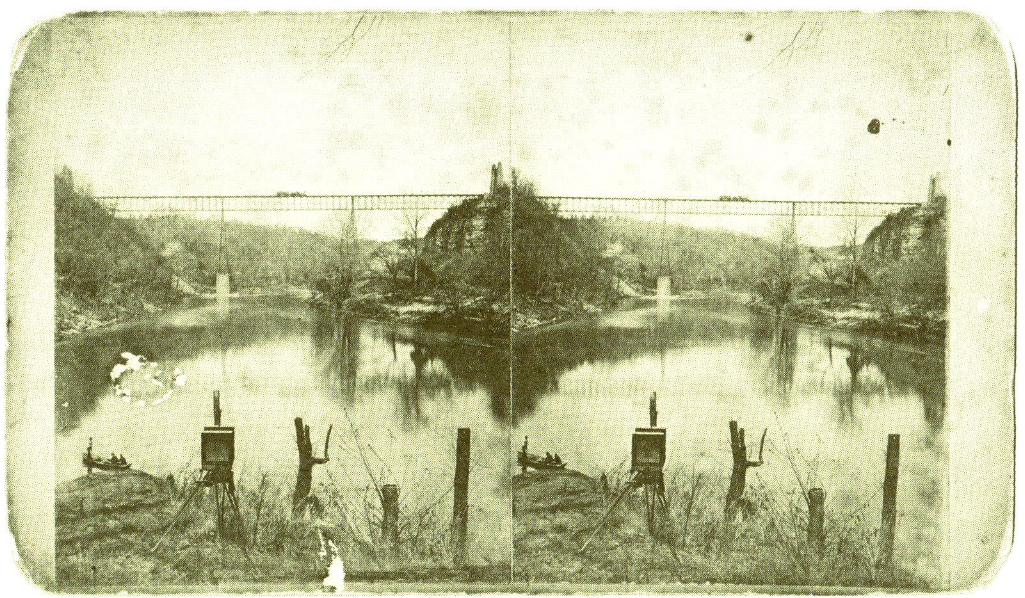

Figure 49. James Mullen, *Kentucky River Bridge. Finished Bridge from Mouth of Dix River*. 1877. Albumen print stereocard. Courtesy of the Archives and Special Collections, University of Louisville.

dateless, featureless, yet more profoundly real than the sharpest of portraits traced by a human hand."[48]

Although Holmes usually refers to the two photographs on a stereo card as "pictures," he sometimes calls them "views."[49] As we have already seen, when users of the optical camera obscura began thinking of themselves as "takers" rather than "receivers" of the world's luminous self-portraits, they also talked about "views"; that was what they "took." The word was important for Niépce as well; he repeatedly tried to extract an image from his camera obscura that corresponded to what he saw when he looked out of his workroom window. And sometimes he says "*point of view*," thereby embedding his optic within what he was attempting to photograph. When Holmes refers to the two photographs on a stereo card as "views," he attests to the impossibility of this project. Even if we were the only spectator in the world, there would always be at least two views, and at least two points of view.

One of the reasons the stereoscope was so easily domesticated is that it is a device for *viewing* these "views," rather than for *making* them. It consequently evades the thorny issue of agency. The stereoscope's user may have been forced to acknowledge his own binocularity, but nothing prevented him from attributing what he saw to the photographer's look. The latter was not so fortunate. Some of the "twin pictures" on nineteenth-century stereo cards were produced with a single-lens camera; the two photographs were made consecutively, with slightly different camera setups, or carved out of the same negative, through artful framing. Most of these photographs, though, were created with a stereo camera. Unlike a conventional camera, which has monocular "vision," which is hard to align with the human look, the stereo camera "sees" binocularly, and is all too easy to align with the human look. I say "all too easy" because as two contemporaneous essays show, the stereo camera cannot be reconciled with the Cartesian dream.

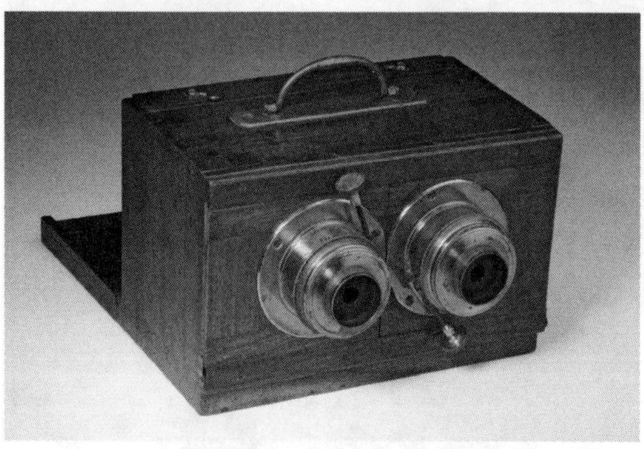

Figure 50. Jamin stereo camera. Courtesy of the George Eastman House, International Museum of Photography and Film.

In September 1869, *Harper's New Monthly Magazine* published an essay by Austin Abbott called "The Eye and the Camera."[50] The human look cannot be compared to an "ordinary camera," Abbott argues there, since we have two eyes, and it has a "single eye."[51] If we want an optical device that resembles human vision, we must turn to a different kind of camera: the *stereo* camera. The caps that fit over the "two round tubes in front" that contain the lenses are like our eyelids, and the diaphragm that regulates the side of the aperture is like our pupils, which expand and contract "according to the degree of light."[52] This "double instrument" makes "two pictures at the same instant that differ from each other just as the images received by one eye differ from those received by the other in an observer standing at the same place." This is not a flattering comparison, to say the least; instead of humanizing the camera, it mechanizes the human look. The analogical "fit" is also so tight that it would be impossible for anyone using the stereo camera to deny that his vision is "two-sided." And since being binocular means not just receiving two slightly different retinal images, but also not being able to perceive either of them, the stereo photographer could not even claim that he is "in charge" of what he sees, let alone what his camera registers. In both cases, all that he could really purport to be is a "viewer."

The September 1869 issue of *Harper's New Monthly Magazine* also contains another essay about photography, which speaks directly to this point. The essay, which is called "Photographs from the High Rockies," was written by John Samson, who accompanied Timothy O'Sullivan on his High Rockies expedition. Since it recounts the story of that expedition, the "photographer" to whom Samson refers is presumably O'Sullivan, who worked with both a conventional camera and a stereo camera. As Rosalind Krauss notes, the word "view" figures prominently in "Photographs from the High Rockies," but its meaning keeps shifting.[53] Sometimes a view is something that the photographer "takes," at other times it is something that he "makes," or "works up," and in one astonishing passage, it is something that he "views." "In speaking of the Humboldt and Carson sinks," this passage reads, "our photographer remarks: 'It was a pretty location to work in, and *viewing* there was as pleasant as could be desired.'"[54]

IN 1860, the French scientist J. M. Taupenot began experimenting with collodion dry plate.[55] His exposures were extremely slow—six times the length of the collodion wet plate—but in 1864, B. J. Sayce and William Blanchard Bolton cut this time in half, and other "improvements" followed. In 1871, Richard Leach Maddox replaced the collodion with gelatin, allowing the plates to be sensitized in advance and developed later, and in 1878 gelatin dry plates began to be industrially produced. Photographers no longer had to travel with a darkroom and chemicals, prepare their own plates, or wait for the gradual development of an image.[56]

The single-lens reflex camera also returned in a new guise in the 1880s. It was called the "Monocular Duplex," and it was marketed as an extension of the photographer's look. The camera "enables the Operator to see the picture non-inverted, and the full size of the plate the very instant of making the exposure," one advertisement proclaimed. It dispenses with all of the extraneous "impediments" that have prevented this "fascinating amusement" from realizing its full potential, a second declared. E. W. Smith issued another promise through the camera's name: the promise that it would allow the viewer to see "double" with a single eye, instead of "single" with two eyes, as stereoscopy had mandated—to preside over both stages of the photographic event, without undergoing an internal division. And by describing the Monocular Duplex as an "Artist Camera," the advertisements also bestowed another power on the viewer—one that recalls the purpose for which Hooke designed his 1694 camera obscura.

The ocularization of chemical photography reached its zenith in 1888, when George Eastman began manufacturing dry, transparent, flexible, photographic film and released the first Kodak camera. He marketed the camera under the slogan "You Press the Button, We Do the Rest." The last word in this slogan covered a lot of things. The camera was "fitted with a rectilinear fixed-focus lens" that gave a "sharp definition of everything beyond 8 ft," and it had only "one speed and a fixed stop." It arrived "loaded" with enough film for one hundred exposures, and when they had all been used it was sent back to Eastman with the film still in it so that the negatives could be processed, printed, and mounted. The camera was reloaded, and returned to the owner with the prints.[57]

The ostensible purpose of these innovations was to make the camera a more democratic apparatus—one available to amateur as well as professional photographers. "Today photography has been reduced to a cycle of three simple operations," the "primer" proclaimed. "1. Pull the String. 2. Turn the Key. 3. Press the Button. This is the essence of photography and the greatest improvement of them all; for where the practice of the art was formerly confined to those who could give it

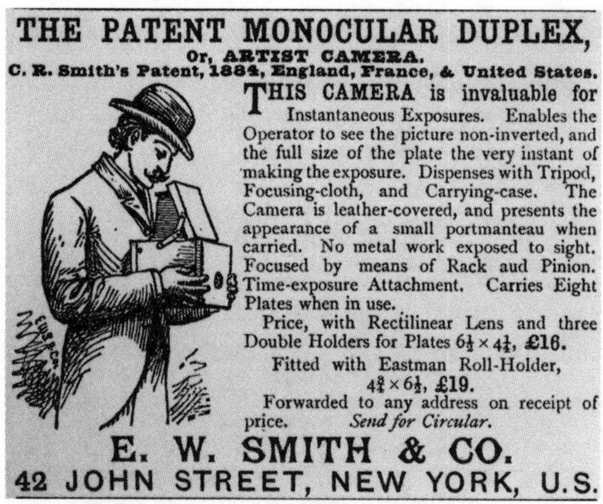

Figure 51. Newspaper advertisement for Smith's Monocular Duplex Camera, 1886.

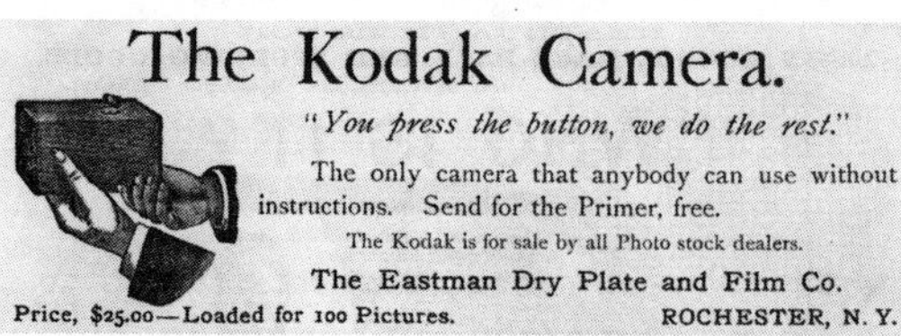

Figure 52. Newspaper advertisement for the Kodak camera, 1889.

study and time and room, it is now feasible for *every body*." And because "the mechanical act of taking the picture . . . is divorced from all the chemical manipulations of preparing and finishing pictures which only experts can perform," anyone of "ordinary intelligence" can "learn to take good pictures in ten minutes."[58]

But by reducing photography to three predefined steps, George Eastman substituted the Kodak system for the "pencil of nature." By releasing the photographer from "the chemical steps of the process," he also sealed off photography's liquid intelligence. Finally, by printing as well as developing the negative at the factory, Eastman created the illusion that the photographs that arrived in the mail were the exact

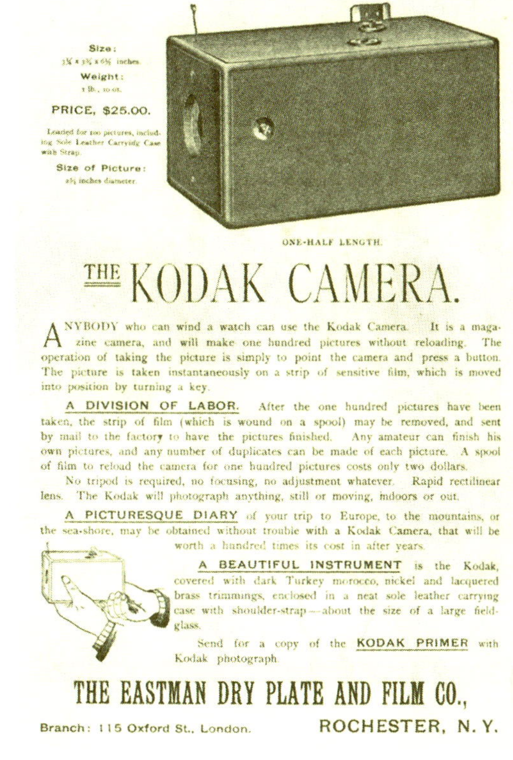

THE KODAK CAMERA.

ANYBODY who can wind a watch can use the Kodak Camera. It is a magazine camera, and will make one hundred pictures without reloading. The operation of taking the picture is simply to point the camera and press a button. The picture is taken instantaneously on a strip of sensitive film, which is moved into position by turning a key.

A DIVISION OF LABOR. After the one hundred pictures have been taken, the strip of film (which is wound on a spool) may be removed, and sent by mail to the factory to have the pictures finished. Any amateur can finish his own pictures, and any number of duplicates can be made of each picture. A spool of film to reload the camera for one hundred pictures costs only two dollars.

No tripod is required, no focusing, no adjustment whatever. Rapid rectilinear lens. The Kodak will photograph anything, still or moving, indoors or out.

A PICTURESQUE DIARY of your trip to Europe, to the mountains, or the sea-shore, may be obtained without trouble with a Kodak Camera, that will be worth a hundred times its cost in after years.

A BEAUTIFUL INSTRUMENT is the Kodak, covered with dark Turkey morocco, nickel and lacquered brass trimmings, enclosed in a neat sole leather carrying case with shoulder-strap—about the size of a large field-glass.

Send for a copy of the KODAK PRIMER with Kodak photograph.

THE EASTMAN DRY PLATE AND FILM CO.,

Branch: 115 Oxford St., London.   ROCHESTER, N. Y.

Figure 53. Newspaper advertisement for the Kodak camera, 1888.

positive equivalents of the negatives that were in the camera when it was shipped off—that the governing principle of photography is "sameness."

IN THE CONCLUDING sentences of "Photography and Liquid Intelligence," Wall offers yet another account of the latter concept. This time he associates it with a number of human qualities—thought, intention, agency, the capacity to look back—but locates it outside us. Wall presents this part of his argument through an extended analogy: "In Andrei Tarkovsky's film *Solaris*, some scientists are studying an oceanic planet. Their techniques are typically scientific. But the ocean itself is an intelligence which is studying them in turn. It experiments on the experimenters. . . . I think this was a very precise metaphor for, among other things, the interrelation between liquid intelligence and optical intelligence in photography. In photography, the liquids study us, even from a great distance."[59]

Initially this external site appears to be chemical photography, but the last sentence suggests that it is much "bigger." So does the expansive nature of the analogy; the signifier (the oceanic planet) radially exceeds what it is supposed to signify (the fluids in chemical photography). And immediately before

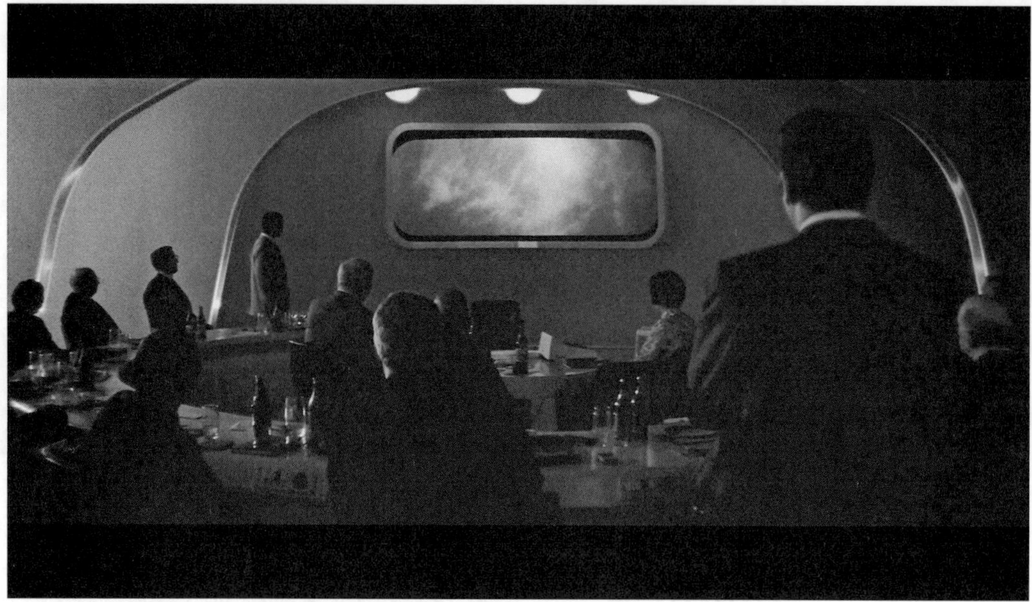

Figure 54/Colorplate 9. Andrei Tarkovsky, *Solaris*, 1972 (film still).

declaring *Solaris* to be "a very precise metaphor" for the relationship "between liquid intelligence and optical intelligence in photography," Wall differentiates the oceanic planet from the vehicle through which it communicates with the scientists. The ocean experiments on the experimenters through images, he writes—by returning their memories to them "in the form of hallucinations,

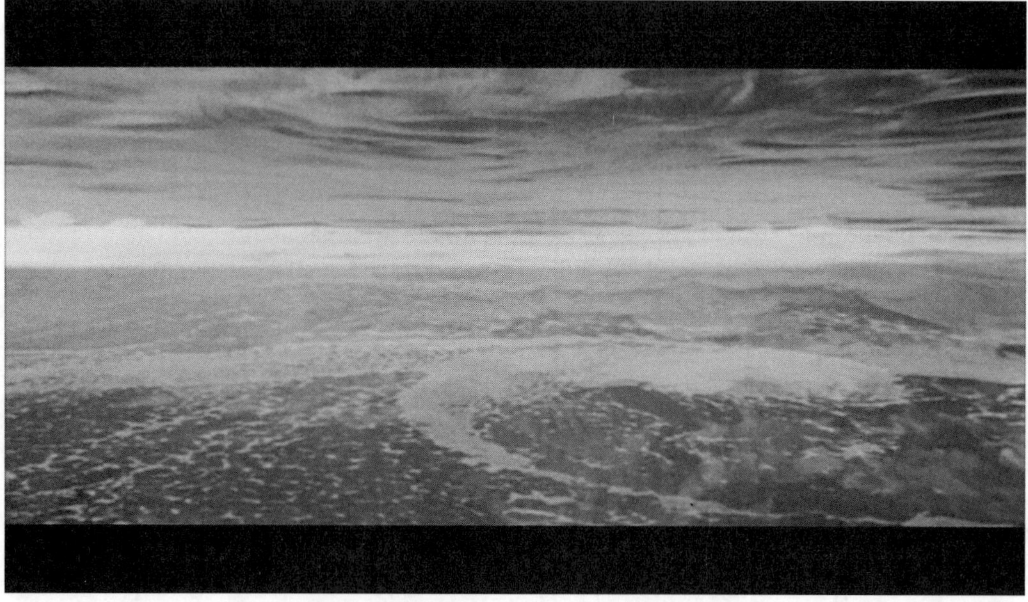

Figure 55/Colorplate 9. Andrei Tarkovsky, *Solaris*, 1972 (film still).

perfect in every detail." It shows the scientists people from their past so that they will relate to these people again, "maybe in a new way."

Like Tarkovsky's scientists, we have secured ourselves "behind a barrier of perfectly engineered glass," so that we can "study" an oceanic planet without getting "wet." This planet is as "intelligent" as the one in *Solaris*, and it also communicates with us through images. Like the hallucinations in Tarkovsky's film, these images are ontological calling cards: a summons to relationality. This oceanic planet, however, is our world, and it is through photography—rather than hallucinations—that it speaks to us.

Chapter 4

A KIND OF REPUBLIC

NOT SURPRISINGLY, photography's early viewers and practitioners didn't know how to classify its images. Although Fox Talbot titled his 1844–46 book *The Pencil of Nature*, and sometimes referred to its photographic plates as "drawings," he often used a more all-purpose noun, like "images," or "pictures."[1] His contemporaries employed a wide variety of other designators: "painting," "engraving," "imprint," "copy," "mirror," and "double."[2] Several authors weren't even sure that a photograph is an entity. At one point in his review of available photographic processes, the anonymous author of "Photogenic Drawing, or Drawing with the Agency of Light" declares every photograph to be "an authentic chapter in the history of the world" and the medium of photography to be "a gift to all nations."[3]

Lady Eastlake makes a number of equally tantalizing claims. In one passage in her 1857 essay, she maintains that the photographic image is not a letter, a message, or a picture, but rather "a new form of communication between man and man,"[4] and in another that it ushered in a new kind of relationality: one based on "brotherhood." Photography "unites men of the most diverse lives, habits and stations" into "a kind of republic," she writes, whose members follow a "new business," practice "a new pleasure," and speak "a new language."[5] It also "fills up the space" between them.[6] These claims point to another dimension of photography's saving power—one that is social as well as ontological. The photographic image not only analogizes the external world, but also links us to one another through a particularly binding and democratizing kind of analogy: the one called "chiasmus."

According to *The Oxford English Dictionary*, a chiasmus is "a rhetorical or literary figure in which words, grammatical constructions, or concepts are repeated in reverse order, in the same or a modified form,"[7] such as John F. Kennedy's "Ask not what your country can do for you—ask what you can do for your country." But chiasmus is also operative in other domains. The brain is able to fuse the two dimensional images that light inscribes on the retinas of two-sighted people into one three-dimensional image because half of the optic nerve fibers carrying visual "information" from each retina to the brain cross at the optic chiasm.[8] "Chiasmus" is also Merleau-Ponty's name for the ontological thread stitching the seer to what is seen, the toucher to what is touched, and sight and visibility to touch and tactility.[9]

We are all both seers and part of the spectacle of the world, the philosopher argues in *The Visible and the Invisible*. Each of us also touches, and is touched, and there is a "reciprocal insertion and intertwining" of the visual in the tactile, and the tactile in the visual.[10] Since these faculties belong to the same body, we cannot separate them, but we also cannot weave them into a seamless whole by exercising all of them at once, or by being simultaneously the seer and what is seen, the toucher and what is touched. We shuttle back and forth between these aspects of our Being, at one moment a seer or toucher, and at the next moment what is seen or touched.

If we were alone in the world, there would be no communication between these "selves," and our non-identity would be a source of perpetual unhappiness. Since, however, we share this world with others, who also see and are seen, and touch and are touched, they provide the "rejoinder" for which we would otherwise wait in vain, and we do the same for them. We see because they are visible, and we are visible because they see us. Through their gaze, we are also able to see our own, and when gazing at them, to experience our own visibility. Merleau-Ponty metaphorizes this relationship as "two mirrors facing one another [in which] two indefinite series of images [...] arise which belong really to neither of the two [mirror] surfaces." Through the images reflected in them, he adds, these mirrors form a "couple," which is "more real" than either of them could be alone.[11] This couple has no fixed constituency, and its members belong to many other couples. I invoke it here not to suggest that it is the building block of society, but rather to make the following point: we are not "ourselves" when we are isolated from others. Two is the smallest unit of Being.

Chiasmus is also operative within a closely related domain: that of personhood. "Consciousness of self is only experienced by contrast," Emile Benveniste writes in *Problems in General Linguistics*. "I use *I* only when I am speaking to someone who will be a *you* in my address. It is this condition of dialogue that is constitutive of *person*, for it implies that reciprocally *I* becomes *you* in the address of the one who in his turn designates himself as *I*."[12] Personhood consequently depends on the utterance of these two reversible and mutually defining pronouns. This pronominal chiasmus is closely related to the one described by Merleau-Ponty. Giving and receiving the "you," as Martin Buber puts it,[13] is one of the most important means we have for affirming our ontological kinship with another human being.

The Oxford English Dictionary's definition of "chiasmus" can be effortlessly applied to the camera obscura. As Martin Kemp explains, the latter device was "founded on the principle that rays of light from an object or scene will pass through a small aperture in such a way as to cross and re-emerge on the other side in a divergent configuration."[14] When this configuration is "intercepted by a flat screen, a reversed and inverted image is formed." Although most accounts of the pre-optical camera obscura focus on the reversed and inverted stream of images inside the device, the stream of images on the other side of the aperture form an ongoing "recto" to this "verso." The crossing of the rays of image-bearing light at the aperture also analogizes the crossing of the optic nerve fibers at the optic chiasm.

At first glance, Merleau-Ponty's and Benveniste's definitions of the chiasmus have no bearing on the camera obscura, since they involve two players, instead of one, and none of the definitions of the chiasmus seems applicable to chemical photography. Although the photographic negative reverses the light values of its so-called referent, and the positive prints those of the negative, these reversals are generally assumed to be non-reciprocal. We also subordinate the negative to the positive print; it is the template from which photographs are generated, but it is not a photograph itself.

However, the similarities between the camera obscura and the eye led Leonardo and Kepler to conclude that human perception originates in what is seen, rather than in the seer.[15] They consequently anticipated one of Merleau-Ponty's most important claims: the claim that "it is as though our vision were

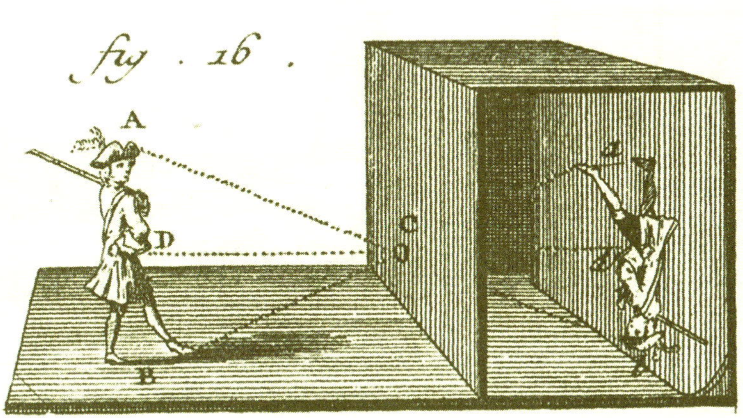

Figure 56. Illustration from Diderot's *Encyclopédie*, 1772.

formed in the heart of the visible, or as though … the vision we acquire of them seems to come from them."[16] Although the pre-optical camera obscura was primarily used to view natural and man-made things, there was also nothing to prevent another person from entering the field of vision, and then inviting the viewer to exchange positions with him. Both of these things were, in fact, an ever-present possibility, since they were implied by the structure of the device. Merleau-Ponty seems to have been imagining this kind of enclosure when he wrote that we are "from one side" a seer, and from the other "a thing among things."[17] And this reversal would have prepared the way for the one described by Benveniste.

When the camera obscura was equipped with lenses and mirrors, and transformed into a box into which the viewer peered, rather than a room into which he entered, it lost the capacity to show him that his visible body "subtended" his look, but it recovered this power through Talbot's photographic process. Unlike Daguerre's photographs, which were singular positives that morphed into negatives when viewed from a particular angle, all of Talbot's camera photographs were laterally reversed until 1839.[18] He clearly understood from the very beginning that he could make positive prints from these negatives, since he mentions the possibility in an 1835 notebook entry, but he did not act on this knowledge for years.[19] This was in part because he liked the way the negatives looked; in 1839, he sent a package of photographs to his friend John Herschel, with a note explaining why all but one of them were negatives. "In the little packet of photogenic drawings which I send today by the Railway," this note reads, "there is a [positive print] of a fern leaf; [such prints] are easily made but in the estimation of most people are less pretty then the first or white images."[20] But it was also, as the same note shows, because he saw the negative as a full-fledged photograph, and not merely as the template from which to produce one.[21]

Talbot wasn't disturbed by the fact that the "first or white image" was laterally reversed, because he wasn't striving to duplicate worldly forms; he sought, rather, to preserve the portraits they made of themselves. He also clearly understood that although these self-portraits were *like* their authors, they were not identical. He attributed his decision to begin experimenting with photography to two thoughts. The first was that it would be "charming" if he could find a way of "caus[ing]" the inimitably beautiful pictures of nature's paintings that appeared inside the camera obscura "to imprint themselves durably, and remain fixed upon the paper!" The second was that the resulting images would have "a *general resemblance* to the cause which produced [them]" (my emphasis).[22] Since worldly forms imprinted themselves on Talbot's sensitized paper in a

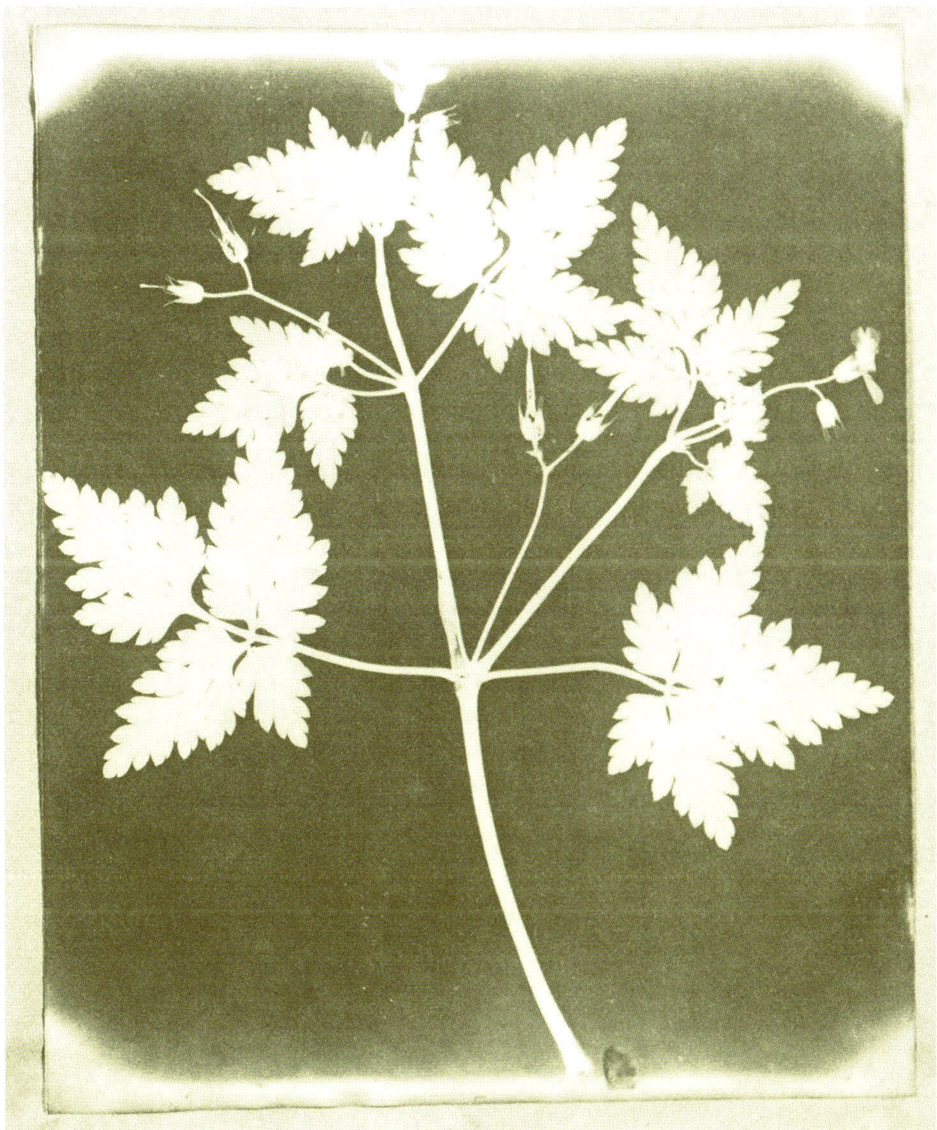

Figure 57. Henry Fox Talbot, salted paper print from a calotype negative, ca. 1838. Courtesy of the National Media Museum/SSPL.

negative form, and he understood photography to be about similarity, rather than sameness, he did not see this reversal as something to be corrected.[23] The negative/positive distinction comes not from him, but rather from Herschel, the inventor of the fixative agent, "hypo."[24]

Talbot sought to preserve two kinds of photogenic drawings: those created in a camera obscura, and those created by placing an object directly on the paper and exposing it to light. He describes the second procedure in *The Pencil of*

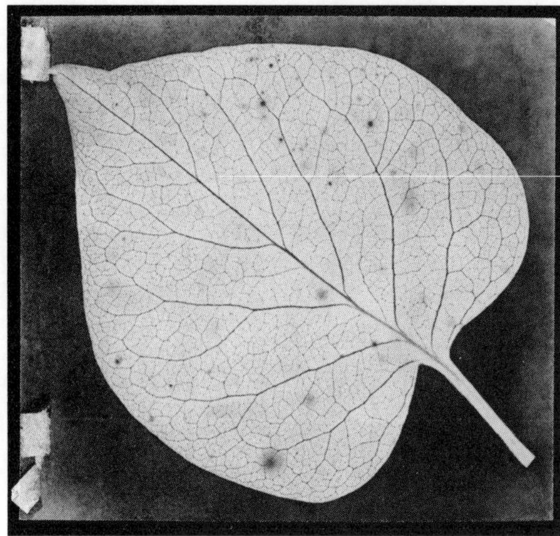

Figure 58. Henry Fox Talbot, *A leaf*, ca. 1840. Photogenic drawing negative. Courtesy of the National Media Museum/ SSPL.

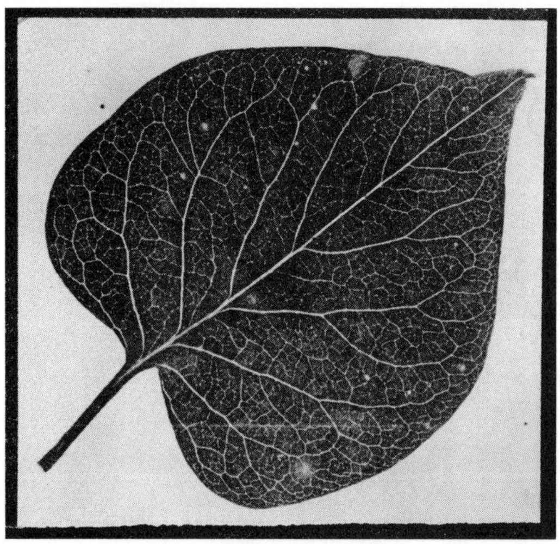

Figure 59. Henry Fox Talbot, *A leaf*, ca. 1840. Salted paper print. Courtesy of the National Media Museum/SSPL.

Nature, on the page next to plate 13. "The ordinary effect of light upon white sensitive paper is to *blacken* it. If therefore any object, as a leaf for instance, be laid upon the paper, this, by intercepting the action of the light, preserves the whiteness of the paper beneath it, and accordingly when it is removed there appears the form or shadow of the leaf marked out in white upon the blackened paper; and since shadows are usually dark, and this is the reverse, it is called in the language of photography a *negative* image."

Talbot used the same method to make positive prints from his camera obscura negatives, but instead of placing an object directly on a piece of sensitive paper before exposing it to light, he put the negative there. Since he waxed it first, so that its white areas were transparent, the light blackened the corresponding areas of the underlying paper. The darkened areas of the negative did the opposite. What was dark in the negative image was consequently light in the print, and vice versa. Talbot thought of this process as a reversal of the negative's reversal. "If the paper [that is used for the negative] is transparent," he wrote in 1835, "the first drawing may serve as an object to produce a second drawing, in which the lights would be reversed."[25]

Talbot used a similar formulation five years later, when describing the positive prints in an 1839 exhibition; they were "reversed images," he wrote, that "require[d] the action of light to be TWICE employed."[26] Because these double reversals were effected through direct contact between the first image and a piece of sensitized paper, they showed those who were prepared to see that

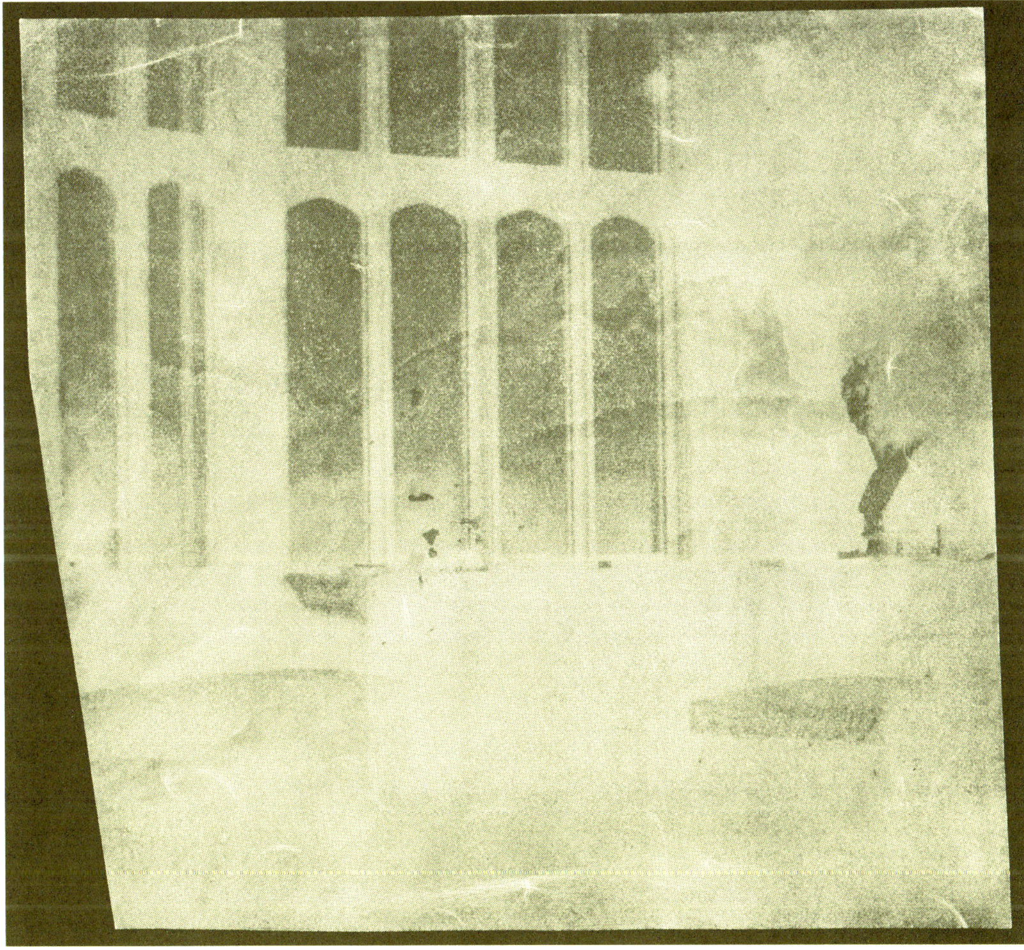

Figure 60/Colorplate 10. Henry Fox Talbot, *Oriel Window, South Gallery, Lacock Abbey*, April 1839. Photogenic drawing negative. Courtesy of the National Media Museum/SSPL.

"every visible is cut out in the tangible, every tactile being is in some manner promised to visibility, and that there is encroachment, infringement . . . between the tangible and the visible."[27]

Talbot's photographs also correspond with Merleau-Ponty's late philosophy in another way: chromatically. Most of his negative and positive prints are red, purple, yellow, brown, or black. These colors are neither representative nor representational; they are singular, and we experience them directly. Some of them also have a curious texture. This is in part because Talbot continued to use ordinary paper, rather than switching to calotype paper. Each sheet of this paper was slightly different from every other, and since there was no emulsion on which the image could form, it sank into the fibers of the paper. Each sheet of paper also reacted differently to the chemicals that were applied to it, and

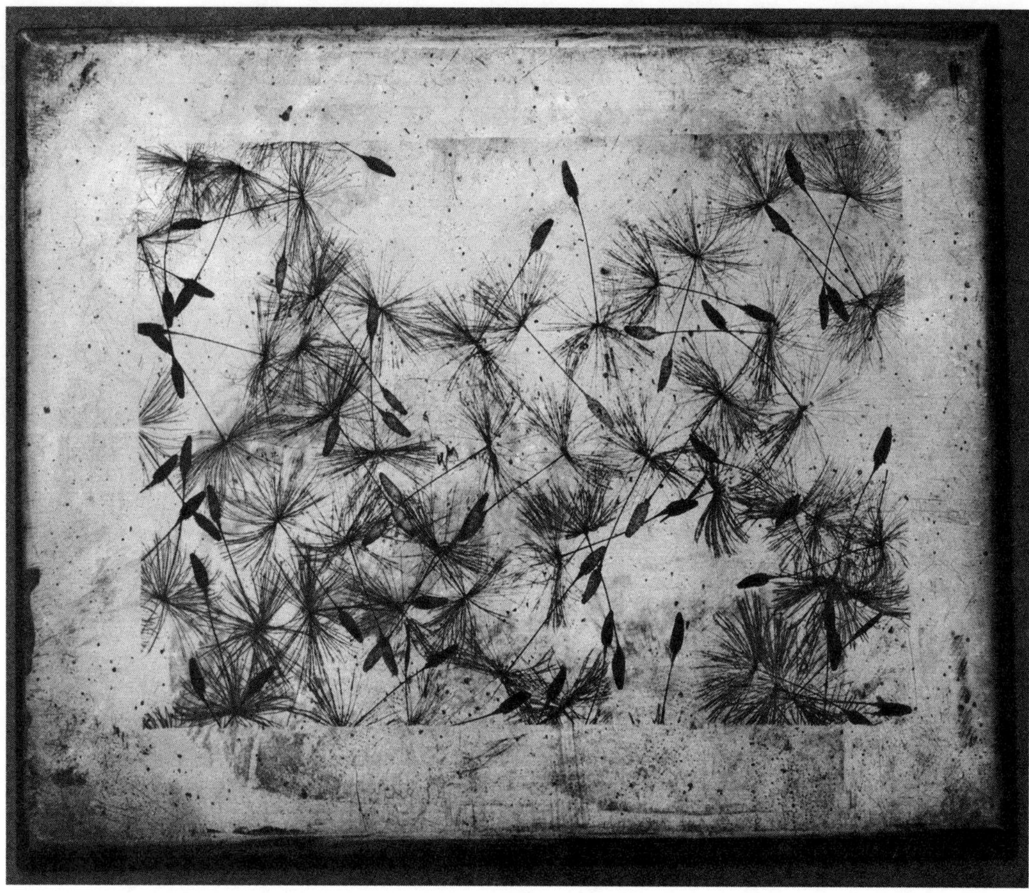

Figure 61/Colorplate 11. Henry Fox Talbot, *Seeds*, 1853. Photogravure. Courtesy of the National Media Museum/SSPL.

the chemicals themselves were also variable, as were the amounts used, and the mode of application. The sun, as Larry J. Schaaf puts it, was an even bigger "variable." "Depending on the density of the particular negative, and even more on the fickle nature of the English sun," he writes in *The Photographic Art of William Henry Fox Talbot*, "the exposure time for the print might vary from a few minutes up to many tens of minutes. This had profound effects, not only on productivity, but more importantly on the tonal range and color of the final print."[28]

The images in *The Pencil of Nature* are actual photographs, and the photographs in one exemplar often differ chromatically from those in another. Talbot talks about these differences in "Brief Historical Sketch of the Invention of the Art," an essay included in *The Pencil of Nature*. The prints made from the same negative are "almost facsimiles of each other," he writes there, "but there is some variety in the tint they present." The phrase with which he describes their relationship to one another—"almost facsimiles"—anticipates the one through which an artist powerfully attuned to the analogical basis of the photographic image would later characterize photography's relationship to the world. A photograph is "almost nature," Gerhard Richter observed in 1989.[29]

It might be possible to "render" the tints of his prints more "uniform," Talbot writes in the same essay, "if any great advantage appeared likely to result" from this "uniformity." But in order to regularize the colors, he would have to establish a "norm," and those with whom he discussed this matter had differing notions of what the norm should be. Since the photographic process "presents us spontaneously with a variety of shades of color," and different viewers are drawn to different shades, this diversity must be an integral part of the calotype, so Talbot decided to admit all the tints "that appeared pleasing to the eye." He concludes his essay by commending the photographs in *The Pencil of Nature* "to the indulgence of the Gentle Reader." Since commendations like this were a convention of the day, this would be an insignificant detail if it were not for one thing. Although Talbot addresses us as readers, it is for our visual rather than our literary indulgence that he asks. Dear Readers, he effectively says to us, be gentle with my photographs; don't expect all of the prints that I have made

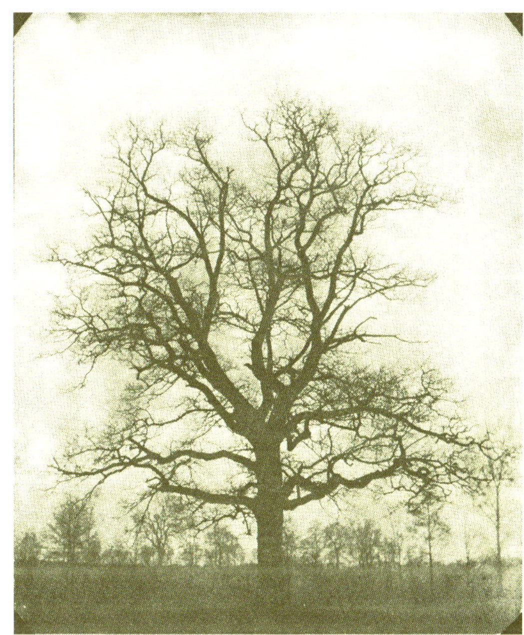

Figure 62/Colorplate 12. Henry Fox Talbot, *Tree in Winter*, ca. 1842. Salted paper print from calotype negative. Courtesy of the National Media Museum/SSPL.

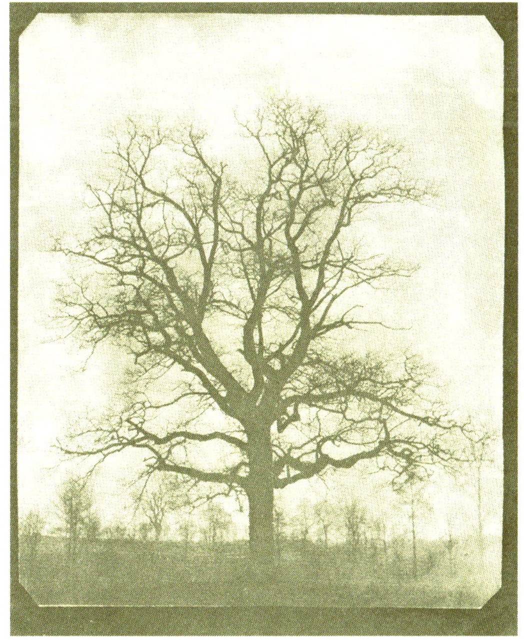

Figure 63/Colorplate 12. Henry Fox Talbot, *Tree in Winter*, ca. 1842. Salted paper print from calotype negative. Courtesy of the National Media Museum/SSPL.

from the same negative to be the same color. Although they all reverse the tonal values of the "first image," each does so in a different way. They are siblings, not identical twins, and the same is true of the look to which each print appeals.

Merleau-Ponty introduces the topic of color early in the last chapter of *The Visible and the Invisible*, describing it in ways that are surprisingly congruent with Talbot's account of his "tints." Color is neither a "pellicule of being without thickness," he asserts, nor "a chunk of absolutely hard, indivisible being, offered all naked" to our look. It is, rather, thick, "atmospheric," and textured; our eyes sink into it, and wander around inside it. It is also "a sort of straits between exterior horizons and interior horizons." We are drawn to the colors that are the equivalent "on the outside" of what we are "on the inside"—the ones with which we are in a relation of "pre-established harmony."[30] These colors are "for our vision and our body"; they are unavailable to other looks. There is consequently something within the chiasmus that is not reversible. Since every seer "envelops" and "palpates" a color that is for his vision and his body, what each of us perceives is only the "surface" of an inexhaustible "depth." This alterity enlivens what would otherwise be a deadening universality, and renders the world unplumbable.[31]

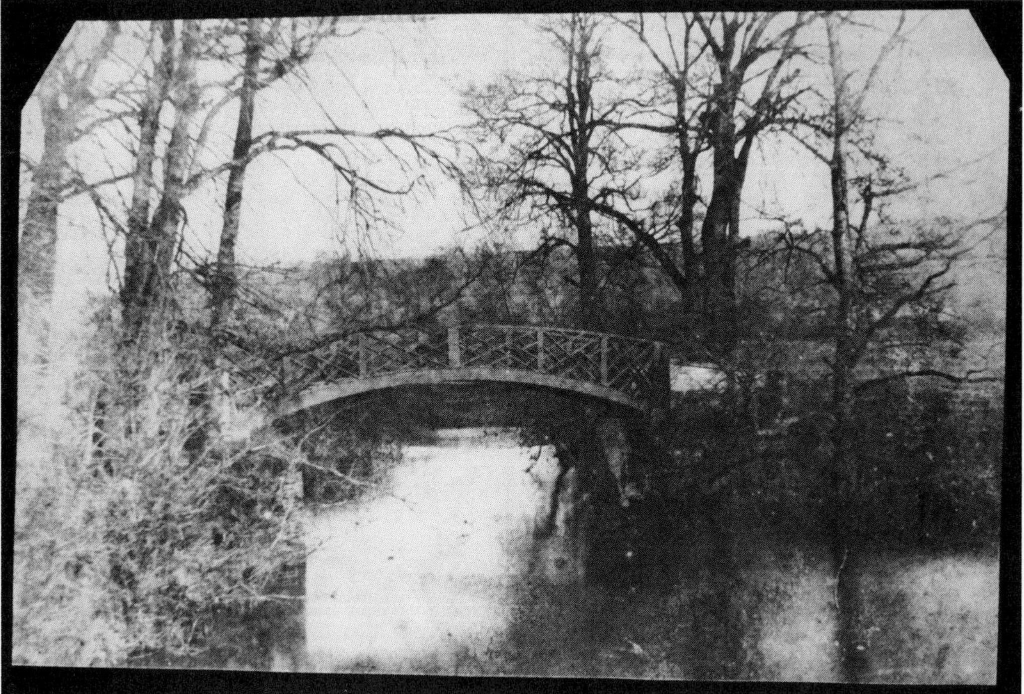

Figure 64/Colorplate 13. Henry Fox Talbot, *China Bridge at Lacock Abbey*, 1841. Salted paper print. Courtesy of the National Media Museum/SSPL.

TALBOT WASN'T THE ONLY PERSON who worked with color in the early years of photography. Between 1843 and 1854, Anna Atkins produced hundreds of exquisite cyanotypes of British algae. She made them available to a select circle of viewers through *Photographs of British Algae: Cyanotype Impressions*, a handmade book consisting of twelve serial parts, which she assembled into two- and three-volume presentation albums.[32] Atkins was the daughter of John George Children, a celebrated chemist, zoologist, and mineralogist, and the head of the Royal Society in 1839, when Talbot unveiled his discovery.[33]

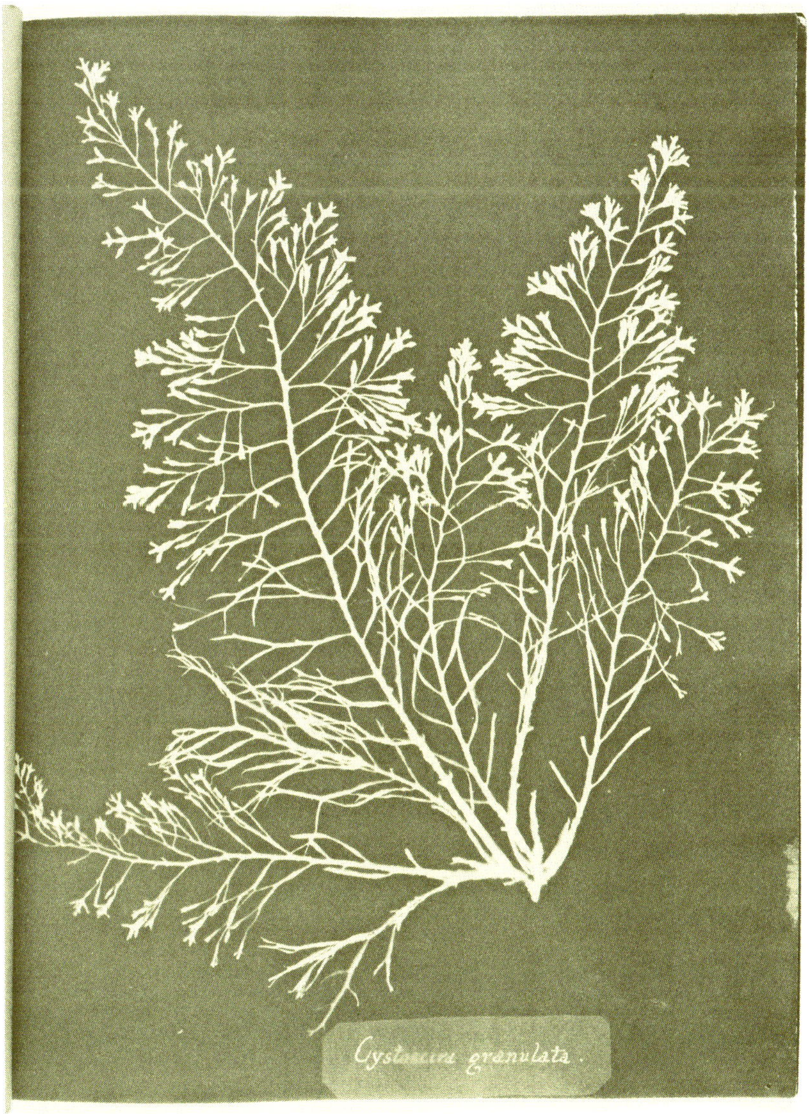

Figure 65/Colorplate 14. Anna Atkins, *Cystoseira granulata*, from *Photographs of British Algae*, 1843. Cyanotype. Courtesy of the National Media Museum/SSPL.

Atkins learned about photogenic drawing through her father's conversations with Talbot, and about the cyanotype process directly from Herschel its inventor.[34]

There are very few words in *Photographs of British Algae*, and most of them are names. In the preface to her book, Atkins identifies William Henry Harvey's *A Manual of the British Algae: Containing Generic and Specific Descriptions of All the Known British Species of Sea-weeds, and of Conferae, both Marine and Freshwater* (1841) as the source of these names. However, she also notes that she has "intentionally departed from [the] systematic arrangement" of Harvey's book. As Carol Armstrong shows in *Scenes in a Library*, color is the place where this departure is most marked.[35] Harvey divides British algae into distinct groups on the basis of their colors, which he identifies as grass-green, olive-green, and red. He does so, he tells us, because algae's colors are "indicative" of their "structure" and "natural affinities."[36] He uses the same colors both to visualize these types and to distinguish them from one another in an illustrated edition of his book. Every engraved plate contains multiple numbered figures, and the numbers are correlated with names at the bottom of the page. Harvey renders this system hyper-legible by positioning the figures against a cream-colored background.

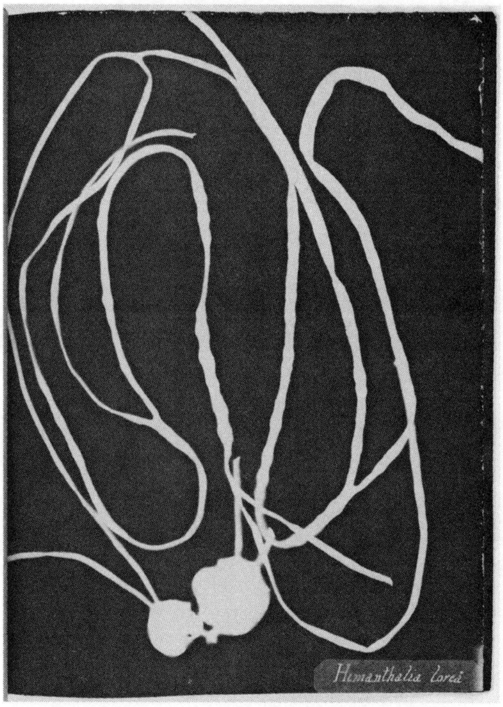

Atkins's cyanotypes, on the other hand, are monochromatic; she produced them by placing specimens of algae on sensitized paper and exposing them to sun. There is only one figure in most of the resulting images, and since these images are contact negatives, it is white, and the surrounding field is deep blue. And not only do these cyanotypes reverse the usual light/dark relationship, but they also blur the distinction between the two parts of the image. In some of them the dark blue of the field seems to have seeped into the area occupied by the specimen. In others, as Armstrong observes, the color seems to have drained out of the specimen and into the paper, as so often happened when an actual

Figure 66/Colorplate 15. Anna Atkins, *Himanthalia lorea*, from *Photographs of British Algae*, 1843. Cyanotype. Courtesy of the National Media Museum/SSPL.

specimen was mounted on paper. The plant also seems to have returned to the "oceanic habitat" in which it was colored.[37]

The name of the species to which each plant belongs appears below it, in a small box, but the box is inside the cyanotype, and the name is handwritten. Both the name and the box also participate in the photograph's "color scheme"; the former is white, like the figure, and the latter a slightly lighter shade of blue than the field. There is no other "information," and nothing whatever to suggest that the plant pictured in the cyanotype represents a group, or that it is ontologically different from any of the other plants. Last but not least, Atkins's photographs are *pictures*, in the strong sense of the word; we look at them not because they satisfy our desire to know, but because their blues are "so blue that only blood would be more red."[38]

Although Atkins used a photographic process developed by Herschel, her relationship to photography is much closer to Talbot's. Like him, she regarded a contact negative as a full-fledged photograph. This was, in fact, the only kind of photograph she ever made; instead of generating the photographs for her book by striking numerous positive prints from the same negatives, she produced new negatives. Atkins also privileged "becoming" over "being." She relied on the same specimen to make numerous contact negatives, and since plants are perishable objects, they changed over time, and her prints registered those changes. *Photographs of British Algae* was also itself forever-in-the-making; Atkins constantly withdrew photographs, added new ones, and altered the order in which her photographs appeared.[39]

Finally, Atkins was as interested as Talbot was in analogies—those through which her photographs were made, those that emerged when the photographs were brought together, and those through which they continued to develop, long after they had been chemically "fixed." She describes her algae cyanotypes as

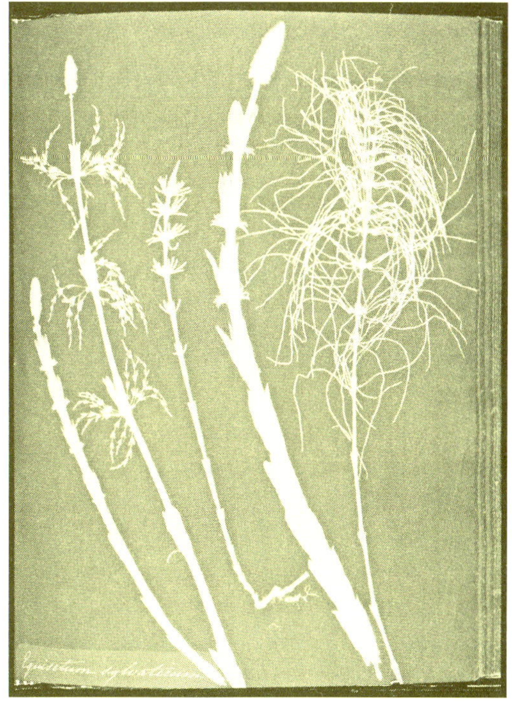

Figure 67/Colorplate 16. Anna Atkins, *Equisetum sylvaticum*, from *Cyanotypes of British and Foreign Ferns*, 1853. Cyanotype. Courtesy of the Open Content Program of the Getty Museum, Los Angeles.

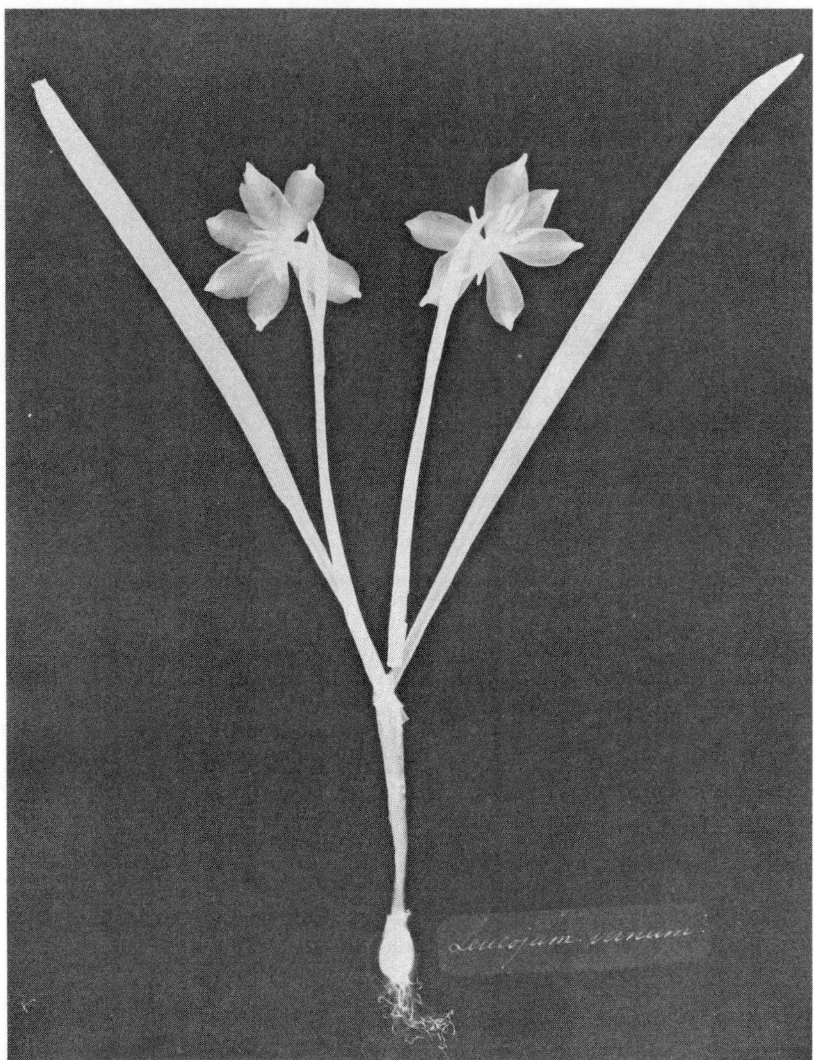

Figure 68/Colorplate 17. Anna Atkins, *Leucojam varium*, from *Cyanotypes of British and Foreign Ferns*, 1853. Cyanotype. Courtesy of the Open Content Program of the Getty Museum, Los Angeles.

"impressions of the plants themselves,"[40] and one is constantly struck as one turns the pages of her book by the echo in one of the formal attributes of another—echoes that show no respect for the boundaries established by Harvey. The figures in these photographs also correspond in mysterious ways with the words that are written beneath them. The script in which each specimen's name is written seems to come from the plant world, and Atkins reinforces this point by forming the words "British Algae, Vol. I" on the title page of the first volume of *Photographs of British Algae* out of bits of seaweed, in a similar script. These are—as Carol Armstrong elegantly puts it—"signs made by Nature and out of

Nature's things,"[41] and the same is true of the photographs in a related book, *Cyanotypes of British and Foreign Ferns* (1853), which Atkins co-produced with Anne Dixon.[42]

Since Atkins limits herself to cyan blue, instead of admitting all the tints "that appeared pleasing to the eye,"[43] her relationship to color might seem the opposite of Talbot's. It is, however, impossible to look at the images in *Photographs of British Algae* without thinking of the ocean, not just because algae are ocean flowers, but also because of the depth and expansiveness of their blues. These blues liquefy the categories that conflate one plant with a number of other plants, and separate it from the rest; all of the algae swim in the same great sea, and their by-now-personal names float with them, carried on tiny rafts. And although Talbot privileged the relationship that links each seer to a specific color, he too thought about his botanical contact negatives in oceanic terms.[44] In a February 1839 letter to *The Literary Gazette*, he wrote that a photograph of one blossom is as "essential" a part of "the same wonderful Whole" as a photograph of a thousand.[45]

ONCE THE DISTINCTION between the "negative" and the "positive" was firmly established, it became almost impossible to perceive the "first image" as a reversal, and the second as a reversal of this reversal. Not only did these terms seem to relate to each other in a binary fashion, but they also evoked a series of other oppositions: light/dark, white/black, good/evil, truth/falsehood. Holmes satirizes this tendency in "The Stereoscope and the Stereograph." The "perverse and totally depraved negative" appears to be the creation of a "magic and diabolic power" that has "wrenched all things from their proprieties," he writes, transforming "the light of the eye" into "darkness" and gilding "the deepest blackness . . . with the brightest glare." It stands for our imperfect world, whose "shadows" a "better world" will turn to "light."[46] The gradual standardization of color also encouraged viewers to think about the photographic image in more black-and-white terms.

However, as one contemporary artist has recently proven, both of these things still have the capacity to show us that each of us calls for an other. In 2008, Hiroshi Sugimoto began making large-format gelatin-silver positive prints of early Talbot photographs—photographs that we would call "negatives," but that predate the negative/positive distinction, and that in some cases have only ever existed in this form. Sugimoto refers to the works in the series the way Talbot referred to his own early photographs: as "photogenic drawings." He also gives each of them two dates: the one when Talbot made the negative, and the one when he himself made the positive.

Figure 69/Colorplate 18. Hiroshi Sugimoto, *Roofline of Lacock Abbey, Most Likely 1835–1839*, 2009. Toned silver-gelatin print from calotype negative. © Hiroshi Sugimoto, courtesy Pace Gallery.

Sugimoto published some of the prints in a bilingual exhibition catalogue,[47] whose layout recalls *The Pencil of Nature*, but instead of displaying his photographs on the left page, and the accompanying remarks on the right, as Talbot does, he positions his photographs on the right page and the accompanying remarks on the left.[48] In the little essay that he wrote for the catalogue, he also describes the series as a return journey—a pilgrimage back to the place from which the negatives came.[49] Through this trans-temporal chiasmus, Sugimoto shows us that a negative really is a reversal, and a positive the reversal of this reversal. He also helps us to see that much more is at issue here than two pieces of paper.

Sugimoto used nineteenth-century recipes for his "tones," and applied them as they would have been applied a hundred and fifty years ago, but he didn't try to reproduce the color of the negatives "bequeathed" to him by Talbot, nor did

Figure 70/Colorplate 19. Hiroshi Sugimoto, *Louisa Gallwey and Horatia Feilding, at Lacock Abbey, August 29, 1842*, 2009. Toned silver-gelatin print from calotype negative. © Hiroshi Sugimoto, courtesy Pace Gallery.

he limit himself to red, yellow, purple, brown, and black. Instead, he adhered to the principle enunciated in *The Pencil of Nature*: he admitted "tints" that are "pleasing" to other eyes. The four prints that are most pleasing to my eyes— *Stem of Leaves and Flowers, circa 1834–1839* (2008), *Piece of Lace, circa 1839* (2008), *Botanical Specimen (Erica Mutabolis), March 1839* (2009), and *Roofline of Lacock Abby, circa 1835–1839* (2009)—are deep blue, like the contact prints in *British Algae*. They please me not only because they make room within this trans-temporal chiasmus for Atkins, but also because cyan blue is—quite simply—the color that I most "espouse."

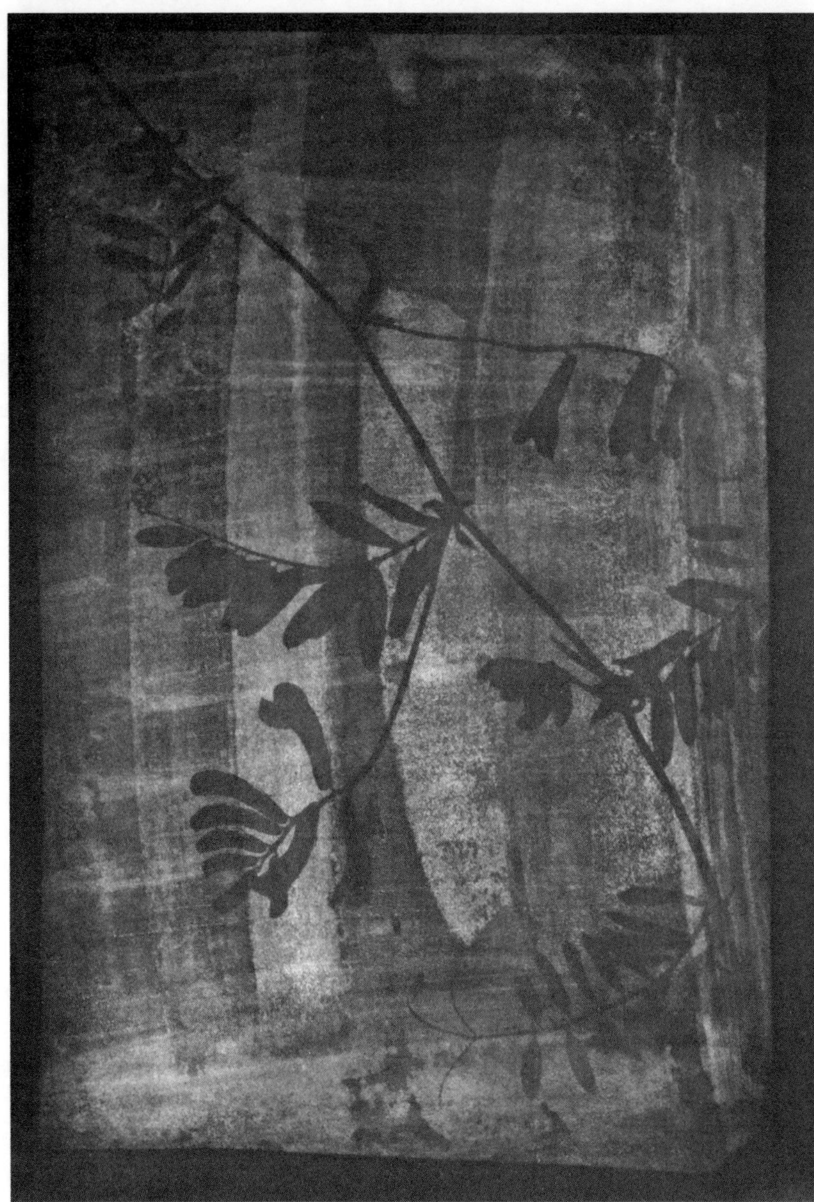

Figure 71/Colorplate 20. Hiroshi Sugimoto, *Stem of Leaves and Flowers, ca. 1834–1839*, 2008. Toned silver-gelatin print from calotype negative. © Hiroshi Sugimoto, courtesy Pace Gallery.

HOLMES DOESN'T JUST SATIRIZE the moralization of the negative/positive distinction; he also reinstates Talbot's definition of these terms. The negative is a "reversed picture" of the *object*, he writes; it has "the right part of the object on the left side of the picture, and the left part on its right side."[50] The positive is a reversed picture of the *negative*; it has the right part of the negative on the left side of the picture, and the left part on its right side.[51] It is also created through direct contact with the negative. Consequently, although everything about the negative may seem "just as wrong as it can be," Holmes wryly observes, "the relations of each wrong to the other wrongs are like the relations of the corresponding rights to each other in the original natural image." And although "every given point of the picture" may seem "as far from the truth as a lie can be, in traveling away from the pattern it has gone round a complete circle, and is [therefore both] as remote from Nature and as near as possible."[52]

Holmes devotes so much time to the distinction between the negative and the positive in an essay about the stereoscope because the stereoscopic image also has a recto and a verso, and because it, too, alerts us to a much more primordial reversibility: the one that is activated every time we see or touch another body. It is with this last relationship that Holmes begins his essay. "Democritus of Abdera . . . taught that all bodies were continually throwing off certain images like themselves, which subtle emanations, striking on our bodily organs, gave rise to our sensations," he writes in the opening paragraph of "The Stereoscope and the Stereograph." These images "are perpetually shed from the surfaces of solids, as bark is shed by trees."[53] This passage recalls Leonardo's description of the constant flow of images through which the world presents itself to us.

In the next paragraph, Holmes encourages us to look at the images that we "shed," as well as those we receive from others—to view ourselves from the outside, as others see us, as well as from the inside, where we see them. "These evanescent films may be seen in one of their aspects in any clear, calm sheet of water, in a mirror, in the eye of an animal by one who looks at it in front," he observes, "but better still by the consciousness behind the eye in the ordinary act of vision."[54] The body described in these two paragraphs is strikingly similar to the one that Merleau-Ponty would later describe. It sees in response to an external solicitation, which is both tactile and visual, and it solicits a similar response from other perceivers.

A few pages later, Holmes identifies another corporeal aspect of human vision: binocular disparity. As we have already seen, the right retina of a two-sighted person receives a slightly different image than the left. Both of these images are flat, but the brain construes these differences as depth, and fuses them into a single three-dimensional image. Since this image is produced by the brain, it might seem a figment of our physiological "imagination." Holmes, however, draws the opposite conclusion. He argues that its depth is our body's way of countering the most dangerous of all optical illusions: the illusion that the world is immaterial. The three-dimensional image that our brain produces by fusing two almost identical flat images allows us to *feel round* what we see, to "clasp an object with our eyes, as with our arms, or with our hands, or with our thumb and finger."[55] When we look at something in this way, Holmes adds, we "know it to be something more than a surface"—something more, in other words, than a physical or mental representation.

Before chemical photography, it was easy to divorce form from matter, since the images that bodies were "continuously throwing off" perished instantly, but the daguerreotype "[held] them as a picture."[56] Because it was so manifestly a gift from the world to us, the early photographic image was also deep; its space extended backward, toward its source. The more photography was "humanized," the flatter it became, but the stereoscope has restored its depth. "A stereoscope," Holmes declares, "is an instrument which makes surfaces look solid." When looking at the stereo card through its lenses, our mind "feels its way into the very depths of the picture."[57]

As other commentators have already noted, the stereoscopic image has a different kind of depth than we are used to perceiving. It is what Jonathan Crary calls "an assemblage of local zones of three-dimensionality, zones imbued with a hallucinatory clarity, but which taken together never coalesce into a unified field."[58] When looking at it, we also have "an insistent sense of 'in front of' and 'in back of.'"[59] Holmes does not address Crary's first point, but he does talk about the second. In a striking passage midway through his 1859 essay, he suggests that some things in the stereoscopic image not only seem to be emphatically in front of other elements, but to be approaching us, and even on the verge of touching us. "The scraggy branches of a tree in the foreground

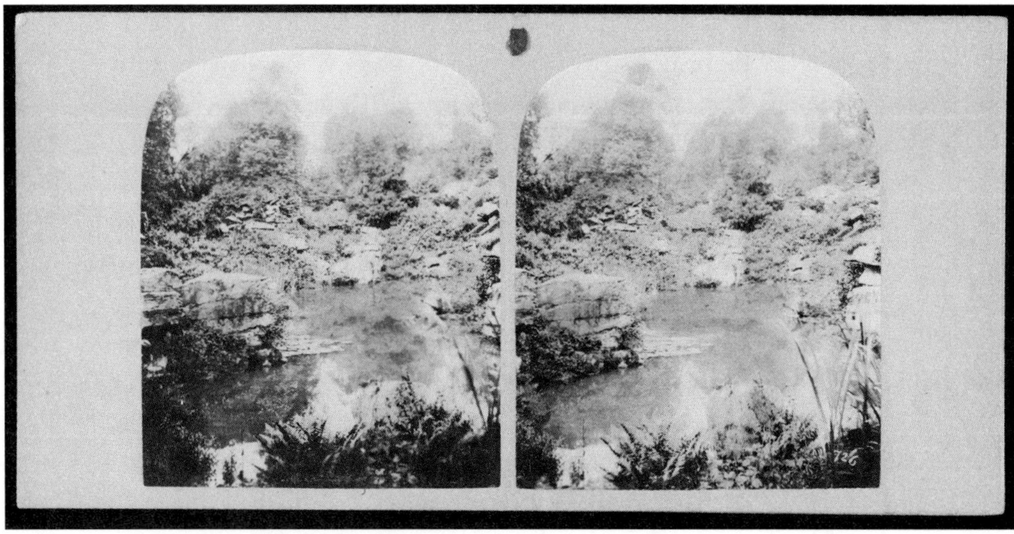

Figure 72. Unknown photographer, *View of the Rock Pond, below the Stride, Chatsworth Pleasure Grounds*, ca. 1859. Albumen print stereocard. © Victoria and Albert Museum, London.

run out at us as if they would scratch our eyes out," he writes. "The elbow of a figure stands forth so as to make us almost uncomfortable."[60]

Holmes also refuses to treat this image as a purely human construction. When we are looking at it, he observes, we have "the same sense of infinite complexity [that] Nature gives us."[61] It also shows us that the boundary separating our body from other bodies is traversable—and in both directions. Not only can we "feel round" what we see, but other bodies can extend into the space we occupy. They are able to cross these borders for the same reason we are: because each of us is already on both sides. Here, too, there are profound affinities between Holmes's argument and Merleau-Ponty's phenomenology. The body "unites us directly with [things] through its own ontogenesis," the philosopher writes in his last book, "by welding to one another the two outlines of which it is made, its two laps: the sensible mass it is and the mass of the sensible wherein it is born by segregation and upon which, as seer, it remains open."[62]

Holmes happily crosses over the boundary separating him from the picture—not just once, but over and over again. "I creep over the vast features of Ramses, on the face of his rockhewn Nubian temple," he enthuses in a passage devoted to the delights of stereoscopic viewing. "I scale the huge mountain-crystal that calls itself the Pyramid of Cheops . . . I stroll through Rhenish vineyards, I sit under Roman arches."[63] When he is inside the picture, he is also keenly aware of the materiality of the world. He marvels over the marks left on a doorway by the "rubbing of [people's] hands and shoulders" in three photographs of Anne Hathaway's cottage, and wonders whether some of them are "scales of epidermis" from "the trembling hand" of "Hathaway's young suitor, Will Shakespeare."[64]

However, Holmes is considerably less enthusiastic about incursions from the other side. He finds the tree branches that extend into his space threatening, and the protruding elbow makes him "uncomfortable." It is perhaps for this reason that he often seems weirdly attached to the oppositions he seeks to dismantle, and that he characterizes the stereoscope as the instrument by means of which form "make[s] itself seen through the world of intelligence" when introducing the device.[65] But although there are numerous points in the essay where Holmes deviates from the argument I have been parsing, nothing prepares us for the last section, which contains the passage that I quoted in the introduction to this book—the one that begins "*Form is henceforth divorced from matter*. In fact, matter as a visible object is of no great use any longer, except as the mold on which form is shaped."[66]

This passage is unabashedly metaphysical, and it shows nineteenth-century rationalization to be the logical extension of the values celebrated by Descartes.

Far from challenging this idealism, photography is now the star in its crown, and the means through which it penetrates other domains. A photographic event is like a hunting expedition, Holmes declares; we participate in it only for the "skin." After we extract it from the world, we abandon what remains, which is of "little worth." Soon we will have enough of these "skins" to create "a comprehensive and systematic stereographic library, where all men can find the [one that] they particularly desire to see as artists, or as scholars, or as mechanics, or in any other capacity."[67] This library will be even more useful when we have standardized our photographic practice, because when we look at stereographs of similar objects that were shot from the same distance and with the same kind of camera lens, we will be able to study them dispassionately, and not be misled by "partialities." This standardization will also allow us to create a vast "system of exchanges." The stereograph will become a "universal currency," minted for us by the sun.[68]

In the penultimate paragraph of the essay, Holmes identifies another of the things that photography is "good" for: capturing and immortalizing iconic images from the battlefield. "It is asserted that a bursting shell can be photographed," he writes. "The time is perhaps at hand when a flash of light, as sudden and brief as that of the lightning which shows a whirling wheel standing stock still, shall preserve the very instant of the shock of contact of the mighty armies that are even now gathering. . . . The lightning of clashing sabres and bayonets may be forced to stereograph itself in a stillness as complete as that of the tumbling tide of Niagara as we see it self-pictured."[69] Never have the lethal consequences of the medium's rationalization been more evident. It would also be hard to think of a better way of describing the violence we have done to photography itself.

Every time I read this section of "The Stereoscope and the Stereograph," I ask myself the same question: is Holmes speaking in his own voice here, or is he ventriloquizing someone else? The last time I searched for the answer to this question, I realized that I had been looking in the wrong place. It resides not in the passage I have just summarized, but in the two sentences that precede it. "What is to come of the stereoscope and the photograph we are almost afraid to guess," Holmes writes there, "lest we should seem extravagant. But, premising that we are to give a *colored* stereoscopic mental view of their prospect, we will venture on a few glimpses at a conceivable, if not a possible future."[70] These sentences are full of equivocations and *double entendres*, which I will not attempt to unpack, but they permit us to say one thing with absolute certainty. Holmes is not describing photography as it exists in the final section of his essay, or even photography as it will later look; he is describing, rather, an imaginable but *unrealizable* future.

Holmes returns to this future in the final sentence of "The Stereoscope and the Stereograph." "Before another generation has passed away," he proclaims, "it will be recognized that a new epoch in the history of human progress dates from the time when He who 'never but in uncreated light / Dwelt from eternity' took a pencil of fire from the hand of the 'angel standing in the sun,' and placed it in the hands of a mortal."[71] This sentence is densely packed with literary and visual references to a light that does not belong to man, but that he has in at least one case appropriated. It alludes to the myth of Prometheus, in which fire is stolen from the gods and given to mortals; Milton's Prologue to *Paradise Lost*,[72] in which the blind poet appeals to God for illumination, so that he can recount two other stories of "overreaching"—Satan's expulsion from heaven and the fall of Adam and Eve; Turner's *An Angel Standing in the Sun*, in which the Angel of the Apocalypse appears in a great circle of light, brandishing a fiery sword; the passage from Revelation that Turner appended to his painting, that begins with the words "And I saw an angel standing in the sun; and he cried with a loud voice, saying to all the fowls that fly in the midst of heaven, Come and gather yourselves together unto the supper of the great God"; and—finally—the pencil of light, with which nature draws the photographic image, but which man is now beginning to arrogate to himself. This is hardly a ringing endorsement for the "new epoch in the history of human progress" that began when the "pencil of fire was placed in the hands of a mortal." On the contrary: there is a strong sense of impending doom.

Since the future as it is described in the last sentence of the essay closely resembles the past, it is easy to see why it should be "conceivable." The claim that this future is "not possible," though, is perplexing, since history seems to have proven otherwise. Holmes wrote "The Stereoscope and the Stereograph" approximately two years before the start of the American Civil War, whose bloody battles and massive casualties decimated the nation, and compounded the oppositions on which it was founded. Over the four years of the war, most of what Holmes describes in the last section of "The Stereoscope and the Stereograph" became a reality.

In 1862, Mathew Brady mounted an exhibition of photographs from the first battle of the Civil War, and a *New York Times* reviewer urged his readers to go and see "the fearful reproductions," which were "for sale" in Brady's gallery, and acquire some for themselves. They were, he added, "of a size convenient for albums."[73] The photographers who worked for Brady continued to produce war photographs for his gallery, and Alexander Gardner's photographers did the same after he stopped working for Brady and established a rival gallery.

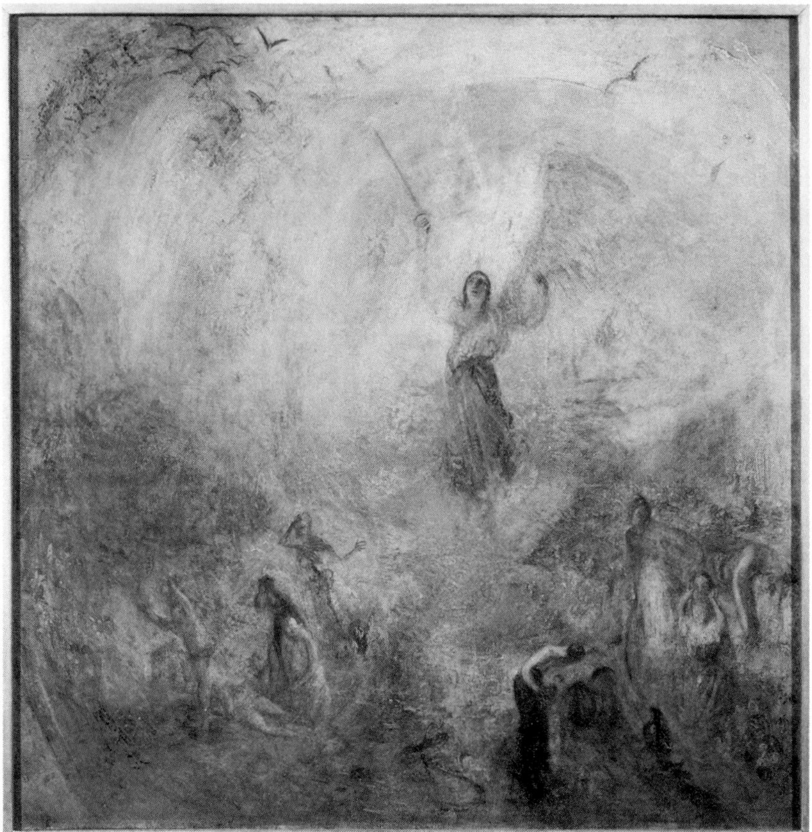

Figure 73/Colorplate 21. J. M. W. Turner, *An Angel Standing in the Sun*, 1846. Oil on canvas. The Tate Britain, London. © Tate, London 2014.

Gardner advertised his business with the words "Views of the War," and by 1865 he had accumulated nearly three thousand glass negatives, one hundred of which he published in *Gardner's Photographic Sketch Book of the War*.[74] Many of these photographs show corpses that were abandoned after their metaphoric skins had been removed.

Most of Brady and Gardner's "views" were available both as large silver albumen photographs and as stereo cards, and priced accordingly. Thousands of other photographers turned a handsome profit on war portraits, which were aggressively marketed to both soldiers and their families. They were also available in many different forms, which became increasingly standardized, and were pegged to different socio-economic groups. As a contemporary reviewer noted, the American Civil War industrialized both death and photography, and often in tandem. "America swarms with the members of the mighty tribe of cameristas," he wrote, "and the civil war has developed their business in the same way that it has given an impetus to the manufacturers of metallic air-tight coffins and embalmers of the dead. The young Volunteer rushes off at once to the studio when he puts on his uniform, and the soldier of a year's campaign sends home his likeness that the absent ones may see what changes have been produced in him by war's alarms."[75] In 1862, the United States began taxing photographs, making them a rich source of national as well as personal revenue, and eventually this "vast treasury" of images[76] found its way into the archives for which they were always destined.

But Holmes was right to say that the nightmarish account of photography that he presents in the last section of "The Stereograph and the Stereoscope" is unrealizable, because none of this has anything to do with the pencil of nature. No matter how many cameras we train on the world, it will never "scale off its surface for us," stamp our "banknotes" with the great seal of the sun, or "send us stereographs of battles." Nor did it stick around when we began arrogating the photographic image to ourselves, and using it as a tool of conquest. Although the world continued speaking to us through individual photographs, most of its self-portraits took other forms in the decades that followed.

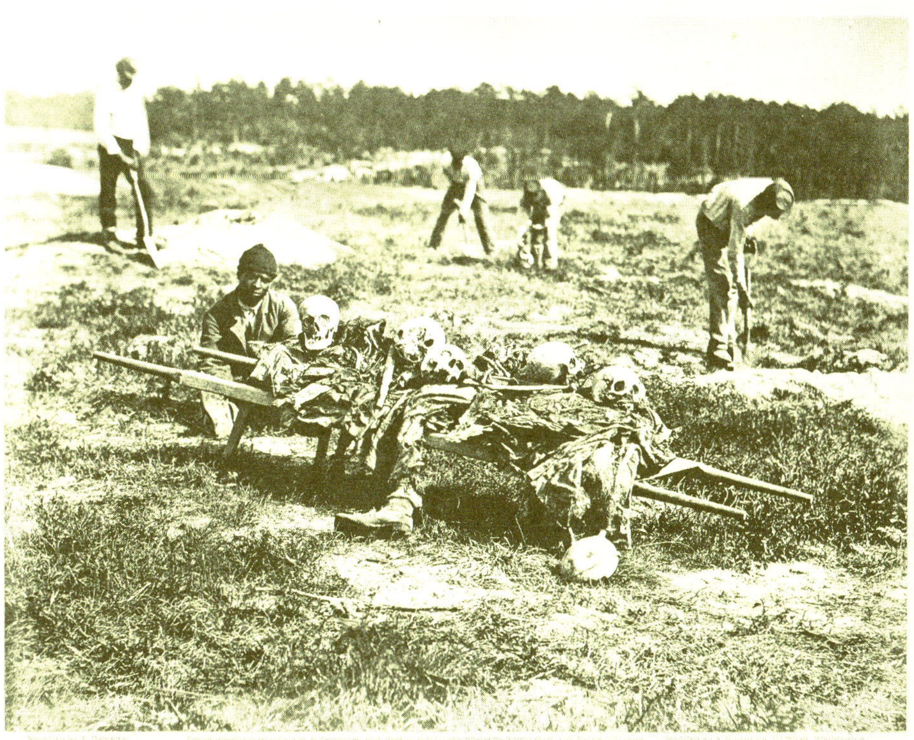

Figure 74. John Reekie and Alexander Gardner, *A Burial Party, Cold Harbor, Virginia*, 1865 (printed 1866). Albumen print from collodion wet-plate negative. Courtesy of the Open Content Program of the Getty Museum, Los Angeles.

In the next chapter, I will discuss some of the means through which photography lived on after the industrialization of the chemical medium, but I want to conclude this one with a powerfully disclosive photograph from the 1860s: John Reekie's *A Burial Party on the Battle-Field of Cold Harbor* (April 1865). The five figures in this photograph are engaged in a grim task: burying the remains of thousands of Union soldiers, who were killed in two battles the preceding year, both of which were fought on this site. Since they have been lying there for a long time, these remains are sparse: some bleached skulls, a jumble of other bones, a boot, and tattered bits of clothing. They are piled on an angled stretcher in the foreground of the photograph, behind which one of the men is crouching. He looks directly out at us, from the left side of the photograph. The skull that is most proximate to him also faces us. The other men have shovels and are dispersed across the field that extends from the stretcher to the trees at the rear of the image. Three of them appear to be digging graves, and the fourth is standing beside a mound of earth. They all look down at the ground, from which they came, and to which they will one day return.

The photograph speaks volumes about America's still-palpable racial divide. The men in the burial party are all African Americans, and they are interring the remains of Northern soldiers in Virginia, a slave state. Although they are not slaves,[77] they are working in a field, and doing a job that the local residents refused to do, or even command their slaves to do. One of the men is wearing a Union Army uniform, indicating that he is a soldier, and suggesting that this may also be the case with the other men. However, although the ostensible goal of the Civil War was the eradication of slavery in the remaining slave states, African Americans were not allowed to join the Union Army until 1863, and when they were finally admitted they were relegated to separate units, and discriminated against in numerous ways. Finally, most—if not all—of the men whose remains they are burying were white.

Burial Party is one of the hundred photographs in Gardner's *Photographic Sketchbook of the American Civil War*. Gardner credits the negative to Reekie, and the positive to himself, just as Sugimoto does with Talbot's photographs in his *Photographic Drawings*. Like Sugimoto, Gardner also positions the photograph on the right page and the commentary on the left. He wrote this commentary, and its first sentence is as remarkable for what it doesn't say as for what it does. Gardner refuses to utter the adjective on the basis of which certain Americans were deemed to be "slaves," or were relegated to a segregated military unit. He identifies the men in the photograph simply as "soldiers."[78] He also characterizes their relationship to the fallen men in a surprising way. He writes that they are "in the act of collecting the remains of their comrades."[79]

With the last word in this sentence, Gardner declares them to be equal with and ontologically connected to the dead men. The photograph itself goes even further. As Elizabeth Young observes, the "dismembered foot" in the foreground of the photograph "seems an extension of the live African American bodies,"[80] and the skulls lined up in a row on the stretcher undo *all* binary oppositions—not just "white" and "black," but North and South, rich and poor, and slave and freeman. The skull that faces us also shows us that we are as deep inside this picture as Holmes was in the pictures of Anne Hathaway's cottage when he noticed the rub marks on her doorway.

The skull, however, cannot cross over to our side, because its sockets are empty. The real center of the photograph is not it, but the man whose shoulder it seems to touch. He invites us to join the republic for which he stands "by using [our] own being as a means of participating in [his]."[81] His look is "undiminished by time," as Eleanor Jones Harvey puts it,[82] because it does not belong to the past. It is headed toward the present: toward the here and now in which a potentially infinite series of later looks will both meet it and greet it.

Chapter 5

JE VOUS

IN THE FINAL DECADES of the nineteenth century and the first decades of the twentieth, the tropes that had earlier been associated with the pinhole camera, the camera obscura, and chemical photography began appearing in some surprising places: in painting, literature, and psychoanalysis. When Cézanne described himself as a "recording machine,"[1] and Rilke wrote that *The Sonnets to Orpheus* had been "dictated" to him by a non-human agency,[2] they echoed what Pope said about the camera obscura and Talbot about the calotype: "It is not the artist who makes the picture, but [rather] the picture which makes ITSELF."[3] They also indicated that they themselves were receivers.

Cézanne and Rilke sought to receive what the world gave them on the "surface" of their psyches, which they conceptualized as a photographic plate. The painter "must silence all the voices of prejudice within him, he must forget, forget, be quiet, become a perfect echo," Cézanne told Joachim Gasquet. "And then the entire landscape will engrave itself on the sensitive plate of his being."[5] "Paris this time was just as I had promised it to myself, difficult," Rilke wrote Lou Andreas-Salomé in 1913, "and I seem to myself like a photographic plate which is exposed too long, in that I still lie open to what is here, this powerful influence."[4] They attempted to transmit what they received to others through their work, just as Leonardo did in the fifteenth century. Unfortunately, though, Cézanne and Rilke weren't always able to accept what was given to them, because something within them wanted the exact opposite: isolation and autonomy.

Freud also compares the psyche to a photographic plate on which light inscribes images, describes the human subject as the receiver of these images, and talks about an opposing force: one that seeks to exclude the world and replace it with a mental representation. Conscious vision begins with the influx of perceptual stimuli from the external world into the psyche, he writes in *Interpretation of Dreams*. These stimuli are "receive[d]" at the "sensory end" of the psyche, and pass into the unconscious, where—as in the darkened chamber of a photographic camera—they inscribe enduring images. Most perceptual stimuli move from there to the preconscious, and then on to the perception-consciousness "system." Since this system is incapable of retaining anything, they quickly disappear, making room for new perceptions.[6]

In *Introductory Lectures on Psycho-Analysis*, Freud compares the enduring images that light inscribes on the unconscious to a photographic negative, the unconscious to a room in which negatives are stored, and the images that reach consciousness to a positive print. "Every mental process . . . exists to begin with in an unconscious stage or phase and that it is only from there that the process passes over into the conscious phase," he observes, "just as a photographic picture begins as a negative and only becomes a picture after being turned into a positive." Not every negative "becomes a positive," though, "nor is it necessary that every unconscious mental process should turn into a conscious one."[7] It is also not *possible* for every unconscious mental process to become conscious. Perceptions arrive at consciousness in a "cut-up" form, Freud writes, since only one image can enter at a time.[8] And some never arrive; they are confined to the unconscious because they are associated with forbidden wishes.[9]

In a 1924 essay, Freud compares human perception to another implicitly photographic device—one that recalls the pencil of nature, and the kind of "openness" to which Rilke and Cézanne aspired. This device is the "Mystic Writing-Pad," a children's notebook with an erasable top layer and an underlying waxy support that retains the traces of what is inscribed with a stylus on the top layer. The unconscious resembles the underlying layer, Freud observes, because its capacity to receive is limited by what has already been inscribed on it. The perception-consciousness system is like the top layer, which retains nothing, but has "an unlimited receptive capacity for new impressions."[10] A psychic agency with an "unlimited capacity for new impressions" is one into which "fresh 'vital differences'"[11] are constantly flowing—i.e., one similar to the camera obscura and early photography. And although Freud usually privileges the unconscious over the perception-consciousness system, here his sympathies are clearly with the latter.

Elsewhere, though, he associates the psyche with a different kind of photography: the kind that emerged through the industrialization of the medium. Sometimes an image becomes stuck in the "defile" of consciousness, he writes in *Studies in Hysteria*, which prevents new perceptions from entering. It "remains in front of the [subject]," so that he "sees nothing of what is pushing after it, and forgets what has already pushed its way through."[12] Human desire also resembles a printing press, Freud remarks in "The Dynamics of Transference"; it is continually reproducing the same image. "Each individual . . . has acquired a specific method of his own in his conduct of his erotic life—that is, in the preconditions to falling in love that he lays down, in the instincts he satisfies

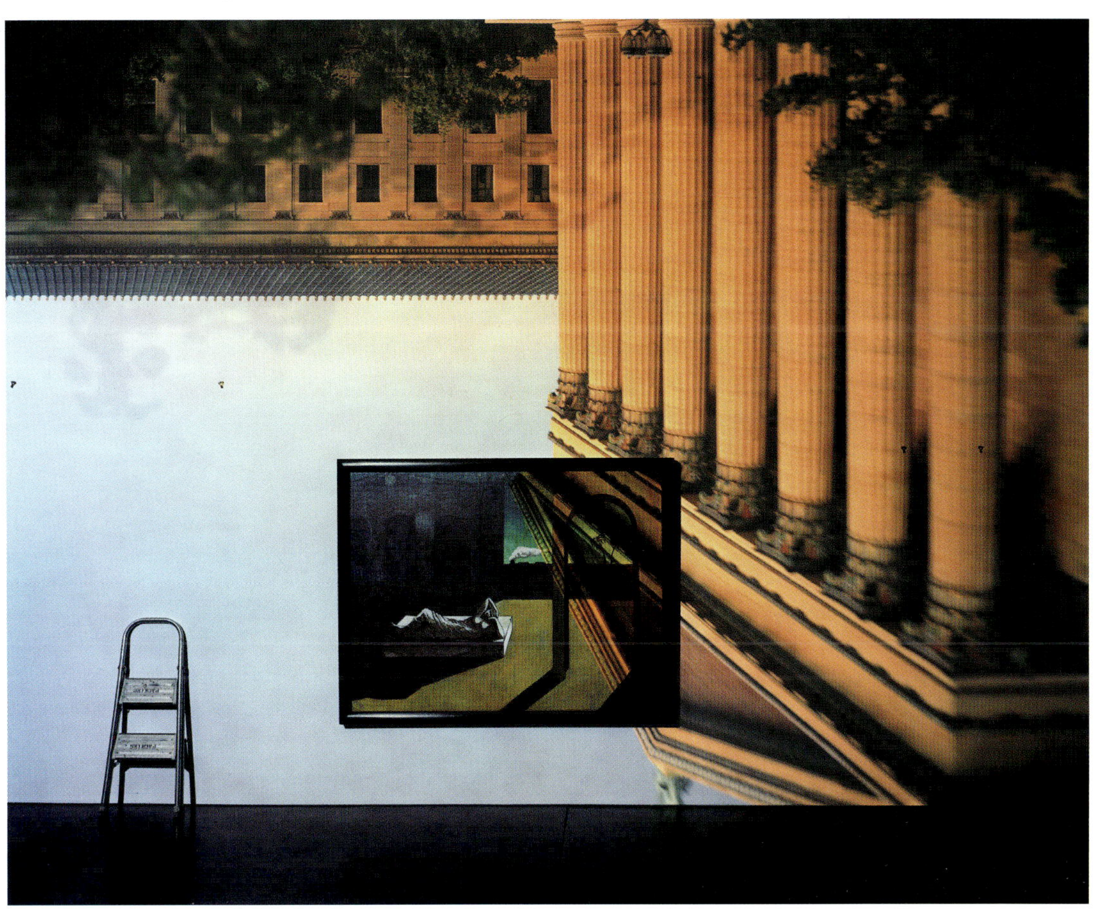

Colorplate 1/Figure 20. Abelardo Morell, *Camera Obscura: The Philadelphia Museum of Art East Entrance in Gallery #171 with a de Chirico Painting*, 2005. Inkjet print. Image © Abelardo Morell, courtesy of Edwynn Houk Gallery, New York.

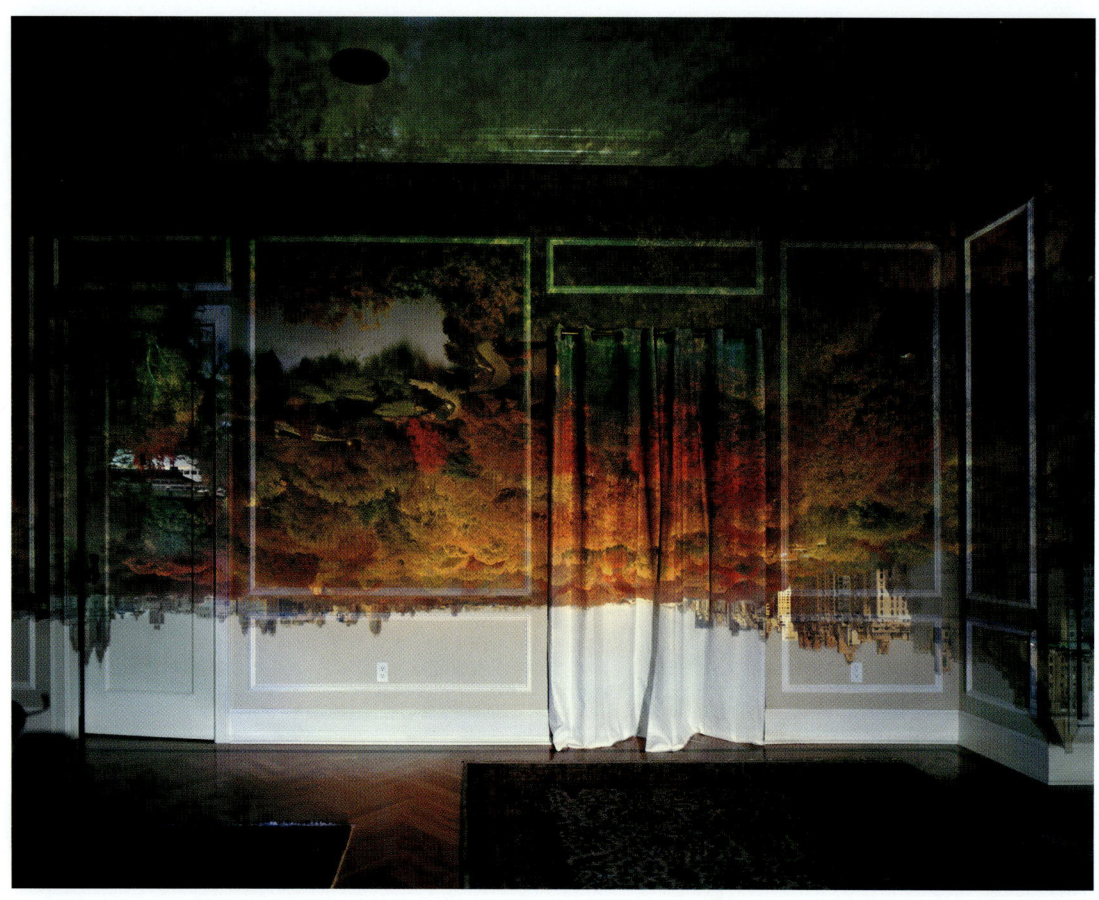

Colorplate 2/Figure 21. Abelardo Morell, *Camera Obscura: View of Central Park Looking North— Fall*, 2008. Inkjet print. Image © Abelardo Morell, courtesy of Edwynn Houk Gallery, New York.

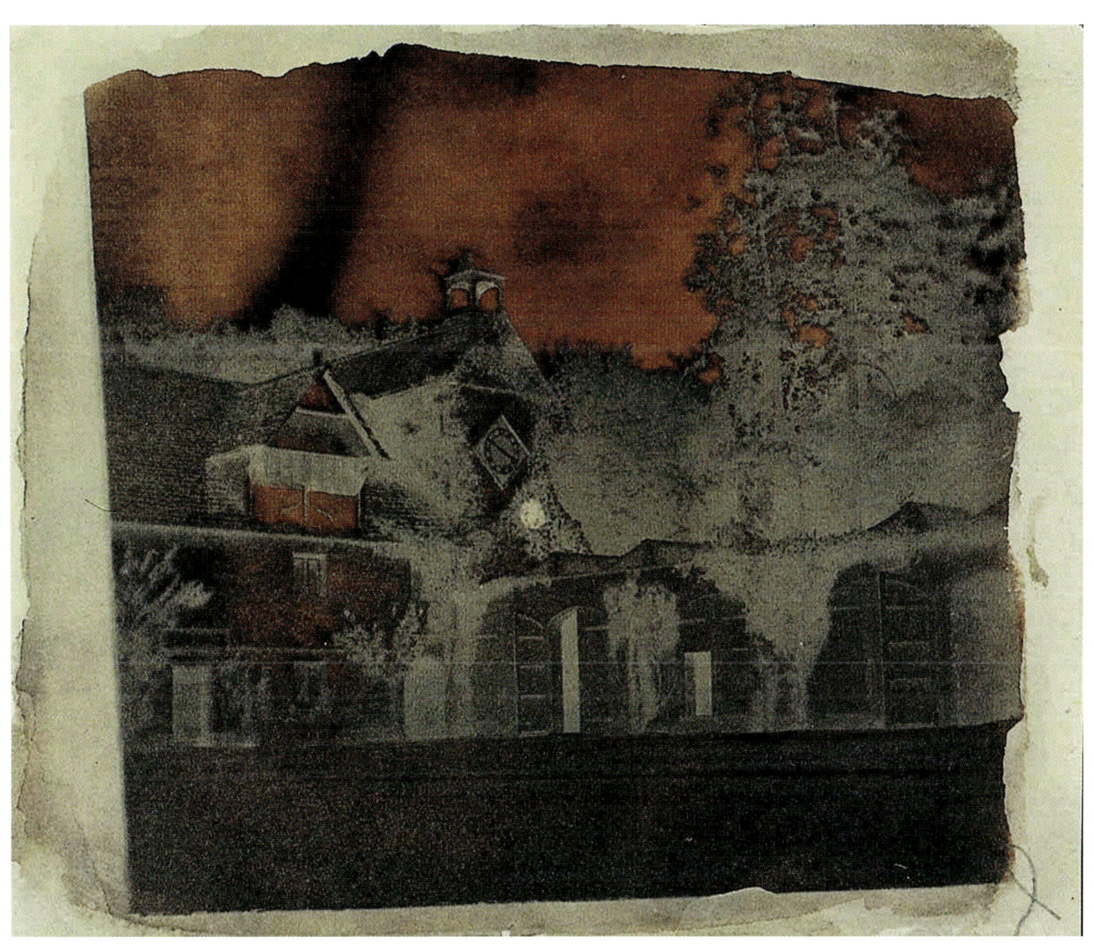

Colorplate 3/Figure 28. Henry Fox Talbot, *The Stable Court, Lacock Abbey*, ca. 1841. Calotype negative. Courtesy of the National Media Museum/SSPL.

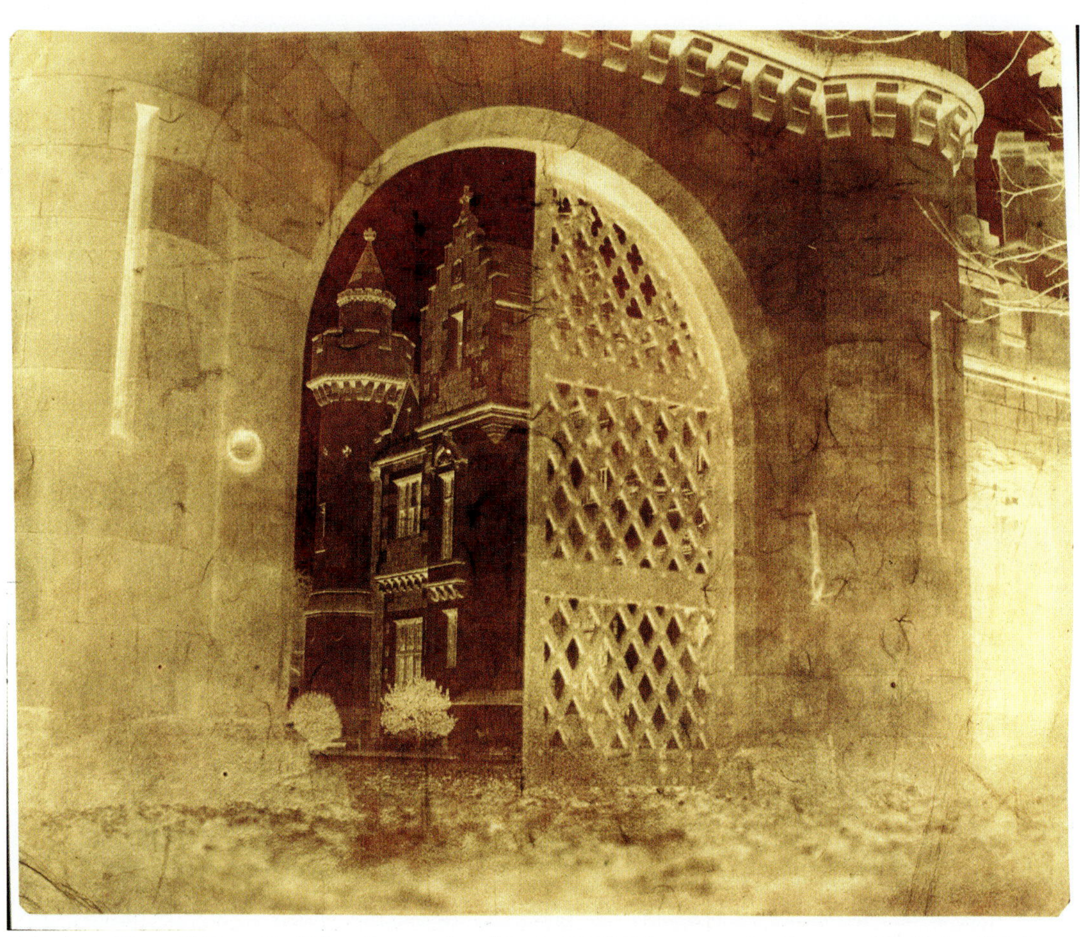

Colorplate 4/Figure 29. Henry Fox Talbot, *Entrance Gate, Abbotsford*, 1845. Calotype negative. Courtesy of the National Media Museum/SSPL.

Colorplate 5/Figure 33. *View from the Window at Le Gras* in its original frame. Courtesy of the Harry Ransom Center at the University of Texas at Austin.

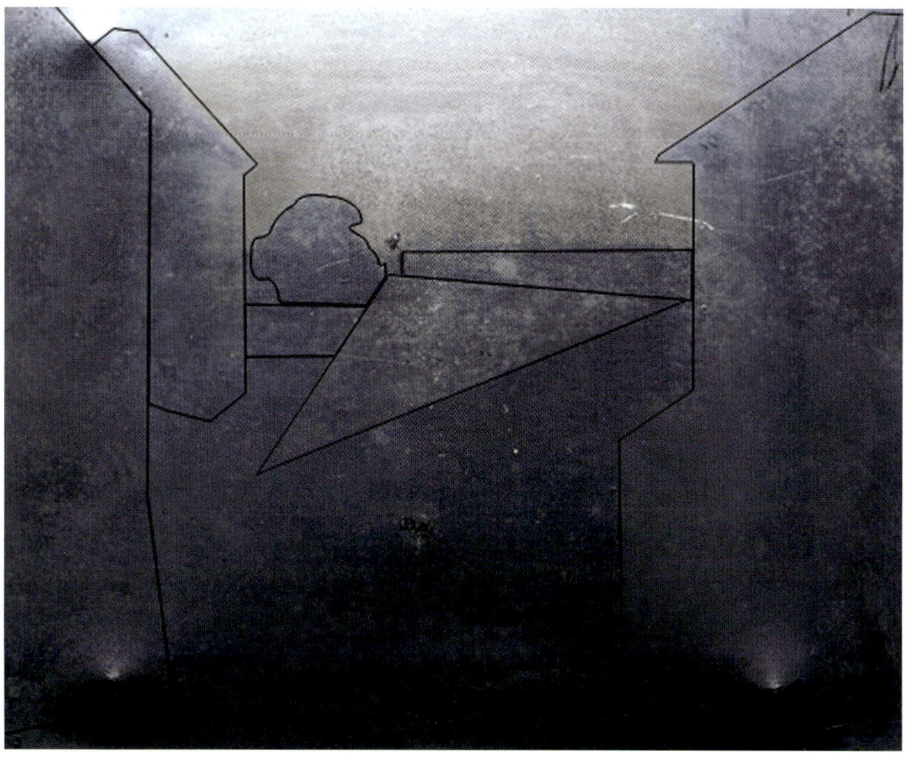

Colorplate 5/Figure 35. *View from the Window at Le Gras* with Gernsheim's pencil drawing superimposed. Courtesy of the Harry Ransom Center at the University of Texas at Austin.

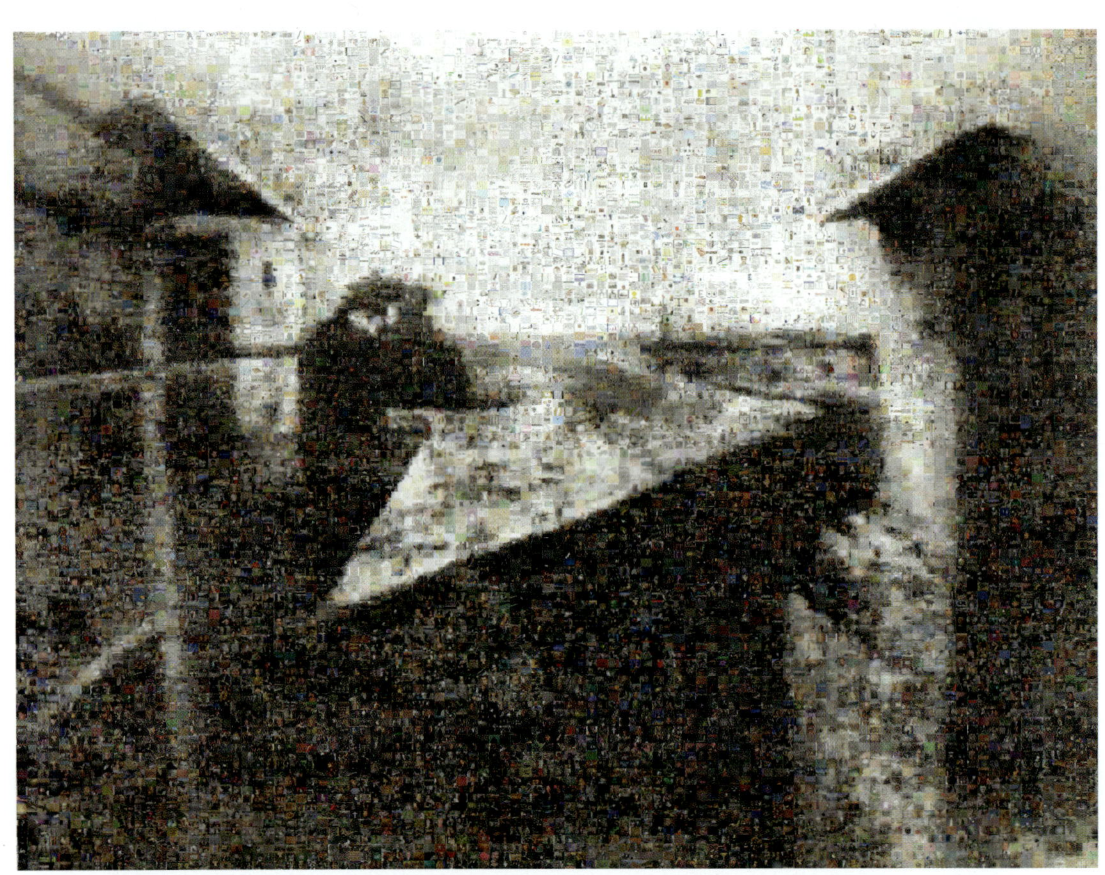

Colorplate 6/Figure 36. Juan Fontcuberta, *Googlegram: Niépce*, 2005. Chromogenic print. Courtesy of the artist.

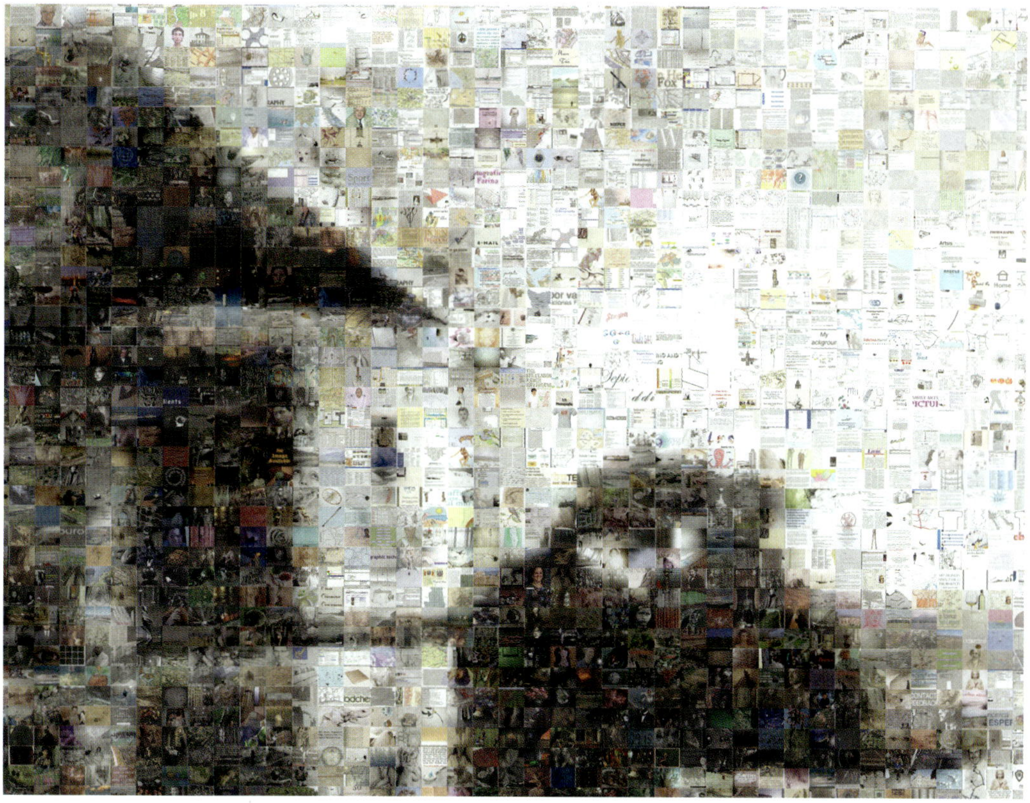

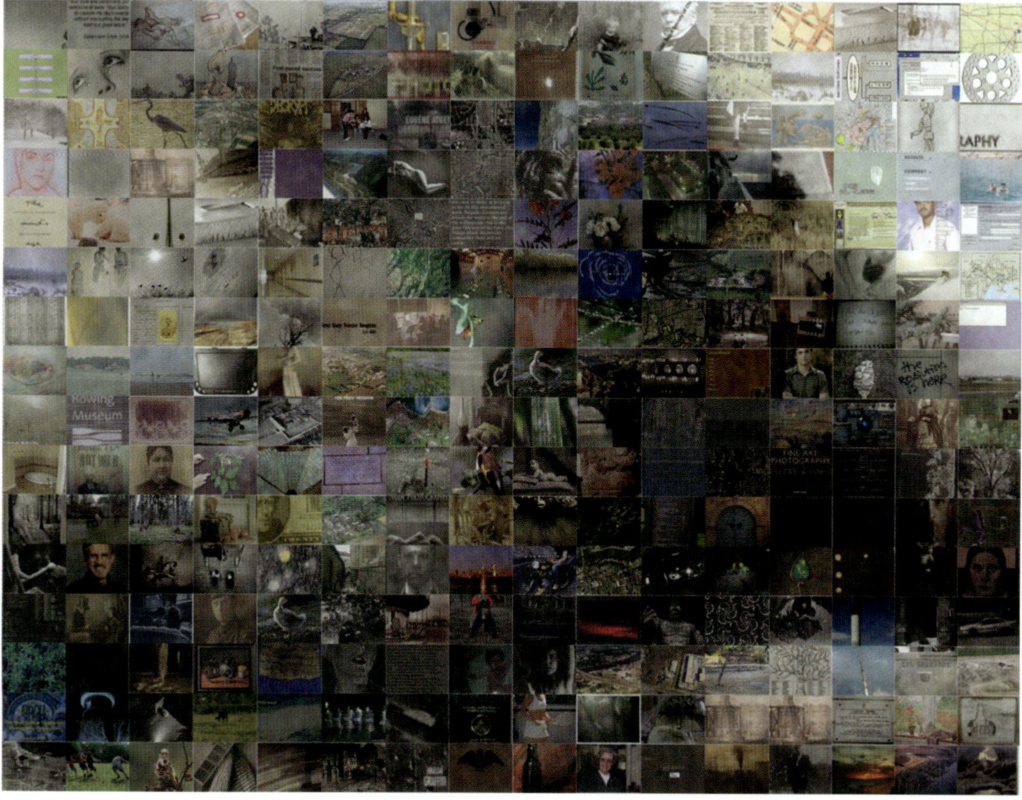

Colorplate 7/Figures 37 & 38. Juan Fontcuberta, *Googlegram: Niépce* (details). Courtesy of the artist.

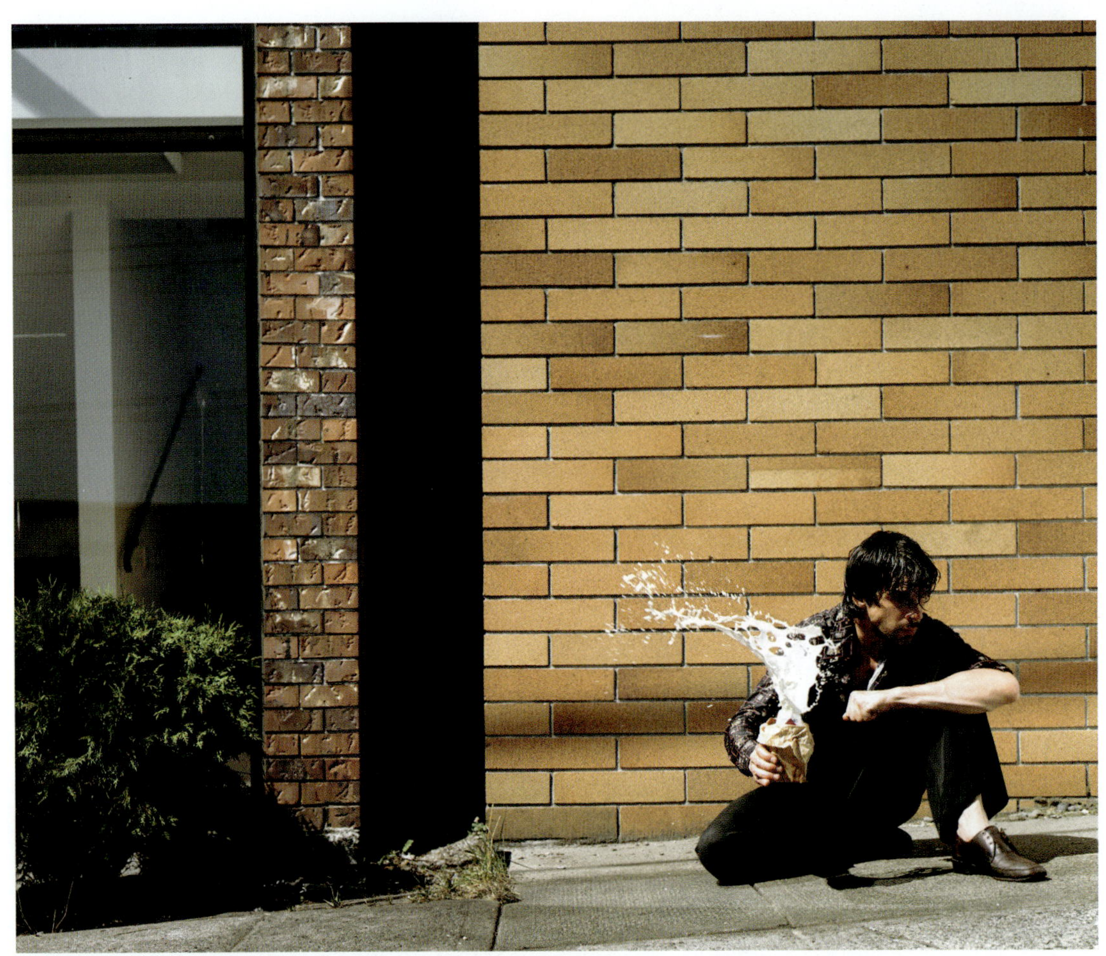

Colorplate 8/Figure 39. Jeff Wall, *Milk*, 1984. Transparency in light box. Courtesy of the artist.

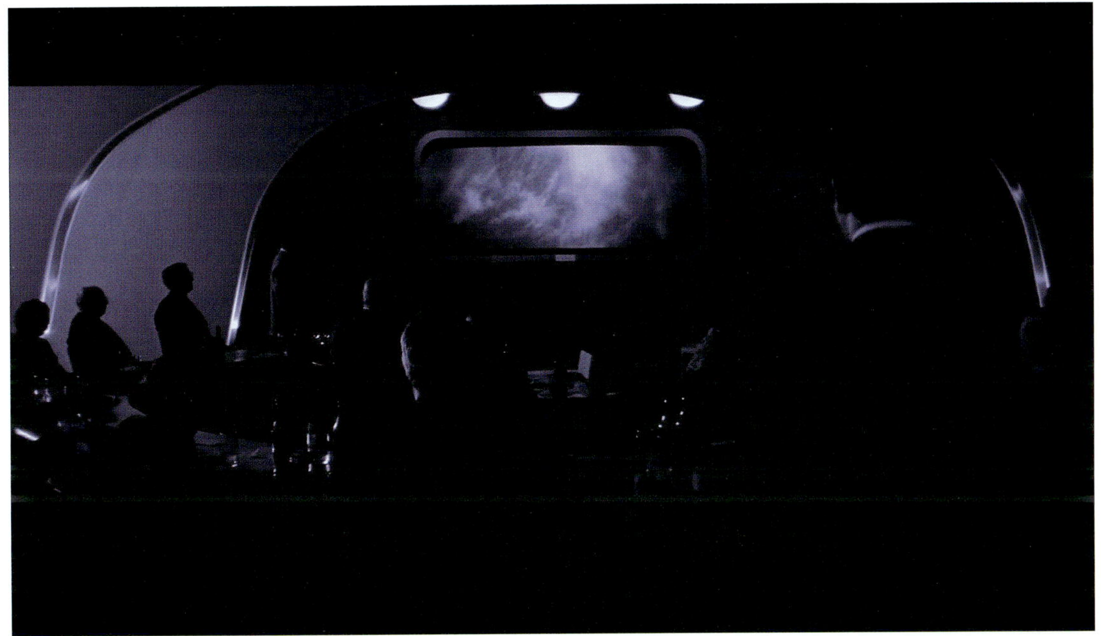

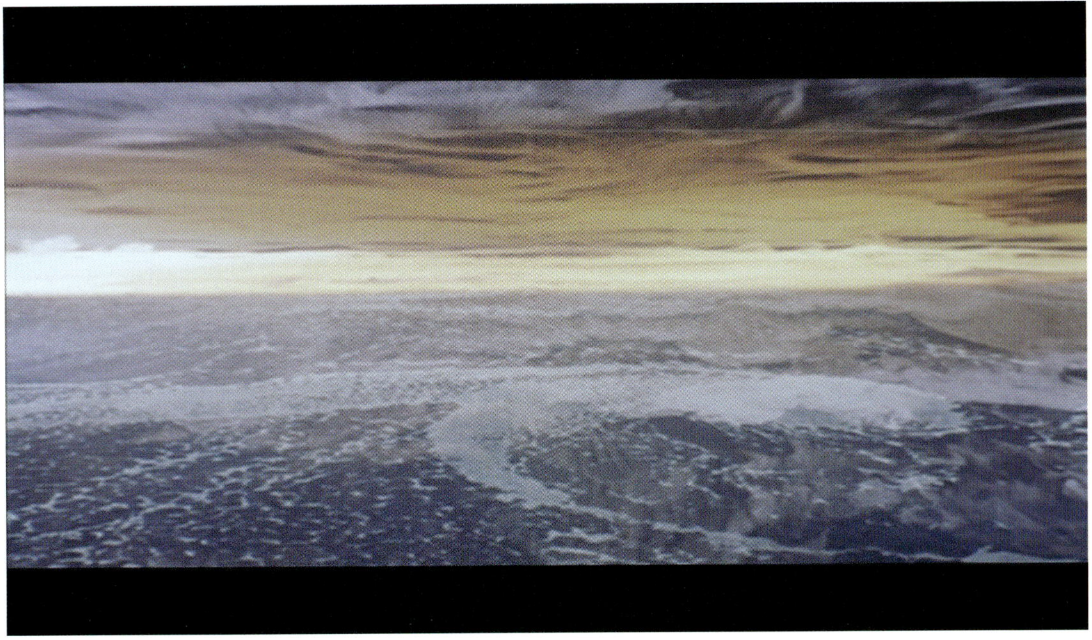

Colorplate 9/Figures 54 & 55. Andrei Tarkovsky, *Solaris*, 1972 (film still).

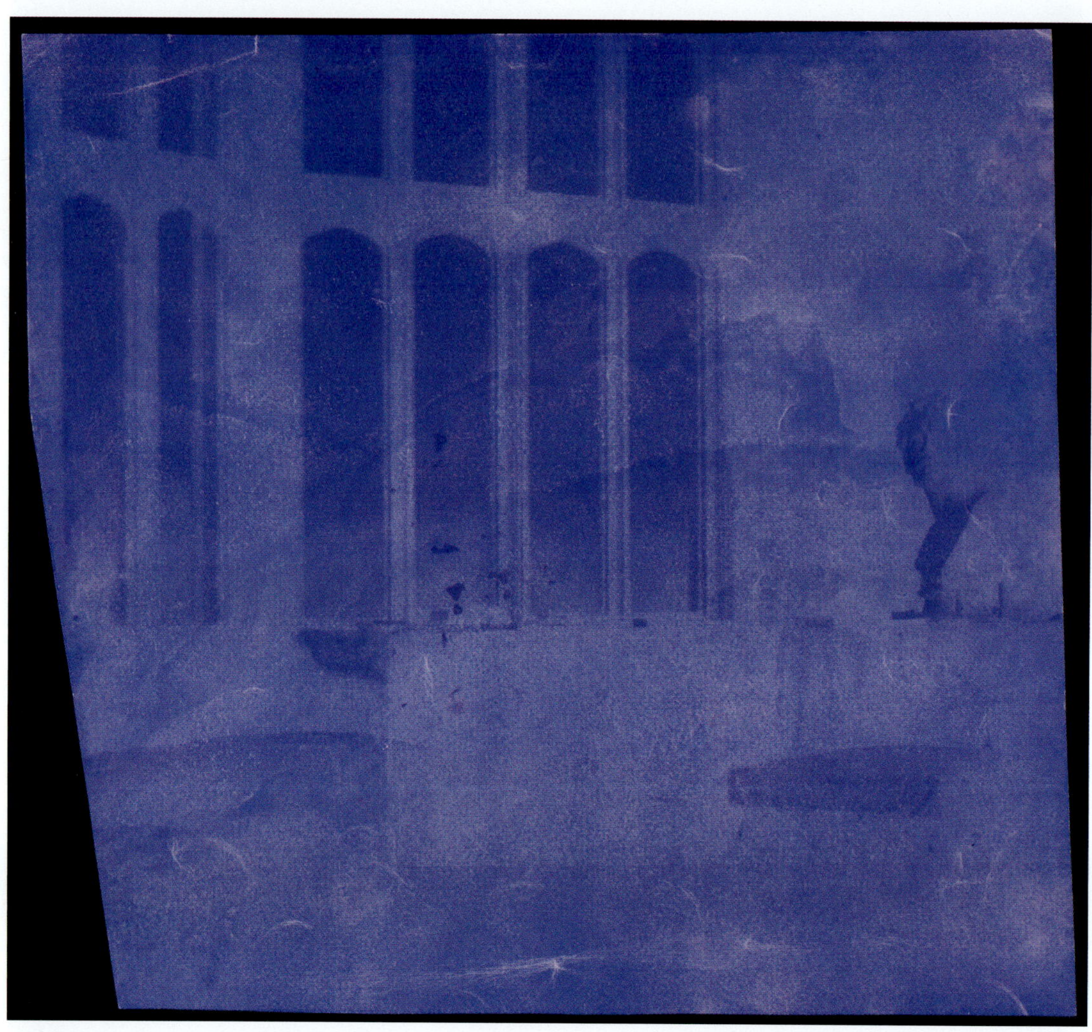

Colorplate 10/Figure 60. Henry Fox Talbot, *Oriel Window, South Gallery, Lacock Abbey*, April 1839. Photogenic drawing negative. Courtesy of the National Media Museum/SSPL.

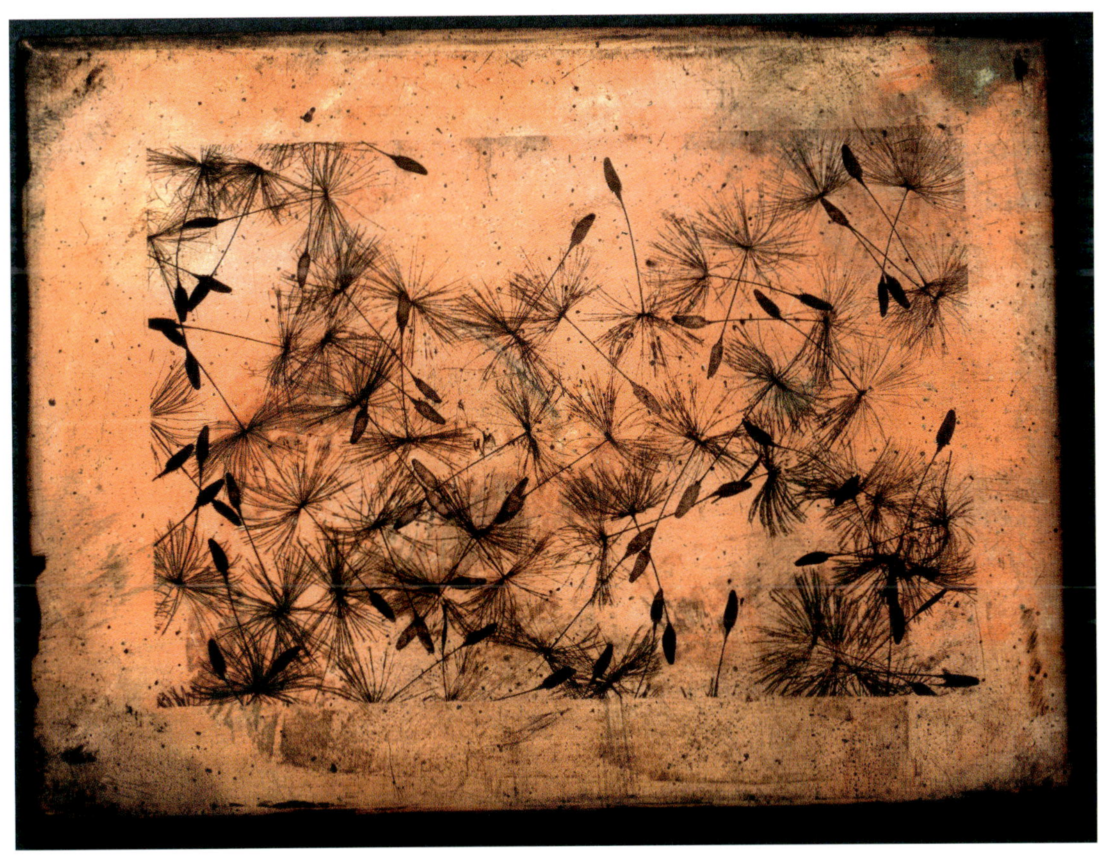

Colorplate 11/Figure 61. Henry Fox Talbot, *Seeds*, 1853. Photogravure. Courtesy of the National Media Museum/SSPL.

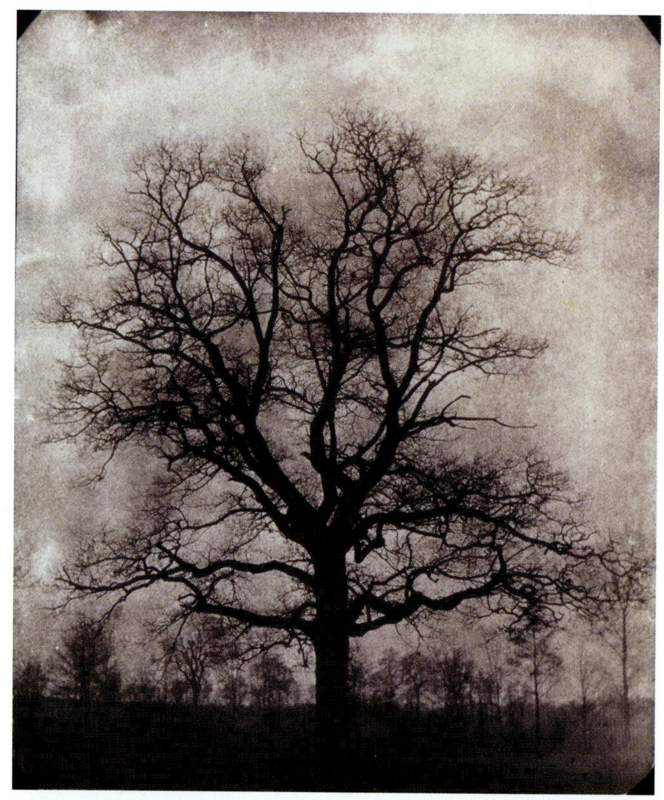

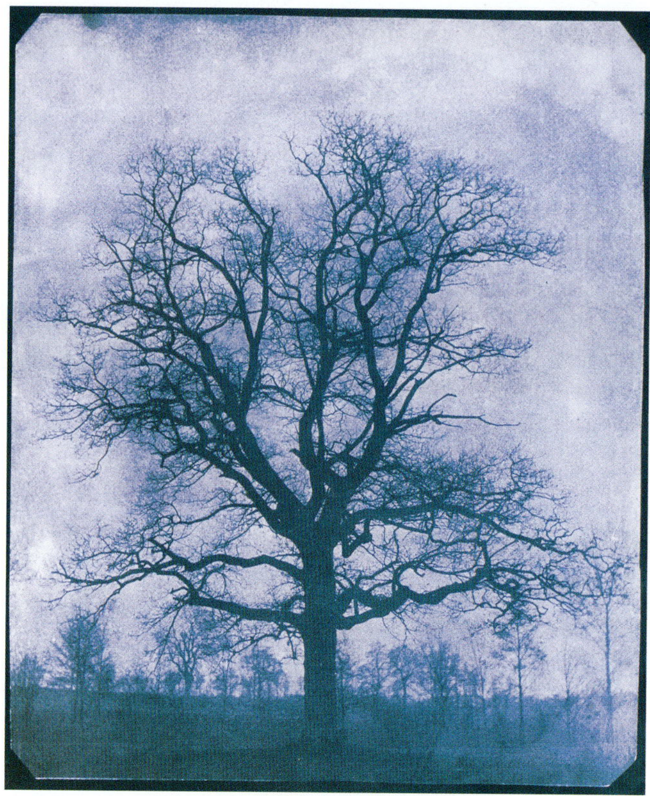

Colorplate 12/Figures 62 & 63. Henry Fox Talbot, *Tree in Winter*, ca. 1842. Salted paper print from calotype negative. Courtesy of the National Media Museum/SSPL.

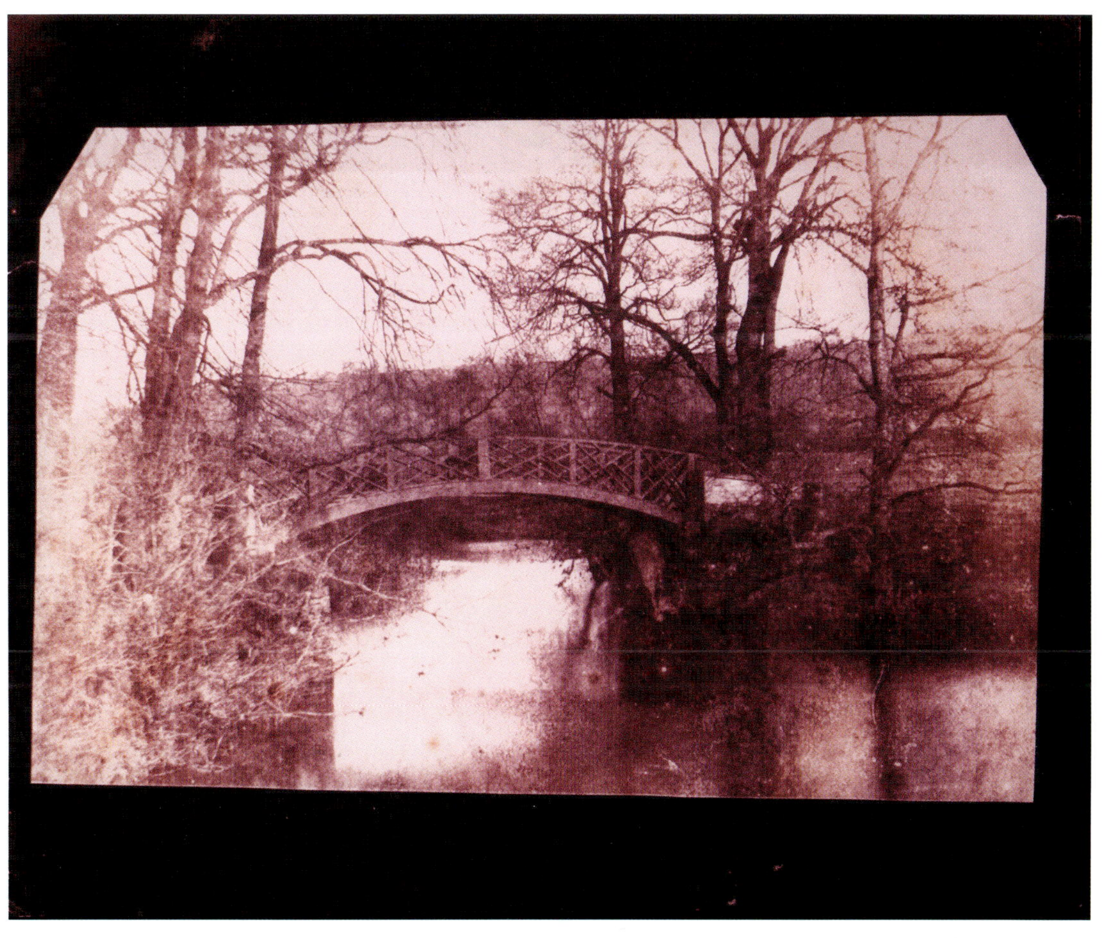

Colorplate 13/Figure 64. Henry Fox Talbot, *China Bridge at Lacock Abbey*, 1841. Salted paper print. Courtesy of the National Media Museum/SSPL.

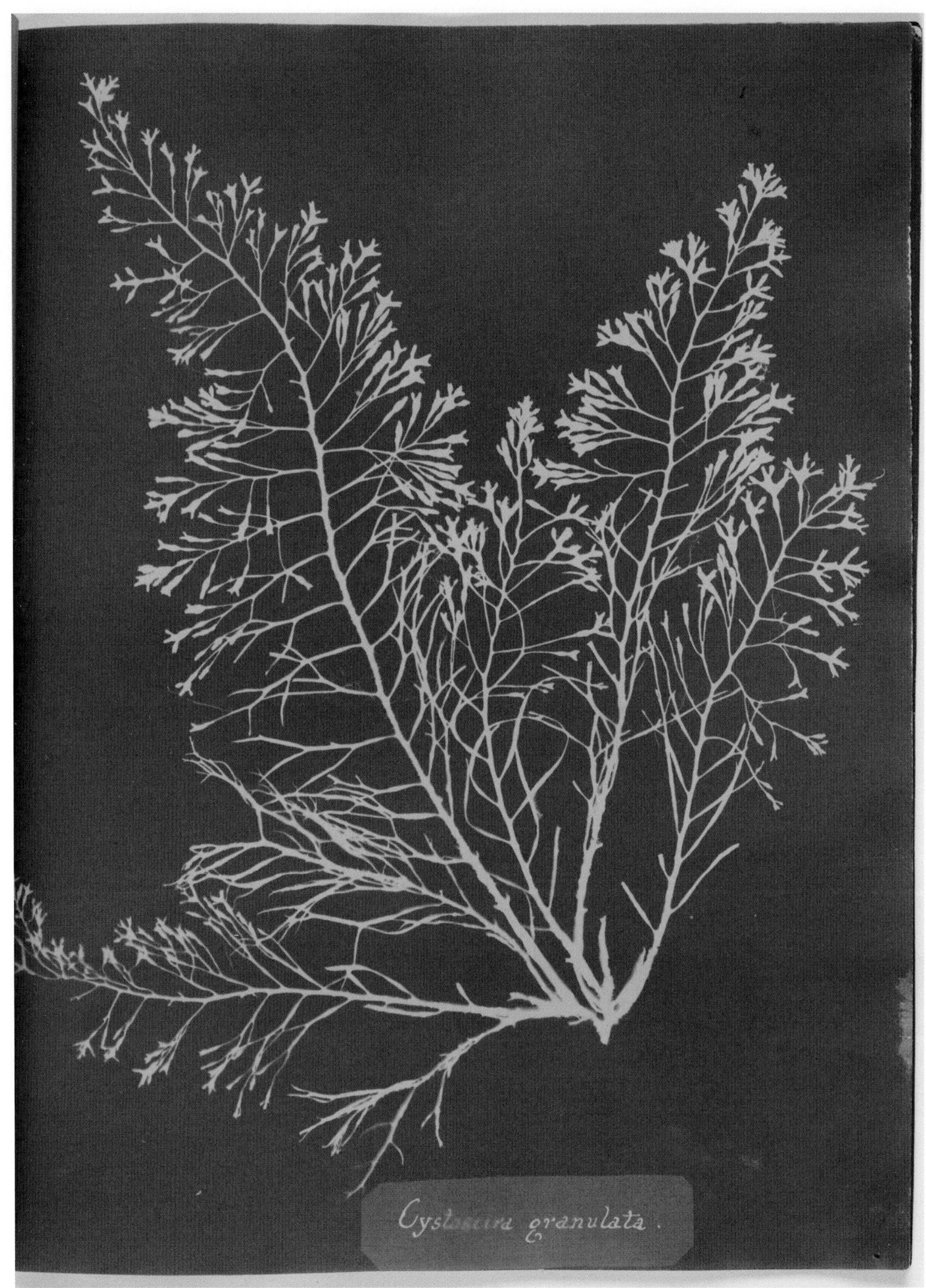

Colorplate 14/Figure 65. Anna Atkins, *Cystoseira granulata*, from *Photographs of British Algae*, 1843. Cyanotype. Courtesy of the National Media Museum/SSPL.

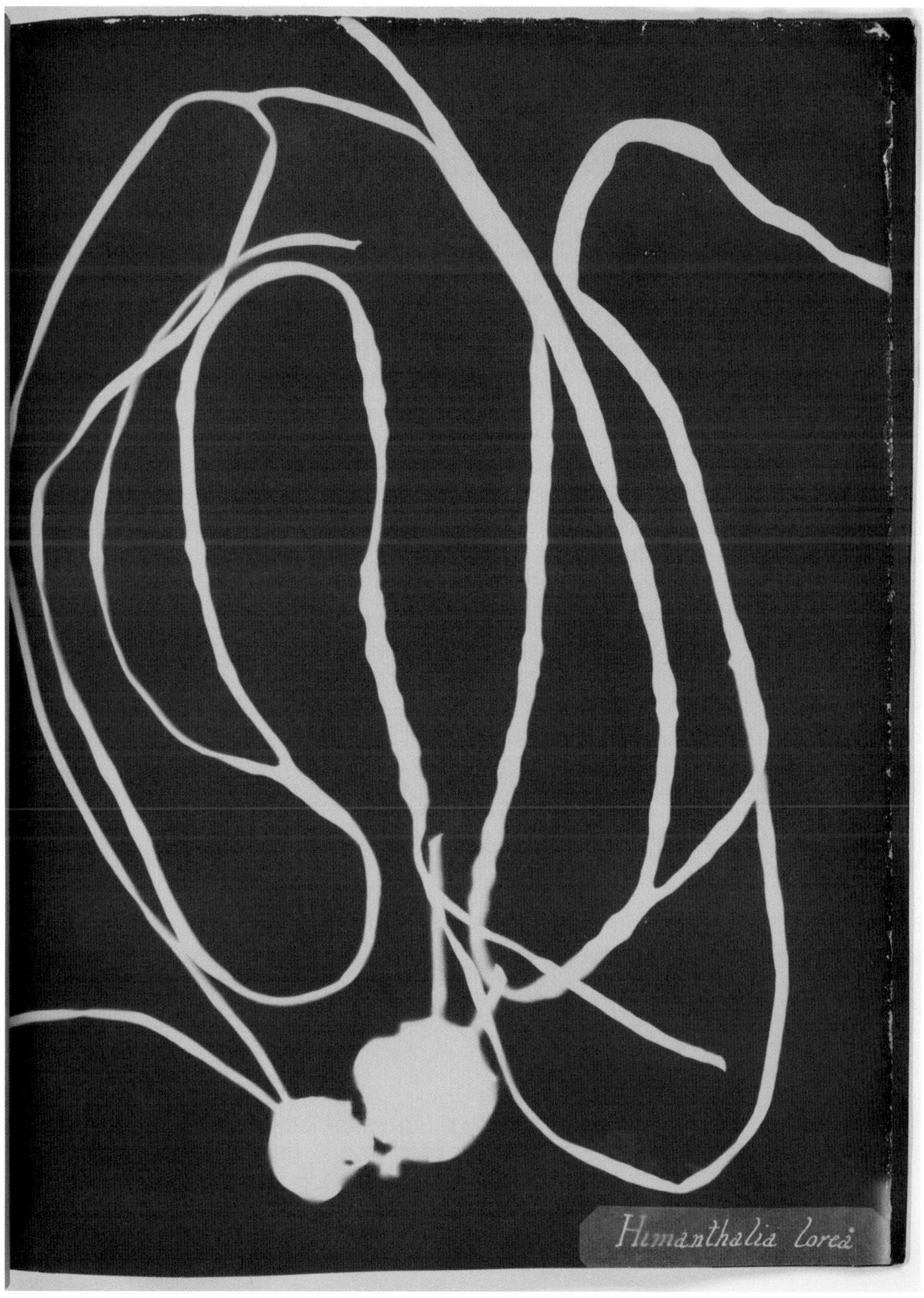

Colorplate 15/Figure 66. Anna Atkins, *Himanthalia lorea,* from *Photographs of British Algae,* 1843. Cyanotype. Courtesy of the National Media Museum/SSPL.

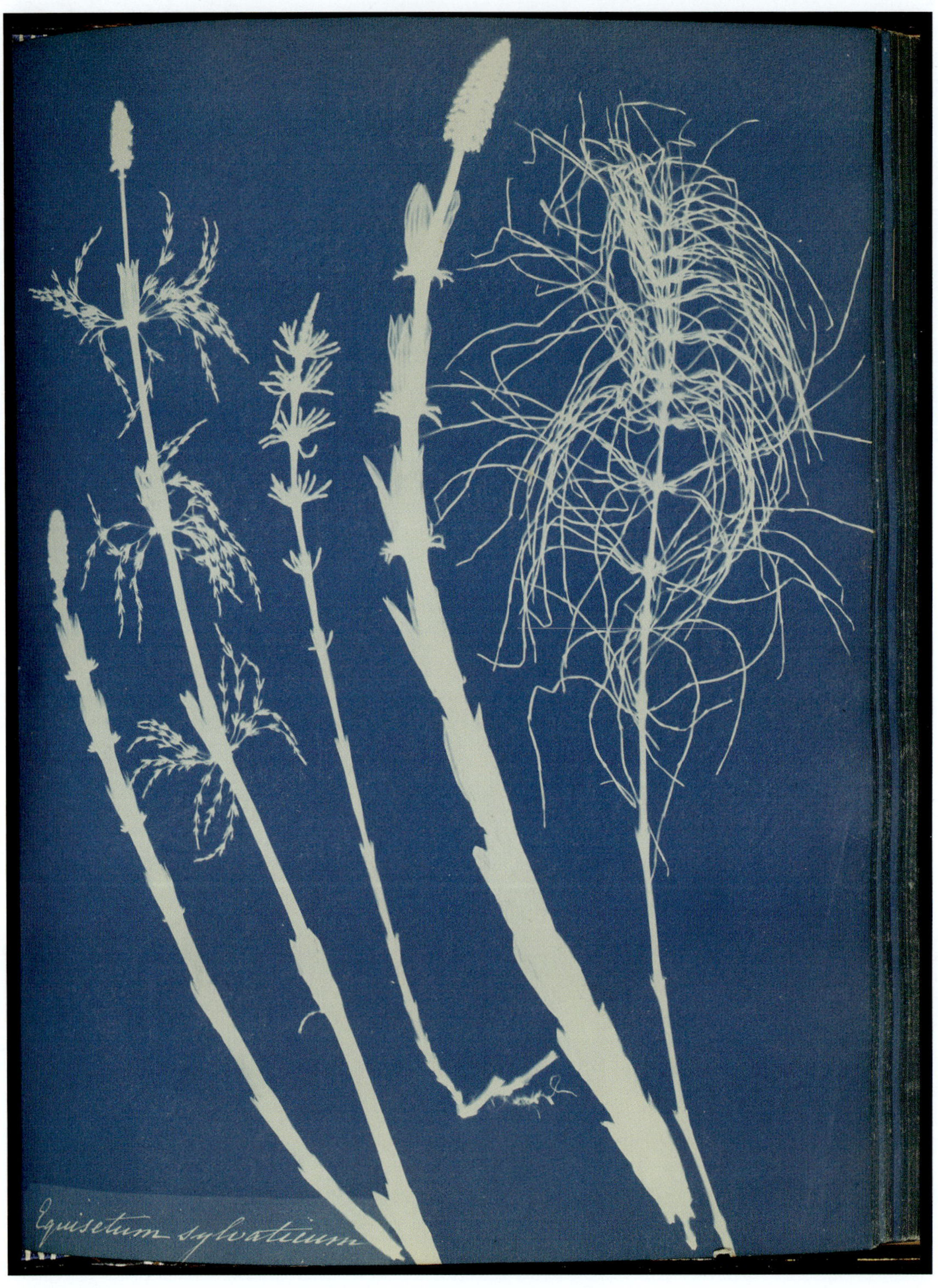

Colorplate 16/Figure 67. Anna Atkins, *Equisetum sylvaticum*, from *Cyanotypes of British and Foreign Ferns*, 1853. Cyanotype. Courtesy of the Open Content Program of the Getty Museum, Los Angeles.

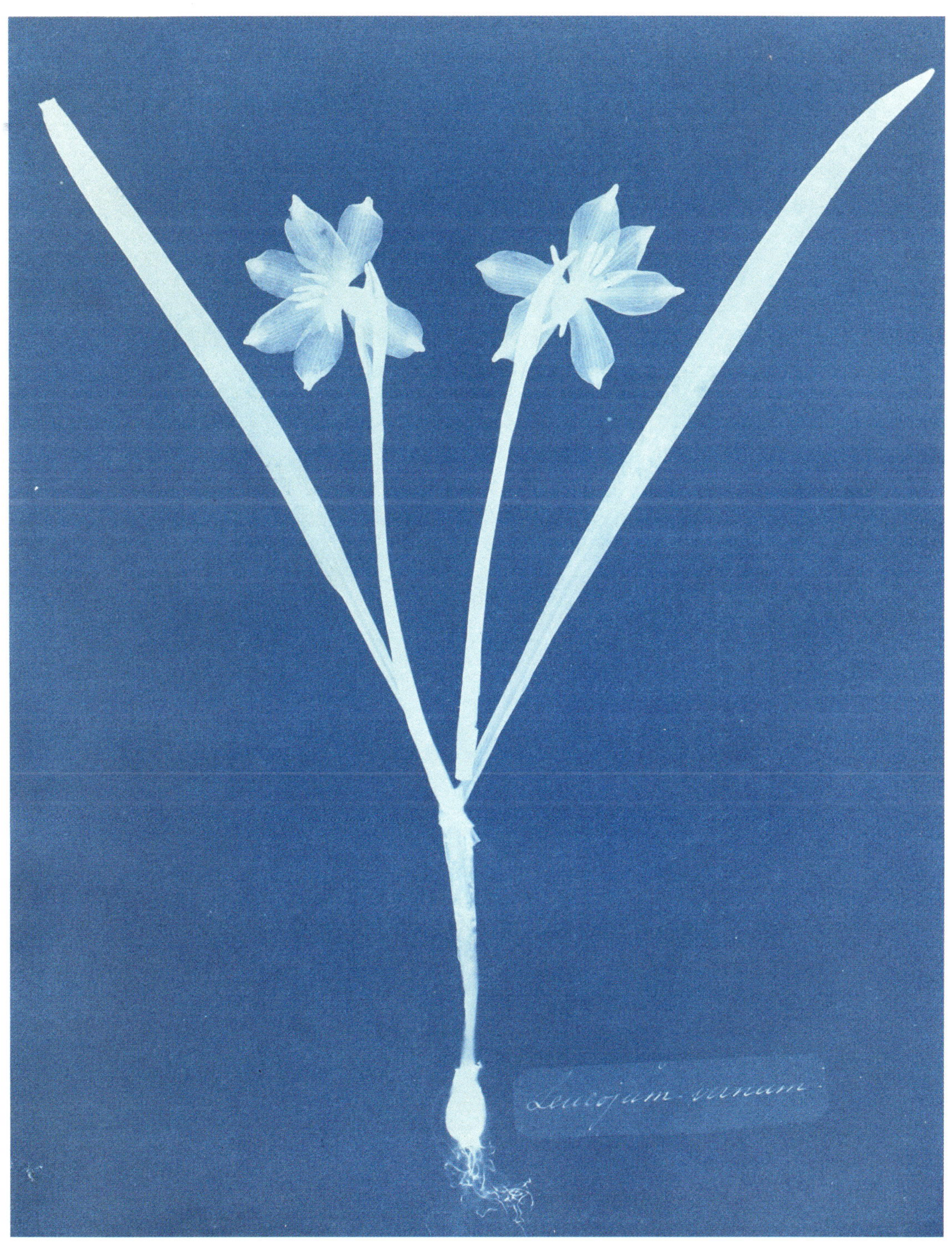

Colorplate 17/Figure 68. Anna Atkins, *Leucojam varium*, from *Cyanotypes of British and Foreign Ferns*, 1853. Cyanotype. Courtesy of the Open Content Program of the Getty Museum, Los Angeles.

Colorplate 18/Figure 69. Hiroshi Sugimoto, *Roofline of Lacock Abbey, Most Likely 1835–1839*, 2009. Toned silver-gelatin print from calotype negative. © Hiroshi Sugimoto, courtesy Pace Gallery.

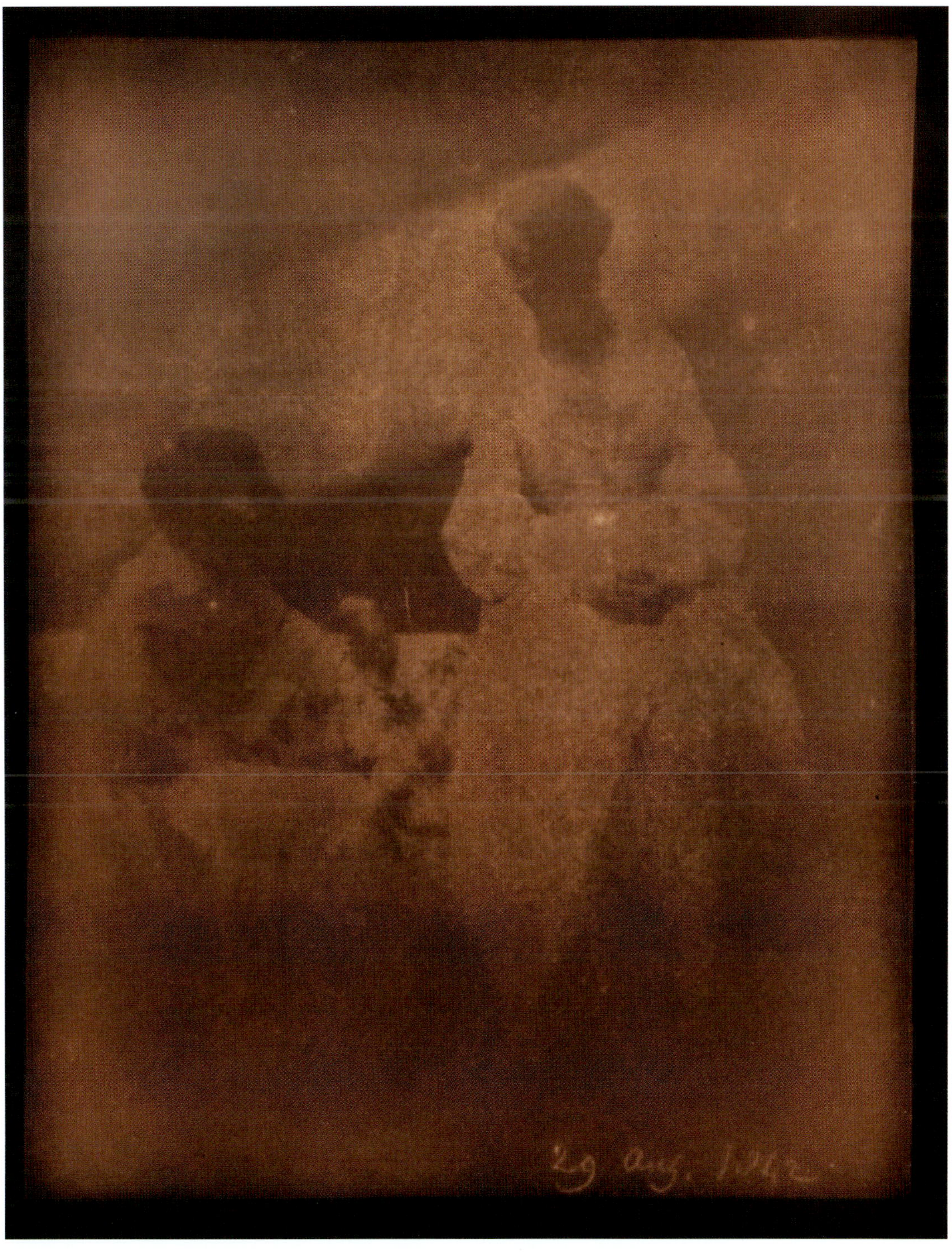

Colorplate 19/Figure 70. Hiroshi Sugimoto, *Louisa Gallwey and Horatia Feilding, at Lacock Abbey, August 29, 1842*, 2009. Toned silver-gelatin print from calotype negative. © Hiroshi Sugimoto, courtesy Pace Gallery.

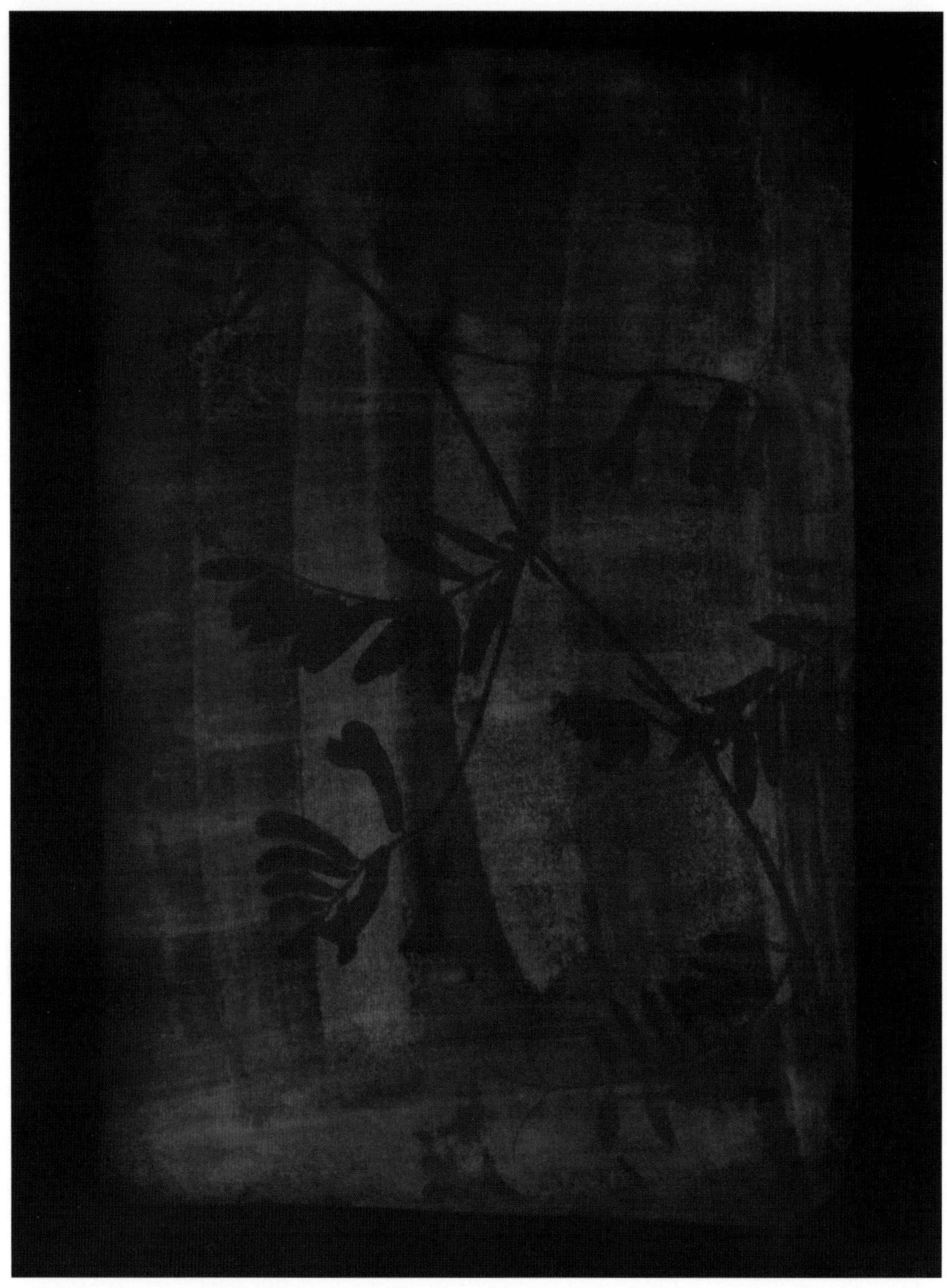

Colorplate 20/Figure 71. Hiroshi Sugimoto, *Stem of Leaves and Flowers, ca. 1834–1839*, 2008. Toned silver-gelatin print from calotype negative. © Hiroshi Sugimoto, courtesy Pace Gallery.

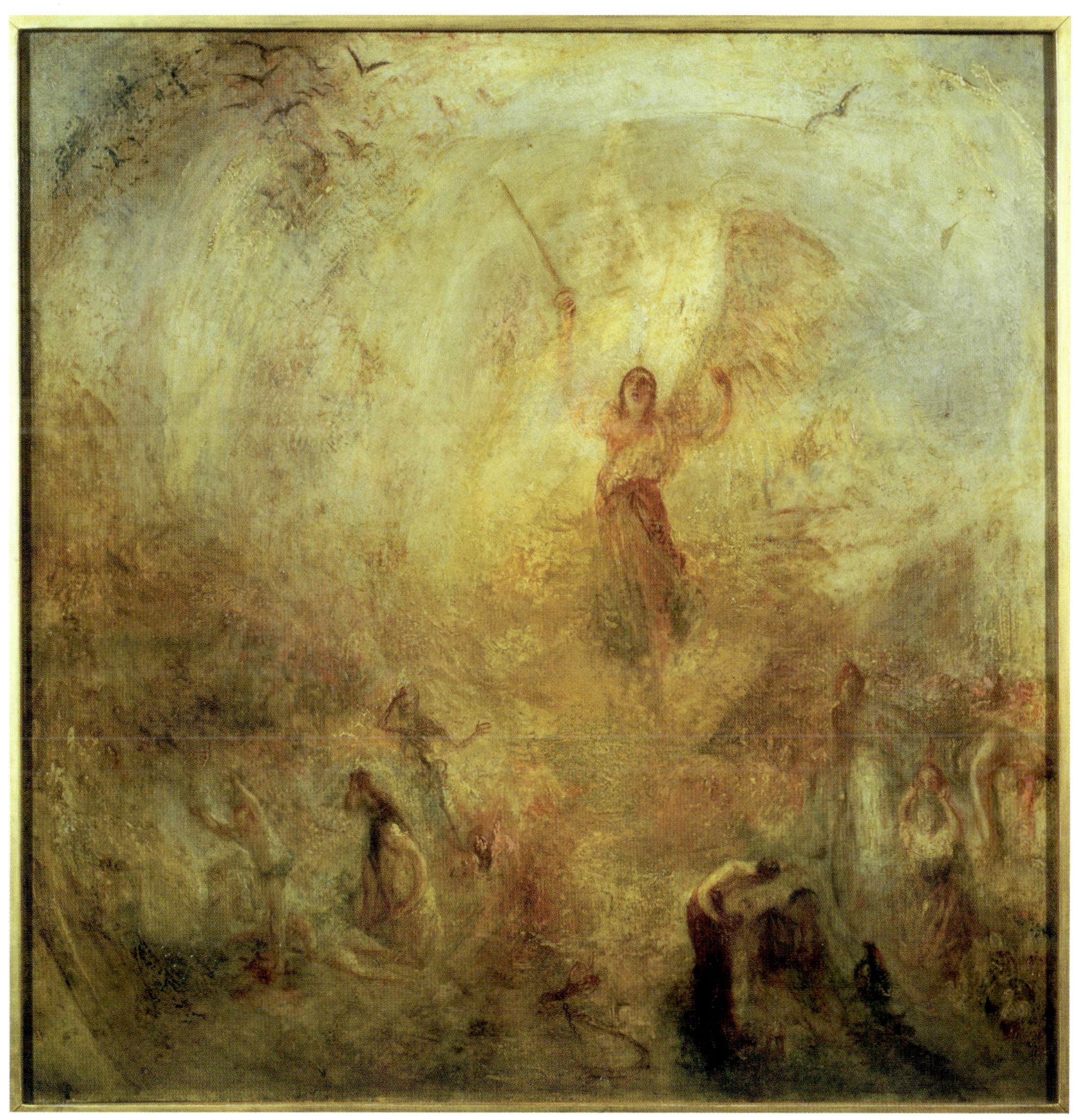

Colorplate 21/Figure 73. J. M. W. Turner, *An Angel Standing in the Sun*, 1846. Oil on canvas. The Tate Britain, London. © Tate, London 2014.

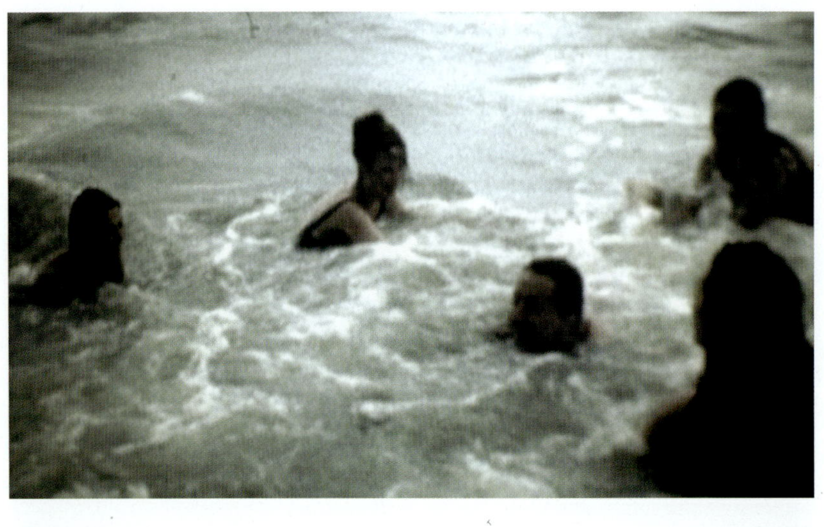

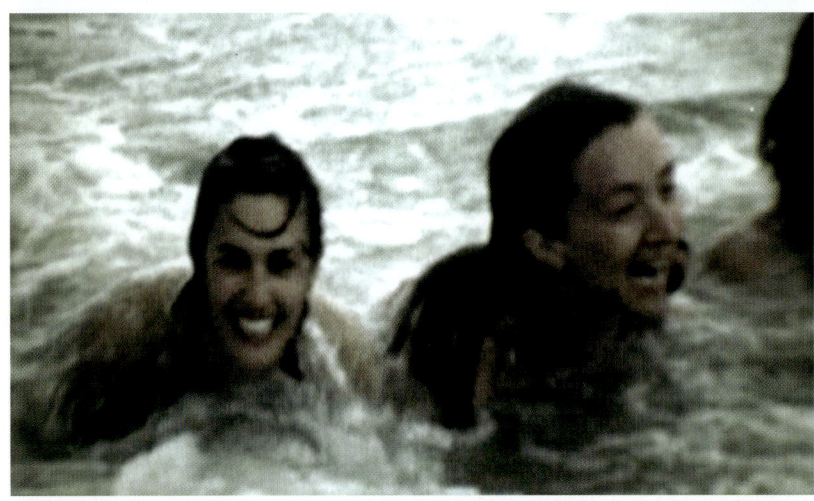

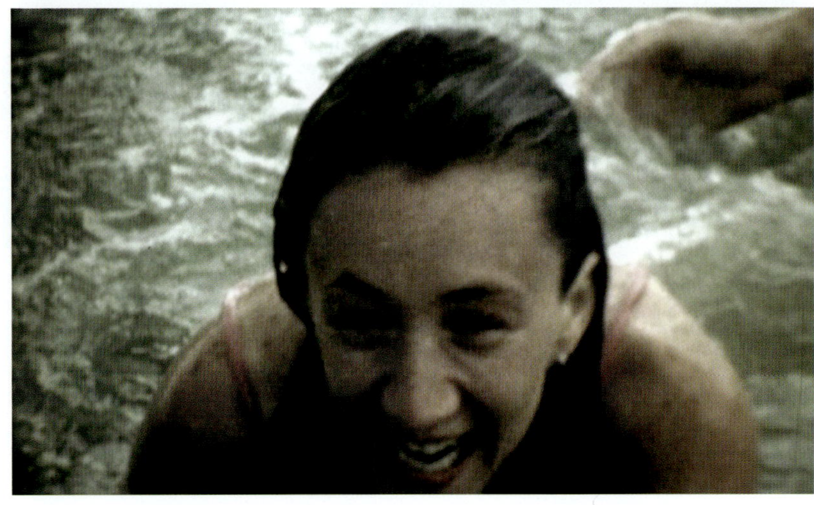

Colorplate 22/Figures 75–77. Chantal Akerman, *La Captive*, 2001 (film stills).

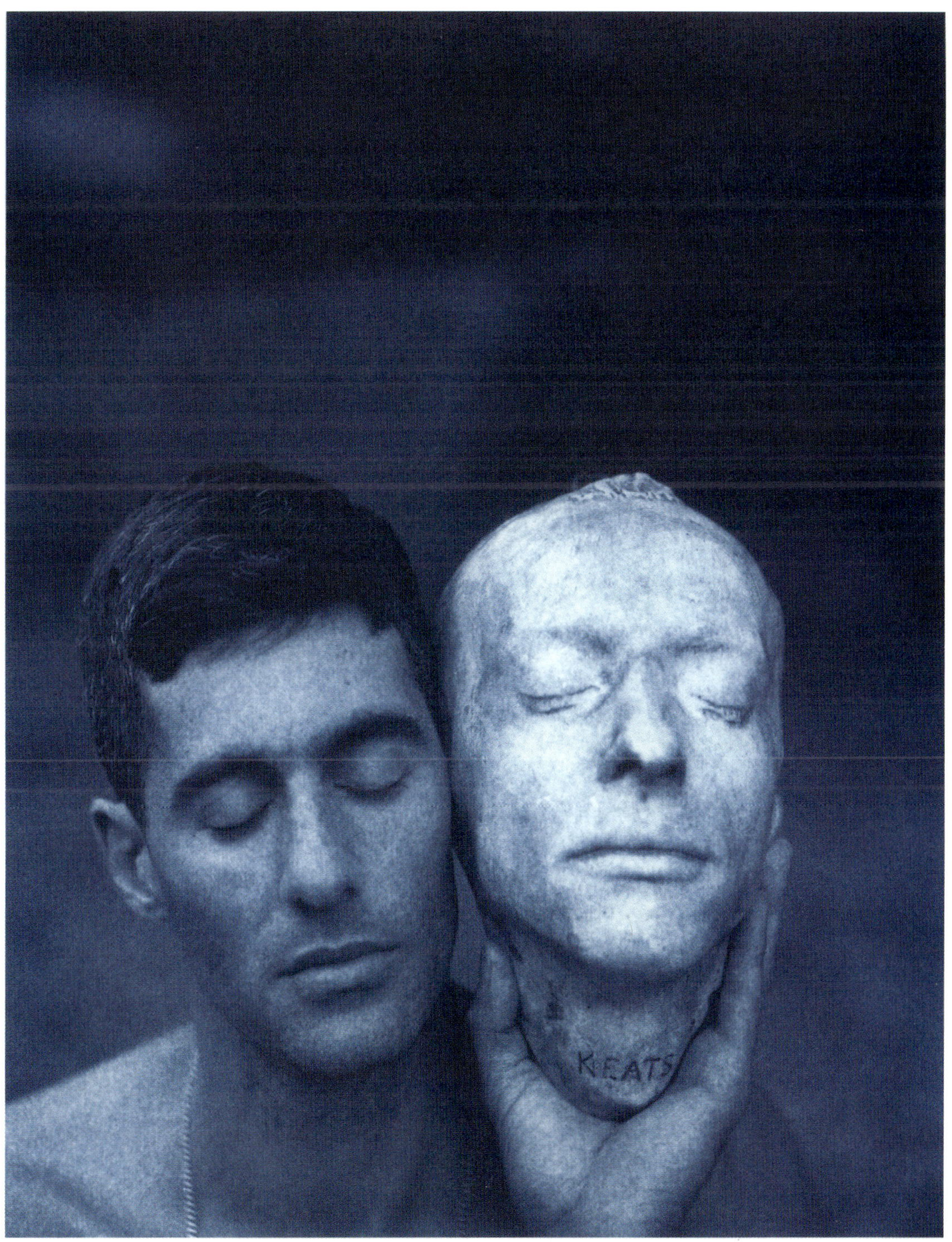

Colorplate 23/Figure 94. John Dugdale, *Death Mask of John Keats*, 1999. Cyanotype. Courtesy of the artist.

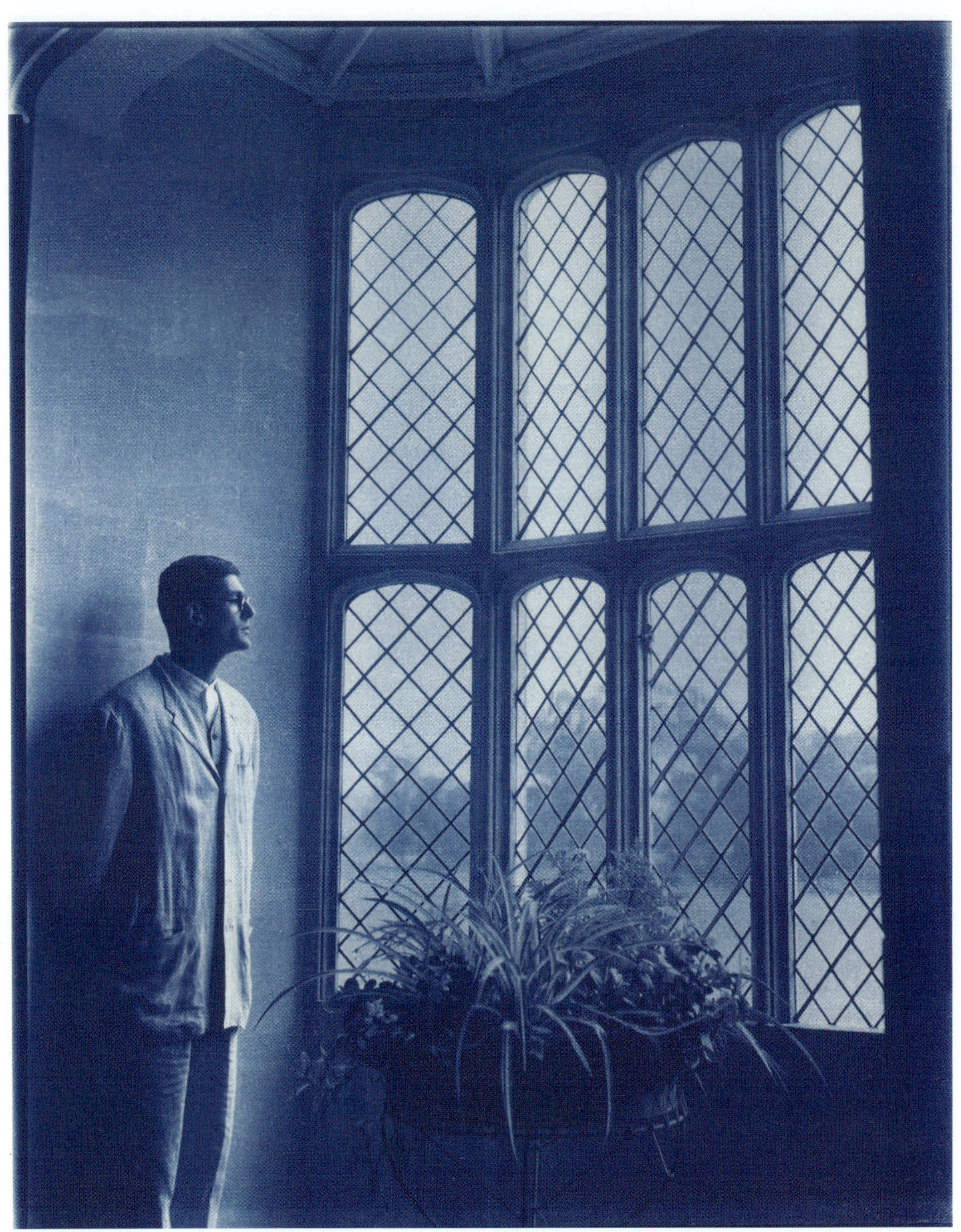

Colorplate 24/Figure 95. John Dugdale, *Self-Portrait at Oriel Window*, 1998. Cyanotype. Courtesy of the artist.

and the aims he sets himself in the course of it," he writes. "This produces what might be described as a stereotype plate (or several such), which is constantly repeated—constantly reprinted afresh—in the course of the person's life."[13]

These two kinds of fixity come together in Lacan's account of the ego, which builds on Freud's. The ego is the fantasm through which the modern subject attempts to prove that it is sovereign and self-constituting, he argues in several early essays. It is created through a series of unsustainable identifications with external images, which "situate" the subject "in a fictional direction," which will "only ever asymptotically approach [his] becoming."[14] The "shadow" of his ego also falls on his objects, rendering his relationship to others narcissistic and rivalrous, and leading to bizarre misrecognitions. A child who beats another child says that he was beaten, and a child who sees another child fall behaves as if he had fallen.[15] The introduction of a third term compounds the problem. The subject now desires "an object desired by someone else," which not only mechanizes desire, but also diminishes "the special significance of any one particular object." It becomes "equivalent" to many others,[16] like an industrial photograph. The "rigid structure"[17] of the ego also leads him to project "permanence, identity and substance" onto his objects—qualities that are "very different from the gestalts that experience enables us to isolate in the mobility of the field constructed according to the lines of animal desire."[18] Lacan characterizes what happens to the phenomenal world when it is perceptually frozen as "formal stagnation," and compares it to "the faces of actors when a film is suddenly stopped in mid-frame."[19]

The concepts associated with early photography figure even more prominently in *À la recherche du temps perdu*. Like the Freudian psyche, the one described by Proust—and dramatized by his narrator—is a receptive surface, like a photographic plate, on which sensory "impressions" are traced. These impressions are invisible until we are "back at home" and able to illuminate them with the "lamp" of voluntary memory, and even then our vision is limited, because it casts only a narrow pool of light.[20] The stream of images that enters the sensory end of the psyche is as labile as the one that enters the camera obscura, and it retains this lability at the level of the unconscious, or what Proust calls "involuntary memory." However, it is inert by the time it reaches consciousness because voluntary memory "begins at once to record photographs independent of one another" and to eliminate "every link" and "sequence between the scenes portrayed in the collection which it exposes to our view."[21] It also displays only one image at a time, and replaces that one with another only after a long interval; voluntary memory is like a shop in whose window "now one," and "now another photograph of the same person" is exhibited, and in which each new photograph is "for some time the only one to be seen."[22] Voluntary memory tries to subsume the world to these fixed images. Marcel asks his mother, his grandmother, Gilberte, and Albertine all to play the "leading part" in a play whose plot, incidents, and lines have achieved an "unalterable form."[23] Consequently, not merely can he visualize only one "photograph" at a time, but it is always the same "photograph": one structured through and through by an Oedipal logic. "When I lay awake at night and revived old memories of Combray," the narrator confides, "I saw no more of it than this sort of luminous panel, sharply defined against a vague and shadowy background . . . broad enough at its base, the little parlor, the dining room . . . the hall through which I would journey to the first step of that staircase, so painful to climb . . . and, at the summit, my bedroom, with the little passage through whose glazed door Mama would enter." It is always summer, and it is always 7 p.m.[24]

Only "the miracle of an analogy" can lift this spell, and reanimate what the psyche has mortified.[25] There is nothing in *À la recherche* that does not rhyme with many other things, but a miraculous analogy requires more than similarity. One half of these double impressions, as Proust calls them, is "sheathed" in an object, and the other half is "prolonged in ourselves."[26] They also link the present to the past, and the psyche to the world. Last, but not least, miraculous analogies issue from a non-human source and reveal themselves to us through a sensory experience that we can neither anticipate nor control. "Whether I considered reminiscences of the kind evoked by the noise of the spoon or the taste of the madeleine, or those truths written with the aid of shapes for whose meaning I searched in my brain," Proust writes, "where . . . they composed a magical scrawl, complex and elaborate, their essential character was that I was not free to choose them, that such as they were they were given to me."[27]

These "hieroglyphs," whose "patterns are not traced by us," form a "book." Although we are not the author of this volume, it is "the only [one] that really belongs to us."[28] When it arrives, we are able to read it, but no one else can. In order to make this book legible to others, we must give it a form that allows it to be "prolonged" in them, because "every reader is, while he is reading, the reader of his own self."[29] We must develop it, in other words, into a work of art. Although Proust sometimes suggests that the artist has more agency in the aesthetic domain than in the perceptual, at other times he uses the same terms to describe both of them. "I had arrived . . . at the conclusion that in fashioning a work of art we are by no means free," he writes in an important passage in *Time Regained*, "that we do not choose how we shall make it." The work "preexists" us, and we are obliged "to do what we should have to do if it were a law of nature—to discover it."[30]

The most famous of Proust's miraculous analogies is of course the one activated by the taste of the tea-soaked madeleine, and it establishes the template for the others. When the adult Marcel connects the tea and madeleine that his mother brings him on a rainy Parisian day with the tea and madeleine that his aunt Léonie used to give him in Combray, the parts of her house that he had previously been unable to see rise up "like a stage set" and attach themselves to the "isolated segment" that he could see, "and with the house the town, from morning to night and in all weathers," and "all the flowers in [his family's] garden and in M. Swann's park, and the water-lilies on the Vivonne and the good folk of the village and their little dwellings and the parish church and the whole of Combray and its surroundings."[31]

IN *The Mottled Screen: Reading Proust Visually,* Mieke Bal refers to the structuring role played by Marcel's "mental vision" in his narration of *In Search of Lost Time* as a "focalization," and she shows that many passages in the novel are focalized through the lens of an imaginary camera. "The photographic mechanism can be seen at work in the cutting-out of details, in the conflictual dialectic between the near and the far, and in certain 'zoom' effects," she writes. "It can also be seen in the effects of contrast, which prevent or enable the under- or overexposed image to be seen. It appears in the focusing, when the image oscillates between clarity and indistinction."[32]

In an essay that was the starting point for this book, which I wrote for a volume devoted to Bal, I argued that there are two focalizers in *À la recherche,* "both of whom use the first-person pronoun, have the same name, and are closely related to each other: the Marcel who used to go to bed early, and the one who reflects upon this phenomenon from a subsequent moment in time."[33] I still think that there are two focalizers in the novel, but I believe that they can be better described through the distinction that I introduced in chapter 3 than the one I used earlier: the distinction between an optical intelligence and a liquid intelligence. I take these concepts from Jeff Wall, who associates optical intelligence with "the projectile or ballistic nature of human vision when it is augmented and intensified" by glass and machinery, and liquid intelligence with "the archaism of water, of liquid chemicals," that connects photography to memory, the past, and "ancient production-processes."[34] As Wall intimates, optical intelligence is a specifically *human* intelligence. Liquid intelligence is photographic, but it also courses through our psychic veins, and it is the great ocean in which we all swim.

As Brassaï points out in his wonderful Proust book,[35] when the narrator likens the cup of tea in which he dips his madeleine to the bowl of water in which the Japanese place "little pieces of paper" that are "without character or form" when they are dry, "but, the moment they become wet, stretch and twist and take on colour and distinctive shape, become flowers or houses or people,"[36] he is implicitly comparing both of them to the developing bath. The "uneven cobblestones, the stretched napkin, the boot, the spoon tapping a plate, [and] the copy of *François le Champi*" are also "developers."[37] These miraculous analogies have a profound effect on Marcel's subjectivity. In the opening pages of *Swann's Way*, in which he details some of the memories that were recovered through the tea and madeleine, he, too, stretches and twists, and becomes flowers and houses and people. "For a long time I would go to bed early," the narrator recounts. "Sometimes, the candle barely out, my eyes closed so quickly that I did not have time to tell myself: 'I'm falling asleep.' And half an hour later the thought that it was time to look for sleep would awaken me; I would make as if to put away the book which I imagined was still in my hands, and to blow out the light; I had gone on thinking, while I was asleep, about what I had just been reading, but . . . it seemed to me that I myself was the immediate subject of my book: a church, a quartet, the rivalry between François I and Charles V."[38] During this astonishing meditation, which continues for several pages, there are no "beings," only multitudinous "becomings."

Albertine is another instantiation of liquid intelligence. The first few times Marcel encounters the band of girls, he registers their features, but he has difficulty determining to whom they belong. "Except for one, whose straight nose and dark complexion singled her out from the rest," he confides, ". . . they were known to me only by a pair of hard, obstinate and mocking eyes, for instance, or by cheeks whose pinkness had a coppery tint reminiscent of geraniums; and even these features I had not indissolubly attached to any one of these girls rather than to another."[39] Later Marcel "deals" these features into little "heaps,"[40] attaches names to them, and identifies Albertine as the object of his desire, but she proves as elusive in isolation as she was in the group. Sometimes she is "thin, with a grey complexion, a sullen air, and a violet transparency slanting across her eyes." On other occasions, "happiness [bathes her] cheeks with a radiance so mobile that the skin, grown fluid and vague, [gives] passage to a sort of subcutaneous glaze," or her face draws his desires "on to its varnished surface," but prevents them from "going further."[41]

Marcel is "refreshed" by this "spectacle of forms undergoing an incessant process of change," that "recalls that perpetual re-creation of the primordial elements of nature which we contemplate when we stand before the sea,"[42] and once again it "liquefies" his own ego. "I . . . developed the habit of becoming a different person," Marcel confides, "according to the particular Albertine to whom my thoughts had turned: a jealous, an indifferent, a voluptuous, a melancholy, a frenzied person."[43] So heterogeneous are "the selves who . . . thought about Albertine," he adds near the end of this passage, that each ought really to have a different name; "I ought still more to give a different name to each of the Albertines who appeared before me, never the same, like those seas . . . that succeeded one another and against which, a nymph likewise, she was silhouetted."[44]

PROUSTIAN DEVELOPMENT not only resurrects the dead and reanimates the living; it is also conjunctive. The word "and" appears so many times in the periodic sentence with which the madeleine passage ends that we eventually see that there is nothing that could not emerge from Marcel's famous cup of tea. As both Rilke and Benjamin note, this and many other passages in *À la recherche* also connect the novel's readers to the narrator and one another. In a 1914 letter, Rilke describes what would happen if a group of people were to read *Swann's Way* together. "One person or another would read aloud what especially struck home to him out of the inexhaustible pages and would hold it out in a specific way to the general opinion," he writes, ". . . [and] to many a one his own childhood would appear out of half-oblivion, and one would pass from tale to tale far into the summer night, but also far into the mutually true, rich and alive."[45] Benjamin arrives at a similar conclusion in "The Image of Proust." "When Proust in a well-known passage described the hour that was most his own," he observes, "he did it in such a way that everyone can find it in his own existence. We might almost call it an everyday hour."[46]

But important as this community is, it is not the republic for which we have been waiting. Only those who are willing to embrace an even more miraculous analogy are admitted to this republic: the one called "chiasmus." Marcel acknowledges that the relationship between himself and Albertine is reciprocal and reversible in the passage with which I ended the last section, but he refuses to affirm it. Although he "*ought*"—as he puts it—to give a different name to each of the Albertines who appeared to him, and each of the selves who thought about her, he does not do so. And in a related passage, in which the narrator uses the distinction between a negative and a positive photograph to describe the similarities that link him to Gilberte and Albertine, thereby showing that he sees the "recto/verso" as a relational principle, he represents himself as the author of this analogy. "If in this craze for amusement Albertine might be said to echo something of the old original Gilberte," he observes, "that is because a certain similarity exists, although the type evolves, between all the women we successively love, a similarity that is due to the fixity of our temperament . . . They are, these women, a product of our temperament, an image, an inverted projection, a negative of our sensibility."[47]

Proust also turns in making this argument to a different definition of photography: the one established through the industrialization of the medium. Suddenly the photographic image is a representation instead of an analogy, a human construct instead of a photogenic drawing, and fixed rather than dynamic. The distinction between the positive and the negative is also absolute, and the development process irreversible. The narrator denies that this is a reciprocal relationship in another way as well: by claiming the first person pronoun not just for himself but for all other men, and by using the third-person pronoun to designate the many women desired by this male monolith.

This is not the only occasion on which the narrator attempts to negate the chiasmus, or that he turns for this purpose to industrial photography. In another passage in *Within a Budding Grove*, Saint-Loup offers to take a photograph of Marcel's grandmother. Since she knows that she will soon die, and sees this as a way of providing her grandson with a lasting image of herself, she accepts his offer "with a joyful air," and searches for a flattering hat and her "nicest dress."[48] Marcel is extremely irritated by his grandmother's "vanity," but rather than accepting her offer to forgo the photograph, he encourages her to have it taken, and then ruins it with a few "sarcastic and wounding words."[49] As Bal points out, this story resurfaces a number of times,[50] and on one of the occasions when Marcel returns to it he admits that what really angered him was not his grandmother's vanity but rather the fact that she was orienting herself toward Saint-Loup's look—a look to which he had no access. To make matters worse, the unknowable person she was on her way to becoming would be authenticated and immortalized by the camera, and this would prove that his grandmother was not "created solely" for him.[51] He tries to recover his egoic footing by producing a counter-photograph.

In a related passage, Marcel enters the drawing room and sees his grandmother absorbed in thoughts that she has never allowed him to "see." For a moment, he becomes a "spectator to [his] own absence"; he realizes that she continues to exist when he is not there, and that even when he is with her, he is not seeing all of her. This alarming thought yields to the bizarre fantasy that a stranger has just entered the room, and is photographing his grandmother as she would appear if he were not there to protect her. What this imaginary camera sees is a "red-faced" woman sitting on a sofa beneath a lamp, who is "heavy and vulgar, sick, day-dreaming, [and] letting her slightly crazed eyes wander over a book."[52] Although this apparatus is clearly a fantasmatic extension of his own look, Marcel spends most of the rest of the paragraph deploring the photographer's cruelty. He also maintains that the unflattering photograph is *objectively* true.

Albertine's look denotes an even more radical alterity—and one that includes Marcel, thereby making him a stranger to himself. "'If she had seen me, what could I have represented to her?'" he asks himself later in the same volume. "From the depths of what universe did she discern me? . . . If we thought that the eyes of such a girl were merely two glittering sequins of mica, we should not be athirst to know her and to unite her life to ours. But we sense that what shines in those reflecting discs . . . [are] the dark shadows, unknown to us, of the ideas that the person cherishes about the people and places she knows."[53]

Although there are no explicit references to photography in this passage, Marcel expresses his desire to plumb the depths of this "universe," and he later attempts to satisfy this desire by kissing her. When he approaches Albertine for this purpose, she turns not just into a grainy photograph, but one that can be viewed from a potentially infinite number of angles, only one of which can be occupied at a time. "At first, as my mouth began gradually to approach the cheeks which my eyes had recommended it to kiss," Marcel writes, "my eyes, in changing position, saw a different pair of cheeks; the neck, observed at closer range and as though through a magnifying-glass, showed in its coarser grain a robustness which modified the character of the face."[54]

In all of these passages, what activates the narrator's anxiety and motivates him to aim a mental camera at the world is the discovery that there are blind spots in his field of vision. He reaches for a Pistolgraph instead of a pistol because these visual occlusions are part of what Benjamin would later call the "optical unconscious." At its most rudimentary, the optical unconscious consists of those aspects of the visible world that are too small for us to see, or that occur too quickly for us to register, but which photography and film make available through close-ups and slow motion. But photography also reveals another kind of optical unconscious: it shows us that the world presents itself differently to the camera than to the human eye.[55]

If the world discloses a different side of itself to the camera than it does to us, then we can see only what it permits us to see. It must also present different aspects of itself to different looks, and since we are part of the world, we—too—must reveal dimensions of ourselves to others that are unavailable to us. We cannot neutralize the threat that this poses to our unity and autonomy by underscoring the subjectivity of human vision, because perspective is not something we bring to visual phenomena. It is internal to their Being, and it dramatically restricts what we can know about ourselves and the world. The optical unconscious proved considerably more difficult for the modern subject to assimilate than the discovery that the photographic image derives from an external source, and even some of the most ardent practitioners of photography by other means were unable to accept it.

IN THE PARAGRAPH after the one in which Marcel compares Albertine to a constantly changing photograph, he talks about photographs into which multiple viewpoints have been crammed, presumably so as to overcome the limits of human vision. He emphasizes the absurdity of this project by comparing it to his own attempt to get behind Albertine's eyes by kissing her, and by suggesting that the photographic image has a directly contrary effect upon the human eye. "I can think of nothing that can to so great a degree as a kiss evoke out of what we believed to be a thing with one definite aspect the hundred other things which it may equally well be," he wryly observes, "since each is related to a no less legitimate perspective."[56]

Proust also tries to make room for others in the last volume of his novel by abstracting away from sensory experience to universal laws, but this leads to a generalization of the first-person pronoun, rather than a greater accommodation of the second.[57] A new Marcel also emerges in some passages in *Time Regained*—one whose perceptual coordinates are closer to "radiography" than to photography. As the narrator suggests in *Within a Budding Grove*, this is a mortifying optic; it peels away the "tiny particles of epidermis whose varied combinations form the florid originality of human flesh" to reveal the "joyless universality of a skeleton."[58] Marcel recoils from this kind of looking in the second volume of *In Search of Lost Time*, but he later justifies it as the necessary condition for art making. A book is "a huge cemetery in which on the majority of the tombs the names are effaced," he writes in *Time Regained*.[59]

There is one passage in the last volume of Proust's novel, though, where the narrator not only acknowledges that the world reveals different aspects of itself to every seer but also expresses the desire to leave his cork-lined room, and re-enter the "loud, clamoring, semi-visible world."[60] He stops talking about art as the purveyor of universal truths and begins thinking of it as the agency through which looks that would otherwise remain completely sealed off might somehow communicate with one another. "Through art alone are we able to emerge from ourselves," Proust writes in *Time Regained*, "to know what another person sees of a universe that is not the same as our own and of which, without art, the landscapes would remain as unknown to us as those that may exist on the moon."[61] And although he is no closer to uttering the second-person pronoun here than he is when he characterizes Albertine as "a product of [his] temperament," he is clearly trying to make the first-person pronoun a lot more capacious.

THE REVERSE FIELD that was disclosed through the negative/positive distinction did not disappear after the industrialization of photography; it remained stubbornly in place, and although neither Sartre nor Merleau-Ponty links it to the so-called "medium," they are obsessed with it. Both philosophers also respond to the passage in which Proust attempts to make room for other landscapes and looks. In chapter 3 of *Being and Nothingness*, Sartre tells a story about a man who visits a public park. The man is alone at first, and everything seems to radiate out from his look, but then someone else enters the park, who perceives it from a different position, and toward whom the "raw green" of the lawn turns a different "face."[62] The "whole universe" slides away from him, and toward the interloper.[63] The man tries to recover his equilibrium by reasoning that since he sees the latter, he is still the perceiving subject, and the Other the object of his look, but he is prevented from doing so by an even more distressing realization: the realization that the Other is also looking at him. What is true of the "raw green" of the lawn is also true of him; he turns a different face to the Other than he does to himself, and it will forever elude him.

This is a reversible but not a reciprocal relationship; either one sees or one is seen. The same principle obtains at the level of language; Sartre narrates the story from the first man's perspective, in direct discourse, and he refers to the second man with the third-person pronoun. At the outset, "I" means "the one who sees," and "he" means "the one who is seen," but at a certain point the speaker realizes that "the truth of 'seeing-the-Other'" is "'being-seen-by-the-Other.'" Since this is an unavoidable objectification, "I" must signify the one who is seen. "Thus I, who in so far as I am my possibles, am what I am not and am not what I am—behold, now I am somebody!" he exclaims. "And the one who I am—and who on principle escapes me—I am he in the midst of the world in so far as he escapes me."[64] But the first-person pronoun is nothing without the second, and it soon devolves into the third.

Merleau-Ponty responds to this section of *Being and Nothingness* as well as to the passage which Sartre attempts to rebut in *The Visible and Invisible*. He begins by not only agreeing with a number of Sartre's claims but strengthening them. If two men entered a park, he writes, the "raw green" of the landscape would indeed turn a different "face" to each of them, since we all have our "own depth," and this depth is "backed up" by what we see. We "espouse" the aspects of the visible world with which we are in "pre-established harmony"—with the things that are the equivalent "on the outside" of what we are "on the inside."[65] What the second man saw when he entered the park would also escape the first. The face that the world turns toward us is "only for our vision and our body"; it cannot be seen by anyone else. And since it shows different aspects of itself to other seers, what each of us sees is only the "surface of an inexhaustible depth."

But once he has detailed these points of commonality, Merleau-Ponty parts company with Sartre and aligns himself with Proust. He extends what the novelist says about art to speech, and he makes this linguistic mediation one of the cornerstones of his phenomenology. Our perceptions are not hermetically sealed, Merleau-Ponty argues, because language allows us to share them with one another. When I look at a landscape with someone else, and each of us describes what we see to the other, "the individual green of the meadow under my eyes invades his vision without quitting my own," and I "recognize" his green in mine. Our landscapes "interweave," and we realize that "it is not *I* who sees, or "*he* who sees," but rather a "vision in general" that sees, and that "inhabits" both of us.[66]

Merleau-Ponty clearly grasps the significance of the pronominal antithesis that figures so prominently in Sartre's account of the look, because he emphasizes it here. He also makes dialogue the agency of its resolution. Oddly, though, he does not utter the word on which all dialogue depends; instead of replacing the third-person pronoun with the second, he leaps to "vision in general." He thus inadvertently promotes *impersonality*, instead of *relationality*, just as Proust does in the final volume of his novel. I want to end this chapter with a work that satisfies all three definitions of the chiasmus, and that will help us to see how interdependent they are: Chantal Akerman's filmic "renovation"[67] of *In Search of Lost Time*, *The Captive* (2001).

THE CAPTIVE opens with credits over a 35mm nocturnal shot of the sea. This shot—which comes slowly and moodily into focus—is accompanied by the sound of crashing waves. The transition from it to the film "proper" is unusually smooth, since the first scene also begins with a frontal shot of a seascape, accompanied by the sound of waves. Now, though, the sun is high in the sky, and a group of girls are playing in the water. This shot is also grainier than the one that precedes it, and it is followed by a series of handheld and equally grainy shots of the girls and the water. The sound of a film projector competes with—and eventually replaces—the sound of waves, and from time to time we hear the "click" of a still camera.

Two girls leave the water and approach the camera: Ariane and Andrée, Akerman's Albertine and Andrée. They pause briefly in front of the camera, allowing the photographer to study their faces, and their friends gather around them. Then the girls begin playing with a soccer ball on the beach, and the image becomes once again hard to read. The photographer attempts to follow their movements, but the jerkiness of his handheld camera renders them even less intelligible. Eventually he manages to isolate Ariane from the others, and he moves from a close-up to an extreme close-up of her face.

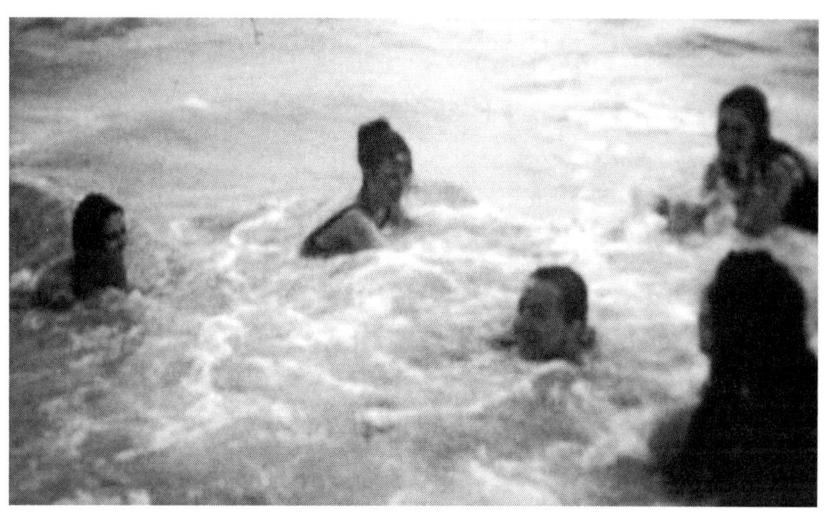

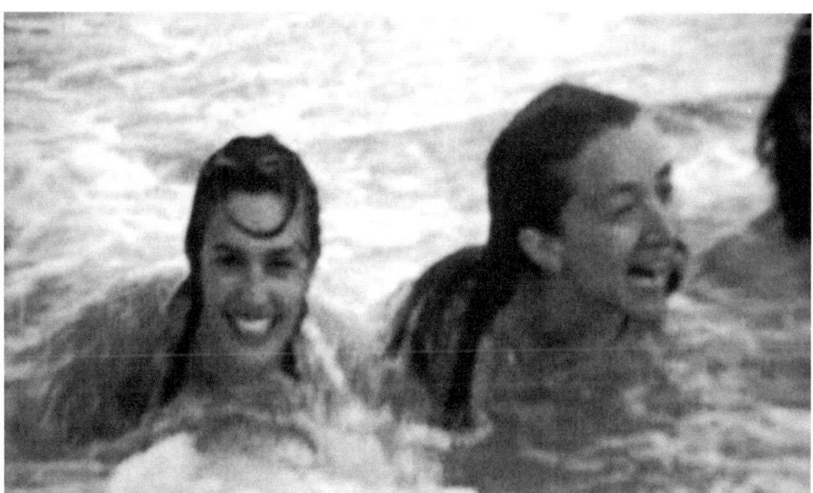

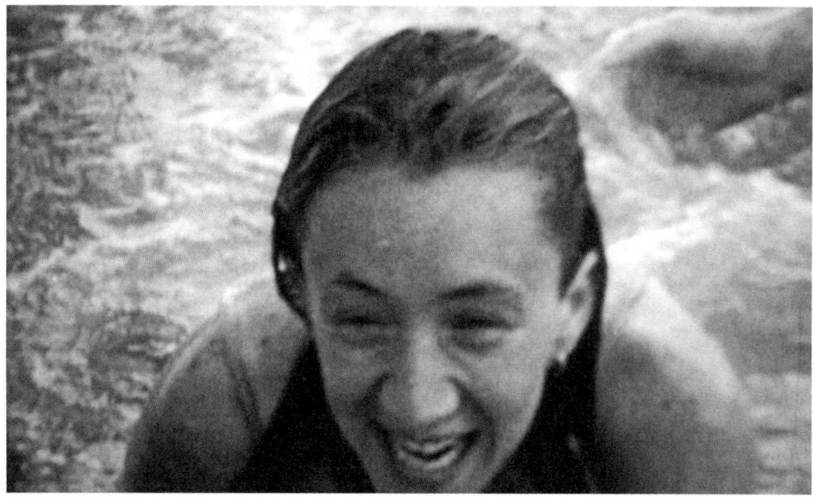

Figures 75–77/Colorplate 22. Chantal Akerman, *La Captive*, 2001 (film stills).

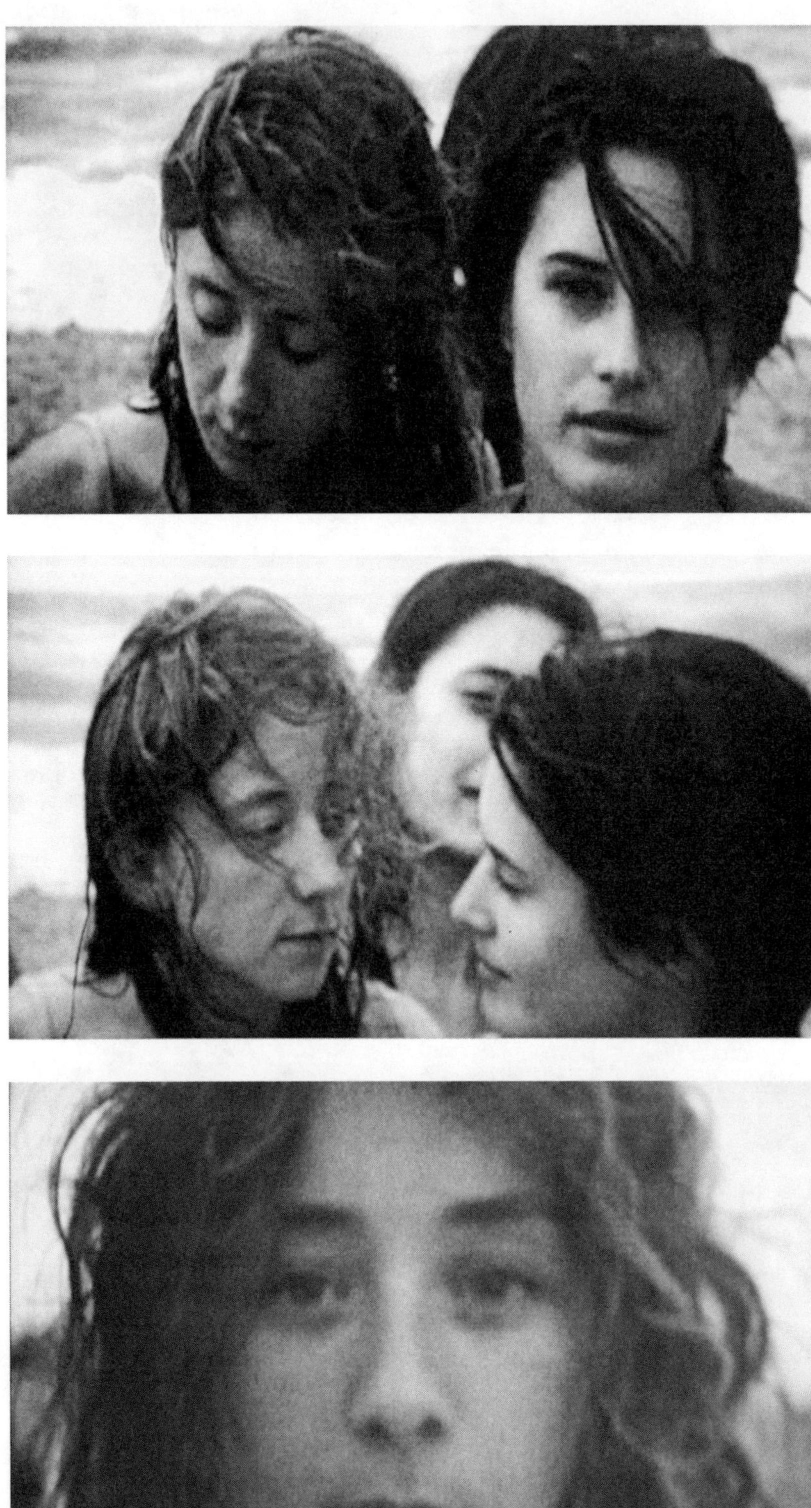

Figures 78–80. Chantal Akerman, *La Captive*, 2001 (film stills).

Akerman cuts away from this close-up to a 35mm shot of Simon, the counterpart in her film for the narrator in Proust's novel. He stands beside a projector, which he is using to screen a film. It is a home movie, presumably shot by him, and the source of the grainy images at which we have been looking. The projector permits us to identify the mechanical "whirr" that competes with and eventually drowns out the crashing waves. At first, it also seems responsible for the mysterious "click," since Simon repeatedly stops the projector and rewinds a bit of film, and each time he does so, we hear this sound. Before long, though, it becomes evident that the "click" is the auditory exteriorization of a *mental* camera. Akerman also treats the amateur camera and the film projector as perceptual metaphors. She uses the blur that results when unpredictable movements are filmed with a handheld camera, and then re-photographed with a higher-resolution camera, to depict the "spectacle of forms undergoing an incessant process of change"[68]; the clicking sound to dramatize Simon's perception, which transforms this mobile beauty into a series of still photographs; and the stopping and starting of the projector to suggest another sort of arrestation—that through which the ego attempts to stabilize itself, and master the world.[69]

As the camera holds on Simon, he says, "*Je . . . je . . . je . . . vous.*" Since he looks at Ariane as he utters these words, she is obviously the referent for one of them, but it is impossible to determine which, since he could be speaking either for her or for himself. These pronouns become even shiftier when the camera cuts back to the home movie. Ariane and Andrée stand together on the beach, against the backdrop of the sea. They are wrapped in towels, and lean into each other like lovers, but—because they stand with their backs to the sun—their faces are difficult to make out. As we look at this ambiguous shot, we hear

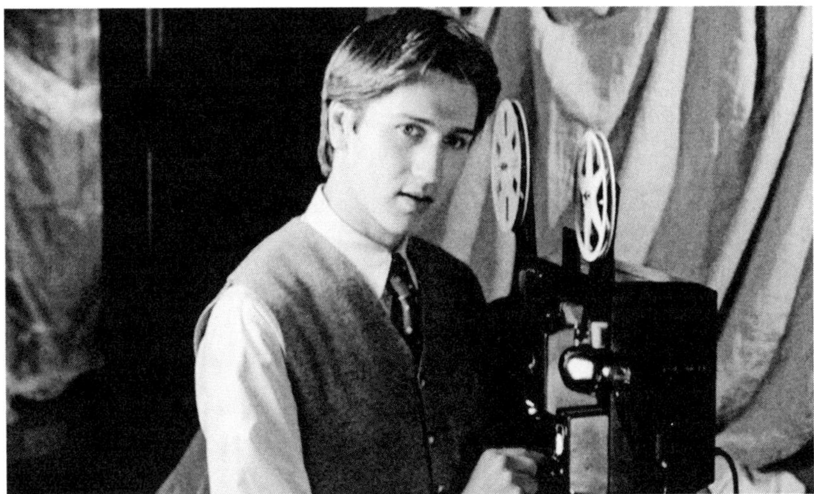

Figure 81. Chantal Akerman, *La Captive*, 2001 (film still).

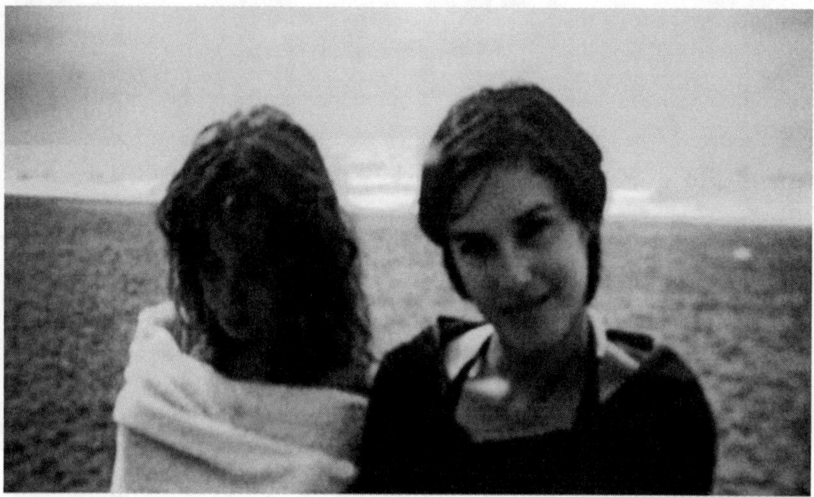

Figure 82. Chantal Akerman, *La Captive*, 2001 (film still).

Simon utter the following words, from an off-screen position: "*je . . . je vous . . . je vous . . . je vous aime bien.*"

Since "*vous*" is the plural as well as the formal version of the second-person pronoun in French, its field of possible referents now expands to include Andrée. Initially, this expansion seems to secure Simon in the position of the "*je*," but before long another possibility emerges: the possibility that the first- and second-person pronouns are reversible designators for Ariane and Andrée. The camera returns to Simon, who repeats these words, but this time he smiles as he speaks, and there is a lilt to his voice. It then cuts back to the home movie, and remains facing in this direction until the end of the scene. Simon approaches the screen, sits down in front of it, and presses his face against Ariane's image. His head forms an oversized shadow in the lower-left frame. From this strange position, which is simultaneously inside and outside the home movie, Simon again says, "*Je vous aime bien.*" The emphasis now falls as much upon the last two words as the first two. In this iteration, "*aimer bien*" means not only "to love a lot," but also "to love well."

In *The Captive*, as in the novel it analogizes, the central male character derives erotic gratification from pressing against the female body. Proust represents this as a masturbatory sexuality, but in *The Mottled Screen* Bal links it to "the image of the breasts of two women pressed flat against one another" that Marcel sees while watching Albertine and Andrée dance together, and that "plunges" him into "jealous rage."[70] As we have already seen, physical contact is also an important part of Talbot's photographic process, and of Merleau-Ponty's chiasmus, which is tactile as well as visual. Akerman retains this aspect

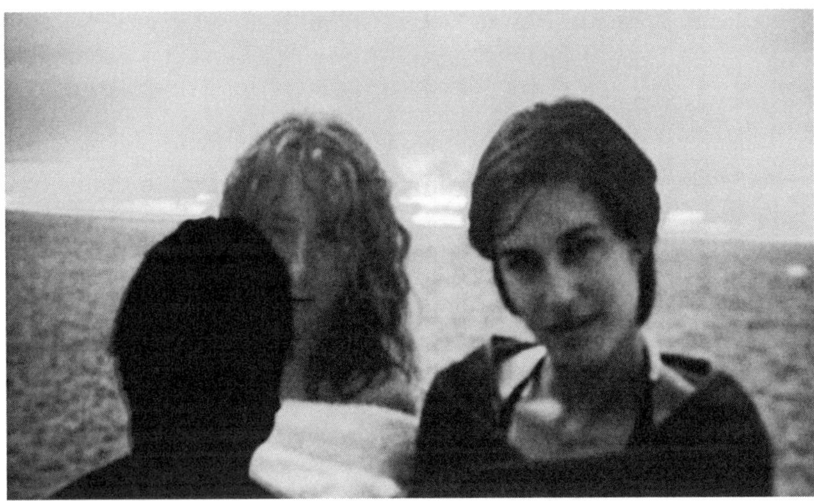

Figure 83. Chantal Akerman, *La Captive*, 2001 (film still).

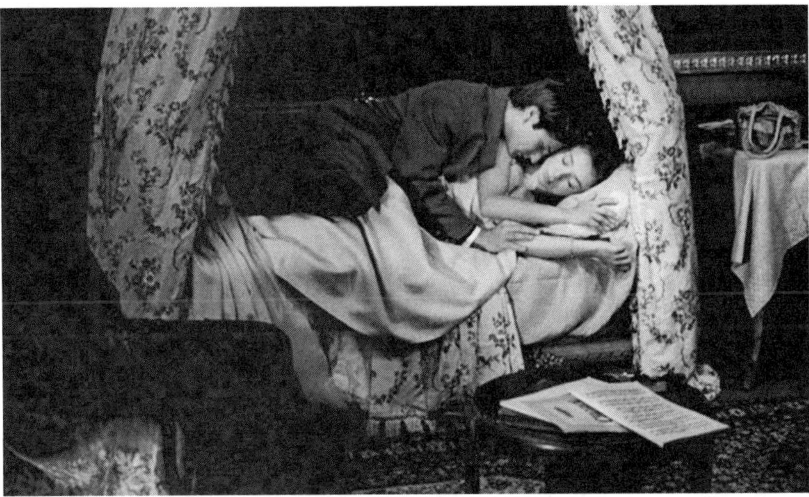

Figure 84. Chantal Akerman, *La Captive*, 2001 (film still).

of the Proustian narrative, but she makes it a source of female as well as male pleasure.

Simon climaxes twice while pressing against Ariane's body, and both times she also manifests extreme sexual pleasure. She enjoys this activity, she explains later in the film, because it is non-invasive—because it does not encroach upon her physical or (even more importantly) her psychic interiority. She is therefore free to think about Andrée while experiencing corporeal pleasure with Simon, i.e., to be with both of them at the same time.[71] The second time he says "*Je vous aime bien*," he acknowledges that his own pleasure derives from the same source—that he loves Ariane because she and Andrée love each other.

The third time, he goes even further: he affirms their right to address these words to each other. And since by doing this, he loves them *well*, he also finds his own way back to the "*je*."

This scene relies heavily upon the shot/reverse shot formation. Since this device is often used within normative cinema to construct sexual difference and conceal the presence of the camera, Akerman ostentatiously avoids it in two of her most celebrated films, *Jeanne Dielman* (1975) and *News from Home* (1976). This is not, however, the role for which it is "destined." The shot/reverse shot is structurally linked to the recto and verso of the camera obscura's image stream and Talbot's double reversals, and it houses the same power. Akerman mobilizes this power here, through another "renovation." Ariane and Andrée are separated from Simon by the fourth wall, so they shouldn't be able to return his look, but they miraculously *do*. After he acknowledges the interdependence of his desire for Ariane, and hers for Andrée, and affirms the girls' right to say "*je vous aime bien*" to each other, they respond by smiling first at each other, and then at him. And when Simon walks over to the screen, and presses his head against Ariane's image, *he* responds to *their* response.

Akerman often signals her authorial presence by correlating the height of the camera to her own look—i.e., by positioning it lower than usual.[72] She follows this practice when filming Simon, but because these shots establish him as the source of the home movie, this is easy to miss. However, in the last shot of this scene, Akerman alerts us to the fact that there is a second focalizer in a number of different ways: by not moving her camera when Simon does; by continuing to film the screen from a standing position after he sits down;

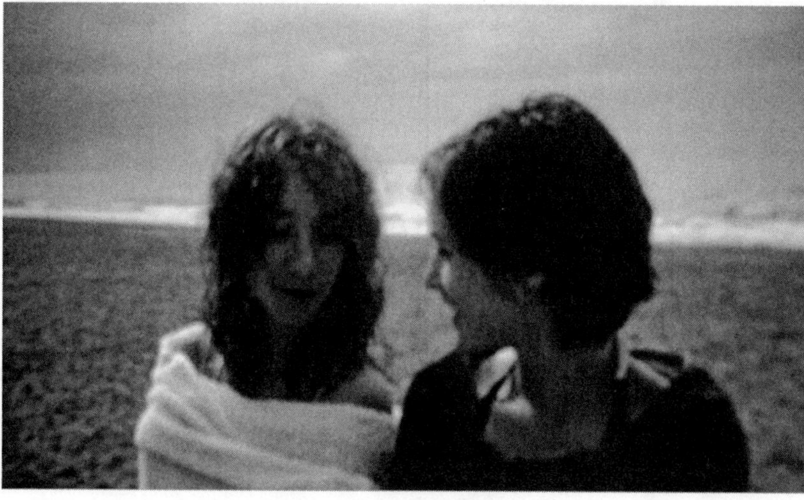

Figure 85. Chantal Akerman, *La Captive*, 2001 (film still).

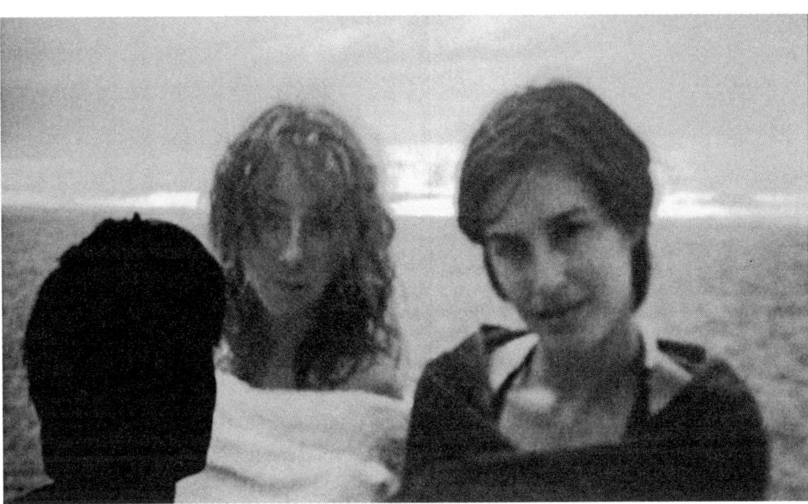

Figure 86. Chantal Akerman, *La Captive*, 2001 (film still).

by dramatizing the lateral distance separating him from the camera by situating his head in the left corner of the image; and by showing Ariane and Andrée looking away from him, toward another seer.

We recognize this focalizer from other Akerman films—not just as a formally rigorous eye, but also as a person named "Chantal," who is Jewish, Belgian, and a lesbian. The parallels between *The Captive* and *Je tu il elle* (1974) are particularly striking. In the latter film, Akerman plays a lesbian who seduces a former girlfriend, and during their lovemaking the two women press their bodies passionately together. The title of the film also consists entirely of pronouns. Chantal is the only character who appears in every scene, which might seem to entitle her to the "*je*," but there are also two other claimants to this position, and times when she is more closely aligned with one of the other pronouns. In the second part of the film, she is picked up on the side of a road by a truck driver. He commandeers the first-person pronoun by doing most of the talking, thereby assigning the second-person pronoun to her. Chantal later gives him a "hand-job," at which point she could be a "you," a "she," or an "I," and he a "you," a "he," or an "I." In the scene in which she visits her former girlfriend, each exercises power, and then has it wrested away from her by the other. The "I" and "you" shift positions at a dizzying rate, both literally and metaphorically, and the surprisingly frank way in which Akerman films their lovemaking marks both of them as a "she." As Ivone Margulies so elegantly puts it, the four pronouns in the title of the film "seem to be on call, performing rituals of abeyance."[73]

Things are every bit as labile in *The Captive*, both within the fiction and at the level of the enunciation. Here, however, Akerman is less contestatory. She

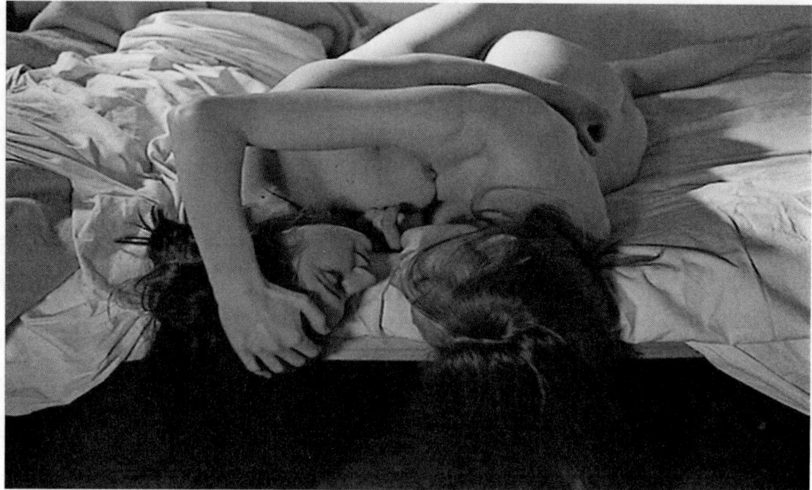

Figure 87. Chantal Akerman, *Je tu il elle*, 1976 (film still).

emphasizes the impossibility of replacing Simon's look with hers by depicting it as a blind spot within her own field of vision. She also presents her look as a *second* vantage point from which to observe and desire the band of girls, rather than an alternative to it. Last, but not least, Akerman shows these two looks meeting at the site of Ariane's body, like the landscape invoked by Proust, Sartre, and Merleau-Ponty. If we were to translate this meeting into language, it would read: "*je ... vous ... je vous*." This chapter is the site of a similar exchange. In it, two old friends meet each other through a book they both love, and give and receive the "you."

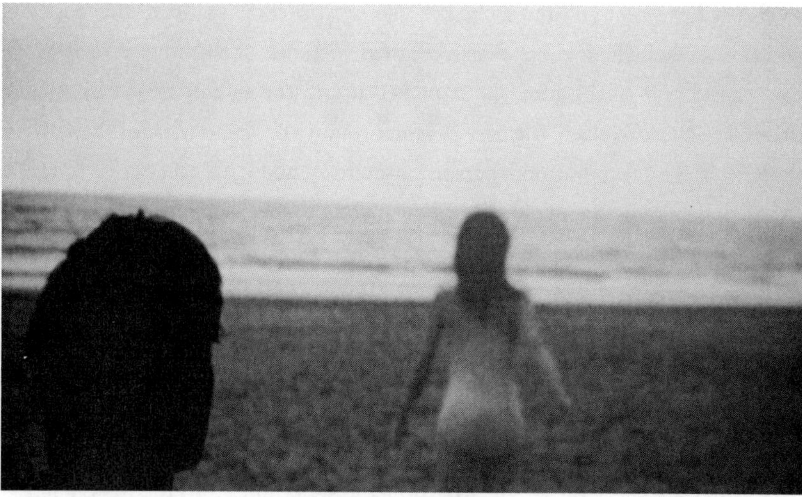

Figure 88. Chantal Akerman, *La Captive*, 2001 (film still).

POSTHUMOUS PRESENCE

IN 1936, Walter Benjamin produced the theory for which George Eastman's 1888 camera seemed to call. The photographic image isn't analogical, he announced in "The Work of Art in the Age of Its Technological Reproducibility," and it doesn't originate in the world; it is, rather, a reproduction, generated by a machine. The medium is also a tool for us to use as we see fit: for generating evidence, disseminating images, expanding the field of human knowledge, and effecting political change. Benjamin's relationship to photography is so unquestioningly instrumental that he even emphasizes the essay's own use-value in its 1938 version. "In what follows," he writes in the introduction, "the concepts which are introduced into the theory of art differ from those now current in that they are completely useless for the purposes of fascism. On the other hand, they are useful for the formulation of revolutionary demands in the politics of art."[1]

In *The Promise of Social Happiness*, the companion volume to this book, I will trace the torturous train of thought that led Benjamin to this argument, and explore its consequences for leftist thought and art making. I will also talk about three moments in the postwar period in which the photographic image recovered its saving power: the one in which Susan Weil and Robert Rauschenberg made their cyanotype photograms and Rauschenberg his early combines; the one in which a group of artists began using the photographic image as the basis for a new kind of figurative painting; and the one in which large-format photographs began appearing on the walls of museums and galleries. In the concluding chapter of this book, I want to show how alien "The Work of Art" is to Benjamin's own thought, and to explore his *other* theory of photography—the theory that he develops in an earlier essay.

The central concept in Benjamin's 1936 definition of photography, and the vehicle through which he links it to the "masses," is "sameness." "The stripping of the veil from the object, the destruction of the aura, is the signature of a perception whose 'sense for sameness in the world' has so increased that by reproduction it extracts sameness even from what is unique . . . ," he proclaims in "The Work of Art." "The alignment of reality with the masses and of the masses with reality is a process of immeasurable importance."[2] Before writing this essay, though, Benjamin was concerned with a very different concept: *similarity*. He returned to it again and again in the 1920s and early 1930s, and defined it in ways that recall Proust's analogies.

This was not entirely fortuitous. In 1925, Benjamin accepted a commission to translate part of the fourth volume of Proust's great novel, *In Search of Lost Time,* and between 1926 and 1930, he and Franz Hessel co-translated three and a half more volumes.[3] During this period, Proust was—as Marcus Bullock and Michael W. Jennings put it—"never far from his mind."[4] Benjamin was absorbed in *The Guermantes Way* throughout his 1927 stay in Moscow, and discussed passages from it and other volumes with Asja Lacis and Bernhard Reich.[5] He also talked about *In Search of Lost Time* with André Gide during a 1928 visit to Paris, and he devotes a large part of his "Conversation with André Gide" to this exchange.[6]

In 1929, Benjamin published an essay about Proust's "impassioned cult of similarity." "The similarity of one thing to another which we are used to, which occupies us in a wakeful state," he writes there, "reflects only vaguely the deeper similarity of the dream work in which everything that happens appears not in identical but in similar guise, opaquely similar to itself."[7] Every day these analogies "unravel," and every night they are "woven anew." Proust didn't want any of these "intricate arabesques" to "escape him," so he turned his days into nights.[8] Although Benjamin goes to great lengths to separate himself from the novelist in the second half of this essay, it is clear from this and many other passages in the first half that he is a devoté of the same cult.

In the *Moscow Diary* he not only acknowledges as much, but also compares his own project to Proust's. The passage on Giotto's *Charity* in *Swann's Way* "corresponds at every point to what I myself [try] to subsume under the concept of allegory," he wrote on January 18, 1927, and the novel's "lesbian scene"—which hinges on a photograph—to the "thrust of my baroque book."[9] There are also many echoes of Proust's novel in *A Berlin Chronicle*, Benjamin's first version of his childhood story. The narrators of both works—as Katja Haustein notes—talk about going to the theater, playing in the park, reading, speaking on the telephone, waiting for an absent mother, and "sleeping, dreaming and awakening in [a] dark room."[10]

In 1930, Benjamin conducted two important conversations with Adrienne Monnier, an anonymous writer and the owner of a Parisian bookstore, Aux Amis des Livres, and he describes both of them in his "Paris Diary." In the first, which occurred on February 4, he noted how much easier it is to "enjoy" works of art in photographs than in person, since their complexity is diminished. Monnier defended photographic reproductions of works of art through an argument that Benjamin would later make his own. "Great creations," she told him, "cannot be thought of as the works of individuals. They are collective objects, so powerful that a condition of enjoying them is to reduce them in stature. In the last analysis, the methods of mechanical reproduction are a technique for reducing them. They allow people to obtain the degree of domination over the works without which they cannot enjoy them."[11]

Benjamin was clearly struck by Monnier's response, because he remarks in the final sentence of this entry that her "theory of reproduction" may prove "valuable" to him, but he was not yet ready to replace similarity with sameness. In the second conversation, which took place six days later, Monnier said that she was revolted by Proust's "transfigur[ation]" of "high society," and the sexual ambiguity of his characters. She spoke "with fanaticism, almost hatred, of Albertine," Benjamin writes, "who was so absurdly like *ce garçon du Ritz*—Albert—whose burly body and masculine gait she could always sense in Albertine."[12] "The hundred doors that offer an entry into his world have remained unopened . . . ," he responded. "In order to understand Proust, it is vital to realize that his true subject is the *reverse side*."[13]

Benjamin seems to have been thinking as he uttered these words about two kinds of Proustian reversal: the gender reversal through which Albertine was created, and the sexual "inversions" through which (according to the doctrine of the day) a man comes to love men, instead of women, and a woman to love women, instead of men. But there are also two other kind Proustian reversals—the one that lies at the heart of the photographic image, and that Marcel associates with perception, and the one towards which he gestures when he says that Albertine is an "inverted projection" or a "negative" of his "sensibility." As we saw in the previous chapter, the second of these reversals is reversible, but Marcel tries to arrest it; he refuses to acknowledge that he is also the "inverted projection" or "negative" of Albertine's "sensibility."[14]

Benjamin was clearly thinking of these reversals as well, either during his conversation with Monnier, or in the months that followed, because in an astonishing May 6, 1931, diary entry, he does what Proust's narrator is unwilling to do. He confesses that the relationship between himself and the women in his life is a two-way street. "Genuine love makes me resemble the woman I love . . . ," he writes. "This transformation into the realm of the similar . . . was something that I experienced most powerfully in my relationship with Asja, with the result that I discovered many things in myself for the first time . . . [but] I have come to know three different women in the course of my life, and three different men in myself."[15] And in *A Berlin Chronicle*, Benjamin compares the process through which an unconscious memory becomes conscious to the development of a negative,[16] just as Proust does in *Time Regained*.

But *A Berlin Chronicle* also contains a passage in which Benjamin admonishes himself *not* to indulge his predilection for similarity—i.e., *not* to be like Proust. "He who has once begun to open the fan of memory never comes to the end of its segments," this passage reads. "No image satisfies him, for he has seen that it can be unfolded, and only in its folds does the truth reside . . . and now remembrance progresses from small to smallest details, from the smallest to the infinitesimal, while that which it encounters in these microcosms grows ever mightier. Such is the deadly game that Proust began so dilettantishly."[17] Benjamin wrote *A Berlin Chronicle* while staying in Ibiza for the first time, a period during which he realized that he would soon have to leave Germany. He summoned the memories that would be most likely to awaken homesickness in his exiled psyche, as he explains in the 1938 version of *Berlin Childhood*, in the hope of "inoculating" himself against it. Since a vaccine works only when administered in small quantities, he sought to "limit" the "effect" of these memories by telling himself that the world they represented was not just *personally* unavailable, it was *socially* "irretrievable."[18] The analogies that connected each of these memories to a host of other memories rendered that task impossible, as did their capacity for entering into new ones.

Benjamin was consequently unable to heed his own admonition. He returned to the topic of similarity again in 1933, through what he calls "natural correspondences."[19] Like Proust's analogies, these correspondences are dynamic and unmasterable, and they "flash up fleetingly out of the stream of things," at a particular moment in time, and then "sink down once more."[20] They also call for a response from us, and "awaken" the faculty through which we provide it: the mimetic faculty.[21] Although Benjamin cannot prevent himself from pursuing the similarities that link everything to many other things, he again tries to "limit" their "effect," this time by mobilizing a linguistic shield. Our "mimetic powers" are much weaker than those of our predecessors," he argues, so we do not apprehend similarity the way they did: through the senses.[22] We experience it, instead, through language,[23] the agency through which we "master" our perceptions and our memories.[24]

SINCE THERE ARE no references to photography or Proust in "Doctrine of the Similar," and Benjamin subsequently adopted Monnier's account of the medium, she might seem to have had the last word in both of their conversations. Three of the most celebrated passages in the essay are, however, at odds with its primary claims. The one that begins "What then is the aura?" locates the beholder in a landscape, instead of a fascist rally or a prestigious museum, and interweaves three sets of ostensibly opposed terms through a kind of call and response between the beholder and the landscape: time and space, proximity and distance, and the human psyche and the physical world.[25]

The beholder is distant from the mountain and the bough of the tree because he knows that they are not a figment of his imagination; they are real, solid, and unassimilable. But he is also as close to them as any of us can be to another being, because he follows their perceptual lead. The bough casts its shadow on the beholder, and the beholder traces the outlines of this shadow; the mountain range exhales its aura into the atmosphere, and the beholder breathes it in. Every time I read this definition of the aura, I think of a passage from *The Visible and the Invisible*. "The look . . . envelops, palpates, espouses the visible things, as though it were in a relation of pre-established harmony with them. . . . ," it reads. "What is this prepossession of the visible, this art of interrogating it according to its own wishes, this inspired exegesis?"[26]

Benjamin describes the aura in similar terms in another passage from the second version of "The Work of Art," and this time he attributes an even more active role to the perceptual world: that of beckoning. He also suggests that photography was once the vehicle of this appeal, instead of the agency through which it was silenced. "In the fleeting expression of a human face, the aura beckons from early photographs for the last time," Benjamin observes. "This is what gives them their melancholy and incomparable beauty."[27] If these two passages constituted everything that he had to say about the aura, his call for its destruction would be incomprehensible. Most of us would not rush to sever the connection between the beholder and the landscape, or greet the withdrawal of the human face with joy. It is not only that the prohibition on beauty is no longer politically justifiable; it is also that the narrative enacted in the first passage and described in the second is dispiritingly Cartesian. Agency is wrested away from perceptual forms, so that it can be transferred to the human look, and this transfer leads to the triumph of instrumental reason, and the derealization of the phenomenal world.

The passage in which Benjamin discusses the optical unconscious is as rife with contradictions as these two accounts of the aura. It begins with a startling claim: the claim that the camera has thrown us off balance, and that the "social function" of film is to help us reestablish our equilibrium. In the middle of the next paragraph, we learn why photography is so destabilizing. The world discloses different aspects of itself to the camera than it does to us. "Clearly, it is another nature which speaks to the camera as compared to the eye," Benjamin writes. "'Other' above all in the sense that a space informed by human consciousness gives way to a space informed by the unconscious."[28] As the frame around the photographic image also compels us to see, every disclosure is a partial disclosure—the world vastly exceeds our capacity to see it, even with the assistance of the camera. Benjamin refers to this invisibility at the heart of all visibility as the "optical unconscious," and he likens it to the "instinctual unconscious."

These three passages feel out of place because they are remnants of an earlier essay, "Little History of Photography" (1931). The second half of this essay is a dry run for "The Work of Art"; it offers a technological account of photography, opposes the medium to art, and associates it with the destruction of the aura.[29] Benjamin also treats photography as a tool, and associates the long exposures of early photography with the seemingly limitless amounts of time enjoyed by its bourgeois clients.[30] And in the last paragraph of "Little History," he transforms the camera into a weapon, and turns it against the world. "It is no accident that Atget's photographs have been likened to those of a crime scene," he writes there. "But isn't every square inch of our cities a crime scene? Every passer-by a culprit? Isn't it the task of the photographer ... to reveal guilt and to point out the guilty in his pictures?"[31] It would be hard to find a clearer articulation of the aesthetics of exposure, or a more vivid dramatization of the politics on which it is based.

However, in the first half of "Little History" Benjamin distinguishes industrial photography from preindustrial photography, instead of art, and privileges the latter, rather than the former. "The fog that surrounds the beginnings of photography" is not "quite as thick as that which shrouds the early days of printing," he writes in the opening sentence of the essay, since the time was "ripe" for its invention; the camera obscura had been around for centuries, and scientists began trying to "capture" its images long before several of them succeeded in doing so. In spite of our familiarity with the prehistory of photography, though, we know little about the early history of the medium itself, since it was industrialized as soon as its patent problems were solved, and its "rapid ongoing development has long precluded any backward glance."[32]

The motor force behind the technological innovations that have prevented us from looking back is capitalism; the product with which industry made its initial "inroads" into the medium was the calling card, and its first manufacturer became a "millionaire." Capitalism discouraged us from looking back because it relies on technological "progress." There may also have been something in early photography that pointed in a different direction—something incompatible with capitalism. "It would not be surprising if the photographic methods which today, for the first time, are harking back to the preindustrial heyday of photography had an underground connection with the crisis of capitalist industry," Benjamin enigmatically observes.[33] But whether or not this was the case, one thing is undeniable: it was in the decade before its industrialization that photography "flowered." If we want to know what the medium is, we need to look back, and Benjamin does that in more than one way in the next paragraph.

This paragraph, which is one of the most important passages that he ever wrote, begins with a description of the daguerreotype that emphasizes its uniqueness, its non-reproducibility, and its elusiveness—i.e., everything that distinguishes it from mechanical reproduction. "Daguerre's photographs were iodized silver plates exposed in the camera obscura," he writes, "which had to be turned this way and that until, in the proper light, a pale gray image could be discerned. They were one of a kind."[34] Although it is not marked as such, this description of the daguerreotype comes from *Der Geist meines Vaters*, Max Dauthendey's memoir of his father, Karl Dauthendey.[35] This is the first of a series of authorial transpositions that demonstrate how central the "mimetic faculty" was to Benjamin's thought.

Karl Dauthendey was both one of the first German daguerreotypists and an early calotypist, and *Der Geist meines Vaters* documents his life as a photographer and his thoughts about the medium. Although he began his career in Leipzig, he spent most of his adult life in St. Petersburg, and married two Russian women of German descent. The first wife was Jewish, as we learn in Max's memoir, and her family rescued Karl from penury. She committed suicide soon after the birth of their sixth child. The second wife was eighteen years younger than her husband, and also died at a very young age. Max Dauthendey, the last child from Karl's second marriage, was a writer and impressionist painter. I mention all of this because Benjamin is in close dialogue with both Dauthendeys throughout this paragraph, and because Karl's marital history figures prominently in the dialogue.

Although Benjamin looks back to the daguerreotype instead of the calotype at the beginning of "Little History," most of the photographs he discusses are calotypes, and he also echoes many of Talbot's claims. Photography is neither a human representation nor a tool, he argues, but rather one of the primary means through which the world discloses itself to us. What it reveals is uninformed by human consciousness—not just because it exceeds our optical capacities, but also because nature "speaks" a different language to the camera than it does to the human eye: one based on analogy. Photography shows us that the "horse willow" reprises "the forms of ancient columns," that the "ostrich fern" resembles a "bishop's crosier," that "chestnut and maple shoots" recall "totem poles," and that the "fuller's thistle" is like "gothic tracery." The language that nature speaks to the camera is also "physiognomic." Photography shows us that the qualities that we associate with the human face are present even in the "smallest things."[36]

"Something new and strange" also surfaces in early photographs—a non-human agency that authors them from the inside. David Octavius Hill did not attribute any independent value to his photographs, Benjamin writes; they were merely props to be used in painting. It is, however, the "unpretentious

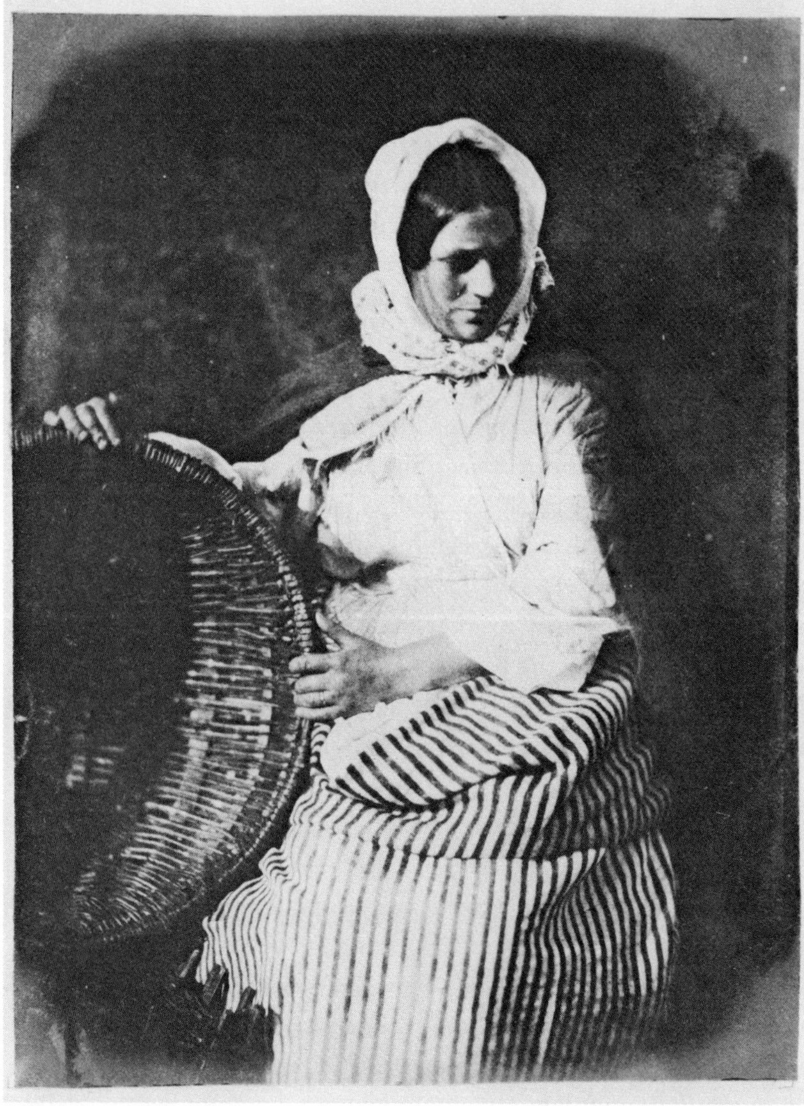

Figure 89. David Octavius Hill and Robert Adamson, *Mrs. Elizabeth (Johnstone) Hall, Newhaven fishwife*, 1843–1847. Salted paper print from paper negative. Courtesy of the Metropolitan Museum of Art, New York.

makeshifts" that he and Robert Adamson generated for "internal use" that have given him "a place in history," not the paintings over which he labored.[37] This a-subjective intentionality makes itself felt through the urge that the photographs awaken in us: the urge to look at what they show us. In Hill's and Adamson's photograph of Mrs. Elizabeth Johnstone Hall, Benjamin observes, "there remains something that goes beyond testimony to the photographer's art, something that cannot be silenced, that fills you with an unruly desire to know what her name was, the woman who was alive there, [*who also really is still here*,] and will never consent to be wholly absorbed in 'art.'"[38]

This description of the relationship between Mrs. Hall, her photographic portrait, and the viewer recalls not just Talbot's writings but another of the passages discussed in the first chapter. "Ye artists of all denominations that have so vilified nature as her journeymen, see how she rises up against you, and takes the staff into her own hands," this passage reads. "Your mistress now, with a vengeance, she will show you what she really is. . . . Every church will show itself to the world without your help. It will make its wants visible and known on paper."[39] Like the author of this anonymous essay, Benjamin associates the demonstrative force he ascribes to early photography with presence. This gets lost in translation in the Harvard edition, which renders "*die auch hier noch wirklich ist*" as "who even now is still real," instead of "who is also really still here." There is, as we will see, no necessary connection between presence and reality. Something can be real but not present, or no longer real but nevertheless present.

Benjamin attributes the disclosive power of preindustrial photography to the length of its exposures, which "caused the subject to focus his life in the moment rather than hurrying on past."[40] Because he inhabited the here and now in such an intense way, the sitter "grew" into the picture, and took "the space in which [he] lived" with him.[41] The long exposures also led to more aesthetically realized photographs than those that came later, and because they resembled "well-drawn or well-painted pictures," they made "a more vivid and lasting impression on the beholder."[42] Consequently, although those who posed for their portraits in the early years of photography were forced to wear neck clamps and knee braces, they were "at home" in the resulting pictures.

But it is not only that preindustrial photography was "congruent" with the sitter's being,[43] and that its pictorial strengths made it easier for the viewer to see what was shown; what "cannot be silenced" in the photograph of Mrs. Elizabeth Johnstone Hall, Benjamin tells us, is the look implied by the "indolent" and "seductive modesty" of her "downcast eyes."[44] "How did the beauty of that hair, / those eyes, beguile our forebears?" he asks through the Stefan George poem to which his meditation leads.[45] Although language once again plays a central role, this passage confers a new meaning on the act of looking back, one based on the *reversibility* of the visual relationship between the sitter and the viewer: the sitter looks back at the viewer and invites him to reciprocate.

Benjamin also discusses another photograph in which there is "something that cannot be silenced," and again he links it to a sitter's look. The photograph is *Karl Dauthendey (Father of the Poet), with his Fiancée* (1857), and it features two people: Dauthendey and Fraulein Friedrich, to whom he was engaged, and whom he later married. Benjamin saw this photograph in Helmuth Bossert and Heinrich Guttman's book, *Aus der Frühzeit der Photographie, 1840–1870.* According to the editors of this book, it was taken on September 1, 1857, in St. Petersburg, and the following caption is printed beneath it, in German, English and French: "The photographer Karl Dauthendey with his betrothed Miss Friedrich after their first attendance at church."[46] I don't know who wrote the caption, which associates the photograph with an even more specific moment in time, but it is clearly congruent with Dauthendey's wishes, because he tried to burn the same time stamp into the photograph. Although he and Friedrich are sitting on what appears to be a loveseat in an interior space,[47] both are wearing their coats, as if they have only just returned from church and haven't had time yet to remove them. She also holds a hymnal, and he his top hat.

Dauthendey's attempt to anchor the photograph to a particular moment in time presumably has something to do with his engagement—with his desire to experience and preserve the longed-for "now" in which Friedrich, who was much younger, and reluctant to marry him, was fully and completely what the caption declares her to be: his betrothed. But the photograph was shot in a studio, instead of a place to which we could imagine the couple going after church—Dauthendey's house, the home of Friedrich's parents, the domicile of a friend. It was also carefully staged. The loveseat with its curved sides was clearly chosen because it fits perfectly inside the oval shape of the photograph, rather than for comfort, since it's too small for two people in street clothes. Dauthendey's coat has also been artfully arranged, so as to provide a full view of his elaborate collar and tie, and a partial view of his vest, watch chain, and sumptuous top hat. The portrait's careful construction and the manifest irreality of its "here" completely de-realize its "now."

The photograph also divides the couple, instead of uniting them. It is split into two parts by the lightness of Friedrich's clothing and the darkness of Dauthendey's, an effect that is compounded by the lighting and consolidated through the divergence of their looks; he gazes directly and authoritatively at the camera, but she gazes past both him and the camera, at something unseen and perhaps even unseeable. Finally, the fact that Dauthendey and Friedrich

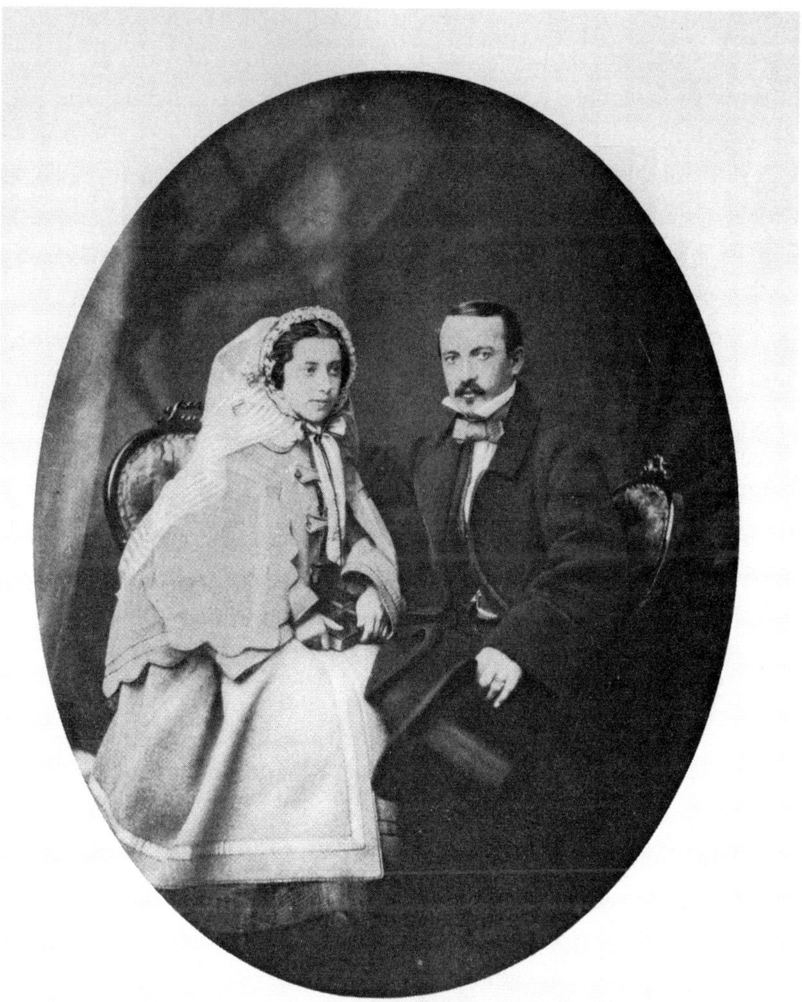

Figure 90. Karl Dauthendey, *The Photographer Karl Dauthendey with his betrothed Miss Friedrich after their first attendance at church*, 1857.

are wearing street clothes in an interior space blurs the distinction between the inside and the outside, and suggests that the photograph may also be serving another function.

Benjamin thinks that the woman in the portrait is Dauthendey's *first* wife, Anna Olswang, who committed suicide in 1855, and he interprets the photograph accordingly. Although we can see from her look that she was already halfway out of the world when the portrait was made, he writes, Dauthendey doesn't notice; "her gaze passes him by . . . absorbed in an ominous distance."[48] In actuality, though, as André Gunthert has recently pointed out, the photograph was taken two years after Olswang's death, and shows Dauthendey with the woman who became his *second* wife. Benjamin makes this mistake, Gunthert reasons, because he confuses *Karl Dauthendey and his Fiancé*e with another photograph—a photograph of Dauthendey with his *first* wife.[49]

This second photograph, which exists only as a description, derives from the same source as Benjamin's account of the daguerreotype: *Der Geist meines Vaters*. "The youngest of my step-sisters still has in her possession an image that shows this young woman, her mother, on the veranda of a Russian country estate . . . ," Max writes at a key juncture. "My father stands outside in a leather hunting suit at the railing of the wooden balcony. He shoulders a gun and a hunting pouch . . . [and] stands there very slim and towering, as the woman in a wide crinoline skirt . . . who is sitting on the veranda, watches him with intelligent eyes. There is no trace of her unhappy future in this image, only that my father's sinister, hard and manly look betrays a juvenile brutality, capable of hurting this woman, who observes him submissively."[50]

Gunthert's first claim is indisputable: Benjamin was clearly thinking about this passage when he looked at *Karl Dauthendey and his Fiancée*. He was drawn to the story about Dauthendey's first wife, I believe, because he had recently spent time in Moscow, the city that he mistakenly substitutes for St. Petersburg; because he, too, was Jewish; and because he, too, had been contemplating suicide.[51] This does not mean, though, that Benjamin didn't see the photograph in front of him, or that he subordinated it to Max's description of his sister's photograph. Benjamin thought of the latter while looking at the former because of their structural similarities. Although Olswang's eyes are fixed on her husband in the photograph described in *Der Geist meines Vaters*, instead of an unseeable "elsewhere," he no more meets her gaze than he does Friedrich's in the engagement photograph, because his eyes rebuff her. And although he is embracing Friedrich in *Karl Dauthendey and his Fiancée*, rather than repudiating her, the look that he directs toward us and the camera is "sinister, hard and manly," like the one he directs at Olswang. If a look can kill, it probably will, Benjamin is effectively saying—and we know that this one can, because it has done so before.

Max Dauthendey describes the veranda photograph after a long and seemingly exculpatory account of his father's refusal to satisfy his wife's desire for love and romance, which was (he implies) the reason for her suicide.[52] He is so closely identified with Karl throughout this passage that he almost seems to be "channeling" him. When Max comes to the photograph of Dauthendey and Olswang, though, he adopts a very different point of view: one aligned with his stepsister and her mother. The word with which he characterizes Olswang's eyes—"intelligent"—cancels out the preceding passage, with its belittling account of her romantic desires. The metaphoric connection between Dauthendey's gun and his look also renders the final sentence affirmative; there *is* a trace of Olswang's unhappy future in this image, and it is her husband's sinister, hard and manly gaze. Benjamin also adopts this vantage point: he looks at the engagement photograph the way Max and his sister looked at the photograph of Karl's first wife.

Max's description of this photograph is closely related to three other passages in *Der Geist meines Vaters*, all of which are direct quotes from Karl. In the first, Karl describes his initial encounter with the woman in the engagement photograph, and in the second his subsequent life with her. Both passages revolve around the same thing: Friedrich's "large eyes and silent doe-eyed look," which caused him to fall instantly in love with her, and became the emblem of her exemplary wifely compliance. She was "the softest woman in the world," he repeatedly says, and "[although] I was often violent with her . . . she never uttered a violent word in return. In fact, she said nothing. [She just looked at me with] her large, silent, timid eyes," that were "more soothing than any word."[53] We have all encountered eyes that speak volumes, thereby compensating for their owner's reticence, but Dauthendey does not say that Friedrich's eyes were more eloquent than words. He says, rather, that they were "timid" and "silent"—i.e., that they communicated nothing. In the third passage, which comes shortly after the other two, Karl says to Max: "You have your mother's eyes, which really worries me. A man should have hard eyes. Try to steel your heart instead. Then things will never go badly for you."[54]

The gender binary could not be more sharply delineated—and it is also highly visible in the engagement photograph. We see not only the "hard eyes" that a man "should" have, but also the "soft eyes" that allowed Karl to love his second wife. These looks cannot meet, because they have been rendered *irreversible. Der Geist meines Vaters* is also a one-way street. Karl asked Max to write a memoir based on his father's memories and stories, instead of his own. Most of the book is a paraphrase of Karl's oft-told stories and his unpublished memoir. There are also many direct quotations, some of them so long that it is hard to tell whether the speaker is Karl or Max. The book begins with the sentence "Today I visited my Father's grave."[55] The last one should be: "And I took his place, so that he could live again."

BENJAMIN RETURNS to the topic of the sitter's look at the end of the paragraph, through another quotation from *Der Geist meines Vaters*. The passage is a paraphrase of things that Karl said to Max, but he treats it as a direct quotation from Karl. "We didn't trust ourselves at first to look long at the first pictures he developed," it reads. "We were abashed by the distinctness of these human images, and believed that the tiny little faces in the picture could see *us*, so powerfully was everyone affected by the unaccustomed clarity and the unaccustomed fidelity to nature of the first daguerreotypes."[56] As we learn in the passage from which this quotation comes, Karl is not just talking about how it felt to be an early viewer of photographic portraits; he's talking about how it felt to be an early viewer of his *own* photographic portraits.[57] He was "astonished" by this experience, Max tells us, and we can see why: it catapulted him from the position of the photographer to that of a viewer, thereby stripping him of his authorial credentials. The "little faces" in these pictures also made him feel *seen*. They looked back at him as his ontological equals, and invited him to return the favor.

Dauthendey reacted the way Sartre's voyeur does when he thinks that he is being observed from the place of the Other:[58] he was ashamed of *himself* and he didn't trust *himself* to return the look. I italicized "himself" because Dauthendey uses reflexive verbs to describe both responses (*sich vertrauen* and *sich scheuen*), and because this helps us to see just how self-referential those responses were. When he felt himself seen by the faces in early photographs, he realized that he was not what he had imagined himself to be: a sovereign subject.

It is odd, to say the least, that someone so unnerved by the faces in his early photographs should have devoted his life to photographic portraiture. It is not only that Dauthendey must have been exposed on an almost daily basis to looks that he did not trust himself to return, but also that the mysterious intentionality that emanated from those looks must have repeatedly challenged his claim to be the source of his photographs. He tried to solve the first problem by rendering the look irreversible—hence his insistence on the "hardness" of the male gaze and the "softness" of its female equivalent. He attempted to solve the second by authoring *Karl Dauthendey and his Fiancée* from the inside, as well as the outside. With his commanding look, Dauthendey tries to occupy two positions at once: that of the photographer and that of the sitter. Now we understand the photograph's spatial and temporal equivocations: why Karl is wearing a coat and holding his top hat when sitting on a loveseat in an interior space, and why the photograph claims both to issue from a single moment in time and to be the product of a long exposure.

There is no place within this aspirational economy for Friedrich, and she makes no effort to be in the photograph that Dauthendey is trying to make. She sits where he presumably told her to sit, and looks in the direction he presumably told her to look, but she doesn't strike a pose, or assume a role.

Dauthendey doesn't appear in this photograph either, because it was never made. When he looked through the viewfinder at the scene he had so carefully constructed, the space next to Friedrich was empty, and when he sat down next to her, he vacated his position in front of the viewfinder. I can't help but think that the breathlessness conveyed by the caption has less to do with being just back from church than it does with his haste in moving from the camera to the sofa. But even if Dauthendey had been able to bridge the gap between those two subject-positions, he wouldn't be the sole author of the engagement portrait. That agency through which the sitter "presences" in early photographs can't be accessed through human consciousness or supplanted by will; it is, indeed, highly resistant to both. Benjamin's eyes were drawn to Friedrich's look rather than to Dauthendey's because it is *unstaged*: because, as Roland Barthes said of his mother, she "lent" herself to the photograph, instead of trying to control it.[59]

Benjamin clearly saw all of this, because he concludes his reading of *Karl Dauthendey and his Fiancée* with a meditation on the radically different kinds of agency that are at work within it. He also indicates yet again where his own allegiances lie. "No matter how artful the photographer," he writes, "the beholder feels an irresistible urge to search such a picture for the tiny spark of contingency, of the here and now, with which reality has . . . seared the subject, to find the inconspicuous spot where in the immediacy of that long-forgotten moment the future nests so eloquently that we, looking back, may rediscover it."[60]

MY GOAL HERE is not to prove that Dauthendey was a "bad" person, or even that he made both of his wives unhappy. It is, rather, to show that the issues that Benjamin addresses in the first half of "Little History" are ontological as well as pictorial, and that they have profound social consequences. Although nothing is more fundamentally egalitarian than touch and sight, there are more power lines in the field of vision than in the New York subway system. Every culture attempts to colonize the field of vision—to determine who is visible, who is invisible, who is "allowed" to see, and what visibility, invisibility, and vision signify. This colonization has real consequences; we are psychically and socially constrained by the visual categories into which we are slotted. It has particularly deadly consequences for women, since gender is almost always the vehicle through which the chiasmus is first repudiated. The heterosexual couple is also frequently used the way Karl Dauthendey used it: to "prove" that two *isn't* the smallest unit of Being.

Since the early photographic portrait was the ontological extrusion of its sitter, it revealed both aspects of his visual being. He gazed out from it, as well as appearing within it, and his look showed the viewer that he, too, was part of the visible world. And because the photographic image emerged so slowly in the first decades of its history, and was so manifestly developmental, often changing in tandem with the world, it could not be relegated to the past. It said "this is," rather than "this was." It consequently not only lit the pathway leading back to the world, and demonstrated that there is no thought without sensory perception, it also invited its viewers back into the relationship described by Merleau-Ponty: one in which "the seer and the visible reciprocate one another and we no longer know which sees and which is seen."[61]

Since Benjamin was not born until 1892, he could not meet Friedrich in the here and now, but because of how the engagement photograph was created, another kind of chiasmus was available to him: a trans-historical chiasmus. During the relatively long period in which she sat in front of the camera, Friedrich grew into the picture, and this allowed her not only to "presence," but also to continue "presencing" long after she ceased to exist. The engagement photograph journeyed into the future, in search of a viewer who would do what Dauthendey had failed to do. Fifty-nine years after Friedrich's death, it found him. By looking back at her both retrospectively and reciprocally, Benjamin rendered her *posthumously present*. He did the same for Mrs. Elizabeth Johnstone Hall.

As Benjamin shows in the second half of "Little History," the industrialization of chemical photography stripped the photographic image of its capacity to render its sitter present—first by transforming it into a representation, and then by typologizing it. He wholeheartedly embraces the second of these developments, in a passage that anticipates his 1936 account of photography. "Whether one is of the Left or the Right," Benjamin enthuses, "one will have to get used to be looked at in terms of one's provenance. And one will have to look at others in the same way."[62] Those who don't know how to do this should consult August Sander's *Face of Our Time*, which is an "instruction manual" for "comparative" looking. He is highly critical, though, of the first development, partly because it aestheticizes photography, and partly because it severs the sitter from the viewer.

Benjamin blames the transformation of the photographic portrait from an ontological extension of its sitter's being into a man-made representation on a transitional generation of photographers, who approached portraiture as a business, but marketed their photographs as art. This generation "simulated" the "aura" that was destroyed by industrialization by dressing their clients in elaborate costumes, positioning them in artificial settings that were full of "artistic" props, and retouching the resulting images, to make them more "atmospheric."[63] Benjamin's primary example of this kind of portrait is a childhood photograph of Franz Kafka that was made around the same time as the first mass-produced camera. The boy in the photograph is dressed in a "humiliatingly tight child's suit overloaded with trimming, in a sort of greenhouse landscape," whose "upholstered tropics" are rendered "even stuffier and more oppressive" by the "inordinately large broad-brimmed hat" that he holds in his left hand.[64] Kafka would be utterly "lost in this setting," Benjamin observes in the final sentence of the paragraph, "were it not for his immensely sad eyes, which dominate this landscape predestined for them."

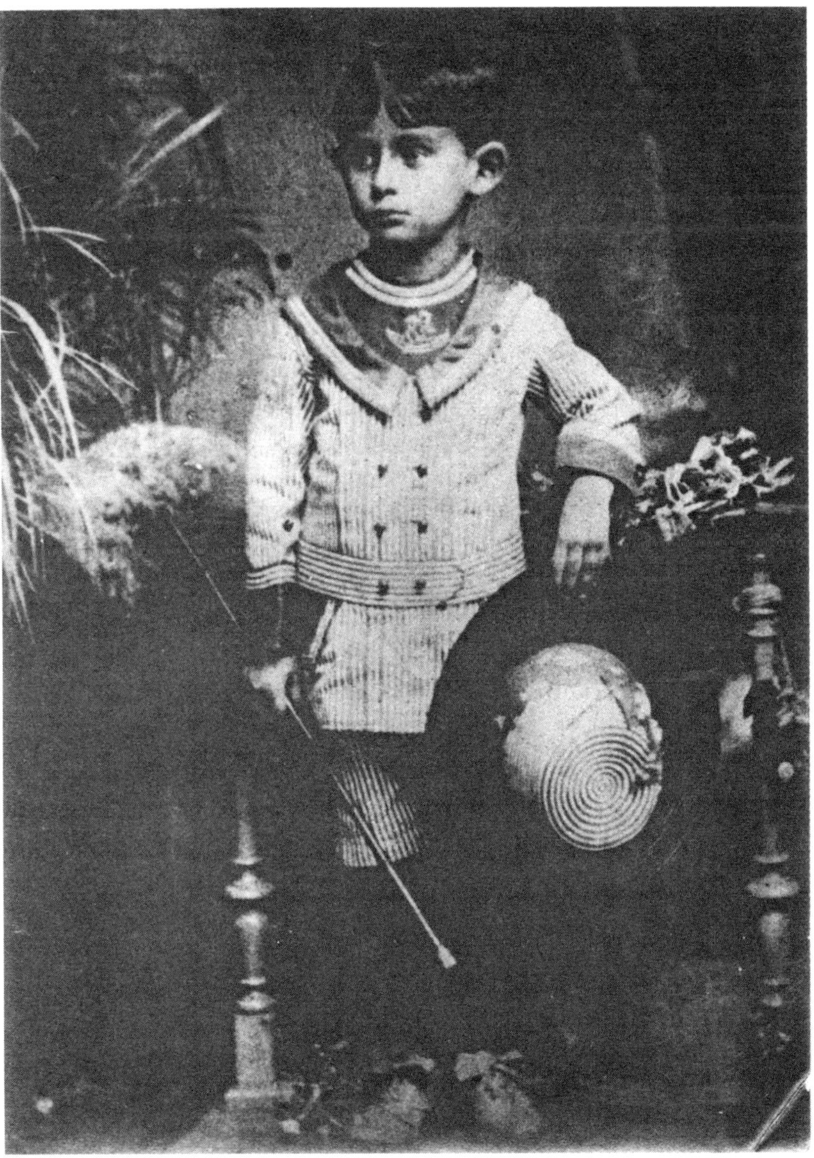

Figure 91. Franz Kafka, about four years old, 1887. Courtesy of the Klaus Wagenbach Archiv, Berlin.

In the next paragraph, Benjamin contrasts Kafka's eyes with those that peer out of earlier photographs. Unlike the gaze of those who sat for their portraits in the preindustrial period, which was "full" and "secure," he writes, the boy in this portrait looks out "at the world" in an "excluded and godforsaken . . . manner."[65] Benjamin's characterization of the first kind of look may seem surprising, since Fraulein Friedrich's look is neither "full" nor "secure," but he is talking about a series of midcentury portraits of male representatives of the "rising class," such as *The Philosopher Schelling* (ca. 1850), whose aura extends even to the creases in their clothing,[66] and whose gaze has the qualities that so unnerved Dauthendey.

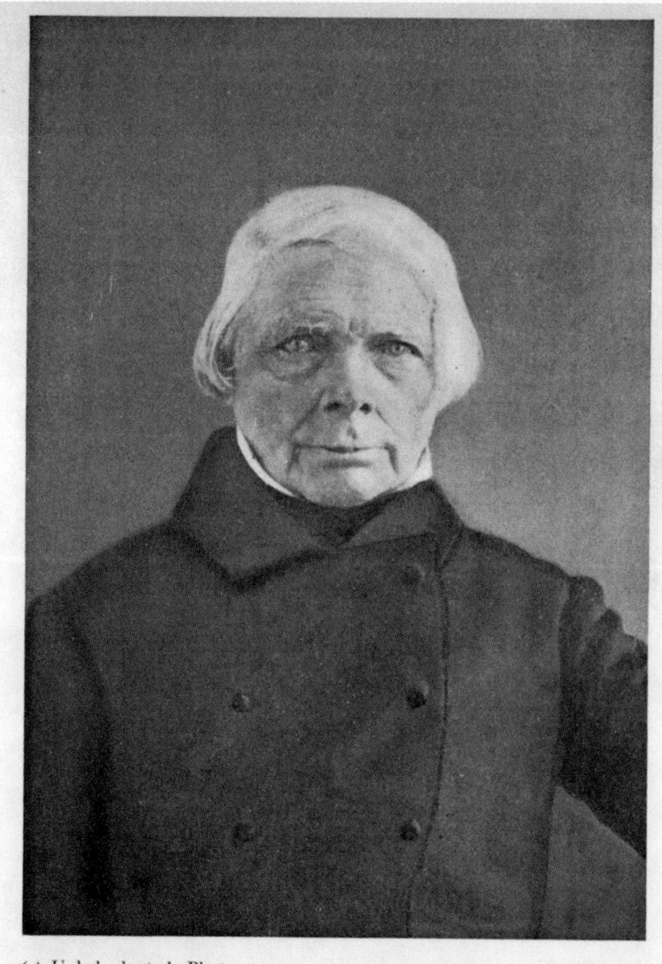

Figure 92. Friedrich Wilhelm Joseph von Schelling, ca. 1850.

But the industrialization of photography cannot prevent a detail in an individual photograph from striking an answering chord in a particular viewer, and Kafka's eyes clearly had this effect on Benjamin. He returns to the Kafka photograph in his 1934 essay about the novelist, and again emphasizes the "sadness" of his look and the mysterious "dominance" that it exercises over the artificial setting.[67] The photograph also resurfaces in the first version of *Berlin Childhood Around 1900* (1932–1934). In an entry called "The Mummerehlen," a neologism based on a childhood misunderstanding, Benjamin talks about the two very different kinds of similarity that he experienced as a child. The first, which he associates with language, gave him a "foothold on life," and "lit up paths to the world's interior."[68] It also embedded him in the nineteenth century, like a mollusk in its shell. The second kind of similarity, which he associates with industrial portrait photography, pried him out of that shell. Inserted into a prefabricated picture, and asked to "resemble" the props in his studio surroundings, Benjamin experienced a kind of "fading" of his "being."[69] "I saw myself surrounded by folding screens, cushions, and pedestals which craved my image much as the shades of Hades craved the blood of the sacrificial animal," he writes. "In the end, I was offered up to a crudely painted prospect of the Alps, and my right hand ... cast its shadow on the clouds and snowfields of the backdrop."[70]

However, the real distinction here is not between the similarities enabled by *language* and those mandated by industrial photography; it is between the similarities enabled by *early photography* and those mandated by industrial photography. A mollusk's shell is "ektoskeletal": an extension or outgrowth of the mollusk itself. It is also through this extension that the creature comes into contact with other beings. A mollusk's shell consequently cannot be compared to language, even when the latter assumes a "magical" form. The only likeness that "behaves" the way it does—that is generated by what it analogizes, and that connects this thing to other things—is a photograph of the kind described in "Little History": one into which the referent has "grown."

The passage that precedes the mollusk comparison also suggests that although industrialization marks the end of analogical photography and the beginning of representational photography, it may sometimes be possible to reverse this chronology: to analogize an industrial photograph. It begins with a description of a studio photograph of Benjamin, standing in front of an "Alpine" backdrop, dressed as a "little mountaineer." This image is partly modeled on a *carte-de-visite* photograph of Benjamin and his brother, which shows two boys posed before a similar backdrop, dressed as mountain climbers and holding rustic walking sticks.[71] But no sooner does it emerge than it begins to

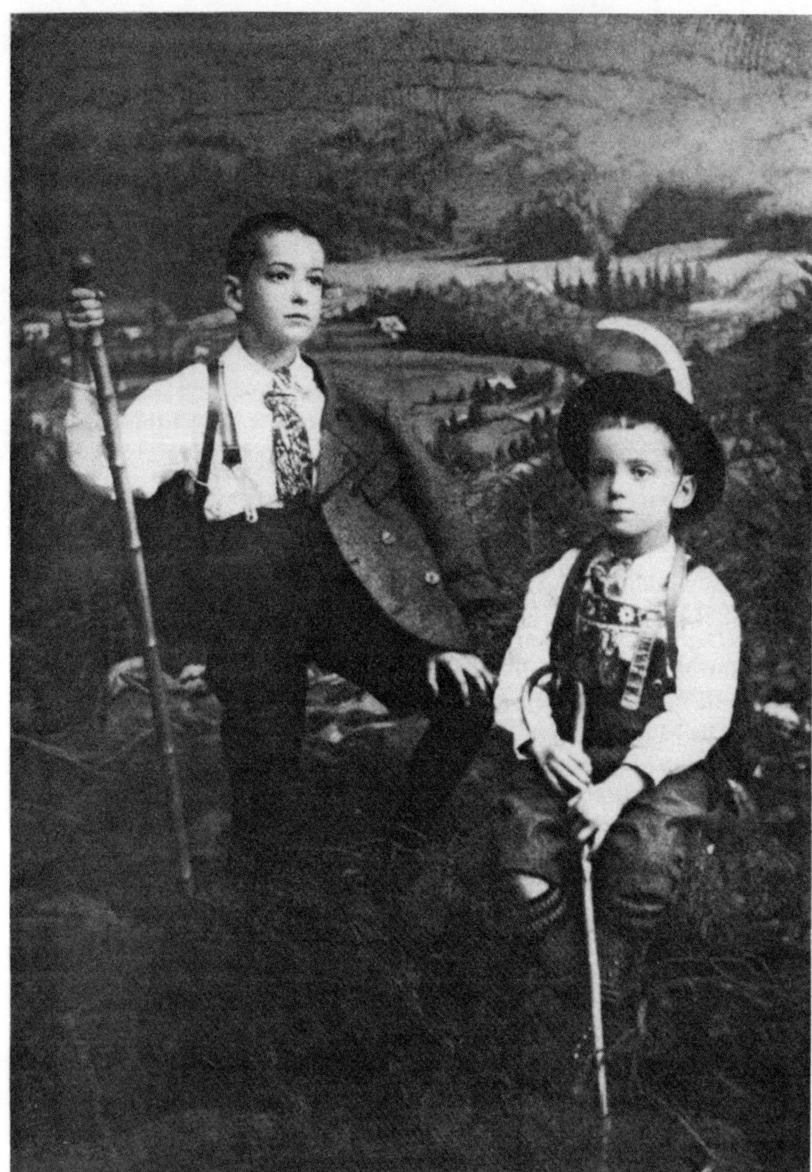

Figure 93. Carte-de-visite photograph of Walter Benjamin with his brother Georg, circa 1902. Courtesy of the Österreichische Nationalbibliothek, Vienna.

morph. A "kidskin hat" makes its way into the boy's right hand, and a "giant sombrero" into the left. A potted palm appears on one side of the photograph, and a garden table with a "cluster of ostrich feathers" on the other. No surviving photograph of Benjamin corresponds in any way to this new image. The ostrich feathers, garden table, potted plant, and giant sombrero all come—as others have already noted—from the Kafka photograph.[72]

The "Mummerehlen" chapter of *Berlin Childhood* ends with the story of a painter who entered one of his pictures, and was never seen again.[73] The metamorphosis of the Benjamin photograph into the Kafka photograph seems destined to end in a similar way: with the disappearance of one of the boys. Surprisingly, though, that does not happen, because shortly after the garden table and ostrich feathers appear, Benjamin's mother enters the picture, and what seemed a single image resolves itself into two similar—but not identical—images, like those on a stereo card.

This analogy emerged out of another analogy. Benjamin felt a profound sense of kinship with Kafka, just as he did with Proust. Some of these affinities were biographical; both men were Jewish writers who were products of, but intellectually estranged from, the late-nineteenth-century bourgeoisie. Others were ontological; Kafka was someone whose "style of Being" rhymed with his own.[74] The look in the boy's eyes activated these correspondences, allowing Benjamin to transform the childhood photograph from a representation into an analogy. He effected this transformation by elaborating the extra-photographic similarities between himself and the novelist in photographic terms. Although the resulting "stereo card" does not render Kafka posthumously present, it does give him a more attenuated kind of presence: what might be called "past presence."

SIMILAR RESCUES have been enacted countless times since Benjamin wrote *Berlin Childhood*, some of which Barthes describes in *Camera Lucida*, and on the foundation of which he erects his theory of photography.[75] Twentieth-century artists have also analogized industrial photographs in other ways, and these analogies have opened the door to a new kind of photographic image: one that allows the viewer and the sitter to meet in the here and now. But these are matters for another book, and it is time to bring this one to a close. I will do so through a brief discussion of the photograph on its cover.

This cyanotype, which is called *John Keats's Death Mask* (1999),[76] is by John Dugdale, a contemporary artist who makes photographs in preindustrial ways, and who calls Julia Margaret Cameron his "godmother,"[77] and Talbot an "old soulmate."[78] The artist appears in the lower left side of the image, facing the camera, and the eponymous death mask occupies a similar position on the right. Dugdale supports his plaster companion, and grazes the latter's cheek with his own. Like *Dauthendey and his Fiancée, John Keats's Death Mask* is thus both a self-portrait and the portrait of a couple. This photograph, however, was not shot in a studio, under tightly controlled conditions. Instead, Dugdale stood at the edge of the woods near Maurice Sendak's home in Ridgefield, Connecticut,

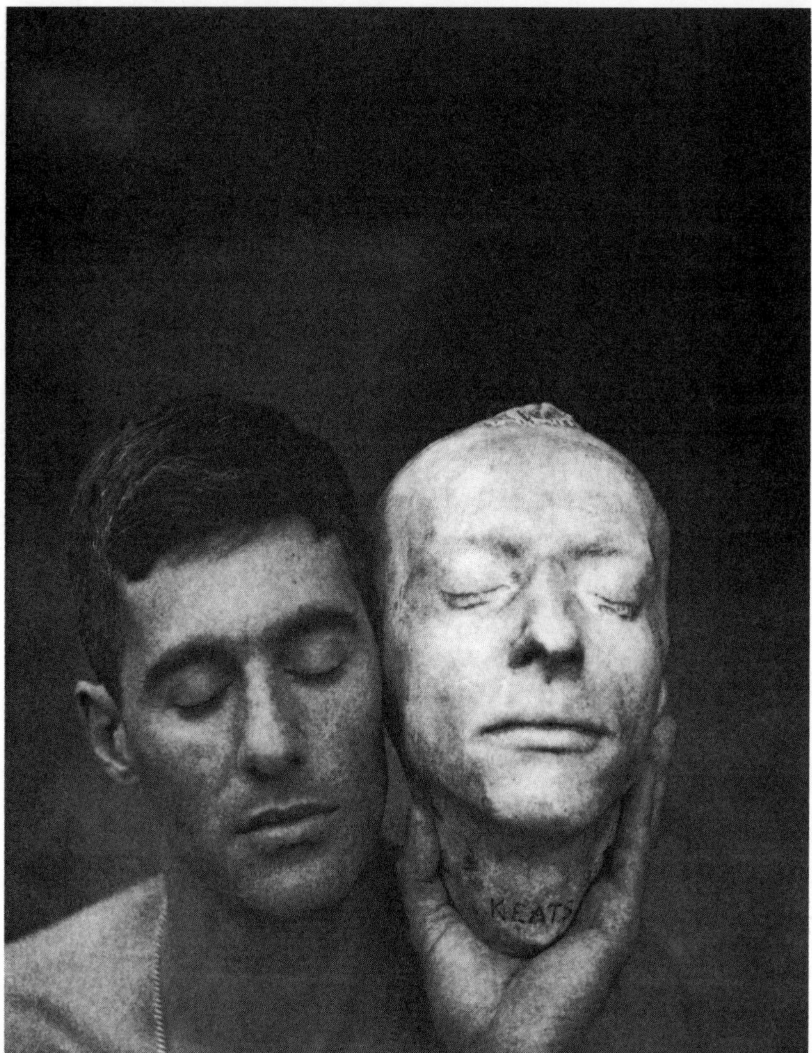

Figure 94/Colorplate 23. John Dugdale, *Death Mask of John Keats*, 1999. Cyanotype. Courtesy of the artist.

at twilight one evening in 1999, while someone else exposed the negative.[79] And rather than directing a "hard, manly look" at the camera, the artist shut his eyes.

Dugdale's eyes are closed in this and many of his other photographs because he is blind. He lost all of his vision in one eye and eighty percent of his vision in the other in 1994, as a result of a cataclysmic series of health crises precipitated by the human autoimmune deficiency virus. He lost his remaining vision in 2010. But Dugdale's eyes would also be closed if this were not the case, because he knows that they are not the locus of vision. "Sight does not exist in your eyes," he declares in *Life's Evening Hour*, his first book of photographs. "[It] exists in your mind and heart."[80] He also knows that the camera isn't an extension of his look. Photography means "drawing with light," he observes in another passage in *Life's Evening Hour*—and the photographer is the recipient, not the creator, of the resulting images.[81]

The passage that I have just quoted accompanies a cyanotype that was made at Lacock Abbey, and that references Talbot's earliest extant photograph: *Oriel Window*. Standing in front of this window, Dugdale recounts in the same passage, he felt "light falling on his body," just as it had fallen on Talbot's sensitized

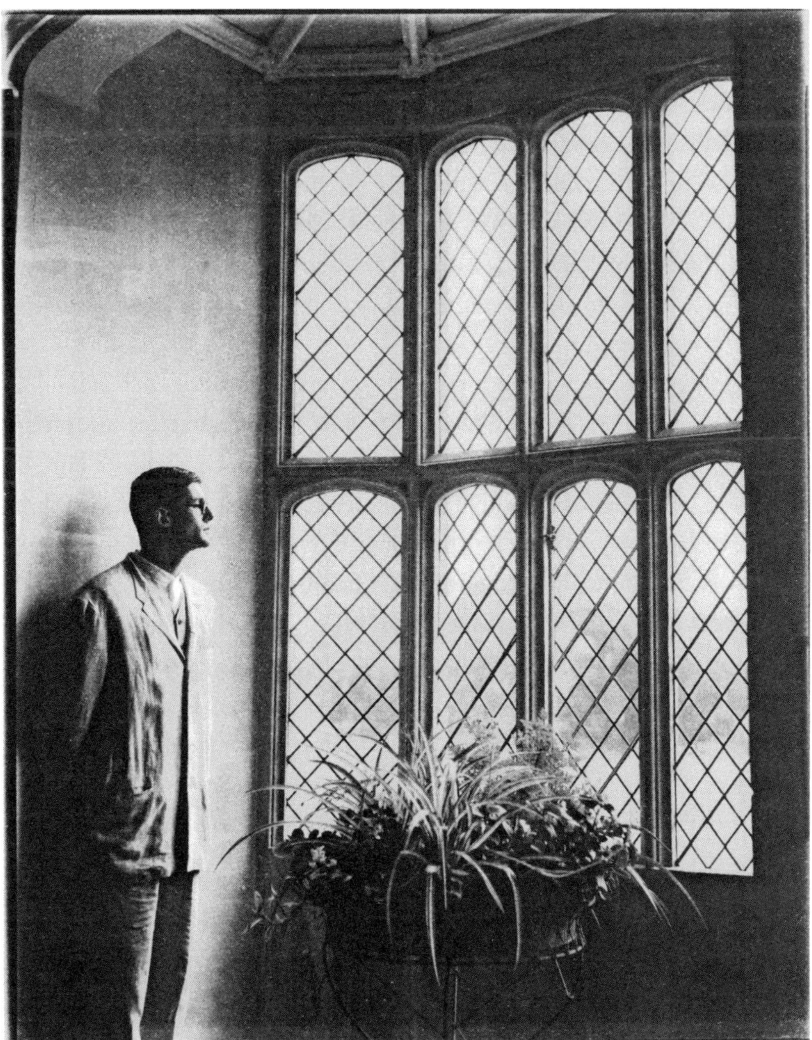

Figure 95/Colorplate 24. John Dugdale, *Self-Portrait at Oriel Window*, 1998. Cyanotype. Courtesy of the artist.

paper. The artist's comparison of his body to a photographic negative is the physical counterpart of the concept mobilized by Cézanne, Rilke, and Proust to describe the receptivity of their artistic practice: the concept of the psychic photographic plate.[82] Dugdale characterizes himself as a receiver in another way in a gallery statement, writing: "The quietude that people respond to in my pictures is, in part, because of the way the pictures are made: no flash; no harsh electric light; not even the sound of the shutter—just a lens cap removed, and then gently replaced."[83]

Dugdale refers to the photographs in *Life's Evening Hour* as "likenesses."[84] Since these photographs are staged, and his sitters often assume fictional personae, their similarity might seem to be the kind to which Benjamin objects, and which he associates with the transitional generation of industrial photographers. Dugdale, however, always introduces us to his models, so that we know whose likeness we are observing, and he often describes the situation out of which the photograph emerged. And not only is *John Keats's Death Mask* a likeness of the artist holding a death mask, but the mask itself is also a likeness of John Keats, and of a very particular kind. Like Talbot's photogenic drawings, which resemble their "cause," and the shell described by Benjamin, which extends outward from and conforms to the mollusk, a death mask analogizes the face that shaped it.

John Keats's Death Mask also discloses other resemblances that cannot be attributed to a human author. Dugdale's features and the shape of his face are strikingly similar to those of his plaster companion, and the latter's eyes are also closed. Although the photograph is a monochrome, and therefore chromatically non-representative, the field of cyan blue that fills the upper third of the photograph resembles the light that created it. "The twilight," Dugdale told me, "is what gives the picture its soft glow." The chemicals used in the cyanotype process have also sprinkled delicate freckles over the bodies of both figures, transforming plaster into flesh, and making Dugdale's hand seem like the organic extension of the mask's face. And instead of rending asunder what analogy has joined together, the composition reinforces these connections. Not only are both figures located in the lower part of the image, with the one on the left occupying a comparable position to the one on the right, but both are "busts," their heads are level, and they are sheltered beneath the same sky.

Finally, instead of banishing other intentionalities, as Dauthendey attempts to do, Dugdale invites them in. Some of these intentionalities are "objective"; they originate in the phenomenal world, and enter with the light. Others, though, are emphatically human. "The heartfelt grace and love that people bring to my pictures when viewing them is a gift to me of inestimable value,"

Dugdale writes in *Life's Evening Hour*, ". . . a gift that keeps me whole and alive."[85] He provides a similar account of his models. "When the floodlight is on and I focus the camera on people," he confides in another entry, "I find they're touched by inspiration and our session becomes a give and take between the photographer and the subject. We're orchestrating, creating a picture together, a process I cherish."[86] Instead of telling his sitters what to do, Dugdale "directs" them by adopting the position that he wants them to assume, and he sometimes asks *them* to focus the camera.[87]

Since Dugdale is the only person in *John Keats's Death Mask*, it might seem less chiasmatic than the photographs described in the previous paragraph. However, the death mask belonged to Sendak, and it was at his request that the cyanotype was made.[88] Although neither Dugdale nor Sendak may have realized this, the photograph is also a visual antiphon to one of Keats's own utterances. "Tender is the night," the poet remarks in "Ode to a Nightingale," and there has never been one more tender than this. And although there is usually nothing more redolent of absence than a death mask, this mask functions like an early photograph; it is the vehicle through which Keats "presences." Finally, when placed side by side with eyes that not only cannot see, but that—unlike them—cannot open, something even more miraculous happens: Dugdale's closed eyes become a return look. Since these transformations occur within the frame of a cyanotype, they reactivate chemical photography's own presentational powers—its capacity to disclose the world, and to solicit a response. As we gaze at *John Keats's Death Mask*, the medium becomes again what it was in 1839: the highest form of *poiēsis*.

NOTES

INTRODUCTION

1. Martin Heidegger, "The Age of the World Picture," in *The Question Concerning Technology and Other Essays*, trans. William Lovitt (New York: Harper and Row, 1977), 128 and 134.

2. René Descartes, *Discourse on Method and Meditations on First Philosophy*, ed. David Weissman (New Haven: Yale University Press, 1996), 70.

3. Charles Sanders Peirce, "What Is a Sign?," in *The Essential Peirce: Selected Philosophical Writings*, vol. 2, *1893–1913*, ed. the Peirce Edition Project (Bloomington: Indiana University Press, 1998), 8.

4. This is also the case with Peirce himself.

5. Roland Barthes, "Rhetoric of the Image," in *Image – Music – Text*, trans. Stephen Heath (New York: Farrar, Straus, and Giroux, 1977), 44.

6. Roland Barthes, *Camera Lucida: Reflections on Photography*, trans. Richard Howard (New York: Farrar, Straus and Giroux, 1981), 96.

7. I am thinking particularly here of Haacke's use of photography in *Shapolsky et al. Manhattan Real Estate Holdings, A Real-Time Social System, as of May 1, 1971*, a work that documents 142 slum properties owned by a few New York City landlords. Haacke adopts a different relationship to photography in a number of his later works, most notably *Oil Painting, Homage to Marcel Broodthaers* (1982). (In 1971, the Guggenheim Museum canceled an exhibition of Haacke's work because it included two pieces that the museum's director, Thomas Messer, deemed to be offensive. *Shapolsky* was one of them. This injustice was rectified by the Whitney Museum in 2007–2008, which included *Shapolsky* in an exhibition of Haacke's work.)

8. Benjamin also maintains that the "hidden political significance" of photography is its capacity to provide "evidence." See "The Work of Art in the Age of Its Technological Reproducibility," in *The Selected Writings of Walter Benjamin*, vol. 3, *1935–1938*, ed. Howard Eiland and Michael W. Jennings (Cambridge: Harvard University Press, 2002), 108.

9. George Baker provides a brilliant discussion of this backward turn in the work of three other important artists—Tacita Dean, Zoe Leonard, and Sharon Lockhart—in "Lateness and Longing," in *50 Moons of Saturn: T2 Torino Triennale*, ed. Daniel Birnbaum (Milan: Skira, 2008), 47–97. This essay provided the nucleus for his forthcom-

ing book, *Lateness and Longing: On the Afterlife of Photography* (Chicago: University of Chicago Press, 2015).

10. Barthes, *Camera Lucida*, 117.

11. Walter Benjamin, "Left Wing Melancholy," in Benjamin, *Selected Writings*, vol. 2, *1927–1934*, ed. Michael W. Jennings (Cambridge: Harvard University Press, 1999), 425–426.

12. See Karl Marx and Friedrich Engels, *The German Ideology: Part One*, ed. C. J. Arthur (New York: International Publishers, 1974), 64–65.

13. Benjamin wrote the first version of "The Work of Art" in 1935, and the second in 1936.

14. I am drawing here on the second version of "The Work of Art," cited in note 8. Benjamin, "The Work of Art," 104.

15. Ibid., 132n37.

16. Ibid., 104.

17. Ibid., 101, 104, 108, 124n10.

18. Benjamin also knows this. "The dialectic of commodity production in advanced capitalism: the novelty of products . . . is accorded an unprecedented importance," he writes in *The Arcades Project*, trans. Howard Eiland and Kevin McLaughlin (Cambridge: Harvard University Press, 1999). "At the same time, 'the eternal return of the same' is manifest in mass production" (331).

19. Benjamin, "The Work of Art," 105.

20. Ibid., 113.

21. Ibid., 103 and 110.

22. Ibid., 102.

23. This claim comes from a closely related passage in an earlier essay, the second half of which is a dry run for "The Work of Art." See Walter Benjamin, "Little History of Photography," in *Selected Writings*, vol. 2, *1927–1934*, ed. Michael W. Jennings (Cambridge: Harvard University Press, 1999), 518.

24. Benjamin, "The Work of Art," 112–113.

25. Ibid., 112.

26. Ibid., 113.

27. Benjamin, "Little History," 510.

28. Walter Benjamin, "On the Concept of History," in *Selected Writings*, vol. 4, *1938–1940*, ed. Howard Eiland and Michael W. Jennings (Cambridge: Harvard University Press, 2003), 390.

29. Ibid., 391.

30. Benjamin, *The Arcades Project*, 474.

31. Benjamin, "On the Concept of History," 391.

32. Benjamin, *The Arcades Project*, 462.

33. Ibid., 482.

34. Ibid., 462.

35. Benjamin makes this claim in both "Doctrine of the Similar," in *Selected Writings*, 2:698, and "On the Mimetic Faculty," in *Selected Writings*, 2:721–722.

36. Benjamin, "The Mimetic Faculty," 721.

37. Benjamin, "Doctrine of the Similar," 698.

38. I recount the narrative of how Richter got from the concentration camp photographs to *Sechs Fotos* in chapter 7 of *Flesh of My Flesh* (Stanford: Stanford University Press, 2009).

39. Oliver Wendell Holmes, "The Stereoscope and the Stereograph," *The Atlantic Monthly* 3 (June 1859): 747.

40. Lady Eastlake, "Photography," in *Classic Essays on Photography*, ed. Alan Trachtenberg (New Haven: Leete's Island Books, 1980), 65 (hereafter cited as *Classic Essays on Photography*).

41. Ibid., 65.

42. Ibid., 41.

43. William Henry Fox Talbot, "Photogenic Drawing," letter to the editor, *Literary Gazette; and Journal of the Belles Lettres, Arts, Sciences, etc.*, no. 1150 (February 2, 1939): 72–75. This would seem the point at which to note that this book has been fifteen years in the making. I planned to write it immediately after *World Spectators*, and published two essays shortly after the latter's completion that were steps toward this goal: "The Author as Receiver," and "*Je Vous.*" However, as my journey continued, my thoughts became too big and unwieldy for a single book, so I divided them into two. *Flesh of My Flesh* is the first of these books, and *The Miracle of Analogy* the second. Like the mothers in Leonardo's *Virgin and Child and St. Anne*, these volumes are joined at the hip, and both sit on their predecessor's "lap." The same thing happened while I was writing *The Miracle of Analogy*; my thoughts about photography continued to expand, and I eventually realized that I was writing a two-volume work.

44. Although I will be focusing on three of the "inventors" of chemical photography—Joseph Nicéphore Niépce, Louis-Jacques-Mandé Daguerre, and William Henry Fox Talbot—another figure warrants mention here as well: Hippolyte Bayard. For an excellent discussion of his work and his place within the history of photography, see Geoffrey Batchen, *Burning with Desire: The Conception of Photography* (Cambridge: MIT Press, 1997), 157–173.

45. Walt Whitman, *Leaves of Grass*, ed. Richard Maurice Bucke, Thomas R. Harned, and Horace L. Traubel (New York: Doubleday, 1902), 2:22.

46. I am paraphrasing one of Heidegger's claims. A work of art, he writes in "The Origin of the Work of Art," "holds open the Open of the world." See Martin Heidegger, *Poetry, Language, Thought*, trans. Albert Hofstadter (New York: Harper and Row, 1971), 45.

47. See *Flesh of My Flesh*, 173–175.

CHAPTER 1

1. Geoffrey Batchen provides a very helpful account of this history in his immensely learned book, *Burning with Desire*, 24–53. See also Helmut Gernsheim and Alison Gernsheim, *The History of Photography from the Camera Obscura to the Beginning of the Modern Era* (London: Thames and Hudson, 1969), 30–64.

2. So, we will see, did Niépce. I draw throughout this section on Gernsheim and Gernsheim, *The History of Photography*, 17–29; John H. Hammond, *The Camera Obscura: A Chronicle* (Bristol: Adam Hilger, Ltd., 1981); Martin Kemp, *The Science of Art: Optical Themes in Western Art from Brunelleschi to Seurat* (New Haven: Yale University

Press, 1990), 167–220; David C. Lindberg, *Theories of Vision from Al-Kindi to Kepler* (Chicago: University of Chicago Press, 1976); Wolfgang Lefèvre, "The Optical Camera Obscura I: A Short Exposition," in Wolfgang Lefèvre, ed., *Inside the Camera Obscura—Optics and Art under the Spell of the Projected Image* (Berlin: Max Planck Institute für Wissenschaftsgeschichte, 2007), 5–12; Philip Steadman, *Vermeer's Camera: Uncovering the Truth behind the Masterpieces* (Oxford: Oxford University Press, 2001), and David Hockney, *Secret Knowledge: Rediscovering the Lost Techniques of the Old Masters* (New York: Viking Studio, 2006).

3. Hammond, *The Camera Obscura*, 1–3.

4. Aristotle, *Problems*, ed. and trans. Robert Mayhew, Loeb Classical Library (Cambridge: Harvard University Press, 2011), 471.

5. The Gernsheims state that the original manuscript is located in London's India Office Library. Gernsheim and Gernsheim, *The History of Photography*, 17.

6. Ibid., 18.

7. Leonardo da Vinci, "How the Images of Objects Received by the Eye Intersect within the Crystalline Humour of the Eye," in *The Literary Works of Leonardo da Vinci*, vol. 1, trans. Jean Paul Richter (London: Samson Low, Marston, Searle and Rivington, 1883), 44, and Steadman, *Vermeer's Camera*, 6.

8. Quoted by Gernsheim and Gernsheim in *The History of Photography*, 19.

9. Henry Wotton, *Reliquiae Wottonianae* (London, 1651), 413. Quoted by Steadman, *Vermeer's Camera*, 11–12, and Norma Wenczel, "The Optical Camera Obscura II Images and Texts," in Lefèvre, *Inside the Camera Obscura*, 22.

10. Jonathan Crary offers a dramatically different account of the camera obscura in his influential book *Techniques of the Observer: On Vision and Modernity in the Nineteenth Century* (Cambridge: MIT Press, 1990). From the late 1500s until the end of the 1700s, he argues, the camera obscura was perceived as a knowledge machine—a device for determining what was "objectively true." It also privatized subjectivity and disembodied the human eye (39). The camera obscura functioned in this way, Crary argues, because it separated the viewer from what he saw, and because it "implie[d] a spatial and temporal simultaneity of human subjectivity and objective apparatus" (41).

11. This passage is quoted in Gernsheim and Gernsheim, *The History of Photography*, 22.

12. Ibid., 17–19; Hammond, *The Camera Obscura*, 8–10; Steadman, *Vermeer's Camera*, 4–5.

13. James S. Ackerman, "Leonardo's Eye," *Journal of the Warburg and Courtauld Institutes* 41 (1978): 100–103; Gernsheim and Gernsheim, *The History of Photography*, 19–20.

14. The camera obscura was of abiding interest to Leonardo; he produced 270 diagrams of the device, and wrote about it often in his notebooks. See Kim H. Veltman, "Leonardo and the Camera Obscura," in *Studi Vinciani in memoria de Nando de Toni* (Brescia: Fratelli Geroldi, 1986), 81–92.

15. Leonardo da Vinci, "Of Painting," in *The Literary Works of Leonardo da Vinci*, 145; Gernsheim and Gernsheim, *The History of Photography*, 19; Steadman, *Vermeer's Camera*, 6.

16. As translated in *The Genius of Leonardo da Vinci: Leonardo da Vinci on Art and*

the Artist, ed. André Chastel, trans. Ellen Callmann (New York: Orion Press, 1961), 205. For Richter's 1883 translation, see Leonardo da Vinci, "A way of developing and arousing the mind to various inventions," in *The Literary Works of Leonardo da Vinci*, 254.

17. Leonardo da Vinci, "Perspective," in *The Literary Works of Leonardo da Vinci*, 38.

18. Leonardo da Vinci, "Painting," in *The Literary Works of Leonardo da Vinci*, 253.

19. Ackerman, "Leonardo's Eye," 114–115. For a much fuller account of this distinction, see Lindberg, *Theories of Vision*.

20. Paul Valéry, "Introduction to the Method of Leonardo," in *Leonardo, Poe, Mallarmé*, trans. Malcolm Cowley (Princeton: Princeton University Press, 1972), 18.

21. This is the title of part 1 of Daniel Arasse's important book *Leonardo da Vinci: The Rhythm of the World*, trans. Rosetta Translations (New York: Konecky and Konecky, 1998).

22. Johannes Kepler, *Paralipomena to Witelo*, in *Optics*, trans. William H. Donahue (Santa Fe: Green Lion Press, 2000), 181.

23. Ibid., 180.

24. Peter Barker and Bernard R. Goldstein, "Theological Foundations of Kepler's Astronomy," *Osiris* 16 (2001): 112.

25. This description was written by Henry Wotton, who visited Kepler. It is quoted in Steadman, *Vermeer's Camera*, 11–12.

26. René Descartes, *Optics*, in *Discourse on Method, Optics, Geometry, and Meteorology*, trans. Paul J. Olscamp (Indianapolis: Hackett Publishing Co., 2001), 91–100. According to Lefèvre, this experiment was also conducted by two other seventeenth-century figures, Christoph Scheiner and Gaspar Schott (*Inside the Camera Obscura*, 8).

27. Descartes, *Optics*, 87.

28. Maurice Merleau-Ponty, "Eye and Mind," in *The Merleau-Ponty Aesthetics Reader*, ed. Michael B. Smith (Evanston: Northwestern University Press, 1993), 130. Norma Wenczel also discusses the schematic nature of Cartesian representation in "The Camera Obscura II," in Lefèvre, *Inside the Camera Obscura*, 25.

29. John Locke, *An Essay Concerning Human Understanding*, trans. A. C. Fraser (Oxford: Clarendon Press, 1894; New York: Prometheus Books, 1995), 107. Citation refers to the Prometheus edition.

30. Crary claims that Leibnitz follows Locke, except for the fact that he attributes "an inherent capacity for structuring the ideas it receives" to the camera obscura; *Techniques*, 51.

31. G. W. Leibnitz, *New Essays on Human Understanding*, trans. Peter Remnant and Jonathan Bennett (Cambridge: Cambridge University Press, 1981), 145–146.

32. Daniele Barbaro, *La pratica della perspettiva* (Venice, 1568), 152. Quoted in Gernsheim and Gernsheim, *The History of Photography*, 22.

33. Giovanni Battista della Porta, *Magiae naturalis*, trans. anonymous (London, 1658), book 17, chapter 6.

34. Hammond, *The Camera Obscura*, 16; Lefèvre, "The Optical Camera Obscura I," 6; Gernsheim and Gernsheim, *The History of Photography*, 22.

35. I quote here from the Barbaro passage I just mentioned, but see also Gernsheim and Gernsheim, *The History of Photography*, 21; Steadman, *Vermeer's Camera*, 8–10; and

Michael John Gorman, "Projecting Nature in Early Modern Europe," in *Inside the Camera Obscura*, 42–43.

36. Hammond, *The Camera Obscura*, 24–26; Gernsheim and Gernsheim, *The History of Photography*, 23–24.

37. Hammond, *The Camera Obscura*, 36; Gernsheim and Gernsheim, *The History of Photography*, 25–27.

38. Gernsheim and Gernsheim, *The History of Photography*, 28–29; Steadman, *Vermeer's Camera*, 8–10.

39. Quoted in Gernsheim and Gernsheim, *The History of Photography*, 26.

40. Eliza Meteyard, *The Life of Josiah Wedgwood: From His Private Correspondence and Family Papers* (London: Hurst and Blackett, 1886), 2:282.

41. Horace Walpole, "September 21, 1777: To the Rev. William Mason," in *The Letters of Horace Walpole, Fourth Earl of Orford*, ed. Peter Cunningham (Edinburgh: John Grant, 1906), 483–485.

42. Ibid., 483–484.

43. Gernsheim and Gernsheim, *The History of Photography*, 26.

44. Heidegger, "The Age of the World Picture," 129–130.

45. Quoted by Gorman in "Projecting Nature in Early-Modern Europe," in Lefèvre, *Inside the Camera Obscura*, 45. As can be seen from the title of this essay, Gorman is critical of such claims.

46. Quoted in Arthur Wheelock, ed., *Johannes Vermeer* (Washington, D.C.: National Gallery of Art, 1995), 25–26.

47. Quoted in Hockney, *Secret Knowledge*, 252.

48. Joseph Addison, "Wednesday, June 25: Pleasures of the Imagination," in *The Works of Joseph Addison: The Spectator*, ed. George Washington Greene (New York: G. P Putnam and Co., 1854), 338; also quoted in Hammond, *The Camera Obscura*, 71.

49. Benjamin Martin, *A New and Compendious System of Optics* (London, 1740), 161; also quoted in Hammon, *The Camera Obscura*, 80.

50. Francesco Algarotti, *An essay on painting written in Italian by Count Algarotti* (London: L. Davis and C. Reymers, 1764), 61–62. Almost a century later, John Ruskin also commented on the aesthetic properties of the camera obscura's image. "I have often been struck, when looking at a camera-obscura on a dark day, with the exact resemblance the image bore to one of the finest pictures of the old masters," he wrote in *Modern Painters* (London: Smith, Elder and Co., 1848), vol. 1, sec. 2, ch. 1, 139.

51. Alexander Pope, "To Blount, June 2, 1725," in *The Works of Alexander Pope*, vol. 6 (London: John Murray, 1871), 383.

52. Algarotti, *An essay on painting*, 60–61.

53. Ibid., 63.

54. Ibid., 62–63.

55. Ibid., 62.

56. Heidegger, "The Question Concerning Technology," in *The Question Concerning Technology and Other Essays*, 27.

57. Ibid., 10–11.

58. Ibid., 34.

59. Ibid.

60. Joseph Nicéphore Niépce, *Notice sur l'Heliographie*, 1827, Harry Ransom Center website, http://www.hrc.utexas.edu/exhibitions/permanent/firstphotograph/history/#top.

61. Louis-Jacques-Mandé Daguerre, "Daguerreotype," in *Classic Essays on Photography*, 12.

62. Ibid.

63. Jules Janin, "La Daguerreotype," in *Court and Lady's Magazine, Monthly Critic and Museum* 17 (October 1839): 436–439. From the research archive of Gary W. Ewer, ed., The Daguerreotype: An Archive of Source Material, http://www.daguerreotypearchive.org.

64. Anonymous, "Fine Arts—Royal Society," *The Literary Gazette; and Journal of the Belles Lettres, Arts, Sciences, etc.*, no. 1150 (February 2, 1839): 75. From the research archive of Gary W. Ewer, ed., The Daguerreotype: An Archive of Source Material, http://www.daguerreotypearchive.org.

65. Edgar Allan Poe, "The Daguerreotype," in *Classic Essays on Photography*, 38.

66. "Photogenic Drawing, or Drawing by the Agency of Art," *The Edinburgh Review* 86, no. 154 (January 1843): 317. Although no author is listed, this essay was apparently written by Sir David Brewster, and I will list him as the author from this point forward.

67. I want both to mention and to endorse the Gernsheims' claim that by 1685 the camera obscura was *"absolutely ready and waiting for photography"*—i.e., that the camera obscura and chemical photography are part of the same history, a history that defies rational explanation (*The History of Photography*, 27). Crary challenges this claim in *Techniques of the Observer*. He argues that there was an epistemological break between the camera obscura and nineteenth-century photography, because the new technology differentiated the camera from the human look by eliminating the distinction between "inner" and "outer," locating its viewer within the world, and embodying the human eye (14–17, 24). It was also a "crucial component [in] a new cultural economy of value and exchange" that abolished referentiality (13). Last, but not least, the medium was "part of the complex remaking of the individual as observer into something calculable and regularizable and of human vision into something measurable and thus exchangeable" (16–17). Crary bases his account of photography on the changes that occurred within the field of optics in the nineteenth century. The invention of photography was "part of the reorganization of the field of vision" that occurred after the discovery that human vision is binocular, subject to afterimages, and afflicted by blind spots, he argues, and therefore both an unreliable source of information about the world and difficult to align with the camera, which is monocular (16).

68. Joseph Nicéphore Niépce, "Memoire on the Heliograph," in *Classic Essays on Photography*, 5–10.

69. Oliver Wendell Holmes, "Doings of the Sunbeam," *The Atlantic Monthly* 12, no. 69 (July 1863): 1–15.

70. Talbot, "Photogenic Drawing," 72–75. This would seem the moment to mention Khalip and Mitchell's edited volume, *Releasing the Image: From Literature to New Media* (Stanford, Stanford University Press, 2011), which contains an excellent introduction to the philosophical questions that are raised by the notion of the "image," and a section called "Origination and Auto-Origination of the Image," which includes a very interesting essay by Peter Gerner. Gerner takes Talbot's claims about the photographic

image seriously, and concludes that not every aspect of this image is a human invention. However, he does not consider the possibility that there may be objective forms of intentionality, and so concludes that "photography would never have come into being without the construction of mobile cameras and light-intensive lenses, without successful experimentation and reflection, without information being passed down, without correspondence or meetings" ("'Self-Generated' Images," 40).

71. This is the name of Talbot's 1844–46 book of photographic plates.

72. See—for instance—Talbot's short preface to part 1 of *The Pencil of Nature* (London: Longman, Brown, Green, and Longmans, 1844).

73. Daguerre, "Daguerreotype," in *Classic Essays on Photography*, 12.

74. Brewster, "Photogenic Drawing."

75. Lady Eastlake, "Photography," in *Classic Essays on Photography*, 52.

76. For an excellent account of the relationship between early photography and drawing, see Carol Armstrong, "Cameraless: From Natural Illustrations and Nature Prints to Manual and Photogenic Drawings and Other Botonographs," in *Ocean Flowers: Impressions from Nature*, ed. Carol Armstrong and Catherine de Zegher (Princeton: Princeton University Press, 2004), 86–165.

77. Sir John Robison, "Notes on Daguerre's Photography," *Edinburgh New Philosophical Journal* 27, no. 53 (July 1839), 155–157. From the research archive of Gary W. Ewer, ed., The Daguerreotype: An Archive of Source Material, http://www.daguerreo typearchive.org.

78. Samuel F. B. Morse, "The Daguerrotipe" [*sic*], *New-York Observer* 17, no. 16 (April 20, 1839), 62. From the research archive of Gary W. Ewer, ed., http://www.dag uerreotypearchive.org.

79. Brewster, "Photogenic Drawing," 317.

80. Talbot, "A Brief Historical Sketch of the Invention of the Art," in *The Pencil of Nature*, n.p.

81. Talbot called his earliest photographs "photogenic drawings." He referred to his later photographs as "calotypes."

82. Anonymous, "Photogenic Drawing," *United States Democratic Review* 5, no. 17 (May 1839): 517.

83. "Editor's Table," *The Journal of Belles Lettres* (March 12, 1839): 2.

84. Brewster, "Photogenic Drawing," 312.

85. Talbot, "A Brief Historical Sketch of the Invention of the Art," in *The Pencil of Nature*.

86. Armstrong also comments on the reflexive properties attributed to the photographic image in the early history of the medium. See "Cameraless," in Armstrong and de Zegher, *Ocean Flowers*, 93–94.

87. Brewster, "Photogenic Drawing," 317.

88. "New Discovery—Engraving and Burnet's Cartoons," *Blackwood's Edinburgh Magazine* 45, no. 281 (March 1839): 382–391. From the research archive of Gary W. Ewer, ed., The Daguerreotype: An Archive of Source Material, http://www.daguerreotype archive.org. This essay serves as both the prologue and the epilogue to a letter to the editor from Talbot. The author of the essay, who was clearly one of the journal's editors, is extremely ambivalent about the medium of photography. He worries in the epilogue

about what he most emphasizes in the prologue: the self-delineation of fields, rivers, trees, houses, and cities. He also does so in ways that anticipate Baudelaire's attack on photography. Photography is disturbing, he declares, because it dispenses with the "human hand."

89. Lady Eastlake, "Photography," in *Classic Essays on Photography*, 57.

90. This story is recounted in Matthew 25:1–13.

91. Lady Eastlake, "Photography," in *Classic Essays on Photography*, 57.

92. Morell describes this process in an interview in *A Camera in a Room: Photographs by Abelardo Morell* (Washington, D.C.: Smithsonian Institution Press, 1995), 7.

93. This is how the title reads in *A Camera in a Room*, n.p.

94. This is how the title is listed in *Camera Obscura: Photographs by Abelardo Morell* (New York: Bulfinch Press, 2004), 14.

95. Morell links his project to Talbot's in several important ways. In 1999, he made a black-and-white photograph of what appears to be one of Talbot's own cameras pointed at the illuminated page of a book displaying one of the latter's early contact negatives. Morell called this photograph *Book and Camera: In Memory of Fox Talbot*, and he couples it with a famous passage from *The Pencil of Nature* in a 2004 catalogue. This passage is the one in which Talbot cites as the inspiration for his photographic experimentation the thought "how charming it would be if it were possible to cause these natural images to imprint themselves durably, and remain fixed on paper" (*Camera Obscura: Photographs by Abelardo Morell*, 78–79). In 2003, Morell also made a black-and-white camera obscura photograph in the room in Lacock Abbey in which Talbot invented the negative/positive photographic process, which I am using as the frontispiece to this book. It superimposes an upside-down image of the exterior of the building on the "recto" of this interior. Morell made a similar photograph of the Cloisters at Lacock Abbey. Both of these photographs are published in the same catalogue, on 76 and 80.

96. *A Camera in a Room*, n.p.

97. This is how the title is listed in *Camera Obscura: Photographs by Abelardo Morell*, 16. The catalogue for a recent retrospective offers yet another variant: "*Camera Obscura: Houses Across the Street in Our Bedroom, Quincy, Massachusetts.*" See *Abelardo Morell: The Universe Next Door*, ed. Elizabeth Siegel (Chicago: Art Institute of Chicago, 2013), n.p.

98. Abelardo Morell, "Camera Obscura," http://www.abelardomorell.net/posts/camera-obscura/.

99. Elizabeth Siegel, "Wonderlands," in *Abelardo Morell: The Universe Next Door*, 16–17. The preposition in the title of this work—*Camera Obscura: The Philadelphia Museum of Art East Entrance in Galley #171 **with** a de Chirico Painting*—also attests to the collaborative nature of its production (my emphasis).

100. Siegel, "Wonderlands," 22, and Morell, "Camera Obscura."

101. Morell, "Camera Obscura."

CHAPTER 2

1. For an excellent discussion of the difficulties faced by early photographers, see Larry J. Schaaf, *Out of the Shadows: Herschel, Talbot, and the Invention of Photography* (New Haven: Yale University Press, 1992), 75–151.

2. "Taking 1826 as the date of this photograph, it is nine years earlier than Talbot's first paper negative (1835) showing the lattice window of his library, and eleven years

prior to Daguerre's first successful result, a still life taken in 1837," Gernsheim and Gernsheim write in *The History of Photography*, 59.

3. In fact, he came to it through lithography, with which he also experimented. See Georges Potonniée, *The History of the Discovery of Photography*, trans. Edward Epstean (New York: Arno Press, 1973), 77–81.

4. I draw here on Geoffrey Batchen's very helpful description of these experiments in *Burning with Desire*, 120–121.

5. Batchen provides a different account of this language than I do; see *Burning with Desire*, 69–70. He connects it to eighteenth- and early nineteenth-century landscape painting and the picturesque.

6. della Porta, *Magiae naturalis*, book 17, chapter 6, also quoted in Steadman, *Vermeer's Camera*, 10.

7. Hammond reproduces this diagram in *The Camera Obscura*, 23, as do the Gernsheims in *The History of Photography*, plate 6.

8. Quoted by Potonniée, *The History of the Discovery of Photography*, 82.

9. Ibid., 83.

10. Ibid., 97–99.

11. For a deconstructive reading of these two "points," see Jacques Lacan, *The Four Fundamental Concepts of Psychoanalysis: The Seminar of Jacques Lacan, Book XI*, ed. Jacques-Alain Miller, trans. Alan Sheridan (New York: Norton, 1981), 67–119, and my *The Threshold of the Visible World* (New York: Routledge, 1996), 125–161.

12. Beaumont Newhall, *The History of Photography* (New York: Museum of Modern Art, 1982), 13; Batchen, *Burning with Desire*, 81.

13. Gernsheim and Gernsheim, *The History of Photography*, 57; Potonniée, *The History of the Discovery of Photography*, 97–98.

14. Goethe discovered the afterimage in 1817. "Goethe's theory challenged the Aristotelian truthfulness of optical perception by tethering the act of observation with the body, fusing time and vision," Robert Hirsch writes in *Seizing the Light: A History of Photography* (New York: McGraw-Hill, 2000), 11. For a fuller discussion of the implications of Goethe's discovery for human vision, see Crary, *Techniques of the Observer*.

15. I discuss this concept in chapter 1.

16. Scholars disagree about the date of the heliograph. Potonniée maintains that it was made in 1822 (*The History of the Discovery of Photography*, 97); Newhall says it was made in 1827 (*The History of Photography*, 15), a claim with which Batchen concurs (*Burning with Desire*, 126); and the Gernsheims argue that it could have been made in either 1826 or 1827 (*The History of Photography*, 59).

17. Gernsheim and Gernsheim, *The History of Photography*, 58–62.

18. Potonniée, *The History of the Discovery of Photography*, 97; Gernsheim and Gernsheim, *The History of Photography*, 59.

19. Both Paul Valéry and Daniel Arasse talk about the dynamic nature of Leonardo's analogies. See Valéry, "Introduction to the Method of Leonardo," 25–26; Arasse, *Leonardo da Vinci: The Rhythm of the World*.

20. Quoted in Gernsheim and Gernsheim, *The History of Photography*, 61.

21. Gernsheim and Gernsheim, *The History of Photography*, 62; Helmut Gernsheim

and Alison Gernsheim, *L. J. M. Daguerre: The History of the Diorama and the Daguerreotype* (New York: Dover, 1968), 63–65.

22. Gernsheim and Gernsheim, *L. J. M. Daguerre*, 63, 67; Batchen, *Burning with Desire*, 121.

23. For a detailed account of the steps through which Daguerre established himself as the source of the photographic image, see Gernsheim and Gernsheim, *L. J. M. Daguerre*, 70–109.

24. Daguerre, "Daguerreotype," in *Classic Essays on Photography*, 12.

25. Ibid.

26. Hippolyte Gaucheraud, "Fine Arts. The Daguerotype," *The Literary Gazette; and Journal of the Belles Lettres, Arts, Sciences, Etc.* 1147 (January 12, 1839): 28. From the research archive of Gary W. Ewer, ed., The Daguerreotype: An Archive of Source Material, http://www.daguerreotypearchive.org.

27. Anonymous, "New Discovery in the Fine Arts. The Daguerroscope," *New-Yorker: A Weekley Journal of Literature, Politics, Statistics, and General Information* 7, no. 5 (April 20, 1839): 70–71. From the research archive of Gary W. Ewer, ed., The Daguerreotype: An Archive of Source Material, http://www.daguerreotypearchive.org.

28. Janin, "La Daguerreotype," 436–439.

29. Ibid.

30. Gernsheim and Gernsheim, *The History of Photography*, 66–74; Hirsch, *Seizing the Light*, 12–13.

31. This is an editorial addendum to an essay whose author is unknown: "Chemical and Optical Discovery," *Journal of the American Institute, a Monthly Publication Devoted to the Interests of Agriculture, Commerce, Manufactures, and the Arts* 4, no. 5 (February 1839): 267–277. From the research archive of Gary W. Ewer, ed., The Daguerreotype: An Archive of Source Material, http://www.daguerreotypearchive.org.

32. This is the date that Batchen assigns it (*Burning with Desire*, 136). Newhall says 1838 (*The History of Photography*, 16–17).

33. Batchen, *Burning with Desire*, 133.

34. Robison, "Notes on Daguerre's Photography," 155–157.

35. Gernsheim and Gernsheim, *L. J. M. Daguerre*, 194; Batchen, *Burning with Desire*, 133.

36. Gaucheraud, "Fine Arts—The Daguerotype," 43–44.

37. Anonymous, "Self-Operating Processes of Fine Art: The Daguerreotype," *Spectator: A Weekly Journal of News, Politics, Literature and Science* 553 (February 2, 1839): 114–115. From the research archive of Gary W. Ewer, ed., The Daguerreotype: An Archive of Source Material, http://www.daguerreotypearchive.org.

38. Morse, "The Daguerrotipe," 62.

39. Gaucheraud, "Fine Arts—The Daguerotype," 28.

40. Batchen notes the strange elision in Morse's account of the person who is shining the man's boots, and finds traces of this figure in the first daguerreotype (*Burning with Desire*, 133–136). Nicholas Jenkins proves that this is indeed the case through a microscopic visual analysis, and argues that there may also be two other figures in the photograph ("Traces," *Day by Day: A Blog* [blog], August 22, 2007 http://www.stanford.edu/njenkins/archives/2007/08/traces.html). Both Batchen and Jenkins relate the

shoeshine's semi-invisibility to the lowliness of his social position. Giorgio Agamben sees the daguerreotype as an "image of the Last Judgment" (*Profanations*, trans. Jeff Fort [New York: Zone Books, 2007], 23–27). Since this reading dictates that there be only one person in the daguerreotype, he elides the shoeshine.

41. Henri Bergson, *Creative Evolution*, trans. Arthur Mitchell (New York: Dover, 1998), 302.

42. Gaucheraud, "Fine Arts. The Daguerotype," 28.

43. Robison, "Notes on Daguerre's Photography," 157.

44. Ibid., 155–157.

45. I draw here on Gernsheim and Gernsheim, *The History of Photography*, 75–83; Larry J. Schaaf, *The Photographic Art of William Henry Fox Talbot* (Princeton: Princeton University Press, 2000); Schaaf, *Out of the Shadows*; and Gail Buckland, *Fox Talbot and the Invention of Photography* (Boston: David R. Godine, 1980).

46. This photograph has almost faded away. The one pictured here was made the same year, from the same position, but with a slightly larger camera.

47. Buckland, *Fox Talbot and the Invention of Photography*, 28.

48. Quoted by Malcolm Daniel, Department of Photographs, "William Henry Fox Talbot (1800–1877) and the Invention of Photography," in *Heilbrunn Timeline of Art History* (New York: Metropolitan Museum of Art, October 2004), http://www.met museum.org/toah/hd/tlbt/hd_tlbt.htm.

49. Buckland, *Fox Talbot and the Invention of Photography*, 33.

50. William Henry Fox Talbot, "Letter to the Editor," *The Literary Gazette*, no. 1258 (February 19, 1841): 139–140.

51. Brewster, "Photogenic Drawing," 327.

52. This passage accompanies plate 13 in *The Pencil of Nature*. As Russell Roberts notes, it prefigures Walter Benjamin's account of the "optical unconscious" ("Specimens and Marvels: The Work of William Henry Fox Talbot," in *Specimens and Marvels: William Henry Fox Talbot and the Invention of Photography* [New York: Aperture Foundation, 2000], 64–65). Although he has a different understanding of truth, Edgar Allan Poe expresses similar sentiments in his essay on the daguerreotype. He writes that "the Daguerreotyped plate . . . is *infinitely* more accurate in its representation than any painting by human hand," and that "the closest scrutiny of the photogenic drawing discloses only a more absolute truth, a more perfect identity of aspect with the thing represented" ("The Daguerreotype," in *Classic Essays on Photography*, 38). Holmes echoes these claims in the following passage from "The Stereoscope and the Stereograph": "A perfect photograph is absolutely inexhaustible. In a picture you can find nothing which the artist has not seen before you; but in a perfect photograph there will be as many beauties lurking, unobserved, as there are flowers that blush unseen in forests and meadows." Even if we were to look at this image a hundred times with the aid of "the best of our common instruments," Holmes adds, we would not really "know" it, because every time we encounter a photograph, we see something new ("The Stereoscope and the Stereograph," 744).

53. Talbot, "Letter to the Editor," *The Literary Gazette*, 139.

54. This passage accompanies plate 6 in *The Pencil of Nature*.

55. For a detailed account of Talbot's relationship to photographic reproduction, see chapter 4.

56. Joseph Nicéphore Niépce, "Memoir on Heliography," published in Gernsheim and Gernsheim, *L. J. M. Daguerre*, 67.

57. "The memoir dated 'Kew, le 8 Décembre, 1827' was accompanied by several heliographs," Gernsheim writes; "these, with the exception of this photograph from nature, were reproductions of engravings. The specimens were all referred to him together with the memoir, for the Royal Society felt unable to take cognizance of an invention, the details of which the inventor was unwilling to disclose"; Gernsheim and Gernsheim, "Rediscovery of the World's First Photograph," 1.

58. Helmut Gernsheim, "The 150th Anniversary of Photography," *History of Photography* 1, no. 1 (1977): 6–7.

59. Gernsheim offers the most detailed account of this discovery in "The 150th Anniversary of Photography."

60. Ibid., 7.

61. Ibid., 8.

62. Gernsheim and Gernsheim, *The History of Photography*, 59.

63. I am quoting here from the Harry Ransom Center website, "Conservation: The First Photograph" (Austin: The University of Texas at Austin, 2003–present), http://www.hrc.utexas.edu/exhibitions/permanent/firstphotograph/conservation/#top.

64. This is how Batchen characterizes the over-painted photograph (*Burning with Desire*, 127).

65. Gernsheim, "The 150th Anniversary of Photography," 8.

66. Ibid., 8.

67. Barbara Brown, "The First Photograph," *Abbey Newsletter* 26, no. 3 (November 2002). Brown is the head of photograph conservation at the Harry Ransom Humanities Research Center, and participated in the Getty Conservation Institute's analysis of the photograph.

68. The Getty Conservation Institute, "Scientific Analysis of World's First Photograph," J. Paul Getty Trust, 2002, www.getty.edu/conservation/publications_resources/newsletters/17_2/gcinews1.html.

69. Eduardo Cadava and Gabriela Nouzeilles included an exhibition copy of this work in an excellent photography exhibition at the Princeton University Art Museum in the fall of 2013, "The Itinerant Languages of Photography." Cadava also discusses it in the exhibition catalogue. Both the exhibition and the catalogue were devoted to the premise that photographs cannot be "fixed in a single time and place," because they "travel from one forum to another," and because "with each recontextualization and rereading, they redefine themselves and take on different and expanding significances." See Cadava and Nouzeilles, introduction to *The Itinerant Languages of Photography*, ed. Cadava and Nouzeilles (Princeton: Princeton University Art Museum, 2013), 17. In the first essay in the catalogue, Cadava writes that "although Fontcuberta stresses the intensification of this circulation and itinerancy today in the era of digitization, he also suggests [through *Googlegram: Niépce*] that this movement has always formed part of the photographic image" (30). Needless to say, I concur strongly with both of these claims.

70. For the sake of clarity, I have described the Google search and the photomosaic program separately, but the two operations happened simultaneously. In fact, Fontcuberta ran the Google search *through* the photomosaic program.

71. Joan Fontcuberta, "Archive Noise," Artist Statement, www.fontcuberta.com.

72. Ibid.

73. Joan Fontcuberta, "Googlegrams," Artist Statement, www.fontcuberta.com.

74. I am of course paraphrasing a famous passage from Benjamin's "On the Concept of History" (390).

CHAPTER 3

1. Jeff Wall, "Photography and Liquid Intelligence," in *Jeff Wall: Selected Essays and Interviews*, ed. Peter Galassi (New York: Museum of Modern Art, 2007), 109–110.

2. Ibid., 109.

3. Ibid.

4. In *Creative Evolution*, Henri Bergson repeatedly likens the instantaneity and fixity of human perception to a "snapshot." See *Creative Evolution*, 302, 273, 306. When we want to perceive movement, Bergson argues, we string these snapshots together like a roll of film, and switch on a mental projector (306).

5. Wall, "Photography and Liquid Intelligence," 109.

6. Ibid.

7. Ibid.

8. Ibid., 110.

9. I am thinking here of two essays: Martin Heidegger, "The Question Concerning Technology," and "The Age of the World Picture," in Heidegger, *The Question Concerning Technology and Other Essays*, 3–35 and 115–154, respectively.

10. Wall, "Photography and Liquid Intelligence," 110.

11. Todd Gustavson, *Camera: A History of Photography from Daguerreotype to Digital* (New York: Sterling Publishing Co., 2009), 101.

12. As George Baker puts it in "Black Mirror," "We know—or feel like we know—that we have lost . . . the labor of photography that was its chemistry, its noisome liquids and its baths. The optical now reigns supreme (indeed we face a triumphalism of 'camerawork' that ties the entire history of photography, analogue or digital, to 'lens-based' aesthetic alone)." See Baker, "Black Mirror," in *Paul Sietsma*, ed. Christopher Bedford (Columbus: Wexner Center for the Arts, Ohio State University, 2013), 4.

13. Gustavson, *Camera*, 9, and Gernsheim and Gernsheim, *L. J. M. Daguerre*, 96–97 and 112–113.

14. Gustavson, *Camera*, 10–11, 13, 15, 16. This is only a cursory account of each of these devices, and only a partial list of the cameras designed between 1839 and 1851.

15. Gernsheim and Gernsheim, *The History of Photography*, 415. Although Sutton was a well-known figure in his day—he was the author of *A Dictionary of Photography* and a number of other books about photography, the editor for eleven years of *Photographic Notes*, and the inventor of the first wide-angle panoramic camera—we have little information about his single-reflex camera.

16. Gernsheim and Gernsheim, *The History of Photography*, 260; Gustavson, *Camera*, 30–31.

17. Gustavson, *Camera*, 30–31, 78.

18. This information comes from the website of the National Media Museum in Bradford, UK, which has a Revolver Camera in its collection. The Colt revolver's

chamber could be fired six times, and the Thompson Revolver Camera's four times. See "Thompson Revolver Camera: Photographic Technology" (Bradford: National Media Museum), http://www.nationalmediamuseum.org.uk/Collection/Photography/Photo graphicTechnology/CollectionItem.aspx?id=1991-5101.

19. Gernsheim and Gernsheim, *The History of Photography*, 415.

20. "Thompson Revolver Camera," http://www.nationalmediamuseum.org.uk/Col lection/Photography/PhotographicTechnology/CollectionItem.aspx?id=1991-5101.

21. "Poetus Photographicus," *The Photographic Journal* (February 21, 1854): 210. Quoted by Gernsheim and Gernsheim, *The History of Photography*, 231.

22. Lady Eastlake, "Photography," in *Classic Essays on Photography*, 55.

23. Gernsheim and Gernsheim, *The History of Photography*, 335–336.

24. Hirsch, *Seizing the Light*, 72–73.

25. Holmes, "Doings of the Sunbeam," 5.

26. Ibid., 5–6.

27. David Falk, Dieter Brill, and David Stork, eds., *Seeing the Light: Optics in Nature, Photography, Color, Vision, and Holography* (Hoboken: John Wiley and Sons, 1988), 210–219; Nicholas J. Wade and Michael T. Swanston, *Visual Perception: An Introduction* (East Sussex: Psychology Press, 2013), 207–209.

28. I discuss these challenges in chapter 1.

29. Wade and Swanston, *Visual Perception*, 204–207.

30. Laura Burd Schiavo, "From Phantom Image to Perfect Vision: Physiological Optics, Commercial Photography, and the Popularization of the Stereoscope," in *New Media: 1740–1915*, ed. Lisa Gitelman and Geoffrey B. Pingree (Cambridge: MIT Press, 2003), 113–138.

31. Ibid., 116.

32. Gernsheim and Gernsheim, *The History of Photography*, 256–257.

33. Schiavo, "From Phantom Image to Perfect Vision," 127.

34. Edward W. Earle, ed., *Points of View: The Stereograph in America—A Cultural History* (Rochester: Visual Studies Workshop Press, 1979), 32.

35. Sir David Brewster, *The Stereoscope: Its History, Theory, and Construction* (London: John Murray, 1856), 36.

36. Lady Eastlake, "Photography," in *Classic Essays on Photography*, 53.

37. Antoine Claudet, "Photography in its Relation to the Fine Arts," *The Photographic Journal* 6 (June 15, 1860), 266.

38. James Ellis, *Progress of Photography, Collodion, the Stereoscope* (London: Bell and Daldy, 1856), 50. Quoted by Schiavo, "From Phantom Image to Perfect Vision," 119.

39. Holmes, "The Stereoscope and the Stereograph," 739.

40. Ibid., 744.

41. Ibid.

42. Holmes, "Doings of the Sunbeam," 10.

43. Oliver Wendell Holmes, "Sun-Painting and Sun-Sculpture," *The Atlantic Monthly* 8, no. 45 (July 1861), 14.

44. Holmes, "The Stereoscope and the Stereograph," 738.

45. Holmes, "Sun-Painting and Sun-Sculpture," 16.

46. Homes, "The Stereoscope and the Stereograph," 743, 746.

47. Ibid., 745.

48. Ibid.

49. See, for instance, ibid., 742.

50. Austin Abbott, "The Eye and the Camera," *Harper's New Monthly Magazine* 39 (1869): 476–482.

51. Ibid., 480.

52. Ibid., 481.

53. See Rosalind E. Krauss, "Photography's Discursive Spaces," in *The Originality of the Avant-Garde and Other Modernist Myths* (Cambridge: MIT Press, 1988), 138–141. Krauss focuses on the naturalization of the stereoscopic "view," the way it becomes embedded in the landscape.

54. John Samson, "Photographs from the High Rockies," *Harper's New Monthly Magazine* 34 (1869): 471.

55. Taupenot's dry-plate process wasn't the first, but it was the most popular (Gernsheim and Gernsheim, *The History of Photography*, 322–325).

56. Ibid., 325–332.

57. Ibid., 422–425, and Hirsch, *Seizing the Light*, 172–173.

58. Gernsheim and Gernsheim, *The History of Photography*, 413–414.

59. Wall, "Photography and Liquid Intelligence," 110.

CHAPTER 4

1. Fox Talbot uses all three words in "A Brief Historical Sketch of the Invention of the Art," in *The Pencil of Nature*.

2. See, for instance, Daguerre, "Daguerreotype," in *Classic Essays on Photography*, 11–13; Poe, "The Daguerreotype," in *Classic Essays on Photography*, 37–38; and Holmes, "The Stereoscope and the Stereograph," 739–748.

3. Brewster, "Photogenic Drawing, or Drawing with the Agency of Light," 330 and 344. See Batchen, *Burning with Desire*, 64, on the long list of possibilities pondered by Niépce.

4. Lady Eastlake, "Photography," in *Classic Essays on Photography*, 65.

5. Ibid., 41.

6. Ibid., 65.

7. *Oxford English Dictionary Online*, s.v. "Chiasmus," accessed December 2013, http://oxforddictionaries.com/definition/english/chiasmus?q=chiasmus.

8. Falk, Brill, and Stork, *Seeing the Light*, 182.

9. I am drawing here on the last chapter of Maurice Merleau-Ponty's *The Visible and the Invisible*, trans. Alphonso Lingis (Evanston: Northwestern University Press, 1968), especially 137–139.

10. Ibid., 138.

11. Ibid., 139.

12. Emile Benveniste, "Subjectivity in Language," in *Problems in General Linguistics*, trans. Mary Elizabeth Meek (Coral Gables: University of Florida Press, 1971), 224–225.

13. Martin Buber, *I and Thou*, trans. Walter Kaufmann (New York: Simon and Schuster, 1970), 84.

14. Kemp, *The Science of Art*, 189.

15. I discuss these similarities in chapters 1 and 2.

16. Merleau-Ponty, *The Visible and the Invisible*, 131.

17. Ibid., 137.

18. This is, at least, what Larry J. Schaaf thinks, and I find him a very persuasive thinker. See *The Photographic Art of William Henry Fox Talbot*, 19.

19. Ibid., 15.

20. Ibid., 19.

21. For Talbot, a negative was "a real object in and of itself," Schaaf writes in *Records of the Dawn of Photography: Talbot's Notebooks P & Q* (Cambridge: Cambridge University Press, 1996), xviii.

22. Talbot, "A Brief Historical Sketch of the Invention of the Art," in *The Pencil of Nature*, n.p.

23. George Baker, "Black Mirror," 6 and 10.

24. Schaaf, *The Photographic Art of William Henry Fox Talbot*, 19.

25. This passage comes from Talbot's *Scientific Notebook*. It is quoted by Michael Gray in "Henry Fox Talbot, 1800–1977," in *First Photographs: William Henry Fox Talbot and the Birth of Photography*, by Michael Gray, Arthur Ollman, and Carol McCusker (New York: powerHouse Books, 2002), 127.

26. Schaaf, *The Photographic Art of William Henry Fox Talbot*, 15 and 19.

27. Merleau-Ponty, *The Visible and the Invisible*, 134.

28. Schaaf, *The Photographic Art of Henry Fox Talbot*, 25.

29. Gerhard Richter, *The Daily Practice of Painting: Writings and Interviews, 1962–1993*, ed. Hans-Ulrich Obrist (Cambridge: MIT Press, 1995), 187. I discuss the role that analogy plays in Richter's art and thought in *Flesh of My Flesh*, 167–221.

30. Merleau-Ponty, *The Visible and the Invisible*, 132–133.

31. Ibid., 133.

32. Carol Armstrong, *Scenes in a Library: Reading the Photograph in the Book, 1843–1875* (Cambridge: MIT Press, 1998), 184.

33. Geoffrey Batchen, *Each Wild Idea: Writing, Photography, History* (Cambridge: MIT Press, 2001), 156.

34. Larry J. Schaaf, introduction to *Sun Gardens: Victorian Photograms by Anna Atkins* (New York: Aperture Foundation, 1985), 24–31.

35. I draw heavily in my account of Harvey's *Manual of British Algae* on Armstrong's illuminating and deeply informed discussion of it in *Scenes in a Library*, 187–208. I am also indebted both here and elsewhere in this section of chapter 4 to another of Armstrong's writings, "Cameraless," in Armstrong and de Zegher, *Ocean Flowers*, 86–165 and 196.

36. These words come from the introduction to the 1849 rather than the 1841 edition of the book.

37. As Kathryn A. Tuma observes in "The Victorian 'Book of Nature': Modeling, Mimesis, and the Community of Forms," Atkins uses the "analogies given readily in the material specificities of her medium" to return "the specimens to something like a native domain" (in Armstrong and de Zegher, *Ocean Flowers*, 201 and 231).

38. This is Merleau-Ponty's paraphrase of a line from a poem by Paul Claudel (*The Visible and the Invisible*, 132).

39. Armstrong, *Scenes in a Library*, 273–275, and Batchen, *Each Wild Idea*, 158.

40. Armstrong, *Scenes in a Library*, 204.

41. Ibid., 268.

42. Two of the cyanotypes that are reproduced here are from *Photographs of British Algae*, and two are from *Cyanotypes of British and Foreign Ferns*.

43. Talbot, *The Pencil of Nature*, 13.

44. I use the word "oceanic" here in the way that I use it throughout *Flesh of My Flesh*: as a designator for the untotalizable totality to which we all belong, and which has no "outside."

45. Talbot, "Photogenic Drawing," 75.

46. Holmes, "The Stereoscope and the Stereograph," 741.

47. Hiroshi Sugimoto, *Nature of Light* (Shizuoka, Japan: Koko Okano, 2009).

48. Schaaf wrote the commentaries. They are printed in two columns—one English and the other Japanese.

49. Sugimoto, "Photogenic Drawing," in *Nature of Light*, 37.

50. Holmes, "The Stereoscope and the Stereograph," 740.

51. Ibid., 740–741.

52. Ibid., 741.

53. Ibid., 738.

54. Ibid.

55. Ibid., 742–743.

56. Ibid., 738.

57. Ibid., 742.

58. Crary, *Techniques of the Observer*, 126.

59. Ibid., 125. Crary finds this last feature of the stereoscopic image unnerving. Things occupy space "aggressively," he writes, and space has "a disturbing palpability." He claims that there is a "derangement" of conventional "optical cues" in the stereoscopic image because it is non-referential—because it is a purely physiological construction. He also maintains that the body produces this image in response to the demands of nineteenth-century capitalism, and that it does so over and over again. Like a worker on an assembly line, the viewer's brain transforms a long series of "dreary parallel images" into "a tantalizing apparatus of depth." And each time it effects this transformation, it "transubstantiate[s]" the "mass-produced and monotonous cards" into a "compulsory and seductive vision of the 'real'" (*Techniques of the Observer*, 131–132).

60. Holmes, "The Stereoscope and the Stereograph," 744.

61. Ibid., 744.

62. Merleau-Ponty, *The Visible and the Invisible*, 136.

63. Holmes, "The Stereoscope and the Stereograph," 745–746.

64. Ibid., 746.

65. Ibid., 744.

66. Ibid., 747.

67. Ibid., 748.

68. Ibid., 747–748.

69. Ibid., 748.

70. Ibid., 747.

71. There are three related passages in Holmes's "Sun-Painting and Sun-Sculpture"; see 14, 16, and 28.

72. As Mark Durden notes in *Fifty Key Writers on Photography* (London: Routledge, 2013), Holmes misquotes the line he takes from Milton. The latter says "unapproached light," not "uncreated light" (127).

73. Jeff L. Rosenheim, *Photography and the American Civil War* (New York: Metropolitan Museum of Art, 2013), 7.

74. Ibid., 1–26.

75. Quoted by Rosenheim, ibid., 147.

76. Ibid., 1.

77. Anthony W. Lee writes that they are "newly emancipated" ("The Image of War," in *On Alexander Gardner's "Photographic Sketch Book" of the Civil War*, ed. Anthony W. Lee and Elizabeth Young [Berkeley: University of California Press, 2007], 45).

78. Alexander Gardner, *Gardner's Photographic Sketchbook of the American Civil War, 1861–1865* (New York: Delano Greenidge Editions, 2001), 198. As Lee notes, Gardner's commentary is "extraordinarily unusual," since most "white observers . . . preferred not to tackle the question of the African American presence after the war" ("The Image of War," in *On Alexander Gardner's "Photographic Sketch Book,"* 47).

79. Gardner, *Gardner's Photographic Sketchbook*, 198.

80. As Young observes, the "dismembered foot" in the foreground of the photograph "seems an extension of the live African American bodies" ("Verbal Battlefields," in *On Alexander Gardner's "Photographic Sketch Book" of the Civil War*, 90).

81. Merleau-Ponty, *The Visible and the Invisible*, 137.

82. Eleanor Jones Harvey, *The Civil War and American Art* (New Haven: Yale University Press, 2012), 96.

CHAPTER 5

1. I am of course referring here to Joachim Gasquet's 1921 account of his conversations with Cézanne in Joachim Gasquet, *Cézanne: A Memoir with Conversations* (London: Thames and Hudson, 1991), 152, rather than to a document produced by the painter himself. It might therefore seem more appropriate to attribute this passage to Gasquet than to Cézanne. However, Rilke describes Cézanne's project in similar terms in an October 21, 1907, letter. See Rainer Maria Rilke, *Letters on Cézanne*, trans. Joel Agee (New York: North Point Press, 2002), 66.

2. Rainer Maria Rilke, *The Letters of Rainer Maria Rilke, 1910–1926*, trans. Jane Bannard Greene and M. D. Herter Norton (New York: Norton, 1947), 289.

3. Talbot, "Photogenic Drawing," 73.

4. Gasquet, *Cézanne*, 150.

5. Rilke, *The Letters of Rainer Maria Rilke, 1910–1926*, 96.

6. Sigmund Freud, *The Interpretation of Dreams*, in *The Standard Edition of the Complete Psychological Works*, vol. 5, trans. James Strachey (London: Hogarth Press, 1953–1974), 536–543.

7. Freud, *Introductory Lectures on Psycho-Analysis*, in *The Standard Edition*, 16:295.

8. Freud, "The Psychotherapy of Hysteria," in Freud and Josef Breuer, *Studies on Hysteria*, in *The Standard Edition*, 2:291.

9. Freud, *The Interpretation of Dreams*, 610–621.

10. Freud, "A Note Upon the 'Mystic Writing-Pad,'" in *The Standard Edition*, 14:227–232.

11. Freud uses this expression in *Beyond the Pleasure Principle* in *The Standard Edition*, 18:55.

12. Freud, "Psychotherapy of Hysteria," 291.

13. Freud, "The Dynamics of Transference," in *The Standard Edition*, 12:99–100.

14. Jacques Lacan, "The Mirror Stage as Formative of the *I* Function as Revealed in Psychoanalytic Experience," in *Écrits*, trans. Bruce Fink (New York: Norton, 2006), 76.

15. Lacan, "Aggressiveness in Psychoanalysis," in *Écrits*, 92.

16. Lacan, "Some Reflections on the Ego," *International Journal of Psychoanalysis* 34 (1953): 12.

17. Lacan, "Aggressiveness in Psychoanalysis," in *Écrits*, 96.

18. Ibid., 90.

19. Ibid.

20. Marcel Proust, *In Search of Lost Time*, vol. 6, *Time Regained*, trans. Andreas Major, Terence Kilmartin, and D. J. Enright (New York: Modern Library, 1993), 300, and *In Search of Lost Time*, vol. 2, *Within a Budding Grove*, trans. C. K. Scott Moncrieff, Terence Kilmartin, and D. J. Enright (New York: Modern Library, 1992), 616–617.

21. Proust, *Within a Budding Grove*, 621.

22. Ibid., 642.

23. Ibid.

24. Proust, *In Search of Lost Time*, vol. 1, *Swann's Way*, trans. C. K. Scott Moncrieff, Terence Kilmartin, and D. J. Enright (New York: Modern Library, 1992), 58–59.

25. Proust, *Time Regained*, 262–263. The title of my book comes from this passage.

26. Ibid., 292.

27. Ibid., 274.

28. Ibid., 275.

29. Ibid., 322.

30. Ibid., 276–277.

31. Proust, *Swann's Way*, 64.

32. Mieke Bal, *The Mottled Screen: Reading Proust Visually*, trans. Anna-Louise Milne (Stanford: Stanford University Press, 1997), 201.

33. Kaja Silverman, "Je Vous," *Art History* 30, no. 3 (June 2007): 453.

34. Wall, "Photography and Liquid Intelligence," 109–110.

35. Brassaï, *Proust in the Power of Photography*, trans. Richard Howard (Chicago: University of Chicago Press, 2001), 136.

36. Proust, *Swann's Way*, 64.

37. Brassaï, *Proust in the Power of Photography*, 136.

38. Proust, *Swann's Way*, 1.

39. Proust, *Within a Budding Grove*, 505.

40. Ibid., 508.

41. Ibid., 718–719.

42. Ibid., 663.

43. Ibid., 719–720.

44. Ibid., 721.

45. Rilke, *The Letters of Rainer Maria Rilke, 1910–1926*, 110.

46. Walter Benjamin, "On the Image of Proust," *Selected Writings*, 2:238.

47. Proust, *Within a Budding Grove*, 647.

48. Ibid.,, 500.

49. Ibid., 501.

50. Bal, *The Mottled Screen*, 196. Bal also discusses many of these passages.

51. Proust, *In Search of Lost Time*, vol. 4: *Sodom and Gomorrah*, trans. C. K. Scott Moncrieff, Terence Kilmartin, and D. J. Enright (New York: Modern Library, 1993), 237.

52. Proust, *In Search of Lost Time*, vol. 3, *The Guermantes Way*, trans. C. K. Scott Moncrieff, Terence Kilmartin, and D. J. Enright (New York: Modern Library, 1993, 183–185.

53. Proust, *Within a Budding Grove*, 510–511.

54. Proust, *The Guermantes Way*, 498.

55. Benjamin, "The Work of Art," 117.

56. Proust, *The Guermantes Way*, 498–499.

57. In a chilling passage in *Time Regained*, Proust maintains that "matter is indifferent," and that "anything can be grafted upon it by thought" (*Time Regained*, 320–321). He invokes this axiom as proof of his "idealism."

58. Proust, *Within a Budding Grove*, 648.

59. Proust, *Time Regained*, 310.

60. I take this phrase from Ralph Ellison, who uses it to describe a chiasmus that is closely related to those I discuss in this book, and to which I will return in *The Promise of Social Happiness*. See his *Invisible Man* (New York: Vintage International, 1995), 574.

61. Proust, *Time Regained*, 299.

62. Jean-Paul Sartre, *Being and Nothingness: A Phenomenological Essay on Ontology*, trans. Hazel E. Barnes (New York: Citadel Press, 1956), 231.

63. Ibid.

64. Ibid., 239.

65. Merleau-Ponty, *The Visible and the Invisible*, 132–133.

66. Ibid., 141–142.

67. Akerman introduces a narrative element into *The Captive* that is not present in Proust's novel and that suggests that the former is a renovation of the latter, rather than an "adaptation": workmen are constantly painting and plastering the walls of Simon's apartment.

68. Proust, *Within a Budding Grove*, 661.

69. Proust claims in *Time Regained* that "nothing is further from what we have really perceived than the vision that the cinematograph presents" (*Time Regained*, 279), but it is difficult to place much credence in this assertion, since associational montage works the same way Proustian analogy does; both privilege resemblance over temporal contiguity. As Bal argues in *The Mottled Screen*, *In Search of Lost Time* also evokes a certain kind of avant-garde film: the kind where the diegesis is based on vision rather than narrative (*The Mottled Screen*, 213). *The Captive* provides both an instantiation of, and a reflection upon, this last sort of cinema.

70. Bal, *The Mottled Screen*, 8.

71. Simon is later overcome by the desire to know what Ariane is thinking about, and this desire proves fatal for her.

72. Akerman reflects upon this practice in an interview with the editors of *Camera Obscura*: "Delphine [Seyrig] said, 'Why do you use such a low angle?' I said, 'That's my size.' She said, 'It's better from a little higher up.' And I said, 'No, I don't want to do that. That's not how I see the world.' *[Jeanne Dielman]* was never shot from the point of view of the son or anyone else. It's always me" (Chantal Akerman, *"Jeanne Dielman, 23 Quai du Commerce, 1080 Bruxelles," Camera Obscura*, no. 2 [1977]: 119).

73. Ivone Margulies, *Nothing Happens: Chantal Akerman's Hyperrealist Everyday* (Durham: Duke University Press, 1996), 116.

CHAPTER 6

1. Walter Benjamin, "The Work of Art in the Age of Its Technological Reproducibility," in *Selected Writings of Walter Benjamin*, vol. 4, *1938–1940*, ed. Howard Eiland and Michael W. Jennings (Cambridge: Harvard University Press, 2003), 252.

2. Benjamin, "The Work of Art," *Selected Writings*, 3:105.

3. Benjamin's translation of volume 4 was never published, and has been lost. Volumes 1 and 2 were published by Verlag Die Schmiede in 1927 and 1930, respectively, and volume 3 by Piper Verlag in 1930. See Benjamin, *Selected Writings of Walter Benjamin*, vol. 1, *1913–1926*, ed. Marcus Bullock and Michael W. Jennings (Cambridge: Harvard University Press, 1996), 513. Gary Smith provides a somewhat different account of this translation project in Walter Benjamin, *Moscow Diary*, trans. Richard Sieburth, ed. Gary Smith (Cambridge: Harvard University Press, 1986), 38 n. 6.

4. *Selected Writings*, ed. Bullock and Jennings, 1:513.

5. Benjamin, *Moscow Diary*, 38, 94–95.

6. Benjamin, "Conversation with André Gide," in *Selected Writings*, 2:93–94.

7. Benjamin, "On the Image of Proust," in *Selected Writings*, 2:239.

8. Ibid., 238–239.

9. Proust, *Swann's Way*, 94–95.

10. Katja Haustein, *Regarding Lost Time: Photography, Identity, and Affect in Proust, Benjamin, and Barthes* (London: Modern Humanities Research Association and Maney Publishing, 2012), 74.

11. Benjamin, "Paris Diary," in *Selected Writings*, 2:348.

12. Ibid., 348–349.

13. Ibid., 349.

14. Proust, *Within a Budding Grove*, 647.

15. Benjamin, "May–June 1931," in *Selected Writings*, 2:473.

16. Benjamin, *A Berlin Chronicle*, in *Selected Writings*, 2:632–633.

17. Ibid.,597.

18. Benjamin, *Berlin Childhood around 1900*, trans. Howard Eiland (Cambridge: Harvard University Press, 2006), 37.

19. Benjamin, "Doctrine of the Similar," in *Selected Writings*, 2:695.

20. Ibid., 698.

21. Ibid., 695.

22. Ibid.

23. Ibid., 697.

24. Although Benjamin does not mention Freud in this essay, he is clearly drawing on the psychoanalyst's discussion of the "binding" properties of language in *Beyond the Pleasure Principle*, a book he invokes both in "Toys and Play" (1928) and in "On Some Motifs in Baudelaire" (1940). See Benjamin, *Selected Writings*, 2:120, and *Selected Writings*, vol. 4, *1938–1940*, 316–319; and Freud, *The Standard Edition*, 18:12–23.

25. Benjamin, "The Work of Art," *Selected Writings*, 3:104–105. Both here and in the remainder of this chapter, I quote from the second version of the essay.

26. Merleau-Ponty, *The Visible and the Invisible*, 133. As Miriam Bratu Hansen notes in her superb essay "Benjamin's Aura" (*Critical Inquiry*, no. 34 [Winter 2008], 342), the Benjaminian aura often seems to imply "a phenomenal structure that enables the manifestation of the gaze"—a structure based on reciprocity. Kathrin Yacavone makes a similar observation in *Benjamin, Barthes, and the Singularity of Photography* (New York: Continuum, 2012), 57. Both Hansen and Yacavone invoke the passage in "On Some Motifs in Baudelaire" in which Benjamin explicitly links the aura to the possibility of a return look (*Selected Writings*, 4:338–340). This possibility is foreclosed in "On Some Motifs in Baudelaire," through Benjamin's discussion of Baudelaire's "Passante."

27. Benjamin, "The Work of Art," 108.

28. Ibid., 117.

29. Benjamin, "Little History," in *Selected Writings*, 2:517–528.

30. Ibid., 517.

31. Ibid., 527.

32. Ibid., 507.

33. Ibid.

34. Ibid., 508.

35. Max Dauthendey, *Der Geist meines Vaters: Ein Lebensbild* (Hamburg: Tredition Classics, n.d.), 35.

36. Benjamin, "Little History," 512.

37. Ibid., 510.

38. Ibid.; my emphasis.

39. Anonymous, "New Discovery—Engraving and Burnet's Cartoons," 382–391.

40. Benjamin, "Little History," 514.

41. Ibid., 514 and 519.

42. As Benjamin notes, he's quoting Emil Orlik here. The editors of volume 2 of *Selected Writings*, identify the source of the quotation as Orlik, *Kleine Aufsätze* (Berlin: Propyläen Verlag, 1924), 38 ff.

43. Benjamin, "Little History," 517.

44. Ibid., 510.

45. The poem is "Standbilder, das Sechste," and comes from Stefan George, *Der Teppich des Lebens und die Lieder von Traum und Tod* (Berlin: Georg Bondi, 1921).

46. Helmuth Th. Bossert and Heinrich Guttmann, *Aus der Frühzeit der Photographie, 1840–70* (Frankfurt am Main: Societäts-Verlag, 1930), n.p.

47. As Michael Ann Holly suggested to me, it may also be two contiguous chairs.

48. Benjamin, "Little History," 510.

49. André Gunthert, "Le complexe de Gradiva: Théorie de la photographie, deuil et résurrection," *Etudes photographiques*, no. 2 (May 1997): paragraphs 10–12.

50. Dauthendey, *Der Geist meines Vaters*, 121.

51. In a 1931 diary entry, Benjamin described his "growing willingness" to take his own life (Benjamin, *Selected Writings*, 2:470). As Hansen points out in "Benjamin's Aura," 341, the story also anticipates his actual death, which was self-induced.

52. Dauthendey, *Der Geist meines Vaters*, 118–120.

53. Ibid., 23.

54. Ibid., 24.

55. Ibid., 7.

56. Benjamin, "Little History," 512.

57. Dauthendey, *Der Geist meines Vaters*, 49–50.

58. Sartre, *Being and Nothingness*, 235–237.

59. Barthes, *Camera Lucida*, 67.

60. Benjamin, "Little History," 510.

61. Merleau-Ponty, *The Visible and the Invisible*, 139.

62. Benjamin, "Little History," 520.

63. Ibid., 514–517.

64. Ibid., 515.

65. Ibid.

66. Ibid., 517.

67. Benjamin, "Franz Kafka," in *Selected Writings*, 2:800.

68. Benjamin, *Berlin Childhood*, 130–131.

69. I am echoing, but also reformulating, Jacques Lacan's account of "aphanisis"— associating it with representation, rather than the entry into language, and questioning its inevitability. See *The Four Fundamental Concepts of Psychoanalysis*, 203–227.

70. Benjamin, *Berlin Childhood*, 131–132. Eduardo Cadava also talks about this "disappearance" in *Words of Light: Theses on the Photography of History* (Princeton: Princeton University Press, 1997). "The *Berliner Kindheit* . . . presents itself as an epitaph for the 'one' who, now dead, still speaks," he writes (126). Carolin Duttlinger provides a similar account of this passage in "Imaginary Encounters: Walter Benjamin and the Aura of Photography," *Poetics Today* 21, no. 1 (Spring 2008), 91.

71. Yacavone discusses the relationship between the two images in *Benjamin, Barthes, and the Singularity of Photography*, 63–64.

72. See, for instance, Cadava, *Words of Light*, 76–115; Yacavone, *Benjamin, Barthes*, 75–80; and Duttlinger, "Imaginary Encounters," 92.

73. Benjamin, *Berlin Childhood*, 134.

74. In *The Visible and the Invisible*, Merleau-Ponty writes that there is "a style of being wherever there is a fragment of being" (139).

75. I am referring, of course, to *Camera Lucida*, and the notion of the "punctum."

76. I want to thank James Sawyer for drawing Dugdale's work to my attention, and Khalip for showing me *John Keats's Death Mask*, which he has the privilege of owning, and for introducing me to the artist. (The only other print of the cyanotype is in the permanent collection of the Metropolitan Museum of Art.) Khalip recently curated an

exhibition of Dugdale's work at Brown University ("My Friend is Mine: The Photography of John Dugdale," 2014) and will also be writing about this photograph.

77. The artist made this observation in conversation with Khalip and me.

78. John Dugdale, *Life's Evening Hour* (New York: Arno Press, 2000), from Dugdale's commentary on figure 25, *Talismanic China* (1997). Because this book is unpaginated, I will identify all of the passages that I quote from it through the photographs to which they are linked.

79. The artist conveyed this information to me through an e-mail message.

80. From Dugdale's commentary on figure 2, *Our Minds Dwell Together* (1999).

81. From Dugdale's commentary on figure 27, *Self-Portrait in Oriel Window* (1997).

82. See chapter 5 for a discussion of this concept.

83. Quoted on the website of the Scheinbaum & Russek LTD gallery, www.photographydealers.com/artists/john-dugdale/.

84. From Dugdale's commentary on figure 52, *Self-Portrait in Summer Haze* (1999).

85. Ibid.

86. From Dugdale's commentary on figure 7, *Expulsion* (1996).

87. Ibid.

88. Dugdale described Sendak's role in his conversation with Khalip and me.

REFERENCES

Abbott, Austin. "The Eye and the Camera." *Harper's Magazine* 39 (1869): 476–482.

Ackerman, James S. "Leonardo's Eye." *Journal of the Warburg and Courtauld Institutes* 41 (1978): 108–146.

Addison, Joseph. "Wednesday, June 25: Pleasures of the Imagination." In *The Works of Joseph Addison: The Spectator*, edited by George Washington Greene, 336–340. New York: G. P. Putnam and Co., 1854.

Agamben, Giorgio. *Profanations.* Translated by Jeff Fort. New York: Zone Books, 2007.

Akerman, Chantal. "*Jeanne Dielman, 23 Quai du Commerce, 1080 Bruxelles.*" *Camera Obscura*, no. 2 (1977): 115–121.

Algarotti, Francesco. *An essay on painting written in Italian by Count Algarotti.* London: L. Davis and C. Reymers, 1764.

Anonymous. "Chemical and Optical Discovery." *Journal of the American Institute, a Monthly Publication Devoted to the Interests of Agriculture, Commerce, Manufactures, and the Arts* 4, no. 5 (February 1839): 267–277. From the research archive of Gary W. Ewer, ed., The Daguerreotype: An Archive of Source Material, http://www.daguerreotypearchive.org.

———. "Editor's Table." *The Literary Gazette; and Journal of the Belles Lettres, Arts, Sciences, etc.* (March 12, 1839): 2.

———. "Fine Arts—Royal Society." *The Literary Gazette; and Journal of the Belles Lettres, Arts, Sciences, etc.*, no. 1150 (February 2, 1839): 75. From the research archive of Gary W. Ewer, ed., The Daguerreotype: An Archive of Source Material, http://www.daguerreotypearchive.org.

———. "New Discovery—Engraving and Burnet's Cartoons." *Blackwood's Edinburgh Magazine* 45, no. 281 (March 1839): 382–391. From the research archive of Gary W. Ewer, ed., The Daguerreotype: An Archive of Source Material, http://www.daguerreotypearchive.org.

———. "New Discovery in the Fine Arts. The Daguerroscope." *New-Yorker: A Weekly Journal of Literature, Politics, Statistics, and General Information* 7, no. 5 (April 20, 1839): 70–71. From the research archive of Gary W. Ewer, ed., The Daguerreotype: An Archive of Source Material, http://www.daguerreotypearchive.org.

———. "Photogenic Drawing." *United States Democratic Review* 5, no. 17 (May 1839): 517.

———. "Poetus Photographicus." *The Photographic Journal* 1 (February 21, 1854): 210.

———. "Self-Operating Processes of Fine Art: The Daguerreotype." *Spectator: A Weekly Journal of News, Politics, Literature, and Science*, no. 553 (February 2, 1839): 114–115. From the research archive of Gary W. Ewer, ed., The Daguerreotype: An Archive of Source Material, http://www.daguerreotypearchive.org.

Arasse, Daniel. *Leonardo da Vinci: The Rhythm of the World.* Translated by Rosetta Translations. New York: Konecky and Konecky, 1998.

Aristotle. *Problems.* Edited and translated by Robert Mayhew, Loeb Classical Library. Cambridge: Harvard University Press, 2011.

Armstrong, Carol. *Scenes in a Library: Reading the Photograph in the Book, 1843–1875.* Cambridge: MIT Press, 1998.

Armstrong, Carol, and Catherine de Zegher, eds. *Ocean Flowers: Impressions from Nature.* Princeton: Princeton University Press, 2004.

Baker, George. "Black Mirror." In *Paul Sietsma*, edited by Christopher Bedford, 3–21. Columbus: Wexner Center for the Arts, Ohio State University, 2013.

———. "Lateness and Longing." In *50 Moons of Saturn: T2 Torino Triennale*, edited by Daniel Birnbaum, 47–97. Milan: Skira, 2008.

———. *Lateness and Longing: On the Afterlife of Photography.* Chicago: University of Chicago Press, forthcoming.

Bal, Mieke. *The Mottled Screen: Reading Proust Visually.* Translated by Anna-Louise Milne. Stanford: Stanford University Press, 1997.

Barbaro, Daniele. *La pratica della perspettiva.* Venice, 1568.

Barker, Peter, and Bernard R. Goldstein. "Theological Foundations of Kepler's Astronomy." *Osiris* 16 (2001): 88–113.

Barthes, Roland. *Camera Lucida: Reflections on Photography.* Translated by Richard Howard. New York: Farrar, Straus, and Giroux, 1981.

———. "Rhetoric of the Image." In *Image–Music–Text,* translated by Stephen Heath, 32–51. New York: Farrar, Straus, and Giroux, 1977.

Batchen, Geoffrey. *Burning with Desire: The Conception of Photography.* Cambridge: MIT Press, 1997.

———. *Each Wild Idea: Writing, Photography, History.* Cambridge: MIT Press, 2001.

Benjamin, Walter. *The Arcades Project.* Translated by Howard Eiland and Kevin McLaughlin. Cambridge: Harvard University Press, 1999.

———. *Berlin Childhood around 1900.* Translated by Howard Eiland. Cambridge: Harvard University Press, 2006.

———. *A Berlin Chronicle.* In *Selected Writings*, vol. 2, *1927–1934*. Edited by Michael W. Jennings. Cambridge: Harvard University Press, 1999.

———. "Conversation with André Gide." In *Selected Writings*, vol. 2, *1927–1934*. Edited by Michael W. Jennings. Cambridge: Harvard University Press, 1999.

———. "Doctrine of the Similar." In *Selected Writings*, vol. 2, *1927–1934*. Edited by Michael W. Jennings. Cambridge: Harvard University Press, 1999.

———. "Franz Kafka." In *Selected Writings*, vol. 2, *1927–1934*. Edited by Michael W. Jennings. Cambridge: Harvard University Press, 1999.

———. "Left Wing Melancholy." In *Selected Writings*, vol. 2, *1927–1934*. Edited by Michael W. Jennings. Cambridge: Harvard University Press, 1999.

———. "Little History of Photography." In *Selected Writings*, vol. 2, *1927–1934*. Edited by Michael W. Jennings. Cambridge: Harvard University Press, 1999.

———. "May–June 1931." In *Selected Writings*, vol. 2, *1927–1934*. Edited by Michael W. Jennings. Cambridge: Harvard University Press, 1999.

———. *Moscow Diary*. Translated by Richard Sieburth. Edited by Gary Smith. Cambridge: Harvard University Press, 1986.

———. "On the Concept of History." In *Selected Writings*, vol. 4, *1938–1940*. Edited by Howard Eiland and Michael W. Jennings. Cambridge: Harvard University Press, 2003.

———. "On the Image of Proust." In *Selected Writings*, vol. 2, *1927–1934*. Edited by Michael W. Jennings. Cambridge: Harvard University Press, 1999.

———. "On the Mimetic Faculty." In *Selected Writings*, vol. 2, *1927–1934*. Edited by Michael W. Jennings. Cambridge: Harvard University Press, 1999.

———. "On Some Motifs in Baudelaire." In *Selected Writings*, vol. 2, *1927–1934*. Edited by Michael W. Jennings. Cambridge: Harvard University Press, 1999.

———. "Paris Diary." In *Selected Writings*, vol. 2, *1927–1934*. Edited by Michael W. Jennings. Cambridge: Harvard University Press, 1999.

———. *Selected Writings*. Vol. 1, *1913–1926*. Edited by Marcus Bullock and Michael W. Jennings. Cambridge: Harvard University Press, 1996.

———. "Toys and Play." In *Selected Writings*, vol. 2, *1927–1934*. Edited by Michael W. Jennings. Cambridge: Harvard University Press, 1999.

———. "The Work of Art in the Age of Its Technological Reproducibility." In *Selected Writings*, vol. 3, *1935–1938*. Edited by Howard Eiland and Michael W. Jennings. Cambridge: Harvard University Press, 2002.

———. "The Work of Art in the Age of Its Technological Reproducibility." In *Selected Writings*, vol. 4, *1935–1938*. Edited by Howard Eiland and Michael W. Jennings. Cambridge: Harvard University Press, 2003.

Benveniste, Emile. *Problems in General Linguistics*. Translated by Mary Elizabeth Meek. Coral Gables: University of Florida Press, 1971.

Bergson, Henri. *Creative Evolution*. Translated by Arthur Mitchell. New York: Dover, 1998.

Bossert, Helmuth Th., and Heinrich Guttmann. *Aus der Frühzeit der Photographie, 1840–70*. Frankfurt am Main: Societäts-Verlag, 1930.

Brassaï. *Proust in the Power of Photography*. Translated by Richard Howard. Chicago: University of Chicago Press, 2001.

Brewster, Sir David. *The Stereoscope: Its History, Theory, and Construction*. London: John Murray, 1856.

Brewster, Sir David (attributed). "Photogenic Drawing, or Drawing by the Agency of Art." *The Edinburgh Review* 86, no. 154 (January 1843): 309–344.

Brown, Barbara. "The First Photograph." *Abbey Newsletter* 26, no. 3 (November 2002).

Buber, Martin. *I and Thou*. Translated by Walter Kaufmann. New York: Simon and Schuster, 1970.

Buckland, Gail. *Fox Talbot and the Invention of Photography*. Boston: David R. Godine, 1980.

Cadava, Eduardo. *Words of Light: Theses on the Photography of History*. Princeton: Princeton University Press, 1997.

Cadava, Eduardo, and Gabriela Nouzeilles, eds. *The Itinerant Languages of Photography*. Princeton: Princeton University Art Museum, 2013.

Claudet, Antoine. "Photography in its Relation to the Fine Arts." *The Photographic Journal* 6 (June 15, 1860): 259–267.

Crary, Jonathan. *Techniques of the Observer: On Vision and Modernity in the Nineteenth Century*. Cambridge: MIT Press, 1990.

Daniel, Malcolm. "William Henry Fox Talbot (1800–1877) and the Invention of Photography." In *Heilbrunn Timeline of Art History*. New York: Metropolitan Museum of Art, October 2004. http://www.metmuseum.org/toah/hd/tlbt/hd_tlbt.htm.

Dauthendey, Max. *Der Geist meines Vaters: Ein Lebensbild*. Hamburg: Tredition Classics, n.d.

della Porta, Giovanni Battista. *Magiae naturalis*. Anonymous translator. London, 1658.

Descartes, René. *Discourse on Method and Meditations on First Philosophy*. Edited by David Weissman. New Haven: Yale University Press, 1996.

———. *Optics*, in *Discourse on Method, Optics, Geometry, and Meteorology*, translated by Paul J. Olscamp, 91–100. Indianapolis: Hackett Publishing Co., 2001.

Dugdale, John. *Life's Evening Hour*. New York: Arno Press, 2000.

Durden, Mark. *Fifty Key Writers on Photography*. London: Routledge, 2013.

Duttlinger, Carolin. "Imaginary Encounters: Walter Benjamin and the Aura of Photography." *Poetics Today* 21, no. 1 (Spring 2008): 79–101.

Earle, Edward W., ed. *Points of View: The Stereograph in America—A Cultural History*. Rochester: Visual Studies Workshop Press, 1979.

Ellis, James. *Progress of Photography, Collodion, the Stereoscope*. London: Bell and Daldy, 1856.

Ellison, Ralph. *Invisible Man*. New York: Vintage International, 1995.

Falk, David, Dieter Brill, and David Stork, eds. *Seeing the Light: Optics in Nature, Photography, Color, Vision, and Holography*. Hoboken: John Wiley and Sons, 1988.

Fontcuberta, Joan. www.fontcuberta.com.

Freud, Sigmund. *Beyond the Pleasure Principle*. In vol. 18 of *The Standard Edition of the Complete Psychological Works*. Translated by James Strachey. London: Hogarth Press, 1953–1974.

———. "The Dynamics of Transference." In vol. 12 of *The Standard Edition of the Complete Psychological Works*. Translated by James Strachey. London: Hogarth Press, 1953–1974.

———. *The Interpretation of Dreams*. Vols. 4–5 of *The Standard Edition of the Complete Psychological Works*. Translated by James Strachey. London: Hogarth Press, 1953–1974.

———. *Introductory Lectures on Psycho-Analysis*. Vols. 15–16 of *The Standard Edition of the Complete Psychological Works*. Translated by James Strachey. London: Hogarth Press, 1953–1974.

———. "A Note Upon the 'Mystic Writing-Pad.'" In vol. 14 of *The Standard Edition of the Complete Psychological Works*. Translated by James Strachey. London: Hogarth Press, 1953–1974.

———. "The Psychotherapy of Hysteria." In Sigmund Freud and Josef Breuer, *Studies on Hysteria*. In vol. 2 of *The Standard Edition of the Complete Psychological Works*. Translated by James Strachey. London: Hogarth Press, 1953–1974.

Gardner, Alexander. *Gardner's Photographic Sketchbook of the American Civil War, 1861–1865*. New York: Delano Greenidge Editions, 2001.

Gasquet, Joachim. *Cézanne: A Memoir with Conversations*. London: Thames and Hudson, 1991.

Gaucheraud, Hippolyte. "Fine Arts. The Daguerotype." *The Literary Gazette; and Journal of the Belles Lettres, Arts, Sciences, Etc.* 1147 (January 12, 1839): 28. From the research archive of Gary W. Ewer, ed., The Daguerreotype: An Archive of Source Material, http://www.daguerreotypearchive.org.

George, Stefan. *Der Teppich des Lebens und die Lieder von Traum und Tod*. Berlin: Georg Bondi, 1921.

Gernsheim, Helmut. "The 150th Anniversary of Photography." *History of Photography* 1, no. 1 (1977): 3–8.

———. "Section A." *The Photographic Journal* (May 1952): 118–120, 129.

Gernsheim, Helmut, and Alison Gernsheim. *L. J. M. Daguerre: The History of the Diorama and the Daguerreotype*. New York: Dover, 1968.

———. *The History of Photography from the Camera Obscura to the Beginning of the Modern Era*. London: Thames and Hudson, 1969.

———. "Rediscovery of the World's First Photograph." *Image: Journal of Photography at the George Eastman House* 1, no. 6 (1952): 1.

The Getty Conservation Institute. "Scientific Analysis of World's First Photograph." J. Paul Getty Trust, 2002. www.getty.edu/conservation/publications_resources/newsletters/17_2/gcinews1.html.

Gray, Michael, Arthur Ollman, and Carol McCusker. *First Photographs: William Henry Fox Talbot and the Birth of Photography*. New York: powerHouse Books, 2002.

Gunthert, André. "Le complexe de Gradiva: Théorie de la photographie, deuil et résurrection." *Etudes photographiques,* no. 2 (May 1997): 115–128.

Gustavson, Todd. *Camera: A History of Photography from Daguerreotype to Digital*. New York: Sterling Publishing Co., 2009.

Hammond, John H. *The Camera Obscura: A Chronicle*. Bristol: Adam Hilger, Ltd., 1981.

Hansen, Miriam Bratu. "Benjamin's Aura." *Critical Inquiry,* no. 34 (Winter 2008): 336–375.

Harry Ransom Center. "Conservation: The First Photograph." Austin: The University of Texas at Austin, 2003–present. http://www.hrc.utexas.edu/exhibitions/permanent/firstphotograph/conservation/#top.

Harvey, Eleanor Jones. *The Civil War and American Art*. New Haven: Yale University Press, 2012.

Harvey, William Henry. *A Manual of the British Marine Algae*. London: John van Voorst, 1849.

Haustein, Katja. *Regarding Lost Time: Photography, Identity, and Affect in Proust, Benjamin, and Barthes*. London: Modern Humanities Research Association and Maney Publishing, 2012.

Heidegger, Martin. *Poetry, Language, Thought.* Translated by Albert Hofstadter. New York: Harper and Row, 1971.

———. *The Question Concerning Technology and Other Essays.* Translated by William Lovitt. New York: Harper and Row, 1977.

Hirsch, Robert. *Seizing the Light: A History of Photography.* New York: McGraw Hill, 2000.

Hockney, David. *Secret Knowledge: Rediscovering the Lost Techniques of the Old Masters.* New York: Viking Studio, 2006.

Holmes, Oliver Wendell. "Doings of the Sunbeam." *The Atlantic Monthly* 12, no. 69 (July 1863): 1–15.

———. "The Stereoscope and the Stereograph." *The Atlantic Monthly* 3 (June 1859): 738–748.

———. "Sun-Painting and Sun-Sculpture." *The Atlantic Monthly* 8, no. 45 (July 1861): 13–29.

Janin, Jules. "La Daguerreotype." *Court and Lady's Magazine, Monthly Critic and Museum* 17 (October 1839): 436–439. From the research archive of Gary W. Ewer, ed., The Daguerreotype: An Archive of Source Material, http://www.daguerreotype archive.org.

Jenkins, Nicholas. "Traces." *Day by Day: A Blog* (blog). August 22, 2007. http://www .stanford.edu/njenkins/archives/2007/08/traces.html.

Kemp, Martin. *The Science of Art: Optical Themes in Western Art from Brunelleschi to Seurat.* New Haven: Yale University Press, 1990.

Kepler, Johannes. *Paralipomena to Witelo.* In *Optics,* translated by William H. Donahue. Santa Fe: Green Lion Press, 2000.

Khalip, Jacques, and Robert Mitchell, eds. *Releasing the Image: From Literature to New Media.* Stanford: Stanford University Press, 2011.

Krauss, Rosalind E. *The Originality of the Avant-Garde and Other Modernist Myths.* Cambridge: MIT Press, 1988.

Lacan, Jacques. "Aggressiveness in Psychoanalysis." In *Écrits,* translated by Bruce Fink, 82–101. New York: Norton, 2006.

———. *The Four Fundamental Concepts of Psycho-Analysis: The Seminar of Jacques Lacan.* Book XI. Edited by Jacques-Alain Miller. Translated by Alan Sheridan. New York: Norton, 1981.

———. "The Mirror Stage as Formative of the *I* Function as Revealed in Psychoanalytic Experience." In *Écrits,* translated by Bruce Fink, 75–81. New York: Norton, 2006.

———. "Some Reflections on the Ego." *International Journal of Psychoanalysis* 34 (1953): 11–17.

Lee, Anthony W., and Elizabeth Young, eds. *On Alexander Gardner's "Photographic Sketch Book" of the Civil War.* Berkeley: University of California Press, 2007.

Lefèvre, David C. *Theories of Vision from Al-Kindi to Kepler.* Chicago: University of Chicago Press, 1976.

Lefèvre, Wolfgang, ed. *Inside the Camera Obscura—Optics and Art under the Spell of the Projected Image.* Berlin: Max Planck Institute für Wissenschaftsgeschichte, 2007.

Leibniz, G. W. *New Essays on Human Understanding.* Translated by Peter Remnant and Jonathan Bennett. Cambridge: Cambridge University Press, 1981.

Leonardo da Vinci. *The Genius of Leonardo da Vinci: Leonardo da Vinci on Art and the Artist.* Edited by André Chastel. Translated by Ellen Callmann. New York: Orion Press, 1961.

———. *The Literary Works of Leonardo da Vinci.* Vol. 1. Translated by Jean Paul Richter. London: Samson Low, Marston, Searle and Rivington, 1883.

Locke, John. *An Essay Concerning Human Understanding.* Translated by A. C. Fraser. Oxford: Clarendon Press, 1894. Reprint, New York: Prometheus Books, 1995.

Margulies, Ivone. *Nothing Happens: Chantal Akerman's Hyperrealist Everyday.* Durham: Duke University Press, 1996.

Martin, Benjamin. *A New and Compendious System of Optics.* London, 1740.

Marx, Karl, and Friedrich Engels. *The German Ideology: Part One.* Edited by C. J. Arthur. New York: International Publishers, 1974.

Merleau-Ponty, Maurice. "Eye and Mind." In *The Merleau-Ponty Aesthetics Reader,* edited by Michael B. Smith, 121–149. Evanston: Northwestern University Press, 1993.

———. *The Visible and the Invisible.* Translated by Alphonso Lingis. Evanston: Northwestern University Press, 1968.

Meteyard, Eliza. *The Life of Josiah Wedgwood: From His Private Correspondence and Family Papers.* Volume 2. London: Hurst and Blackett, 1886.

Morell, Abelardo. *A Camera in a Room: Photographs by Abelardo Morell.* Washington, D.C.: Smithsonian Institution Press, 1995.

———. *Camera Obscura: Photographs by Abelardo Morell.* New York: Bulfinch Press, 2004.

Morse, Samuel F. B. "The Daguerrotipe" [*sic*]. *New-York Observer* 17, no. 16 (April 20, 1839): 62. From the research archive of Gary W. Ewer, ed., http://www.daguerreotypearchive.org.

Newhall, Beaumont. *The History of Photography.* New York: Museum of Modern Art, 1982.

Orlik, Emil. *Kleine Aufsätze.* Berlin: Propyläen Verlag, 1924.

Peirce, Charles Sanders. "What Is a Sign?" In *The Essential Peirce: Selected Philosophical Writings.* Vol. 2, *1893–1913.* Edited by the Peirce Edition Project, 4–10. Bloomington: Indiana University Press, 1998.

Pope, Alexander. *The Works of Alexander Pope,* volume 6. London: John Murray, 1871.

Potonniée, Georges. *The History of the Discovery of Photography.* Translated by Edward Epstean. New York: Arno Press, 1973.

Proust, Marcel. *In Search of Lost Time.* Vol. 1, *Swann's Way.* Translated by C. K. Moncrieff, Terence Kilmartin, and D. J. Enright. New York: Modern Library, 1992.

———. *In Search of Lost Time.* Vol. 2, *Within a Budding Grove.* Translated by C. K. Scott Moncrieff, Terence Kilmartin, and D. J. Enright. New York: Modern Library, 1992.

———. *In Search of Lost Time.* Vol. 3, *The Guermantes Way.* Translated by C. K. Scott Moncrieff, Terence Kilmartin, and D. J. Enright. New York: Modern Library, 1993.

———. *In Search of Lost Time.* Vol. 4, *Sodom and Gomorrah.* Translated by C. K. Scott Moncrieff, Terence Kilmartin, and D. J. Enright. New York: Modern Library, 1993.

———. *In Search of Lost Time*. Vol. 6, *Time Regained*. Translated by Andreas Major, Terence Kilmartin, and D. J. Enright. New York: Modern Library, 1993.

Richter, Gerhard. *The Daily Practice of Painting: Writings and Interviews, 1962–1993*. Edited by Hans-Ulrich Obrist. Cambridge: MIT Press, 1995.

Rilke, Rainer Maria. *Letters on Cézanne*. Translated by Joel Agee. New York: North Point Press, 2002.

———. *The Letters of Rainer Maria Rilke, 1910–1926*. Translated by Jane Bannard Greene and M. D. Herter Norton. New York: Norton, 1947.

Roberts, Russell, ed. *Specimens and Marvels: William Henry Fox Talbot and the Invention of Photography*. New York: Aperture Foundation, 2000.

Robison, Sir John. "Notes on Daguerre's Photography." *Edinburgh New Philosophical Journal* 27, no. 53 (July 1839): 155–157. From the research archive of Gary W. Ewer, ed., http://www.daguerreotypearchive.org.

Rosenheim, Jeff L. *Photography and the American Civil War*. New York: Metropolitan Museum of Art, 2013.

Ruskin, John. *Modern Painters*, vol. 1. London: Smith, Elder, and Co., 1948.

Samson, John. "Photographs from the High Rockies." *Harper's Magazine* 34 (1869): 465–475.

Sartre, Jean-Paul. *Being and Nothingness: A Phenomenological Essay on Ontology*. Translated by Hazel E. Barnes. New York: Citadel Press, 1956.

Schaaf, Larry J. *Out of the Shadows: Herschel, Talbot, and the Invention of Photography*. New Haven: Yale University Press, 1992.

———. *The Photographic Art of William Henry Fox Talbot*. Princeton: Princeton University Press, 2000.

———. *Records of the Dawn of Photography: Talbot's Notebooks P & Q*. Cambridge: Cambridge University Press, 1996.

———. *Sun Gardens: Victorian Photograms by Anna Atkins*. New York: Aperture Foundation, 1985.

Schiavo, Laura Burd. "From Phantom Image to Perfect Vision: Physiological Optics, Commercial Photography, and the Popularization of the Stereoscope." In *New Media: 1740–1915*, edited by Lisa Gitelman and Geoffrey B. Pingree, 113–138. Cambridge: MIT Press, 2003.

Siegel, Elizabeth, ed. *Abelardo Morell: The Universe Next Door*. Chicago: Art Institute of Chicago, 2013.

Silverman, Kaja. *Flesh of My Flesh*. Stanford: Stanford University Press, 2009.

———. "Je Vous." *Art History* 30, no. 3 (June 2007): 451–467.

———. *The Threshold of the Visible World*. New York: Routledge, 1996.

Steadman, Philip. *Vermeer's Camera: Uncovering the Truth behind the Masterpieces*. Oxford: Oxford University Press, 2001.

Sugimoto, Hiroshi. *Nature of Light*. Shizuoka, Japan: Koko Okano, 2009.

Talbot, William Henry Fox. "Letter to the Editor." *The Literary Gazette; and Journal of the Belles Lettres, Arts, Sciences, etc.*, no. 1258 (February 19, 1841): 139–140.

———. *The Pencil of Nature*. London: Longman, Brown, Green, and Longmans, 1844–46.

———. "Photogenic Drawing." Letter to the Editor. *The Literary Gazette; and Journal of the Belles Lettres, Arts, Sciences, etc.* no. 1150 (February 2, 1839): 72–75.

Trachtenberg, Alan, ed. *Classic Essays on Photography.* New Haven: Leete's Island Books, 1980.

Valéry, Paul. "Introduction to the Method of Leonardo." In *Leonardo, Poe, and Mallarmé,* translated by Malcolm Cowley, 3–63. Princeton: Princeton University Press, 1972.

Veltman, Kim H. "Leonardo and the Camera Obscura." In *Studi Vinciani in memoria de Nando de Toni,* 81–92. Brescia: Fratelli Geroldi, 1986.

Wade, Nicholas J., and Michael T. Swanston. *Visual Perception: An Introduction.* East Sussex: Psychology Press, 2013.

Wall, Jeff. "Photography and Liquid Intelligence." In *Jeff Wall: Selected Essays and Interviews,* edited by Peter Galassi, 9–10. New York: Museum of Modern Art, 2007.

Walpole, Horace. September 21, 1777: To the Rev. William Mason." In *The Letters of Horace Walpole, Fourth Earl of Orford,* edited by Peter Cunningham, 483–485. Edinburgh: John Grant, 1906.

Wheelock, Arthur, ed. *Johannes Vermeer.* Washington, D.C.: National Gallery of Art, 1995.

Whitman, Walt. *Leaves of Grass.* Edited by Richard Maurice Bucke, Thomas R. Harned, and Horace L. Traubel. New York: Doubleday, 1902.

Wotton, Henry. *Reliquiae Wottonianae.* London, 1651.

Yacavone, Kathrin. *Benjamin, Barthes, and the Singularity of Photography.* New York: Continuum, 2012.

INDEX

Page numbers in italics refer to illustrations.

RENDED SOULS

BOOK THREE OF THE DARK HEART CHRONICLES

DREZHN

PUBLISHING

RENDED SOULS

Published by Drezhn Publishing LLC
PO BOX 67458
Albuquerque, NM 87193-7458

Print Edition – December 2019
Version 1.8 – June 2023

Cover design by Drezhn Publishing LLC
Cover illustration by Jonathan Myers

HARDBACK (DUST JACKET) ISBN: 978-1-947328-27-3
HARDBACK (CASE LAMINATE) ISBN: 978-1-947328-73-0
PAPERBACK ISBN: 978-1-947328-28-0

CENTAURIA
THE ANCIENT REALM

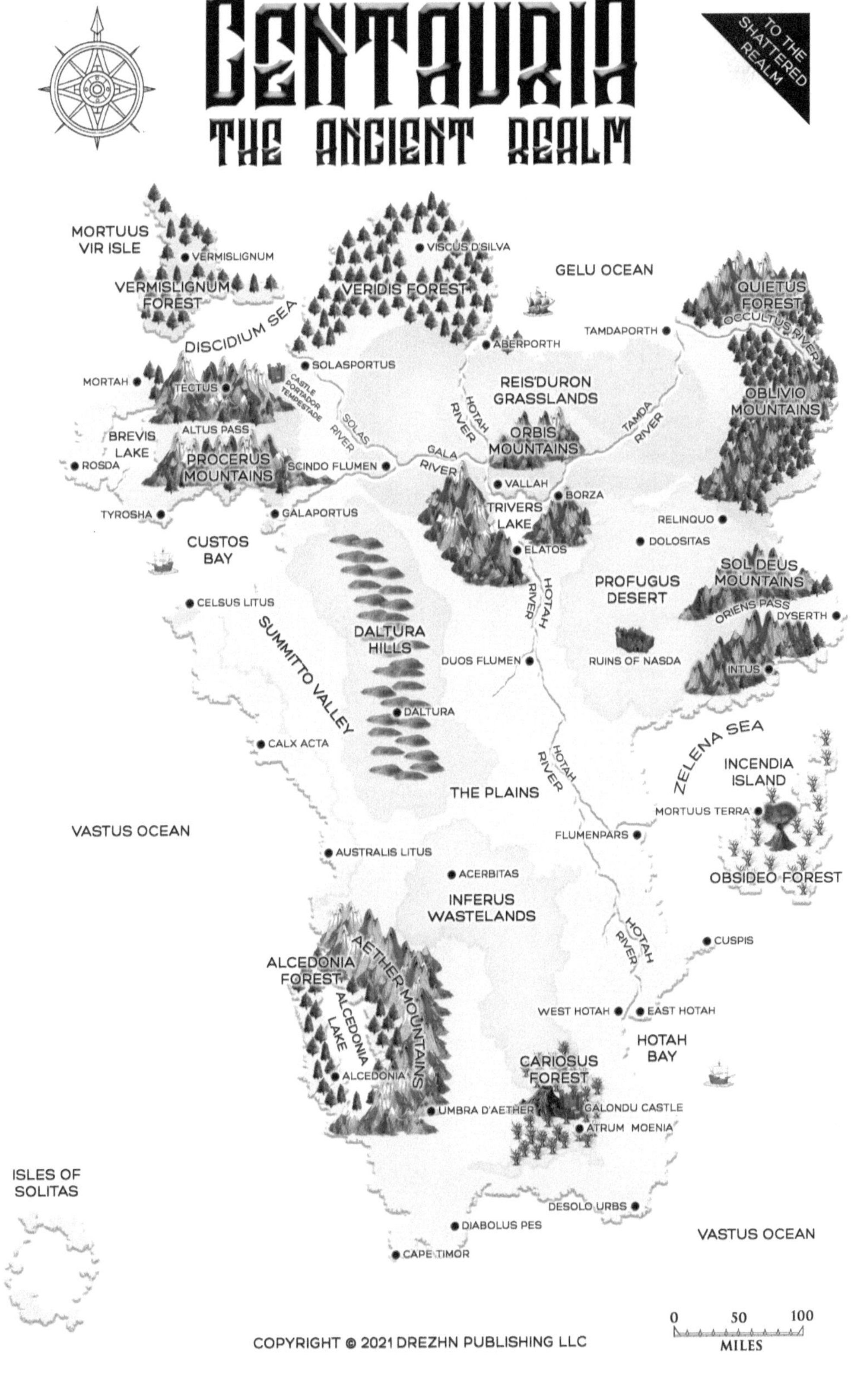

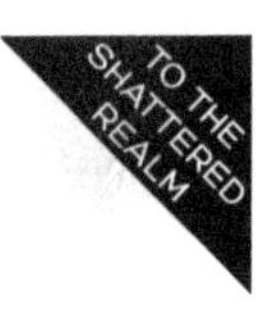

COPYRIGHT © 2021 DREZHN PUBLISHING LLC

READ *SCOURGE* FOR FREE

Do Eshtak's tattoos hold the key to the between?

danielkuhnley.com/become-a-conqueror

Sign up and read *Scourge*, A World Of Centauria Novella. Be the **FIRST** to get sneak peeks at my upcoming novels and the chance to win **FREE** stuff, like signed books.

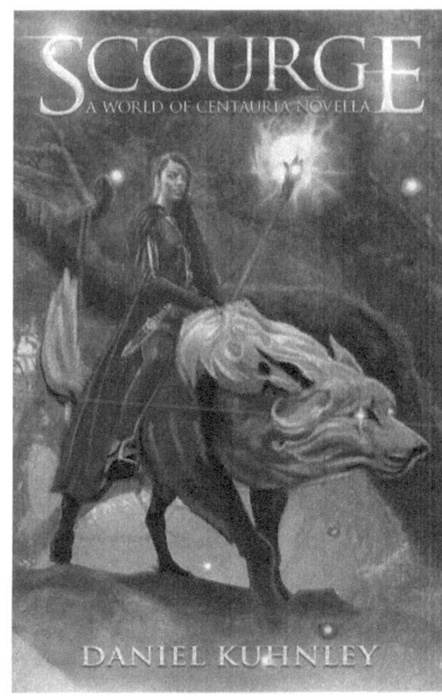

Never use persuasion magic on a powerful wizard.

That was Emorith's hardest lesson to learn. Right from that fateful moment, Magus forced her to use her manipulative sorcery to further his evil purposes. She regretted everything he put her through with one exception: their son Illian. Him, she loved with all her heart.

Magus demanded she cast an apocalyptic curse and destroy an unsuspecting city. She steeled herself to refuse him… but then he threatened the life of her beloved child.

With Illian's life on the line, what choice did she have? She wanted to protect the city and its citizens, but her son would always come first. No, there must be another way. Will she be able to thwart Magus and save them all in time? Or is their fate already sealed?

Scourge is a prequel novella to *The Dragon's Stone*, the first book in *The Dark Heart Chronicles* epic dragon fantasy series. If you like thrilling adventures and terrifying magic, then you'll love Daniel Kuhnley's enthralling tale.

BOOKS BY DANIEL KUHNLEY

EPIC DRAGON FANTASY

<u>The Dark Heart Chronicles</u>
*†The Dragon's Stone
*Reborn
*Rended Souls
True Heir

Scourge (novella)

SUPERNATURAL SERIAL KILLER

<u>Alice Bergman Novels</u>
*Birth Of A Killer (novella)
*The Braille Killer
*The Night Mauler
*The Chrono Slasher

CHRISTIAN YA SCI-FI/FANTASY

<u>VR Academy</u>
Kiara Kole And The Key Of Truth

* - Also available as an audiobook
† - Previously released as Dark Lament

Visit Daniel's website to find these books and more!
danielkuhnley.com

This book is dedicated to you, the reader. Thank you so much for sticking with me along this long journey. I hope you enjoy reading this continuation of *The Dark Heart Chronicles* as much as I enjoyed writing it!

Geoff and Steve, thank you for your feedback!

Last, but never least, all glory goes to Jesus Christ, my Lord and Savior. Through Him all things are possible!

THE DARK HEART CHRONICLES

RENDED SOULS

3

DANIEL KUHNLEY

CHAPTER ONE

Nardus knelt in the middle of the Great Library, surrounded by chaos and eyed by a beast intent on spilling his blood. He trembled with fear and elation—fear of an impending death and elation over the majestic beauty of the beast.

He breathed deep and exhaled evenly, releasing his pent-up fear with the breath. His pulse slowed, and the wild bird trapped within his chest settled. He held out his right hand; it trembled like a leaf in the spring wind for several moments before stilling.

The beast stalked forward, her ears pinned back against her head and her tail held low. Her beige fur glistened in the pale light as her muscled form moved effortlessly across the remains of torn books, demolished wooden shelves, and shattered crystal chandeliers.

Her yellow eyes locked onto his. He didn't recognize her transfigured body, but those eyes he knew. He'd never forget them. Never thought he'd see them again.

Theyn.

Nardus leaned forward and stretched his arm out as far as he could. "Theyn, it's me." His voice didn't waver, but his fear returned as flashes of Berggren's mutilated stomach and chest pummeled his mind.

His pulse raced and his mind reeled as questions bombarded him. *Where's Gnaud? Were there tufts of fur in the rubble? Dried blood? Is Gnaud dead, buried amongst the remains of the books?* His eyes grew wide. *Did she eat him?* He quickly pushed the thought from his mind, unwilling to contemplate it further.

The beast paused, sniffed the air, and growled deep in her throat. She crouched down, ready to pounce, but she didn't move.

It's me, Theyn. You know me... better than most.

Time itself stood still as they held each other's gaze, neither willing to blink or look away. Each passing moment proved more difficult than the last for Nardus to breathe, and his thoughts failed to make sense.

Had the air been sucked from the room, or had he forgotten how to breathe? He didn't know, but either way the air pressed down on him and suffocated him like a thick pillow over his face. His arm fell to his side, the act of holding it out any longer unbearable.

The beast lunged from her crouch like a wound spring unloaded, and she hit Nardus square in the chest before he had a chance to react or brace himself. The impact forced out what little air he'd held in his lungs, and it knocked him backward and onto his back. He grunted as her full weight settled on top of him.

She pinned him down; her claws pressed into the fleshy part of the backs of his arms. Her claws didn't break the skin, but they would if he moved. She snarled, her fanged teeth dripping with saliva. She opened her jaws wide, howled like no other creature he'd ever heard, and then went for his throat.

Instinct pulled Nardus's eyes closed, his body turned rigid, and he grimaced. Her fangs rested against either side of his neck. *It's me, Theyn. Don't do it. You love me.* Theyn applied pressure, and her fangs sank into his skin like four arrowheads.

Nardus gasped and swallowed hard. His pulse raced, and beads of sweat formed on his brow as droplets of warm blood slid down the sides of his neck. Moments they'd shared flashed through his mind: long looks, subtle touches, shared smiles, the night at Joriah's, the vision of their future when their minds had interlinked.

Nardus opened his eyes. *Our minds...*

With no understanding of how it worked or if he had the ability to do so, Nardus opened his mind and reached out to Theyn. *"I know you don't want to kill me. You love me. Remember that. You love me, Theyn."*

Theyn's jaws tightened, and her claws dug into his arms. Nardus winced as fresh blood trickled down the sides of his neck.

Damn. Guess that didn't work. What had he expected? Mezhik? The idea sickened him.

Theyn's words pierced his mind and left him stunned. *"I do. But do you love me?"*

Do I love her? Attracted to? Yes. Enamored with? Perhaps. But love? Preposterous. How could he? To love Theyn would betray his love of Vitara, wouldn't it?

Theyn bit down harder, and Nardus groaned.

"Don't think too long on it," she said in his mind.

Tell her what she wants to hear… even though it's a lie.

Nardus gritted his teeth. "I do love you, Theyn—" The words burned his heart like acid. "—but I never wanted to."

In his mind's eye, Nardus grabbed the arrow that had pierced Vitara's throat. He twisted it violently and shoved it in deeper. He tensed, balled his fists, and screamed within his mind. *Forgive me, my love! They're only words, nothing more. I don't love her. I swear it!* But even he didn't believe his own lie.

Theyn's claws retracted, and she released his throat. She purred as she stroked the wounds on his neck with her sandpaper tongue.

Even her tongue? "Huh…" He'd never contemplated it changing in her transfigured state, but it made sense. Everything about her had changed.

Theyn rubbed her furry jaw against his. *"I knew you loved me. It's about time you admitted it. Had you been anyone else, I would've killed you. Until you spoke to me in my mind, my thoughts were purely animalistic. Thank you for coming back for me. I've longed to be with you since we separated. Never have I felt so alone."*

Theyn rubbed against him and kneaded his arms with her claws.

Nardus jerked. "Ouch! Can you please stop with the claws and let me up? I think there's a book crushing my spine."

Theyn growled, but she rose and moved to the side. *"Don't make me regret not killing you."*

Nardus sat up and rubbed his neck; the puncture wounds Theyn had left were little more than pricks. Leaning over, he wrapped his arms around her neck and held her for several moments. "I thought you were dead, Theyn. We all did. I didn't know what had happened. I stepped through the mirror, Pravus placed another collar around my neck, and then Berggren started cursing at me.

"If Joriah hadn't been there to restrain him, he would've killed himself trying to attack me through the mirror. I couldn't see the ground where you'd been standing, and I thought I might've killed you like I did Shaul. Then the mirror went dark and Pravus wouldn't let me go back."

"How did I get here? Where exactly is here? And how do we escape? There are no doors, and the windows are too high to climb out of. Trust me. That's why most of the bookshelves are toppled over." She looked around. *"The rest of this chaos I can't explain."*

Nardus scratched the back of his head. "I think I know what happened, but I'm surprised it did. When Joriah removed the silver collar from my neck and placed it on yours I thought I'd be able to finally escape and return here—Nasduron. What I didn't realize at the time was that the stone prevented me from returning here, not the collar.

"You must've been touching me when I stepped forward to return here. Unfortunately, I only phased in and out from here as I did on the boat, but you remained here. In that brief moment, you must've let go of me.

"No one there knew about this place or that I could travel here, so they assumed that I'd killed you like I did Shaul. You cannot comprehend the sorrow I experienced in that moment and in every one since then until I came here and found you alive. I'd lost everything, Theyn. Again. I begged for death." Tears welled in his eyes, and he blinked them back.

Theyn sat back on her haunches. Her tail whipped the air, and her upper lip rose, exposing her fangs. *"If you thought I was dead then you didn't come back for me."* She growled. *"Why did you come here?"*

Nardus huffed. "To escape from Pravus and Cinolth, but now that I know you're alive, I'll do everything I can to help you get back to your human form."

"Cinolth? As in the dragon Cinolth the Dark? Cyrus Nithik killed him 1200 years ago."

Nardus sighed. "Yes, the same one. The stone I retrieved for Pravus didn't resurrect the dead—as he'd told me it would. Instead, it brought Cinolth back to life. It wasn't a stone that I'd retrieved. It was Cinolth's heart. Dragons are apparently difficult—if not impossible—to kill. So, I've basically ensured the destruction of the world."

Theyn shook her head. *"I can't believe you've brought the most evil being to have ever walked this world back into it. You may as well have brought Dizäfär here."*

"Yeah… lesson learned: never trust an evil wizard, even if they've promised to raise your family from the dead." Nardus chuckled, more from nervous guilt than amusement. "Anyway, Cinolth was about to kill me. That's why I came here."

He glanced toward the ceiling and frowned. "To be honest, I'm not sure how I escaped. Based on the rules of traveling here, I should've been prevented from coming. You cannot travel here as a means of escaping death, and I most certainly did. Then again, those rules seem to have no relevance or hold over me. I've broken more than one of them on multiple occasions."

Theyn cocked her head. *"What else have you lied to me about, wizard?"*

"Wizard?" Nardus spat on the floor and pointed his finger at Theyn. "Don't you dare accuse me of being something so vile. I'm as much a wizard as you're a spectre." He spat again.

"You walk between places—across great distances in the blink of an eye—and you don't believe you do so with the power of mezhik?" Theyn laughed, but it sounded like small bursts of growls. *"What else would it be?"*

Nardus frowned as he thought about it. No answer came to mind. He shrugged and shook his head slowly. "I can't explain how I'm able to do it, but it's certainly *not* mezhik. Don't you think I'd know if I were a wizard and could wield mezhik? My life would've turned out much different. I would've shielded my family from the arrows and destroyed the bastards who attacked us with a single thought."

"You're a strange man, Nardus. It's just one of the many reasons why I love you."

Love… Everything I've done for it has repaid me with grief.

Nardus surveyed the room again. "Speaking of strange men, where's Gnaud? You didn't eat him, did you?" He laughed.

"I…" Theyn lowered her head. *"Forgive me, Nardus."*

Nardus swallowed hard and clutched his stomach. "My God, Theyn…"

Theyn's cat-like eyes misted. *"Please listen before you judge me."*

Gnaud… Nardus closed his eyes and nodded, lost for words.

Theyn continued, *"For the first few days I held my condition in check, clinging to my identity with thoughts of you. But my condition raged within. Several times I blacked out for many minutes, waking to find myself surrounded by destruction and Gnaud in a panic.*

"I warned him to keep his distance from me, but he'd convinced himself that he could find an answer as to how to cure or control my condition. Then, as before, my last thread of sanity snapped, and I lost control. My condition consumed me within a few minutes. From that moment, I've remembered nothing until your arrival."

Nardus exhaled, stood, and dusted off his trousers. He looked at Theyn and held her gaze for several minutes. *It's not your fault. It's mine.*

Nardus rubbed the scars on his left bicep. "I'm the last person that would ever have the right to judge you."

Theyn rose and sniffed the air. *"The wood shelves and leather-bound books overpower almost every other scent, but I do smell traces of blood as well.*

Nothing of death, but this place is massive. He could be anywhere or gone."

Nardus shook his head. "Gnaud would never leave this place. This is his home. He's gotta be here somewhere."

Theyn moaned softly. *"If he's dead, I'll never forgive myself."*

And I might never forgive you.

Nardus looked to his right. The destruction impressed him. Nary a shelf still stood, nor a book unrent. *Gnaud, if you're still alive, will you forgive us?*

Nardus cleared his throat. "Gnaud, it's Nardus," he yelled. "If you can hear me, answer me. Or make some noise if you can't talk."

A minute passed in silence.

"Gnaud!" Nardus's voice thundered through the Great Library.

Theyn bounded up and over two mounds of carnage and stopped abruptly atop a third. She looked back at Nardus, her tail tucked between her hind legs and her head low. Nardus scrambled over the piles, tripped, fell, and gouged his hand on the splintered end of a chair leg. He cursed loudly, picked himself back up, and pushed forward.

The wound stung his hand, but the thought of Gnaud dead stung his heart. *Ɂäṯūr, don't let him be dead.*

Nardus reached Theyn and stopped next to her. He met her gaze briefly, but then his gaze locked onto the tufts of fur and the pool of dried blood at the bottom of the mound they stood atop.

Nardus's hands dampened, his breathing shallowed, and he dropped to his knees. Pain ripped into his heart, a feeling he'd experienced too many times in his life.

Theyn's voice quivered in his mind. *"I'm so sorry, Nardus. I don't remember any of it. Forgive me."*

Nardus clenched his fists. *Forgive you? How could I?* Anger welled in his stomach, swelled in his chest, rose into his throat, and burst from his lips as a bone-chilling, guttural scream.

Theyn slunk back. *"Kill me if you must. I will not fight you. I deserve nothing less."*

Nardus rose to his knees and shook his fist at her. "No! I've been down that road. Killing the men who took the lives of my wife and youngest daughter brought me no satisfaction. I've suffered endlessly since that day. Nothing I did brought them back, and nothing ever will."

His chest convulsed, and he sobbed. *Have I lost hope? Will I never see you again Vitara? Savannah? And what of you, Shardan? Do you still live, or did I bury you with your mother?*

Nardus took a deep breath, wiped his eyes, and looked down at Theyn. "So no, I'm not killing you, Theyn. I've lost almost everyone I've ever cared about or loved. I'm not losing you, too. Do you hear me? Whether I choose to forgive you or not is irrelevant. I will not abandon you."

We'll be damned together.

Theyn crawled over to Nardus. *"How will I live with myself knowing that I ate your friend? I can't even fathom having done so."*

Nardus couldn't wrap his mind around it either. He pulled his hair back and groaned. "I don't know. Every time I think my life can't possibly get worse it does." He punched the remnants of a book next to him.

Theyn jerked upright and craned her neck forward. She blinked several times and then howled. *"At the far end of the room, there's a door with a bloody handprint on it!"*

Nardus jumped to his feet. He squinted but couldn't even find a door let alone discern that a bloody handprint marred its surface.

He looked down at Theyn. "Are you certain?"

She nodded. *"I can see for miles. How do you think I spotted you in the middle of the lava fields on Incendia Island?"*

Nardus ignored the question and bolted ahead, Theyn at his side. "Gnaud!"

CHAPTER TWO

Nothing in life could've prepared Aria for the experience of riding a dragon. The speed alone frightened her, and the weightless sensation while diving recklessly toward the ground drove her stomach into her throat and frayed her nerves, but the sense of complete freedom it provided left her begging for more when Cinolth landed atop the southern rampart of Galondu Castle.

She slid from Cinolth's neck and down his long arm, landing on her feet, but the rain-slicked stone and her wobbly legs tumbled her to the ground. She grunted as pain flashed in her knees and spread the length of her legs. They'd flown perhaps ten or fifteen minutes, but the toll it took on her inner thighs and her buttocks would certainly present itself in the form of bruises by the evening; the next morning at the latest. Despite the pain and fear, she wouldn't hesitate to take flight again.

Aria had seen Rídärz Drezhn depicted on tapestries and paintings throughout the castle, each sitting in a saddle fashioned for the dragon they rode. They certainly looked like they'd be more comfortable than sitting on rock-hard scales and hugging a long, bony spike.

Perhaps I'll commission a saddle of my own. But would Cinolth allow me to use it on him?

After spending several days with him in her head and understanding the depth of his pride and arrogance, she doubted it. Still, she'd find a way to broach the subject, but not until she understood him and their bond better.

When the time comes to go to war, he'll understand the need of it. At least she hoped he would.

"Today, chaos will rain down on the Ancient Realm." Cinolth's presence and his voice in her head startled Aria and pulled her from her own thoughts.

Having no experience communicating with dragons, she didn't know if she should answer back in her head or aloud. Commonsense told her to speak aloud, but he'd chosen to speak to her mind. Should she do the same, or did he have a reason for doing so?

Can he not speak aloud?

"*I can,*" said Cinolth in her mind again. "*However, you may find my speaking voice both harsh and difficult to decipher, so I chose to mindspeak for brevity and clarity.*"

Mindspeak…

She'd never heard the term before, but it lent itself to a clear understanding of what it entailed. But could she mindspeak with anyone or just dragons?

"*You may speak to me as you wish. My hearing is quite good. Far better than yours. Be aware that you can mindspeak with me at far greater distances than your voice would allow as well. If you can feel my presence, you can mindspeak with me.*"

Can he always read my thoughts? She gasped. *Can others?*

"*Have you learned nothing yet?*" Cinolth's condescension grated her nerves.

Heat shot up her neck and warmed her cheeks. She crossed her arms and gazed up at the brooding clouds, but the rain proved too heavy. Instead, she focused her eyes on Atrum Moenia far below. "Pravus promised to teach me how to use my powers, but he never has time to do so. Also, it's hard to learn anything when I've worn *zäbräzär* since before I knew I had mezhik."

"*Never let that collar touch your skin again.*"

"But Pravus says I'm a danger to everyone until I learn how to control and use my mezhik."

Flames shot from Cinolth's mouth and lit the dark sky. The rain sizzled as it evaporated. It reminded Aria of frying bacon. "*He's a liar. That collar leeches your mezhik energy and stores it, even when you're not trying to use your mezhik.*"

"I don't understand." She fingered her neck where the collar had been for so long. "What purpose does it serve?"

"*Pravus accesses that stored energy to enhance his own mezhik abilities. He is nothing but a weak and pathetic man without you. That is why he married you and insisted that you bind your soul with his. Don't you see? Through the use of prophecy and deception, he created you. His agenda has nothing to do with love for you. I warned you about him, but you chose to marry him and spread your legs for him.*"

Had Pravus used her? Paranoia gripped her as her mind spun through memories of her past. How *had* he known about her and where to find her?

"You've haunted my dreams for years," Pravus had said when they'd first met in Dragnus's office.

But he'd saved her from Dragnus, hadn't he? She took his word at face value, but she'd always had reservations about his intent and doubted he disclosed everything to her despite assuring her that he would. Every time she discovered something new about him or something he'd done, he never denied it, but he kept more secrets than a pack of tongueless thieves.

"Do you know this about Pravus, or are you just guessing?"

"The man reeks of weakness and seeks power wherever he can find it. If you doubt my word, ask Wizard Wrik."

Aria sighed and waved her hand dismissively. "No matter the reason or intention, I'm bound to him. There is one thing that troubles me though. Can he read my thoughts as you can?"

"When I'm in your mind, can you feel my presence?" asked Cinolth.

"Yes."

"Good. This will be true of anyone entering or probing your thoughts. Only dragons, wizards, and sorceresses have the ability to force-enter another's mind. You must learn to guard your mind against it, especially when it comes to your foes. Imagine how easy it would be for your enemy to kill you if they knew your every thought and move. Even worse, imagine if they controlled your actions and turned you against your allies."

Aria turned and peered up at Cinolth. "Will you teach me?"

Smoke bellowed from Cinolth's nostrils. *"I will, but only because we share a bond through your blood."*

She had a feeling that the reason was far greater than a simple bond, but she didn't press Cinolth on the matter.

Less than a half hour later, she'd mastered the techniques of guarding her mind and thoughts from her enemies. However, she sensed Cinolth retained access to her mind beyond what she felt, and her shoulders tensed with unease. Cinolth denied it with a scoff, so she let it go.

"Thank you," said Aria.

Aria's white, rain-soaked shirt clung to her sides, its buttons still undone from the stone ceremony. With wet, exposed breasts she should've been freezing in the cold rain, but Cinolth produced an aura of heat that warmed her and the surrounding air. A belly full of fire had many uses.

Aria pulled her shirt closed and began buttoning it. "What did you mean earlier when you said that chaos would rain down on the Ancient Realm today?"

Cinolth roared and spewed a column of fire skyward. *"There are a hundred thousand humans across the realm who are lying in a comatose state and will awaken at my command. They will rise up and slaughter everyone around them, both friend and foe."*

Alderan's face flashed in Aria's mind. She tensed. "Not just how is that possible, but what is the purpose of the attacks?"

"Humans are a plague that devastates our world with every thought and action. When I lived before, two factions of humans warred: the zhiftäd and the ʊnzhiftäd. The ʊnzhiftäd believed that any person or creature that possessed the ability to wield mezhik should be imprisoned and, in some cases, eradicated.

"I fought alongside the zhiftäd to bring justice to the world, but a select few of the zhiftäd known as Ūrdär Dhef Ձäfn Dhä betrayed us. Those traitors killed my servant, Magus Carac, and then tried to kill me by removing my heart, but they didn't have the means to destroy it. So, they took my heart and locked it up in a place where no one could ever retrieve it."

Aria nodded with understanding. "Until Nardus came along."

"Yes." Cinolth crushed the top of the rampart barrier in his clawed hand. *"So, now I will do everything in my power to bring the human race to its knees and plunge it toward extinction."*

"I understand why you think this will satisfy you, but your plan is flawed."

Cinolth's head snaked down to her level. Rage pulsed in his red, reptilian eyes, each the size of her head. "You question my intelligence?" His thick, gravelly voice shook the rampart. Her shirt and hair dried instantly from the heat of his breath.

Aria backed away with her arms raised. She choked on the sulfuric fumes from his breath. "Never!"

"Then what?"

"First off, *I* am human."

"And I'll let you live." His voice returned to her head.

"You and I both know that you have no choice in that."

Cinolth's eyes narrowed. *"Do not fool yourself, girl. If I kill you, you will stay dead, but I can be resurrected again."*

Aria hadn't thought of that, and she didn't want to dwell on it, so she pressed on. "I agree that many humans are evil, but not *all* of them. Pravus and I have gathered an army of our own. There are gnolls, orcs, zheballin, giants, ogres, and humans that will fight for us. We will march on the Three Kingdoms soon and gain control of the Ancient Realm.

"Would it not make more sense if we were to join our forces? A coordinated attack would prove far more effective than random acts of violence throughout the realm.

"Not only that, but word of a risen dragon will have traveled far and wide already. There are many people who will see these attacks and quickly conclude that you're the one behind them. They will come after you with everything they have and drive you back down to the pit you crawled out of."

"I'd love to see them try."

"Trust me when I say that I have the capacity to be the greatest mage to ever live. Teach me everything you know, and we will be unstoppable."

"You are full of yourself."

"Perhaps, but there are many prophecies written about me. Together, we can fulfill them."

"To what end? What would I gain from it?"

Aria needed to stroke Cinolth's ego and knew just how to accomplish it. "It's simple. Instead of killing all the humans, we'll enslave them and force them to worship you as a god and make daily sacrifices to you."

Cinolth stared into the distance. Raindrops sizzled on his scales, producing a barrier of fog around him and her. *"To humans, I'm already a god."*

Aria brooded. "Then what will satisfy you? What is it you seek?"

Cinolth said nothing, but memories flashed through Aria's mind. Not her memories, but his. A legion of dragons. They stood opposed to him. Banished him from his home. She'd never felt such hatred and rage. Humans had only been the tipping point. A name entered her thoughts: *Quldrai.*

Aria rested her hand on Cinolth's leg. His red eye narrowed as he glanced down at her. His voice shook her. "And what is it you think you understand? What brings that smile to your lips?"

Aria stared into his eyes for several beats before speaking. "Do this for me. Join our forces, and I will ensure your revenge against Quldrai."

Cinolth stomped the rampart, and it trembled beneath Aria's feet. Smoke and fire joined the words from his curled lips. "And what do you know of that beast?"

"Only what you've shown me." Aria closed her eyes. "Together, we will bring her reign to an end, and you'll take your rightful position as king of the dragons."

When Aria opened her eyes again, she stared right into Cinolth's right eye. His hot breath billowed her shirt. Her heart thundered in her ears as she stood her ground and awaited his response.

An eternity of moments passed before he mindspoke to her. *"My forces will join yours, and we'll take the Ancient Realm by storm. In a few hours, my followers will awaken and begin their journey here."*

"Thank you," she mindspoke. *"You've made a wise decision, as I knew you would. Quldrai will not live another year."*

"Disappoint me, and it will be the last thing you ever do. Now, I must go feed. Twelve hundred years without food is far too long." His mind withdrew from hers.

I must learn how to do that.

Aria smiled to herself. "Very well. I will let Pravus know your decision."

Cinolth snorted and took to the sky, his wings a gale force in her face. Aria covered her eyes and stumbled backward. Rain poured down, soaking her once again. She pushed her matted hair behind her ears. Cinolth's presence faded from her mind as he disappeared into the blackened sky.

Cinolth would join them. She'd never been happier of anything.

Pravus will certainly be pleased... but I'll never trust him again.

CHAPTER THREE

Rayah stretched her arms and legs and yawned. The haze of sleep still lingered, and the morning sunlight filtering in through the front windows didn't help. She rolled onto her side and slid right out of the rocking chair. She landed hard on the wooden floor and grunted, every bone jarred.

She sighed. *A perfect start to the day.*

She rubbed the sleep from her eyes and stared at the vaulted ceiling suspended above her. Three large oak beams stretched the distance from the front of the living area to the back wall that separated it from the kitchen. She didn't know how someone could've moved such large beams into place without the use of mezhik.

Mezhik ruled the world—at least it did hers. Would the world she knew exist without it? She doubted it, and the thought of it left her cold. She'd heard tales about the far reaches of Centauria banning mezhik and sacrificing any who were caught wielding it. Such rumors circulated every few years like seasons, but their absurdity didn't prevent her mind from lingering on them.

How would she cope without her mezhik? More to the point, how would she cope without her wings? *Love. Nothing else matters.* She'd know soon enough.

The impending change scared her, but she understood the sacrifice she'd be making. She knew exactly what she'd be giving up for Alderan the moment she had realized that they'd bonded.

Everything. I'll sacrifice everything for you, Alderan.

How would she tell him though? How would she explain it to him in a way he'd understand? Could she do so? Would he still marry her if he knew the cost she must pay?

Should I tell him now, or wait until after it cannot be undone?

She brooded over the fallout she'd face from Alderan no matter which path she chose.

No. I cannot keep this from him. He'd never forgive me if I did. He must know, and I must tell him while I still have the courage to do so.

Rayah sat up. "Alderan? Are you awake?"

He didn't answer. *Maybe he's still asleep.* She turned around to check on him, but his rocking chair sat empty. She stood, pressed her hands against the middle of her back, and leaned backward until her back finally popped. A sigh of relief escaped from her lips.

She walked over to the couch. Eshtak wasn't there either. The door to Savric's room stood wide open. She walked over to the doorway and peeked inside the room. *Empty… where is everyone?*

Jealousy bubbled in her mind like a festering wound. She balled her fists. *Why didn't they wake me?* She stormed across the living area, yanked the front door open, and stepped out onto the porch. Birds chirped and sang, and leaves rustled in the trees, but the porch and yard were empty.

The crisp morning air caressed Rayah's bare arms and legs, transforming her skin from a silky-smooth porcelain to bumpy gooseflesh. She raised her shoulders, squeezed her arms tight to her body, and trembled for a moment, forcing warmth back into her bones. She scowled.

Have you abandoned me too, Spring?

Rayah turned around and marched back into the house, through the living area, and into the kitchen. Stacks of books littered the counters and covered the small kitchen table. She rounded the table and gasped. "Zerenity!"

Zerenity lay on the floor on her side. Her hair covered her face, and black veins spiderwebbed across her arms and legs. Rayah gasped again.

Dear Ƶäṭūr! When had she become infected?

Rayah knelt next to Zerenity and gingerly turned her onto her back. Zerenity's head flopped to the side, exposing more black veins that ran the length of her neck and marred her face like cracked pottery. She lifted one of Zerenity's eyelids and confirmed that her entire pupil and iris had turned black.

Just like in Alderan's dream.

Zerenity's chest rose and fell, and the black veins in her neck pulsed.

Rayah patted Zerenity's cheek. "Can you hear me?" Zerenity didn't respond, so Rayah patted her cheek a bit harder. Still, she didn't respond.

Rayah huffed. *You never listen to me.*

She took a deep breath, pulled her hand back, and slapped Zerenity hard on the cheek. *Smack!* Zerenity didn't even let out a peep, but a red handprint bloomed on her cheek where the black veins didn't surface. Shame washed over Rayah like an ocean wave.

I'm sorry, Zerenity. I don't know what came over me.

Rayah massaged Zerenity's cheek, but the red mark lingered. Laughter came from beyond the kitchen. *Eshtak!* Rayah jumped up and ran into the living area.

Savric patted the top of Eshtak's head. "You are a strange lit—"

"It's Zerenity!" Rayah's chest tightened, and she erupted with sobs.

Savric moved toward her. "My dear girl, what has happened?"

Rayah gathered herself and pointed toward the kitchen. "She's on the floor. I tried to wake her, but she didn't respond." She couldn't bring herself to tell him about the black veins.

Savric's eyes widened, and then he disappeared in a flash.

"Bugger-bees!" Savric's shout came from the kitchen.

Eshtak ran past Rayah and into the kitchen, but she just stood in the middle of the living area, rooted to the floor with fear. She couldn't stomach seeing Zerenity like that again. Understanding as to why Alderan's dreams had disturbed him so much filled her.

Ƹäṭūr, save her, and give me the strength to face what must be done.

She looked around the room and that's when it hit her. All Alderan's things were missing: his bow, his pack, and his clothes. Bitterness swelled in her heart.

Even after our talk you still went home?

She nearly cursed his name, but then a revelation came to her. *He knew about Zerenity.*

"That's why you were so adamant about finding a cure." Rayah sank to the floor.

Without her, who will train him? How can he possibly save the world on his own?

Another thought, dark and without hope, hit her like a brick to the face.

Can the world still be saved, or is it too late?

Rayah's heart pounded as despair rose in her throat like bile. She quickly gathered her things and headed into Zerenity's room.

"Where is girl?" Eshtak's call came from the living area.

She slipped into Zerenity's closet and eased the door shut. Her pulse raced, and perspiration moistened her palms. Guilt squeezed the air from her lungs and left her breathless.

Forgive me, Master Savric. I'll return as soon as I can.

She struggled through many rows of clothing before reaching the mirror at the back of the closet. She wrapped her hand around the mirror's ornate wooden frame and pressed her forehead against it.

You can do this, Rayah. Master Savric will understand.

The closet door cracked open, spilling light into the dark closet. "Wizard man needs girl."

Rayah stood still and held her breath.

Go away, Eshtak. I must find Alderan.

Twice in her life she'd traveled through a mirror. The first time was when Silas dragged her through the mirror in Alderan's basement and into the burning castle. It'd happened so quickly that she didn't have time to process the experience. Fear for her life had muddled her memory of it as well.

The other time came the day she, Alderan, Master Savric, and Zerenity had traveled from Alderan's house in Viscus D'Silva to Zerenity's house in Tyrosha. She remembered everything about it: the static shock of mezhik when she touched it, the cold, liquid glass caressing her skin, and the sense of detached limbs when she stuck her arms through it.

She cleared her mind and concentrated on Alderan's house. She placed the palm of her left hand against the mirror's surface. Immediately, the surface turned from warm-and-hard to cold-and-wet, and her palm sank into it until she couldn't feel it anymore.

Through the mirror she saw the room where she'd been captured by Silas, lit like the heavens by the mirror's frame. She gasped and then quickly covered her mouth. She'd forgotten the depth of its majestic beauty. Butterflies fluttered in the pit of her stomach.

On her side of the mirror, Zerenity's closet brightened and several grunts shattered the silence. Rayah glanced back over her shoulder and froze. Clothes swayed on wooden hangers and filled the closet with soft moans as the hangers rubbed against the wooden dowels that kept them suspended.

The last row of clothes parted and Eshtak stepped through them. Rayah's hand pulled away from the mirror as her arm dropped to her side. Eshtak's glowing, lime-green eyes glistened with tears.

She met his gaze, but only held it for a moment. She turned and focused her attention back on the mirror. Her heart ached with guilt, and her pulse rose.

Now or never, Rayah.

She took a deep breath, but her hand didn't move from her side.

"Eshtak cares for lady. Eshtak not lose lady." Eshtak grabbed Rayah's shoulder and gently pulled on it. "Eshtak take girl to wizard man."

The room through the mirror faded, and her own ghostly reflection replaced it. She closed her eyes.

I cannot abandon my duty. Master Savric needs me, and I know Alderan will return.

Telling Alderan the truth about everything would have to wait. It always did. She opened her eyes and met Eshtak's gaze through the mirror's reflection. She reached up and patted the back of his hand. "Let's go see what we can do for Zerenity."

† † †

Distance. Only distance separated Zerenity from her dark master. Her creator. The Dark One.

Time. How long would it be until he called her to serve him? She didn't know, but the desire to be in his presence consumed her every thought, and the anticipation of meeting him face-to-face left her nerves frayed.

Darkness. Cold, forlorn, and swaddled in darkness, she waited. Nothing else in the world existed. Nothing else needed to. Soon, her master would extinguish the light and usher in an age of darkness for all eternity. And, in that darkness, he'd reign forever. A god to all who would bow to him, and a reaper to all who would defy him.

Longing. Zerenity reached into the darkness and spoke to him through her mind. *"Call upon me, my dark master. You are the Ancient One. The Dark One. The Fire Breather. A god to all men, women, and beasts. I am your slave, willing to serve you until death takes me. Allow me to do your bidding. I beg it of you. Denying me would be worse than death itself."*

† † †

Savric leaned back against the kitchen cabinets and rested his eyes. *Dear Ɛäṭūr, tell me what to do. How can I stop this poison from killing my brother and the love of my life? Mezhik does nothing for them now, and I fear I am useless.*

How many more of those he loved would meet the same fate? Would anything be able to stop it, or did they fight an impregnable enemy? *Have I lost faith in the prophecy? In the boy? In us all?* He dug deep within himself, but only a sputtering spark remained of the eternal flame of hope he'd carried for so long.

"Master Savric, tell us what to do. How can we help?"

Sweet, innocent Rayah. Savric opened his eyes. She and Eshtak stood to his right, their arms interlocked.

Savric peered over the pair and frowned. "Where is the boy?"

Rayah eyed the floor. "I don't know. I mean… I think I know, but I can't be certain. He was gone when I woke up this morning. All of his things are gone too."

"Gone… Heavens, dear girl." Savric stroked his beard but it failed to comfort him the way it often did. "And where might you surmise he has ventured off to?"

Rayah released Eshtak's arm and twirled one of her chestnut curls around her finger. "I'm pretty sure he's gone back home. He told me that there might be a book in his basement that could help Master Qotan."

Savric cocked his head. "A book to help Qotan and Reni?"

Rayah shook her head. "I don't believe so. Zerenity mentioned that she'd read a book about what had happened in Intus. I think he's trying to figure out a way to make Qotan whole once more."

Savric groaned. "I cherish his enthusiasm and relish the thought of having my brother back with us all again, but this affliction upon Reni and Qotan must be dealt with first. If the boy had known Reni suffered as well, he would not have left."

Rayah looked up at him, her hazel eyes glistening with moisture. "Now that I think back on it, I'm certain he's aware of Zerenity's condition. Perhaps that's why they both desperately sought a solution in these books."

Savric curled his stiff fingers into a fist. Arthritic pain pulsed within his whitened knuckles. "I trust that you are correct." He relaxed his hand. "I will go find him and bring—"

Zerenity rose from the floor. "Yes, my master. I'm coming."

"Reni!" Savric rushed to her side and put an arm around her shoulders. Heat radiated through her clothes.

Zerenity's black eyes stared at nothing, and her blackened lips moved in silence. Savric's arm dropped to his side as Zerenity moved forward through the kitchen without glancing at any of them. Rayah and Eshtak stepped out of the way when Zerenity reached their position.

Savric, Rayah, and Eshtak followed Zerenity out of the kitchen and into the living area. Movement to his left froze Savric mid-stride. Qotan lumbered out of his room, a blanket wrapped around his ankle. He shook it off as he made his way toward the front door.

"Brother?" Savric's voice croaked from his mouth.

Zerenity opened the front door and stepped out onto the porch. Savric teleported from where he stood to the front porch in a blink, just behind Zerenity. He grabbed Zerenity by the shoulder and pulled her back around to face him. She didn't resist. In fact, she did nothing but stare ahead. Savric shook her but she didn't respond.

Vapor plumed from Zerenity's skin and clothing, creating a hauntingly beautiful aura of yellow-and-orange around her. It unsettled Savric. He gazed into the dark inkwells where her eyes used to be.

Savric reached out to Zerenity with his mind. *"Reni, can you hear me?"*

Hatred and an infinite darkness lashed out at him. Pain erupted in his temples as he fought back the sudden attack. He pulled his mind back and erected protective barriers, but a deep cold ached his bones and sorrow wracked him.

It took every bit of his strength to stay upright and rein in his emotions. He closed his eyes and prayed to his God—the one true God.

Ɂäṭūr, I ask for Your strength. Help me gain understanding of the affliction they suffer. How can I help them? My God, I beg of you, tell me what to do!

Savric opened his eyes just as Qotan walked past and brushed his shoulder. Qotan traversed the steps down into the yard, vapor plumes trailing him. Rayah and Eshtak joined them on the porch, their faces paler than normal and their eyes wide.

Savric shook Zerenity by the shoulders. "Reni!" She didn't even blink. He released her, and she turned and followed Qotan through the yard and beyond the tree line.

"What should we do?" asked Rayah, her eyes still wide and full of fear.

Savric's mind spun as he stood on the porch like a statue. What could they do? He needed to delve into the prophetic writings further, but time didn't favor them; it favored no one. His stomach lurched as a thought entered his mind. He didn't like it, but nothing else presented itself.

He pulled on his beard. "Rayah, you will go find Alderan. Eshtak and I will follow Reni and Qotan."

Rayah frowned. "Wouldn't it be safer for Eshtak to go with me?"

Savric stomped his foot. "Feathers, girl! We do not possess the time to argue this further. I am uncertain if Eshtak would survive going through the mirror with you."

"Eshtak uses mirror. Leaves home through mirror long ago."

Savric cocked his head as he eyed Eshtak. "As you say, but it is of no consequence. I may need your assistance in keeping track of Reni and Qotan if they should split up."

Rayah nodded, her cheeks flushed. "I'll take my book and send you a message when I find Alderan so that we can meet up with you."

The book. Savric sighed. "It will do you no good. I am no longer in possession of its twin."

Rayah gasped. "What—"

Savric raised his hand. "A tale for another time, dear girl. However, I must insist you give me yours. I may need it for purposes as of yet unknown. As for how I will locate you, we must find another solution."

Eshtak tugged on his sleeve. "Eshtak mirror?"

Savric rubbed the top of Eshtak's bald head. "Perhaps we can use your mirror, but I am unfamiliar with its mezhik and its range. We will need another solution as well."

Eshtak ran back inside, pirouetting through the open door.

Savric eyed the two fir trees through which Qotan and Zerenity had disappeared into the forest. *We must go before we lose them.*

Rayah stepped out onto the porch. "Can you track me with a spell?"

Savric shook his head but smiled wearily. "Tracking spells cannot be used on flesh. However, they can be attached to inanimate objects such as your brooch. Their reliability is questionable at best though."

Eshtak returned to the porch, two brass-handled mirrors in one hand and Qotan's staff in the other. He handed the staff to Savric and one of the mirrors to Rayah.

Eshtak eyed the mirror and spun in a circle. "Eshtak sees girl."

"And I see you." Rayah set the mirror down on the bench, unpinned her brooch, and stared at it for several moments. "I shall pray that Ɂäţūr makes my brooch reliable." She handed it to Savric with a trembling hand. "Do what you must."

"You have nothing to fear, dear girl. The spell will not harm the brooch." Savric closed his eyes and searched his memories for the right spell. The word finally arose from the thick fog shrouding his mind. *Thank you, Ɂäţūr.*

He held the brooch in his right palm and concentrated his mind on it. *"Ţräíɀ."* The warmth of mezhik seeped from his open palm, and a faint, yellow light surrounded the brooch. The light pulsed for several moments and then faded, along with the warmth.

Savric handed the brooch back to Rayah. "This must suffice. Whatever you do, do not lose it."

Rayah shook her head as she pinned the brooch back onto her shirt. "I won't." She looked back up at him, her hazel eyes brimming with moisture.

Savric cupped Rayah's cheek. "My dear girl, everything will be as it should."

Rayah pulled away. Her gaze fell to the porch as tears streaked her cheeks. "But there's something I didn't tell you…"

"We have but a few moments." He peered back at the forest. "Make haste with your words."

"I think one of the vines bit me too. My side has been sore and itchy ever since I discovered them. I've been too afraid to look at it."

"Bugger-bees! Why have you kept this knowledge to yourself until now?"

"Everyone had so much stress already with Master Qotan and Zerenity. I didn't want to make things worse."

Savric eyed Rayah. His heart ached for her. "What you intended to say is that Alderan would have abandoned everything to try and save you."

Rayah sniffed and wiped her nose. "Am I going to become like Zerenity and Master Qotan?"

"If what you say is true, you would have been bitten before Reni." He stroked his beard. "Lift up your shirt and let me examine your wound."

Rayah pulled up her shirt. "Is it bad?"

Savric bent down. The wound on Rayah's side looked similar to what Qotan had described of the one he'd suffered. However, Rayah's wound showed no signs of black, spiderwebbed veins. Instead, a puffy, dark-red ring encircled the wound.

"Looks as though you might have scratched yourself on a branch or something, but there are no signs of you being infected like Qotan and Reni."

Rayah exhaled loudly. "Thank Ꙅäʈūr."

"Indeed. Hold still, and I will speed up your recovery." Savric placed his hand over the wound and drew upon his mezhik. A warm, yellow light emanated from his palm and penetrated Rayah's side.

Rayah giggled. "That tickles and prickles."

Eshtak took a deep breath. "Eshtak smells sunshine." He twirled off the porch and danced around in the yard.

The yellow light faded and Savric straightened. "I believe that will help your discomfort."

Rayah hugged Savric. "Thank you." She pulled back. "I know you must leave now, but what do you want me to do once I've found Alderan?"

Savric pulled the hood of his cloak over the top of his head. "Pray he has found a cure to this poison and a way to make Qotan whole again. We will meet back here soon." He turned and took the steps down to the yard. "Eshtak, come."

He didn't look back as he crossed the yard and headed into the vast sea of fir trees. Zerenity, his heart and soul, trudged through the forest ahead of them, and he'd rather be damned than lose track of her.

† † †

Rayah went back inside Zerenity's house, gathered her belongings, and returned to the back of Zerenity's closet. She stared at the girl in the mirror and the glimmering wings at her back. *Will this be the last time?* The thought rent her to the core.

Every last one of them had sacrifices to make, some bigger than others, but it would all be for naught if Alderan didn't save the world. *He can't save the world without me.* The thought startled her and warmed her cheeks, but she couldn't deny the truth of it.

The girl in the mirror would soon fade from existence, but she would survive. She must. *I am his protector.* The world rested on Alderan's shoulders, but she lightened his load with her unyielding love and dedication to him.

She placed her hand on the mirror. *I am coming, my love.* Her reflection faded as the mirror's surface grew wet and cold, and what lay beyond it left her breathless and petrified.

A dim corridor stretched before Rayah, its breadth wide. Black stone walls, floors, and ceilings extended beyond her vision. Black metal sconces hung from the walls at evenly spaced intervals, alternating from one wall to the other. Torches burned, popped, and smoked in the sconces but offered little light to brighten the corridor.

Alderan?

A man dressed in black armor stepped into the corridor ten paces away. He glanced Rayah's way and then took two steps in the opposite direction before wheeling back around. He squinted at her and lowered his pike.

"Halt!" He stormed toward her, his armor clanking together and his boots pounding the stone floor with each step.

He nearly came upon her before she roused from her stupor. She backed away from the mirror, ripe with fear. "Don't come any closer." Her voice croaked.

He poked his pike through the mirror, its tip little more than a foot from her midsection. "You dare bark orders at me?"

Rayah stepped back until her back touched the closest row of clothes. "Are you so foolish? I'm trying to save your life!"

The man snarled and stepped through the mirror. "You're—"

His eyes widened, and his pike dropped from his hand, thumping against the wooden floor. His armor followed suit, piling on the floor with a loud crash. In a blink, nothing remained of him but a charred pile of ash.

The mirror's surface returned to a reflection of the closet.

The stench of singed hair and burned flesh assaulted Rayah's nostrils and stung her eyes. She gagged and coughed and shook her finger at the ashes. "This isn't my fault. I warned you."

Rayah huffed, stepped around the pile of armor, and faced the mirror once again. She raised her hand but couldn't bring herself to touch the mirror again. Twice, she'd been attacked through a stupid mirror.

The closet started spinning as her past reared its ugly, forked-tongue head. Her eyes rolled back in her head, and her heart thundered in her ears, drowning out the world.

Buckled knees pulled Rayah to the floor as Sardis's scaly arm slithered out of the past and wrapped around her throat. His clammy hand clamped over her mouth.

Sardis's voiced hissed in the back of her mind. *"He'sss dead."*

"No!" she screamed.

CHAPTER FOUR

Calen stood in front of the cold hearth, staring into the depths of darkness and blackened logs. The fire had died out several days ago, but he didn't care. A fire might warm his extremities, but it'd do nothing for his cold and broken heart.

Three weeks ago, Master Savric had disappeared without so much as a parting word. He'd never done that before, and it both scared and hurt Calen. Soon after that, Calen's aunt fell ill after tilling the garden under. Her skin began turning white, and her blue and purple veins turned black. In the last few days, she'd become unresponsive, keeping to her room and mumbling with incoherence. After several failed attempts, Calen finally persuaded the town's natural healer, Erlich Mann, to come examine his aunt.

"Calen?"

Calen turned around and faced Healer Mann. "What's wrong with her? What can I do?"

Healer Mann stood across the small room, his fingers lodged in his thinning, peppered hair. "Look, son, what I'm about to tell you will be hard to hear. As you might've heard, there are more than a hundred cases like your aunt's in Daltura alone. What's more disturbing is that it seems to be a widespread problem, daily reports coming in from across the Ancient Realm bearing similar news."

Calen wiped his nose. "I know, but I need my aunt. What can you do for her?"

Healer Mann removed his spectacles and wiped his eyes and brow with a kerchief. His slumped shoulders dropped farther as he eyed Calen. "I must be brutally honest with you. It would be unfair otherwise." He returned his spectacles to his face. "There's nothing to be done because no one knows what's wrong with them."

Calen stalked forward with his hands clenched at his sides. Anger brewed in the pit of his stomach and rose into his chest, tightening it. "There must be *something* you can do for her."

Healer Mann's gaze fell to the floor and his head shook slowly. "You should prepare yourself for her death, son."

Calen stopped dead in his tracks, his anger abated. *Death?* His pounding heart sounded in his ears, shaking him with every beat. He nodded, his throat so tight he couldn't talk or breathe. Tears streaked his face.

Healer Mann stepped forward and patted Calen's shoulder twice. A fly would've landed harder. "I'll leave you to it." He stepped back and eyed the door. "As you can imagine, I'm quite busy. Because of the circumstance, I won't charge you for the visit." He exited the house, closing the door behind himself.

Calen dropped to his knees. *I don't want you to die, Aunt Tahmara. I still need you. I've started to become a man, but fourteen name days aren't enough to be on my own. Please don't leave me.*

The worst case Calen had ever contemplated involved living with Master Savric if his aunt died, but what would he do now that Master Savric went missing too? Calen had very little to his name. To be exact, he possessed a small coin purse with four copper coins and a few silver ones that he'd earned doing chores for Master Savric.

Calen didn't have enough to live on for long. They were running out of food already. Aunt Tahmara hadn't eaten anything in the last three days. If she had, they'd probably be out of food now. He didn't know how much longer she'd survive without eating or drinking, but so far, she didn't seem worse for wear other than the black veins, pale skin, and lack of interaction. Her ignoring him hurt more than seeing her in such a state.

The floor squeaked behind Calen. He whipped around to find his aunt standing a few feet away.

"Aunt Tahmara?" Calen's voice shook.

Tahmara didn't look Calen's direction or seem to notice him at all. She walked over to the door and opened it. She wore few clothes, not even a jacket, and stepped out into the cold morning. Heat rose from her in vaporous plumes. Calen yelled for her to come back, but she kept walking.

Calen grabbed his coat and ran out the door after her, not bothering to close or lock it behind himself. What he saw outside disturbed him. Dozens of people walked down the road like a mob, none of them speaking or carrying anything except what was on their backs. All of them had pale skin and black veins covering the exposed skin that Calen could see. Several people he didn't know but recognized were amongst the horde. Others, uninfected like him, watched in horror.

Calen ran back inside the house and gathered what little food remained and stuffed it into his pack, along with a blanket. He collected all the coins he could find stashed around the house and stuffed them into his coin purse. Then he grabbed the dagger and scabbard from his aunt's room and rushed back outside. The horde had traveled a full block down the road, but they moved slow.

Calen caught up with his aunt and tried to shake her out of her stupor even though his heart told him it would do no good. Tahmara didn't fight back, but she didn't respond to Calen either. When he released her, she continued walking north with the others. Calen trailed her all the way through Daltura and to the northern town gates. Several people stood at the gates, watching the mass exodus of the infected.

"Good riddance," said an elderly woman. She gestured with two fingers. Calen's cheeks warmed. "Never thought I'd rid myself of the old coot. I pray the gods don't return him."

"Mother wait!" cried several children.

A man spat on the ground. "Ɂäʈūr has cursed them. They travel toward *Ef Demd Dhä*."

Dozens of other people wailed while still others cried. Most people hung back at the gates, wrought with fear, but many children chased after one or both of their parents with abandon.

The road out of Daltura curved toward the northwest, but the horde of infected didn't stick to it. Instead, they headed northeast, trampling through the tall grass. Many stumbled over the uneven ground, several falling to their knees and a few all the way to the ground, but all of them got back up and continued their march. Calen didn't understand what drove them all in the same direction and why they didn't stick to the road. It would've been a far easier path, especially for the children and the elderly.

Is something controlling them? He gasped. *Or someone?* The thought prickled his skin. *Just don't think about it.*

Calen needed to press on before he lost his nerve, the horde, and his aunt. He tried to move forward, but his legs refused to respond, his feet rooted to the ground.

I can't do this. I can't do this. I can't do this.

Nothing in his life had prepared him for a moment like this. In fact, he'd been groomed for the opposite. His mother had died when he was four. His father, a drunken bastard with a streak of rage that rivaled any other, rotted in jail for killing her. If not for Master Savric and Aunt Tahmara, Calen would've lived in the alleys.

Maybe it would've served me better. I'm just a scared, fat kid. What can I possibly do to help them?

Calen scrunched up his face and pulled on his hair. Master Savric would reprimand him for such thoughts. He knew better. Ɛäṭūr had a plan for everyone, even him.

That thought sparked a memory from a month prior. The words of the wizard he'd met at the gates rose in his mind: *"...they will look to you in the time of their greatest need."*

Had that time come? "Is this the moment he spoke of?" Calen could think of no greater need than the one presenting itself right then, but his feet stayed rooted to the ground.

He stared at his feet. Oversized for his height. Perhaps he'd grow into them, but he had his doubts since his father wasn't a tall man. Then again, he bore little resemblance to his father at all.

Don't fail me, feet. I don't want to be nothing forever. And I don't want to be my father.

Calen took a deep breath. He'd never ventured more than a few dozen paces from the town gates before, and the thought of doing so shook him to the core. His arms and legs trembled, both covered in gooseflesh. He'd planned on venturing out one day, but not like this; not in pursuit of a horde of infected people. He'd always imagined embarking on an adventure with Master Savric.

Where are you, Master Savric? I need you.

Calen's throat tightened and tears formed in the corners of his eyes. He blinked them back and gritted his teeth.

I can't be a baby anymore. Aunt Tahmara needs me.

In truth, he knew it to be the other way around, but he couldn't change the situation. He drew another deep breath, but his hands wouldn't steady. The world before him blurred. He wiped his eyes with his sleeves.

Calen balled his hands. "No more. They need me." He stepped beyond the gates with apprehension.

A hand latched onto Calen's shoulder and spun him around. "Auh!" His stomach leapt into his throat.

"Calen, where do you think you're going?" He knew the woman's voice.

He wiped his eyes once more, and his vision cleared. "Mrs. Dougett?"

"It's not safe out there for a boy like you."

A boy like me? Did she know something about him?

No, her eyes mirrored the fear that threatened to consume him. Nothing more than that. He didn't blame her.

Calen tried to shrug her hand away, but her taloned fingers held firm. "I have to follow my aunt. I don't think she knows what she's doing."

Deep ruts formed between Mrs. Dougett's eyes, flanking the bridge of her slender nose. "You're in no shape to follow them. You'll freeze to death, and your aunt will be no better off than she is right now."

Calen groaned. "My aunt wouldn't know the difference either way right now."

"Well then perhaps you should stick with me." She smiled a knowing smile, but it faded just as quickly as it had appeared. "My husband is among the infected as well. We can use my carriage to follow them. It will be far safer and more efficient than trying to follow them on foot."

Calen glanced back at the retreating mob. "But they're not using the roads. How will a carriage be able to follow them?"

Mrs. Dougett tapped her chin with her middle finger and nodded. "I see your point." Her eyes brightened. "We could just use the horses then."

Calen shook his head. "I don't know how to ride a horse, and I don't think this is a good time to learn how to do so." He pulled away from her grasp. "I need to go. I've already lost sight of my aunt."

Mrs. Dougett frowned. "We'd be better together, Calen. *Safer*. There are so many dangers out there. Creatures and people who aren't friendly."

He sniffed loudly. "I know, but it doesn't matter. I've no one left but my aunt. If she dies, I'll have no one."

Pangs of despair wracked him.

"What about Master Savric? Isn't he your friend?"

"Yes, but he's been gone for many weeks. He even missed my name day. He's never done that before. I think something might've happened to him as well."

Calen's chest tightened just thinking about it. He didn't have time to waste anymore. He turned to leave.

A mournful, bone-chilling sound filled the air. Calen had never heard such a sound, but it reminded him of someone blowing a ram's horn. *But who would be blowing a horn right now?* The sound morphed into a chorus of horns and grew louder.

Several people screamed, "Zhebəllin!"

Mrs. Dougett grabbed Calen's hand. "Back inside! They'll kill us all!"

Calen jerked his hand away. "I'm not your responsibility!"

"Close the gates!" yelled a man.

"Hurry! Before they overrun us!" exclaimed another.

People rushed back toward the gates, trampling several others who had lost their footing amidst the panic and chaos. Projectiles flew through the air, taking down others. Sick, twisted snarls joined the screams in a rising symphony of madness. Men and women shoved past Calen, several yelling at him to get out of their way, but his feet stayed rooted in the ground.

Calen's eyes bulged as hideous, humanoid creatures poured out of the surrounding hills like a plague, their swords sheathed and strange yellow tubes hanging between their lips. Little man-beasts, no more than three-and-a-half-feet tall. He'd never seen such creatures with his own eyes, but he'd heard many tales growing up.

Zhebəllin. Fear coursed through him in waves.

Each zhebəllin sported a mouth full of small, sharp, yellowed fangs. Their flattened faces drew back from broad noses and stretched into long foreheads. Beady, red eyes, deep-set under thick, white eyebrows, brimmed with hatred as they scanned what had become a battlefield. Elongated and pointed ears pinned back against stretched skulls akin to those of hellhounds. Dark, orangish-brown colored skin served as a backdrop to small bones strung around their thick necks. Dark leathers stained with who knew what covered their lower extremities, and spiked gauntlets wrapped their forearms. A repulsive stench of feces and death preceded them as they stalked closer.

Animalistic war cries rose from deep within the throats of the zhebəllin. Calen couldn't pull his gaze from them, even as they drew ever closer. Never had he seen so much chaos and bloodshed. It'd all happened in the space of a minute, a thousand souls sent to meet their maker.

The zheballin didn't seem to care for their own kind, shooting an assortment of projectiles at everything that moved. Calen started as the town gates slammed shut behind him with a loud *thud*. The noise pulled him from his thoughts and set his mind and feet into action.

In that moment, Calen did something he never though he could do. He unsheathed his dagger, screamed a battle cry with such ferocity that he didn't recognize his own voice, and then stormed through the grass, giving chase to the horde of infected.

Several zheballin broke away from their assault on Daltura and gave chase to Calen. Calen slashed at anything that came close, connecting several times with jarring blows. Warm fluids splattered his face and arms as he pressed forward, but he didn't allow his mind to think about what it was that covered him and dripped from his eyes and chin. His eyes burned, both with tears and the fluids that sprayed them.

Within minutes, his lungs burned, and his legs ached. He could hardly see through blurry vision. He fell so far behind that he didn't know where his aunt had gone.

He stopped for a moment and drew several ragged breaths, his chest heaving. "Aunt Tahmara!" He yelled her name several more times, knowing she wouldn't respond even if she stood next to him.

What would he do if he couldn't find her again? How would he continue living without her? She'd saved him from his father and from living in an orphanage or in the alleyways. He'd do anything to save her. He'd travel across the Ancient Realm on foot if he must. Nothing would stop him from doing so, not even the zheballin or whatever else might be lurking out there in the wild, open world.

Calen wiped his face with his shirt and continued on, trudging through the mud, snow, and dead grass. He spun several people about looking for his aunt, but she seemed to have disappeared. He couldn't think straight or do anything but press on looking for her. She had to be somewhere among them.

A wretched grunt sounded behind him. He turned quickly, dagger slashing, but his reaction came moments too late. A crude club struck him on his left side, right in the ribs. Bone cracked. Pain shot through his chest and across his back. His dagger fell from crippled fingers. The ground rushed toward him and smashed into the side of his head before he had a chance to brace for impact. He rolled onto his back and clutched his left side, the pain far greater than anything he'd ever experienced. Each breath ratcheted the pain up another level.

Three zhebəllin surrounded him. They growled at each other, perhaps in a language Calen couldn't understand. Wicked grins parted their thin lips.

CHAPTER FIVE

Wizard Wrik lumbered down the corridor, looking over his shoulder now and again to make sure no one followed him. Spies came in every shape and form, even shadows. His future—no, the world's future—hinged on events that would unfold over the next several days. He'd leave nothing to chance.

Ten paces ahead, two steel doors, each three feet wide, ten feet tall, and nearly a foot thick, capped off the corridor. Thick, fire-resistant, black steel framed the doors and extended several feet into the rock walls on either side, into the ceiling, and down through the floor, creating a nearly impenetrable room beyond.

Wrik stopped in front of the two doors, turned around, and watched the shadows for more than a minute, listening for any noises beyond his own breathing and heartbeat. Satisfied he hadn't been followed, he turned and faced the doors.

In his mind's eye, he envisioned the runes he'd used to conjure the trespass ward that protected the room beyond the doors from even the most skilled of wizards. Anyone who stepped beyond the doors' threshold without removing the ward would be cut into pieces as though they'd walked through a grid of thin, razor-sharp wires. Non-wizards wouldn't even know the ward existed and would have no warning before meeting their death.

Wrik didn't like the idea of killing innocent people, but he couldn't risk anyone finding the items contained within the room, some of them more powerful than even Ƨţōn Dhef Dädh.

With a finger, he began drawing runes in the air. Tendrils of blue flame followed his finger and ignited each rune as he drew them. The runes ebbed and flowed like blue spectres, each lingering for several moments before fading out of existence.

In all, he drew seven of them. A tabletop with two outward-curving legs:

π. A lowercase letter 'p': ρ. A lowercase letter 'o': o. A capital letter 'T' with a forward-facing tail: τ. A curvy 'e' or an 'm' on its side: ε. The letter 'x' with tails on the top left and bottom right: χ. And last, another capital letter 'T' with a forward-facing tail: τ.

Thin beams of blue light, crisscrossed and woven together like a spider's web, emerged from the darkness, covering the entire door. The beams separated and turned until they paralleled each other, and then they pulled together and formed a single beam of light. Then the beam of light shrank until nothing remained of it.

Wrik reached into an inner pocket of his robes and pulled out a ring of thick, black keys. He selected the largest key and shoved it deep into the lock on the left door until only the bow protruded. With a clockwise, half-turn, a loud *click* sounded. After several moments, gears began churning within the doors. *Click, clack, clank, pop!*

He waited until the last gear ground to a stop before turning the key a full turn-and-a-half counterclockwise. More gears wound for several moments, another loud *pop* sounded, and then the right door swung inward. Darkness lay beyond the door.

Wrik removed the key from the lock and placed the ring of keys back inside his inner pocket. He stepped across the dark threshold and pushed the door closed behind him. Once again, gears ground together, and large steel bars slid into place across the backs of the doors. The locking mechanism engaged with a final *pop*, and the gears halted.

Wrik breathed deep and gathered his thoughts. With his finger, he drew the same seven runes as he had on the other side of the doors, only backward—the last one first, and the first one last. A blue beam of light formed across the doors, separated into numerous beams, and those beams turned and wove themselves into a web of light. The web sank into the doors and disappeared.

Wrik moved to his right and flipped a switch attached to the wall. Across the ceiling, glass tubes affixed to metal fixtures buzzed and flickered before fully coming to life and filling the entire room with light. No amount of candlelight could ever compare to the light the glass tubes produced. No matter how many times he flipped that switch, its power stole his breath away.

He'd found a book several years ago by a man named Derrik Spencer describing a technique that used gases inside glass tubes. Applying what they'd called "electricity"—a source of energy like stored lightning—to the trapped gases caused the tubes to glow and produce a bright light. A watermill deep underneath Galondu Castle provided the "electricity" to the room. Derrik had called this and many other things "technology," but Wrik understood it to be mezhik of another kind.

White-washed walls, ceilings, and floors made the room appear even brighter, but they also left the space devoid of character and charm. At its center, the twenty-foot-square room contained a rectangular table carved from a single piece of golden oak, a chair made of the same wood, and several stacks of books.

Wrik moved past the table and over to a steel door inset in the wall on the far left side of the room. A hinged steel bar secured the door. He lifted the end of the bar and flipped it backward, clearing it of the steel, U-shaped clamp that held it in place. The door moaned as he pulled it open. He stepped backward.

Wrik swept his arm outward. "Please come into the light, my young friend. I'm sorry to have kept you here for so long, but other matters that couldn't wait have occupied my time. Alas, your arrival here was… *unexpected.*"

A young man stepped out of the small room and into the light. Blonde hair hung past his shoulders, front and back, some of it tucked behind his rounded ears. Red veins fissured the whites of his eyes, but his green irises shone brightly, miniature glass tubes reflected in them.

The young man stared intently at Wrik, his forehead creased, and his eyebrows angled down over the bridge of his slightly curved nose. His squared jaw set, and thin red lips pursed, he said nothing. Not a single hair lined his chin or jaw, but a long, bright-red scar ran across his throat.

Wrik pointed at the scar. "A recent injury?"

He absently rubbed his neck, his nostrils flared. "Let me go, and I won't kill you."

"Kill me?" Wrik chuckled. "Oh, I'm certain you possess the power to do so if you really wanted to, but I don't think that's who you are. In fact, I'd venture to say that's *exactly* who you're not. Isn't that right, Alderan?"

† † †

Alderan circled the large, dark-skinned man. "You know me, do you?

Then you also know what I'm capable of."

The man grinned and held out his hand. "I am Wizard Wrik."

Alderan stared at the large hand. It dwarfed his own by more than a length. "I don't care who you are. You've no right to keep me—" He looked around the strange room and at the ceiling. "—wherever we are." The odd, light-filled tubes overhead mesmerized him.

What are those?

Wrik pointed at the tubes. "Fascinating, aren't they? They're powered by electricity."

Alderan nodded but frowned. "I've never heard of electricity."

"Few have." Wrik folded his arms behind his back. "Suffice it to say it's equivalent to lightning."

Lightning?

Alderan scratched his head. "How do you put lightning into tubes?"

Wrik chuckled. "It's technology, my friend. A type of mezhik, if you prefer."

"I don't think we're speaking the same language."

"Check this out." Wrik walked over to the far wall where a metal handle protruded from it waist-high. He pulled the handle down and the tubes of light dimmed overhead. Then the room fell into total darkness and silence.

Alderan had wondered where the incessant buzzing had come from. Now he knew, but it didn't matter. He didn't have time to waste. Zerenity and Qotan needed him.

He took a deep breath. "Look, Wrik. All of this is fascinating, but I've got somewhere to be."

Click!

The glass tubes flickered, buzzed, and sprang to life with light once again. "I promise I won't keep you much longer, but there are a few questions that need answered first." He motioned toward a chair with his hand. "Please take a seat."

Take a seat?

Alderan snarled and willed the electricity flowing through the tubes to leap into his hands but nothing happened. *Why would it? I'm pathetic.*

He walked over to the chair and sat down with a huff. "What do you want from me?"

Wrik sat on the edge of the table to Alderan's right. Despite the height of the table his feet stayed planted on the floor with length to spare in his legs. He folded his hands over his stomach. "Let's start with why you're here."

Alderan raked his fingers through his hair. "First of all, I don't know where *here* is."

Wrik nodded. "Fair enough. Where were you headed when you opened the mirror portal?"

Alderan tilted his head back and stared at the tubes of light. Something swirled inside them. "Home, I guess. I don't know."

"And where is this home of yours?"

Alderan straightened and eyed Wrik. The man's smile revealed the whitest teeth he'd ever seen. Perhaps his dark skin contrasted them further, but his teeth weren't his most interesting feature. No, that title belonged to the golden eyes glowing behind his wire-rimmed spectacles.

Alderan eased down in the chair. "Viscus D'Silva."

Wrik nodded knowingly. "Northernmost town on the continent, just edging out Vermislignum for the title." He chuckled. "There are few other places in the Ancient Realm that would place you farther from home than where you are now."

Alderan huffed. "Not surprising. I always wind up right where I don't want to be. Where are we?"

Wrik smacked his lips. "You've found your way inside Galondu Castle. It lies on the northeastern edge of Atrum Moenia."

Alderan shrugged. "Never heard of it. Why would the mirror take me here when I wanted to go home?"

"Were you thinking of something or someone before you touched the mirror?"

"Only home… well sort of." Alderan scratched his head. "I was thinking about my twin sister Aria as well."

Wrik lifted his head and breathed deep through his nostrils. "Ah, that explains it."

Alderan frowned. *Did I miss something?* He straightened in the chair. "Explains what?"

Wrik lowered his gaze and met Alderan's. "How you came to be here. It was dark when I grabbed you through the mirror, but even then I thought you looked familiar. Your likeness to Aria is remarkable."

Alderan sprung to his feet. "You know Aria? Is she here? Can I see her?"

Wrik held up a finger. "I'll make arrangements for you to see her when we're finished here."

"Arrangements?" Alderan thrust his arms in the air. "She's my sister!" His voice echoed in the room. "She'll want to see me. She called to me before I went through the mirror."

Surprise flashed in Wrik's eyes, or so Alderan thought. He could've been wrong though. "You must understand that the current atmosphere of Galondu Castle is... *delicate.* I fear your arrival here will not be welcomed by most."

Alderan paced back and forth. "Why? What have I done? Why does it seem like everyone wants me dead?"

Wrik stood, straightened his silver robes, and adjusted his spectacles. "It's not a matter of what you've done but of what you're destined to do. People fear that which they don't understand. Prophecy is a fickle friend to some and an enemy to most."

Alderan stopped pacing and leaned over the chairback. "Who are you and what do you know of prophecy?"

Wrik smiled wryly. "I am a friend of your sister's and a friend to you by extension."

"But why are you here? What role do you play in her captivity?"

Wrik laughed aloud. "Captivity? Is that what you think has become of her?" He shook his finger. "No, no, no. You've got it all backward, my friend. She rules this castle and everyone in it with her deadly charm."

Aria ruling a castle? That's not possible.

He rounded the chair and sat back down. His dream of her standing atop the castle wall flooded his mind and left him adrift in its wake. The room tossed him about like a ship in rough waters.

How much have I missed?

He closed his eyes, leaned forward, and placed his head in his hands. "She does this under your authority?"

"*My* authority? Nothing could be farther from the truth. I am employed by Lord and Lady Rosai. Lord Rosai is the figurehead, but his will and ear bend to all of Aria's desires."

Lady Rosai?

It took several moments for Alderan to wrap his mind around the context of those words, but then understanding shot his eyes open and him upright in the chair. "Aria… she's… married?" The bitter words lingered on his tongue like dandelion paste and plunged a dagger deep into his heart.

Has she forsaken me?

Wrik said something, but the room spun around Alderan. Darkness crept into his vision until he could no longer hold onto consciousness.

† † †

Wrik retrieved a bottle of hartshorn oil from one of the cabinets at the back of the room and returned to the chair where Alderan slumped over the table unconscious. He pulled the stopper from the bottle and held it underneath Alderan's nose.

Alderan's nose wrinkled, and he snorted several times before his eyes fluttered open. He gasped and pushed Wrik's hand away. "What are you trying to do to me with that stuff?"

Wrik returned the stopper to its bottle and placed the bottle on the table. "You passed out, so I revived you with it."

"It smells terrible." Alderan sat up and rubbed his nose.

"I believe that's the point." Wrik glimpsed a mark on the inside of Alderan's left wrist. *A wizard, just like his sister.* "It's made from the horns and hooves of red-tailed deer."

"I've killed many deer in my life, and none have ever smelled so foul."

"And you've never ground the horns and hooves and distilled them either. The process brings out a distinct smell akin to urine, and it's perfect for reviving a person."

"I think I'd rather stay unconscious than smell that again." Alderan rose from the chair and grabbed the edge of the table to steady himself. He squeezed his eyes shut for a moment and shook his head. "It's time you took me to see Aria."

Wrik held up a finger. "One last thing before we depart."

Alderan huffed. "What now?"

Wrik looked down at Alderan's left arm. "I see that you're a wizard, like your sister. May I look at your marking?"

"Aria's a wizard too?" Excitement filled his voice.

"Yes, of course, but I've yet to see her abilities manifested since she wore *ʒäbräʒär* until recently."

"What is *ʒäbrä*—whatever?"

"*Ʒäbräʒär*. It's a silver collar that traps and suppresses mezhik. Often, the collar is placed on an individual who manifests mezhik abilities right after their sixteenth name day to keep them from harming themselves and others until they can be trained to use their mezhik properly. Some find the practice of using the collar barbaric. I can see both sides of the argument, especially when the individual possesses great potential, like your sister."

"Aria has great potential?" He shook his fist. "I knew it! She must be the one who saves the world, not me."

"Don't discount yourself. Power comes in many forms."

"I can't even—" Alderan grimaced.

"You can't control your mezhik yet. That's understandable. Many find it difficult to master at first. Given time, you will find your way. Now, let me see your wrist."

Alderan pulled up his sleeve and stuck his arm out, palm up. "Be my guest."

Wrik leaned over and examined the inside of Alderan's wrist. "A gray scroll..."

Where have I seen that before?

"I don't remember what it's called, but it allows me to see events of an object's past."

Wrik smirked. *Mustapha.* How long had it been since he'd seen the old hag? He couldn't recall. "*Fizärd Mämärä*."

"Yes, that's it." Alderan lowered his arm.

Interesting. "A memory wizard. With time and practice your power will grow well beyond seeing events."

Alderan shrugged. "Maybe. I have a mark on my other wrist as well."

Wrik nearly choked on his own saliva.

Another mark?

He finally understood Lord Rosai's fear of the boy. *He's the first mage in over twelve hundred years.*

Then, another thought occurred to him. *Aria is exceptional, but Lord Rosai went to far greater lengths to retrieve her than he would have done for anyone or anything else. She must be a mage as well.*

But what does it mean?

He leaned closer to Alderan. "May I see that one as well?"

Alderan pulled up his right sleeve and held out his arm. An opened, transparent-purple book marked his wrist. "This one allows me to read books in languages I don't even know."

"*Nealläzh.*" Jealousy swelled within Wrik's chest and tightened his jaw. He glared daggers at Alderan. "Do you understand the rarity of this gift?"

Alderan shrugged. "I've been told so by others, but it doesn't change the way I see it. Everything is new and rare to me."

He grabbed Alderan's shoulder and shook him. "Two entire millennia have passed since that mark has been seen."

Alderan groaned. "I get it, but you don't need to hurt me."

"Entire languages have been lost!" Wrik released Alderan's shoulder and stood. He smacked his fist into his palm. "You must stay here and help me translate some of the books of prophecy."

Alderan rotated his arm and rubbed his shoulder. "And why would I do that?"

Wrik knew the answer. Given the fact that Aria had called out to Alderan and he'd heard her, the two of them must share a bond stronger than any he'd witnessed before. He folded his hands behind his back and smiled. "For your sister."

Alderan crossed his arms. "Take me to her, and we'll see what she has to say."

Wrik smacked his lips. "Deal." He retrieved a strip of black cloth from within his robes and offered it to Alderan. "Wrap this around your head and cover your eyes with it."

Alderan snorted. "I'm not putting that on."

"You will do as I say, or you'll find yourself locked inside that room again."

Alderan huffed and grabbed the strip of cloth. "You need to work on your hospitality skills."

Wrik shook his head. *He certainly shares Aria's attitude.* "No one knows about this room or its location, and I will do everything in my power to keep it that way. Understood?"

Alderan wrapped the cloth around his head several times and then tied the ends together. "Satisfied?"

"To be certain. Stay right here. It will take me a few minutes to unlock the door."

"Sounds like a ten-second job to me."

"Only if you prefer death."

Alderan swallowed hard. "Take your time then. By the way, where are we headed?"

Wrik walked over to the door. "To my bedchamber. It's where I study and sleep. I'll leave you there while I fetch Aria."

Wrik unraveled the trespass ward surrounding the doorway and unlocked the door with his key. He cracked the door open and peered down the corridor. Nothing moved, shadows or otherwise. Satisfied, he walked over to Alderan and took him by the arm. "Do as I say and don't make a sound until I tell you it's safe. Understood?"

Alderan nodded.

Wrik guided Alderan out of the room and into the corridor, and then he locked the door and conjured the trespass ward again.

Gods, let our path be unobstructed.

CHAPTER SIX

Aria stood out on the balcony that jutted out from the southern side of her and Pravus's bedchamber. Her black robe pulled against her shoulders as it billowed at her back, leaving her naked flesh exposed to the cool, morning air. A few people moved about in the city of Atrum Moenia far below, little more than sewer rats from her vantage.

She couldn't care less if the people below gazed upon her nude body. In fact, she relished the thought. With Cinolth at her side, she'd become their goddess, deserving of worship. She drew upon her mezhik as she rubbed her stomach where Cinolth's heart had once been, intoxicated by her own touch. Gooseflesh prickled her skin.

Pravus lay in bed twenty feet behind her, still asleep. The thought of ravishing him again as she had several times on their wedding night aroused her, but with that memory came sobering thoughts. Her mezhik faded as her mind drifted to Alderan, her brother risen from the dead the previous night. How long had it been since she'd seen him?

Ages. Longer.

She pulled her robe closed and cinched it with its belt, the air no longer refreshing. Her fingers twisted through strands of red-and-blonde hair as she pondered her life and how Alderan would see her now. So many things had changed in the last year. Would Alderan recognize her? Not physically of course, but the person she'd become.

I'm a woman, a wife, and a queen now.

She peered down at the insides of her wrists. Six marks. Six elements. Fire, water, nature, earth, air, and light. Three on the left wrist, and three on the right.

Mezhik came to her with little effort. The bonds she shared with Pravus and Cinolth likely attributed to her quick learning, but she thirsted for more.

Six marks. Five more than Pravus. *The first mage in 1200 years.*

With just a thought, she pulled moisture from the air and formed a puddle in her left palm. She gazed at herself in the puddle's reflection. She hardly recognized herself from the child Alderan knew. Her eyebrows had thickened and darkened significantly since she last looked upon herself. They reminded her of small dragon wings. The ends of her lips curled into a smile.

I am Rídär Drezhn.

Aria closed her eyes. Her heart fluttered and her spirits soared like they had when she'd flown through the skies on Cinolth's back. That moment could've lasted a lifetime and she would've been satiated. Desire to be upon his back filled her once again, a sensual longing akin to the way the touch of mezhik intoxicated her. His presence didn't register in her mind like it normally did. She looked skyward and scanned the gray skies but found no trace of the leathery beast.

Where have you gone without me?

Anger swept through her like a pulse of light, boiling the puddle of water in her palm. Steam rose in the cool air. She cast the water over the balcony and retreated back inside the bedchamber.

She'd given Cinolth life through her mezhik, bonding with him on a level she couldn't begin to comprehend, but that bond didn't afford her control over his thoughts or actions. However, she obsessed over him, his presence ever at the forefront of her mind.

Is it he who controls me?

She shook the thought from her mind. It made little difference. They shared the same desires.

Plush animal pelts tickled Aria's toes as she walked across the room and over to the massive fireplace. Its opening extended above her head and stretched wider than she could reach. A pile of fresh-cut logs lay on its hearth, ready to be consumed by fire. She obliged. *"Zäṭ äbəlläíz."*

A pulsing, orangish-red fireball formed over her palm and leapt onto the logs, setting them aflame. Within moments, heat began leaching from the logs and warmed her hands.

Aria uncinched the robe's belt, and the robe slid off her shoulders and into a pile on the floor. The flames bathed her with their warmth as she drew closer to them. Gooseflesh faded from her skin as the fire drew the cold from her bones.

The scent of pine filled her nostrils, and boiling sap popped as it seeped from the logs. Aria breathed deep. The smell carried her back home to Viscus

D'Silva, her thoughts returning to Alderan.

What has become of you in my absence? Are you a wizard? Or a mage like me?

Assuming him dead for so long, she'd never contemplated such ideas before. How had his life changed apart from her and Red? Had he searched for her? Her eyes filled with moisture, and her chest ached to see him again.

Does Alderan know I'm alive?

She peered up at the stone ceiling, but the answer she sought wouldn't come from a god she couldn't see, hear, or touch. In the past, she'd relied on Ɂäṭūr's guidance over her life, but each passing moment since she'd taken Cinolth's heart from Nardus's chest diminished her need for Him further. Soon, Ɂäṭūr would be nothing more than a faint memory. A false god who takes life without remorse. No, she only needed to look within for the answer, so she did.

Alderan must know.

On her wedding night, she'd felt her bond with Alderan like she had in the past; a familiarity akin to the wind through her hair. Two rended souls united once again. She could've placed his location on a map.

It'd been so long since she had felt the bond that she'd forgotten how much she missed it. Nothing else compared to its warmth and depth. An unbreakable bond.

However, after the commencement of the stone ceremony and the awakening of Cinolth, the bond weakened. She still sensed Alderan's presence in the world, but she could no longer locate him.

She searched the undulating flames before her, but they held no answers. "Where are you, Alderan? How will I ever find you?"

She'd give anything to see Alderan again. Within reason, of course. She needed to find someone she could trust to track him down and bring him to her.

But who?

Aria trusted few people or creatures in the world. It only took a single hand to count them. *Alderan. Amicus. Karraar. Wizard Wrik.*

At one point, she would've placed Pravus's name in her short list, but his constant need to keep her in the dark and lie to her face diminished her view of and respect for him. No doubt she loved him, but love had nothing to do with trust. He might never earn hers again.

Obviously, she couldn't have Alderan find himself. She didn't know where to find Amicus either so that left Karraar and Wizard Wrik. She already owed Wizard Wrik for helping her get down into the dungeon where Pravus had held her father, Nardus. The last thing she wanted was to owe him further. Karraar, on the other hand, had sworn his life to serving her when they were in the wastelands.

Aria twirled a finger in her hair and frowned. *Where is Karraar?*

She hadn't seen Karraar since the night they'd arrived at Galondu Castle. In fact, she'd seen nothing but humans roaming the castle corridors. In truth, the castle stretched farther and wider than she could imagine. She'd seen but a fraction of its glory, but she had a knack and a mind for mapping out buildings and terrain with ease. One day, she'd know every last secret Galondu Castle held within its walls.

Excitement rose in her chest but faded quickly. So many other things took precedence in her life now. She forced her thoughts back to Karraar. For all she knew, Pravus had executed Karraar for nearly getting her killed in the Inferus Wastelands.

To be fair, she'd wanted nothing more than to spill Karraar's blood when they were deep in the wastelands. Had she the strength at the time, she would've. Now, the thought of Karraar lying dead somewhere unsettled her more than she would've thought possible.

She ground her teeth and clenched her fists. *I owe him nothing.* The words echoed in her mind, hollow and meaningless. She'd never escape the truth: she would've died without his help.

How Karraar had weaseled his way onto her good side escaped her. She reminded herself that he'd killed Red, the only father she'd known, but it did nothing to ease her fear of his demise. For reasons she couldn't quite grasp, she'd chosen to believe Karraar had killed Red to end his suffering.

Cold hands slid around her waist. She shivered even as Pravus's voice filled her ears. "Is something troubling you, my love?" He pulled her against himself. His fingers, slivers of ice, worked their way down the sides of her legs.

Aria pushed his hands away, turned, and met his golden-eyed gaze. She found no trace of concern in his lust-filled eyes. She rarely did.

"No," she said.

Pravus lifted her into his arms and pressed his lips against hers as he carried her over to the bed. He set her down on its edge and pushed her onto her back. She wrapped her legs around his waist as he leaned into her.

Several minutes later, Pravus collapsed onto the bed next to her. Sweat glistened on his broad chest and across his brow. He sighed loudly, his breathing labored. "That's just what I needed."

"Thrice last night." She rolled onto her side and stroked his chest. "Are you determined to impregnate me in our first week of marriage?"

He pushed a strand of hair from her face. "Would that be so bad?"

She didn't answer. How could she, knowing she'd never be able to bear him a child? She should have confessed it to him before but never did, so how could she now? Instead, she planted kisses on his lips, his chin, and down the side of his neck. By the time she reached his chest, he grabbed her and pulled her back down.

Aria made love to him once more. This time, he took his time with her. Finished and sore, she rolled to the side and stared up at the crimson canopy overhead.

"Where is Karraar?" she asked.

"Do I know this Karraar?" Pravus's voice betrayed him with a slight but noticeable inflection at the end.

Aria's pulse raced. *Perhaps he did have Karraar killed.*

She pressed him. "The beast who saved my life in the wastelands."

He sat up, his brow creased in a scowl. "Do not concern yourself with his whereabouts."

She covered her breasts with her arm. "Yet I must. I've neglected to thank him for what he did out there."

Pravus's jaw tightened. "He did his job. Leave it at that."

She maneuvered herself to the edge of the bed and slid off of it. "I pray you do not misunderstand me, husband." She faced Pravus and pushed up her breasts. "If you plan on partaking of these again, you'll find him and bring him to me."

Redness crept up his neck. "If you think threatening—"

"It's a promise." She walked back over to the fireplace and snatched her robe off the floor.

"Auh!" The bed rattled as Pravus ejected himself from it. He stalked forward, his finger wagging. "You're lucky I don't squeeze the life from your pretty, little neck."

"Pfft. As if you could." She glared at him. "We both know my mezhik surpasses yours in every way."

Pravus swept his arm toward her. In an instant, the room flashed across Aria's vision. Her body jolted as it slammed against the bed. Her breath caught in her throat as a silver collar wrapped around her neck and strangled her. She convulsed, the air trapped in her lungs.

Another flash, and she stammered backward, nearly falling into the fire. Her chest heaved as she sucked in air, the collar gone.

Everything he did to her was an illusion, and she knew it, yet her mind still couldn't distinguish between it and reality.

"Never test me again," growled Pravus.

Aria massaged her neck as her eyes narrowed. *One of us won't survive this marriage.* "Your little demonstration changes nothing. Bring Karraar to me."

Pravus snorted. "So be it, but it will take several weeks to get Karraar back here." He turned and teleported out of the room before she had the chance to respond.

Aria huffed. "I shan't wait several weeks to find Alderan."

The smell of burning wool stung her nostrils. She looked down at the robe in her hand. Plumes of smoke rose from it. She tossed it into the fire and watched it shrivel and burn. If Pravus thought he'd get away with manhandling her again, it'd be him she'd cast into the flames the next time. She crossed her arms and paced in front of the fire, her anger building. How had talks of war in the war room transitioned to battles in the bedroom?

Was there ever love between us? She chided herself. *You know the truth, Aria. You still love each other.* But would it be enough to hold their marriage together? A kingdom divided would surely fall into ruin. She must do better showing unity with Pravus. Her future depended on it.

Aria stood tall in front of the flames. "I'm a survivor. A warrior. I cannot fail."

She turned from the fire, her mind set on her next task. *Time to find Alderan.*

A smirk crept onto her face. "Looks like I'll owe Wizard Wrik another favor after all."

Other odors besides the fire and charred robe permeated the air. She lowered her head and sniffed herself. "Ugh!" She reeked of sex and sweat, and not just of her own.

Shivers crawled across her skin and shook her. "I'll go see Wizard Wrik *after* I've had a bath."

Aria could easily draw a bath with the aid of mezhik, but what good would it be to have servants if she did everything herself? They'd become lazy and complacent. She'd have none of that. Besides, she had better things to do with her mezhik.

She reached out to Brema with her mind. *"Come draw me a bath at once."*

† † †

Pravus stormed through the castle corridors looking for someone or something to unload his fury upon. "The insolence of that woman," he growled. "I cannot and will not allow her to usurp my kingdom."

He reached out, and the steel doors before him swung outward, banging against the other side of the stone walls. Credan stood on the other side of a massive, rectangular table made of brownish-gray stone. The ruckus caught Credan's attention and drew a gasp from his lips.

Credan bowed, his eyes still fraught with surprise. "Good morning, my lord."

Pravus stilled his anger as he approached the table. "She's not been herself since taking that damned stone from Nardus."

Credan's expression turned from surprise to confusion. "My lord?"

Pravus leaned over the table and eyed Credan. "This is all that wretched dragon's doing."

"I doubt you are wrong, but perhaps you could fill me in on what's happened so that I can gain a better understanding as to the context of the conversation."

Pravus seethed. "Cinolth corrupts Aria's mind and pits her against me." He brought his fist down on the table with enough force to jostle and topple the war pieces laid out across the map of the Ancient Realm spread across its surface. "Every thought she possesses stems from his twisted influence. He must be dealt with before he ruins everything I've built."

Credan drew his hand across the top of his bald head but stopped short from plunging down the side of his face. Instead, his fingers attacked a large, black mole just above his left ear. Pravus wanted to reach across the table and rip the mole off of Credan's head.

"I... don't disagree." Credan shrank back from the table. "However, don't we need his help to defeat the Three Kingdoms?"

Anger and pride rose in Pravus's chest. He pointed a finger at Credan. "And what does he offer us beyond the strife he sows? Nothing. He brings us nothing."

Credan pulled on his shirt collar with a finger. "Forgive me for speaking of rumors, my lord, but they abound."

Pravus grabbed one of the war pieces from the table and palmed it. His eyes narrowed. "Rumors of what?"

Credan folded his hands together and stared at them for several moments before answering. "If true, an army gathers in his name."

Pravus scoffed. "And you believe these rumors?"

Credan nodded.

"Why would he need an army?" Pravus glared at Credan and waited several moments for an answer but only got a shrug out of the man.

Is Cinolth trying to usurp my kingdom?

Pravus shook the thought away. The war piece dug into his clenched fist as he squeezed harder. "There is no basis to these absurd lies. People spread rumors out of fear and nothing more. Cinolth controls no army. I control him."

But if they are true...

"As you say, my lord." Credan paced next to the table, his brow furrowed. "How does one kill a dragon?"

Good question, but he's no ordinary dragon.

Every account Pravus read of Cinolth solidified his fear of the beast. Tightly clustered and stronger than steel, he'd read of no weapon that could penetrate Cinolth's scales. Not only that, but Cinolth's scales resisted most types of mezhik attacks as well.

How had Cyrus defeated him in the Great War?

"I don't have an answer." Pravus tossed the war piece onto the map and rubbed his palm where it had left a dent. "First and foremost, we need to find out if the rumors are true. In the meantime, I'll feign interest in reconciling my differences with the beast."

Credan stopped pacing. "I agree. Turn him, and he'd be a great asset."

"Yes, but only until the war is won." Pravus brooded. "But how?"

"Queen Aria." Credan's eyes twinkled behind wire-rimmed spectacles.

"She seems to have as much influence over him as anyone else."

Pravus sneered. *More than me is what you mean.* He paused and allowed his anger to quell before responding to Credan. After all, the man merely spoke the truth.

"It is true." Pravus began righting the fallen war pieces. "Somehow, she's bound to that beast, and I'm not certain she has the strength to persuade him the way he does her."

Credan stepped over to the table and helped Pravus place the war pieces back where they belonged. "If I've witnessed nothing else, I've seen the strength she possesses. She commands everything in her path. She's a true queen if ever I've seen one."

"Then we shall make a concerted effort to persuade her to influence the beast to join our cause."

"We, my lord?" Credan cleared his throat. "Tell me what needs to be done, and I will make it so."

"Prepare an elegant feast for lunch. Like most men, she has a fondness for lavish food and good wine."

Credan dipped his head. "As you wish, my lord. It will rival that of your wedding feast."

"Good. See to it at once and notify me when it's ready. In the meantime, I've got a war to orchestrate."

Credan bowed low and then exited the room.

Pravus circled the table, viewing the map from every angle. Attacking the Three Kingdoms would prove tough, even if they had the element of surprise. Only three paths led into the Orbis Mountains, each fortified well. An assault from all three directions at the same time would tax their army and spread them thin, but that wasn't the plan. The brunt of their attack would come from the south, through Elatos. Once King Zaridus fully committed his forces there, Murtag would lead a second force south along the Hotah River and attack Vallah, the King's city, to the north. With luck, Murtag would sever the head of King Zaridus's army and force surrender.

Pravus moved the war pieces into position, surrounding the cities of Vallah, Elatos, and Borza. Then he toppled the piece representing King Zaridus. They would have the element of surprise with the second attack. The plan would not fail.

He cracked his knuckles. "Soon, the Ancient Realm will be mine."

CHAPTER SEVEN

It took the better part of an hour for Nardus and Theyn to navigate the debris field of shredded books, toppled shelves, broken tables, and dismantled chairs to reach the door with the blood-smeared frame. By the time they did, water dripped from several new cracks in the ceiling. More water trickled down the walls from several of the high windows. Lying underneath miles of ocean, the Great Library hemorrhaged water like a boat pocked with holes.

This isn't good.

Nardus turned the handle, but the door wouldn't open either direction. He slammed his shoulder into the door several times, but the door didn't budge. "Gnaud must've barricaded himself in there."

Theyn spoke directly into his mind. *"We must breach the door. I see no other way in. Maybe there's an axe or some other tool lying around that we could use."*

Nardus shook his head, anger in his voice. "We don't have the time to search this place for tools. Go see if you can find something to break the door down with." Theyn nodded and trotted away.

He kicked the door and beat it with his fists, but didn't even leave a dent in the thick, hard wood.

Theyn's voice entered his mind again. *"Over here to your left. I think I've found a piece of wood that you could use as a battering ram."*

Nardus stumbled over several mounds of debris before locating Theyn and the long piece of wood that'd splintered from one of the massive shelves. "This might just work."

The piece of wood proved far heavier than it looked, taking most of his strength just to lift it off the floor. With a grunt, he got the piece of wood balanced on his right shoulder. His legs trembled beneath him, but he managed to keep his balance. The door stood forty paces ahead, a far greater distance than he would've liked, but he had no alternative.

Nardus staggered toward the door, his chest heaving and his vision a bit blurred as he hauled the piece of wood across churning chaos. On his second to last step, his boot clipped a chair leg. He stumbled forward, and the piece of wood tumbled from his shoulder. It missed crushing his foot by the width of a hair.

Theyn growled deep in her throat. *"We're running out of time."*

Nardus shook off his fatigue as best he could. He turned toward Theyn, but his words caught in his throat. Water pooled in the valleys between the mounds of debris.

Damn!

Somehow, water had yet to reach the door he hoped Gnaud hid behind. Nardus gathered his strength and lifted the piece of wood back onto his shoulder. He roared and slammed the piece of wood against the door. The jolt sent shock waves of pain down into his toes. Several splinters tore into his hands and arms. He shook off the pain, ignored the splinters, and continued pounding the door, roaring like a beast with each strike.

The sixth blow splintered the door top to bottom with a loud *crack*. Another hit, and the door split completely in two. Nardus dropped the piece of wood, kicked the door all the way in, and climbed through the narrow opening.

The small room contained a single desk that hugged the right-hand wall. Several books sat atop the desk, each in a different phase of repair. Gnaud lay on the floor in the far corner to the left, unmoving. A crimson puddle surrounded Gnaud's midsection, his grey fur matted with blood.

"No!" Nardus hurried over to Gnaud and knelt by his side. Nardus took Gnaud's small wrist between his fingers and felt for a pulse but found none. He pressed a finger against Gnaud's neck. At first, he felt nothing, but then a faint heartbeat lifted his finger ever so slightly.

Nardus exhaled a breath he hadn't realized he'd held. "He's alive, Theyn!"

Theyn nuzzled Nardus's neck. *"Thank the gods!"*

Gnaud's bloodied shirt lay across his abdomen, little more than a shredded rag. Four gashes flayed his fur-covered skin, two far deeper than Nardus would've liked. He shook Gnaud gently, but the little gordak didn't respond.

Nardus turned to Theyn. "I don't think he will last much longer. We've got to get him out of here and to someone who can help heal him."

Theyn gestured at the floor with her head. *"I agree, but we don't have much time either."*

A good two inches of water stood on the floor now. Nardus hadn't noticed that his trousers were soaked through. "Damn!"

They had no time to formulate a plan. Besides, Nardus only knew of one way to leave Nasduron. What he didn't know was what they'd be walking into when they arrived back at Pravus's castle. He'd have to trust fate, Ɛäṭūr, the gods, or whatever else one might rely on to keep them safe.

Nardus lifted Gnaud into his left arm as gingerly as he could, mindful of Gnaud's open wounds. He stood and grabbed Theyn's collar with his other hand.

This had better work.

His gaze met Theyn's. She nodded, and then they stepped out of the library together.

Chapter Eight

Qotan's staff didn't sit in Savric's hand the way his own had. He'd changed hand positions several times during the sixteen-mile journey to Tyrosha before conceding that it would never feel the way his did. Giving voice to his frustrations over it garnered no sympathy from Eshtak either.

The little man seemed oblivious to everything going on around them, skipping and dawdling about throughout the entire journey. He'd chased every moving thing with childlike wonder, except for Qotan and Zerenity of course.

Twice, Savric thought he'd lost Eshtak altogether and admittedly felt a bit of relief in those moments of separation. In truth, he feared bringing Eshtak along might've been a mistake, but that ship sailed long ago. So, he'd prayed that Ɂäʈūr would grant him the patience to stave off his growing frustration toward Eshtak. It hadn't worked, but he did find the strength to hold his tongue.

The docks of Tyrosha ran a good quarter mile along the southern shoreline of Custos Bay. Bony-fingered piers stretched far into the bay, ships of all sizes moored along either of their sides. Savric gazed upon the large ship docked at the end of the longest pier, their gangplanks extended as droves of people boarded it.

Ten yards ahead, dozens of men dressed in black with red, dragon head emblems on their breasts guarded the end of the pier and the ship. Each guard held a rigid, leather switch in their hand as they examined each person, granting passage to only those who were infected.

Many people screamed, yelled, and wailed as the guards separated them from their infected family members and friends. Several tried to fight their way through the line of guards, but the switches proved a great deterrent. Each strike from the switches produced a purple energy arc that cracked the air like thunder and incapacitated the would-be attackers.

Savric couldn't grasp where these men had come from or where they'd gotten the switches. The best he could surmise was that they belonged to some sort of dragon-worshiping cult. It certainly wouldn't surprise him if it were the case. People worshiped just about everything.

As they neared the checkpoint, Savric grabbed Eshtak's arm and pulled them out of the line. They ducked behind a large stack of wooden pallets and empty crates. Savric eyed the ship and pulled on his beard. "We stand no chance of walking past those guards. We must find another way aboard."

Eshtak pulled on Savric's sleeve, but Savric waved him off. "Give me a minute to conjure a plan."

Beyond the checkpoint, the infected formed two distinct lines to board the front and back of the ship. He spotted Qotan halfway up the front gangplank. A minute later, he located Zerenity boarding from the rear gangplank.

At least there is only one ship. But how can Eshtak and I board it unnoticed?

Eshtak tugged his sleeve again. Savric frowned. "I have yet to formulate a plan. As I am certain you are aware, these tasks take time."

Eshtak's lower lip bulged out. "Eshtak has plan."

Savric guffawed. "*You* have a plan?"

Eshtak nodded and pointed at himself. "Eshtak black and white like people. Eshtak walks with others. Friend wizard blinks."

Savric opened his mouth to refute Eshtak's plan but came up with no objections. Instead, he chuckled. "Wizard blinks..."

Eshtak nodded vigorously.

Savric had never heard anyone refer to teleportation as "wizard blinking," but logically speaking it made sense. He peered down at Eshtak with renewed vision. *Perhaps I have exercised haste in judging Eshtak's intellect. Qotan would relish this moment were he present.*

Savric clasped Eshtak's shoulder. "I believe that your assessment of the situation and your plan are both of sound mind. I have no objections. Shall we execute accordingly?"

Eshtak nodded. "Eshtak sees friend on boat."

"Indeed. We will see each other soon."

Eshtak nodded and skipped over to the line of infected people. He glanced back at Savric, winked, and then he turned away, lowering his head and merging into the line.

Savric grinned and looked skyward. "May your creations never fail to amaze me, ʔäṯūr."

A blunt object poked Savric's spine. "Ain't nothin ta see here, old man. Take yer leave before ya meet me friend."

Savric turned and faced the stout man. The man wore the same black outfit as the other guards. His right hand gripped a switch.

"Yes, of course." Savric raised a finger. "However, I do have one question for you." The man grunted but didn't object, so Savric continued, "Are you privy as to the destination of the vessel, per chance?"

The man glared at Savric. "Ain't sayin." He spat on the pier. "Yeh've had yer question. Now git."

Savric dipped his head. "As you wish."

Savric slammed the butt-end of Qotan's staff against the pier and disappeared in a whirlwind. The next moment, he reappeared on the ship's deck. Several guards stood around the deck, each with their back to him. He pulled his hood down low, lowered his head, and concealed his hands within his sleeves. A few others held staffs too.

Once aboard, none of the infected moved or spoke, all their black eyes peering straight ahead, perhaps into another plane of existence or maybe at nothing at all. Their eerie silence and countenance jittered Savric.

A wake with no victim.

Savric leaned against the center mast, easing some of the burden from his weary legs. The walk from Zerenity's house into Tyrosha sapped most of his energy, and the use of mezhik to teleport on board the ship took him to the brink of collapse.

A bite to eat and a quick nap would help build his strength back up, but he had no way of doing either without garnering unwanted attention to himself. Depending on the destination of the ship, he might need to find a place to rest.

The ship rocked gently, weighing down his eyelids and pulling him toward sleep. He fought the urge to give in to his weariness and sleep, electing to stand up straight. But soon, his shoulders drooped, his knees quaked, and his eyelids couldn't be held open.

Savric jerked awake with a jolt. His tailbone ached and his neck angled toward his chest, so stiff that he had a tough time lifting his head back up.

"Outta the way," said a gruff voice with a thick accent.

An islander? Savric blinked away the sting from his eyes.

Large, sun-bronzed arms parted the sea of people that stood before Savric. A man with one small, golden hoop through his left eyebrow and another one through the left corner of his lower lip glared down at Savric.

From Savric's right came another man. The second man had the same piercings as the first, same color as well. The piercings signified rank amongst the islanders. Iron outranked every other metal, then bronze, silver, and gold. The more piercings, the higher the rank as well. These two ranked near the bottom with only two gold hoops each.

Grunts.

"Looks like we got ourselves a stowaway," said the first man.

The second man snarled, his lower lip quaking. "Shark food, says I."

The first man nodded. "Aye." A ghoulish grin warped his face. "On yer feet, dog."

Savric couldn't get his legs to cooperate with his mind, but an escape plan of sorts formed in his head.

"Ya deaf, oldtimer?" The second man nudged Savric with his boot. "Me friend here told ya ta git up."

Savric smiled at the man. "To be certain, my hearing is not what it used to be, but I assure you that my ears work better than my traitorous legs at this present moment. If one of you would be so kind, I fear I need assistance getting to my feet."

The second man spat on the deck and eyed the first man. "Thinks he better than we with fancy talk."

"Aye." A devious grin curled the corners of the first man's lips. "Means he got coin ta give us."

"Let's take im below, Bierch." The second man rubbed his hands together. "Squeeze im fer gold."

Bierch winked. "Aye, Ashter."

The two men grabbed Savric by the arms and hauled him backward through the sea of infected people. He opened his right palm, and Qotan's staff flew into it. He'd need it soon enough. Darkness engulfed the three men as they descended the narrow stairs leading down into the ship's hull.

They dragged Savric a good twenty paces before depositing him on the wood-planked floor. Rusty hinges groaned, and then a latch clicked into place.

"We be back in a shake," said the man named Bierch. "Best yeh find some coin."

It took several minutes for Savric's eyes to adjust to the darkness before he could get his bearings. He sat in the middle of a crude holding cell made of wooden walls and a wooden door with a small, barred opening toward the top. A pair of manacles hung from each of the two sidewalls. Had the men any smarts, they would've at least strung him up.

Savric rose from the floor and retreated to the back of the cell, Qotan's staff clutched in his hand. A minute later, Bierch and Ashter returned.

The cell door creaked open. Light poured into the cell from the torch Ashter held. "Time's up, oldtimer."

Savric shielded his eyes and grinned. "I understand what you just accomplished. I surmise you find your wit endearing?"

Ashter cocked his head, straightening the scar that crossed the bridge of his nose and ran the length of his right cheek. "Think he hit his noggin."

Bierch pushed past Ashter, a glint of steel in his left eye. A patch covered his right one. He took the torch from Ashter and closed the distance between himself and Savric. A short foot remained between them. "Aye. No matter. His coins still be good. Ain't that right?"

Savric shrugged. "Truth be told, I lack any coins."

Bierch stepped back and turned to Ashter. "Search him."

"Don' hafta ask twice." Ashter stepped forward, a snarl on his lips.

Savric drew some mezhik from the crystal orb atop Qotan's staff, giving himself a much-needed boost. He spun in a whirlwind and teleported just outside the cell. He slammed the door shut and slid the lock into place before the two men could puzzle out what had just happened.

Ashter and Bierch yelled a slew of profanities at Savric, several of which he'd never heard before. Their wicked mouths gave meaning to the phrase "cussin like a shipper."

Savric reached out and pulled the light straight from the torch Bierch held, effectively snuffing it out.

"Wizard!" exclaimed Ashter.

Enough of this.

"*Ɛəlläb*," said Savric.

The two men fell silent and slumped to the floor. Within moments, their snores filled the holding cell.

Savric chuckled. "That will keep them occupied for a few hours."

CHAPTER NINE

R ayah set her mind on Alderan's house and touched the mirror's cold, wet surface. The mirror room underneath Alderan's house rippled into view.

She stepped through the mirror and tensed as a memory of Sardis slithered up from the depths of her mind again. A wave of gooseflesh washed over her and shook her shoulders, but she didn't let the memory incapacitate her like it had earlier.

Rayah walked into the adjoining room where the shelves of books and tables sat, but the room lay in darkness. A cold draft filtered down through the shaft that led up into the house, blowing her hair back and leaving her chilled as it swept past. A door slammed in the house above, the jarring noise nearly pulling her out of her skin.

The sound of her own heartbeat drummed in her ears, and her hands trembled. She took a few steps into the dark room as her eyes began to adjust.

"Alderan?" Her voice croaked, no louder than a whisper.

Rayah waited several moments but received no response. She called his name again, louder. "Alderan?"

A gruff voice sounded from the house above. "You shouldn't be here. Go away." The voice wasn't Alderan's, but Rayah knew its owner well enough.

Urza.

Rayah located the ladder across the room and started climbing. Dim light filtered down through the small, square opening in the main floor of Alderan's house. She pulled herself up through the opening and rounded the side of the fireplace.

Urza lay on the floor in the middle of the living area. She didn't even bother to lift her head off the floor when Rayah walked over to her. "I said, 'go away.'"

Rayah's hands latched onto her hips. "I heard you the first time. What's wrong with you, and why are you here?"

Urza closed her eyes. "Doesn't matter. You need to leave before Rakzar comes back inside." Her voice sounded strange. Weak.

Rayah looked around. "Rakzar's here too?" She didn't know what was going on there, but she didn't like it. "What are you doing in Alderan's house? Better yet, what have you done with him?"

"Relax before you go and *soil* yourself." Urza chuckled and then coughed. "Rakzar and I have been here for a few days now, but we haven't seen the *emotional* wizard boy."

He's not here? The thought pierced Rayah right through the heart and made her chest ache. *If he didn't come home, then where did he go?*

The dark corridor and the soldier that came through the mirror rose in her mind. Her pulse raced faster.

Where was that place? Why did you go there, Alderan?

"You need to leave, *dryte*." Urza sounded just like Rakzar.

Rayah scoffed, ignoring Urza's attempted insult. "*I* need to leave? Why? I have as much right to be here as you do. More so in fact. Why don't *you* leave?"

"If you'd step outside of your self-absorbed world for a moment, you might clue in on the fact that I'm not feeling well."

"Don't you dare—" Rayah paused.

Had things changed with Urza?

Rayah crouched next to Urza and truly looked at her for the first time since entering the room. Several things about Urza differed from when she'd seen her just a few weeks ago. Urza's fur didn't shine like it had before, and her eyes sank farther into her skull than Rayah remembered. Also, Urza's nose didn't have its normal wet sheen, and her arms and legs had tufts of fur missing.

A hint of concern crept into Rayah's voice. "What's wrong with you?"

Urza turned onto her side. "It's a long story. Suffice it to say that I'm dying. Now get out before you find yourself dying as well."

Dying?

Rayah beat her wings and slid back several feet. She swallowed hard. "Are you contagious or something?"

"No, it's nothing like that. Leave now, and you'll be fine."

Rayah stood. "I'm not leaving until you explain what's going on. I have the right to know since you're holing up in Alderan's house."

Urza groaned. "Alright, but you must agree to two things. Don't repeat what I tell you to anyone, and when I've finished telling you what's going on, you must leave. Agreed?"

Rayah crossed her arms and huffed. "Fine… If what you say warrants me leaving."

Urza opened her eyes. Her irises, previously a deep yellow, looked washed out and faded. Perhaps a bit milky.

"Rakzar is cursed," Urza said flatly. "Anyone who comes into contact with him will die. That's why I'm dying. Good enough for you?"

"No!" She moved closer to Urza. "What do you mean he's cursed?"

Urza sighed. "When he went after Murtag, there were two sorceresses there. They cast a spell on him they called sickle. It marked his soul. Anyone who comes into contact with him will die a slow, agonizing death. I refused to leave his side after I rescued him, and now I'm dying. So, get out of here before he comes back, or you'll find yourself on the verge of death as well."

Rayah couldn't wrap her mind around what Urza said. Rakzar was a sadistic, twisted beast to begin with. Now, everyone around him would die?

Heat rose in Rayah's cheeks. "Alderan should've killed Rakzar when he had the chance."

"Maybe you're right, but it makes no difference now. To make matters worse, the spell keeps him from killing himself."

A thought occurred to Rayah. "Wait a minute… was Eshtak with you and Rakzar *after* the spell was cast on Rakzar?"

"Yeah, why?"

"Eshtak was still fine this morning."

"Perhaps the spell doesn't affect those around him unless they stay with him like I did."

Rayah recalled Amicus telling her that mezhik didn't seem to affect Eshtak the way it did others. "Or Eshtak's immune to it."

Urza grunted. "Either way, I don't think you want to stick around to find out just how it works."

Why didn't Alderan listen to me? Rakzar should've died on that beach.

Rayah groaned. "He'll never be anything but a killer."

"As I said before, you know nothing about him. He's not who you think he is."

"He's tried to kill me more times than I can count."

"You're lying to yourself." Urza rolled onto her other side. "How about I tell you the story of how Rakzar saved a baby dryte?"

Rayah swallowed hard. The thought of Rakzar doing anything for anyone but himself didn't register in her mind. The beast she knew had no compassion for anyone. Anything Urza said to the contrary would be a pack of lies. But she wanted to hear it anyway.

Rayah settled on the floor next to Urza. "Sure. What did he do?"

Urza closed her eyes and took a deep, ragged breath and then began her story. "Many years ago, there was a terrible fire in the Oblivio Mountains. As you probably know, Rakzar loves fire, so he went there to watch it all burn.

"Animals and creatures of all kinds fled the forest in a frenzy as the flames spread through the underbrush. While admiring the destructive nature of the fire, Rakzar heard a cry from deep within the forest. He rushed into the smoke and flames without a second thought.

"He searched the forest for a dozen minutes and almost gave up before hearing another cry not far from where he stood. A minute later, he found a baby girl dryte lying on the forest floor, surrounded by a wall of flames. The baby's mother lay at her side, charred and dying.

"Rakzar grabbed the baby dryte and her mother and carried them through the flames. By the time they reached a safe place, the mother had died, but the baby dryte survived.

"Rakzar knew he couldn't and wouldn't take care of her, so he took her to the one place he knew she'd be safe and cared for: the home of a hamadryad named Shalaidah. He left her there and never looked back.

"That was you, Rayah. He saved your life and tried to save your mother's as well."

Rayah's cheeks swam beneath a river of tears. *How could Rakzar have done something so selfless? Why?*

He couldn't have done it without reason, could he?

No. He's incapable. But then what did he gain from it?

None of it made sense. She wanted to believe that Urza lied, but no one knew the truth about her past other than Alderan. No one knew Shalaidah had raised her.

Rakzar saved me... The truth of it sank in. Shook her world.

Shalaidah had told Rayah that her mother had abandoned her all those years ago. Why had she lied to her? What else had she lied about?

No, no, no! She took me in. Gave me a home. Treated me as her own.

What difference would it have made if she'd told me the truth about my mother?

She knew the answer in her heart, but she couldn't let herself think about it. *Let it stay in the past.*

Rayah wiped her cheeks and sniffed. "I... I can't believe Rakzar would do such a thing. How could someone like him—a beast with no heart—do something so selfless?"

Urza forced air from her nostrils. "He has a bigger heart than you can imagine, even if he doesn't show it. He saved me as well when I was just a pup."

"He did?" Perhaps she didn't know him as well as she thought she did.

Ɂäţūr, have I been wrong about him all this time?

Urza peered up at Rayah through slitted eyelids. "He's not the monster you believe him to be. Killing was a means for him to survive, not what his heart truly desired. He saved Alderan from that castle fire as well. Don't you see? He does care. He saved us all."

Rayah suddenly felt sick to her stomach. She'd practically begged Alderan to kill Rakzar several times. *Yet he didn't.*

Alderan, the prophesied savior of the world, strove to preserve all life, even of those that sought to end his. He'd taken the lives of two gnolls to save hers on that hill. Had that selfless act tainted his soul?

Rayah groaned. *I started the fight that led us onto that hill.*

Would Alderan still save the world, or had her jealousy over Aria ruined everything?

No! I can't believe that. Ɂäţūr, tell me there's still hope!

Rayah needed to find a way to stave off her jealousy and focus on the needs of those around her. She couldn't allow her selfish desires to rule her mind anymore. She'd change, starting right then.

Rayah reached out and stroked Urza's yellow, fur-covered forearm. She wondered what had happened to the spring-loaded sheaths Urza normally wore on her forearms but decided not to ask. Urza growled but didn't pull away. Maybe she didn't have the strength to do so. Or perhaps she liked the attention. Rayah couldn't be certain.

Her mind returned to the problem at hand. "How can Rakzar break the spell?"

Urza yawned. A long, grayish-black tongue curled into her mouth and then unwound. "As far as I know, there's no way to do so."

Rayah moved closer and stroked Urza's back. "There must be some way for him to break the spell."

Urza growled. "What do you think you're doing?"

Rayah withdrew her hand. "I don't know. Trying to help I guess."

"Well, you're not. I'm no dog."

Rayah nodded. "I know. I'm sorry. It's just that Shalaidah used to rub my back when I didn't feel well. It always made me feel better. I thought it might make you feel better too."

"I'm slowly dying, not sulking."

"Right. Sorry." She twirled her finger into her hair. "Can't all spells be broken or countered? If they've been cast, there must be a way to remove them."

"I know little of mezhik or how it works, so I'm no help there."

Rayah stared at the blackened hearth. "Maybe he can get the sorceresses to remove the spell."

"You really are stupid, aren't you? They'll never reverse the spell. They'd rather die."

The jab stung, but Rayah let it slide. It actually felt good doing so. The thought of the sorceresses dying sparked an idea. "Why doesn't he find them and kill them? Maybe the spell will die with them."

"That's absurd."

"Why? You have a better suggestion?"

Urza closed her eyes. Her chest rose and fell slowly, and she wheezed with each breath. "No. Maybe you're right. Maybe he could kill them and break the spell."

"Then tell Rakzar to do it."

"Why are you trying to help him? I thought you hated him and wanted him dead."

"I do." Rayah frowned. "Or I did." She shrugged. "I don't know. Perhaps he's changed. Maybe he's not as bad as I thought. I don't know."

"Perhaps it's you who has changed. Or at least your view of him."

How cold is it in here?

Rayah hugged herself and rubbed her arms, but the rigid little bumps that speckled her skin remained. "Would you like me to build you a fire before I go?"

Urza nodded. "I'd like that."

Rayah took some logs from the pile next to the fireplace and placed them inside the hearth. She stuffed kindling between and underneath the logs and then found a match to light it. The kindling burned hot, quickly catching the logs on fire. Within a few minutes, the fire pumped much needed warmth into the room.

Urza crawled closer to the hearth and curled up. "Thank you."

Rayah rose. "You're welc—"

A noise outside the front door startled Rayah.

Urza's eyes shot open. "You must go now! If you don't, you won't survive."

"I'll come check on you again. I promise."

"If you do, make sure Rakzar isn't here first."

"Right. I'll call for you through the mirror."

The door handle rattled.

Rayah flew around the side of the fireplace and descended the ladder as fast as she could. The front door shook the house just as she reached the last rung. She jetted through the lower room and into the side room with the mirror.

Zerenity's closet appeared through the mirror when Rayah pressed her hand against its surface. She pushed herself through the mirror's cold, wet surface and stepped around the pile of ash on the floor. Had she not seen the soldier combust with her own eyes, she wouldn't have believed it to be more than dust.

Through rows of hanging clothes came a faint light. She followed that light into Zerenity's room and shut the closet door behind her. She leaned against the door and exhaled. Her pulse raced.

What would she do now? Master Savric wanted her to find Alderan, but she had no idea where to look for him. The mirror frightened her.

The dark corridor she'd seen through the mirror might be where Alderan went, but she couldn't be certain and had no idea where the corridor led. Even if she did find that same corridor, she might not be as lucky as the first time. Anything or anyone could be waiting on the other side of it, including those that wielded mezhik.

For the first time in her life, Rayah felt helpless. She didn't know what to do or where to go, so she knelt, closed her eyes, and prayed to her God.

Ɂäṭūr, I am Your servant. Tell me what to do, and I will obey. Guide me by Your hand as a shepherd guides his sheep. I will follow. Give me a way to be useful and contribute. I surrender.

A toppled tree flashed in Rayah's mind. She remembered it well. Sickly, dark-grey vines with orange thorns and leaves grew up from the black soil where the tree once stood. The vines produced a pungent odor that stung her nostrils, and a loud hissing noise filled her ears.

A pit of vipers.

Rayah opened her eyes. What would she find there if she went back? Would the vines have spread and infected the entire forest, or had they shriveled? She didn't know, and it scared her to think about it.

A strong urge to visit the forest rose within her, followed by an urgency she couldn't explain. Sweat dampened her palms, and her heart drummed in her ears. Wings fluttering, her feet lifted off the floor. She paced in the air.

I must go back to that spot.

✝ ✝ ✝

Rakzar stood just inside the door for several moments, inhaling the tantalizing aroma of burning wood. Little else gave him pleasure since Amicus's death. Fresh snow pellets clung to his cloak. He brushed them off and watched as they melted into dozens of miniature puddles across the warm floor.

Urza lay on the floor in front of a blazing fire, her back to him.

"Did you start the fire?" he asked, but she ignored him.

Rakzar's forked tongue flicked the air. "I can smell the dryte. Is she still here?"

"No." Urza didn't move. "Rayah just left."

Rakzar removed the cloak Eshtak had given him, stuffed it into the brown sack flung over his shoulder, and tossed the sack on a chair. "Good, but why was she here?"

Urza rolled over and faced Rakzar. "She came looking for the boy."

"The White Knight?" He breathed deep but didn't detect Alderan's scent. "He was here too?"

"No, she just thought he might've come here."

Rakzar moved over to the fire. Its warmth felt good on his smooth skin, but the skin didn't feel good on him. He removed the lizard's eye ring from his finger and braced for the transformation. It came in convulsing waves, as it always did. His body contorted, twisted, and morphed from a disgusting lizard creature back into his normal, seven-foot-tall gnoll form. He hated the ring, but it allowed him to move freely amongst his enemies. He placed it on the mantle.

Urza stared up at him, a slight smile parted her snout.

"What?" he growled.

"Your fur has started to fill in nicely. You can hardly see the scars anymore underneath it."

Rakzar eyed his stomach. White fur grew over the scars, a stark contrast to the red fur that covered the rest of him. "I don't care about the scars."

"I know, but I do." Her voice broke as tears rolled down her fur-covered cheeks. She took a deep breath and regained her composure. "I gave them to you, and I hate myself for it."

Rakzar gazed into the flames. "You followed Murtag's orders. He gave you no choice. If you hadn't, neither of us would be alive."

"Would that be so bad? I won't be here for much longer anyway."

"Don't talk like that." He bent down and rubbed her nose with his. "I will find a way to undo this damned spell. You just need to hold on a bit longer."

Urza lifted her head and tried to lick Rakzar's cheek, but her dry tongue caught in his fur. She sighed. "For better or worse... I think that's part of what makes the spell so horrific. I believe I'll hang on for quite some time yet, and you'll have to watch me waste away to nothing." She lay her head back on the floor and closed her eyes. "You should just kill me now and save yourself the pain. Save me the pain."

"No!" Rakzar stood and roared. "There's no way I'd ever take your life, Urza."

But I could strangle you right now.

The irony of the thought gave him pause. He looked down at his hands. How many lives had they taken over the years? How much blood had they spilled? He deserved death. Why hadn't the White Knight let him die on the beach?

If Urza dies, I'll blame you, White Knight.

"You would've done so a few weeks ago without a second thought. Now isn't the time to be soft. End me before I suffer further."

"You know I can't and *won't* do that. I'll find a way to save you if it's the last thing I do. You're all I have left."

"That isn't true. Never lose sight of what's around you." Urza coughed and cleared her throat. "Several others care about you just as much as I do."

Rakzar snarled, "Your sickness has made you delusional. Face the truth. We. Are. Alone."

Forever.

He retreated to the kitchen and leaned on the table, his mind swimming. Cold, dark waves crashed all around him, and the ocean's undertow threatened to pull him under once again. Emptiness and despair suffocated him like the water had that day. A loneliness, so deep and complete, ravaged him and pulled him to the floor.

His hands trembled, and his eyes stung with tears. Agony rose in his throat and manifested in a deep groan. On his knees, he bowed his head.

Zäṭūr, if You're there, do what You must with me, but I beg of You, don't let her death be by my hands. She deserves so much more. A full life. I can't handle losing her. I will gladly suffer anything else.

Snot hung from his snout and tears clung to his fur, but his moment of despair had passed. He wiped his face and snout with his forearms and rose from the floor. An empty bowl sat on the table's edge. He took the bowl and filled it with water.

Returning to the living area with the bowl of water, Rakzar set it on the floor next to Urza's head. "Drink it. It'll make you feel better."

Urza lifted her head and pulled the bowl closer. She lapped at the water until most of it had been drunk. She pushed it away with her snout. "Thank you." Her voice sounded better than it had earlier. Less gravelly.

Rakzar curled up next to Urza. "What am I going to do? How can I save you from this fate?"

Urza rested her head on his arm. "Rayah had a suggestion."

"You told the dryte about me?" He slammed his fist into the wooden floor. Several planks jumped in a rippling effect, and a small dust cloud rose in its wake.

Urza lifted her head and sneezed twice. "She wouldn't leave until I explained the situation to her, and I didn't want her here when you came back. I didn't think you'd want to look after two dying friends."

Friends... The dryte hates me. But could he blame her?

Rakzar growled, "And what did she suggest? I pray to ʒätūr about it?" He already had, but he'd never admit it to Urza or anyone else for that matter.

Urza cocked her head. "What? Why would she suggest that?"

"Never mind. Go on."

"She said that you might be able to break the spell by killing Käíeʑ."

Rakzar rose onto his elbows and glared at Urza. "And you believe I hadn't thought of that?"

She glared back. It was the first time Rakzar had witnessed fire in her eyes in more than a week. Hope welled in his chest.

"I'm not saying you didn't, but Rayah had a good point," said Urza. "Kill Käíeʑ and maybe the spell dies with her… or them."

Rakzar rolled over and stared at the ceiling. The patch he'd made to the roof still held. "And what am I supposed to do? Leave you here? You know I can't do that."

Urza grabbed his arm. She still had strength. "You must. If you just stay here with me, I will certainly die. Is that what you want?"

Rakzar flung her hand off and jumped to his feet. He pointed a finger at her and spoke through clenched jaws. "I told you to stay away from me to begin with. *This* is *your* fault."

"It doesn't matter who's to blame, Rakzar. We're in this situation now." She rose on all fours. "Deal with it. Man up. Do something about it instead of just lying around complaining." She turned and headed toward the front door.

He met her at the door and flung it open. "Fine. I'll go get myself killed trying to kill Käíeʑ."

Urza was right, and he hated her for it. Not so much hated her but hated that she knew him better than he knew himself at times. He couldn't just sit around and do nothing. His nature wouldn't allow it. He knew nothing but action.

How in the world can I kill a creature like Käíeʑ?

She could phase in and out of solidity, and that would be an issue. He had no idea how to overcome that, but he'd do everything possible to figure it out. He had no choice. Urza's life depended on him succeeding.

What if I kill her but it doesn't break the spell?

He pushed the thought from his mind.

I won't allow Urza to die.

Urza walked outside and into the snow.

He followed her. "Where do you think you're going?"

She looked back over her shoulder. "To relieve myself. You coming to watch?"

"Not a chance." He went back inside, grabbed the brown sack off the chair, and then retrieved the ring from atop the fireplace mantle. He dropped the ring in the bag and slung the bag over his shoulder. Satisfied he had nothing else to take with him, he headed back outside.

Urza rounded the far corner of the house and headed back toward Rakzar and the front door. "I know you're not stupid enough to go get yourself killed without a plan, so where are you off to?"

"I need to go for a run so that I can think."

"You're not going to wear the ring then?"

"Not for this. I'm faster in my natural form. Besides, it's disgusting walking around as a saurian." The thought sent tremors racing through him.

Urza snorted. "Can't be as bad as the way you smell when you turn into one."

Rakzar shook his head. "Nice. I'll be back in an hour or two. Will you manage while I'm gone?"

Her left eyebrow rose. "I'm not dead yet. Besides, Rayah said she'd drop in again to check on me."

What kind of game is that dryte playing?

He didn't have the time or desire to think about it. "Fine."

Rakzar dropped on all fours and headed into the falling snow without saying another word. Each step propelled him toward a destiny he could no longer avoid. Urza needed him, and he wouldn't let her down.

I don't know how I'll save you, but I'll die trying.

† † †

About thirty minutes later, Rakzar found himself on the same beach where he'd died a few weeks ago. When he left Alderan's house, he hadn't planned on returning to that spot, yet there he stood. That day, after Zerenity and Alderan had brought him back from the depths of darkness and despair, he'd vowed to be better. To serve a penance for all the bloodshed he'd caused. To redeem his soul—if he actually had one. However, his efforts only led to more death.

First Amicus. Urza will follow soon.

How many more lives would he take before death came for him? How would he find the answer to defeat Käíez without jeopardizing more lives? He'd read through every book under Alderan's house—at least the ones in High Centaurian—and found nothing.

An answer must exist.

He kicked the sand and growled at the incoming waves. "Why didn't you kill me when you had the chance?"

"Are you talking to me or the waves?"

Rakzar knew that voice, and his fur stood on end, but he refused to turn around and face his approaching dark demon. "I buried you with your family, Shadowman."

"You certainly did, and I appreciate it," said Amicus.

"Then why are you here?" he growled. "I've got enough on my mind without you rising from the dead. Go be with your family."

Amicus stopped just beyond Rakzar, facing the ocean. "Would if I could, but you and I must have some unfinished business."

Rakzar looked down at Amicus. A thin, scarlet line circled Amicus's neck. Memories of Amicus's death played in Rakzar's mind: Wibble's wire ripped through Amicus's flesh again, and Amicus's head tumbled from his narrow shoulders. Then Amicus, his severed head on a pike, blamed Rakzar for getting him killed.

"No, we don't." Rakzar glared skyward. *I don't need this. Do you hear me, Ɂäṯūr? Have I not suffered enough?*

Amicus shrugged. "If we don't, then why did you bring me here?"

Rakzar growled. "I didn't. You're dead. Now get out of my head before I detach yours."

Amicus rubbed his neck. "Ouch!" He turned and gazed up at Rakzar, a hint of hurt in his eyes and voice. "Don't you think it's a bit too soon for comments like that? I've only been dead a short while, my friend."

Rakzar regretted the comment, even to a dead man haunting him, but he'd never own up to it. Instead, he matched Amicus's stare and crossed his arms but said nothing.

A grin spread Amicus's lips. "I'm just playing with you. Lighten up, you furry beast. You act like you're the one who's dead." He reached out and grabbed Rakzar's elbow.

Rakzar jerked his arm away, not expecting to feel Amicus's touch. "How did you do that? You're dead."

"Everything I do and say comes from *your* head. The mind is a powerful thing. It's obvious you need to work through something. Ah, yes, Käíeƹ." Amicus sat down in the sand and patted the spot next to him. "Sit down, and let's figure it out together."

Rakzar plopped down on the cold, damp sand and stared at the Gelu Ocean. "After you died, that wretched thing cursed me. Now Urza is dying because of it, and there's nothing I can do to stop it."

"A solution always exists, but you must dig deep to find it."

"Dig deep?" Rakzar dug his hand into the sand and grabbed a fistful of it.

Amicus chuckled. "Physically is one approach."

Rakzar squeezed the sand until his knuckles ached. When he opened his hand, the sand didn't sift through his fingers. Instead, it just sat there, clumped together in a misshapen ball. The pressure he'd applied to it, combined with the ocean water, held it together.

Rakzar stared at the ball of sand. *If only it were Käíeƹ's neck.* He chucked the sand ball into the encroaching waves. "This is useless."

"On the contrary, my friend. You are far cleverer than you let on." Amicus reached down, grabbed a fistful of sand, and squeezed it into a ball. He held it up and examined it. "There must be a way to keep Käíeƹ in her solid form."

Understanding rocked Rakzar. "Like the sand..." His mind raced to find a solution. "But what could do that?"

Amicus scratched his chin. "Perhaps some sort of spell or containment field would do the trick."

"A weapon... or an object." Rakzar swept his arm through the sand and flung the sand at the waves. "But how can I find the answer?"

"You have resources. Use them. After all, what are friends for?" Amicus winked at him.

"That's creepy," growled Rakzar. "Don't ever do it again."

Amicus laughed aloud. "All in your head, my friend!"

Rakzar knew someone who might have an answer. Or at least Rayah did. *But why would the dryte help me?*

A deep, dark, hideous thought crept into Rakzar's mind.

Infect her, and she'll have no choice.

He boxed his ears and roared at the ocean. "No! I will not risk another life."

"Life is precious, especially that of friends, but sometimes you must take risks that endanger them in order to save others."

"I got you killed!" roared Rakzar.

"I knew the risks going into that cave." Amicus grabbed Rakzar's arm again. "You didn't drag me in there. I chose to go. Besides, it led me right where I belong."

"But the dryte hates me." Rakzar stood and approached the incoming tide. "She'll never agree to help."

"You tried to kill her and Alderan on several occasions," yelled Amicus, "but I think she'll come around. She has as much heart and pride as you. You're more alike than you may think."

Clarity came to Rakzar in the form of another dastardly thought, but far less hideous than the first. "Rayah will help me if she thinks Shalaidah's life is in danger."

Amicus suddenly stood next to Rakzar. "And what do you think she'll do when she finds out you lied to her?"

"It's not a lie. If Rayah doesn't come along, I will be forced to go see Shalaidah myself, putting her life in danger."

"Sounds dishonest to me."

Rakzar retreated several paces as the tide drew near. "No one asked you, Shadowman."

Amicus laughed. "Then why am I here?"

Rakzar brushed the sand from his fur, satisfied with his plan. He glanced back at Amicus and growled, "Don't follow me."

"Wouldn't dream of it." Amicus winked at him again.

Rakzar shuddered, dropped onto all fours, and tore across the beach.

I know I can save you, Urza.

CHAPTER TEN

Alderan moved past Wizard Wrik and entered the bedchamber. The drab room was cozy if not cramped and smelled of fresh-cut cedar. A large bed and a small desk, too small for even Alderan, lined the opposing wall.

To the right of the door sat a table and two chairs, shoved into the corner. The hearth inset in the wall between the table and bed lay dormant. Four logs sat on its stone surface, three propped up on one another and the other between the three. A small pile of cut wood stacked to the right side of the hearth.

The room leeched warmth from Alderan like a soul-sucking wraith. His teeth chattered, and gooseflesh prickled his skin. He rubbed his arms with fervor. "Do you mind if I build a fire?"

"Build a fire? How archaic," jested Wrik. "Are we not wizards?"

Heat rose in Alderan's cheeks. "I don't know—" Rayah's words about keeping his weaknesses to himself filled his mind. He started again, "I prefer to use mezhik only when necessary."

Wrik pointed at the hearth. "*Ɛäṭ äbəlläíz.*" A ball of purple flames shot from his hand, streaked across the room, and struck the four logs on the hearth. The logs caught fire, and the flames transitioned from purple to blue-and-orange.

Alderan shook his head. *Showoff.* He moved in front of the hearth and warmed his hands. He peered back over his shoulder. "Thank you."

Wrik frowned. "I trust that you'll touch nothing while I'm away?"

Alderan gave Wrik a curt nod and returned his gaze to the fire. He grinned. *Nothing that doesn't interest me.*

"Very well. I'll return within the hour with Aria." Wrik exited the room and closed the door. The locking mechanism clicked as it engaged.

Alderan stood before the fire until it chased the last of the chill from his cold bones. He could've used something to eat, but it didn't look like Wrik stocked food in the room. His stomach would have to wait.

Piles of papers and books covered every inch of the table's surface. Alderan pulled out a chair and sat down. After twiddling his thumbs for a solid minute, he decided to peruse the closest stack of papers. He grabbed the top piece of paper.

"*Fädinzh dhä Ballek…* could be interesting." The first few sentences captivated him, so he read through the rest of it. By the time he reached the end, he found himself frostbitten with fear.

The Black Wedding. I wonder if the prophecy's been fulfilled.

He grabbed the next piece of paper, read the first sentence, and tossed it aside. "Boring."

He snatched one of the books off the table and rifled through it, but it didn't grab his attention. However, the title of one of the other books in the pile did. He yanked it out from underneath three other books, and the entire pile tumbled off the table and thwacked the granite floor.

Good job, Alderan.

He bent down to pick up the books, but his sudden movement rustled several papers. One of them drifted off the table and right into the fire. Alderan reached into the flames and snatched the paper back. He patted down the blackened edges and pieces of it crumbled away. He shoved the paper underneath several others, hoping Wrik wouldn't notice it until much later, if at all.

Just put everything back and stop snooping.

He gathered the books from the floor and re-stacked them on the table. When he sat back down, he noticed something red on the floor underneath the table. He scooted the chair back and bent down to retrieve the object.

A feather?

He picked it up and sat back down on the chair.

Six inches long, the feather was like none he'd ever seen. Its thick quill stood out with a dark, crimson hue, and the barbs on the vane alternated between dark oranges and deep reds. As a woodsman and hunter, Alderan knew the wildlife well, at least around Viscus D'Silva. He had no clue as to what kind of bird that feather came from though.

The golden chain attached to the end of the quill interested him further. Thin, tightly woven links comprised the chain, and it weighed less than the feather. No hand could've crafted such a chain.

He pulled the chain over his head and moved his hair out of the way.

Shorter than the leather necklace he wore, it hung inside of the leather necklace. The feather itself hung at his breastbone and tickled his skin. When he reached for it, the feather and chain burst into flames and disintegrated. His chest tingled with mezhik for several moments afterward.

Alderan gasped. "What just happened?"

He pulled the front of his shirt down. The leather necklace with his mother's small, brass ring still hung around his neck, but the other necklace had vanished. Well, sort of. A six-inch-long red mark discolored his skin and matched the feather perfectly. He rubbed his chest, but the mark remained.

"Whoa." His fingers slipped from his shirt. "What have I done?"

Wrik's gonna kill me.

† † †

Wrik glided down corridors, hallways, and stairs, his mind preoccupied with the young man waiting in his bedchamber and how his presence affected the world. Just in the last several weeks, Wrik could count a handful of fulfilled prophecies, a few of which he'd personally witnessed.

Those moments drove him down his own path. Fed his obsession. He thrived on the anticipation and calculated guess as to which path a given prophecy would take. Oft, his guesses paid off. He served Lord Rosai at Castle Galondu for one such reason: the prophecy of Ɂţōn Dhef Dädh and the twins.

Wrik understood the prophecy of Ɂţōn Dhef Dädh better than anyone and had anticipated the resurrection of Cinolth The Dark. Lord Rosai had not. His pride had blinded him from the truth. Wrik smiled.

And he'll never see what's coming next.

Up ahead, Master Credan strode toward Wrik, his brow scrunched, and his gaze captured by the floor. Torchlight glinted off his bald head.

Just the man I'm looking for.

Wrik halted in the corridor and awaited Credan's approach. To Wrik's surprise, Credan walked right past him without a moment's glance and pressed on down the corridor.

Wrik turned back and called to him. "Master Credan." His deep voice boomed and echoed off the high ceilings.

Credan jerked upright so quickly that he nearly toppled over. He swung around, his eyes wide and his spectacles crooked on his face. "Wizard Wrik! Where the gods did you come from?"

Wrik closed the distance between them in three quick strides. "You must be about some important business to have missed a man as large as me." He towered over Credan by a good eighteen inches. Perhaps more.

Credan straightened his spectacles and craned his neck. "I am. As I'm sure you're aware, Lord Rosai is not a patient man." He waved his hand. "Never you mind that. How may I be of assistance?"

"Do you know where I might find Lady Aria?"

"Lady Aria…" Credan scratched his head, his fingers focused on a particularly large liver spot right on his left crown. "Last I heard, she sought the open air. I'm certain you'll find her strolling about atop the southern rampart."

Wrik dipped his head. "Very good, Master Credan. Your assistance is most appreciated. I won't keep you from your business any longer."

Credan held up a finger. "Might I ask a favor of you?"

"A favor?" Wrik clasped his hands behind his back and smiled. "It would be an honor."

"When you've located Lady Aria, let her know that Lord Rosai requests her presence in the main dining hall in two hours."

"Consider it done."

"Good. Now—"

Wrik cut him off. "However, do not hold me responsible if she arrives late… or not at all."

"Yes, of course." Credan nodded curtly. "Good day." He turned and strode away.

Good day, indeed.

✝ ✝ ✝

Aria stood atop the southern rampart of Galondu Castle and gazed into the distance. Without a single cloud to obstruct her view, she could just make out the Vastus Ocean on the horizon, its deep-blue hue rising up to meet the faded, blue sky.

"How far do you think we are from the ocean?" she asked.

Cinolth stood next to her. His forearm dwarfed her entire body, his clawed hand large enough to crush her in his palm. "Seventy-five miles." His demonic voice prickled her skin.

A light breeze ruffled her hair. The late winter air still bit a little, even with the sun fully overhead. She pulled her cloak tight. "I want to see it up close. Take me there."

"You're still a foolish, young girl. Will you never learn your place? I am no beast of burden that you can summon for a ride every time you get a whim. Try and treat me as such, and you'll never take flight again."

Foolish?

Aria seethed. "I brought you back to life. I can send you back to the grave just as quickly."

Cinolth stomped the parapet, leaving a crack two feet long down the inside of it. "Do not fool yourself." The heat of his breath caused Aria's clothes to smoke. She stepped back with a slight cringe. "Your blood, and the blood of the others, pulled me from a great sleep. We are bound together by that blood, but I am the one who has control. Never forget that."

Aria closed her eyes and concentrated on the soothing rhythm of her heartbeat. "Like mezhik, I feel your presence coursing through my veins. I can summon you with my mind, talk to you without words, and track your location across great distances. I feel what you feel. My desires are yours." She looked up at him. "Tell me that's not control."

Cinolth laughed, a deep, reverberating rumble. Plumes of smoke rose from his nostrils and bellowed out the sides of his massive jaws. "You know nothing of control. Let me give you a demonstration of what true control looks like." He turned his hand palm-up. "Climb on."

Aria climbed onto Cinolth's hand, and he lifted her onto his back.

"Hang on," he said in her mind.

She barely had time to grab hold of one of the spikes on his back before he took to the sky with the thrust of his wings. No matter how many times she witnessed it, the size and power of his wings left her astonished. They stretched a good thirty-five feet in both directions.

The air whooshed and snapped with every beat as they climbed high above the castle. Like lightning, they streaked across the sky with a southeast heading. Within ten minutes, they'd traveled two-thirds of the distance to Desolo Urbs. Cinolth dove, and the ground streaked toward them in a blur. Aria laughed as her stomach rose into her throat. Impact certain, Aria braced herself, but Cinolth leveled them out at the last moment. Two streaks of dust trailed them, Cinolth's wings kicking it up from the dry ground.

Cinolth reared up, halting their forward momentum. He settled on the ground.

"Why have we stopped," she asked.

His voice entered her mind. *"Look around us."*

A sea of people ambled across the rugged terrain. Most of them didn't take notice of the giant dragon in their midst. Several of the ones who did shrieked with fear and scattered. A few others drew weapons and retreated several dozen paces.

"I don't understand. Why are they all headed toward the castle?"

"Because I've summoned them."

Summoned them?

Aria's mind traveled back to the conversation she'd had with him earlier that morning.

This is his army?

Aria looked closer. Many of the people wore little clothing, or at least far less than they should've, given the temperature. Each of them bore pale skin, almost a chalky-white, and black veins covered the portions of exposed skin she could see. Arms, legs, necks, faces. Everything.

"Are they infected?"

"In a sense, yes. But not how you think. Let me demonstrate. See the woman passing by on the left in the green shirt?"

"Yes. She doesn't seem to know we're here."

"I'll have her attack the man with the red cloak in front of us. Watch close."

Aria focused on the woman with the green shirt. The woman halted, turned around, and walked straight toward the man with the red cloak. The man backed away several steps as the woman approached him. The tip of his sword touched the ground, his face full of confusion.

The man raised his arm. Fear lit his eyes. "What is it you want?"

The woman reached him, pulled the knife from the sheath on his belt, and drew it across his neck before he had a chance to react. Blood sprayed from his neck. He screamed, but it only lasted a few moments before blood erupted from his mouth. The man clutched his throat, dropped to his knees, and then collapsed onto his side.

Aria gasped. "Dear Ʒäțūr!"

"Do you now understand what it means to have control?"

Aria nodded, her eyes fixed on the woman in the green shirt. The woman dropped the knife, turned, and started walking toward the castle again. Blood covered her clothes, arms, and face. She made no attempt to wipe it off.

Another man rushed to the first man's side, shouting curses at the woman as he checked for a pulse.

"Tell them to go back home, or they will all die this day."

Aria sat up straight. Many of the people looked to her. *I am their queen.* She must get used to addressing them with authority.

She cleared her throat, but no words came to mind. How could she explain something that she herself didn't understand? How did the beast control them?

A heat flash swept through Aria, head-to-toe and down into her bones, and then words poured from her mouth. "Citizens of Desolo Urbs, you may not know me yet, but you soon will. I am Aria Rosai, your rightful ruler as Queen of the Ancient Realm. Listen to what I have to say and heed my words."

Aria swept her arm toward the flowing sea of infected people. "As you have witnessed, these people are sick of mind. They are infected with a disease that can only be cured by means of mezhik. The process of cleansing them is arduous, and it will take many months for them to recover.

"Because of this, we have summoned them to the castle where they can be properly cared for and healed. Do not hinder them. Do not follow them. Return to your homes. I promise that your loved ones will return to you if the disease is successfully purged from them.

"However, there is no guarantee of recovery. If they've failed to return to you within a year, consider them dead. Do not come seeking them. Their bodies will be burned to prevent the disease from spreading.

"If you fail to comply, we bear no responsibility to your wellbeing. In all likelihood, you will suffer the same fate as the man before me. You have been warned. Return to your homes."

"You're not our queen!" shouted a man.

Cinolth trembled beneath her, the scales on his neck turned red with heat, and then flames poured from his mouth. The smell of sulfur rose in the air, and screams filled Aria's ears. The crowd scattered in a fit of chaos. Several people lost their footing or were shoved to the ground, trampled under foot.

Aria gasped as though waking from a nightmare, her lungs burning for air. Her heart knocked against her ribcage, her eyes misted with tears. The words she'd spoken hadn't originated from her mind. Somehow, Cinolth had used her as his mouthpiece, and the implications of what it implied drove fear into her heart.

In her mind, she traced back through several recent memories. In many of them, she'd demonstrated a level of rage she'd never attained before. With Pravus. Her father, Nardus.

Am I truly under his control?

Her stomach gurgled, and bile rose into her throat. She closed her eyes and forced it back down.

"Hold on," said Cinolth in her mind. She complied, wrapping her arms around one of his long spikes and squeezing her thighs against his muscled shoulders.

Cinolth took to the sky in a flurry of dust and wings, circling as they climbed ever higher. Far below, several people attended to the wounded and dead left in the wake of chaos. Many others turned and headed back to Desolo Urbs, but a few of them didn't heed Cinolth's warning. She knew they'd be put to death when they arrived at the castle.

Aria looked to the heavens. *What have I done?*

Fifteen minutes later, they landed atop the southern rampart of Galondu Castle once again. Wizard Wrik stood a good distance from them, just outside the third tower entrance. He held his hands behind his back. A grin parted his lips, and his white teeth beamed against his dark skin. Sunlight glinted off his wire-rimmed spectacles and his hairless head.

Aria slid down Cinolth's shoulder and arm and landed on her feet.

Cinolth's presence entered her mind. *"I must hunt. When I return, I will show you how to truly use your mezhik."*

"As you wish." She didn't look back. If she had, he would've seen the fear in her eyes. As it were, she likely reeked of it. In her heart, she knew the truth.

He is part of me. I can hide nothing from him.

Whoosh-whoosh. Whoosh-whoosh-whoosh.

Aria's hair blew in her face as Cinolth took to the sky. She swept her hair out of her face and tossed its ends over her shoulders. Cinolth's presence faded as the distance between them expanded. Her fear dissipated, she turned her attention toward the hulking man waiting patiently for her by the third tower.

Aria approached him. A smile curled her lips. "Wizard Wrik, you're just the man I need."

† † †

Aria approached Wrik, her red-streaked, blond hair in disarray. He first noticed her unusual gait and how gingerly she stepped. Then he noticed her eyes, not particularly the vibrant-green hue of her irises, but more so the shade of red that tinted the whites of them.

Windblown? Or is it something more?

A sadness belied the smile she wore, yet her beauty still shone.

A beacon of light.

Aria stopped before him and offered him her hand. He took it and bent over as he brought it to his lips. Uncovered, her skin was ice on his lips.

"Lady Aria." He eyed her over the tops of his wire-rimmed spectacles, her face reduced to splotches of colors and shapes. "I've sought your company as well." He released her hand and stood tall.

"My company?" A bit of color returned to her cheeks. "For leisure or business?"

He chuckled. "A bit of both, perhaps."

"Walk with me." She offered her arm, and he took it.

Wrik sensed Aria needed time to process what she'd come to ask, so he clung to her arm in silence as she led him along the wide path of the ramparts. He didn't mind it though, her presence more than enough to occupy his thoughts.

After some distance, she halted, just in front of a large crack on the parapet. He'd walked the ramparts several days ago and hadn't noticed the crack then. It must've happened recently.

Aria turned to him and peered into his eyes. "You've done so much for me in the last few weeks, and I hate to ask anything else of you, but there are few people in this world that I can trust, especially with the task I need done."

"I too trust very few people." He took her hand in his, and his mind fired warnings of overstepping forbidden boundaries, but withdrawing now would prove far more awkward, so he forged ahead on his steep slope of regret. "Ask anything of me, and I'll do everything in my power to accomplish it."

Aria withdrew her hand from his, but not with malice. She turned toward the parapet and gazed into the distance. "On my wedding night, Pravus removed *zäbräzär* from my neck so that I could fully experience the… throes of passion."

Throes of passion. Those were the last words Wrik wanted to hear from her lips in reference to Lord Rosai. He cringed at the thought of her elaborating further. He placed his hands atop the parapet and looked skyward.

Gods, let this conversation take another path. Do not make me suffer thinking about that vile man violating her.

Aria continued, "Later that night, while Pravus slept in my arms, a bond I'd all but forgotten sparked back to life." She turned and placed her hand over his.

Wrik looked down at her dainty, pale hand. Ghostly white against his black skin. Her entire hand, fingers and all, fit on the top of his hand with room to spare. His gaze met hers. Tears wet her cheeks, but a smile parted her lips.

The fingers from Aria's other hand wrapped around Wrik's forearm. "After thinking him dead for nearly a year, I finally felt the bond again that I'd always shared with my twin brother, Alderan. As when we were children, in that moment I knew his exact location. Far to the northwest, outside Tyrosha."

Aria absolutely beamed, the sadness he'd witnessed in her eyes before vanquished. He smiled with her. "That is marvelous news! Your happiness is a welcome sight."

She squeezed his arm. "Yes, but the stone ceremony changed everything."

Wrik frowned. "How so?"

"I don't know for certain, but I believe the bond I now share with Cinolth somehow weakened the bond I have with Alderan." She closed her eyes for a moment. "I can still sense his presence in the world, but I cannot locate him anymore."

May the gods continue to show me favor.

Wrik smiled. "I'm certain I can be of assistance in this matter."

Aria nodded. "Yes, I believe you can be. Do this for me, and I will be indebted to you yet again."

He wagged his finger at her. "No, Lady Aria, this I'll do as your friend." He took her hand, bowed low, and kissed the top of it. "Consider it done."

Aria wrapped her arms around his waist. "Thank you!"

Wrik held Aria for a moment, and the world felt as it should, but then demons from his past rose from the depths of Ef Demd Dhä and into his mind. Once, he'd gotten too close to a woman, and it'd nearly killed him. In that moment, he'd vowed never to do so again. His shoulders shuddered as he pulled away from her and stepped back.

Aria didn't seem to notice. "Now, you said you were looking for me as well. What is it that I can do for you?"

"Ah, yes. There are two things, actually. First, Master Credan asked me to inform you that Lord Rosai requests your presence in the dining hall for lunch." He looked up at the sun's location in the sky. "I'd say you have less than an hour now."

"Very well. And the second?"

"The second is a bit of a surprise, actually. Accompany me to my bedchamber, and I'll show you."

Aria gasped. "Wizard Wrik! Have you no shame?"

Wrik's cheeks caught fire and his tongue tied in his mouth. "Mistress… Lady… I didn't mean—"

Aria snorted. "Relax, my friend. I didn't know you'd get so worked up about a little joke. Forgive me."

"No, no. I…" Wrik rubbed the back of his neck.

She took his arm in hers and pulled him around toward the third tower. "Let us go to your bedchamber and put this moment in the past."

He nodded, still too flustered to speak without tripping over his tongue.

Gods, I'm a fool.

† † †

Alderan woke to the sound of voices in the corridor outside Wrik's bedchamber. The left side of his face ached, and when he lifted his head from the table a piece of parchment came with it, stuck to his cheek with saliva. He yanked the parchment from his face and tossed it on the table.

The fire in the hearth smoldered, the coals still red with heat. A single log remained intact, the others reduced to lumps of ash. The candle atop the desk burned low, but he didn't remember how much of it had remained when they'd arrived.

How long have I been asleep? A crick in his neck clued him in. He tried rubbing it out, but it proved as stubborn as him.

Across the room, Alderan spotted a small water basin perched atop a narrow pedestal. He didn't recall seeing it there earlier. A large bucket half-filled with water sat next to it on the floor. He drew some of the water from the bucket with a small, wooden cup and poured it into the basin bowl. The water sparkled in the candlelight but held no secrets of the future.

Alderan refreshed himself and returned to the chair at the table. He leaned back in the chair, disengaging its front legs from the floor. Nerves squirmed in the pit of his stomach as the minutes passed. So much had changed.

Lady Rosai.

The title had a ring to it for certain, but it only heightened his anxiety thinking about it. How should he address her? He'd never met a lady before.

She's your sister, you oaf. You've known her your entire life.

He raked his fingers through his hair. *But she's a lady now. I'm nothing. Will she even want to see me? Will she recognize me?*

He swallowed hard. *Will I recognize her?*

A key rattled in the door and sent him crashing to the floor. He rolled his head forward and narrowly avoided splitting it against the stone floor. The door lock disengaged.

Alderan scrambled to his feet and righted the fallen chair. He pulled his hair behind his ears and smoothed his shirt. Stains soiled it. He couldn't have looked less presentable, especially for a lady.

He gripped the chairback, his nerves frayed and his legs weak. Wrik entered the room first, followed by a woman he hardly recognized. His knees buckled, but he held fast to the chair.

"Alderan!" squealed the woman. She nearly knocked him over as she embraced him.

It took a moment for Alderan's mind to catch up with what his heart already knew. He wrapped his arms around Aria and lifted her off her feet. "I... I hardly recognized you."

Alderan had visualized finding Aria and embracing her so many times over the last year, but never had he imagined these specific circumstances. Rayah's presence in that moment had seemed certain.

Rayah! Alderan's stomach lurched. *She must be out of her mind with worry. She's probably gonna kill me when I get back to Zerenity's.*

"You look just as I remembered you," said Aria.

Focus, Alderan. Be content in the moment.

"I'll leave the two of you with some privacy for a time," said Wrik. "I'm sure you have many things to discuss."

"We'll certainly speak later about how you came upon Alderan," said Aria.

Wrik nodded, stepped out of the room, and closed the door.

Alderan released Aria and stepped back. "Turn around. Let me have a look at you."

Aria twirled around, her beige cloak flowing at her back. White, skin-tight trousers wrapped her legs and disappeared underneath black, shin-high, leather boots with several straps and silver buckles. A white blouse with a ruffled neck hugged her slender curves and dipped low between her breasts, revealing more skin and cleavage than Alderan cared to see. A necklace with a dragon pendant hung at her breastbone, and several rings hung on her fingers. Extravagant earrings of gold and diamonds swayed from her earlobes, sparkling in the light.

Everything about her spoke to the fact that she'd become a lady in his absence, but the locks flowing from her head and down her shoulders attracted his attention the most. "What happened to your hair? Why is it streaked with red?"

Aria stroked her hair. "Do you like it?" She grinned.

"Yeah, sure. It's just... different." Alderan craned his neck forward and frowned. "Your teeth. They were crooked before, right? I didn't just imagine that?"

"Pravus, my husband, fixed them for me. In fact, he fixed a lot of things for me." Aria's eyes glossed over, and her lower lip quivered.

Alderan took her arm and led her over to Wrik's bed. The two of them sat on its edge. "Tell me everything, Aria. What happened to you after they captured you and killed our father? And how did you wind up getting married to a lord?"

Aria daubed the corners of her eyes with a kerchief and then delved into a twisted story so frightening that Alderan had a hard time sitting still and listening to it. Anger, sorrow, frustration, and despair tossed him about with every turn of her tale.

Alderan pulled on his hair. Everything she told him about her bondage, rape, and torture left him sick with guilt and brimming with rage, but one question kept rising to the surface of his thoughts. He voiced it, as much to himself as to Aria. "Why did Dragnus send the gnolls to capture you but kill me?"

Aria wiped her eyes. "I don't know, but it wasn't what Pravus told him to do. Pravus would never wish you dead."

"Speaking of your husband, how did you wind up marrying a lord?"

Aria smiled as she looked down at her hands. "He saved me from Dragnus and promised me a future by his side. Our union was prophesied about. Destiny."

The thought of prophetic destiny turned Alderan's stomach. Given that it was his prophetic destiny to save the world, he wondered how often the prophecies were wrong. He pushed the thoughts to the back of his mind and focused back on Aria and Pravus.

"So Pravus is the one who freed you from the dungeons?" he asked.

"No. By the time he arrived, I was locked in a tower." She pulled him back into her story and told him about how Amicus had saved her from a man she called One-Eyed Jess.

Hearing everything Amicus did for her with such selflessness tore at his heart. Guilt festered in his mind, and he broke down and sobbed.

This time, Aria consoled him. "Talk to me, Alderan. What are you thinking and feeling?"

How far Alderan and Aria had come in the last year, but not for the better. They'd known each other intimately for most of their lives, sharing thoughts, feelings, and so much more because of their bond, yet now they sat on the edge of Wrik's bed as strangers. Disconnected. It hurt him more than knowing he hadn't been there for her during her darkest hours.

I must learn everything about her again and show her who I've become as well.

Alderan pulled himself into the past. Into the cell where Rakzar had bound him. He removed the faded, yellow and green bracelet from his wrist and held it up. "I almost killed Amicus over this. The instant I saw it around his wrist I knew it was yours. I assumed he'd killed you and took it. I'd never felt so much rage. If Rakzar hadn't stopped me, I would've killed him."

Aria grabbed Alderan's arm and shook it. "You know Amicus? How is he? How is his family?"

Alderan gazed into her beautiful, green eyes, but even they'd changed. Red tinted the fringes of her irises.

He searched for the right words to tell Aria that her friend and his family had died, but his silence answered her questions just as well.

She dug her nails into his arm. Mezhik tingled in her touch. "They're dead? How?"

Alderan recounted everything, from the castle fire to the demise of Amicus's family to the beheading of Amicus. By the time he finished, Aria sat next to him, stunned and speechless. He peeled her fingers off of his arm and placed his arm around her shoulders. He pulled her to him and rested his head against hers, but she didn't respond as he would've thought.

She pushed his arm away and stood. "It doesn't matter. In the end, they would've died anyway. Every last one of them will." A coldness he'd never known her capable of laced her words.

Alderan sat back, stunned. Did he know the woman who stood before him anymore? He didn't need to search far for an answer. Her eyes held the truth, and his heart ached for her.

He rose from the bed. "What do you mean by that? Every one of who?"

Aria walked over to the fireplace and then faced Alderan. The flickering flames at her back gave rise to the hairs on Alderan's arms. He hadn't connected everything when she'd first come into the room, but now he understood.

Ɂäţūr, my God... Aria's the woman from my nightmares!

✝ ✝ ✝

Fear filled Alderan's eyes and face and gave Aria pause. Had what she said been so harsh? She'd only told him the truth, yet guilt rose in her throat.

"Alderan, are you okay?" Aria took a step forward and Alderan stuttered backward.

"Is it true?" Alderan's voice quavered.

"Is what true?" She took another step. "That so many people will die?"

Alderan shook his head slowly. "The dragon... You have one?"

Aria froze and then her eyes narrowed. "Who told you about Cinolth? Wrik?"

Alderan reached back and probed for the bed as he continued to stare at her with wide eyes. Having located it, he sat back down. "No. I've had visions... err... nightmares for many months. The face of a beast haunts me. Although I've never seen one myself, I knew it had to be a dragon."

Could it be true? Is Alderan a prophet? A seer? She must know what he saw.

Aria moved closer and knelt before Alderan. "Tell me about these visions of yours. What all did you see?"

Alderan drew a deep breath and closed his eyes. He crossed his arms over his chest and buried his hands in his armpits. Visually, he trembled, so Aria placed her hand on his thigh to calm him.

Alderan's voice quavered when he spoke, "The day was dark and grim. Black clouds filled the sky. I stood outside the castle in an unfamiliar town peering up at the ramparts of a black castle. People gathered on the roads all around me, their skin white as sheets. Black veins pulsed underneath paper-thin skin and black eyes gazed at nothing.

"I grabbed several of them by their arms and shouted at them, but they were all unresponsive. They all stood there looking up at a woman dressed in red. Her blonde hair, streaked with red, billowed in the wind. Two red orbs—evil eyes—floated over her head and black leathery wings spanned a great distance on either side of her. The people seem to be awaiting instruction."

Alderan's eyes moved rapidly behind his eyelids for several moments, and then his eyelids sprang open. Moisture glistened in them. "You may not be dressed like her, but you are that woman, Aria."

Aria recalled the horde of infected people she'd seen traveling toward the castle earlier that morning and knew Alderan's words to be true. She leaned back on her heels and then stood. Sweat moistened her palms, and her heart raced in her chest.

She retreated to the fireplace and stared into the flames. *How much more does he know?*

"What have you done?" he asked.

She crossed her arms and scowled. "I've done nothing wrong, Alderan. You should know that. I'm still your sister."

"Are you?" Alderan's voice held no trace of accusation, but the question cut Aria deep.

She turned around and lashed out at Alderan with venomous words, unable to control herself or her mouth. "What have I done? Survived! Everything I've done has been out of necessity. You weren't there for me, so don't judge me." Mezhik rose into her palm, and lightning crackled at her fingertips, arcing between them.

Tears streaked Alderan's cheeks as he stared at her hand. "You think I wanted it that way? Despite everyone telling me to give up hope and the voice in my head telling me you were dead, I never stopped searching for you." He gazed into her eyes. "I love you, Aria. What do you think brought me here?"

Aria's mezhik withdrew as her anger dissipated. "Our bond?"

"Yes and no. Two nights ago, I felt our bond for the first time since we'd been separated."

"Me too." Aria closed the distance between herself and Alderan once more. "I hadn't realized how much I'd missed it until I felt it again. Until that moment, I thought you were dead. I'd given up on ever seeing you again. Do you know how hard that was? Part of me died with you."

Alderan ran his fingers through his hair. "Then why does our bond feel so different now? You're distant, and I don't know what you're thinking or feeling."

Aria took Alderan's hands and held them. "It feels different for me too."

Alderan frowned. "But why? What has changed?"

"Several things have changed. When I married Pravus, he joined our souls together. That bond is unbreakable. Also…"

Alderan released one of her hands and lifted her chin. "What is it? You know you can tell me anything."

Alderan's eyes sparkled. She'd forgotten how beautiful they were. A faint smile flashed upon her lips. "Through a blood sacrifice, I gave life to Cinolth. Because of that, we are also bound together. All of these things have changed me. Changed us."

"So how do we move forward? How do we get back to the way things were? I don't ever want to lose you again."

"Nor I you." She reached up and rubbed a tear from his cheek with her thumb. "We will find a way, starting with you meeting my husband."

"And what of Cinolth? Can I meet him too?"

"Soon—"

The door creaked open. Wizard Wrik's head popped around the corner. "Lady Aria, I believe it's time you head to the dining hall."

Aria nodded. "Agreed. All three of us."

Wizard Wrik's eyebrows rose, and his mouth opened, but Aria cut him off before he had a chance to protest. "It's not a request."

Wizard Wrik nodded. "As you wish."

Aria offered her elbow to Alderan. "Shall we?"

Alderan dipped his head, a wry smile upon his lips. "Your wish is my command, my Queen, but then I must return home to check on Rayah."

"You will return, right?"

Alderan leaned over and kissed her cheek. "How could I not? I've only just found you." He smiled, took her arm, and led her out of Wrik's bedchamber.

With each passing hour, Aria grew fonder of the day. Finally, the skewed world righted itself once again. She couldn't help but smile.

† † †

Pravus sat at the end of the long, rectangular table in the dining hall, awaiting Aria's arrival. A lavish spread of meats, both local and exotic, a dozen types of cheeses, fruits, nuts, and breads, and more desserts than Pravus could count filled the table. Another table held three tankards of ale, six types of both red and white wines, an assortment of spiced and non-spiced teas and coffees, and a variety of fruit and vegetable juices.

Credan outdid himself.

He leaned back in the iron chair and gazed up at one of the three massive chandeliers suspended thirty feet overhead. Cobwebs hung from many of the candle holders, their silk webbing draped between the candles like lace ruffles on a dress. Credan would be scolded, and one of the servants would pay with their life.

Blood is cheap, especially a servant's.

That simple thought gave rise to a dark desire he thought he'd moved beyond after binding his soul with Aria's. Images of Tilly and the other women he'd brutalized and killed flooded his mind. A coppery, iron taste rose in his throat and bathed his tongue. He found himself aroused. Not for sex but for blood. Perhaps both.

He gripped the armrests. Willed the moment to pass.

I will not allow this obsession to rule me. Centauria will soon be mine. Nothing will stand in my way.

Except Nardus.

Pravus groaned. The man gouged his side like a thistle. He'd never forgive himself for failing to kill Nardus when he'd had the chance. He wouldn't fail again.

He urged himself to concentrate on how he'd persuade Aria to align Cinolth to his plans, but his thoughts kept returning to Nardus. Or Cyrus. Nothing explained how the man could've disappeared from the atrium unless his memory and mezhik had begun to return to him. No other rational explanation existed.

If it's true, then the memory spell must be wearing off.

He rapped his knuckles on the tabletop. Could a spell wear off? He'd never contemplated such a notion. Many spells had a natural end, but did they all?

Perhaps a spell can run out of energy.

No matter the reason, Nardus presented an immediate threat if he knew the truth of what Pravus had done. If he did, how long would it take for him to return? When he did, would he try to kill Pravus?

Certainly not... if he understands the cost of such an action.

Nardus loved Aria. Pravus saw it in his eyes and in his actions. Nardus would never do anything that would harm her. Not after everything he went through to get her back from the dead.

He's not a threat but a liability.

Pravus must deal with Nardus once and for all. Even without his mezhik, Nardus proved resourceful. Killing him would be a dangerous task. Then again, Cinolth seemed to hate Nardus more than Pravus did.

They've got far more history than he and I. Maybe I'll just let Cinolth deal with him.

Another thought about the failing spell popped into Pravus's head.

Perhaps the spell didn't wear off but somehow broke when we resurrected Cinolth. Yes, that must be it.

He didn't quite understand how the two events could be tied together, but it made far more sense than the notion of a spell just wearing off. Besides, he'd never read a book that talked about spells having some sort of expiration date.

Absurd. The world would crumble.

Footsteps echoed on the granite floor and pulled Pravus from within his head. A moment later, Aria entered the dining hall from the far end, her face aglow and a smile on her lips. She didn't come alone. Wizard Wrik followed her, and another person trailed him, but Pravus couldn't see more than an arm around Wrik's large frame.

Pravus rose from his chair, his anger steeping. Balled hands hung at his sides, and sharp fingernails dug into his palms. He still couldn't identify the third person, and it infuriated him further.

Why did she bring Wrik with her? Or anyone else for that matter? This was supposed to be a private affair. Had Credan not told her?

When Aria reached Pravus, she rose on her tippy-toes and kissed his cheek. "My love, I have a special surprise for you."

Pravus's eyes narrowed. Something had altered Aria's foul mood from earlier. He didn't like it.

Wizard Wrik stepped aside, exposing the young man who stood behind him. The young man stared at Pravus. Pravus's breath caught as recognition came to him. Had Pravus had food in his mouth, it would've lodged in his throat when he failed to swallow properly. The young man looked so much like Aria. He could be none other than Alderan, Aria's brother.

Rage filled Pravus, and the heat of mezhik burned in his palms. His jaw tightened, and his left eyebrow twitched, but he held himself together. Kept his rage concealed.

Murtag said the boy had been killed. Why did he lie to me about it? And how did the boy find his way here?

Pravus looked up at Wrik, and the large man smiled. A knowing, spiteful smile.

That bastard had something to do with this. Why does he continually betray me? He must be dealt with.

Pravus drew a deep breath and exhaled his anger. He turned his attention to the boy. "And who might you be?"

"This is my brother, Alderan." Pravus hadn't heard such excitement in Aria's voice in a long time.

Pravus steepled his fingers. "Yes, of course. I can see the family resemblance."

Alderan nudged Aria in the ribs with his elbow. "You didn't tell me that you'd married an old man."

Aria's cheeks flushed red. They matched the streaks in her blond hair. "Alderan!"

Alderan laughed. "Don't be so uptight. It was only a jest. Someone had to break the tension in here."

Wizard Wrik's jovial laugh filled the dining hall. "The tension has indeed been broken."

Alderan offered Pravus his hand. Pravus stared at it for several moments before taking it.

Soft hands for someone so keen on the outdoors.

Alderan shook Pravus's hand hard but didn't squeeze the life from it. "A pleasure."

Pravus retracted his hand and casually wiped it on his robes. "I'm certain it is. Welcome to our home."

Alderan smiled a big, dumb smile. "Thank you. It exceeds all imagination."

"Yes, it does. Galondu Castle once served as the home of the Ancient Realm's great king, Magus Carac. One day, it will serve as the central point of the realm once more."

A servant entered the dining hall and added two place settings to the table. Pravus nodded at the woman and then gestured toward the spread of foods. "I am quite famished. Shall we dine?" None protested.

A minute later, the four of them had filled their plates with various breads, meats, cheeses, and fruits and sat around the end of the table in silence, focused on their plates of food.

Beast trotted into the dining hall and settled on the floor a few feet from Pravus's chair. Pravus took several pieces of roasted boar from his plate and tossed them to the massive dog. Beast caught them all mid-flight and downed them without chewing.

Pravus smiled. *May our enemies suffer the same fate.*

CHAPTER ELEVEN

Calen woke to a dim world filled with agony. Every muscle ached, and each breath pierced his left side with shards of pain. His mind struggled with every thought, shrouded by a thick fog he couldn't seem to break through. He sat up, and the world tilted to the side. Or rather the wooden-shafted cage he sat in did.

He looked down and wished he hadn't. His chest heaved, and a loud gasp escaped from his dry lips. Not only did he sit in a cage suspended over a deep pit, but shrewd, wooden poles filled the pit below him, each sharpened with an uneven point.

Suddenly, the shafts of wood that made up the cage seemed far too thin and frail to support his weight, and the strands of grassweed twine that bound the cage together looked like they'd been tied by a three year old. He tried to stand up but knocked his head against the top of the cage. It didn't come close to accommodating his height even though he stood just five feet tall.

Calen slumped back down and leaned against the side of the cage. Tears slid down his cheeks and blurred his vision. In the last few weeks, his life had turned to shambles, and he didn't understand what went wrong. How had he wound up in this moment? So many questions swirled through his mind.

Where am I? What do the zhebəllin want with me? Why did Master Savric abandon me? What happened to Aunt Tahmara and all those other people? Why didn't it happen to me? Why wasn't I infected? Why did the zhebəllin attack the town? Why didn't they kill me like they did so many others?

Each question led him back to himself and all his inadequacies.

Because I'm fat and worthless. I'm nothing.

Several tales of the zhebəllin rose in his mind, and he thought he knew his purpose a little better.

They're going to eat me. The thought terrified him and sent his mind racing down another hole full of questions and despair.

Will they kill me first, or cook me alive? Do they even cook their food? Will they keep me alive and slowly snack on my arms and legs before digging into my soft center?

He squirmed as sharp little teeth gnawed on his plump, sausagie fingers. He knew it only happened in his mind, but that didn't stop the pain from manifesting. He squeezed his hands into fists.

Several sobs pulled Calen from his thoughts. He rubbed his eyes with fisted hands and peered around the poorly lit room. No, it wasn't a room. More like a cave or cavern. Somewhere underground. As his eyes accustomed to the dim light, he noticed several more cages suspended over pits of their own. Each of the other cages held several people, some with four or five.

Why did they put me in a cage of my own?

The answer punched him in the gut. *Because I'm fat.*

When he took a closer look, he noticed that all the other cages held only children.

Not a single adult.

Furthermore, he seemed to be the oldest of the bunch—by several years in fact. His throat tightened and his heart sank. What chance would any of them have for survival? Tears formed in the corners of his eyes again, but he wiped them away before they had the chance to fall.

I can't let them see my fear. They're more scared than I am.

But what could he do? How could a fat kid from Daltura do anything? The conversation he'd had with Master Savric about not being special bloomed in his mind and twisted his stomach with guilt.

Savric's words echoed in his head, *"2āṭūr does not make anyone insignificant. People choose to be so. You will find your purpose."*

Then, he remembered the words of the wizard he'd met outside of the town gates several months back. *"…one day, I believe, they will look to you in the time of their greatest need,"* the man had said of Calen.

He eyed his hands. Soft and uncalloused. They wouldn't remain that way for long. "Is this it?" he whispered. "Will they look to me?"

It certainly didn't feel like a moment where he'd become some sort of hero. In fact, he felt far more scared and far less heroic than he ever had before. But perhaps that was the point. Bravery didn't require nerves of steel, did it? Could he be the hero those children needed? He didn't know, but who would save them if he sat back and did nothing?

No one.

"You can't just sit here and let them all die." As though imbued with mezhik, Calen's own words lit a flame of courage within himself. "You can do this, Calen."

Calen rolled over onto his hands and knees to see if he could get a better understanding of their situation. He peered through the slats in each direction and took note of anything that might help them escape. Several observations gave him pause, but the most alarming of them had to be the sheer number of cages.

At least fifteen other cages hung from the cavern ceiling. If each cage contained just three children that would put the count at forty-five, and he knew some of them held more. Even if he found a way to free himself from his cage, how could he free all the others and manage to help them escape without getting caught? To complicate matters further, more than a dozen tunnels led away from the cavern. Freeing the children without knowing what they might face in the tunnels could do them more harm than good.

As far as Calen could tell, no zhebəllin stood guard. His stomach gurgled. If the zhebəllin didn't fear them escaping, what chance did they really have of doing so?

None.

He chided himself. "I can't think like that anymore." He rolled back over and leaned against the cage. "Master Savric believes in me. I must believe in myself."

Calen needed a plan, but where would he even begin? No life experiences or schooling had prepared him for such a task, but he knew one thing that would help. He squeezed his eyes tight and offered a quick prayer to Ɂäṭūr for strength, courage, and guidance.

By the time his eyes fully opened, a deep sense of peace filled him and purged his mind of negativity. He took a deep breath and focused on the first task: freeing himself from his cage.

Calen understood that he couldn't just untie the bindings that held the cage together. If he did, he'd certainly plummet straight into the mouth of the pit below and impale himself on the sharpened poles. The thought sent chills racing across his skin and a shudder into his shoulders.

He peered up at the four lengths of twine attached to each corner of the top of the cage. Those lengths converged a good five feet above the cage and twisted together. From there, the twine rose several more feet where it twisted around a large, rusted hook. The hook attached to another length of twine that climbed to the ceiling, through an eye bolt, and back down to another hook that jutted out from the nearest wall, about three feet above the ground. Every cage was suspended in the same manner.

Calen knew very little about momentum and trajectory, but he wondered if he could get the cage to swing on the hook far enough to clear the pit. If he could, how would it help him free himself? He had nothing to cut the bindings with, and, even if he did, his timing would need to be perfect.

He twisted his finger in his ear. *What would Master Savric do?*

Use his mezhik. But if he didn't have mezhik… Calen grinned. *He'd solve one problem at a time.*

"First things first." He hunched over as he stood. "Let's see if I can get this cage swinging."

Calen grabbed a slat with each hand on opposing sides of the cage and started pushing and pulling, shifting his weight from side-to-side as he did. At first, the cage hardly moved, but with every grunt and strain the cage began to swing back and forth, slowly gaining momentum.

The bindings groaned as they slid and contracted around the slats, causing the entire cage to shudder violently. Calen stopped feeding his energy into the swinging cage, perhaps a few moments too late.

Snap!

One corner of the cage jerked and dropped a good foot as the twine that held it broke. Calen lost his balance and fell to the cage floor. The cage creaked and moaned as it swung wildly and spun out of control.

Snap!

A second twine broke, sending Calen face-first into one of the sides of the cage, which now served as its bottom. The cavern spun around him and the pit below drew closer as it swung in and out of view.

Snap!

Chaos and madness jolted Calen every which way. Nausea twisted his stomach, and bile rose in his throat. He didn't know if the motion or his teary eyes caused it, but everything blurred. The taste of blood filled his mouth, and the side of his tongue pulsed with pain.

Snap!

Calen cried out as the cage lurched, and his stomach leapt into his throat. He clutched the cage slats, braced for impact, and prayed that death wouldn't catch him in its snare.

CHAPTER TWELVE

The atrium at Galondu Castle phased into view and Nardus stood in front of its center section. Gnaud lay limp in his left arm, but Theyn didn't stand by his side. Nardus turned in a circle, but she didn't come through.

Damn! Can I only take one person with me, or did the collar prevent her from coming through?

Gnaud groaned. He'd have to worry about Theyn *after* he found help for Gnaud. But who would help him? Pravus?

Not a chance. He'd probably try and kill us both.

However, Wizard Wrik had been cordial enough with him before the wedding. *Perhaps he could help. But how will I find him? This place is as big as an entire city.*

"Nardus." The deep voice came from the left.

Wrik. Nardus sighed with relief. *Żäṭūr's with us today, Gnaud.*

Nardus turned and eyed the large, black man. Wrik's wrinkled brow and set jaw piqued Nardus's concern, but he might be Gnaud's only hope of survival. Wrik's long legs carried him across the atrium at a quick pace, but not quick enough for Nardus.

"What've you got there?" asked Wrik.

Nardus met Wrik halfway between the atrium's center and the northeastern set of large, steel doors. "This is my friend Gnaud. As you can see, he's badly injured. Do you think you can help him?"

Wrik turned around and started walking back toward the doors he'd come through. "Follow me," he said over his shoulder. "If someone spots the two of you, you'll have more to worry about than just your friend's wounds."

Several minutes later, Wrik led them through a set of tall, wooden doors. Light from the corridor failed to penetrate the darkness of the room. Wrik closed and locked the doors behind them, casting them into total darkness.

A moment later, a purple ball of flames lit Wrik's face, hovering just above his outstretched hand. Nardus tensed, still distrustful of the wizard despite the risk he took in helping them.

Wrik thrust the fireball across the small room. A stack of logs erupted with blue and yellow flames within the fireplace hearth, casting shadows throughout the room.

Damned mezhik. Nardus refrained from spitting on the floor.

With smaller flames, Wrik lit several candles that stood atop pedestals spread throughout the small room, bringing its interior fully out of the darkness. The room contained a brown, three-cushioned couch and two white, overstuffed chairs with burgundy pillows. Bookshelves lined the three walls flanking and opposite the fireplace.

"Lay him on the couch, and I'll see what I can do."

Nardus carefully lay Gnaud down. "I can't lose him, Wrik." He rubbed the inside of his left bicep where the arrow had pierced him a lifetime ago. "I've lost too many close to me already."

Wrik knelt on the floor next to the couch. "In truth, Lord Rosai would be better for the job. He has far more experience in healing wounds. However, I realize he'd be more likely to kill you both."

"Agreed, and we don't have the luxury of time either."

"True." Wrik pointed behind Nardus. "Retrieve one of those candles and bring it over here so that I can see what I'm dealing with."

Nardus grabbed the closest candle holder and held it where the light bathed Gnaud. "Good?"

Wrik nodded. He placed his hands over Gnaud's wounds, his thumbs outstretched and touching, creating three sides of a square between them and his forefingers. He muttered some words Nardus didn't recognize, and then a warm, purplish glow emanated from his hands and drifted down into Gnaud. The four gashes across Gnaud's stomach began to knit themselves back together. Wrik repeated the words several more times, and each time Gnaud's wounds became less severe. After the fifth time, Gnaud's eyelids fluttered and then opened.

Gnaud took a deep breath and winced. "Oh, my."

"Pace yourself, little fellow." Wrik leaned back on the balls of his feet. "You suffered quite the nasty wounds. I'm sure it'll take some time before you're feeling normal again."

Gnaud squinted up at Wrik, his bushy white eyebrows hunched over the bridge of his thin, elongated nose. "And who are you?"

"My name is Wizard Wrik, but you can call me Wrik."

"Thank you for saving my life, Wrik. I'm Gnaudius L'Dorak, but you can call me Gnaud." He touched his stomach and groaned. "How did you find me in the Great Library?"

"I did, Gnaud."

"Nardus, is that you?" Gnaud felt his own face. "Can't see a thing without my spectacles."

"It is indeed me, my furry little friend," said Nardus. "You gave me quite the scare."

Gnaud patted the couch aimlessly. "Are my spectacles lying about? Perhaps on the desk?"

"Not sure where your spectacles are at the moment." Nardus touched Gnaud's shoulder but thought better of squeezing it. "I'm sure we'll find them once we return to the library."

Gnaud gasped and peered in Nardus's direction, his orange eyes wide. "You've taken me from Nasduron?"

Wrik cocked his head. "*The* Nasduron?"

Nardus waved Wrik off. "Yes, but not now," he grumbled. "Gnaud, your wounds gave me no choice. If I'd left you there, you'd be dead right now."

"You don't understand." Gnaud tried to sit up but grimaced after just a slight movement. "I need to get back. Nasduron won't survive without me for long."

Nardus and Wrik shared a concerned glance and then leaned closer. "What do you mean?" they both asked.

"The Great Library and Nasduron are tied to me in ways you cannot fathom. They are as much a part of me as I am of them. The books, maps, and resources contained within the walls of the Great Library cannot exist outside of it. Think of them as memories. *My* memories. If I die, all of that knowledge dies too. Do you understand now? We must return before it's too late."

"Are you saying—"

Gnaud cried out, cutting Nardus off. Fresh blood surfaced over Gnaud's wounds and clumped his fur. "Oh... my."

Nardus glared at Wrik. "What in *Ef Demd Dhä* is going on? I thought you healed him."

"I did." Wrik tilted his head. "What did you say caused these wounds?"

Nardus rubbed his left bicep again, a ritual he'd come to rely on when dealing with painful memories and difficult or awkward situations. "Wasn't there when it happened, but I'm certain the wounds were created by the claws of a…" Theyn's beautiful, furry face filled his mind. "…large cat."

Wrik nodded knowingly. "Many nasty bacteria thrive underneath claws and fingernails. I believe Gnaud's wound is infected with one such strain called *kǝllääʐtridäm*. It prevents the wound from ever fully healing and causes it to easily reopen. If I'm right, and it's rare I'm not, then mezhik will only prolong the inevitable—Gnaud will eventually die from his wounds if they aren't properly treated. He'll require a regimen of *zíerōfūʈär*, a special plant known to kill the bacteria. You'll need to get your hands on the entire plant to make a salve. Nothing else will work."

Nardus thrust his hands in the air. "And where am I supposed to find whatever *that* is?"

"*Zíerōfūʈär* is a rare and expensive plant. It grows exclusively at the bottom of Alcedonia Lake."

The bottom of a lake? Nardus shook his head. *This just keeps getting better.*

Nardus returned the candle holder to its pedestal. "Fine, but first I must go check on Theyn. She forgets herself when I'm not with her. I won't be gone more than a few minutes. When I return, you can tell me what I need to do to retrieve the plant. In the meantime, make sure you keep Gnaud alive."

"I'm guessing this Theyn is the one who inflicted the wound?" asked Wrik.

Nardus nodded. He focused his mind on the Great Library and stepped forward, but nothing happened. He stepped forward again with more determination. The Great Library didn't even phase in and out like it did when he'd had the stone in his chest. His palms dampened, his pulse rose, and his stomach lurched.

Theyn? Have I lost you for good this time? The thought unsettled him and gave rise to his anger.

"No, ʕäʈūr!"

"Is there a problem?" asked Wrik.

Nardus growled, "I can't go back to Nasduron."

They both looked down at Gnaud.

"He's still alive," said Wrik.

Nardus leaned over the back of the couch. "Gnaud? Can you tell if the library still exists?"

Gnaud didn't open his eyes, but his lips moved. Nardus missed what he said though.

Nardus moved around the couch and knelt next to Gnaud. "Please, Gnaud. Tell me Nasduron is still there. Tell me Theyn is still alive."

"You left her there?" asked Wrik.

Nardus rubbed his left bicep. "I'm not sure what happened. She was with us when we left the Great Library, but she didn't arrive here with us."

Gnaud talked through gritted teeth, his voice barely audible. "Did she arrive there with you to begin with?"

"No. Why?"

"As you know, traveling to and from Nasduron is special." Gnaud's eyelids fluttered and cracked open. "You must come from and go to the exact same location. Where did she come from?"

Nardus recalled the morning Berggren delivered him to Pravus. *The sewers of East Hotah.* He'd thought Theyn had died that day. His heart ached thinking about it. *She must've returned there.*

"I need to get to East Hotah as fast as I can." Nardus stood. "Wrik, can you take me to the mirror?"

Wrik folded his arms. "I can, but your friend here will die while you're gone. Is Theyn's wellbeing more important than Gnaud's? Are you willing to live with his death?"

Nardus nearly exploded, his face flushed with heat and his hands balled at his sides, trembling. "We don't have time to argue about this! I must get back to Theyn before she kills everyone she comes into contact with. Or, worse yet, before they kill her. How can you not understand that?"

"Oh, I understand your dilemma, but I have my own affairs to attend to," said Wrik.

"Name your price, and I'll find a way to pay it. Just keep Gnaud alive and retrieve that plant for me while I go find Theyn."

Wrik's eyes narrowed, and the left corner of his mouth rose. "I believe I have the perfect solution. It will serve us both well. You show me how to get to Nasduron, and I'll do what needs to be done to save your friend."

Gnaud reached toward Nardus. "No," he whispered.

Nardus brooded. "We've no other choice."

Gnaud grimaced and clutched his stomach. "Let. Me. Die."

Daggers of guilt plunged into Nardus's chest. "I brought this upon you. I cannot allow you to die for it. I won't." He shot a glare toward Wrik as he stood and then offered his hand. "We have an accord."

Wrik clasped Nardus's hand and shook it. "Perfect."

Nardus retracted his hand and stepped back. "There's no time to spare. Take me to the mirror."

Wrik nodded. "Certainly, but first I must heal Gnaud's wounds again before they consume him."

Nardus moved out of Wrik's way. "Yes, yes, just make it quick."

Twenty minutes later, Wrik and Nardus stood in front of a full-length mirror at the end of a long corridor. Nardus's gaze fell not upon the mirror but through it—back to the past. His stomach twisted and his throat tightened as Berggren raged at him for killing Theyn.

"How is it that you're able to use the mirrors if you're not a wizard?" Wrik's voice pulled him from the past.

Nardus eyed Wrik through the mirror. "Don't know and don't care. I just know it works."

Wrik smiled. "Yes, but only with mezhik."

Nardus spat on the floor. "Mezhik be damned."

Wrik nodded and chuckled. "As you say." He pushed his spectacles up his broad nose. "Use the mirror to get to East Hotah. Come back when you've found Theyn, and we'll complete the final task of our accord."

"Agreed." Nardus cocked his head and frowned. "So how do I use the mirror? I've never traveled through one by myself before. Or at least I didn't set its destination."

"Ah, it's simple. All you need to do is think of the place you want to go and then touch the mirror's surface. So, think of East Hotah."

Nardus's gaze met Wrik's. "I can think of anywhere and it will take me there?"

"Not anywhere. There must be a mirror close to where you're trying to go, and some mirrors have wards upon them to prevent unwanted travelers from using them. They can be quite deadly if you're not careful."

Nardus spat. *I hate mezhik.*

He sighed. "And how will I find you when I come back?"

"Return to the room where we left Gnaud." Wrik reached into the folds of his robes and produced a silver chain. A black key hung on the chain. He handed the chain to Nardus. "I've placed a ward on the door—not a deadly one. I'll know if anyone enters or leaves the room."

"Good." Nardus pulled the chain over his head and tucked the key into his shirt.

He looked back at Wrik. "If I get back and find Gnaud dead, I'll kill you. Am I clear?"

"Perfectly." Wrik folded his arms behind his back. "I will retrieve the plant from the elves and heal Gnaud, but from the sounds of it, you'd better hurry. We don't want Nasduron destroyed. Items are located there that I'm certain I need."

Nardus thought about Gnaud's reaction to the accord. *And I'm sure the world doesn't need you to have them.*

As he had with the stone, he'd deal with the consequences of his decision at a later time. Theyn and Gnaud both needed him, and he'd rather be damned than let either of them down.

Nardus set his mind on East Hotah, took a deep breath, and then reached out and touched the mirror. Its surface changed from neutral and solid to cold and wet. His and Wrik's reflections faded, the mirror's surface rippled, and then a small, rectangular room phased into view through the mirror. He remembered it well—a hidden room deep within the sewers of East Hotah.

Where I thought Theyn had died.

Nardus stepped through the mirror and into the small room in East Hotah. He didn't look back but headed straight for the door and into the sewers beyond it. The smells of rancid water, feces, and death hit him hard as he stepped through the mezhik barrier, gagging him. He spat into the center channel of water and cursed the foul place.

He shook off the nausea as best he could and set his mind on the task at hand: a rescue mission of sorts, but he wasn't sure of whom. In the end, no matter the situation or how many bodies she'd left in her wake, he wouldn't give up on Theyn. No harm would come to her.

Unless it already has.

The thought gutted him and drove him through the sewers.

Hold on, Theyn. I'm coming for you.

† † †

After Nardus disappeared through the mirror, Wrik returned to check on Gnaud before heading up to the northern ramparts of Galondu Castle. The little gordak slept, every breath a wheeze through parted lips. Four red lines wet the fur across his abdomen once more. Wrik healed them again and prayed that the gods kept Gnaud alive during his absence.

Wrik turned and teleported down to the ice room in the lower kitchen. Dozens of shelves lined the walls of the small room, each holding many packages of various colors and sizes. He grabbed a white, paper-wrapped package and stuffed it inside his robes. He'd need it soon enough.

From the ice room, he teleported up to the easternmost stairway, one of several that led up to the northern ramparts of Galondu Castle. He would've teleported all the way to the ramparts, but the aquatic elves were fierce and unpredictable in their moods, especially Forlin, their king. He'd need to preserve as much of his mezhik as possible just in case things went sideways. They had before, but he didn't have time to reflect on it.

At the top of the stairs, Wrik headed west along the southern edge of the northern ramparts. These ramparts spanned the length of the castle's northern wall, their breadth thrice that of the southern, eastern, and western ramparts combined.

Red canvas tarps stretched across the tops of fifteen-foot-tall poles and hung down the northern edges of the ramparts, creating a windbreak from the vicious northern winds. The edges of the tarps snapped in the wind, a barrage of fireworks on a cold, blustery day. From the tops of the poles, the tarps stretched southward, across about half of the ramparts themselves, forming what they called "open-air stables" for the nítfinzh.

Wrik halted about two-thirds of the way across the rampart, right in front of a stall that housed one of the most beautiful creatures he'd ever laid his eyes upon. Underneath the flapping, snapping, red tarp, Blackwind lay on a bed of straw.

Thin but sturdy, dark-purple membranes folded against Blackwind's sides, powerful wings that could carry her to the heavens. Black skin, smooth as obsidian, stretched over bony vertebrae and thick muscles. A long, thick tail wrapped around the side of her slender body, and its trident-tipped end thumped the ground. Razor-sharp claws protruded from long, bony toes and fingers, splayed like fans. She kneaded the air.

Wrik loathed waking Blackwind from a good dream, but time was precious—more so than usual. He knew of only one way to rouse her without risk of getting the business end of her claws through his gut.

From within his robes, Wrik pulled out the package he'd retrieved from the ice room. Blackwind faced away from him, but her head rose from the straw, and her nose probed the air before he'd unwrapped the package.

Bright yellow eyes, wide and short and split vertically by lightning bolt-shaped, black irises, shone from a face so dark, they seemed to float in shadows. Sharp, white teeth gleamed underneath raised lips all along her elongated snout. Two short horns, dark purple like her wings, rose from the front of her skull.

She snorted at the package.

Wrik chuckled as he continued to struggle with the twine that bound the package. "I should've come more prepared." Finally, he undid the last knot. The white paper fell open, revealing a platter-sized chunk of pink flesh. Blackwind favored salmon above all other fish. Wrik offered it to her, and she snatched it off the paper in a flash. One gulp, and the fish disappeared. She nudged Wrik's shoulder, looking for more.

"Take me to Alcedonia, and then we'll talk about more food."

Blackwind snorted but bobbed her head. Wrik saddled and mounted her. She rose on all four limbs and crawled from underneath the tarp. In two swoops of her wings, she had them skyborne.

Wrik directed Blackwind toward the west with his mind. She banked that way and then she darted through the sky. He hadn't ridden her in so long that he'd forgotten the sensation of it. Exhilaration left him feeling giddy, and the wind on his bald scalp felt glorious, despite its frigidness. He must get out more often instead of staying cooped up within his bedchamber and secret room.

Blackwind was among the fastest of the nítfinzh. By horseback, it would've been a good six day's ride to get from Galondu Castle to the Alcedonia Forest, but on Blackwind it would consume just two hours.

Wrik hunkered down in the saddle, leaned forward, and stroked her slender neck.

Make haste, my black beauty.

CHAPTER THIRTEEN

"One stupid tree," exclaimed Rayah. "How hard can it be to find one stupid felled tree?"

She couldn't recall any distinct markers, and all the trees and underbrush looked the same to her. Considering that she'd lived in the forest her entire life, she should've been more adapt at tracking and remembering locations, but it just wasn't the case. She'd never been good at it. In her defense, as weak of an excuse as it was, she hadn't grown up in this particular forest.

She'd searched for the tree half the day and passed the point of giving up more than an hour ago, but her gut told her that it lay just beyond the next ridge. Several times before, her gut had told her the same thing. Odds are she'd eventually be right, but her gut proved it couldn't be trusted. She had nothing else to go on, so she let her pride and deep-seeded stubbornness rule her mind and drive her forward.

Her wings gave out long ago, so she trudged through the forest on her feet. She crested a small ridge, certain she'd finally found the correct spot, but the felled tree wasn't there. She kicked the leaves, frustrated.

"Alderan would've walked right to the tree without even blinking," she huffed.

Rayah turned to leave, but something dark and sinister flashed in the corner of her eye. She gasped and jerked around, her arms raised to cover her face from an attack, but one never came. What she'd caught sight of turned out to be nothing more than some sort of black ash or dust underneath the bed of leaves.

Bending down to investigate further, Rayah brushed a section of leaves away with her hand. The band of black looked to be about three feet wide. She swept more leaves away in both directions, and the black streak continued. With a moment's thought, realization widened Rayah's eyes.

"The tree... How could it have rotted and disintegrated so quickly?"

She followed the black streak back to the point where the tree's base had lain. Leaves and other debris filled the shallow hole where the venomous vines had grown. She knelt close, but fear kept her hand from brushing the leaves away. The area smelled of death and wrinkled her nose.

What if the vines are still here, hiding underneath the debris, just waiting for someone like me to disturb them?

The last thing she wanted was to become infected and walk off to who knows where. She took a deep breath, closed her eyes, and just listened to the sounds of the forest. Birds chirped and sang high in the trees as they prepared nests for the coming spring. Squirrels chattered far in the distance, most likely arguing about the discovery of some sort of acorn or nut. The trees creaked and the dead leaves rustled as a light breeze swept through the forest.

The thing Rayah didn't hear was what counted most. *No hissing.*

Before, the vines had hissed at her and Zerenity when they'd gotten close.

Have the vines died as well?

That question needed an answer. A lump rose in Rayah's throat. She swallowed hard, but the lump persisted.

Be more like Alderan. Dive in with abandon.

Her hands didn't move, but her pulse spiked. She loathed the thought of digging through the leaves and debris with her hands, but what other choice did she have?

There's only one way to find out for certain.

Rayah opened her eyes, set her jaw, and dug into the pile before she changed her mind. A nidorous odor permeated the leaves and soil like a two-day-old cadaver but she found no evidence of one. In fact, she found little evidence of anything in the blackened soil.

She sat back and stared at her hands. Soil stuck to them and caked under her fingernails. She'd never felt such a strange sensation. As a soil dryte, dirt and soil had never stuck to her before. Then again, it had never smelled so bad either.

She rang her hands, but the soil stuck well. She took a deep breath and regretted it as her stomach lurched with nausea. "Ugh. I don't think the stink is going to wash off."

She stood and wiped her hands on her blouse. The shallow pit glared up at her. Taunted her. What had she accomplished?

Nothing.

Rayah turned to leave but a thought niggled at her. "I'm not going to do it," she huffed. She took several steps and then stopped. She hung her head for a moment and then looked skyward with defiance.

Is this really what you want me to do, Ɂät̪ūr? Manipulate the dirt?

She didn't need an answer. She turned and glared at the pit. "Fine, you win. Doesn't mean I have to like it though."

Rayah approached the pit and bent down next to it again. She raked her fingers through the black soil. The thought of that thick, disgusting, stinky dirt covering her twisted her stomach in knots, but she must find out if anything remained of the vines. Too many questions surround the vines, but the most important one was where did they come from?

With spring around the corner, and an unusually warm day, the ground had softened enough that she could manipulate it. She didn't want to do it, but if it meant finding an answer to help save Zerenity and Qotan she had no choice. It did.

Rayah took a deep breath and sank into the soil. Other than its nauseating stench, breathing through the soil didn't present an issue. However, because of its strange makeup and stickiness, she found it difficult to see through. She must rely on her sense of touch.

Many rocks and roots littered the soil, and she'd nearly given up on finding something beyond the ordinary when her fingers slid across an object she couldn't identify. Larger than she'd first thought, she had to use both hands to grasp the mostly flat object. Once she secured it in her hands, she rose to the surface with it.

The daylight did little good in helping her understand what it was that she held. She tried to wipe it off with her sleeves and trousers, but the black soil clung to her and to it too well. She'd have to take it back to Zerenity's and wash it off before she could determine what it was.

She spread her wings, but the soil clung to them as well and weighed them down to the point that she'd never get off the ground no matter how hard she flapped them. "A bath is so in order."

Satisfied with her find, she didn't mind walking back to Zerenity's house. She only hoped she could find the way. Before nightfall.

An hour later, Rayah pushed through the last of the trees and stumbled into Zerenity's yard. A well sat at the opposite end of the yard, and she headed straight for it. She set the object down on the dead grass and used the well bucket to draw some water from the well.

It took quite a bit of scrubbing to remove the soil from the object, and when she'd finished, she still didn't understand what she'd dug up. She took the object inside and set it on the kitchen table. Its black color and smooth texture reminded her of obsidian, but its iridescence and slightly flexible composition ruled it out. It had a slight curve to it, kind of like a seashell, but it wasn't that either. Initially, she thought it might be shale, but it proved far more durable, easily resisting a good beating from a hammer she'd found in one of Zerenity's kitchen drawers.

Rayah had hoped to contact Savric with an answer as to what had created the vile vines. Instead, she had more questions than she'd started with. Frustrated, she grabbed the stupid object and stormed into the living area.

She retrieved the brass-handled mirror from her pack and held it up to her face. The girl who stared back sickened her. Not the girl herself, but the disgusting black soil that covered her. Black soil matted Rayah's hair and streaked her face.

Rayah imagined she could pass for one of those backwater people from Mortuus Vir Isle—the mud people. Or at least if she'd been topless and held a spear or some other hand-carved weapon, according to legend anyway. She'd never actually seen a mud person, but the stories she'd heard filled her mind with vivid images akin to her current state. She thanked Ϛäṭūr that she wasn't gazing at a full-length mirror. She didn't think she could handle seeing her entire body covered in such filth. As it was, her arms, legs, and face itched something fierce, and her mind ran wild with disgusting possibilities.

Please don't let there be anything that's crawled somewhere it shouldn't have. She squirmed a little at the thought.

Beyond her physical state, she had other problems as well. In the morning rush earlier, she'd forgotten to ask Eshtak how the mirror actually worked. She'd never witnessed him contact someone, so she did what seemed natural. She stared intently at the mirror and said, "Master Savric?"

Rayah's reflection twisted and swirled and stretched, distorting her face until it became an unrecognizable mess. She waited several minutes, mesmerized by the mirror's undulating rhythm. Finally, the swirling ceased, and Savric's face appeared in the mirror.

Savric peered into the mirror, and his grim expression changed to one of surprise in an instant. "Dear heavens, girl! Dare I ask what you have been up to?"

Rayah scratched her nose. "Since I couldn't find Alderan, I decided to go back into the forest and search for the source of those vile vines."

The lines across Savric's brow deepened. "The vines were in the middle the forest and not the swamp, were they not?"

"Yes, and I think I found something buried deep in the soil beneath the vines." Rayah grabbed the black object and held it in front of the mirror. "This is what I found, but I don't know what it is. I thought it might be shale or a seashell or something, but it doesn't seem to be either."

Savric cocked his head and pulled on his beard. "Can you turn it over and let me see the other side?" Rayah did so. After several more turns of the object, Savric shook his head. "I daresay, you and that rock of yours have me quite confounded. Perhaps I could identify it were I there, but I am uncertain as to the date of my return." Savric looked up for several moments before returning his gaze to Rayah. "Perhaps I can arrange for a friend to come have a look at it. Bear with me while I contact her." Rayah nodded and Savric's face disappeared from view.

She returned to the kitchen and set the object on the kitchen table. When she tried to sit down on one of the chairs, she found the task more difficult than usual. The layer of soil caked on her arms and legs stiffened them to the point where they nearly refused to bend.

I need to get all this washed off before I wind up cocooned in here.

Savric's face returned in the mirror. "We are indeed in luck, but you will need to do a bit of traveling in the morning. Morcinda is currently in Tamdaporth and can meet you east of the Veridis Forest, on the shores of the Gelu Ocean, tomorrow morning."

"I've never heard you mention Morcinda before. How will I recognize her?"

Savric's eyes twinkled in the faint light. "I daresay she will be unmistakable with her blue hair, pale skin, and pointed ears." He chuckled. "She will be sailing a ship with a mermaid on its front."

"There's a lot of coastline on the eastern side of the Veridis Forest. Not only that, but most of it is sheer cliffs."

"Am I mistaken? Are those not wings at your back?"

Rayah's cheeks burned. Thankfully, the soil covered her embarrassment. "Yes, sir. I will take the object and meet this Morcinda in the morning. Hopefully, she'll be able to shed some light on what it is."

Savric nodded. "Very good. Now, I must move on before the horde gets too far ahead of me."

"Master Savric, there's one other thing I wanted to tell you. Rakzar was cursed with a spell called sickle. Have you ever heard of it?"

"Sickle?" Savric stroked his beard. His eyes blinked several times. "I do not recall hearing of such a spell."

"It's terrible. Anyone who comes into contact with him becomes sick and weak and eventually dies. Urza's sick now." Tears formed in her eyes and she blinked them back. Never in her life did she think she would've become so emotional over a beast like Urza, but with each passing moment she found it more difficult to control her emotions. "I want to help figure out how to save her, but I don't know what to do." A tear rolled down her cheek.

"It disheartens me that I cannot instruct you in this matter, my dear girl. You must ask Ɂäʈūr for guidance." Savric looked away from the mirror for a moment. When his gaze returned, his eyebrows were angled toward the bridge of his nose and a fire burned in his eyes. "I must go. We will converse again soon."

Rayah opened her mouth to say goodbye, but the mirror's image froze, and then Savric's face vanished in a swirl of darkness. An instant later, Rayah's reflection returned. Tears clung to her eyelashes. She raised her arm to wipe her face with her sleeve but thought better of it when she noticed how disgusting and soiled it had become.

She set the mirror on the kitchen table and exhaled. "It's time for that bath."

She looked down at her clothes. Not a clean spot remained on them, and they clung to her skin like giant leeches. Her nose wrinkled when she caught a whiff of them. "No amount of scrubbing is going to get rid of that stench. They will definitely be going into the fire."

Forty minutes later, Rayah settled into a copper tub filled with steaming water. She'd cleaned herself up with a rag before getting into the tub, but it had only worked so well. The black soil still clung to her hair. The hot springs up north would've been a better choice given her state, but she didn't have time for that. She scrubbed her hair as best she could, and the water blackened.

A dull crash sounded from across the house, and Rayah froze.

† † †

Alderan stepped through the mirror and into Zerenity's dark closet and proceeded to kick and stumble over an assortment of metal objects piled on the floor. One of them clanged against the wall and rang in his ears as he fell to his hands and knees with a grunt. The torchlight faded as the mirror's portal closed, blanketing Alderan in the closet's perfect darkness.

Alderan groaned, "Graceful as always, you big oaf."

He rose on his knees and pushed his hair back behind his ears. Swinging around the other direction, he probed the darkness for the objects he'd tripped over. The first object he located felt like some sort of metal glove. There were two of them, along with several articles of clothing he couldn't quite identify, each made of a mix of leather, metal ringlets, and fabric. After locating a large metal plate and a long pole with a razor-sharp end, recognition came to him.

The guards at Galondu Castle wear armor like this.

But how a set of armor found its way onto the floor of Zerenity's closet escaped him. "Who would've left these here?" He scratched his head. "And why?"

The closet door squeaked open, sending a chill through Alderan. He held his breath and slowly turned to face the direction of the door. A dim, flickering light filtered through the rows of hanging clothes. It reminded him of the morning sun penetrating the canopy of a dense forest.

"Is anybody in there?" a voice whispered.

Alderan rose to his feet. "Rayah?"

"Alderan!" Rayah squealed.

Pushing his way through the rows of clothes, Alderan moved toward the front of the closet. When he parted the last row, a gasp parted his lips. "For the love of Ɂät̪ūr, Rayah! What were you planning on doing with that hammer?"

His cheeks warmed and then caught fire as his gaze fully took her in. Deep shadows obscured everything below her waist, yet he'd never seen so much of her. Desire swelled within him. He shook his head and forced his gaze to meet hers again. "And why are you nearly naked?"

Rayah glanced down at herself. "I was taking a bath when I heard a crash. The shawl and hammer were the only two things I had time to grab."

Alderan wove his fingers through his hair and pulled it back on his scalp. "And what if it had been someone else that came through the mirror? Did you think about that?"

Rayah shook the hammer at him and scowled. "That's what *this* is for."

"You should've hidden somewhere until you knew it was safe." He stepped closer to her and wrinkled his nose. "Ugh. What is that horrendous smell?"

Her scowl deepened and her nostrils flared. "It's me." She shook the hammer at him again. "You make any comments about it, and you'll find this hammer soaring at your head."

Alderan raised his hands submissively. "Whoa, there's no need to threaten me with violence. I won't say anything about how wretched you smell. Or how bile climbs higher in my throat with each breath. The wall paint that curls in your wake. The wood rotting at the touch of your feet. Your—"

The corners of Rayah's mouth twitched as a smile fought to overtake her frowning lips. She giggled. "You're impossible."

Her face glowed in the candlelight, highlighting her exceptional beauty. Butterflies stirred in Alderan's stomach as he closed the distance and lifted Rayah's chin. He pushed the stench from his nostrils and his mind and kissed her voluminous lips. Her lips parted and their tongues met for the briefest of moments.

He wanted more. *Needed* more. But pulled away. Rayah moaned softly.

Alderan wiped his mouth on his shoulder. "How about we head into the living area and sit down. You can explain what happened to you and why there's a guard's uniform on the floor in here."

Her eyebrows rose. "Me explain?" She handed him the hammer and then pulled the shawl wrapped around her midsection tighter. "We've got plenty of things to talk about, including where you've been for the last day or so. You've worried me sick."

While Rayah finished her bath and got dressed, Alderan piled several pieces of wood on the fireplace hearth, stuffed the spaces between the pieces with kindling, and brought it to life with a few sparks from a flint rock. Satisfied that the fire wouldn't fizzle out, he joined Rayah on the couch.

Alderan wrinkled his nose, the pungent odor still prevalent. Several feet separated him from Rayah, but several more would've been better. He started to say something about it again, but the look on her face stilled his tongue.

"Explain yourself." A hardness he'd never known filled her voice. "Where've you been, and why did you leave without telling me or saying goodbye?"

Alderan sat back and recounted the events that led to his capture, the reunion with his sister, Aria, and meeting her husband, Pravus.

"She's *married*?" Rayah said, her face full of exasperation. "All this time you've insisted we wait until your sister could be present for us to marry, but she had no qualms in marrying without your blessing or presence."

Alderan scooched over on the couch and took Rayah's hand. "Look, Rayah, it's not like that."

"Oh no?" She pulled her hand away and crossed her arms over her chest. "Then tell me, what is it like?"

Alderan raked his fingers through his hair. "She thought I was dead, Rayah. She'd given up hope, and I don't blame her. So many times, I nearly gave up on her as well. You know that. In fact, you're the one that told me that I should stop looking for her because she was dead. So don't sit there and pretend that you're shocked and offended that she moved on when that's all you wanted me to do."

Rayah's features softened. She reached out and reclaimed Alderan's hand. "You're right. My love for you is so deep that it blinds me at times. All I want is to be with you and protect you."

Alderan stared at Rayah's hand in his. Her dainty, porcelain fingers barely reached his first knuckles. How such small hands could wield so much power flabbergasted him, yet he knew their strength surpassed his own. Everything about Rayah surpassed him. Her will, determination, loyalty, love, and resolve. More to the point, she completed him. Every aspect he lacked or fell short on she excelled at. Together, they were an unstoppable force. Nothing and no one in the entire world could diminish or take away the love he felt for her.

Not even you, Aria.

The thought struck him like a blow to the gut. Not so long ago, he never would've entertained such a thought. Rayah hadn't replaced Aria in his heart, but she consumed more of it. His heart was big enough for them both.

He leaned back and stared at the ceiling. "I know, and I feel the same way about you. Given the choice, I would've come back to you sooner."

Rayah crawled on top of his lap and kissed his exposed neck. "I believe you."

Alderan coughed and pushed Rayah away. "Okay, I've done my best to ignore the stench, but I need some room to breathe." He stood and paced. "Now it's your turn to answer some questions. The first question I have is what in Ɛ̌äṭūr's name did you get all over yourself?"

"It's soil. I scrubbed my entire body twice. Imagine how I feel. I can't get away from the stench. It follows me everywhere."

Alderan stopped pacing, stared at Rayah for a moment, and then busted up laughing. Rayah quickly joined in. He laughed until his side hurt and his vision blurred with tears.

"I've never smelled soil like that." He collapsed back down on the couch. "Are you certain you weren't rolling around in a mud pit with some wild boars? Or perhaps the soil was actually a mound of bear scat."

Rayah shook her head. "You think you're funny, but you're not."

"Then why are you beaming?"

"Because I missed you." Her smile faltered. "To be honest, it's far more disgusting than either of those. I couldn't find you, and I didn't want to just sit around here waiting for you to come back, so I decided to go find those vines again and see if I could find anything else out about them."

Alderan jumped to his feet, his heart pounding. "Rayah! You went back there even after knowing what those disgusting things did to Zerenity and Qotan? You could've been bitten as well." He scanned the room, paused, and frowned. The fire crackled and popped on the hearth and several birds chirped outside, but he heard no other sounds.

Concern crept into his voice. "Where is everyone?"

"I was getting to all of that. If you'd just sit down and listen, you wouldn't have to ask so many questions."

Alderan sighed loudly and dropped back on the couch. "Fine. Tell me everything that's happened since I left. And leave nothing out."

† † †

Rayah flew back and forth, her wings pummeling the air with fury. Her mind pulled her in so many directions that she found it impossible to think clearly. She still hadn't told Alderan about Rakzar. Even if she were to, he wouldn't hear her right now. For the last ten minutes, he sat on the edge of the couch, his attention captured by the shiny black object in his hands.

Over and over he turned the object, examining every inch and every angle. "This was buried underneath the vines?"

Rayah descended to the floor with a light touch and stood before Alderan. "Yes, and I'm certain the vines grew out of it."

Alderan cocked his head. "But what is it?"

"I don't have the faintest idea, and neither did Master Savric." She settled on the couch next to Alderan. "I'm supposed to take it to a woman named Morcinda tomorrow morning. Savric's certain she'll know what it is. You can come with me now that you're back."

"Tomorrow morning?" Alderan sighed. "I thought you'd want to come with me so that you could meet Aria."

"Come with *you*?" Rage thrust her from the couch and back into the air. She clenched her fists and spun back around to face Alderan. "You just came back!"

Alderan's gaze fell to the floor and his head slumped forward. "I understand, but I've no choice." He peered up at her. "I must go back."

Jealousy and frustration fueled the scream that erupted from her. Her entire body shook as the sound echoed through the house. "You'd rather be with her, is that it?" She shook her finger at him. "I won't have it. There's no way I'm letting you out of my sight again."

Alderan set the black object on the couch and stood. He reached for her hand, but she retreated. "Rayah, it's not what you think," he pleaded.

"Isn't it? You've always loved her more than me, and you probably always will." She turned in the air and flew over to one of the large windows. Beyond the edge of the porch roof, she eyed the thick, dark clouds. They darkened the sky the same way Aria darkened her heart.

She should've stayed dead.

Tears of guilt swelled in Rayah's eyes. *Ɛäţūr, I didn't mean that.*

"She's my sister, Rayah. Of course I love her, but not the way I love you. The two of you share my heart but in different ways. It's not one or the other. It never has been and never will be."

In the faint reflection of the window glass Rayah watched Alderan rake his fingers through his hair. She knew she was being obtuse, but she didn't understand how he could just run off again without her. Rayah wiped her eyes and flew back over to Alderan.

She took his hand in hers. "If it's not what I think, then explain it to me. Why is it so important that you return to her tonight? Why can't you at least wait until tomorrow?"

Alderan scratched his head and averted her gaze. "I… I may have left out a few details when I told you about everything that happened back at the castle."

"What details?" When he didn't answer Rayah rung his hand. "Tell me, Alderan. What did you leave out?"

Alderan took a deep breath and let it out slowly. "My dreams… they're… coming to life. The woman I saw with blonde hair and red streaks…" He sucked in a ragged breath. "… it's her. That woman is Aria."

Rayah gasped. "What?" Her mind couldn't process the information. "Are you certain? I thought the woman in your dreams was the enemy you'd save the world from."

Tears streaked Alderan's cheeks. His eyes, hollow and distant, gazed beyond her. "So did I." Alderan dropped to the floor and pulled her down with him. "Do you understand now?" His voice broke, and he sobbed.

She pulled him close and stroked his head. *Aria's the enemy? Ɂäṭūr, how can this be? No, no, no. This isn't right. Ɂäṭūr… what have you done?*

Rayah's eyes grew wide. "And what about the red eyes and wings you saw behind her?"

Alderan sucked snot back into his nose and nodded slowly. "All of it. It's all true." He looked up at her. Fear filled his eyes. "She has a dragon," he whispered.

A coldness like nothing she'd ever felt settled in her bones. Her throat constricted, and she struggled for air as convulsions wracked her chest. The room blurred through streams of tears. She managed just one word with each breath. "What. Can. We. Do?"

Alderan pulled on his hair. "If I can't talk some sense into her, we've already lost."

They sat there in silence for several minutes. After Rayah regained control of her breathing she leaned back against the couch. Her eyes stung with tears, and her head ached. "Then you must go back, but I can't go with you. I must follow up with Morcinda on the object that I found, but—" She started to tell Alderan about Rakzar but hesitated.

Alderan looked at her and frowned. "But what? What are you not telling me, Rayah?"

Rayah shook her head. *Just tell him the truth.*

She closed her eyes. "It's Rakzar... he's... cursed."

"What you mean Rakzar is cursed? What happened? When did you see him?"

"He's at your house with Urza, but I didn't see him. If I had, I'd be slowly dying right now."

Alderan grabbed her and shook her. "What do you mean you'd be dying? What's going on?"

She looked into his eyes. Concern filled them, and she knew why. Yesterday, she wouldn't have understood why he cared for the beast, but now she did, and it pained her thinking about it. "I don't know exactly, but some sorceress cast a spell on Rakzar that causes anyone that comes into contact with him to slowly die. Urza knew this but refused to leave his side, and now she's paying the price."

Alderan's brow wrinkled. "How slow of a death are we talking? Days? Weeks? Months?"

Rayah shrugged. "Not sure. At least weeks, but maybe months. We won't really know until Urza dies."

Tears fell from her eyes again at the thought of losing a friend. She cried harder realizing that she did consider Urza her friend. *Ƶäţūr, save her.*

Alderan let out an exasperated breath. "Will we ever get to a point where things start to go right for us?"

"I don't know... But I've decided I'm going to try to help Rakzar figure out how to break the spell and save Urza. I know it sounds crazy, but don't try to stop me. It's something I know I must do."

"Since when? Last I checked, you hated Rakzar. In fact, you practically begged me to kill him."

"I know, but things have changed. I've come to realize that life happens in shades of grey, not just black and white. You taught me that, Alderan." She lifted his hand to her lips and kissed it.

Alderan put his arm around her. "I guess it's settled then. You go try and save Rakzar, and I'll try to save Aria from herself."

"And what about us? Are we destined to be apart?"

"I don't know—" He leaned over and kissed her on the forehead. "—but

I'll never stop loving you or fighting to be with you."

She pulled him close and wrapped her arms around him. "Promise me you'll come back."

"Ɂäṭūr willing, I'll see you soon." He pushed her back and gazed at her. The corner of his mouth rose. "Hopefully, you'll smell better by then."

She harrumphed and ribbed him. "Keep it up, and you'll never see what's underneath these clothes."

"A dead squirrel," he said, barely getting the words out through bouts of laughter.

She ribbed him again and then tackled him. They both giggled as they rolled around on the floor, but the moment quickly faded. Neither of them had an easy road ahead, each destined to face theirs alone, but she had faith that everything would work out in the end.

It must.

† † †

Rakzar stood in front of the fireplace, his fur wet with snow. Had his fur been grown in, the cold would not have bothered him, but he still had several bald patches from Urza's hack job that leeched warmth from his body. He shivered and rubbed his paws together.

Yesterday, Rakzar had devised a plan to deceive Rayah into helping him, but as the hours passed his determination and resolve faltered. He grabbed the sides of the stone hearth and growled deep in his throat. His inaction would kill Urza, but what guarantee did he have that she'd live even if he did find a way to kill Käíeɀ?

He dug his claws into the mortar that held the hearth stones together. *None.*

But he couldn't just sit there and do nothing. As much as he hated to admit it, he needed Rayah's help. He reached deep into his mind and his dark heart, searching for the callused, hateful beast he knew himself to be, but no matter how far he descended, he found nothing that remained of his former self. The White Knight had changed him atop that hill. It seemed a lifetime ago.

Rakzar stared into the fire. Flames leapt and danced across the burning logs, creating several streams of rising black smoke. Rakzar closed his eyes for a moment and breathed deep, drawn to the burning sap and the aroma of charred wood. The combination of the two mesmerized him and pulled him into the past.

When Rakzar opened his eyes, he stood in the middle of a burning forest. Flames engulfed centuries-old trees and swept across the underbrush in waves of violent, brutal destruction. Birds and animals of every kind fled the area, but Rakzar moved closer, drawn to the flames.

Fire scorched the earth, leaving nothing in its wake but blackened, charred remains of everything it touched. Amidst the fire's roar Rakzar heard something else. Not a cry for help but just crying. The longer he ignored it, the greater his desperation became to seek out its source. The sound reminded him of the pups he'd tried to save so long ago.

Rakzar bolted into the flames, all thoughts of self-preservation lost with the rush of energy pumping through his veins. He leapt over felled trees and dodged others as they crashed to the ground with thunderous volume.

Hold on, little one. I'm coming for you.

"Someone's in the basement."

The forest faded, and the hearth filled Rakzar's vision. He turned and looked down at Urza. Her ears stood tall.

"Someone's in the basement," she repeated.

"I know, and I heard you the first time." He hadn't actually heard any noises, but Urza didn't need to know that.

"Leave, and I will take care of it." Urza rose on all fours.

Rakzar looked out the window. "There's a foot of snow out there already, and it's still falling."

Urza walked over to the opening behind the fireplace and glanced back at Rakzar. "I'm not asking you to leave the house. Just leave the room." She crouched down. "Rayah, if that's you, don't come up here. It's not safe."

"I need to speak to Rakzar." Rayah's voice echoed in the basement below and sounded hollow. "I'm coming up."

Rakzar cursed and knocked one of the rocking chairs over. *Damn that dryte.*

"Don't be a fool," he growled. "You need to leave. We don't know how this damned curse works."

Many questions about the spell bombarded him. Did he have to physically touch the person to curse them? Or did it get passed through his eyes? Perhaps the spell was based on proximity. How close was too close for one to get to him? Did walls protect a person from him? How about the mirror? If the dryte stood on the other side of the mirror would she still be cursed? Or maybe it could be his voice.

She might be cursed already.

"You have no control over what others do," said Amicus. "Why don't you let her decide what she wants to do."

"Nobody asked you, Shadowman," snarled Rakzar. "I told you to leave me alone."

Urza looked over at Rakzar, her face twisted with confusion. "Who are you talking to?"

Rakzar looked to his left, where Amicus stood. "No one."

"Didn't you say you needed her help?" asked Amicus. "Have you forgotten the sand already?"

Rakzar scowled at Amicus. "You of all people should know that I can't do that to her."

"What the gods is wrong with you?" Concern strained Urza's voice. "You haven't been the same since you came back yesterday."

Urza jerked back. "Rayah!"

The dryte peered around the corner of the fireplace, her porcelain face framed in golden curls. Rage filled Rakzar. He grabbed the second rocking chair and threw it across the room. It slammed into the wall with a loud crash and splintered into several pieces.

Rakzar trembled with fury, his gaze locked on Rayah. "Your death will *not* be on my hands!"

Rayah smiled. "There is no certainty that I'll live through this day. The burden is mine to carry."

"As I said, it's her choice, my friend," said Amicus.

"You're not helping," growled Rakzar. He kept his focus on Rayah.

Rayah crossed her arms, defiance flashing in her hazel eyes. "Try and stop me."

Rakzar's eyes narrowed. "I wasn't talking to you, *dryte*."

Rayah and Urza shared a look and then they both turned their gaze on Rakzar, their heads cocked slightly to the left. "Then who were you talking to?" they asked in unison.

"Doesn't matter." Rakzar walked away from them and righted the first rocking chair he'd knocked over. He sat down and leaned back in it. The chairback hit him right below his shoulder blades. It would've risen above a normal-sized person's head. He stared up at the thatched roof and the two-foot-square patch of lighter straw just above him to the right. "Why did you come here and damn yourself to death, dryte?"

"You saved my life once, and I'm indebted to you for it."

He remembered the day Brux and Creeb broke in through the ceiling. It was a brilliant idea for two imbeciles. He turned his head to the left and stared at the two women. "Urza's filled your head with fantasies. I never saved your life. Now I've taken it."

Urza laid down in front of the fire, but Rayah flew over to him and settled on the floor next to the chair. "Deny it all you want, but I know the truth. There's a heart buried underneath your cold exterior."

"You need her," said Amicus. "Let Rayah help you. You've got nothing to lose and everything to gain."

Rakzar eyed Urza. He couldn't deny the changes in her face—skin stretched over bone once hidden underneath a layer of muscle and fat. She'd lost several pounds, and her fur lacked the sheen it once held.

He grabbed his head and gritted his teeth. "I've lost everything."

"You know nothing of loss," said Amicus. "But you will if you sit there and do nothing." Amicus shook him by the shoulders. "Pull yourself together before you run out of time. Tell Rayah about Käíeʑ and the sand."

"How can you say that?" asked Rayah. "Your sister lies before you, still breathing. She needs you, and so do I."

Rakzar peered down at Rayah. "You don't know the enemy I face. She cannot be stopped."

"Everyone has a weakness." Rayah touched his arm. "Together, we will find hers and exploit it."

"Käíeʑ is like nothing I've ever seen. She transitions between solid and smoke without effort. How can any weapon harm smoke?" He thought about the sand. "If I could find a way to keep her solid, even for a moment, I might have a chance at killing her, but I know of nothing that can accomplish this. However, there is one person who might be able to point me in the right direction."

"Shalaidah," said Rayah.

Rakzar nodded and returned his gaze toward the ceiling. "I know she won't talk to me, but she'll talk to you."

Rayah sighed. "I wouldn't be so certain of her willingness to talk to me.

We parted on unfavorable terms, and I haven't spoken to her or seen her in years." She stood and stretched her arms. "But I can't think of another place to start, so we shall seek her out in the morning, after I've met with someone on the eastern shore."

"The morning?" growled Rakzar.

"We both need rest. It will be a long journey, and I'm certain it's only the beginning."

"We can't—"

Urza cut Rakzar off. "Leave it be, Rakzar. Waiting one more night will make little difference. I'm not on my last leg yet."

"Fine." Rakzar stood and walked over to the single window. "Bring a warm coat. Winter isn't finished with us yet."

CHAPTER FOURTEEN

Thanks to Blackwind's blinding speed, Wrik made great time, reaching the edge of the Alcedonia Forest in just under two hours. Minutes later, a small clearing came into view, just east of Alcedonia Lake. Using mindspeak, Wrik directed Blackwind to land there. Blackwind touched down in the knee-high grass, soft as a feather landing. Wrik dismounted.

His feet had barely touched the ground when the presence of several elves bombarded the defenses of his mind. Had he not been prepared for the assault, they would've paralyzed him. As it was, they surrounded him, deep-blue, watersteel weapons drawn. He made no sudden moves and ordered Blackwind to fly beyond the forest and wait until he called upon her. Blackwind looked back at Wrik, snorted, and took to the sky with a leap.

One of the elves stepped forward, a male. His stark-white skin and dark-blue hair contrasted the yellows, browns, and greens of the surrounding forest. The patches of black hair in front of his pointed ears signified his position among the clan, a leader of the warriors. Wrik recognized him immediately despite him no longer being a young boy. They called him Tuular.

Tuular spoke in an elvish tongue that Wrik knew. "Why have you trespassed on our land? Your kind are not welcome here." He spat on the grass.

He doesn't remember me.

Wrik bowed to the tall, slender man and spoke in his native tongue. "I seek Noella."

"Noella takes no visitors." The gills on the sides of Tuular's neck opened and closed tirelessly.

"Agreed, but she'll take me. We've known each other for many years." He folded his arms behind his back. "Tell her that Wizard Wrik seeks an audience with her."

A beautiful, slender woman emerged from the shadows. Her long, blue hair, woven into a single braid, rested over the front of her left shoulder. A few loose strands curled down either side of her narrow face, offsetting her porcelain skin and enhancing her beauty. Pointed ears, capped in silver, nearly reached the top of her head. A silver line traced her light-blue lips, and a silver nose ring hung from her right nostril, signifying her place amongst the äəllf äkfeṭik: royalty.

"Ah, Princess Noella." Wrik greeted her with a smile and bowed low, all the while keeping his gaze trained on her. "It is a pleasure to see you again."

Noella's large eyes, bright-blue and deep-set, grabbed his attention and held him prisoner. Her heated glare would melt the southern icecaps if she were to turn it upon them. "I cannot say the same of you."

Wrik straightened. "Forgive my intrusion into your sacred kingdom, but there is something I desperately need from you. Some herbs that can only be found at the bottom of Alcedonia Lake."

She circled Wrik. He turned with her, his gaze locked with hers. "You've come to the wrong place, wizard. Be gone before I give the signal for them to gut you."

"Make no mistake, princess. I come bearing a gift you'll want to see." He smiled wide.

Noella's weapon, a double-sided, curved knife, glinted in the fading light. He hadn't noticed it in her hand before. She gripped its blue bamboo handle firmly, her white knuckles nearly transparent. Its six-inch, curved blades could kill nearly anything within minutes with the smallest cut. The watersteel's unique properties caused wounds inflicted by it to leech water, dehydrating the victim.

Her eyes narrowed. "You've come here to try and bribe me? Have you not already insulted us enough with your mere presence?"

"The gift I bring comes from beyond our shores. Beyond our realm." He leaned forward for effect and whispered, "Beyond our world."

Intrigue flashed in Noella's eyes, but her face revealed nothing of the like. "Take him to the palace and lock him up."

Wrik held out his hands. Water cuffs encircled his wrists and linked to each other. "This will be worth your *time*." He winked at her. "I swear it."

Ten minutes later, Wrik sat inside a cell far below the surface of Alcedonia Lake. He'd been there several times, many years ago, but his last visit hadn't been a pleasant one. Unlike that last time, he brought something with him that he thought would be of great worth to the elves, and the item meant very little to him. An easy exchange for the herbs and access to Nasduron.

I'd pay any price to reach Nasduron.

After waiting several minutes, the cell door opened and Noella entered. She closed the door behind herself and ordered the guards to leave. They did without question, and she turned her wicked grin toward him. She met him in the center of the cell, removed his water cuffs, and threw her arms around his waist.

"Wrik, I am so happy to see you alive. My father told me that he'd had you tortured and killed when you came here the first time. It devastated me."

"It was nothing, truthfully. I've suffered far worse and would do so again to see your beautiful face."

She kissed his left cheek and then his right and then pulled away. From one of her pockets she produced a small bag and handed it to him. "Here are the herbs you requested."

"You are a life-saver." He stuffed the bag in one of his robe pockets. "How will I ever repay you?"

Her eyes widened and her cheeks glowed. "Show me this thing you claim is from another world."

Wrik reached into his robes and withdrew a folded kerchief. "Close your eyes and hold out your hand." She did.

He unwrapped the item and placed it in her hand. "Tell me what you hear. What do you feel?"

Noella breathed deep. Her eyes moved rapidly back and forth underneath her eyelids. "I hear… ticking. Each tick jolts the item ever so slightly. Almost undetectable. It's cool to the touch and rough." She closed her hand over it and stroked it with her fingers. "A round surface. Smooth like glass."

Wrik nodded with excitement. "Yes! Do you know what it is?" Noella shook her head. "Then open your eyes and see what it is that you hold."

When Noella opened her eyes she gasped, the gills on her neck spread wide. "It's… beautiful." She held it in front of her face and scrutinized it further, twisting and turning it between her fingers. She cocked her head and listened closely, the item pressed against her ear. She shook it several times.

"Why does it tick? What's its purpose?" Her eyes widened. "Is it dangerous?"

Wrik grinned. "As I understand it, it's called a wristwatch."

"A wrist-watch?" She frowned. "Why would you need something to watch your wrist? And how does it watch? Does it have eyes?" She examined it again. "The ticking is its heart?"

"No, no, nothing like that. The wristwatch isn't alive."

"Then how does it watch?"

"It's a mechanical chronograph. Those hands underneath the glass signal the time of day. Its original owner calibrated it to work in our world."

"A chronograph…" Her eyes narrowed. "What are the letters around the circle for?"

"Those are called Roman numerals. They signify the hours of the day in one-hour increments." He looked at the face of the watch. "According to the watch, if I'm reading it correctly, it is half past the ninth hour in the evening."

Noella nodded. "As you say."

"It is called a wristwatch because you wear it around your wrist."

She slid her hand through the band. The watch hung loosely. She wiggled her arm and the watch slipped off. She grabbed it with her toes before it hit the floor and lifted it back up to her hand. "It's too big."

"I believe there's a way to adjust it, but you'll have to figure it out on your own. Now, I must get back and save a friend's life before it's too late."

She took his hand. "Will I ever see you again?"

"To be certain, provided I'm not truly killed this time." He winked at her. "It is so good to see you, Noella."

"Likewise." She eyed the wristwatch. "Thank you so much for the gift. I will fully understand its purpose by the time I see you again."

Wrik held up a finger. "Ah, yes. I almost forgot. I brought several pages of notes with me that pertain to the wristwatch." He reached into his robes, withdrew a sizable stack of parchment, and handed it to her. "You will be an expert in no time." He chuckled. "See what I did there?"

She sighed. "Your words aren't as funny as you might think."

"In *time*, you will get it."

She smiled. "Let me show you the way out before you've overstayed your welcome."

When they emerged from the cell, Noella's attitude toward Wrik returned to indifference. She didn't join the escort that took him back to the clearing in the forest but instructed them to leave him unharmed as long as he left immediately. By the time they reached the clearing, Blackwind awaited him.

Wrik stroked Blackwind's neck after he approached the magnificent beast. He turned to say farewell, but the elves had already faded into the forest. He mounted Blackwind and they took to the sky.

"*Home,*" he mindspoke to Blackwind. Blackwind banked east and headed toward the Cariosus Forest and Galondu Castle.

We must return before death pays Gnaud a visit.

Chapter Fifteen

Dusk had settled in about an hour earlier, leaving Custos Bay shrouded in deep shadows. The sparse lights of Celsus Litus waned in the distance, an echo of Savric's grim mood. Neither Qotan nor Zerenity had moved much during the last twelve hours, opting to lay on the ship's deck with all the other infected people most of the time.

Twice, Savric narrowly avoided detection by members of the ship's crew, ducking down and burying himself amongst the infected. On three other occasions, he avoided capture by subduing the overzealous crew members with the help of Eshtak and a touch of mezhik. All of them now resided in the cell down in the ship's hold with the first two men, and he was certain the cell wouldn't hold anyone else.

Twenty minutes later and without further incident, the ship came into port in Celsus Litus. Another ten minutes, and they had the ship moored to the pier. Gangplanks extended from the ship deck to the dock, one at the front of the ship and one at the back. The horde of infected rose from the deck in unison, a disquieting act to say the least. Savric teleported off the ship and into the shadows of another vessel farther down the docks.

"Blech. More of 'em."

Savric spun around so quick that he lost his footing and fell back onto the dock. Pain erupted in his tailbone and shot up the length of his spine. All thoughts of defense escaped his mind. "Feathers!" Savric glared up at the shadowy figure. "You scared the wit from my mind."

A red circle of light the size of a large coin glowed and lit the man's face as he toked the thick cigar hanging between his lips. The burly man made no move to attack Savric or to help him up. He only frowned. "Don' look at me like that. You're the one popped in from outta nowhere."

Savric groaned as he pulled himself to his feet. His bones protested as well, cracking and popping with every move. "*ǝllíṭ ʊb.*" The top of Qotan's staff burst to life with white light, chasing away the deep shadows that hung between Savric and the burly man. "Pray tell the meaning of your words."

The man cocked his head and scratched his chin with chipped, dirty nails. They dragged through a good day's worth of brown stubble. "Few wielders 'round these parts."

Wielders. Although not an archaic term for wizards, Savric hadn't heard anyone use it in several decades. Then again, he hadn't traveled the western coast in several decades either. The beachers—a self-given title for those that lived along the coastline—spoke with the same dialect as the northerners, but their vocabulary differed greatly.

Savric stroked his beard. "To be certain. Now, were you referring to the infected before?"

The man yanked the cigar from his mouth, smoke streaming from his nostrils and billowing from his lips. "Infected?" he scoffed. "Crazy coots more like it. Migratin' southeast just as winter comes to a head. Never in my life I've seen such nonsense."

Savric waved the cigar smoke away from his face. "Then you have seen more of them?"

The man nodded, shoved the cigar back in his mouth, and took a long drag. The cigar's end glowed red-hot again. "Live 'cross town. Just outside." His cigar wagged in his mouth when he spoke.

It looks as though he has swallowed a puppy. Savric chuckled to himself.

The man frowned but continued, "Was up at the break with the pigs this mornin' when a whole heard of 'em wandered right on through my pasture. Not a care between the lot of 'em."

"Do you know where they came from?"

"City folk. Country folk. No difference. Two hands up and left. Lucky I hadn't paid 'em yet."

This situation is far worse that I had imagined.

Savric dipped his head toward the man. "Thank you for your time, good sir. Now, I must attend to some urgent matters."

The man grunted and walked away, disappearing into the shadows of the night.

Several questions swirled in Savric's head, none of which he had answers for.

Qotan would have had answers. Although they might not have matched my questions.

He desperately missed their exchanges. Who could he lean on for answers now? A woman with blue hair and pale skin came to mind.

Morcinda.

Savric smiled. The elves, no matter their race or faction, always held the answers to unfathomable questions. He harbored no doubts as to whether or not Morcinda would as well. Savric slammed the butt-end of Qotan's staff against the dock and removed his hand. The staff stayed upright on its own.

Calen would have been impressed with that.

Heartache filled his chest. He'd been away from Daltura for weeks and hadn't contacted Calen once. Now that he thought about it, he'd missed Calen's name day as well.

I promise I will make it up to you, my boy.

Another thought crossed his mind. *If this infection is as widespread as it seems, there are likely many infected people in Daltura as well.*

He gasped. "Calen…"

What if the boy had been infected as well? Losing Calen would devastate him just as much as losing Qotan or Reni. He couldn't be in two places at once, so what could he do? In that moment, the best and only thing he knew to do was pray, so he did.

Ꝛätür, I pray that Calen is not among the infected. Please keep him safe until I can go check on him.

Certain Calen would be okay, Savric set his mind to the task at hand. He reached into the folds of his robes and pulled out the small, leather-bound book he'd taken from Rayah. A thick layer of dust covered it. He brushed the dust away with his sleeve, revealing the symbol of light and freedom embossed on its cover: Ꝛäəll Dhef Ꝛäfn Dhä.

"The Seal of the Seven." It filled him with pride and wonder every time he gazed upon it. He imagined it did for the seven who created it as well.

Three parts comprised the seal, layered within one another. The outermost layer looked like a golden iris and symbolized the eye of Ꝛätür, the one true, all-knowing God. The second layer, a vibrant-blue heptagram, filled the center of the iris where one might normally find the eye's pupil. The heptagram, a seven-pointed star, represented Ūrdär Dhef Ꝛäfn Dhä— The Order of the Seven. Without the order, all would've been lost in the Great War. A yellow lightning bolt, the third and final layer, sat in the center of the heptagram. It symbolized their resolve to do what needed to be done and the manner in which they chose to do it: strike randomly but with precision, meaning they would fight without a discernible pattern, but their strikes would prove deadly.

A small, golden clasp on the book's right-hand side held the book closed. It had no keyhole or release mechanism. Savric nodded knowingly and placed his hand over the seal. *"In əllíṭ Hiz."*

Click!

The clasp fell open. Savric opened the book to the first page, a blank one, and then retrieved the fountain pen from within the small pouch located on the book's inside cover. He pressed the pen's tip to the page and thought a moment about what he intended to say to Morcinda.

He began writing: *"Greetings, Morcinda. I write to you with a heavy heart and great despair. In the last day, I followed a large group of infected people onto a ship in Tyrosha. Each of them exhibits white skin with black veins, and black inkwells fill their eyes. When confronted they are unresponsive. They have gathered in mass and march toward the southeast, but to where and for what purpose, I am uncertain. In light of this news, I have two questions for you. Have you seen this phenomenon happening elsewhere, and does it affect more than just humans? I look forward to your response. In əllíṭ Hiz. - Savric"*

Savric tapped the page with the fountain pen, and the words faded. He didn't know how long it would be before Morcinda responded, and he didn't have the luxury of waiting around. It could be minutes, hours, or days. He stuffed the fountain pen back in its pouch and closed the book.

Ɂäəll Dhef Ɂäfn Dhä pulsed with blue light on the book's cover. Could Morcinda have responded so quickly? He yanked on the cover, but the clasp had already locked itself. He placed his hand over the seal, said the words of mezhik, and yanked the book open. He grabbed the fountain pen from its pouch and tapped the first page with its tip.

Words formed on the page in black ink. He read them as fast as they appeared. *"Master Savric, as you know, I travel the Ancient Realm frequently. Every town and city I have been to is overrun with infected people. However, this virus or disease does indeed seem to affect only humans. Thank Ɂäṭūr I am äəllfin. -Morcinda"*

He tapped the page with the fountain pen and began writing even as Morcinda's words faded. *"I do not know the evil forces behind this, but I am certain no good will come of these events. I am in a position to find out exactly what is happening and will keep you apprised as events unfold. In the meantime, are you willing to take this information to King Zaridus? I believe his kingdom is in danger. In əllíţ Hiz. -Savric"*

Savric tapped the page and the words faded. A moment later, new words appeared. *"In most human affairs, the äəllfin choose to abstain from taking sides. We are a highborn and proud people. However, I do not share the sentiments of my kinfolk. As you know, most of the jobs I do revolve around humans and their affairs. After I meet with Rayah I will take your concerns to King Zaridus. Let me know the moment you have further information. -Morcinda"*

Hopefully, King Zaridus will heed her words more than he did mine.

Savric returned the fountain pen to its pouch and closed the book. Many prophecies foretold of a time such as this, but words on paper never do reality justice. They also never specified that this affliction would only come up on humans. Savric feared the events of the coming months and the helpless feeling growing deep within. In the end, how would any of them survive? How could anyone fight an infection on such a large scale?

He peered over his shoulder. Dozens of people still poured from the ship he'd arrived on.

As far as he could tell, no order had been established in Celsus Litus like it had been in Tyrosha. Fires burned across the city, lighting up the night sky. Locating Qotan, Reni, and Eshtak again would prove difficult until they moved outside the city.

Savric sighed deeply. *Have we already lost the fight before it has begun?* Such thoughts were unbecoming of him, and he chided himself for it. *I shall solve one problem at a time.*

He stuffed the book back into the folds of his robes, grabbed Qotan's staff, and marched down the dock toward the horde of infected. A single question burned in the back of his mind.

To whom do they serve?

CHAPTER SIXTEEN

Aria stood in the center of the atrium with her hands raised above her head. The wind pulled at her hair and fluttered it at her back. Cinolth stood in front of her, a mass of muscle and devious cunning.

"Concentrate on your surroundings," said Cinolth. "Tell me what you feel."

Aria closed her eyes. "I feel the sand between my toes and the rocks around me. The trees speak to me in a language I don't understand, and the wind beckons me."

"Good. Concentrate on the wind. Imagine it flowing underneath your feet and pushing up against the bottoms of them."

Aria stood there and willed the wind to blow against the bottoms of her feet. The chilled air tickled her toes, and her legs trembled.

"Good. Now, imagine yourself light as a feather and allow the air to lift you off the ground."

Aria gazed skyward and gave in to the sensation of weightlessness. The sky above moved toward her, and she gasped. Her concentration broken, she crashed to the ground in a heap.

Alderan cheered from afar. "Good show, sister!"

Cinolth growled with disgust. "You must concentrate, or this won't work."

"I know what I'm doing." She sat up and pulled her hair back. "It just scared me a little when I realized that I'd actually risen off the ground."

"Then do it again, but this time don't give in to your foolish fears or let it break your concentration."

"Fine." Aria stood, closed her eyes, and summoned the wind once again. The air caught under her feet once more and lifted her off the ground. She opened her eyes. The ground was several feet below her. She wasn't sure what to do from there though.

"What now?" she asked.

"Do what feels natural. Walk through the air or allow the wind to help you soar. Just remember that every moment you're in the air, you're expending mezhik. When your mezhik expends you'll tire. When that happens, you'll be vulnerable to attacks. So, make sure you understand your limits and how to determine when you've reached them before it causes you to become weak."

Aria settled back on the ground and giggled. "I never thought anything like that would've been possible. I wish I had these powers when I was a girl. Life would've been so much fun."

"Papa would've been alive still too," said Alderan. "You could've killed all of those gnolls that destroyed our village."

"You could've too, Alderan. Come over here and practice with me."

Alderan stood and Cinolth growled. Cinolth took to the air with whooshing wings, kicking up a cloud of dust in his wake. He quickly disappeared into the night sky, a shadow in the darkness.

Alderan coughed and fanned the air. "How do you put up with him?"

Aria shrugged. "He's not so bad once you get used to him. Besides, it's good to have him around for protection."

"Protection?" He turned in a circle, arms raised. "From what?"

"Everything." Her stare hardened until his smile faded. "There are threats all around us. We are constantly on the defensive. I nearly died three times just getting to the castle. We were attacked multiple times. Twice in the carriage and then again in the wastelands. If it hadn't been for Karraar, I'd be dead."

Alderan ran his fingers through his hair. "I can understand you being attacked while traveling, but here in the castle? Where would this threat come from? Who would want to attack a lord and lady?"

Aria scowled, more at the world than Alderan. "People vie to gain the power that Pravus and I possess. Jealousy is a driving factor and a great motivator."

She'd missed him so much. How she'd survived all those months thinking him dead escaped her. She never wanted to be separated from him again, and she'd do just about anything to make that happen.

Unless he becomes a threat.

The thought jarred her and left her unbalanced. She plopped down in the sand. Alderan joined her on the ground and took her hand in his. He squeezed it, but not very hard.

She leaned her head on his shoulder. *My little brother. How could he ever be a threat?*

Alderan lay back and pulled her down with him. "Will you always be by my side?"

"Where else would I be?" She laughed. "Someone has to save you from yourself."

He frowned. "You're not the only one who thinks that. You've always been stronger than me."

"That was a jest, Alderan." She latched onto his arm. "You've always sold yourself short, but you're far stronger than you know."

"I am?"

No matter his meaning, Aria took those two words as more of a statement than a question. She let them stand, and the silence between them grew.

A vast sea of stars spanned farther and deeper than she could ever see, twinkling in rhythm to music only they could hear. Her mind drifted to thoughts of what life might be like after the war. If Cinolth got his way, only a handful of humans would remain. Would she be content with that?

Do I have a choice?

Fingers snapped. Twice. "Aria."

Her eyes burned. When had she last blinked? She did so several times before her eyes finally blurred with moisture. She sat up. Pravus approached from the northeast path, a glowing ball of red light preceding him.

Pravus stopped in front of her and offered her his hand. "Come with me."

She looked back at Alderan. He still lay in the sand, a smile on his lips. He waved her on.

"Have no fear, I'll still be here in the morning."

She scowled at him. "You'd better be." She took Pravus's proffered hand, and he pulled her to her feet.

Pravus addressed Alderan. "Master Credan will show you to your bedchamber when you're ready. You'll find him waiting just inside the southern doors."

"Very good. Thank you for your hospitality."

Pravus nodded curtly and then led Aria back the way he'd come. Aria glanced over her shoulder and smiled when Alderan waved. She mouthed him "goodnight" and turned her focus to Pravus.

"Where are we headed?" she asked.

"To plan a war." A hint of a smile touched his lips. "We march tomorrow at dawn."

Her stomach twisted in knots as fear and anticipation battled for dominance.

And so, it begins…

† † †

Pravus stood over the table, eyeing several maps of the Ancient Realm. Elatos, the southernmost city of The Three Kingdoms, lay directly north of Galondu Castle and Atrum Moenia. The distance between them measured roughly 430 miles. It would take several months for an army to traverse that kind of distance. He didn't like the thought of waiting that long to claim the throne and his place as ruler of the Ancient Realm, but what choice did he have? No other route would get them there any quicker.

Credan stood on the other side of the table, next to Aria. "When do you plan on marching north, my lord?"

"Tomorrow. We've wasted too much time already. Summon those who are loyal to me and have them gather their men outside the northern walls of the castle by sunrise tomorrow."

Credan bowed. "My lord, consider it done." Credan left the room.

"We begin our march toward Elatos five hours from now?" asked Aria.

Pravus eyed Elatos and shook his head. "No, twenty-nine hours from now. However, it will take a considerable amount of time to get there."

Aria picked up a miniature soldier and rubbed it with her thumb. "I have good news, my love."

He looked up at her. Whatever she had to say curled the ends of her lips upward, enhancing her beauty. "And what is your news?"

"I've convinced Cinolth to join his army with ours."

Pravus stared at her for several moments. She'd confirmed the rumors of the dragon having an army and had convinced Cinolth to join forces. Her interference alleviated his need to beg for the same result and prevented him from showing any signs of weakness. He resisted the urge to smile.

This could not have worked out better.

"An unnecessary alliance." He looked back down at the maps. "However, it may afford us a quicker victory."

"Without question." Aria slammed down the miniature soldier. "His army is one hundred thousand strong."

Pravus swallowed hard. How had Cinolth gathered such a great army in a single day? He felt his father's kingdom slipping away once again.

Cinolth must die once victory is assured.

"In light of your news, we will gather our forces with those of Cinolth's here." He pointed to a spot on the map just northwest of Duos Flumen. "Make sure Cinolth understands this. If he's foolish enough to attack the Three Kingdoms without our army, then he will have done nothing but destroy the cities. We must be there to claim victory."

Aria moved a miniature dragon onto the map and placed it on that spot. "Cinolth is anything but foolish. He will heed my words."

Pravus cracked his knuckles and steepled his fingers. "Good. We cannot afford any missteps. I've waited far too long for this moment."

Pravus studied the maps a few moments longer. Elatos would be the first city to fall. Then Borza and finally Vallah. He'd rather cut right to the heart of the Three Kingdoms and attack Vallah straight away, but the Orbis Mountains made such an attack nearly impossible. King Zaridus would have several weeks to gather his army by the time Pravus's army reached Vallah, but it would prove futile. King Zaridus stood no chance against an army with a dragon, especially one so fierce and ruthless as Cinolth. The war would certainly end just as quickly as it started.

Excitement tingled his fingers and toes. "I sense my father's bones stirring in their grave. House Rosai begins its ascent tomorrow."

"He would be proud of you, were he here."

Pravus nodded and moved on to another section of the table with detailed diagrams of Elatos and all its defenses. Aria followed him.

"You're certain these diagrams are correct?" asked Aria.

"To the last detail. I paid good coin to get them drawn up and even more to verify their accuracy."

"Cinolth will need to see these before we attack."

"Yes, and there will be plenty of time for him to do just that when we meet up outside Duos Flumen."

"Very well."

Beast trotted into the room and nuzzled Aria's open hand. "There's my good boy," she said.

Pravus sneered at the dog. "Traitor."

Aria peered up at Pravus, a hint of steel in her eyes. The edges of her mouth curled upward. "Are you talking about him or me?"

Pravus shrugged and focused on the diagram of Borza. "Take your pick."

Beast whined. Aria bent down and hugged him. "Papa doesn't mean it. He's just jealous that I love you more than him."

Pravus stiffened. *Does she?*

He stole a glance at her. It didn't matter. Regaining his father's kingdom far outweighed any thoughts as to whether his wife loved him. Besides, he had far more pressing matters to sort out.

Like that damned dragon.

But how could he remove Cinolth from the picture? He loathed the dragon and the influence he had over Aria. It sickened him.

Aria's my wife and mine to control, not Cinolth's.

Only one being existed that Pravus knew of that could take on Cinolth, other than Cyrus: *Käíeᴢ*. Her mezhik ability, dark and beautiful, came directly from Diᴢäfär himself. What he wouldn't give to wield her power.

Once this is over, I will find a way to drink her blood.

Like a spring renewed, the thirst he'd all but forgotten swelled inside of him. His vision darkened as his eyes narrowed into slits. He stared at Aria. At the vein on the side of her neck. It pulsed with life. Power. Mezhik. His hand reached for her throat before the impulse registered in his mind. Aria looked up. Fear flashed in her haunting, green eyes like miniature bolts of lightning.

Pravus struggled within himself. Fought for control.

I cannot take her blood. It will kill us both.

But the thirst couldn't be reasoned with. A sacrifice must be offered. Soon.

Pravus stormed out of the room, leaving Aria gasping in a state of shock. He stalked the corridors, a predator on the hunt. The castle teemed with people ripe for bloodletting. The next person he encountered would relinquish their life and bolster his.

† † †

Alone in the atrium, Alderan still lay in the large circle of sand at its center, staring up at the massive dragon poles. He wondered how big some of the dragons had to have been in order to need such large, thick poles. Cinolth was big enough, his head nearly the size of Alderan's entire torso.

Aria had said that Cinolth would continue to grow for several more months, until he reached the size he'd once been. The thought terrified him.

Until he'd met Cinolth earlier, Alderan had never imagined dragons to be sentient creatures, let alone ones so cunning and deviously intelligent. According to Cinolth, the dumbest dragon could easily outwit the smartest human. Given Cinolth's loathing of humans, Alderan didn't buy it. He did wonder if other dragons still lived or if Cinolth was the last of his kind.

Alderan wove his fingers together and placed his hands behind his head. The glorious sea of stars shimmered, blurred, and then faded as his eyelids grew impossibly heavy. He closed his eyes for a single moment, and when he opened them again, he found himself trapped inside a living nightmare.

Before Alderan could even warn her, a stray arrow caught Aria right between the eyes and dropped her like a sack of turnips. Pravus stood next to her, his face ashen. The center of his forehead turned red and then blood gushed from a hole that hadn't been there a moment before. He dropped to his knees and then fell face first in the mud next to Aria.

Alderan rushed toward Aria, tripping over the trampled grass, mud, and broken bodies as he made his way across the valley floor. A shadow covered the land between them and grew rapidly. Alderan stopped abruptly and looked skyward just as Cinolth came crashing to the ground a few feet in front of him. The large dragon snorted smoke, and then grew still, the fire in his red eyes extinguished.

One arrow. Three deaths.

A man whose face Alderan recognized but couldn't place walked up next to him, his white shirt billowing in the wind. The man held a strung bow in his right hand. "My arrow stayed true." Tears glistened in his eyes.

The arrow wasn't stray, thought Alderan.

This man, whom he knew, had killed his sister. Alderan turned to the man, rage in his eyes. "Why did you kill her?" he growled.

"Sacrificing my daughter was the only way to kill Cinolth and end this war."

Alderan staggered backward and dropped to his knees. "Your... daughter?"

The man bent down next to Alderan. "Yes, my son."

The sky blackened as did Alderan's heart. Mezhik tingled in his fingertips. "I'm no son of yours!"

Alderan thrust his hand straight into the man's chest like a sword and ripped out the man's beating heart. He squeezed the heart until it burst and tossed it to the ground. The man toppled over and grew still.

Alderan rose to his feet and scanned the field. He alone stood. Soon, he'd be the only one left alive as well. He walked through the valley, turning each body over as he checked for survivors. When he found one still alive, he thrust his dagger into their ear and said, "Your death will be forgotten."

Alderan jolted awake, a hand upon his shoulder. He blinked several times before his eyes finally focused on the face of a balding man with wire-rimmed spectacles.

The man smiled and stood. "My name is Master Credan." He proffered his hand. "I believe it's time I showed you to your bedchamber."

Alderan's pulse raced. Sweat beaded his brow and wet the pits of his arms. No matter how hard he tried, he couldn't get the image of Aria out of his mind.

He closed his eyes for a moment. *I won't let them kill you, Aria. No matter what.*

Alderan took Credan's hand, and the man hauled him to his feet. "Thank you. My name is Alderan, Aria's brother."

The man bowed. "Indeed, you are." He swept his arm to the left. "Shall we?"

Alderan nodded and followed the man into the castle, his mind set on finding a way to save Aria and the world, even if it meant sacrificing his own life.

† † †

Pravus stood in the middle of the corridor, blood dripping from his chin. Raw power coursed through his veins, a strength he hadn't felt in weeks. A broken body lay at his feet, suspended in a pool of blood. Male. Young. Perhaps a year or two older than Aria, but no more. Little more than skin and bones remained of him.

The boy certainly had a name, but Pravus didn't know it. He never had, nor did he care to know it now. It wouldn't bring the boy back to life. Oddly, the boy hadn't resisted or struggled, even as his life slipped away.

True bravery.

Pravus wiped his chin with the sleeve of his robes. The blood soaked into the dark fabric and left no trace behind. The boy's body would prove more difficult to dispose of, but he'd leave that job for the person who stumbled upon it.

He turned and teleported out of the corridor and into the war room on the other side of the castle. Aria remained at the table, still studying the maps. She looked up briefly, hardly acknowledging his return.

She's still upset with me.

He couldn't blame her for being cross with him after his blatant loss of control and near-fatal episode earlier, but it didn't matter. He had things to do that didn't require her assistance. At the table, he refocused his mind on the myriad of tasks that needed to be completed before the morning sun rose in the west.

His thoughts returned to the issue of Cinolth and what must be done. Once they arrived outside of Duos Flumen, he'd notify Murtag to send Käíeƨ his way. Using her power, he'd find a way to take the dragon out.

Thinking of Murtag reminded Pravus of his failure to kill Aria's wretched brother. He'd deal with that issue once they'd secured the throne. Right now, he needed to send a message to all those bound to him by blood. Because of that bond, he could speak directly to them. However, in order for the message to reach such great distances, it would take an offering of blood and a special map to spread it upon. Both items were right there in the war room.

Pravus leaned over the table, his arms spread wide to prop himself up. "Take your leave, my love."

Aria looked up, her eyes red and her eyelids drooping. "I've yet to finish studying all the maps and diagrams."

Pravus shook his head. "There's no need to commit them to memory. We will take them with us."

She yawned and nodded. "Then I will retire." She headed straight for the door without a backward glance.

No kiss good night.

He straightened and cracked his knuckles. "Close the door on your way out." She did.

Nearly everything had been set for the morning, but one task remained. "Time to gather my army."

Pravus shuffled through several tubes of rolled parchment before locating the one he sought. He spread the four-foot-by-three-foot map out on the table and used several lead stones to keep the map from curling back on itself. This particular map of the Ancient Realm was unlike any other map he'd ever seen. The cartographic relief depictions matched those of other maps, but this one gained its uniqueness by the intricate runes drawn at the center of each of its four edges, one for each of the four directions of the compass.

An unadorned, ivory-handled dagger lay at the end of the table in a tan leather sheath. He retrieved the dagger and unsheathed it. Its thin, narrow blade glinted in the candlelight. In one swift motion, he drew the blade across his left palm. He winced, but only slightly as the blade proved extremely sharp.

Blood ran around the side of his hand and dripped from his fingers. The map hissed with each droplet of blood that spattered it, and the blood soaked into the yellowed parchment, leaving no trace behind. Pravus squeezed his hand over each of the four runes, applying six drops of blood to each. When the final drop touched the fourth rune, all four runes lifted from the map and glowed bright red. Then they circled and converged over the map's center, forming an altogether different rune. The rune's red glow turned orangish-yellow, bright as the sun, and then it lowered back down to the map. As it touched the parchment, the rune shattered into a thousand shards of light, creating a concussive wave of light and energy that swept outward from the center of the map. Parchment rustled, his robes billowed, and every candle in the room flickered and blew out, casting the room into total darkness. But then a green pinpoint of light pierced the darkness. The pinpoint of light grew into lines, waves, and other shapes as the cartographic details of the map came to life.

With the rune spell activated, Pravus could see those bound to him by blood on the map. He located Kaja, king of the zhebəllin, and mindspoke to him in the native zhebəllin tongue. *"The time for war is at hand. By your sworn oath and the blood that binds you to me, I command you to gather up your warriors and march toward the human city of Duos Flumen."*

Kaja's voice filled Pravus's mind. *"As you command, my lord."* The last two words dripped with venom.

Insolent little bastard. I'll deal with him after the war.

"Stay out of sight, and await my arrival outside of the city," said Pravus.

"We will travel by night and seek cover in the daylight," said Kaja.

"Perfect. Make sure you control your warriors with an iron fist and put down any who fail to comply."

"Yes, my lord."

Pravus withdrew his mind and focused on the map again.

Several more times, he located others bound by blood and delivered similar messages. By the time they arrived outside Duos Flumen, a formidable army would be gathered. Zhebəllin from the Daltura Hills and the Profugus Desert, mountain and forest giants from the Oblivio Forest and Sol Deus Mountains, scores of gnolls from across the realm, and even a few ogres and trolls.

Murtag and his band of orcs would continue to hide in the valley north of the Orbis Mountains. They would serve a different purpose.

Pravus nodded to himself, pleased with how everything had fallen into place. He'd spent decades preparing for this moment, manipulating events and rolling with setbacks and changes as best he could.

He folded his arms across his chest and grinned. "Everything will be as it should. I will rule the world as a god."

† † †

Aria sat straight up in bed, wide awake. Pravus lay next to her, his chest slowly rising and falling. A light snore rumbled from his lips. She didn't know when he'd come to bed.

A sliver of moonlight filtered in through the crack between the lengths of heavy drapes. She rose from the bed, careful not to disturb Pravus, and snuck out onto the balcony. Frost covered the stone floor and railing and froze her bare feet and hands.

Aria recalled the look in Pravus's eyes earlier in the war room and the way it had left her heart cold. She hugged herself, but it did little to ease her troubled mind.

What kind of madness lurks within him?

If for no other reason, she thanked the stars for the bond they shared. As mad as he might be at times, he'd never do anything that would harm himself. So she should be safe.

Unless it can be undone.

Pravus had assured her otherwise, but he'd been wrong about other things that he'd been certain of.

Like the stone.

For now, she could do nothing about it, so she need not waste her thoughts on it. Instead, she returned to her conversation with Cinolth the morning before. Pravus took the news of Cinolth's army joining theirs in stride and played it off as something of insignificance, but she'd detected a hint of elation in his eyes. He'd never fool her.

He must be pleased with what I've accomplished.

Aria reached into the night with her mind and located Cinolth. He hunted in the mountains to the west. Close enough that she could mindspeak with him.

"Direct your followers to head north and gather outside of Duos Flumen," said Aria. *"Our armies will meet them there."*

Cinolth responded, *"Any of my followers north of Cuspis will head that way. The rest will gather at the castle."*

"As you say. Thank you." Aria released her link to Cinolth.

The Three Kingdoms won't know what hit them until it's too late.

Gooseflesh covered her from head to toe, and her feet grew cold and numb. She returned to the room and to the large bed. Under the covers, she pressed her cold body against Pravus's warm, naked flesh. She would never trust him again, but it didn't mean she couldn't use him for warmth and pleasure. She roused him from his slumber with a single touch.

He pulled her into his arms, and soon the quiet night erupted with sounds of passion.

CHAPTER SEVENTEEN

Zerenity trudged through the sand, her mind set on one single goal: getting to Galondu Castle. Whatever her dark master commanded of her she'd do. Nothing else mattered. The world ceased to exist beyond her desire to please him.

Sounds ceased and sights blurred beyond what lay right in front of her.

She rested only when the others did.

She ate only when the others did.

Happiness overwhelmed her when her master's presence filled her and he mindspoke to her. He didn't speak to her specifically but to all of his chosen, but it made no difference. In her mind, he only spoke to her. She was his chosen one.

"Head toward The Plains," said her master. *"Between Duos Flumen and Elatos."* An image of a map with an "X" marking the spot filled her mind, replacing the one she'd been heading to over Galondu Castle.

"Yes, my dark master," she said in her mind, her voice nearly panting.

As one, Zerenity and the other chosen switched direction and headed east.

"Use every resource at your disposal and do not delay in getting there. If anyone tries to stop you or slow you down, spill their blood."

"Yes, my dark master," she said.

"Good. I will meet you there." His presence faded.

Pleasure coursed through Zerenity's veins at the prospect of meeting her master face-to-face.

I am coming, my dark master.

Chapter Eighteen

Many hours had passed since Calen freed himself from the cage, and he'd spent a good portion of it trying to find a way out of the maze of tunnels. He knew there must be some sort of pattern or markings that led to an exit, but he'd failed to find any thus far. No matter which tunnel he took, it eventually led to a hub of more tunnels or came to a dead-end. Strangely, he'd come across no zhebəllin, no living quarters, or any other functional room. That frightened him almost as much as the zhebəllin themselves.

The zhebəllin took all of Calen's possessions when they'd captured him, including his money, food, water, and knife. Now, thirst dried his mouth and throat, and his stomach quaked with hunger. He looked down at his stomach. It bulged several inches beyond the belt at his waist. Missing several meals would do him little harm, but he needed to find something to drink before he dehydrated. He imagined the other children were hungry and thirsty as well.

He pushed onward through the tunnels for another hour, more out of obligation than self-preservation. The Dalturan children needed him to succeed in order to survive, and he'd assured them that he'd come back for them once he found a way out, but he'd begun to lose hope and questioned his ability to do so.

His heart raced, and he wheezed with each breath. Stopping wasn't an option, but each step took him closer to failure. How many deaths would be on his head if he failed?

Too many to count.

Calen marked the walls with a white stone as he traversed what felt like miles of tunnels, but he never crossed any of his markings again. Either the tunnels ran throughout the entire length of the Daltura Hills or someone followed behind him and erased his marks as quickly as he made them.

You're alone, Calen. Don't be afraid.

Those words repeated in his head every few minutes, but he knew them to be a lie. A dozen times, the pitter-patter of bare feet spun him around, but he never found anyone or anything following him when he backtracked. He chalked the occurrences up to nerves, but his heart knew better.

Scrape!

Metal on stone. Calen whirled around so quickly that he nearly threw the torch he held. Rusted steel glinted in the flickering torchlight as the zhebəllin spun the blade in its fingers. Beady red eyes, filled with hate, stared up at Calen.

"Stay back, or I'll hurt you!" yelled Calen. He poked his torch at the creature.

The zhebəllin's snarl morphed into a wicked grin, revealing a mouth full of pointy, yellow teeth. It made a series of noises and grunts as it stocked closer. Calen wasn't sure if it had spoken to him or not. Either way, Calen didn't speak its language.

Calen swung his torch wildly, but the zhebəllin wouldn't be deterred. It didn't seem to be afraid of fire. Calen retreated several steps but quickly found his back against a wall and nowhere else to go. The zhebəllin closed the distance to just three feet.

Now or never, Calen.

Calen screamed as loud as he could and lunged forward, catching the zhebəllin off guard. The zhebəllin dropped its blade and raised its arms to protect its head but not quick enough. The torch thudded in Calen's hand when it struck the side of the zhebəllin's head, reverberating all the way up his arm. The blow dropped the zhebəllin straight to the ground, out cold.

Calen dropped to his knees, stunned at his accomplishment. *Thank you, Ɂäṭūr.*

Using the zhebəllin's blade, Calen cut strips of fabric from his trousers and used them to tie the zhebəllin's hands behind its back. He bound its ankles as well but left enough slack so that the creature could still walk. There's no way he could carry the creature no matter how little it might've weighed. Once it woke up, he'd find a way to communicate with it in order to find the children again and then the exit. He pocketed the blade.

It didn't take long for the zhebəllin to come to, and when it did, it struggled against its restraints for several minutes before realizing it stood no chance of escape. Calen had taken several classes in school on tying knots and was better at it than most of the other kids in his class. It was the one thing he had confidence in.

"Can you understand me?" asked Calen.

The zhebəllin glared at him for several moments but then nodded.

"Good." Calen chewed on his lower lip. "I'm Calen. What do they call you?"

"Lupaak." Its voice shrieked with a high pitch.

Calen looked around. They were still alone as far as he could tell. "Where are all the other zhebəllin?"

"Gone," said Lupaak.

"Gone? Why didn't you go with them?"

Lupaak grinned wickedly. "Stay behind. Kill children. Eat them." He licked his lips and sneered, "Tasty."

Calen wanted to smack Lupaak, but he needed his help. "You will take me back to the children so that I can free them, and then you'll lead us back to the surface."

"No," said Lupaak.

"I don't want to hurt you, but I will," said Calen. "Do what I ask, and I'll let you go."

"Enemy lies. I show. You kill me."

Calen had no intention of killing Lupaak, but he needed the zhebəllin to think so. He took the blade from his pocket and pushed its point against Lupaak's throat until it pierced Lupaak's thick skin. A line of black blood ran down Lupaak's chest.

Calen gritted his teeth and glared into Lupaak's beady red eyes. "You don't show me, and I'll kill you right now." His voice shook. He hoped it conveyed malice and not the terror running through his veins and trembling his hands.

Lupaak swallowed hard and eyed the blade. "Trust enemy."

Calen lowered the blade. "I'm not your enemy."

"All humans are enemies. Drive us into the ground. Eat from the scraps left behind."

Despite the situation, Calen found himself feeling sorry for Lupaak. Had the humans driven them underground? He didn't recall history telling of such a story, but history often lied to cover up atrocities. Perhaps this was one of them. Either way, it didn't matter right then. He had dozens of children to rescue.

"You have my word. Show us the way, and you'll be free to go."

Lupaak nodded. "Follow me."

Calen had a hard time keeping up with Lupaak even with Lupaak's ankles bound. By the time they reached the cavern with all the suspended cages, Calen sucked wind hard. His lungs burned with fire, and he fought to catch his breath. He bent over and placed his hands on his knees and waited until he could breathe evenly again.

He tied Lupaak to one of the twine ropes and then set about freeing the children from their cages. He had to rest several times before freeing all of them. Fifty-four children in total.

About an hour later, they surfaced through a tunnel hidden amongst the trees and hills. The sky overhead shown in hues of blues, purples, yellows, reds, and oranges as the new day sun peeked up from the west. He guessed they were about six miles north of Daltura, but he'd never really ventured outside the town gates more than a few dozen paces, so nothing looked familiar.

Lupaak pointed them in the direction of Daltura and Calen ordered Glenn, the oldest of the bunch after himself, to start leading the children that way. Once the children were out of sight, Calen cut Lupaak's restraints.

"If I ever see you again, I will kill you. Understood?" asked Calen.

Lupaak grunted, nodded, and disappeared into the tunnel they'd come out of.

Calen took a deep breath. He wanted to celebrate his victory, but first he needed to get the children back to the safety of Daltura. No telling what other creatures or threats lurked in the shadows. He took off through the tall, yellow aspen trees and quickly caught up with the children.

Several hours later, they crested a hill and the northern gates of Daltura came into view. Relief swept through Calen when he saw that Daltura still stood. A gathering of people stood outside the gates by the time they arrived. Cheers and cries of joy filled the air as several children ran into the arms of their parents and loved ones. Others wept with realization that their parents were either gone or dead.

Word of Calen's bravery and accomplishment swept through the town. They hailed him as a hero, but he didn't feel like one. In fact, as the minutes rolled on, he grew further distraught over his aunt. He looked around. So many faces he knew were missing. To make matters worse, he had no idea where the horde of infected went.

How will I ever find Aunt Tahmara?

He pushed through the crowd and made his way back to the northern gates. They'd already been drawn shut and secured. He dropped to his knees and cried. A hand rested on his shoulder. He looked up through blurry eyes, and, just for the briefest moment, thought the hand belonged to his aunt.

He knew better. Knew it couldn't be her. But it devastated him further nonetheless when he finally recognized Mrs. Dougett.

"Calen, I'm so glad you're safe. And the children!" She bent down and hugged his neck. Tight. So tight he couldn't breathe. He tapped her arm several times before she relinquished her death grip. "Oh, my! I'm so sorry! Your bravery just got me so worked up." She kissed his cheek.

Calen wiped the wet from his cheek. "I need to get back out there. My Aunt Tahmara needs me."

Mrs. Dougett stood back up. "I won't stop you, Calen, but perhaps you'd like a warm meal, something to drink, and some supplies for your journey."

He'd forgotten about his dry throat and empty stomach, but the thought of food set his stomach rumbling again. "I'd appreciate that. But it needs to be quick. I've lost so much time already."

"Of course. I've got a smattering of breakfast items prepared already. I'm so used to Mr. Dougett always being there that I made enough for him as well. Speaking of Mr. Dougett, please look out for him as you search for your aunt."

Calen nodded. "Yes ma'am."

She proffered her hand. "Come with me. Regain some strength and then go do what you must." Calen took her hand, and she helped him to his feet.

Twenty minutes later, Calen had a full belly and a pack with enough food for a good week slung over his shoulders. A bedroll sat atop the pack, attached to it with leather straps. He wore a new pair of trousers, or at least new to him. They were Mr. Dougett's, and fit surprisingly well after rolling the cuffs a few times. Two sheathed daggers hung from his belt, along with a small coin purse with enough money for additional supplies, if needed.

At the town gates, he said his goodbyes to the dozen or so people gathered to see him off and promised to send word once he located the infected horde of Daltura citizens. One of the townsmen unbarred the gate and opened it just wide enough for Calen to slip through. No one offered to accompany him, nor did anyone offer him a horse for his potentially long journey. He didn't expect either and held no sort of grudge or resentment toward the people for not providing them. As it was, he'd received far more support than he deserved from Mrs. Dougett. He'd never forget her kindness.

Calen stepped through the gates. They slammed shut behind him, sending his pulse soaring. He walked north on shaky legs for a hundred yards before his feet stopped moving. A flurry of activity stirred in his stomach as doubt crept into his mind. He looked north and then east, unsure of where he should go. The hills blocked his view in both directions, and footprints and trampled grass and bushes marred the landscape everywhere he looked. His heart sank.

Aunt Tahmara… How will I ever find you again when I don't know which way you've gone? Ɂäʈūr help me.

CHAPTER NINETEEN

Through the evening and into the night, Nardus traversed the dirt roads of East Hotah, but found no sign of Theyn. In fact, he found few signs of any sort of activity. Most of the houses remained dark through the starless, moonless night, turning the roads into an inkwell of shadows and darkness. East Hotah housed the poor and elderly, so it hadn't surprised him to find it so. Most couldn't afford spare candles.

As the morning sun crept up from the west, he made his way across the long and narrow bridge that connected East Hotah with West Hotah. In his single past experience, West Hotah had crawled with people and activity, but few people moved about that morning. Not that much time had passed since he last set foot on her roads, but she seemed to be a much different city than he remembered.

Merchants kept close to their stands, caution in their eyes and fear in their voices when they spoke of the many things they sold. Many of them openly brandished weapons, and some of the shop keepers kept their doors closed. Had he not recognized the city, he might've thought he'd come through the wrong mirror.

Many people went about their business, but the throngs of people he remembered wading through seemed to have disappeared. The further he walked, the harder he listened to the whispers and murmurs and hushed talk exchanged between merchants and customers. When asked, they told him nothing. They knew he didn't belong there. An outsider.

But I'm here to help. He knew it made little difference.

Nardus began to wonder if Theyn had come here at all or if she'd become stuck between places—between worlds. But then a familiar tale caught his ear. A young woman spoke of a wild beast roaming the night and tearing people apart, limb by limb. She had no firsthand knowledge or many details of the attacks, so he continued his search.

As he neared the heart of the city, the rumors of this wild beast became more detailed. Several people described the beast as a large cat with a tan coat and sharp claws. Blood-stained jaws and front paws. If the stories were to be believed, as Nardus did, the cat hunted people both day and night, singling out those known for their nefarious endeavors. A relentless nightmare.

To compound matters, he heard disturbing rumors of an infection that had spread throughout the city, turning people into pale, black-veined vegetables, their eyes black and distant. But then yesterday, all the infected rose from their beds and started leaving the city, toward the west. None of them were responsive when confronted, and none could be kept from heading toward some unknown destiny unless restrained. Those who were restrained cried out for their master ceaselessly. The thought terrified Nardus more than Theyn did.

To whom do they cry for?

Finally, Nardus came across a merchant who claimed that a wizard with fiery red hair had taken down the beast and dragged it off. Immediately, he knew that the man spoke of Joriah. If true, Theyn would be safe.

But is Joriah?

Nardus traversed roads and hills until he finally recognized Joriah's house atop a distant hill, its red door a beacon of familiarity among a sea of houses with yellow and blue doors.

He made his way over to the small hill it stood upon and traversed the stone path that led from the gate to the front of the cottage. He pummeled the door with his fist. After a minute or so, Joriah answered the door, far more unkempt than normal with a red beard several inches long hanging from his jaws.

Joriah's kind, teal eyes flashed with recognition. "Nardus! What brings you back to West Hotah?" He proffered his hand, but Nardus didn't take it.

Nardus peered around Joriah's slim frame and into the single-room home. "You know why I'm here, Joriah. I've come for Theyn."

"Theyn?" Joriah scoffed. "You and I both know she's dead."

Nardus shook his finger at Joriah, his patience all but gone. "She's not dead, and you know it. What have you done with her?"

"I don't understand. We all saw her die."

Nardus couldn't read Joriah's face, but the man had to be lying. "Step aside, or I will force you to."

Joriah shook his head and stepped aside. "I assure you that Theyn isn't here. As far as I know, she died the day we took you to Pravus. So, why is it that you're really here?"

Nardus stepped past him, purposely knocking Joriah a step backward with his shoulder. "Open the basement, or I will tear this house down."

"You won't find what you're looking for down there."

"Then open it up and prove it."

Joriah sighed and obliged. The floor moved away and revealed the stairway leading down into the basement of the house. Nardus descended into the darkness, Joriah right on his heels.

Joriah snapped his fingers and the basement lit up. "I assure you she's not here."

A room with its door closed sat in the far back corner. Nardus guessed Joriah held Theyn there. He rushed over to the door and tried the handle, but it was locked. "Unlock the door."

"She's not in there," Joriah insisted.

Nardus glared at Joriah. "Unlock the damned door before I kick it in!"

Joriah sighed and unlocked the door, but then he hesitated. He peered up at Nardus, steel in his eyes. "You will speak to no one about what you see in there. Understood?"

"What have you done to her?" Nardus tried to push Joriah out of the way, but the man held his ground.

A look of dark determination hung on Joriah's face, and mezhik crackled and arced across his fingertips with orange light. Nardus didn't think Joriah capable of such malice, but how well did he know the man?

Not well at all.

Joriah's jaw tightened. "Agree, or you will *not* enter this room."

Nardus took a deep breath and staved his anger. "As you wish."

The orange light faded from Joriah's fingertips. "After you." The door swung open and Joriah stepped out of the way.

Nardus entered the dark room. Something lurked in the shadows across the room, massive and hulking. Ragged, drawn-out breaths sounded from the beast. Irregular. Forced.

Joriah stepped into the room and snapped his fingers. Light filled the room, chasing away all the shadows. A cage with thick, iron bars stood two feet from Nardus, but that wasn't what caught his breath. The beast lying on the far side of the cage did.

No, not a beast. A man.

Nardus's mind couldn't process the images relayed through his eyes. He turned toward Joriah but kept his eyes on the man in the cage. "What in *Ef Demd Dhä* have you done?"

† † †

"Don't you dare try and lay the blame of this on me!" shouted Joriah.

Nardus leaned against the wall and slid down until his butt reached the floor. He pulled his hair back and stared at the ceiling. "Then explain what happened. How did Berggren wind up in a cage in your basement?"

"Don't you get it? Theyn's death drove him over the edge. Imagine losing both of your children in a matter of weeks." Joriah glared at Nardus. "By the hand of *one* man. He roamed the roads like a drunken bear, leaving a path of destruction everywhere he went."

Nardus rubbed his left bicep. He knew all too well what something like that could do to a man. Oddly enough, their situations were quite similar. They both thought they'd lost a daughter that turned up alive. But Berggren didn't know. Couldn't be reasoned with in his current state.

"So Berggren's the beast that people saw you subdue…"

"I'm certain that's the case. As I said, until you walked through my door, I was certain Theyn had died. Now, given your determination to find her, I'm not so sure."

"For what it's worth, I'm sorry about Berggren, but you must realize that I wasn't responsible for Shaul's death. Nor Theyn's since she's not dead."

"Then we must find her before someone else does." He stuck out his hand. "We've no time to waste."

Nardus took Joriah's hand and pulled himself up. "Do you know the places she might go?"

Joriah cocked his head. "There are only a few I can think of. Perhaps three."

"Good. We should split up."

"Agreed. You can search Baker Road on the lower westside of West Hotah, and I'll search the other two in the heart of the city."

"Baker Road? How will I find it?"

"Simple. Head southwest from here and let your nose guide you. The smell of freshly baked bread is like no other."

Nardus stood with his arms akimbo. "Fine, but why do you get to search two locations?"

"There are many reasons beyond the odd number of three. For one, I'm a wizard and can travel much quicker than you. I also know where these places are. You'd certainly get lost trying to find them." Joriah smiled smugly. "Is that good enough reason, or should we waste more time arguing about it while Theyn's out there possibly terrorizing people or perhaps being hunted."

Nardus brooded but nodded. "As you say. We'll meet back here?"

"Yes." Joriah reached into one of his many pockets and withdrew a foot-long zabatana, a quiver with four three-inch-long darts, and a bottle of grayish-blue liquid. "Use these to subdue her." He handed the items to Nardus. "Be warned that it'll take a few minutes to take effect though. Rest assured, she'll be torqued off about it."

Nardus slipped the blow tube into his right trouser pocket and strung the small quiver onto his belt. The bottle intrigued him. He held it up to the light. "What's in this?"

"A liquid form of Nízhäíd bəllū. It's extremely potent." Joriah smiled wryly. "From what I've heard, you're familiar with its effects. Quite the sedative, wouldn't you say?"

Nardus understood and ignored Joriah's jab. Theyn had used nízhäíd bəllū on him several times on the boat ride from Incendia Island to West Hotah. "It is." He smiled to himself as he pocketed the bottle.

A bit of payback, if necessary.

He followed Joriah out of the room and back upstairs.

Joriah faced Nardus, his face as grim as the reaper himself. "Baker Road. Don't forget, and be careful."

Nardus nodded. "You as well." He grabbed for his coin purse, but it didn't hang from his belt. He reached over his shoulder and couldn't locate the familiar hilt of Brinzhär Dädh either. In fact, he didn't have any of his things. Panic held him in its grasp for several seconds before he remembered all the events leading up to this moment.

Pravus has everything. Damn him.

"Is there a problem?" asked Joriah.

"I seem to have left all my things with Pravus, including coin."

Joriah smiled and reached into his coin purse. He withdrew four copper pieces and handed them to Nardus. "That should afford you a sizable chunk of bread and a bit of cheese."

"I can't—"

Joriah waved him off. "Think nothing of it. See you back here soon." Joriah disappeared in a flash of his twisting red cape.

"Mezhik," Nardus snarled. He shook his head but refrained from spitting on Joriah's clean floor. He pocketed the coins and headed out the door.

The cool morning air brought a touch of life back into his bloodshot eyes and tired lungs. He didn't know how long it'd been since he'd slept, but it didn't matter. His friends were in peril and nothing would keep him from doing what was necessary to rescue them, not even sleep.

With dogged determination, he marched down the hill and toward a place named Baker Road.

But will I find Theyn there?

† † †

Nardus loved Theyn. Not quite like he did Vitara, but Vitara was his first love. How could he expect to ever love Theyn in the same way?

I never shall.

For some reason, the thought of seeing them both in the next life left him feeling dirtier than he already did. But would they both be there? Would he? He hadn't reconciled his differences with Ɂät̪ūr yet, but he'd begun to understand that some things in life are driven by evil and not sanctioned or condoned by Ɂät̪ūr.

But He allows that evil to thrive.

Or… am I the one who allowed it? Had I been faithful, would things have turned out differently?

He pushed the thought from his mind and focused on his surroundings. Something smelled ripe with sweat. Upon further inspection, he found the source of the stench to be himself. He desperately needed a bath and a shave. His face and neck itched something fierce.

Nardus rubbed his left bicep. The scar remained, but the memory faded with every season. Reuniting with Shanara, his daughter who now went by Aria, had changed him. Changed his priorities. From that moment in the cell, he began focusing on what he had and not what he'd lost.

Shanara will eventually come around. She must.

Nardus wouldn't settle for anything less.

He pushed his hand through stringy, oily hair. When had he last bathed? An image of the old woman in the pool filled his mind, the tops of her long, wrinkled breasts bobbing on the water's surface. He shuddered as her hand latched onto the inside of his thigh once again. Her words rang in his ears. *"Stave your anger, hold your tongue, and opportunity will present itself."*

The opportunity couldn't come quick enough. Pravus needed to die. The bastard had a hand in all the strife in Nardus's life.

One day, he will pay for everything he's done. He'd make sure of it.

Nardus stuffed the last bit of bread in his mouth. The bread helped return some of his energy and drove away his hunger pangs, but it did nothing to ease his mind. He'd had no luck finding Theyn thus far and hoped Joriah's fortune had fared better.

Screams and shouting erupted somewhere down the road from where Nardus stood. He rushed forward, swallowing the bread as he ran. The shouts grew louder as he neared an intersection with another road. He slid to a stop as he rounded the corner, his heart thrashing in his chest and his lungs afire.

A blonde-haired woman lay in the road in a pool of blood. She didn't move, her throat torn open and her head at an awkward angle. Nardus's first thought was that the woman was Theyn, but he knew better. His eyes moved farther down the road. Two men held ropes, stretched taut in opposite directions.

Nardus moved closer. The ropes secured a large cat around its throat.

"Theyn!"

The two men looked Nardus's way. Blood spattered their faces. Nardus froze when he spotted a third man approaching Theyn from the side of the road. The man carried a sledgehammer over his shoulder.

What is he doing?

The man stopped in front of Theyn's head and raised the sledgehammer above his head. Nardus's heart thundered in his ears. He ran toward Theyn and the three men, but he knew he wouldn't reach her in time to save her.

The man looked up at Nardus as the sledgehammer arced downward. Rage filled the man's eyes, and he roared with fury.

"Stop!" screamed Nardus, lurching to a halt.

An arc of golden light shot down the road, expanding outward as it traveled. The event ceased just as quickly as it had begun, in just a fraction of a second. Nardus stood there in shock, the tingle of mezhik fresh on his skin. His mind couldn't comprehend what had just happened.

So many things begged for his attention all at once. It left him breathless and his feet rooted to the road. The man with the sledgehammer stood hunched over, the head of his sledgehammer just inches from Theyn's head. But the man didn't flinch. In fact, nothing did. Trees stood stoic along the road, not a leaf twitching. A piece of parchment hung in the air to Nardus's left, a fixture upon a wall.

Nardus stepped cautiously toward the suspended parchment and poked at it. It moved with his force but stayed wherever he put it. "My God…"

Nardus circled, his gaze searching for the source of such mezhik, but nothing and no one moved no matter where he looked. He didn't understand what could've caused such an event and why it didn't affect him, but he had little time to think about it.

He turned and stared at Theyn. She lay with her back to him. He took a step forward and stopped. His heart pounded in his chest so hard he could scarcely think. His hands trembled and his legs quaked, but he forced himself to take another step.

"Enough of this," he growled.

Nardus rushed forward and knelt next to Theyn. The ropes were impossibly tight around her neck, one above and the other below her silver collar. With a few moves, he made quick work of the simple knots and tossed the ropes aside. He pulled Theyn's head from underneath the sledgehammer and pulled back the fur where the ropes had been. The skin was crimson with broken blood vessels, but he found no abrasions.

He gathered himself and reached out with his mind. *"Theyn, wake up."*

When he did, Theyn sprung to her feet and rounded on him. She crouched back, ready to pounce. A low growl escaped through her wicked teeth. Nardus rose and took several steps backward, distancing himself from her. Theyn stalked forward, her golden eyes locked onto his. Or did they eye his throat? He couldn't quite tell. Either way, he knew he had made a mistake waking her up.

Theyn lunged, and Nardus dove to the side, grunting as he drove his right shoulder into the solid road. Theyn tumbled several times, but it didn't stop her. She sprung back on her feet and stalked toward him once more. Nardus crawled backward with his elbows. Theyn lunged again, and Nardus rolled once more, but she caught his right shoulder with her claws. Pain erupted through his shoulder, and fresh blood peppered the air. He swallowed a yelp and rolled twice more, but he had no chance of escaping her.

Theyn pounced on top of him with crushing weight, her right paw poised to take a swipe at his neck. She did, and Nardus screamed. Theyn flew backward and tumbled across the road. She slumped to the ground and didn't move. A gash ran above her left eye, red with blood.

What in Ef Demd Dhä was that?

Nardus rose to his feet and crept toward Theyn, his left hand holding his right shoulder. Theyn's eyes fluttered open for just a moment, and then she fell limp.

Nardus squatted next to Theyn and lifted her head in his hands. She didn't stir. He parted her eyelids, but her eyes didn't move or dilate.

She's out cold.

He sat back and took a deep breath. Nothing in the last ten minutes made any sense. He searched the roads and buildings again with his eyes, unsure of what he thought he might find. No one lurked in the shadows as far as he could tell, but someone must've. They'd saved Theyn's life and his, so why didn't they come forward?

"Hello?" His voice sounded ragged. No one answered, but what had he expected?

Nardus bent over and kissed the wound over Theyn's eye. He stroked the side of her face and spoke to her through his mind. *"You're such a beautiful creature."*

Memories of the night she came to him at Joriah's house, nearly transfigured, flooded his mind. Her soft fur rubbed against his skin, and she'd purred like a kitten. That night had changed him. Changed the way he saw her and felt about her.

"Where am I?"

Theyn's voice in his head startled Nardus, jolting his eyes open. He didn't remember closing them. She stared up at him, the animalistic rage from before extinguished. He smiled and stroked her head. "We're in West Hotah, somewhere off of Baker Road. When we left Nasduron we got separated. You came here when I went back to Galondu Castle, so I came here to find you."

Theyn rose on all fours and shook her head. She looked around, but her gaze stopped on the woman lying in a pool of blood. *"Did… Did I do that?"* She and Nardus both looked down at her paws. Blood caked the fur.

"I didn't see what happened to her, but I'd guess it was probably you based on everything that was happening."

Theyn's eyes glistened. *"I can't keep doing this, Nardus. I can't live this way."*

Nardus grabbed her chin and looked her in the eye. "This wasn't your fault, Theyn. You weren't yourself when this happened, and you know it."

"How can you sit there and say that? Look around. I'm a monster."

"No, you aren't, and don't ever say that again. If anything, this is all my fault. I never should've left you, and I never will again."

"Your shoulder—"

"Don't worry about it, it's barely more than a scratch." Nardus stood.

Theyn looked around. *"Why is everything frozen?"*

Nardus shrugged. "I'm not sure. Someone saved us both."

"I still don't understand. Why did you come back for me?"

"You know why, Theyn." He glared at her for a moment, but her beautiful eyes softened him. "You knew before I did. I'm in love with you. I refuse to spend another day without you."

"So what we do now?"

"We head for Joriah's. There's something you need to see before we head back to Galondu Castle." He looked back at the dead woman. "And we need to get as far away from this as possible."

Theyn nodded. *"Follow me, I know a shortcut."*

✝ ✝ ✝

People stood like statues in the roads and shops for several blocks before Nardus and Theyn reached an area where life flowed freely again. Questions about the event filled Nardus's head. Had these people just awoken, or had they ever been frozen at all? How long would the others stay frozen, or did they move freely now as well? Did the ones notice the others? Had anyone other than him and Theyn noticed?

Theyn's voice entered his head and disrupted his thoughts. *"Keep your feet moving. We're almost there."*

Nardus hadn't even noticed he'd stopped. For the moment, he needed to shove those questions to the back of his mind and contemplate them when no other lives hung in the balance. Gnaud needed him, and so did

Theyn. Perhaps even Berggren.

Ten minutes later, Nardus and Theyn walked through Joriah's red front door. Moments later, Joriah appeared in a whirlwind of red fury.

"How do you do that?" asked Nardus. "We literally just walked through the door."

"Yes, you did—" Joriah winked at him. "—but a wizard never reveals his secrets."

Joriah's gaze moved to Theyn, and his smile faded. He took several steps backward as he reached into his pocket. Nardus quickly moved in front of Theyn. "There's no need for that. Theyn is herself again, albeit in the form of a cat."

Joriah frowned, the lines in his forehead deepening. "How?"

Nardus shrugged. "Honestly, I don't know. Somehow, I'm able to connect with her and bring her back when she's fallen into her madness." Skepticism painted Joriah's face. Nardus moved to the side and presented Theyn to Joriah. "See for yourself. Talk with her through your mind."

"Mindspeak with her?" Joriah stood up straight, his eyebrows arched high above his eyes. "You've done this?"

Nardus crossed his arms and brooded. "You doubt that I have?"

"You realize that only wizards and sorceresses have that ability, do you not?"

"That's a lie. I'm no wizard, and I wield no mezhik." Nardus spat on the floor and cringed. "Sorry about that. I know it's a bad habit." He bent down and wiped up the spit with his hand. "I swear I'm trying to break it."

"See that you do," said Joriah.

Nardus stood. "Dragons can mindspeak as well."

"I'm sure you're right, along with a few other mezhik creatures and beings." Joriah turned his attention back to Theyn. "Now, give me a moment to speak with her."

"Knock yourself out." Nardus walked over to one of the chairs that sat in front of the fireplace and sat down. Nothing remained on the hearth other than grey ash and a few chunks of charcoaled wood. Nardus rested his eyes as his mind drifted to thoughts of the beast in the basement.

How is Theyn going to react when she sees him?

He supposed it didn't matter. She needed to know and would find out one way or another. He preferred keeping no secrets from her.

"What did you need to show me?" asked Theyn in his mind.

Nardus opened his eyes. Theyn sat in front of him. Watched him. But for how long? Sleep must've snuck up on him. *"Give me a minute,"* he said to her with his mind.

Joriah sat in the chair next to him, his hand over his mouth as he stifled a yawn. "Mind if I take a look at that shoulder of yours? You don't want those wounds getting infected."

"I'd be lying if I told you I felt anything at all." Nardus rubbed his shoulder with his thumb but felt no wound underneath his bloody, shredded shirt. He frowned. "That's curious."

Joriah rose from his chair and examined Nardus's shoulder. "Curious, indeed. You don't even have a scratch."

"Huh. Come to think of it, I do remember it tingling a bit on the way back here. Didn't really think much of it at the time."

Joriah grinned. "Like it or not, you're a wizard."

"Damn you, Joriah. Quit accusing me of such foul things. I swear to you, I'm no wizard." Nardus lifted his sleeves and showed Joriah his wrists. "Look!"

Joriah hardly glanced at them. "If you say so."

Nardus stood and eyed Joriah. "We must leave soon, but there's two things you need to do first."

Joriah straightened the red cape draped over his left shoulder. "And those things are?"

"First, you need to remove Theyn's stupid collar."

Joriah opened his palm, and the collar slid right through Theyn's neck and into his hand. Nardus gasped and Joriah smiled wickedly. "And the second?"

"Show Theyn what's in your basement."

Joriah's smile turned into a scowl in an instant. "There's nothing down there for her to see."

Nardus poked Joriah in the chest with his finger. "It's not a request."

"You don't know how she'll react. The situation could turn deadly in a moment. Are you prepared for that?"

"Say the word, and I'll gut him," said Theyn in Nardus's head.

"There's no need for violence, Theyn." Nardus stroked Theyn's head. "Joriah's just about to do what I've asked of him." He looked at Joriah.

"Aren't you?"

Joriah glared at him for several moments and then sighed loudly. "As you wish, but I refuse to take any responsibility for what might happen."

"Not asking you to. Now open the floor."

Joriah flicked his wrist toward the center of the floor, and the floor opened up, revealing the stairs down to the basement. The three of them descended the stairs and headed straight to the room in the far corner.

Joriah unlocked the door and stepped aside. "Don't say I didn't warn you."

Nardus opened the door and led Theyn into the dark room. Joriah snapped his fingers, and the room brightened. Theyn sniffed the air and backed away from the cage.

She looked up at Nardus, her eyes narrowed. *"What is that?"* she asked in Nardus's mind.

"That's… your father. Berggren."

A low growl escaped from Theyn's throat. *"Wake him."*

Nardus turned to Joriah, who still stood outside the room. "Theyn wants you to wake him up."

"Very well, but I fear nothing remains of his mind." Joriah stepped into the room. "Step back from the cage as far as you can get. Iceberg has a long reach."

Nardus and Theyn moved back against the wall. Joriah teleported inside the cage, touched Berggren's shoulder and mumbled something Nardus didn't understand, and then teleported back outside of the room's doorway. Berggren stirred, stretched, and then roared. He rolled off the bed, grabbed it with one hand, and threw it against the bars. It felt like the impact shook the whole room, and the thunderous clang rang in Nardus's ears.

Berggren rammed the bars with his shoulder and roared. Madness swirled in his eyes. He rammed the bars repeatedly, and Nardus swore they bent a little more with each hit.

Theyn backed away. *"That isn't my father,"* she said in Nardus's head. *"Is that how I become when I can't remember myself?"* Her fear nearly crushed Nardus.

"Don't even think about it, Theyn. It will do you no good." Nardus took a step toward the cage. Berggren rammed the bars again and then reached through them, swiping at Nardus like a bear. Nardus stepped closer, just a few inches out of Berggren's reach.

"I'm here to help," said Nardus.

Berggren roared again and shook the cage. Nardus reached out to him with his mind, hoping to find some semblance of the Berggren he knew, but the only thing he found was a madness that he knew all too well—one he'd carried with himself for so long.

I know your pain.

Nardus opened his mind and allowed the madness to tether itself to him. He drew it into himself, tendril by maddening tendril, until nothing remained within Berggren's mind. He severed the link, and Berggren collapsed to the floor.

Madness drove Nardus to his knees, and he wailed with the pain of loss and the fury of hatred. He grabbed the sides of his head and dug his fingers into his skull.

"You will not control me again!" he screamed.

A light, dim at first but brightening quickly, entered his mind. In that light he found solace. Warmth. A love like none he'd ever felt before. Through that light came the face of an angel. White hair, camel skin, and yellow eyes.

Theyn.

The light exploded in his mind, driving away the darkness and the madness. Nothing remained but her presence. He opened his eyes as tears streamed down his cheeks. Theyn licked his face and nuzzled his chin. Nardus wrapped his arms around her neck and held her for what felt like an eternity, lost inside the moment and never wanting it to end. But as with everything, it couldn't last forever.

Nardus released Theyn and wiped the tears from his eyes. He stood on shaky legs and held fast to one of the cage bars.

Berggren lay on the floor inside the cage, his chest heaving. Tears wet his cheeks. He sat up and stared at Nardus. "You've got a lot of nerve showing your face."

Nardus exhaled a breath he didn't realize he'd held. "It's good to have you back, *Iceberg*."

"Only my friends call me that." Berggren rolled onto his hands and knees and then stood. He approached Nardus, but Nardus didn't back away.

"I'm aware of that."

Berggren reached through the bars and proffered his hand. Nardus hesitated for only a moment before taking it. Berggren pulled him against the bars and wrapped his other arm around Nardus. "It's always good to have another friend."

Theyn's mind entered Nardus's. *"Tell him I said hello."*

"Theyn says hello." Nardus could barely get the words out with Berggren squeezing him so tight.

Joriah moved past Nardus and unlocked the cage. "Not a wizard," he chuckled.

Not a wizard... Am I? Disgusted by the notion, he nearly spat in Berggren's face. *Never.*

Berggren released Nardus and threw his arms around Joriah. "Thanks for not giving up on me."

Joriah coughed and wheezed. "Afraid I did, my friend. This was all Nardus's idea."

"Even so," said Berggren. "I appreciate it." He released Joriah and Theyn pounced on him, knocking him back a few steps. She wrapped her front paws around his neck. Tears streaked Berggren's face again. "Theyn, my beautiful daughter. I thought I'd lost you."

Nardus smiled and walked out of the room, his heart fuller than it had been in a long time. By the time he reached the stairs, reality set in. He and Theyn needed to get back to Galondu Castle. Gnaud's life and Nasduron depended on it.

He reached out to Theyn with his mind. *"We must go."*

Three thunderous bangs sounded from upstairs. "Joriah Treyfus, I am Sgt. Pike, of the City Guard. We're on good authority that you're harboring a murderer and his large cat. Open this door at once, or we'll be forced to break it down!"

Damn!

CHAPTER TWENTY

R akzar paced through the living area and kitchen in Alderan's house. "The little dryte is late, and she's wasting my time. I should just leave without her."

Urza patted the floor next to her. "Come sit down, and stop being so pretentious. A few extra minutes will make little difference. Besides, I'm sure she's preparing for the journey."

"What's she got to prepare for? It's only a few hours away." Rakzar settled on the floor, but he didn't like it.

He didn't like being close to Urza. Not because he disliked her but because he found it difficult carrying the guilt of her situation. He swore he could sense death settling upon her. A subtle stench, but nevertheless there.

"Shalaidah." Urza rested her head on his arm. "They've been at odds for a long time. Go easy on her."

"And why should I go easy?" growled Rakzar.

"She's doing this for us as much as herself. More so, actually. She chose to curse herself for our sakes. Remember that every time you're about to open your big yap and say something stupid or hurtful."

Rakzar expected Urza's words to send him into a rage, but he realized she had a point. He focused so much on his problems that he rarely considered the problems of others. He'd strive to be better but would promise nothing to Urza.

"Admit it. You like the spunky little dryte." Rakzar glanced back at the rocking chair. Amicus sat in it, a smile beaming on his face.

"Stay out of my business."

"I'm only trying to help," said Urza. "You don't need to be rude to me as well."

Rakzar glared at Amicus. "Sorry."

Amicus laughed. "Sooner or later, you're going to have to tell someone that you're talking to me. Or to yourself. You can decide that on your own."

Rayah flew around the corner of the fireplace. "Sorry I'm late."

"It's about—" Urza ribbed him in the side. "It's fine. Let's go before the entire day is wasted." Rakzar rose on all fours.

Rayah said goodbye to Urza and headed out the door.

Rakzar growled, "Don't you dare die on me while I'm gone. I'll return as soon as I've ripped her heart out."

Urza rose, grabbed his snout, and rubbed her nose against his. Hers was as dry as desert sand, and the implications of what it meant scared him. He couldn't think about it though. Doing so might get him killed.

"Be safe, and don't do anything stupid," she said.

What part of this half-baked plan isn't stupid?

He nodded and then headed out the door, too afraid to take one last backward glance.

You'll see her again.

† † †

Rayah waited at the edge of the bluff for her rendezvous with Morcinda while Rakzar stayed hidden in the trees. She held the black, shiny object in her hands and studied it further. It reminded her of a seashell, but much larger and solid black instead of a tannish-white color with hues of pinks, yellows, and oranges.

When Rayah looked up, a boat sat on the water below. She hadn't even seen it arrive. She returned the item to her pack and was about to fly out toward the boat when she witnessed something most peculiar. From her vantage high on the bluff, she watched as a woman with blue hair walked to the edge of her boat, looked down at the water below the boat line, and then stepped out beyond the boat's edge. But the woman didn't fall. Instead, the water rose to meet her feet. And as she continued to walk across the water, the spouts of water shot higher and lifted her up toward the cliff edge. The woman easily stepped from the water and onto the bluff. Rayah stuttered backward, jaw slacken and completely lost for words.

The woman spoke, her voice soft yet commanding. "You must be Rayah." She proffered her hand and Rayah took it. "I am Morcinda. Savric said you'd have something for me to look at." She looked around. "Where is it?"

Rayah stood there, anchored to the woman by her hand. She'd never seen such a strange yet beautiful woman before. As with most people, she'd assumed the whispers of aquatic elves existing we're nothing more than legend, yet one stood before her and spoke to her.

"Well? Are you unable to speak?" asked Morcinda. She pulled her hand away from Rayah's.

"I... um... I have it right here." Rayah dropped her pack from her shoulder and rummaged through it.

What am I looking for? She'd never been so scatterbrained in her life. *Alderan must be rubbing off on me.*

Morcinda pointed at a large black object. "I'm guessing that's what you're looking for."

Rayah blushed. "Yes, of course." She withdrew the black object from her pack and handed it to Morcinda. "It's certainly not fragile. I took a hammer to it and didn't even scratch it."

Morcinda chewed on her lower lip as she examined the object. "Of course you didn't. Very few things could damage this."

"Then you know what it is?" Rayah moved closer, not wanting to miss a word.

"I do." Morcinda turned to walk away, so Rayah grabbed her arm.

That was certainly a mistake. Rayah found herself laid out on the ground before she could blink. She sat up as Morcinda walked away.

Frustrated, Rayah jumped to her feet. "That's it? You're gonna just walk away with it and not give me an explanation?"

Morcinda turned back, her eyes ice blue and her gaze as cold as the sea. "I will return *after* I've spoken with Savric."

Rayah grabbed the brass-handled, hand-held mirror from her pack and thrust it at Morcinda. "No need to go anywhere. You can talk with him face-to-face through this mirror."

Morcinda snatched the mirror and examined it for several moments. When her gaze fell back on Rayah it'd softened a little. "And where did you find such a rare object?"

"It belongs to a sorceress named Zerenity. I borrowed it so that I could contact Master Savric when necessary."

"I see." She handed it back to Rayah. "Contact him. We shall see his reaction together."

Rayah stared into the mirror. "Master Savric?"

Several moments passed and Rayah was about to give up when Savric's face finally appeared in the mirror. He smiled wide, but Rayah could see how weary he'd become since departing from Zerenity's. Dark circles underscored his tired eyes.

"My dear girl, it is a pleasure to see your face." He pulled on his beard. "I fear I am out of sorts."

Morcinda snatched the mirror from Rayah and stared into it. "There's no time for mindless chatter. We've got much bigger problems than we had first imagined."

Savric's smile faded as he stroked his beard. "Graver than hordes of infected humans? Pray tell."

Morcinda held the black object up to the mirror. "This is a dragon scale."

Savric and Rayah both gasped. Rayah looked at the object with renewed vision and wonder.

A dragon scale…

For a few moments, she became lost within her own thoughts and missed a good portion of the conversation.

"…and then Cinolth cursed the world and all the humans in it. His scales shattered and ripped away from his carcass and then shot across the Ancient Realm, spreading across the land to its far reaches and burrowing deep underground," Morcinda finished.

Savric's face had turned ghostly white. "Dear Ɂäʈūr…"

"Yes, you understand the gravity of it," said Morcinda.

"But what does it mean? Where are the people going and why?" asked Rayah.

Savric pulled on his beard. "Time will most certainly tell." He glanced away and grimaced. "Keep me apprised of further developments. I must continue my pursuit of the horde before I lose them again."

Again? Rayah wanted desperately to know what'd happened, but she held her tongue. Another time would be more suitable for asking.

"As do you," said Morcinda to Savric. The mirror went dark and Morcinda handed it back to Rayah. "I will keep the dragon scale. I'm certain it will prove more useful in my hands than yours."

Rayah dared not argue with Morcinda. Besides, she had more pressing matters to deal with, like finding a way to help Rakzar kill Käíeƨ and save her own life. "I'm sure it will."

"Good." Morcinda placed the dragon scale in a leather satchel that hung from her left shoulder and eyed the woods. "Be wary of the company you keep."

Rayah followed Morcinda's gaze but saw nothing.

How does she know about Rakzar?

"It's not what you think. He's—"

Morcinda turned on Rayah, her gaze cold. "Never presume to know what I'm thinking. Even with good intentions, natural instincts are hard to overcome."

A cold streak shot through Rayah. *Did I make the wrong choice?*

Morcinda nodded and then walked away—straight off the bluff. Rayah walked over to the cliff edge and watched Morcinda descend to the ocean's surface on a pedestal of water. She walked across its choppy surface toward her boat, the waves parting around her and giving her a clear path to walk.

Rayah retrieved her pack and headed into the woods where Rakzar waited. She chose to push every negative thought of Rakzar from her mind and focused instead on the events that had just unfolded. Her stomach flipped with excitement.

I can't believe I found a dragon scale! And I met an aquatic elf! Alderan won't believe it when I tell him.

A hundred yards into the dense and dark forest, she found Rakzar leaning against a tall conifer with large pinecones, cleaning under his nails. Morcinda's warning faded in her mind. She walked up to Rakzar, her thoughts still focused on the dragon scale.

"Ready when you are." She couldn't wipe the smile from her face.

"Just what I need. A cheerful dryte," said Rakzar.

"Even you won't be able to ruin this day."

"I won't need to. Shalaidah will bring you back to reality quick enough."

Rayah's mood flattened in an instant. She sighed. "You certainly know how to ruin a girl's day."

"Good. Let's move." He dropped on all fours and headed south through the forest.

Rayah took a deep breath.

This is going to be a long journey.

† † †

About an hour into their almost two-hour journey to see Shalaidah, Rakzar slid to a stop. Rayah came flying up behind him, the sound of her wings akin to a dragonfly's. She settled on the ground next to him, her breathing shallow and quick.

Rakzar sniffed the air and listened intently to the sounds of the forest. He didn't detect anything beyond birds, squirrels, and other small creatures, but his gut told him that something else lurked in the shadows. His hackles rose.

"What's wrong?" whispered Rayah.

"Keep quiet." Rakzar scanned the shadows again, but the thick canopy and dense forest created a plethora of hiding places in the darkness. "We're not alone."

Rayah moved a little closer to him. Too close for his liking. They'd have a conversation about it later. She retrieved a pair of tan gloves from her pack and slipped them on. They helped control the knives that hung from her belt. He appreciated her caution and preparedness.

Snap!

A rotted twig or branch. The sound came from behind them. They both whirled around.

Maniacal laugher filled the air. Came at them from every direction. "Oops." A male voice. Neither gruff nor smooth. Nondescript.

Rayah stood with her hands at her sides, her head on a swivel and poised to loose her blades on anything that moved. Rakzar rose on his hind legs and stood next to Rayah, his double-edged battle axes clutched in his hands.

"Be ready but do nothing unless I say so."

She nodded but kept her focus on the dark forest.

Ten paces away, the shadows moved. A humanoid figure stood within them. No, the shadows moved *with* the figure.

Rakzar gripped his axes tighter. "Show yourself."

The figure stepped forward and shrugged away the shadows surrounding him as though they were nothing more than a cloak. The man dipped his head quickly, sending his curly, raven locks into a bouncing fit around his face and over his shoulders. "Greetings."

The man stood about six and a half feet tall and wore black from head to toe, including a thick, leather coat, a long-sleeved shirt, leather gloves and gauntlets, leather trousers, and leather boots with thick soles and high heels.

"Why are you following us?" growled Rakzar.

"Following you? Oh, no, no, no. You misunderstand. I promise you I'm not the following sort." The man stalked closer, a gleam in his golden eyes and a wicked grin on his face.

Rakzar snarled, "Then explain yourself before the bladed ends of my axes meet in the middle of your neck."

The man chuckled. "Your confidence and enthusiasm are exceptional. I'll give you that. But your confidence is misplaced." He closed the distance by half again, leaving just a handful of paces between himself and Rakzar. "The name's Kendar, and I'm hunting you."

Rakzar motioned Rayah backward. "To the ground, Rayah. This fiend is mine."

Rakzar glanced down. Rayah stood her ground, hands still at her sides. "I've dealt with far worse than a human."

Kendar crossed his arms and smiled. "I'll wait right here while the two of you decide on a plan of battle. I've got all day and nowhere to be."

"Ground. Now," barked Rakzar. "I won't ask again."

"Whatever." She sank into the ground and disappeared.

"You ready now, tough pup?" Kendar winked. "Give me your best shot. I won't even move."

Something about Kendar gave Rakzar pause, and it wasn't just the man's overconfidence. As far as Rakzar could tell, the man carried no weapons.

What kind of fool seeks out a fight without weapons other than a wizard?

Rakzar feared Kendar might be something else entirely. He took a step backward. "Brandish your weapon of choice."

"I assure you that my body is my weapon." He leaned his head to the side and rubbed his neck. "Right here, or anywhere you please. Take your shot, and then I'll take mine."

Enough of this.

Rakzar roared and lunged forward, his arms wide and axes poised to relieve Kendar of his head. Metal struck flesh with a concussive force, cracking like thunder. Fragments of blade exploded outward, a thousand shards of death, nicking and piercing Rakzar's tough flesh. Rakzar retreated. Each of his double-edged axes now only had one edge. Kendar's head remained atop his neck, not a scratch on his flesh.

Kendar threw his head back and laughed. "No weapon can harm me." His smile faded and his jaw tightened. "Now it's my turn." He removed his gloves and stuffed them into his coat pocket.

"Do your worst," growled Rakzar. "You'll find I'm not so easy to kill either."

Kendar squeezed his fingers together with his thumbs, and his hands morphed into thick, long, hooked claws. Then, his arms extended and narrowed into whip-like appendages that stretched all the way to the ground. He whipped them around and they cracked the air.

Rakzar had heard of forest spirits known as the Zhrimɛzhedō that could take the shape of any creature. *Shadowgrym.* As Kendar had stated, weapons could not harm them, but there were other things he'd known about them as well, but he couldn't recall any of them. He retreated several steps and pounded the side of his head with his palm, trying to knock his memories back into place.

Kendar rushed forward, his arms a flurry of motion. Rakzar easily blocked the attack with his axes but hadn't anticipated Kendar's arms wrapping around the ax handles, latching onto them, and ripping them from his grip. He'd never been disarmed so quickly.

Rakzar lunged forward, wrapped his hands around Kendar's throat, and grunted as he squeezed as hard as he could.

Kendar retaliated, wrapping his arms around Rakzar's. His hooked hands sliced right through Rakzar's tough skin, digging deep into the flesh of Rakzar's arms.

Rakzar fought through the pain and found the strength to squeeze harder.

Kendar's eyes bulged, and then his mouth and nose morphed into a sharp, pointed beak. His neck lengthened a good foot, and he pecked at Rakzar's face and eyes.

Rakzar released Kendar's neck and tried to protect his face, but he couldn't escape from Kendar's grip.

Rakzar fell backward, taking Kendar with him, but it only made matters worse. Kendar's weight increased tenfold, crushing Rakzar into the ground.

A question crept into Rakzar's head. *Can I be killed with this stupid curse on my head?*

But the true question that lingered in the back of his mind was whether he was willing to take the chance of finding out. If Kendar succeeded in killing him, would he come back to life?

Saliva dripped from Kendar's beak and landed right in Rakzar's left eye.

It burned like liquid fire, and he couldn't reach his eye to wipe it away.

"Prepare yourself for death," said Kendar.

Death…

How many times had Rakzar been on the brink of death? He couldn't count the times on just one hand.

Memories of those occasions flooded his mind, but then he remembered something else about the Zhrimᴣzhedō.

They are immune to normal weapons, but mezhik weapons can hurt them.

Rayah's knives used some sort of mezhik. He started to call for her but remembered something else.

The Zhrimᴣzhedō heal quickly. Almost as fast as they are injured.

Damn.

Time I faced my death.

Rakzar glared at Kendar, his eyes still full of fire. "I've been prepared for this moment my whole life, yet it always seems to evade me. Don't be surprised if you fail to kill me as well."

Kendar's face returned to a normal state. "I will go slow so that you can savor the moment."

"Bite—"

Rakzar suddenly remembered another detail of the Zhrimᴣzhedō. An important detail.

Rakzar roared, "Now, Rayah! Slit the bastard's throat with your knives!"

Kendar laughed. "Your axes did nothing—"

Two silver blades shot into the air and crossed the front of Kendar's throat.

Kendar's eyes grew wide as two red lines in the shape of an "X" surfaced on his dark, brownish-green skin.

Then those lines opened into gushing wounds.

Kendar's arms unwound from Rakzar's, and Rakzar shoved Kendar to the ground. "Good luck healing those wounds."

Kendar writhed on the ground as he tried to hold his wounds shut, but he couldn't maintain his human form any longer. His torso compacted and his leg shriveled until nothing remained of them. Then his torso retracted into his neck and his mouth and nose formed back into a sharp beak. A third eye appeared over his beak, and a third appendage with a razor-sharp claw sprouted out of the top of his head. All three appendages whipped the air wildly and shook with tremors.

Rayah rose out of the ground and gasped. "What in the name of Ɂätūr is that thing?"

"*Zhrimɛzhedō*," said Rakzar. "Also known as a Shadowgrym in our tongue."

"And why did my knives hurt it when your axes shattered on impact?"

Rakzar rose on his hind legs. "They might be immune to normal weapons, but not ones made of silver like your knives. Silver causes them damage that can only be healed with mezhik."

Rayah shook her head and groaned. "And why didn't we start there? Why did you almost let him kill you before you asked for my help?"

He didn't want to answer her, yet he felt compelled to do so. "I didn't remember until the moment before I yelled at you to attack."

Rayah rose off the ground and matched Rakzar's eye level, her wings a blur of motion at her back. "Is that really what happened, or were you just going to let him kill you and hope that it broke the curse?"

Rakzar snarled, "I can't be killed, remember?" He dropped on all fours. "Stop thinking about it and let's move. We've wasted too much time already."

Rayah looked down at Kendar. "And what about that thing? Are we just going to leave it there?"

"Let him suffer. He'll eventually bleed out."

"Isn't that—"

Rakzar turned and headed south, tuning Rayah out.

I must be mad letting her tag along.

"But she did save your life," said Amicus.

Rakzar growled, "No one asked you, Shadowman."

Amicus chuckled. "I offer my input free of charge."

"Haunt someone else. I'm done with you." Rakzar shook his head to try and rid himself of Amicus, but it only caused him to stumble. He narrowly missed ramming a tree.

"Not a chance, my friend," said Amicus. "We still have issues to work out."

I'm not the one who has issues.

† † †

Rayah stood in the middle of an old chestnut oak grove at the southeastern edge of the Veridis Forest. She hadn't been there in a dozen or so years, but memories came flooding back as she stared at the largest of the oak trees toward the northern edge of the grove.

After leaving Kendar bleeding to death, Rakzar hadn't said anything else the entire rest of the way to Shalaidah's, and Rayah preferred it that way. She didn't need him bringing her down, especially not now. The thought of facing Shalaidah after so many years terrified her enough without his input.

She couldn't recall the argument that'd set her and Shalaidah at odds, but hamadryads were known to have long memories, hot tempers, and little forgiving power. She had no doubt that Shalaidah remembered every last detail, right down to what the two of them had been wearing and what they'd eaten for breakfast that day.

Rayah took a deep breath and pressed her hand against the tree's massive trunk. "Shalaidah, tree spirit of the mighty oak, hear me now and awaken."

Such words were ridiculous and unnecessary, but Shalaidah believed in honoring the old legends of the hamadryads and their role as tree spirits that had been passed down through the ages. She would never come out of her tree or speak to anyone without the words spoken.

The massive tree shuddered, and its branches stretched backward in an exaggerated yawn as a face rose out of the side of its bark covered trunk. "Who calls upon the great..." The eyes narrowed. "Rayah? That is you, is it not?"

Rayah took several steps back, a weary smile upon her lips. "Hello, Shalaidah."

The face scowled at her. "Why are you here? I told you to never return, and I meant it. Go away before I throw you out." The face melted back into the bark.

The last thing Rayah wanted to do was beg Shalaidah for help, but she had little choice. "If you send me away, it will be to my death. Do you want my blood on your hands?"

"Don't be so melodramatic. You survived without me all these years. You can continue to do so." Shalaidah's voice faded.

Rayah beat her fists on the tree trunk. "I demand you listen to me, you wretched woman!"

"Wretched woman?" Shalaidah burst from the tree, peppering Rayah with chunks of bark and knocking her back onto her buttocks.

Shalaidah stood over her, aged but still beautiful. The green streaks in her brown hair had turned silver, along with the green, leaf shapes that surrounded her bright green eyes. Brown, bark-like skin with a hint of silver covered her torso and rose into a V-shape, covering her breasts. Her exposed skin, whitish-beige in color, contrasted the bark quite well.

"I raised you as my own child. Nurtured you and loved you, yet you abandoned me the first chance you had. You are an evil little brat and have no right to call *me* a wretched woman."

Rayah choked back tears as memories she'd worked so hard to forget bombarded her. Shalaidah had raised her as a prisoner, not a child, keeping her hidden away in the darkness of the tree's trunk for most of her first years. As she grew older, Rayah realized that she and Shalaidah were nothing alike. Not even the same species. Shalaidah controlled the tree they lived in but Rayah never could. Rayah knew nothing of her own skills or the power of her wings until she escaped from the tree one day. From that point forward, she refused to live with Shalaidah in the tree, instead building her own home in the soil beneath the roots of the trees.

Rayah stood and wiped herself off. "Couldn't you see that I was never meant to live inside of a tree? I'm not like you, but I didn't abandon you, either." Her gaze fell to the ground. "I'm sorry I called you a wretched woman. I didn't mean it."

"Perhaps not, but it makes little difference." Shalaidah turned away, but not before Rayah caught a glimpse of tears in her eyes. "I'll never forgive you for leaving me."

"You instilled in me a sense of pride and duty to protect our world and the creatures that live in it. Master Savric called upon me to do just that, so how could I have said no? You should know as well as anyone that I had to leave." Rayah reached for Shalaidah's hand, but Shalaidah moved it out of reach. "Show me mercy. Forgive me for what I had to do."

"What you ask of me is impossible." Shalaidah turned back. Teardrops hung from the sides of her narrow jaws. "A broken heart can never be mended. Leave me now before you finish the job."

"I cannot do that. At least not until you've helped me. As I said from the start, your refusal will sentence me to death."

Shalaidah's long, twig-like fingers rapped against her side. "Why? What despicable thing have you done?"

"A friend of mine is cursed with a spell, and anyone who comes into contact with him will slowly start to die. I am one of those."

Shalaidah raised her arms and spread them wide. "Then abandon him. Flee from his side and free yourself of this curse."

"It doesn't work that way. Once cursed, there is no escape. I chose this path of my own free will so that I could help him find a way to break the cursed spell."

"And that choice will be your death. Your blood will not be on *my* hands. Be gone." She turned away and entered her tree once more.

Rayah had one last move, and it wasn't one she'd wanted to make, but Shalaidah had left her no choice. "You will help me, or he will come and curse you as well."

Shalaidah's face rose out of the tree once again. "You would do that to the one who raised you?"

"You are our only hope. There is no other way. I wouldn't be here otherwise. Besides, you know him. He's the one who brought me to you."

"Rakzar?" Shalaidah closed her eyes for a moment and sighed. "If I can provide you with help, I will, but then you must leave and never return. Agreed?"

Rayah lowered her head. "If that's really the way you want it to be then I agree to your terms."

"It must be that way. Now, what can I help you with?"

Rayah spent several minutes explaining everything about the sickle spell and about the creature named Käíez to the best of her ability. When she'd finished, Shalaidah came back out of her tree and sat down on a stump a few yards away.

Rayah followed Shalaidah over to the stump. "Do you know of a way we can defeat her? Trap her with something or turn her solid?"

Shalaidah's gaze focused on the forest or perhaps something far beyond it. Rayah couldn't quite tell. Finally, after several minutes of silence, she spoke. "I heard a legend long ago about a binding crystal that could change any substance, be it gas, air, liquid, smoke, mist, or anything else into a solid."

Rayah waited several moments, but Shalaidah said no more. She rose off the ground and paced in the air, frustrated. "And?"

"That's all I know," Shalaidah said with finality.

Rayah settled on the ground in front of Shalaidah and glared at her. "And where would we find this binding crystal?"

Shalaidah rolled her eyes and sighed. "If it were I with a need to retrieve such an object then I would most likely seek out someone who might be able to confirm or deny its existence."

"Why are you so reluctant to help me?" Rayah crossed her arms. "Just tell me what I need to know, and I'll be gone forever. You said that's what you wanted."

Shalaidah's features softened as she reached out and stroked Rayah's cheek. "A broken heart is full of vengeful words. Ignore them." She smiled. "You've become such a beautiful young woman. It makes me proud."

Heat rose in Rayah's cheeks, but she didn't hide it. "I never thought that I'd hear words like that from you. You don't know how happy that makes me feel."

Shalaidah shrank away and then retreated back to her tree. "Seek out the mountain dwarves in Tectus. If anyone knows, it will be them."

Rayah flew over to the tree and hugged it. "Thank you, Shalaidah. I love you."

A gust of wind blew through the trees and rustled the dead leaves. Rayah swore she heard the words "I love you, too" hidden within the breeze. Her heart swelled in her chest, and tears of joy streamed down her cheeks.

She let go of the tree and backed away.

Such a beautiful old chestnut oak.

Its beauty mimicked that of Shalaidah's.

Until we meet again.

Rayah turned and walked away, an unyielding smile back upon her lips. She wiped her eyes as she headed through the trees. A sense of confidence and determination swelled within her.

The key to everything lies in Tectus.

CHAPTER TWENTY-ONE

Nardus paced in the basement of Joriah's house, his legs fueled by anger. "What in *Ef Demd Dhä* is taking so long?"

It was a rhetorical question, but Berggren must've felt the need to answer it anyway. "You heard what Joriah said when he let those city guardsmen in."

"Yes, I know. There are dozens of guardsmen out there, but that doesn't change the fact that Theyn and I must get going. We've been down here for more than an hour."

"I understand the importance of what you're trying to do but getting yourself killed won't resolve anything."

Theyn's voice entered Nardus's head. *"You know he's right. I could take on several of them, but you and Berggren have no weapons. We wouldn't get twenty feet before they subdued or killed us."*

Nardus growled and spat on the floor. "I rather take my ch—"

The floor above them creaked and moaned as it slid open.

Joriah peered down from above. "I believe it's safe now."

"It's about damn time." Nardus took the stairs two at a time and headed straight for the front door when he reached the top of them.

Theyn's voice screamed in his head, *"Wait!"*

His hand slipped from the doorknob as he turned and glared at Theyn. "What is it now?"

The door creaked open behind him.

As Nardus turned, the years rolled back in his mind. Thirteen of them. Joriah's house faded and the landscape changed. He stood atop his wagon on that fateful day, traveling down a familiar dirt road. The whoosh of an arrow sang in his ears as it soared through the air. His body jerked to the left as it had that day, but the arrow's bite didn't come. Instead, his head snapped back, and white-hot pain erupted in his left shoulder. A great weight slammed into his chest and thrust the air from his lungs.

Nardus blinked several times, stunned. Flashes of white, yellow, and red filled his vision, and the sounds of metal blades drawn from their sheaths rang in his ears, along with grunts, gurgles, growls, and stifled screams.

Someone yelled, "No quarter!"

Nardus shook his head, forcing his mind back into the present. He lay on the floor of Joriah's house, along with two dead bodies—both of them guardsmen. A thick layer of black smoke hung from the ceiling of the cottage and grey haze filled the air. Orange flames consumed the northern wall and most likely a good portion of the ceiling.

Nardus didn't see Theyn or Joriah, but Berggren fought two men on the far side of the room.

A shadow flitted across Nardus's vision, drawing his attention. Sunlight glinted off the shiny yellow armor of a guardsman standing in the doorway. Nardus met the guardsman's gaze, and the guardsman's eyes narrowed. The guardsman stepped inside and raised his brandish sword over his head. Nardus rolled to his left, right over the top of a discarded sword, and narrowly escaped the guardsman's blade as it bit into the wood-planked floor with a thud. The guardsman grunted as he worked his blade free, giving Nardus just enough time to recover the discarded sword and get to his feet.

The guardsman snarled and lunged forward, thrusting his sword at Nardus's midsection. Nardus easily dodged the attack, spun around, and landed a blow to the guardsman's left side, but the blade failed to penetrate the guardsman's thick armor. The blow nearly jarred the sword from Nardus's grip, but he didn't have time to think about it as the guardsman retaliated with a barrage of swift attacks. Nardus managed to block them all but lost a lot of ground in the process. He quickly found himself cornered.

Two more violent blows from the guardsman ripped the sword from Nardus's hand. The sword clanged as it hit the floor. The guardsman spat and grinned. Nardus knew the look in the guardsman's eyes—twisted and animalistic. The man sought to spill his blood, and Nardus had no way of stopping him.

The guardsman raised his sword. "Time ta die."

Nardus flinched as blood exploded from the guardsman's throat. His sword fell from his hand, and he dropped to his knees as he clutched his throat. A hulking shadow stood behind the guardsman, disfigured by the smoky haze.

Berggren.

Berggren drove his sword down through the guardsman's clavicle and into his chest cavity, burying the sword all the way to its hilt. The guardsman gurgled, his mouth full of blood. Berggren ripped the sword back out and the guardsman fell sideways in a heap.

Berggren stepped back, his sword dripping with blood. "Figured I'd return the favor by saving your hide."

"And I thoroughly appreciate it." Nardus bent down and picked up the sword he'd dropped. "We need to find—" Theyn trotted through the doorway, her fur matted with blood. Nardus gasped. "—Theyn! Are you okay?"

Theyn's presence entered his mind. *"Relax. None of the blood is mine."*

"Where's Joriah?" asked Berggren.

"Taking care of the last few guardsmen," said Theyn in Nardus's head. Nardus relayed the information to Berggren as they all headed outside.

Smoke and flames rose from several fires spread over the hilltop. Dead guardsmen lay strewn across the landscape, several with detached limbs and a few without their heads. Others still smoldered, their corpses black and shrunken within their melted armor. Joriah had done a number on them with his fireballs. Nardus counted nearly three dozen bodies in all. The loss of life sickened him, but they'd been left without choice but to defend themselves.

"We need to move," said Berggren. "This mess won't go unnoticed for long."

Theyn lifted her nose in the air and drew a deep breath as she turned in a circle. She snorted and shook her head. *"More of them are on their way now. I believe we will be surrounded if we don't hurry."*

Nardus grimaced. "Theyn says they are coming from every direction."

Joriah pulled his hair away from his face and straightened his cape. "Follow me and stick close. I know this city better than anyone."

The three of them nodded their agreement. Joriah took off down the stone path, surprising Nardus with his agility as he cleared the three-foot-tall iron gate without missing a step. He and Theyn both cleared the gate as well, but Berggren just ran right through it.

For a solid hour, they slowly made their way across West Hotah, narrowly escaping detection on several occasions. Now, the single bridge to East Hotah lay ahead of them, but dozens of guardsmen stood in their path.

The four of them crouched behind a building as they contemplated how to proceed.

Even in the deep shadows Nardus could see that Joriah looked paler than he had earlier. "You okay, Joriah?"

"Just a tad depleted after that fire fight. I'll be fine once we get the two of you to safety."

"I won't allow you to sacrifice yourself for me."

"All of us serve a purpose in life, Nardus. If mine is fulfilled in this act, so be it. Besides, I've not had this much fun and excitement in… well, ever. Don't you dare try to take it away from me."

"Same goes for me," said Berggren. "We're all gonna die at some point."

"Why aren't you saying anything, Theyn?" asked Nardus.

She rubbed her head on his hand. *"Let it go, my love. Neither of us have the power to stop them, nor should we if we had the means to do so."*

"Fine, but you're all fools." He crossed his arms. "Now what?"

Joriah rubbed his hands together and blew into them. "It's time for me to work my mezhik."

"Mezhik." Nardus spat. "What in *Ef Demd Dhä* does that—"

Joriah spun around and disappeared.

Damned fool!

† † †

Joriah removed his cape and tossed it aside, tore his shirt and trousers in several places, and then wiped blood all over himself and his clothes from the rat he'd killed. Satisfied he looked the part, he stepped into the road just west of the bridge. One of the guardsmen from the bridge took notice of Joriah and approached him with his sword drawn. Joriah fell to his knees.

"Help me," Joriah said, his voice weak and broken. "I've been attacked."

The guardsman lowered his sword and knelt next to Joriah. "Who did this to you?"

Joriah grabbed the guardsman's wrist, intent on using his persuasive mezhik, but he hesitated. Decades had passed since the last time he'd used it, and he wasn't sure if he could do so now. Every time he reached within himself to draw upon its power, memories of Nadine bombarded him.

Love of my life! How will I ever forgive myself for what I did to you?

His hand trembled fiercely, but it would play well into what he must do. He swallowed back tears and forced his memories of Nadine back into the box that he kept them in. With a deep breath, he called upon his mezhik, but nothing came.

Don't do this to me. Not now.

"Remove your hand from my wrist before I remove it from your body," growled the guardsman.

Joriah looked into the guardsman's eyes. "I'm sorry sir, but you misunderstand my intentions."

The guardsman's gaze hardened. "Your intentions?"

Joriah nodded slowly as he focused inward. He pictured an ebbing and flowing orange energy within himself welling up like a spring. It seeped from his marrow and poured into his veins. He stared intently at the man as the taste of his persuasive mezhik bloomed on his tongue.

Joriah spoke with intention and direction, pouring every ounce of mezhik energy he possessed into his words. "Three men and a large cat attacked me as they headed north. You know my words are true, and you must convince your fellow guardsmen to head north so that you might cut those fugitives off before they escape. You will be heroes."

"They're heading north..." said the guardsman, his eyes slightly glazed over.

"Yes. You must hurry if you want to catch them." Joriah's hand slipped from the guardsman's wrist as he slumped over on the road.

He closed his eyes, his eyelids far too heavy to keep open.

If there is a God, I beg of you to let this work.

† † †

A loud commotion drew Nardus's attention. He walked over to the corner of the building, crouched down, and peered around its corner, toward the bridge. Something or someone lay in the middle of the road, halfway between him and the bridge. The guardsmen at the bridge hustled around, gathering their gear.

"What's happening?" asked Berggren. His deep, gruff voice barked even at a whisper.

"I'm not sure what Joriah did, but the guardsmen are evacuating their post."

"Knew he'd do something, but where's he now?"

"I don't know, but something's in the road."

Theyn nudged Nardus and spoke into his mind. *"Move out of the way, and I'll take a look. My eyesight is way better than yours."*

Nardus nodded and moved back.

Theyn stepped forward and peered around the corner. *"That's Joriah in the road, and it looks like he's covered in blood. He's still breathing but just barely."*

Nardus turned toward Berggren. "Theyn confirmed that it's Joriah in the road. He's still alive."

Berggren dipped his head. "Best he stays that way too."

"One guardsman stayed behind," said Theyn.

Damn. Never seem to catch a break.

Nardus sighed. "One guardsman hung back."

Berggren straightened, his expression grim. "Leave him to me."

"We'll be right behind you," said Nardus.

Berggren rounded the corner and headed toward the bridge. The guardsman spotted Berggren immediately.

Kinda hard to miss a walking mountain.

Nardus chuckled to himself.

Berggren rushed the guardsman like a bull, closing the distance quickly. The guardsman stuck his pinkies in the corners of his mouth and blew several times but produced no sound. Berggren lowered his shoulder and struck the guardsman square in the chest but not before the guardsman got off one loud whistle.

Theyn and Nardus rushed over to Joriah and knelt next to him. Joriah didn't move or open his eyes. "Joriah, can you hear me?"

Joriah didn't respond.

The sounds of clanking metal armor and stomping boots rose in the distance and grew louder by the moment.

Nardus's pulse raced as he lifted Joriah over his shoulder. He grunted, and his legs shook, but he managed to stand. By the time he reached the bridge he realized there was no way he'd make it across before the other guardsmen caught up with him.

"Give him to me," barked Berggren, seeing Nardus struggle.

What is wrong with me today? First, I couldn't fight, and now I can't carry a man thirty feet? Why am I so exhausted?

Berggren took Joriah from Nardus and started hoofing it across the bridge. Nardus and Theyn flanked him. Two-thirds of the way across, the thunder of boots on the bridge sounded behind them. Berggren picked up his pace but Nardus knew it wasn't quick enough.

They only had two choices ahead of them. Either create a diversion to slow the guards down or find a way to move faster. But Nardus couldn't think of a single solution to accomplish either.

As if on cue, Theyn's presence entered his mind. *"Grab that manure cart on your right. My father can use it to push Joriah instead of carrying him."*

Nardus retrieved the manure cart and caught back up with Berggren. "Throw Joriah on here!"

They stopped and Berggren transferred Joriah to the cart. Nardus looked back. The guardsmen were halfway across the bridge now.

Berggren took off again, this time at a much faster pace. Nardus had trouble keeping up with the big man and quickly fell behind. He sucked air hard, and his lungs burned in his chest. For an instant, his vision went dark, but that's all it took for him to stumble and fall to his hands and knees. He slid several feet on the rough bricks, scraping callouses from his hands and ripping flesh from his knees.

He tried to stand but lacked the strength.

The pounding boots on brick grew louder, nearly deafening. The bridge trembled.

Whoosh!

An arrow sliced through the air and clipped the top of his right ear.

Theyn appeared out of nowhere. *"Get on my back!"* Her voice sounded frantic, even in his head.

Whoosh! Whoosh!

Somehow, he found the strength to climb atop Theyn's back. He wrapped his arms around her neck and his legs around her waist.

Theyn darted to the side and he nearly slipped off her back.

Two arrows ricocheted off the bricks where she'd just stood.

The thunder of boots grew louder. They must've been ten yards back or less. Nardus couldn't hear himself think over the noise.

"Hold on as tight as you can," said Theyn in his head. She bolted forward, nearly throwing him from her back. *"Tighter, dammit! I don't want to lose you."*

Nardus held on for his life and stared straight ahead, barely able to see over Theyn's bobbing head. He dared not look back even as the thunderous noise grew softer. When they reached the end of the bridge and came upon the first crossroad, Theyn banked hard to her right. Nardus had prepared for the turn but hadn't heard or anticipated the arrow that plunged into his right thigh.

He grunted, and his legs slipped from around Theyn's waist. The tight turn, coupled with his shifting weight, sent him and Theyn tumbling across the gravel road. Theyn recovered quickly and was back at Nardus's side, but he couldn't move a single muscle. The throbbing pain in his leg nearly blinded him with each beat of his heart.

"I… can't… move."

Theyn grabbed Nardus by his shirt collar with her teeth and tried to drag him down the road but the deep gravel offered too much resistance. *This isn't working,* said Theyn in Nardus's head.

An old woman exited from a rickety old building to their left. The woman seemed haggard and feeble upon first glance, hunched over with one hand on her hip as she took each step with calculated measure. Little more than rags hung from her stocky frame. She looked nearly as wide as she was tall. A grayish-brown scarf, draped over her head and tied under her double chin, did little to cover her scraggly locks of grey-and-white hair.

But her eyes. Golden brown and full of hope. No trace of fear could be found in them. They erased every preconception Nardus had made of her. He couldn't help but stare at her as she approached.

The old woman bent down in the middle of the road and smiled. "A fine pair you two make."

Nardus had expected her voice to sound stressed and gravelly but it was neither of those. Instead, it was soft but firm and a tinge deeper than he imagined it might've been in her youth. She had a bit of an accent as well, but he couldn't place its origin.

The old woman grabbed him underneath his arms and hauled him up as she stood. Her strength astounded him.

She's so much more than I had first imagined.

Theyn looked back down the road, toward the bridge. Nardus knew what she must be thinking because he wondered the exact same thing. *Those guardsmen should've rounded the corner by now. Why haven't they?*

But then he realized the pounding of their boots had ceased.

Somehow, the old woman knew what they were thinking as well. "You two need not worry. City Guard never enters East Hotah. They be afraid of us. Thinks we be diseased and infectious." She cackled, but not in a sharp and annoying way.

She dragged Nardus across the road and into the building she'd come out of. To the right of the door lay a bed of straw. A dirty and worn wool blanket lay atop it. She gently set Nardus down on top of it, laid him back, and pulled his feet onto it as well. Theyn settled on the floor next to him and rested her head on his stomach. He would've stroked her head, but he didn't have the strength to move his arm.

The old woman talked as she moved toward the back of the room and out of Nardus's sight, "Don't move a muscle, dearie. I've got something that'll fix you right up lickety-split."

Cabinet doors banged and a slew of other noises sounded from the back room as the old woman talked to herself. Nardus closed his eyes and reached out to Theyn with his mind. *"My gut tells me we can trust her, but I fear I'm in no state to make such judgments. What do you think?"*

"Did you not see the bones hanging from the door when we came in? Or all the necklaces, bracelets, and rings she wears? They're fashioned from bones as well."

"She's a cannibal? You think she'll turn us into stew and eat us?"

Theyn snorted. *"Don't be such a fool. She's a healer. I don't think we could be in a better place right now."*

"Galondu Castle. That'd be a better place." Had he really just said that? Several individuals within those castle walls—including a psychopathic dragon—sought his death.

Perhaps my madness is returning.

He knew it wasn't that. However, it seemed like someone wanted him dead no matter where he went. A fugitive of the world.

"I've yet to set foot in that castle, but it certainly doesn't seem like it'd be the best place for us to go."

The old woman returned with a large wooden bowl clutched in her wrinkled and spotted hands. She knelt next to Nardus's head and set the bowl on the floor. Steam rose from the bowl, and its wretched stench stung Nardus's nose. His stomach gurgled with dread.

"What's in the bowl?" he asked.

The old woman chuckled. "Trust me, dearie. It tastes far worse than it smells, but I guarantee it'll get you back on your feet within the hour."

Nardus eyed the bowl. "And how much of that must I consume?"

"You'll need it all." She dipped a deep, wooden spoon into the bowl and then held it to Nardus's lips. "Drink up."

Theyn's head vibrated his stomach.

"Are you laughing at me?" he asked Theyn through his mind. She nuzzled him but didn't respond.

Nardus parted his lips with reluctance, and the old woman poured the liquid in. It wasn't hot, as he had expected it to be, but its taste was fouler than anything he'd ever put in his mouth. The last place he wanted it to go was his stomach, but he couldn't keep it in his mouth any longer. He swallowed the warm liquid down and it burned in his throat like vomit. He couldn't even begin to describe its taste beyond something salty, spicy, rotten, and fermented. Had he tasted rotting flesh and spoiled vegetables he might've likened it to that.

He coughed several times, and his stomach lurched. "What in creation is in that godawful stuff?"

"Eye of newt, tail of dog, wing of bat..." The old woman cackled. "Isn't that what you expected me to say?"

She forced another spoonful between his lips when he opened his mouth to respond.

Sneaky, wretched woman.

Nardus swallowed, and she had another spoonful waiting. By the fourth or fifth spoonful he couldn't even taste the liquid anymore, his mouth and throat raw with fire. When he downed the last spoonful his stomach gurgled several times, but it never threatened to expel its contents.

A few minutes later, heat rose underneath his skin and drenched his entire body with sweat. His hammering heart slowed, and his eyelids grew heavy.

I'll just close my eyes for a moment.

† † †

Berggren never slowed until he reached the sewer entrance. His chest billowed with every inhalation, but he still couldn't catch his breath. He set the end of the manure cart down and rested against its handles.

Joriah's chest continued to rise and fall, but he hadn't moved a single muscle through the entire trip. The side of his face lay in fresh manure, and it clung to his beard. Berggren knew they hadn't had much time, but Nardus still should've emptied the cart.

Lighter load would've made my job a bit easier.

The sun crested overhead, ripening the stench of the manure. Beads of sweat slid down Berggren's bald scalp. He'd expected Theyn and Nardus to be right behind him, but he couldn't see or hear them approaching. He thought nothing of it at first, but as the minutes rolled by, he began to worry more and more.

Where are you, Theyn?

His mind raced with thoughts he didn't want to have but he couldn't help himself. He loved Theyn more than life itself and would do anything to keep from losing her again.

He looked at Joriah and sighed deeply. "I'm sorry my old friend, but Theyn comes first. She always will."

Berggren left Joriah and the cart sitting there and began to retrace his route. Every dozen or so yards he called for her but didn't know what kind of response to expect. The more he thought about it, the more he began to fear she'd slipped back into the monster who'd torn his chest open.

Will I be hunting her, or will she be hunting me?

By the time he reached the main road his throat was raw and his voice hoarse from yelling her name. Something glinted in the sunlight, near where the bridge intersected the road. He hustled down the road, ignoring the fire in his thighs and calves.

Berggren bent down and picked up the broken crossbow bolt. It was definitely the same kind the City Guard used. But where was the other half, and where were Theyn and Nardus? He looked around but found nothing more than some misplaced gravel. Had they been captured? He couldn't stand the thought of it. Besides, the guardsmen were more than eager to kill them at Joriah's house.

His heart sank, and his gaze fell to the ground.

I just got you back, Theyn. I'm not ready to lose you again. My heart can't take it.

Tears welled in his eyes and he let them fall, onlookers be damned. He dropped to his knees and slammed his fists into the wet and discolored rocks. Rage built in his chest. He'd tear every last one of those bastards apart if it was the last thing he ever did.

Berggren stood and wiped his eyes. A girl no older than five or six stood several feet away from him. He glared down at her, and she returned his glare with an unwavering smile. A dimple marked her left cheek. She wore little more than rags and stood on bare feet, and her hands, feet, and face were soiled with so much grime and dirt that he couldn't determine her skin color. Brown, scraggly hair framed her thin face and hung just below her scrawny shoulders.

"Go away," he half barked and whispered.

She walked up to him and took his hand. That simple gesture froze him and left him speechless, but her words spoke right to his heart. "It's okay. I cry sometimes too. Have you lost someone?"

Berggren knelt and looked into her deep brown eyes. "My daughter, Theyn." His voice quavered.

She nodded knowingly. "My father died when I was little, and my mother was gone when I woke up this morning. I don't think she's coming back. I don't think any of them are."

Berggren frowned. "Any of who?"

"The ones with the black veins and pale skin. The infected. My mother was one of them."

Berggren tilted his head skyward. *Zhedäƨ ƨʊn, what is she talking about? How much have I missed?*

He looked around and took notice of the empty road. Surely there would be at least a handful of people out and about by this time of day, wouldn't there? He thought back to their escape from West Hotah and realized they'd had no problems navigating its roads either. He couldn't recall a time in the past when that would've been true. There'd always been throngs of people in West Hotah to tend with.

Berggren stroked the side of the little girl's face with his thumb. "Sorry, little one."

"Niesha. My name is Niesha." She squeezed his hand. "Was your daughter one of the infected?"

"No, but my daughter is… different."

Niesha cocked her head. "Different how?"

Berggren sighed. "Not sure I could explain it in a way that you'd understand."

Niesha let go of his hand and crossed her arms. Her eyebrows drooped over the bridge of her nose and her dried and cracked lips puckered. "I might still be young, but I'm no oaf. I've never been an oaf."

Berggren snorted and raised his hands in submission. "Fair enough. Won't hurt to give it a try I s'pose. Don't think this'll make sense, but she looks like a big cat right now."

Niesha's eyes grew wide. "Beige fur and yellow eyes?"

"You seen her?" Berggren leaned forward.

Niesha nodded wildly. She moved closer, cupped her hand around the side of her mouth, and whispered in his ear. "She was just here."

Excitement filled Berggren's chest and tightened his throat. He could hardly get out his next words. "You see where she went?"

Niesha pointed at a rickety old building on the opposite side of the road and a few doors down. "She went in there with the old witch. They say no one ever leaves her house once they've entered. She hangs their bones on her walls like works of art and sews masks from their skin."

Berggren doubted her words were true, but he still swallowed hard. He stood, clenched his jaw, and stormed toward the building.

No witch will keep me from my daughter or make wall art from her bones. Not this day or any other.

"Theyn!" He pummeled the door with his fist and took it straight off its hinges.

† † †

The door exploded inward, hit the floor with a loud smack, and slid several feet before coming to a rest against the far wall, scraping and grinding as it went. The series of events must've startled Berggren as well because he just stood in the doorway, his eyes wide and jaw slackened.

Nardus eyed the door and then Berggren. "That's one way to make an entrance. Suppose you could've just knocked politely."

Theyn rushed Berggren, tackled him to the ground, and licked his face.

Berggren wrapped his arms around Theyn. "Gods, it's good to see you alive."

Nardus picked up the door and examined it. It seemed to be in fairly decent shape, all things considered. He leaned it against the wall and faced the old woman. "Don't worry, Sorsha. We'll fix the door before we leave."

Sorsha shook her head with a smile and waved him off. "A large breeze could've knocked it over. I've been meaning to get it fixed for some time now. Timing's just never been right."

Nardus checked the hinges. "Looks like today might be that day. You will need some new hinges. We won't be able to fetch those for you, but I'm sure we can scrape enough coins together to pay for it."

Berggren got to his feet and entered the building. He had to turn sideways a bit to fit through the narrow entrance. He dipped his head. "Apologies, ma'am. Tend to get a bit excited when it comes to my daughter's welfare. Swear I had it on good authority that you'd be eating her at some point soon."

Sorsha's hands moved straight to her hips. "Eating her? What gave you that idea?"

"I did." A young girl stepped around Berggren and took hold of his arm. "Until confirmed or debunked, you just never know what to believe around here. Caution is a necessity."

Sorsha cackled. "So it is, dearie. So it is."

"In case you hadn't realized it, that's not Joriah you got on your arm." Nardus pointed at the girl and smirked. "Several degrees cuter I'd say though."

"Puppies are cute, but I'm a girl in case you hadn't realized it."

The girl's got some sass. She reminded him of Shanara, or at least what he thought she would've been like at that age.

Berggren chuckled. "What she said." He reached into the coin purse on his belt and retrieved two silver coins. He handed them to Sorsha. "Believe that will cover your troubles."

Sorsha pocketed the coins. "Yes, and then some." She winked at Berggren. "Feel free to break down my door anytime."

"We need to get moving," said Theyn in Nardus's mind.

Nardus took Sorsha's hand and kissed her knuckles. "I cannot repay you for what you've done for me, and I'll never forget it."

Sorsha blushed or so he thought. "'twas nothing. A wizard needs nourishment to sustain their energy."

Nardus stepped back, stunned. A wave of anger swept through him, curling his hands into fists. "I'm no wizard."

"Of course you're not, dearie." She gave him a long wink. "And I'm no healer neither."

What is wrong with these people?

"Nourishment you say?" said Berggren. "Wouldn't happen to have an extra dose, would you? Got a friend in desperate shape."

Sorsha raised a finger. "As a matter of fact, I do. Let me fetch some for you."

A good hour later, Theyn, Nardus, Berggren, Joriah, and Niesha arrived at the large grate blocking access to the rest of the sewer canal. Berggren carried Joriah over his shoulder, Joriah still unconscious. Once Nardus and Theyn traveled through the mirror Berggren would deal with Joriah and how to get the concoction Sorsha had made down Joriah's throat.

Certain no one had followed them or lurked in the darkness, the four of them stepped right through the grate—an illusion of mezhik created to deter sewer dwellers and the like from stumbling upon the mirror room and potentially getting themselves killed or damaging the mirror. Beyond the grate, they took a left, right through the brick wall, and entered the small room with the mirror.

Nardus could see the pain in Berggren's eyes. The big man didn't want to let Theyn out of his sight again but knew he had no choice because he couldn't travel through the mirror and survive. Nardus shouldn't've been able to either, but something protected him.

No, Nardus must return to save Gnaud and Nasduron, and only he possessed the ability to keep Theyn from losing herself. So, Berggren would stay with Joriah and keep him alive. He didn't have a clue as to Niesha's role in everything, but he'd let Berggren work that one out.

The four of them said their goodbyes—Nardus relaying Theyn's words to Berggren—and then Nardus activated the mirror portal by thinking of Galondu Castle and touching the mirror's surface.

The mirror swirled and grew dark but nothing else happened. Nardus withdrew his hand, thought harder about their destination, and tried again with the same result.

Nardus turned to Theyn. "I don't understand what's hap—"

A hand clamped over Nardus's mouth and pulled him through the mirror's dark, cold surface. A voice whispered in his ear, "Keep quiet."

Theyn lunged through the mirror after Nardus. Berggren stood in the room through the mirror, his face many shades whiter than normal. Niesha clutched Berggren's arm. Berggren started to yell for Theyn, but the portal closed, and darkness surrounded them.

† † †

The beast's yellow eyes glowed in the darkness, and its growl rumbled low like thunder. Wrik kept his distance from it, positioning Nardus between him and it as best he could in the dark. Wrik whispered in Nardus's ear, "Calm your beast, or I'll be forced to use mezhik to subdue it." He moved his hand away from Nardus's mouth.

"She resents the fact that you called her a beast," said Nardus. "Release me, and she'll think about not killing you."

Wrik let go of Nardus. "She's sentient then?"

"Of course she is. Why wouldn't she be?"

"Follow me. We need to get out of this corridor before somebody stumbles upon us. I don't want to have to explain what we're doing together."

"Lead the way."

Wrik pushed one of the folds of his robes into Nardus's hand. "Hold on to this until we get to an area where there's more light. And keep your voice down. Sound travels far in these large, hollow corridors."

They continued to talk quietly as Wrik led them toward the room where he kept Gnaud safe. Wrik glanced back at Theyn. She kept to the shadows between the sporadic areas of torchlight. Her features were striking, especially her yellow eyes.

Wrik peered around the corner at one of the corridor junctures. "Until now, I'd only gotten a brief glimpse of Theyn when the portal opened. I don't think I've ever seen a cat like her before."

"Well, I'd imagine not, seeing as how she's not a cat."

Wrik stopped and turned on Nardus, his gaze sharp. "You specifically told me yesterday that Gnaud was attacked by a large cat."

Nardus avoided looking Wrik in the eye. "Yes, well... I sort of lied to you yesterday. Not really lied exactly, but perhaps I didn't disclose the full truth." He shrugged. "I didn't think it would make a difference."

Wrik pursed his lips and waited for his anger to subside before he talked. "Are you really that dim? Everything matters when it comes to saving a life. You'd better tell me everything now, because Gnaud isn't healing—even with the plant I retrieved from the elves."

"Not healing?"

"No. I need to know everything." Wrik started walking again. Thankfully, most of the castle was deserted since most of the soldiers were busy getting ready for war.

Nardus walked beside Wrik. Theyn followed somewhere behind, still in the shadows. "Suppose the correct term for Theyn would be a shifter."

Wrik exhaled loudly. "A human shifter, I presume?"

"Yes. Does that make a difference?" asked Nardus.

I can feel Nasduron slipping through my fingers. All that knowledge wasted.

"Most certainly." Wrik stopped and unlocked the door. "Humans carry all kinds of infectious diseases underneath their fingernails." He ushered Nardus and Theyn into the room.

Nardus moved over to the couch were Gnaud lay and knelt next to it. "Then what can we do to save him?"

Wrik shook his head. "I'm afraid what you're asking is next to impossible."

Nardus glared up at Wrik. "You don't know the half of what I've been through. Don't you dare tell me that *anything* is impossible."

"What you've been through makes no difference." Wrik removed his spectacles and rubbed his eyes. "The only way to save Gnaud is to find a black level wizard with an innate ability to heal."

Nardus stood. "Point me in the right direction. I'll do anything to save Gnaud."

"You may not like where this path will lead you." Wrik wiped his spectacles and placed them back on his face. "You will never be the same again."

Nardus rubbed his left bicep. "I've not been the same for the last thirteen years. No revelations in my life can change or devastate me further than what Pravus has already done to me."

He doesn't even know how wrong he is.

Wrik crossed his arms. Few things in life gave him more pleasure than watching prophecy unfold, but the chance of gaining access to Nasduron and its knowledge surpassed everything. If Pravus ever found out about him helping Nardus, he'd surely have a fight on his hands. He had no doubt he could take on Pravus, but now that fight wouldn't just affect Pravus. Everything would affect Aria as well, and he could never raise a hand against her.

Yet I have no choice.

"So be it."

† † †

"The Procerus Mountains?" Nardus paced along the couch. "Even if I do find the fabled home of the dragons what makes you think they'll be willing to help me? I've dealt with a dragon before and narrowly escaped with my life." He stopped and glared at Wrik. "You wish to send me to my death? Is that what this is?"

Wrik waved him off. "On the contrary, my friend. What good would that serve either of us?"

Theyn's voice entered Nardus's mind. *"Don't forget about the vision we had together."*

Nardus snapped at Theyn, "You think I could ever forget that?" He took a deep breath. "I'm sorry. I didn't mean to yell at you. Either one of you."

"Think nothing of it," said Wrik.

Nardus sat down on the couch. Fresh blood seeped from Gnaud's wounds, and it reminded him of the dragon's claw protruding from Theyn's stomach. Two terrible paths stood before him. If he refused to go to the Procerus Mountains, he'd be damning Gnaud to a slow and painful death. On the other hand, if he did go, he'd be sealing Theyn's fate. Separating himself from her would drive her back into a pit of madness but taking her with him would surely end her life. How could he choose either path? But he couldn't sit there and do nothing.

Nardus slipped off the edge of the couch and onto his knees. He took Theyn's furry face in his hands and touched his forehead to hers. He spoke to her with his mind. *"Theyn, I must leave you here."*

Theyn pulled away from him. *"That's not an option. Either I'm coming with you or you're not going."*

As he looked into her eyes, tears formed in his. *"I cannot risk losing you."*

She licked his face and rubbed her cheek against his. *"You and I both know that I wasn't a cat in our vision, so there's nothing to risk or fear."*

"I don't know..."

"I do, and my decision is final. Pull yourself together and let's figure out how we're going to get there."

Nardus nodded and wiped his eyes. He stood and faced Wrik. "The Procerus Mountains are what... 600 miles from here? Horseback will take a couple of weeks just to get there. I don't think Gnaud will last another month."

"I can keep him alive a few more weeks at best, but certainly not a month."

Nardus brooded. "You know a quicker way of travel?"

Wrik grinned. "You're not going to like it, but I think I have just the solution. Ever heard of a níţfinzh?"

Dread rose in the bottom of Nardus's stomach. "No, but it sounds like it involves flying."

"Precisely, but it will cut your travel time down to three days."

"How will Theyn ride anything in her current form?"

Wrik frowned. "I thought you said she was a shifter."

"Technically, yes. However, she doesn't know how to control it."

Wrik rubbed his chin. "I think I remember seeing a book on shifters lying around somewhere. I will search for it while you're gone. For the time being, that won't be a problem. The níţfinzh are large enough that they can carry Theyn in their claws. It won't be as comfortable for her, but I'm sure she'll manage."

Nardus looked at Theyn. Her voice entered his mind. *"We have no choice."*

Nardus leaned over Gnaud and stroked his cheek. "Hang on just a little longer, my furry little friend. I will do everything in my power to save you." He straightened and walked over to Wrik. "And when I find this nest of dragons, what am I to ask them? Tell me how to find a black level wizard?"

Wrik's eyes gleamed and his grin widened. "Ask them to help you find Cyrus."

Nardus scoffed. "Cyrus? The wizard of legends? Isn't he dead?"

Wrik patted Nardus's arm. "Yes, but he may yet live again."

Nardus turned and spat on the floor. "Mezhik be damned."

"Indeed, my friend, indeed." Wrik chuckled. "There are a few things you must remember about the níţfinzh. The first is that they can only fly for a couple of hours per day before needing rest and food. And the second is that they can only take you so far into the mountains. The altitude where the dragons are said to live is far beyond anything the níţfinzh can handle. Remember that, and you'll be fine. Also, be aware that they will not wait around for you. Once they drop you off you will be on your own. Understood?"

"Yes. Anything else?"

Wrik tilted his head for a moment. "I don't believe so." He swept his arm toward the door. "Shall we sneak our way up to the northern ramparts?"

"Lead on," said Nardus.

As they made their way up through the castle, Nardus grew more and more apprehensive of what lay ahead.

Flying. Dragons. Theyn. Resurrecting a dead wizard.

So many things could go wrong, and something probably would. His history proved it. He said a quick prayer as they walked in silence, but he had little hope of it being answered. So, he turned to the one thing that had never let him down: *Vitara*.

My rock and my anchor; keep me grounded.

The irony of the last thought wasn't lost on him, given where he was headed. In truth, only one question really mattered.

How does one resurrect a wizard anyway?

CHAPTER TWENTY-TWO

Alderan wandered the castle aimlessly, looking for nothing in particular. He encountered few people in the corridors and thought it strange, but he had no knowledge of how many people resided within the castle walls. For all he knew, it could've been normal.

He'd traversed so many stairs that he'd lost count by the time he found himself walking out onto the southern rampart. A frigid wind swirled and whipped his hair in his face. No matter how many times he swept it back or which direction he faced, his hair found its way back into his face. He finally gave up fighting it.

To the south, far below, sat the town of Atrum Moenia. Torchlight lit up several sections of road through the town but seemed to have no pattern to it. He wondered if some of the other torches had simply blown out or if some other explanation existed. Perhaps he'd explore it further tomorrow evening.

He followed the ramparts around to the east end of the castle, where the main entrance stood. Two lines of tall torch poles stretched far into the distance, their oversized torches giving off significantly more light than the torches in Atrum Moenia. Thankfully, they were nothing more than that. Had they been human torches like the ones he'd seen in his nightmares, he would've screamed with terror.

At the edge of the torchlight, he swore he saw movement. He leaned over the parapet and squinted into the darkness. A figure staggered down the wide road toward the castle. Then another. And another. Hundreds of them. Possibly a thousand. He would've thought that the wind would've carried the noise of conversation to his ears, but he heard nothing but the scrape of sandals and pounding of boots on the compacted gravel road. The sight sent gooseflesh rippling across his arms.

Alderan located the nearest stairwell and traversed the stairs as quickly as he could. Even though many claimed that one could get lost for days within the castle, he found it simple to navigate. Certain patterns existed to its make up, and he'd memorized them quickly. He likened it to his ability to traverse the forests around Viscus D'Silva blindfolded.

By the time he reached the ground level of the castle and the massive eastern doors, they were spread wide. Pravus and Aria stood just outside of them, awaiting the approaching throng of people. Alderan walked over to them and stood next to Aria.

The air cracked like thunder, again and again. Alderan look up just as Cinolth flew around the northern corner of the castle and landed in the middle of the road. Smoke burst from Cinolth's nostrils with each breath, his ribs expanding and contracting rapidly. Blood glistened on his lower jaw, and he picked his teeth with one of his massive claws. Alderan couldn't imagine how much food it must take to fill a dragon's stomach.

The first of the people arrived.

Pale white skin with black veins.

Black eyes.

They looked to Cinolth and spoke as one. "Command us, master."

Alderan stuttered backward. "No, no, no." He reached for Aria's hand, but he'd retreated a bit too far.

Aria turned toward him, a smile upon her face. Her smile faded, replaced with a look of concern. "What's wrong, Alderan?" She moved toward him.

He pointed at the gathering crowd of infected. "Do you not see what's happening here?" Fear and anger drove his words.

She reached out and took his hand. "Yes. Cinolth has called his army to himself."

Alderan couldn't believe his ears. "His army? Look at these people! They are nothing more than peasants, merchants, and farmers."

She stroked the back of his hand with her thumb. "Don't worry. We will provide them with weapons."

What has happened to my sister?

"And who are they to fight? Just look at them. They're sick, Aria. They need help, not weapons!"

Pravus glanced over his shoulder. "Do we have a problem, my queen?"

"Of course not. Alderan just needs some time to understand what's happening before he can think clearly. He'll come around soon enough."

Alderan jerked his hand away from Aria and stormed over to Pravus.

"What have you done to my sister?"

Pravus sneered. "I assure you that your sister acts of her own volition."

Alderan turned back to Aria. "You can't possibly be okay with this!"

"This was all my idea. How could I not be okay with it?" Her twisted smile left him cold.

Tears swelled in Alderan's eyes. "I cannot stand here and take part in this like it's okay. This isn't right. You're sick, Aria. What would Mother and Father think of this?"

"Red and Gretchen were never our parents. How could they have been? They're nothing."

Her words stabbed his heart. "You don't mean that, Aria. Gretchen may not have birthed us, but she and Red raised us and gave us a home."

"Enough," yelled Pravus.

Pravus reached out and Alderan flew across the road and slid on his back. A rash of heat and pain swept across his back. Alderan sat up just as a flash of silver streaked from Pravus's hand. The silver disc or ring flew straight at him. He'd never seen a weapon quite like it.

With little time to react, Alderan reached out to grab or block the weapon, but it sailed right through his hand and hit him square in the throat. He choked and coughed and gagged. He tried to rub his neck, but his fingers met smooth, cold metal, beveled on its edges. The metal disc encircled his neck like a collar and had no seams or clasp or anything. He tried to pull it off in the same fashion it'd been applied, but it only pulled against the back of his neck.

Ɛäṭūr, what's happening? What is this?

Aria walked over to him and knelt. She smiled but her eyes were cold. "Don't worry, the collar's for your own good."

"You can't do this to me!"

"In time, you'll come to realize that this was the only way to bring peace to the realm. We head for war soon, and the Three Kingdoms will fall."

"This isn't you speaking, Aria. He's controlling you. Can't you see that? The realm is at peace now. The only thing you bring is bloodshed."

The red fringe around Aria's green irises glowed like molten metal. "Justice. We bring justice, not bloodshed. If we stand by and do nothing, our kind will be eradicated."

"*Our* kind? Those you seek to destroy are just like us!"

"You know nothing. The *ʊnzhiƒṭäd* plot and scheme daily to eradicate those of us who wield mezhik. Given time and opportunity, they will kill us all."

"Even if that were true, war isn't the answer. There must be another way."

Aria backhanded him. *Whack!* The fact that it came from her stung far worse than the strike to his cheek.

"Your weakness blinds you," snarled Aria. "Don't be such a fool."

Alderan took her hand and pleaded with her. "You don't have to do this, Aria. This isn't you. I'm your brother."

"Relax, Alderan." She bent over and kissed his cheek, and then she whispered in his ear, "You'd be dead already if you weren't my brother."

But you're not the sister I've always known.

In her cold eyes, Alderan found nothing of the brave and selfless sister he remembered.

Does any part of you still remain?

The question crushed him and threatened to drive the life from his lungs. His head raged with pain, but it didn't compare to the pain that rended his heart and soul. He lay back and cried.

Why is this happening to me? How can Aria be the evil that fuels my nightmares? How can I save the world from her? She's my sister, not my enemy.

I can't. I won't.

I've failed you, Ʒäṭūr. I've failed. The world will soon be damned.

† † †

Pravus stood tall, his chest swollen with pride. He'd never been prouder of Aria than the moment after she'd backhanded her brother and put him in his place. Any doubts he still harbored of her dedication and resolve to help him bring down the Three Kingdoms and rule the Ancient Realm dissolved in that moment.

He couldn't love her more. It wasn't physically possible. She captured every piece of his heart that he didn't hold for himself. A mere fraction, perhaps, but still all that remained of it. She completed him.

Aria rose and stood next to Cinolth as throngs of infected people continued to arrive outside the castle gates. Those at the front settled on the ground and awaited further instruction from their master, Cinolth. Pravus hated that Cinolth controlled so many—far more than he did—but knew the war would be shortened by tenfold with Cinolth's help. He could almost grasp his father's kingdom. His hands closed around empty air at his sides, but not for long.

Hundreds of other people accompanied the horde of infected, most lost in fear, anger, and grief over their plight. None comprehended the situation at hand, but many began to gather before Pravus. Soon, the situation would get out of control if Pravus did nothing. But what could be done?

Most of the people seemed too scared to address Pravus directly, but one man in particular found his voice. He held a scythe in his hand and shook it as he spoke. "We give fealty, food, and coin to House Rosai in exchange for protection from all types of threats, but what has it gained us? Nothing."

Mezhik arced across Pravus's fingertips, ready to lash out and incinerate the man, but Pravus held it back. The crowd had quieted and looked to the man as though he held their fates in his hands. Killing him might incite a riot and that's the last thing he needed right before marching toward war.

I'll let the man finish his speech, and then I'll show him the truth of what is happening.

A plan began formulating within his mind. A grand illusion to settle their minds and send them back to their homes. He had the perfect, brilliant idea.

The man spread his arms wide and turned in a circle as he continued, "Look around! Our sons, daughters, husbands, wives, parents, and friends have been stricken with incurable illness and have forgone any and all protections against the elements as they traversed all types of landscapes to assemble here at your doorstep."

The man turned and addressed Pravus directly. "Lord Rosai, explain to us the meaning of all this. What have you done to our people?"

Several people in the crowd echoed the man's words as they began to talk amongst themselves. A few began shouting threats. Aria glanced over at Pravus, malice in her eyes. He raised his hand toward her and nodded.

I've got this under control, my love.

Pravus eyed the crowd and raised a fist in the air. Slowly, the people settled. Folding his arms at his back, he drew a deep breath and turned on the charm. "Citizens of the south, it is with deep regret that I must inform you that your family and neighbors are not only gravely ill but also highly contagious. If you continue to be around them, you will surely suffer the same fate.

"I have identified the unique properties of the illness they suffer from and have determined that they will require a deep cleansing of body and soul to rid them of their affliction."

"Vines of Diӡäfär," hollered a stout woman. "Seen 'em with me own eyes I did."

Pravus glanced up at Cinolth and continued, "Yes, Diӡäfär is the one behind this, not I. But I swear to you that they will be healed if the gods allow it. The process to heal each of them will require a great deal of mezhik and rest. In order to achieve this, they must stay here at Galondu Castle for several months. Perhaps longer."

Several people in the crowd gasped. One woman toward the front fainted.

"And how'll we get along without 'em?" asked a tall, skinny man. The breeze lifted his thin, silvered hair from the top of his bald scalp.

Pravus cracked his knuckles and steepled his fingers. "Simple. Do the work needed to be done."

The first man spoke up again. "And what assurance do you offer us that you will be true to your word and help these people?"

Pravus drew upon his mezhik and the power of his mind. He pictured three massive tents full of beds, supplies, and attendants. Soldiers standing at the entrances to the tents, helping the influx of infected get processed so that they could be assigned a bed. Every last detail passed through his mind's eye, down to the itchiness of the wool blankets that covered the beds and the succulent aroma of rabbit soup wafting from the tents.

He swept his arm to the left, and the peoples' gazes followed. Just to the north of them stood the three tents he'd pictured, as real as life itself. "See the preparations we have made for them? I will spare no expense satisfying their needs and bringing them back to health, the gods willing of course."

"Let us stay with 'em," cried a young girl. "Or take 'em back home."

Pravus stood tall. "Make no mistake. These people have no alternative but death. Do not allow yourselves to join them in their demise. See yourselves home this very night, or you will tax our resources and ability to help the infected. Staying here will hinder our progress, not help it. These people still need food and other provisions, so you must go back home and continue to work your fields, tend to your flocks and herds, and press on. Also, remember to relay this message to all those you encounter on your journey home."

Cinolth's deep, gravelly voice rumbled the ground when he spoke. "Do as Lord Rosai has requested or face my fiery wrath." He roared and spewed fire high above the gathered crowd.

Shrieks and cries filled the night, and the crowd quickly disbanded. The first man who had spoken stood his ground for several moments, eying Pravus intently. Finally, he dipped his head ever so slightly, turned, and walked away.

"Captain Vignar," said Pravus.

A soldier from the castle guard ran up to Pravus and tapped his right fist over his heart. "My lord?"

"Station archers around the castle. If anyone else approaches come morning light, shoot to kill. And burn the bodies."

Captain Vignar nodded once. "As you say, my lord. I will see to it personally."

"See that you do."

Captain Vignar tapped his fist over his heart again and ran off, immediately barking orders to the other guardsmen.

Aria approached Pravus, her face contorted with a scowl. "Why spare their lives when they'll all face death in the end?"

He cocked his head. "And who will be left to rule over if we kill everyone in our path to the throne?"

Aria walked her fingers up his torso and poked his breastbone with a long fingernail. "I will still have rule over you."

Pravus swallowed hard, not because of Aria or her words, but because he feared the woman he'd grown to love would continue to slip between his fingers no matter how hard he held fast to her. In the end, would anything remain of her, or would she be nothing more than Cinolth's puppet?

Pravus took her hand and kissed her knuckles. "As you say, my queen." He turned and walked back toward the castle gates.

Cinolth must be dealt with, but not until the war is guaranteed.

But will Aria survive that long?

† † †

Aria lay atop the southern rampart, staring up at the vastness of space. As the hours and days passed, she found it increasingly difficult to separate herself from Cinolth. At times, she didn't know if her thoughts were solely hers, his, or a mixture of the two of them. To be honest, it scared her to death.

Am I losing myself?

The stars shone bright in the night sky, tiny beacons of light so many used to navigate the land and seas. Other people used the stars to read the future, but Aria had a use for them all her own. When alone and underneath the night sky, she used the stars as a gravitational device, pulling herself toward them and away from the bond she shared with Cinolth.

In those moments, clouded thoughts became clear, and her connection with Alderan grew stronger. But those moments never lasted. Cinolth wouldn't let them. He sensed the disconnect as well and rushed back to her side before long.

It made her wonder if the bond they shared could be broken, given enough distance, but those thoughts always faded into background noise when he returned. Afterthoughts in her mind.

Cinolth landed in front of her on the southern rampart and laid down with his massive head next to her. Sulfur and the stench of death permeated his breath.

"I take it you found a meal," she said.

His mind entered hers, and his words rang in her head. *"For now. I will require more soon."*

"I've been thinking about the war and the fact that all soldiers and all those people you control must march hundreds of miles and still have the strength to fight when we arrive south of Elatos. Not just the distance, but the time it will take to get there. We will lose months and the element of surprise. King Zaridus will have plenty of time to gather his forces and bolster his defenses."

"And where is it that you're going with these thoughts?"

Aria sat up and leaned against Cinolth's neck. Heat radiated from between his scales and chased the chill from her bones. "There must be a quicker way to move our forces such a great distance. Perhaps some sort of portal or gateway."

"Like the mirror portals?"

Aria frowned. "I'm not sure what those are."

"Just as they sound. Mirrors imbued with mezhik that allow the zhiftäd, those who can wield mezhik, to move through them."

Aria patted Cinolth's neck with excitement. "Exactly like that, but on a much, much larger scale. Plus, it'd have to allow the *unzhiftäd* through as well."

"You are far cleverer than I've given you credit. I believe we can achieve building a gateway. It's been done before. But we will need the help of Fizärds Ōírdh. Several of them."

"Earth wizards?" asked Aria.

"Correct. You're a quick learner. Reminds me of Magus."

"And how long do you think it would take to create such a thing?"

"I'd say seven days. But we will need at least two of them."

Aria twirled her finger in her hair. "Fourteen days then... that will still save us several months and many resources."

"For certain."

Aria rose and dusted off her trousers. She'd ditched wearing dresses after her first flight with Cinolth. Her legs still hadn't grown used to riding on him, but she didn't have much choice. The war would come sooner now.

"Good," she said. "I will explain the plan to Pravus and find us some *Fizärd Ōírdh.*"

"Very well. I will return to the hunt. We will start building Zhäíṭfäí Dhä in the morning. And preserve your mezhik. You'll need all that you can get."

Aria nodded and headed for the western stairwell.

Zhäíṭfäí Dhä. She liked the sound of it.

† † †

Pravus marched through the corridors in search of Credan. He hadn't heard a peep or seen anyone or anything regarding the armies his constituents would provide. They must be there by dawn. If Credan failed him, the man would pay with his life, friend or not.

Up ahead, a light shone through the open doorway into the war room.

Credan.

Pravus stormed forward, his tongue full of vitriol and ready to be released. He rounded the corner, entered the room, and came to a full stop as he took stock of the war room table. Anger rushed from his mind, replaced by carnal desire.

Aria sat on the table's edge in a sheer night robe but wore nothing underneath it. Untied and opened in the front, its lengths hung to the sides of her legs, exposing the insides of her voluptuous breasts.

Pravus reached behind himself and shut the door without taking his eyes from his wanton seductress. He left a trail of clothes as he made his way over to the table, stripping off his last sock by the time he reached her. He grabbed her hips, ready to ravish her, but she pushed him back with a hand to his chest.

"Not yet, my love." She smiled deviously. "You think you're aching to get inside me now but wait until I've told you the good news. Once you have, I'm certain you won't be able to restrain yourself."

He took a deep breath and reined in his lust. "This had better be good."

She bit down on her lower lip as she hopped off the table, drawing a drop of blood. Pravus looked away as the *other* lust awakened within him.

Not now, damn you.

Aria turned toward the table and grabbed one of the maps for the Ancient Realm. She rolled it out and placed markers on Galondu Castle and the area northwest of Duos Flumen. She looked back at him, her lower lip dotted with blood. "Roughly 400 miles, correct?"

It took every ounce of willpower for Pravus to maintain focus on Aria's words and not just her lips. "Yes."

"Based on all the equipment and the state of the people under Cinolth's control, we'd be lucky to travel five miles a day."

Pravus nearly danced in place, torn between sexual and blood lusts. "Agreed."

"So, that would put us at eighty days just to reach that point, still another thirty-five miles from Elatos. That march would be another seven days. Perhaps three or four if we doubled the pace."

Pravus closed his eyes. "Where is this leading?"

"Three months. In that time, King Zaridus would have plenty of time to gather his forces and fortify the three cities. In that scenario, the battles will be much bloodier, and we will lose more of our army."

Pravus groaned. "And the alternative?"

She grabbed his arm. Her cold touch soothed his smoldering flesh. "Watch."

He opened his eyes and held her waist as she leaned over the map. Had her night robe not separated them, he would've lost all control. He leaned into her and peered over her shoulder.

Aria took the map and folded the middle of it underneath the ends, joining Galondu Castle with the area northwest of Duos Flumen. "Do you understand now?"

Frustrated and tired of waiting, he pulled her around to face him.

"You've folded the map. This means nothing." He leaned in and kissed the side of her neck.

She pushed him back again. "Restrain yourself, husband, or you'll find yourself in a cold bed tonight."

He grabbed her night robe and pulled it off her shoulders. "Nothing will keep me apart from you tonight."

She covered herself with her arms and glared at him. "Cinolth and I have a plan, but it will require resources I'm sure *you* can easily find."

The name Cinolth nearly drove the lust from him. He straightened. "What kind of plan, and what resources are we talking about?"

"We will build *Zhäítfäí Dhä* between here and there."

Pravus scoffed, "Are you mad? No one has the power..." His voice trailed off.

Aria grinned deviously. "So, you understand then?"

Pravus eyed the map. "And what will it take to build this gateway?"

"We will need two of them. One for each side." She pointed where they'd go. "Each gateway will take seven days to build, but we will need as many *Fizärd Ōírdh* as you can find."

Pravus scratched his head. "Earth wizards... perhaps Wrik can help sort that out."

"Perfect. I will go speak with him now." She pushed past him.

Pravus grabbed Aria's waist, spun her around, and lifted her onto the table's edge. "You're not going anywhere until we've thoroughly defiled this table."

Aria wrapped her legs around his waist and pulled him close. "What are you waiting for, husband?"

† † †

A knock sounded at Wrik's bedchamber door, pulling him from his sleep. He lay there for several moments wondering if the sound had been part of a dream, but then another knock came, louder and more persistent.

Wrik sat up and swung his feet off the bed. Another knock.

"I heard you the first time," he yelled. "Show some restraint."

"*Əllíţ ʊb,*" he muttered. The candle on his desk burst with life. He rubbed his eyes and squinted. The entire room was a blurry mess. He stood and retrieved his spectacles from the desk and placed them on his face. They made his vision marginally better. He always had a tough time focusing his eyes right after waking up.

He grabbed the candle holder and walked over to the door. "Who is it?"

"It's Alderan. I came to say goodbye."

Wrik unbolted the door and cracked it open. "And why would you be leaving at this hour?"

"It doesn't matter. There's nothing left for me here. I'm going back home." The silver collar wrapped around Alderan's neck gleamed in the candlelight.

Ɂäbräʑär.

Wrik opened the door farther. "And where *is* home?"

Alderan looked toward the floor. "It used to be Viscus D'Silva, but the entire town is dead." He scratched his head. "To be honest, I'm not sure anymore. Anywhere but here. Perhaps Tyrosha."

Tyrosha. Its name brought back memories Wrik hadn't thought about in decades. Memories he didn't want to think about. But one could never stop the mind from triggering memories. Names, sounds, smells, and many other things could set it off without warning. The only positive thing he recalled of Tyrosha were its salt baths. But those weren't worth enduring the memories that came with them.

Wrik shook away the rest of the night from his eyes and the thoughts of Tyrosha with it. "Tyrosha is quite some distance from here. Do you plan on walking all that way?"

Alderan looked at him, clearly puzzled. "Walk there? Of course not. I'll use the mirror. Same as I did before."

"You can't. Not with that collar on." Wrik leaned around Alderan and scanned the corridor. Nothing seemed amiss and the shadows looked to be nothing more than just that. Nevertheless, he ushered Alderan inside and closed and locked the door behind them.

Alderan stood next to Wrik's desk and faced him. His eyebrows drooped over the bridge of his nose. "What do you mean I can't?" Alderan's voice boomed and echoed in the small bedchamber.

Wrik glared at Alderan. "Keep your voice down," he whispered. "If Pravus were to catch us alone together it'd be bad for us both."

"He can't do anything to me." Alderan crossed his arms, and it pulled his shirt down a little in the front.

Even in the poor light Wrik saw the red tattoo on Alderan's chest that looked like a feather. He eyed the stack of books on his desk. They sat slightly skewed and out of order. He'd address the thievery in a moment.

"Don't fool yourself. He might not be able to take your life, but there are far worse things than death."

Alderan swallowed hard. "I suppose you're right." He thumbed the collar around his neck. "So why can't I use the mirror with this thing on?"

"That collar is called *zäbrazär*. It blocks you from using your mezhik and stores the mezhik energy you try to use. Because it blocks mezhik, the mirror portal would determine that you are *ʊnzhifţäd* and kill you when you step through it."

"*Ʊnzhifţäd*? What does it mean?"

"Ungifted. Without mezhik."

Alderan pulled on the collar. "And how do I get it off?"

"You won't be able to. Only another wizard can remove it."

"Well then, take it off of me." Alderan stepped closer.

"Although I have the ability to do so, I cannot remove it. It's not worth the consequence of doing so."

"Fine." Alderan tried to move past Wrik, but Wrik blocked him from leaving. "Get out of my way," growled Alderan.

"I'll let you leave as soon as you explain to me how you came to possess my feather necklace."

Alderan's hand shot to his shirt collar, and his face paled several shades. "I... Um... Yesterday. It happened so fast that I didn't know what to do. I swear that I was going to tell you about it, but I completely forgot it'd even happened after you brought Aria here to see me."

"I expressly remember telling you to touch nothing in this room." He scowled at Alderan. "You gave me your word."

Alderan pulled his hair back behind his ears and rubbed the back of his neck. "Yeah, and I'd planned on doing just that, but you were gone a long time and I got bored of just sitting there. I was going to take it off but couldn't figure out how to do so."

"How convenient." Every time Wrik looked at Alderan he noticed a blurry spot on the right lens of his spectacles. He removed them from his face and breathed on them, fogging the glass.

Alderan shrugged. "It's the truth. Please take it back if you know how to."

Wrik wiped his spectacles with a kerchief from one of his pockets and then placed them back on his face. "It's of no consequence. You may keep the necklace."

Alderan looked down at his chest. "But what does it do?"

"What any necklace does." Wrik grinned. "It hangs there and looks nice."

Alderan traced the feather with his finger. "Then why did it sink into my skin and turn it red?"

"Think of it this way. When one raises a puppy from birth, the puppy becomes attached to that person and its loyalty virtually unbreakable. In a way, the necklace is the same as the puppy. I'd been saving it for many decades, waiting for the right moment to use it or the right person to give it to, but fate stepped in and the feather necklace presented itself to you. I will not undo what has been done."

Alderan frowned. "There must be something more to it though."

"Yes. A great friend sacrificed their own life when they gave that feather to me. I'd never cried as hard as I did that day, and I never have since." Wrik wiped a tear from the corner of his eye. "I bound the feather to that necklace so that the feather would never be lost, but I couldn't allow myself to wear it knowing what I'd done."

"I don't understand."

"And I will explain it no further. You are its possessor, plain and simple." Wrik moved over to his bed and sat down. "You may leave now. Go where you wish, but do not attempt to use the mirror. I will not be responsible."

Alderan moved over to the door and unlocked it, but then he turned back. "You seem like a decent fellow, Wrik, so why are you here? Why are you part of this wretched plan to destroy peace and go to war?"

"My obsession is with prophecy and the fulfillment of it. I yearn to see branches trimmed and others fulfilled. How can I see things unfold firsthand without being in the thick of it?"

"Then you wish for the destruction of the Ancient Realm?"

"You misunderstand what I'm saying. I wish to see prophecy fulfilled, no matter the outcome. I do what is necessary to keep myself from influencing any given path."

"And what if you had the chance to save yourself by pushing for a certain outcome? Would you still sit back and let it all play out?"

Wrik nodded. "It's the very nature of who I am. I could never live with myself if I intervened. As I'm sure you know, death is not the end."

"Then you believe in Ɂäʈūr and the afterlife? *Kinzhdm ef Häfn?*" asked Alderan.

"Call it what you will."

Alderan raked his fingers through his hair. "I could never sit back and watch evil run rampant if I knew I could do something to stop it. I'd be compelled to act."

Wrik shrugged. "Then act as you must. I won't fault you for it, nor would I stop you."

Alderan sighed loudly and then left the room, closing the door behind himself as he exited.

Wrik leaned back against the wall and closed his eyes. He didn't know how Alderan played into future events, but the inclusion of the feather necklace intrigued him. He hadn't seen that twist coming.

In the end, who will be left standing?

In his heart, he rooted for Aria to be that one, but Alderan had grown on him as well.

But there cannot be two.

† † †

Fully dressed, Aria strode down the castle corridor toward Wizard Wrik's bedchamber. The late hour made no difference as her desire to get started on the gateway drove her forward. She rounded the last corner before reaching Wizard Wrik's bedchamber and plowed right into Alderan, sending them both stuttering backward.

"I'm sorry," said Aria. "Wasn't expecting the corridor to be occupied at this hour."

Alderan groaned as he walked past her, not saying a word or really looking at her.

She turned and rushed to catch him. "Wait up, Alderan." He marched down the hallway as though he hadn't heard her, but she knew he had.

She grabbed his arm when she caught up to him and pulled him back around.

He glared at her and spoke through gritted teeth. "Let go of my arm."

"What's wrong with you?" She truly didn't understand his hostility toward her.

Rage flashed in his eyes, but he spoke with an even temper. "You cast me aside like refuse and allow that bastard you call a husband to put this collar on me so that I can't leave, and you wonder what's wrong? And that's only part of it. You're willing and ready to sacrifice countless, innocent lives, and for what purpose? Dress yourself up and pretend all you want, but you'll never be a queen. If you take the throne by force, you will never rule the people. They will reject you and revolt. Is that what you want?"

Aria smacked Alderan's face. The pop of the impact echoed through the corridor and stung her hand. It'd happened so fast. She'd never struck him before today. Hadn't ever wanted to. Now, she'd done it twice. But he'd asked for it. Deserved it. So why did she feel so wretched about it when he stormed away?

Tears burned in her eyes. "Alderan, wait…" She knew he wouldn't.

In the morning, she'd seek him out and set things right again. They wouldn't be at odds for long. She'd see to it.

I know you still love me.

Aria patted her eyes dry and squeezed life back into her cheeks. She pounded on Wizard Wrik's door when she arrived and tried the door without waiting for a response. To her surprise, it wasn't locked. She called his name as she stepped inside and closed the door.

"First your brother, and now you. To what do I owe this late-night visit?"

Aria approached Wizard Wrik. "Alderan came to see you?" Her eyes narrowed. "What did he want?"

Wizard Wrik waived her off. "Assistance I could not offer him."

"I see. Perhaps you'll be more willing to assist me."

"Ask, and it will be granted—" He held up a finger. "—if it's within my power, of course."

She sat on the edge of the bed next to Wizard Wrik. "How many *Fizärd Ōírdh* do you think you can round up?"

"Depends. How much time do I have?"

Her hand moved to his knee. "We need them tomorrow. Can you do it?"

Wizard Wrik's gaze fell to Aria's hand. "Perhaps two. No more than that."

"Two will be enough." She stood, leaned over, and kissed his cheek. "Thank you. Have them meet me north of the castle first thing in the morning."

He touched his cheek where she'd kissed it. "You wish them to be free?"

"Yes. We need them to build a large wall of stone. Will that be a problem?"

He rubbed his head. "The situation could be a bit strenuous because they are currently collared and imprisoned here in the castle dungeons."

Aria paced. "Find out why they've been detained. If the offense is minimal, we will offer them their freedom if they agree to help."

"Oh, there's no question as to *why* they reside in the dungeons." The way Wizard Wrik said it drew Aria's attention.

She thought back to the previous night in the war room.

Does this have something to do with Pravus and his rage?

She stopped by the door, exhaled, and crossed her arms. "I assure you that my husband will not stand in the way of this."

Wizard Wrik nodded knowingly. "I'm sure you are right."

He didn't deny Pravus's involvement.

"Good." She left the room and closed the door behind herself.

She set her jaw and marched toward her bedchamber.

No more secrets.

† † †

Aria's breath plumed from her lips as the chilly morning air nipped at her exposed skin. The sun had risen an hour before but still hadn't peeked over the dormant caldera looming over Galondu Castle to the west. Nerves fluttered in the pit of her stomach as she envisioned the gateway they'd be building. She had no idea what it would take to accomplish the task but Cinolth would guide her and her mezhik through the process.

Wizard Wrik had located the two Fizärd Ōírdh as he'd promised, but neither of them seemed too keen to help with the task. It took quite a bit of coaxing and promises—most likely hollow ones—from Pravus to get them on board, but in the end, they knew they had little choice but to help.

Help or die.

With Wizard Wrik's knowledge of containment spells and wards and a boost of mezhik energy from Cinolth, Pravus created a large, secured area in which they would be able to create the gateway. It also served as a prison of sorts for the two Fizärd Ōírdh. They wouldn't be able to leave the area without a ɜäbräɜär on.

Aria watched as Cinolth instructed the two wizards, Mutius and Bardaric. "Dig deep into the earth and pull out the largest stones you can find. This wall must be thick, wide, and tall to withstand the stress of the gateway spell. Every square inch of the wall must support a thousand times its weight."

Bardaric, the older and more skilled of the two, spoke up. "Once we've placed all the stones shall we meld them together? It will strengthen the wall tenfold."

Sulfuric fumes rose from Cinolth's nostrils. "Under normal circumstances, I would advise you to use such a method. However, the spell we will be placing on the wall will sink into the very nature of the stones, and there cannot be any structural defects, or the entire wall will implode with such force that we will all be sucked into its vortex and killed. Is that the way you want to die?"

Bardaric looked at Mutius; the young, bald wizard shook his head vigorously. "No," said Bardaric.

"Very well. Work as long and as quickly as you can. You're the only two *Fizärd Ōírdh* we have, so mind your strength." Cinolth moved closer to the two wizards. His mouth glowed with fire. "But don't think you can be lazy and have it go unnoticed. You have five days to complete the task. Fail, and you will be killed."

The two men nodded and set to work.

Pravus, Wrik, and Alderan looked on from afar. Alderan still hadn't spoken to her since their encounter in the corridor. It troubled Aria. She'd always been capable of reading her brother and getting through to him, but every attempt she'd made that morning to do so failed miserably. Surprisingly, his mind defenses were quite strong.

Cinolth turned to Aria. "We've got work of our own to do. A spell such as what we will attempt to cast requires much preparation, most of which is mental."

Aria gave Alderan one last glance and sighed deeply. "Very well. Show me what must be done, and I will do it."

Cinolth led her away from the others, deep into the heart of the Cariosus Forest. No life remained there. None had since the end of the Great War when Magus Carac cursed the land. After the pending war, once they'd conquered the world, she'd find a way to break the curse and bring life back into the land.

"Wait here," said Cinolth.

He walked another hundred yards into the forest and spun in a circle, bashing and uprooting a large section of the dead trees with his spiked tail. Once he finished, he called her over. Not even a sprig of life grew underneath the layer of black soil and debris.

"Grab a branch and walk with me. You will practice drawing the spell in the dirt until you can replicate it flawlessly."

"Draw it?" Her stomach took a tumble at the thought of sacrificing more wizards and sorceresses for their blood. "It's a rune spell?"

"Yes, but far more intricate than anything you've ever seen. There are more than one hundred layers to the spell, each more difficult to weave than the last. One mistake and you could wind up dead."

"I didn't know spells could be layered."

"Any spell worth casting will have several layers to it. Layering is a way to join not just many types of mezhik but many ideas. Think of it like a recipe. You will need to add all the ingredients in a specific order and use the exact amount or the recipe will fail."

"I think I understand that much of it, but I'm still unsure about the layering of it."

"It's a spider's web. You start with the base or foundation and continue to build on what you started all the way to completion. Remember, this spell will take two full days to weave and there will be no time or rest while doing so. If you pause, even for a few minutes, the base will begin to break apart and the entire process will have to be started again. Do you understand?"

"Yes."

Given her background tracking and tracing everything around her, she knew she'd have success in memorizing the layers of the spell. But would she have the endurance to work through it for two days straight? The prospect frightened her to say the least. Add to that the fear of messing something up and killing everyone and she thought she might be a frayed mess by the end of it.

"You're the only one capable of weaving such a spell. Those around you would have difficulty layering even five of them. Remember who you are. Remember why you're doing this. Remember the stakes. Failure is not an option."

Aria didn't have experience working with or talking to other dragons, but she guessed that none of them would rank high on giving pep talks. It didn't seem like something that would be part of a dragon's nature.

Torture, not nurture.

She snorted and quickly covered her nose and mouth.

Cinolth glared at her and shot smoke from his nostrils. "Then you're ready?"

Aria found a suitable stick for drawing in the dirt and stood before Cinolth. Every day his increased mass astounded her. She'd never seen any creature grow so quickly.

Will he ever stop growing?

"I'm only two-thirds grown," he mindspoke to her. *"Now concentrate on the task. Start by drawing a half circle, five meters in diameter."*

Aria set her jaw and stared at the ground.

"Concentrate on every detail," said Cinolth in her mind. *"Every line. Every circle. Every arc. Every angle. Every dimension."*

Every detail.

She closed her eyes, pictured the half circle, and set to work, letting her heart and mind guide her hand as Cinolth continued to give her instruction. The day wore on and turned into night before they stopped for the evening.

"You have done well for your first lesson." Cinolth turned in a circle and swept all her work away with his tail. *"Tomorrow morning we will start again. You will draw everything you learned today from memory. Make a mistake, and you will be punished with fire. Complete it as instructed, and we will continue to build layers on top of it. Understood?"*

Somehow, the simple task of drawing shapes had worn her down to the point that she could barely keep her eyelids open. Weakness and fatigue riddled her muscles. She nodded. Cinolth took to the sky. The beating of Cinolth's wings moved the air around him with such force that it nearly took her from her feet. She lost her bearings for several moments and stood there with her hands on her knees until she recovered enough to stand upright again. She turned and staggered back toward the castle.

Pravus met her at the castle gates and lifted her into his arms. She snaked an arm around his neck, curled her head into the crook of his arm, and let the night slip away from her.

CHAPTER TWENTY-THREE

Three days of flying for a few hours and then resting the rest of the day left Nardus feeling restless, but it certainly beat the alternative of a fifteen-day horseback ride. As per Wrik's instructions, Berserk and Tailwind—the two nítfinzh that flew them from Galondu Castle to the Procerus Mountains—dropped Nardus and Theyn off right about the snow line, thousands of feet below the towering peaks.

Talking with Theyn and getting to know her better was the one saving grace of them spending so much time waiting around. He'd filled her in on everything that Pravus had put him through, both before and after going to Räəllm Kenzhärd Dhä, and it'd brought them closer together. She'd never liked Pravus to begin with, but now her hate for Pravus matched his own.

Several hours into their hike, the snow depths rose to the tops of many of the trees. Farther up, they found themselves traversing passes formed entirely of snow, the sides of them piled twice as high as Nardus's head. He couldn't help but think of his and Theyn's vision several weeks back. His fingers probed his shirt and found the amulet Tharos had given him. At least they'd be safe from dragon's fire.

From that point on, every additional step farther up the mountain pass increased his uneasiness. The only thing that comforted him was knowing that in the vision Theyn was herself and not a large cat. The pass reflected the vision almost to the last detail, but Nardus made sure that Theyn stayed behind him. He didn't want her getting skewered by a large dragon's claw.

Through several steep passes they climbed higher and higher into the Procerus Mountains. The air grew thinner, and the temperature plummeted. He wore thick furs, but the wind penetrated right through his layers and bit him anyway. He could only imagine what the wind felt like to Theyn, but she didn't complain about it. When he looked back over his shoulder, he noticed that her fur coat had grown several inches over the last hour. Seeing that set his mind at ease.

They went around a bend and the trail ended. A sheer cliff lay ahead, dropping off into a white oblivion. Nardus raised his hand and Theyn halted. He looked around, but there was only the trail they'd traversed, the steep drop-off, and rising, ice-covered walls on either side.

"Where to?" asked Theyn in his mind.

He mindspoke with her, the wind's howling far too loud. *"I'm not sure, but we can't go forward."*

The wind whipped around them with such force that Nardus dropped to his knees to keep from getting swept over the edge of the cliff. Then, just ahead, a large green dragon descended and faced them.

"Behind me!" screamed Nardus.

The rush of flames knocked him backward and on top of Theyn. The flames relented and Nardus rose to his feet with defiance.

The dragon glared at Nardus with a serpentine eye. "How dare you enter our land." His voice vibrated the air and created an avalanche behind Nardus and Theyn. The snow piled dozens of feet high, filling the pass and trapping them.

Nardus stepped forward, right to the edge of the cliff. "My name is Nardus Remison, and this is my… companion Theyn." He immediately regretted his choice of words to describe his relationship with Theyn. He knew he'd hear about it later. "We seek an audience with Tharos the Cunning."

"Then you are in the wrong place. Leave before I kill you both."

"Do not lie to me, dragon. We've traveled a long way to see him and will not be turned away."

"You've wasted your time coming here. Tharos was banished to another world twelve hundred years ago."

"Yes, and I'm the one who freed him from that prison. He told me to come here when I was ready to accept a truth I've long forgotten. I need his help."

The dragon spewed a column of fire again but Nardus braced himself. The flames swept around him and warmed him through his clothes, but they didn't burn him.

"You're wasting your breath, dragon. Take me to Tharos."

The dragon flew up and disappeared around the side of the mountain. Nardus went back to Theyn and held her close. "Are you okay?"

"Yes. You blocked the flames from me."

"Good."

Several minutes passed and then a red dragon swept down from the sky behind them. Nardus whirled around and faced the dragon.

"Ah, it is indeed you. I didn't think you'd ever come."

"Tharos. It's good to see you." The words sounded foreign to his ears and tasted foul on his tongue. Just a month prior, he'd never wanted to see the dragon again.

Theyn rose, along with her hackles, and stood next to Nardus. She growled deep in her throat and spoke into Nardus's mind. *"I don't like dragons."*

Nardus held her head against his leg. "It's okay, Theyn. This is the dragon I told you about on the boat."

Tharos lowered his clawed hand to the ground where it dropped into oblivion. "Climb into my hand and I will take you to our home."

Nardus moved to the cliff edge, but Theyn retreated farther.

He returned to Theyn and stroked the side of her muzzle. "Theyn, it's okay. You can trust him. He won't hurt you. I promise."

Theyn crept forward as Nardus climbed into Tharos's hand. She sniffed Tharos, groaned deep, and climbed into his hand next to Nardus.

"We die, and I'm blaming you," she said in his mind.

"Fair enough, but we're not going to die," Nardus replied.

Tharos closed his hand around them, and they jolted as Tharos pulled back from the cliff edge. Upward they climbed, beyond the cloud barrier. What they saw then took Nardus's breath away. Lush green peaks formed a ring at least fifty miles across in each direction. A valley nestled in between the peaks.

The Valley of Dragons.

The air should've been frigid, but Nardus found it to be quite pleasant and his thick coat unnecessary. Given the altitude, the air should've been quite thin but Nardus had no problem breathing it in.

Dragons of many shapes, sizes, and colors moved about throughout the valley. Some young ones chased each other across the ground and through the air in a game reminiscent of tag. Others gathered in circles and conversed in a language Nardus didn't understand. It seemed to be comprised mostly of gestures and sounds and not actual words. He could've easily been wrong though.

Tharos landed close to the eastern end of the valley and dropped them on the ground. He settled down and eyed Theyn.

"And who is this lovely creature?"

"Her name's Theyn. She doesn't normally look like that. She's a human like me."

"Really? Then why does she not look human?"

"She has a condition that forces her into this form."

"Ah, I see. And why have you come here, son of Ɂäṭūr?"

"I need your help. My friend Gnaud is dying from unhealable wounds, and a wizard named Wrik told me that the only way to save my friend was to find an old wizard named Cyrus Nithik. He said you dragons would know where this Cyrus could be found."

"Your wizard friend is wise. As it turns out, Cyrus Nithik arrived here the exact same moment you did."

"Perfect! Can you take me to him?"

"Are you certain that's what you want?"

"I don't have time for your games, Tharos."

"I assure you that it isn't a game. Do you seek Cyrus and everything that doing so entails?"

"Yes, I don't care what the cost is. I need him to save my friend."

"Very well. I will take you to Quldrai, Lady of the Red. She is our queen. She will either grant you access to Peorvem or she will kill you."

"What is with the hostility from you dragons?"

"You tell me. A thousand years of enslavement by humans and you expect something different of us? We dragons live a long time and forget nothing."

Nardus hadn't thought of it like that. Had the roles been reversed, he'd have a hard time not killing them as well. "Take me to see her."

Tharos nodded. "Good. Your friend may come along as well if she'd like."

"She will not leave my side. Doing so would prove deadly for many."

"Very well. From this point forward, you will say nothing and do only as instructed. If you do not comply you will die."

Nardus nodded. "Understood."

"Make sure your lady friend understands as well," said Tharos.

"She hears and understands every word you speak."

Tharos led them over to a cave with an opening that spanned at least a hundred feet across and high. The cave sloped down at a good pace, burrowing deep into the side of the mountain. A few hundred feet below the surface the cave grew brighter. Torches lined the walls and their flames cast light across the walls and ceilings. Gold and jewels of every shape and color lined the walls like tapestries. Nardus had never seen anything so spectacular in his life. The cave transitioned into a massive chamber that spanned several thousand feet in width, depth, and height. Stones of every color glowed in the walls, floors, and ceiling, turning the chamber into a giant prism of light.

A dragon with fiery red scales laid at the back of the chamber, her mass taking up a sizable portion of the space. She made Tharos look like a dwarf and Nardus an ant. She raised her head and it floated among the gems on a long, serpentine neck. Her head drew close to Nardus, her jaws spread wide. Each of her needle-sharp teeth were the size of Nardus.

Nardus took a step back, but her jaws closed around him in an instant. Her tongue pushed Nardus between rows of teeth. She bit down, but her teeth didn't rip into his flesh. In fact, he didn't even feel pressure around him.

She spat him out and glared at Tharos. "What is the meaning of this? You bring me food I cannot eat?"

Tharos bowed low. "My queen, I have brought you the man who freed me from my prison of solitude. Because of his selfless act, I beg you to give him audience."

Smoke rose from Quldrai's flared nostrils. "And what is it that he seeks?"

Tharos looked at Nardus and grinned his wicked dragon grin. "Cyrus Nithik."

"Cyrus Nithik? The mage of old?" questioned Quldrai.

"The very same," Tharos confirmed.

Quldrai stared at Nardus. "And why has he come here seeking a man who has been dead for more than a millennium?"

"It is a complicated matter, my queen." Tharos shifted his weight several times and looked everywhere but toward Quldrai. Until that moment, Nardus had thought dragons incapable of fear. "With your permission, we will speak with the ancient one, Peorvem."

"No one speaks with him," she roared. "Not even the one with the amulet." She glared at Nardus.

Theyn leaned against Nardus's leg. He'd forgotten she was there. He reached down and stroked her head. He thought better of it after he did, but she purred.

Nardus drew courage from Theyn and broke the rule of silence. "I must see him, your ladyship. I cannot save my friend without his help. I must find Cyrus Nithik."

Quldrai stomped her foot, and the cavern shook. Dust and rock rained down. "You do not speak to me unless permitted. Do you understand? If you do so again, I will eat your furry little friend."

Nardus bowed. *I hate dragons.*

Tharos continued, "My queen, I ask you this one favor. Grant Nardus an audience with Peorvem and my debt to him will be repaid. Then Nardus will leave this place and never return."

Quldrai stood. When she did, her head touched the ceiling. She stretched out her wings and they reached either wall. She yawned and sat back down. "Only because of your debt to him will I grant this. Then he leaves for good."

"Agreed," said Tharos.

Quldrai stomped the ground, and the wall to her left turned to dust. Where it stood was another tunnel, much smaller than the one that had led down to where they stood. Tharos guided them forward and into the tunnel. Little light penetrated this tunnel, and nothing lined its walls other than the blackest obsidian Nardus had seen since the statue of the three-headed snake in the room underneath the ruins of Mortuus Terra.

Another hundred yards of twists and a long descent and they arrived at another chamber. A cold, blue light filled the chamber, just enough light to see that there was a pool of water that stretched a quarter mile or farther. Bubbles and steam rose from the otherwise still waters.

Tharos bowed low, and Nardus and Theyn followed his lead.

"Ancient one, we seek your knowledge," said Tharos.

The waters quaked, and a pale-blue dragon rose from beneath its surface. White strands of hair hung from his elongated snout and white hair clung to the tops of his eyes like eyebrows. Nardus had never seen a dragon with hair. Then again, he'd only ever seen two dragons before arriving there.

"Why have you roused me?" The booming voice shook the ground and Nardus dropped to his knees.

Tharos rose. "Peorvem The Ancient, this man seeks that which cannot be found."

Peorvem drew near the edge of the pool and pulled himself from the water. He stood half as tall as Tharos. He closed his eyes and nodded.

"Yes, I can see the aura of the spell around him."

Nardus blinked. *Spell?*

Theyn looked up at Nardus. *"Do you know what he's talking about?"* she said in his mind.

Nardus shook his head. *"I'm not sure what I've agreed to."*

Peorvem beckoned Nardus with a clawed hand. "Come closer, son of Ɂäʈūr."

Nardus rose and approached the dragon with apprehension. Peorvem took one of his claws and pressed it against Nardus's temple.

Peorvem groaned deep. "This will take some time for sure."

"How many hours?" asked Nardus.

The old dragon laughed. "If only it were that simple. At least a week. Perhaps two. I've never seen a spell rooted so deep." He stroked the hairs underneath his chin. "This will not be without pain."

"I don't understand. What does any of this have to do with Cyrus?" He glanced up at Tharos. "You said Cyrus arrived when I did."

"He did," said Tharos. "Now, Peorvem The Ancient will draw him out of you."

Nardus felt his legs grow weak, and he sank to the ground. Had Cyrus returned with him from the conjured world just as Cinolth had?

How many more souls possess me?

Nardus nodded. "I'll never be ready, so do what you must."

Peorvem took a deep breath and began drawing runes into the rock floor with one of his claws. In all, Peorvem drew twelve runes around Nardus. Then he took a scoop of water from the pool and filled the runes. The water glowed bright-blue and the tingle of mezhik flowed into Nardus. The feeling sickened Nardus, but he couldn't move.

Light from the runes shot into the air with a burst of water and sprayed the ceiling. Pain akin to needles pierced Nardus's temples, and he screamed. The chamber's blue light slowly faded from his vision until nothing remained but darkness.

He searched for Vitara's voice in the darkness but heard nothing. How would he survive without his anchor?

Then, Theyn's voice entered his mind. *"Be brave, my love. I will never leave your side."*

It was the last thing he heard before slipping down into a deep sleep.

But then the sound of beating wings filled his head as his nightmares came to life.

CHAPTER TWENTY-FOUR

Solasportus, a small fishing town and port of the northwest, lay at the bottom of the valley below. Nothing remained of the town but charred, hollowed-out shells of mud and wooden structures. Rakzar growled deep in his throat, not because of the loss of life that had occurred but because of the one who'd inflicted it.

Murtag.

Murtag's name remained at the top of Rakzar's execution list, just below that of Käíeƨ.

"Don't lose sight of what's important," said Amicus. "I did for one single night and it cost me everything."

Rakzar had spent several days trying to get Amicus out of his head, but nothing worked. Amicus's presence persisted, and he made appearances at the most inopportune times. Because of him, Rayah had begun to question Rakzar's sanity even more than usual. Several times in the last few days. Sooner or later, he'd have to tell her the truth.

Rakzar rose onto his hind legs. He towered over Amicus. "Yes, I know. I will see this through before I make a move against Murtag."

Amicus looked down the hill where Rayah sat on a large, flat rock. It was one of the only rocks on the entire hillside. "She cares about you even though she may not show it. Be gentle with her and protect her with your life."

Rakzar huffed. "Don't you think it's kinda late for that advice since I've already sentenced her to death?"

"Trust me, nothing is ever too late until you're dead." Amicus laughed and faded away as his laughter trailed off.

Rakzar dropped on all fours and trotted down to where Rayah sat. She rolled a flower stem between her thumb and forefinger, but her gaze didn't settle on the twirling lavender and yellow flower. Instead, she focused her gaze across the valley. Rakzar followed it over to the burned-out remains of

Castle Portador Tempestade. Dragnus's rotting corpse still hung from the top of its eastern wall—the only wall left standing.

She'd gone through a lot that day. Even now, Rakzar sensed fear pouring from her pores like sweat. So much strife riddled her life, and he'd been the cause for a lot of it. Guilt tore at his insides and threatened to manifest into words of sorrow and regret. He swallowed them down.

He walked past Rayah and purposefully nudged her shoulder. "Let's get to the base of the mountains before nightfall catches us."

She sniffed. He assumed she wiped her eyes as well but didn't glance back to confirm. They trekked down through the valley and up the other side in silence.

A nice change from her constant banter.

Through the castle ruins and along the coastline, Rayah continued to hold her tongue. Rakzar tried to forget about it and slough it off, but it wore on his conscience. Concern built in his gut until he couldn't take it anymore.

Rakzar broke the silence with the stupidest question that had ever crossed his lips. "What's on your mind?"

Amicus laughed in his head.

Rayah paused and looked down toward the Discidium Sea far below. "I've been thinking a lot about our situation. What if there isn't a way to kill Käíeƨ? Or what if you do manage to kill her but it doesn't break the spell? Or what if the spell is broken but its effect can't be reversed?"

There wasn't a specific instance at which Rakzar could point to that defined the shift in his thinking, but it had to exist. He turned back and stood next to Rayah. Words he wasn't even sure he believed spewed from his mouth like uncontrollable vomit. The more he tried to hold them back the more of them that came out.

"You of all people should have no doubt as to what will happen. Your God listens to you, Rayah. I've never known another god that has. He answered your pleas in the dungeon no matter how absurd they seemed at the time. If you've prayed to your God about this path we're on, I know it will lead us to victory over this curse. Nothing will stand in our way."

Rayah hugged his neck. Genuinely hugged him. His first instinct was to toss her over the cliff, and it took a lot of control to keep himself from doing it. But then something strange happened. Something unexpected. His arm slipped around her shoulders, and he pulled her close. She smelled of wildflowers with a hint of mint on her breath. Perhaps a little dust as well.

"Thank you." Rayah cried into his neck.

He held her tight. "You mention this to anyone, and I'll end you. Understood?"

"Tell me I'm not interrupting something."

Rakzar and Rayah released each other and had their weapons drawn by the time they spun around.

Urza stood upright several yards back, her knives twirling in her hands. She smiled deviously.

Rakzar lowered his axes. "That's a good way to get yourself killed."

Urza shrugged. "You've gone too soft, brother. I never would've snuck up on you a few months back."

"Why are you here?" growled Rakzar. "You're supposed to be resting."

"I'll rest when I'm dead. Besides, you clearly need someone to watch your back."

"I'm glad you're here." Rayah sheathed her knives. "I think we *will* need your help."

"Saw your handiwork on that thing in the woods."

"That was Rayah's doing," said Rakzar.

"I know," said Urza. "She's the one I'm talking to."

"Whatever." Rakzar turned and headed south. "Let's find a place in the mountains to camp for the night. The path to Tectus will be too treacherous to travel at night. For a *dryte*."

✝ ✝ ✝

Rayah woke to the sound of chirping birds. The sun hadn't risen in the west yet, but it had begun turning the dark skies shades of purple and blue. She sat up and found herself wedged between Rakzar and Urza. It explained the warmth she felt despite the frigid mountain air that had settled on them during the night.

Rakzar and Urza stirred and were up and moving by the time she wiped the night from her eyes. After a quick breakfast of dried fish and stale bread—at least that's what she ate—they headed toward the mountain trail hidden deep in the forest.

Nearly five hours and several abrasions later, they finally arrived at the cave entrance that led into Tectus. Two dwarves dressed in battle armor and donning several weapons guarded the entrance.

The one to the left sized them up. His long, red beard twisted into a braid below his square jaw and featured several silver and turquoise beads. His bushy eyebrows gravitated toward the center of his face and hovered over a broad nose. The other dwarf looked similar to the first, but his hair was far more orange than red. Both of them were bald.

The dwarf with the red beard pointed his axe at Rakzar and Urza. "Yer kind ain't welcome 'ere."

"Since when?" growled Rakzar.

"Since yeh can' be trusted," said the second dwarf.

"I've never dug my claws into a dwarf before," said Urza. "You wanna make this the first time?"

Rayah stepped between the two dwarves and Rakzar and Urza and held out her arms. "Violence isn't going to solve anything." She turned to the first dwarf. "Would you let them through if someone vouches for them?"

"Not unless it be a dwarf who does so," said the second dwarf. "None ever would though."

The two dwarves chuckled.

Urza bent down and met the dwarves' gazes. If anything, it strengthened their resolve, but then she dropped a name they knew. "Torbrek Stonebreaker."

The two dwarves looked at each other wide-eyed.

"She knows Stonebreaker?" asked the first dwarf to the second.

They both turned back, eyes narrowed.

"What yeh know of 'im?" asked the second dwarf.

"He's a friend," said Urza.

Click-click!

Knives slid into her hands. "Made these for me."

The first dwarf stepped forward and examined the spring-loaded sheathes strapped to Urza's forearms. He grunted several times and then nodded. "That be Stonebreaker's work, alright."

"Then we can pass?" asked Rayah.

The two dwarves looked at each other again for several moments before the first nodded.

"A friend of Stonebreaker is a friend of all dwarves," said the second dwarf.

The two dwarves stepped aside, but the first one scowled at Rakzar.

"Thievin' is punishable by death." He drew his finger across his neck and made a choking noise.

To Rayah's surprise, Rakzar said nothing. The three of them entered the cave and made their way down to the first level of the city, a good twenty-five meters below the cave entrance. As with many of the dwarven cities, Tectus consisted of seven levels.

The first level served as the marketplace and housed the forges and leather workshops. Many wares could be purchased in various shops including clothing, weapons, and armor. Some foods were sold as well, mainly dried meats.

The second level served as housing for the vast majority of the population, and the third they used for anything having to do with agriculture. It also served the entrances to a plethora of mines that ran throughout the Procerus Mountains. Gold, silver, copper, tin, iron, jewels, crystals, and many other elements of worth.

The fourth and smallest of the levels served as the dungeons. No more than fifty cells existed, and less than half of them were occupied. The Tectan Dwarves prided themselves on two things concerning prisoners: reform and death. Few ever survived in the dungeons for more than a year.

The entire army resided on the fifth level, a strategic position used to protect the sixth level, where the king, the treasure vaults, banks, royal advisers, and royalty lived. Several measures of defenses were deployed on the fifth level as well. No enemy had ever breached the fifth level in Tectus's several millennia history and they boasted of it via dozens of sculptures and murals spread throughout Tectus. In truth, the Tectan Dwarves were a mighty and proud people. Some considered them too proud.

A vast space riddled with catacombs lay underneath the sixth level and housed the dead. Royalty, patriarchs, and citizens alike rested there, going back many millennia—far before they'd started recording history.

Rayah, Rakzar, and Urza made their way down to the fifth level where they'd likely find Torbrek Stonebreaker. After several inquiries as to his whereabouts, they finally located him at the back of the armory where he studied the latest techniques of making armor and weapons. They waited there in silence for several minutes until Urza finally cleared her throat.

Torbrek hardly glanced up from the weapon he examined. "Can I help you?"

Urza approached Torbrek while Rayah and Rakzar hung back. "Torbrek Stonebreaker. It's good to see you."

Torbrek laid the weapon down on the table next to him and peered up at Urza. His eyes sparkled, and the depth of their blue hue amazed Rayah. He cocked his head and tapped his foot on the solid rock floor. After a few moments, he wagged a finger at her. "I do know you, don't I?"

Urza held out her arms and showed him her sheathes. Torbrek's eyes brightened with recognition. "I'd never forget such beauty and craftsmanship, especially of my own making." He eyed Urza again and smiled. "Ah, yes. It's coming back to me now. The Butcher. I hardly recognized you without your necklace of death."

The Butcher? Rayah had never heard anyone call Urza that before. Then again, she hadn't known Urza long.

Urza fingered her breastbone, likely the place where it used to hang. "Those days are in the past."

"I see," said Torbrek. "Should I no longer call you *The Butcher* then?"

"Urza," she said flatly.

"As you wish. So what brings you back to Tectus, Urza?"

Urza glanced over at Rayah and motioned with her head for Rayah to join her, so Rayah did.

Torbrek examined Rayah as he would one of his weapons. "My, my, my. So much beauty in such a small package. And what is your name?"

Rayah's cheeks ignited with fire but she couldn't look away. "Rayah," she managed.

Torbrek took her hand and kissed her knuckles. "The pleasure is most definitely mine. How may I be of service to you?"

"We're looking for a crystal that can turn a non-solid object into a solid one. I was told that the only people who might know of such a crystal would be the Tectan Dwarves. That's why we're here." She tugged on one of her curls. "Is this information true, or have I been misled?"

Torbrek leaned against the table and groaned. "You have not been deceived. At least not in the fact that I know of what you speak. It's a crystal known as a binding shard, hence its name, *allzíäezherd*."

"Then you have one?" asked Urza.

"Gods, no." Torbrek pulled down on his face, distorting his otherwise handsome features. "That crystal is rare."

"But won't we need just a small piece of it?" asked Rayah.

Torbrek shook his head. "Perhaps I'm not being clear enough." He held up his arms and balled his fists. "When I say it's rare, I mean that no one has possessed even a sliver of the *əllzíäezherd* in millennia."

"We've no choice but to try and retrieve it. Several lives depend on it—" Rayah looked Torbrek right in the eye. "—and that number grows daily."

She figured he didn't comprehend her meaning but wasn't about to elaborate further. For all she knew, the dwarves would lock them all up or put them to death if they knew the danger Rakzar presented to their entire race.

If we fail, they'll all die, and none of them will understand why.

Thinking about it like that stirred guilt in Rayah's gut, but they didn't have much of a choice. In war—and that's what she considered their fight for survival—, some casualties were unavoidable. She prayed for their success and for haste in eliminating Käíez.

Torbrek crossed his arms. Each of his biceps bulged between bands of leather, accentuating their size. "I needn't know the details. I fear they would diminish my mood further because of the nigh impossibility of attaining what you seek."

"Don't tell us what is or isn't possible," said Rakzar. "Just give us the location of the crystal, and we'll be on our way."

"As you wish." Torbrek lifted himself onto the table and sat on its edge. His feet swung wildly several feet from the floor. "There are a thousand rumors as to the location of *əllzíäezherd*, but I'm certain I know its true location. However, information like this comes with a great price."

Rakzar stepped forward and got in Torbrek's face. "You greedy little—"

Urza pulled Rakzar back by his waist. "Calm yourself, brother." Rakzar pushed her hands away and stormed out of the room.

Urza smiled at Torbrek. "Please forgive him. He's under a lot of stress right now." Torbrek nodded and she continued, "We will gladly pay any price you name."

Any price?

As far as Rayah knew, they had little to no money and only a handful of possessions between the three of them. How would they pay anything at all?

"Yes, of course," said Torbrek. "I trust that you will. However, you must keep in mind that finding the *əllzíäezherd* will only be the first part of your quest. Once you've found it, you must bring it back here so that it can be refined and fashioned as a weapon." He eyed Rakzar who had just reentered the room. "That *is* what you want it for, correct?"

"Yes," said Rayah.

"Good." Torbrek slid off the table and landed with a soft *thud*. "I will tell you the location of the *allzíäezherd after* you've agreed to my non-negotiable terms."

The three of them nodded and Torbrek continued, "First, my brother Normak must accompany you on this quest. He's what some might call a bit off-kilter, but I assure you that there's no better warrior among us."

"No," growled Rakzar. "He'll only slow us down, and I will not be responsible for another life."

"Do you misunderstand the concept of non-negotiable?" scoffed Torbrek. He shook his head. "No, I think you're smarter than that. Besides, I assure you that you will be the ones slowing Normak down."

"Us slower than a dwarf? Impossible," said Urza.

"As you know, nothing is impossible in a world filled with mezhik." Torbrek's eyes sparkled, just like his pearly-white teeth. "My brother possesses a pair of winged boots."

Rayah gasped. "Winged boots?" She'd never heard of such a thing. "Can he fly with them on?"

Torbrek chuckled. "If only that were so. Alas, the boots only provide speed, not flight."

Urza eyed Rakzar for several moments. "Your brother shall accompany us. And your other terms?"

"Other than *allzíäezherd*, my brother will retain any spoils you might find during your quest."

"Agreed," said Rakzar. "Anything else?"

"There is one last thing, but I'm sure you'll find it to your liking all the same." Torbrek motioned them to follow him as he moved deeper into the armory. "I insist on supplying you with better weapons and armor. You're headed to a very dangerous place, and I'd like to see my brother returned alive."

Rayah loved her gloves and knives, so she'd keep them. Unless Torbrek offered her something far superior. But she couldn't imagine what that could possibly be. Rakzar on the other hand desperately needed new weapons after dealing with the zhrimezhedō.

An hour later, Rayah, Rakzar, Urza, and Torbrek stood in a wide circle at the first level of Tectus, just beyond the tunnel entrance. They awaited Normak's arrival. Apparently, he'd gone off to explore a new vein in one of the silver mines. Torbrek assured them that Normak would be along soon enough.

A gust of wind kicked up a cloud of dust and blew Rayah's hair in her face. She pulled her hair out of her face and spat ground rock and hair from her mouth. When she looked up, a young man stood next to Torbrek. The family resemblance was evident in their chiseled faces, but the two of them were otherwise dissimilar.

Torbrek had striking blue eyes, muscular but thin legs, bulging biceps, narrow shoulders and a thin waist, and thick red hair that covered his head and jaws. He kept both long and woven tightly into two braids.

Normak, on the other hand, had wild yellow eyes, stocky arms and legs, a barreled chest and broad shoulders, and unkempt, wiry, yellow hair that spread over most of his chest and back. Two small, black hoops pierced each of his bushy, yellow eyebrows on their outer fringe, and a gnarly scar crossed over his left eye, dividing his eyebrow and disfiguring the side of his nose. Dark-green leathers covered most of his body, fashioned to look like scales, and brown boots that looked a size too big covered his feet and rose to the middle of his calves. A pair of white wings protruded from the backs of the boots, just above the ankle. A large war hammer, a sheathed dagger, and a coin purse hung at his waist from a black belt made of steel ringlets.

"Where we be 'eadin'?" asked Normak, his voice deeper and his accent far thicker than Torbrek's.

Torbrek clapped Normak on the back and smiled. "Hopefully not to your death." He stood a good three inches taller than Normak.

"Aye," said Normak. He gestured with his crotch and grinned. His teeth were surprisingly white. At least the ones that remained. "Still got me some conquestin' ta do if ya catch me meanin'." He turned his head and winked at Rayah.

She rolled her eyes. *Not in this lifetime.*

"Just tell us where we're headed, and we'll be on our way," said Urza.

Torbrek's expression grew dark and grim. "Have you heard of the Ruins of Nasda?"

Urza nodded. "No one enters that place and ever returns."

"Yeh know why that be?" asked Normak, his prior amusement erased from his face.

Click-click!

Urza's blades slid into her hands. "Legends say slithering beasts lurk within its lower regions and lure anything that catches their eye with breathtaking songs."

"Trust me when I tell ya it ain't no legend," Normak replied.

"And what makes you think the crystal is hidden in these ruins?" asked Rayah.

Torbrek leaned into the middle of the group. "A sunken city of sandstone and glass. Need I say more?"

Rayah didn't understand, but the other three seemed satisfied with Torbrek's answer, so she kept quiet.

"From what I've heard, the ruins are a big place," growled Rakzar. "Where is the crystal located?"

Torbrek used his hands when he spoke, motioning wildly at times, but it conveyed his words well enough. "Deep beneath the desert, hidden below a temple dedicated to *Äfäūm*. The place is said to be cursed."

Rayah sighed. She could've lived her entire life without setting foot inside a temple dedicated to some false god. Especially one cursed and buried in the desert. "Perfect."

"Be careful. You will face brutal trials." He slapped Normak on the back. "Keep your wits about yourselves and remember that every problem has a solution."

Normak rubbed his hands together. "Time fer some action!"

Yeah, looking forward to it.

"How about the three of you head on out?" said Torbrek. "I need to speak to my brother about a private matter before he leaves. It won't take but a few minutes."

Rayah, Rakzar, and Urza bade Torbrek farewell and headed to the surface. Outside, the day had worn itself down pretty well with more than half of it gone. According to Normak, the ruins lay roughly four hundred miles to the southeast, a good four day's journey from Tectus. Once they cleared the Procerus Mountains, most of that distance would be easy traveling through the Reis'Duron Grasslands and The Plains. The last fifty or so miles through the Profugus Desert would prove a bit more difficult, but none of it would compare to the trials they'd certainly face once they reached the Ruins of Nasda.

Ten minutes later, Normak appeared out of nowhere. "We be goin' or just sittin' 'ere?"

"Did your brother ask you to do something we should know about?" growled Rakzar.

Normak winked at Rayah. "Secret ta me grave."

Urza looked to Rakzar and swept her arm toward the trail. "Lead the way, mighty Rakzar."

Rakzar led the group through the dense trees, and Rayah fell in behind him. Urza followed her, and Normak brought up the rear. A strange and unlikely band they were, and perhaps the perfect group to accomplish the impossible.

Ƶätūr, guide us and keep us safe.

CHAPTER TWENTY-FIVE

Calen had spent the last five days tracking the horde of infected from Daltura but still hadn't come across any of them. Either they moved too quick, or he moved too slow. Being pudgy and out of shape, he figured it to be the latter.

So many times, he'd wanted to turn around and go back home, but he wasn't even sure where that was anymore. At some point, the horde had changed direction and led him back into the Daltura Hills. He'd missed the transition when it'd happened and had spent several hours sitting on the ground bawling his eyes out thinking they'd just up and disappeared altogether. Once he pulled himself back together and gathered his wits, he'd realized what had actually happened.

Calen had no prior experience tracking anything, and it left him severely disadvantaged. He prayed that Ɂätūr would give him a sign and lead him in the right direction, but the sign hadn't come. With weak legs, an empty stomach, and a setting sun, he found himself somewhere on the fringe of the Daltura Hills where they sloped down to meet The Plains. He leaned against a tall, yellow aspen and took a deep breath.

Never had he seen so far and so little at once. A sea of brown, dead grass stretched from where he stood all the way to eternity. His heart sank in his chest.

You can't do this, Calen. You're gonna wind up dead out there.

A strong wind whipped through the trees and stirred the remains of broken branches and stalks of grass. Birds scattered, squawking and protesting the gale. Calen closed his eyes and listened to the sounds around him. Yes, the wind stirred up many things, but underneath its sound he heard something else. *Footfall.* It sounded almost like a stampede. The low rumble grew until it overtook the sounds of the wind and the birds.

Calen turned toward the Daltura Hills and opened his eyes. A few people marched through the trees. Then more. Many more. Hundreds. All of them looked straight ahead with black eyes, and none of them spoke a word. He gasped and cowered behind the tree as the horde came straight at him, but none of them ran him over. They moved around him and the tree like any other obstacle, all heading toward the northeast.

Based on the drab, colorless attire most of them wore, Calen guessed they must've come from the coast. Most likely from Calx Acta. Beachers he'd heard them called before. Sand, grass, and dried mud covered most of them to their knees, their shoes unrecognizable underneath the many layers of debris. How long had they been walking? They must've departed from their homes around the same time his aunt and the other people from Daltura had.

Ӡäţūr, this must be a sign that You're looking out for me. Thank You.

Despite the fact that the odds of finding his aunt had increased exponentially, Calen allowed himself a small smile. He hadn't given up, and it would pay off in the end. It just had to.

Calen joined the throng as they marched northeast. Excitement to be on his first real quest tightened his chest, but terror of what or whom he might find at its end lurked in the back of his mind—a demon he'd soon face.

After about an hour of marching across the flat plains of dead grass, the horde stopped for the night. The way they all moved and acted as one cohesive entity couldn't have been creepier. It reminded him of how he used to play with wooden figures. A question struck him and put cold fear into his bones.

Does something or someone control them?

It did explain some of their strange behavior, but how could something like that be possible? Where had the infection come from? Why didn't it seem to spread? So many questions raced through his mind.

In some ways, the infected acted just like normal humans. They set up fire pits and cooked food they'd foraged at some point. He supposed everyone needed to eat. Otherwise, they'd die. His heart leapt at the thought, and hope swelled in his chest.

If the infected are eating, then they aren't dead! I can still save you, Aunt Tahmara.

† † †

Savric stood atop a small outcropping in the middle of The Plains, looking out across the vast horde of infected. He leaned heavily on Qotan's staff, his legs far more fatigued than he'd ever remembered. Eshtak stood at Savric's side with his hand firmly attached to Savric's robes. Neither of them spoke. They didn't need to. Dread had found a home in both their hearts.

After making an abrupt turn from their initial southeastern heading five days back, the horde's collective demeanor changed. They transitioned from docile shells of humans when interacted with to violent and deadly adversaries when confronted. Many groups of people had found that out the hard way.

Several such groups bent on exploiting the infected by robbing them of their supplies quickly met their end along the way. Others just trying to corral their loved ones and get them to safety wound up dead or severely injured. Savric did what he could to heal those who survived, but few had. After many events like those, he and Eshtak fell back and trailed the horde. Many others did as well, but their numbers were dwindling. Most had lost hope that their loved ones still remained inside those pale, black-veined bodies and turned back.

From that initial turn, the horde's numbers began to grow, picking up several more here and there as they migrated east. Savric's concern grew with the group's numbers and exploded into an all-out panic about an hour ago when his horde merged with another significantly sized horde, nearly doubling their size.

A scream shattered the night a hundred yards south of where Savric stood, giving rise to the hairs on his arms and his nape. Eshtak huddled closer. He took Eshtak's hand and led them toward the commotion.

Up ahead, a body lay on the ground, gutted and sliced beyond recognition. A young girl knelt next to it.

Savric let go of Eshtak's hand and bent down next to the little girl. "My name is Savric. Did you know this young man?"

"He's my stepbrother, Jonas." The little girl trembled but didn't cry. "He tried to grab my stepmother's arm and take her back home, but she became violent and killed him." She rose to her feet and pulled her brown cloak back over her shoulders.

Savric eyed her but didn't try to give her comfort. He didn't want to scare her away. "I know it might be difficult to understand, but your mother is not in control of herself. None of the infected people are. Try not to blame your mother or your stepbrother for what happened."

The girl nodded. "I do understand. Something evil controls them. I warned Jonas, but he just wanted to go home."

Eshtak hugged the girl. "Eshtak sorry."

The girl wrapped her arms around him and held him tight. "Thank you. My name's Pear. Well, it's not actually Pear, but that's what everyone calls me because my real name is Pearllina. Plus, I love pears."

"Eshtak loves pears!"

Savric smiled. Eshtak had a way of quickly bonding with people and comforting them. He'd relied on Eshtak's companionship several times already and feared he would've been lost without it.

Ƶäṭūr's little helper.

Savric rose. His knees cracked like whips, and pain radiated down his legs and into his shins. How much farther could he go before his old bones finally gave up? Sustenance and rest would do him some good. It'd do them all some good. Some distance from Jonas's dismembered body would do Pear well, too. He'd find a way to bury the kid later.

"Eshtak. Pear. How about the two of you come with me?" Savric swept his arm back toward the outcropping they'd come down from. "We can make a small fire and get some food in our stomachs."

Eshtak broke from Pear's embrace and danced in a circle. "Eshtak hungry!"

Eshtak's love of food rivaled his own. He'd never thought he'd find another like himself, let alone two.

"We ran out of food yesterday," said Pear. "That's why my brother tried to take my mother away."

Savric smiled even though his heart ached for the girl. "You need not worry about that, my dear Pear. We have some food to spare. Perhaps not pears though."

"It's okay. I'm not picky. I can eat anything." Her yellow eyes spoke of wisdom far beyond her years, yet they also contained a rare innocence.

"Hmm." Savric pulled on his beard. "Even pickled socks?"

Eshtak's face turned a shade of green, or at least Savric imagined it did. He stuck his tongue out and wiped it with his fingers. "Yuck! Yuck! Yuck! Eshtak not eat pickled socks!"

Pear giggled. "I think I could eat pickled socks as long as the socks were clean. Dirty pickled socks are definitely out."

Eshtak gagged and dry heaved. "Eshtak not hungry."

Savric and Pear both laughed as they made their way over to the outcropping. For a moment, everything seemed almost normal. He took a deep breath and exhaled the day's trouble with it. With Eshtak and Pear's help, he cleared a six-foot circle of ground where they could have a small fire and then pushed up his sleeves.

But then the night sky lit with mezhik.

† † †

A green ball of fire formed over Zerenity's open palm. It crackled and popped, and its undulating light pushed back both the shadows and the group of men who were rounding up some of her fellow servants. The Dark One would not stand for it, so neither would she.

She targeted one of the men. A scroungy fellow with hate in his eyes. He held up a hand toward her but swung a lasso in his other. She snarled and hurled the fireball. It hit him square in the chest and engulfed him in flames before he had a chance to react. He screamed with agony as the fire melted his skin and burrowed into the center of his chest. She readied another fireball and hurled it at another man before the first man had hit the ground.

Two more. Then another. Each death sent chills racing through her. Nothing would stop her until they all burned.

Even as she continued killing them, she reached into the darkness with her mind and called for him. The Ancient One. *"Are you pleased with my work, my dark master?"*

Pleasure like nothing she'd ever felt before filled her mind and sent tremors through her body. She panted as she dispatched three more of the non-servants. Three of the two dozen remained, and they fled. She gave chase, desperate to finish her task and please her god.

"I will not fail you!"

† † †

The distance between Savric and the flashes of green fire had been too great for his tired, old eyes to recognize the source of the fireballs, but Eshtak confirmed his suspicion and fear.

"Pretty lady shoots fire!" exclaimed Eshtak. He hopped from foot to foot and pulled on his cheeks. "No, no, no!"

"My Reni..." Savric's spirit sank into despair as he lamented over what she'd done.

He would've gone to face her and keep her from killing others, but he knew the fight would be to the death and he couldn't face that truth in his current state. In fact, he didn't think he could face that truth in any state. How could he ever raise a hand against the love of his life, especially knowing she had no control over her actions?

Dear Ʒäţūr, what will I do if I must face her in war?

Would he be able to subdue her without killing her? Would she give him the chance, or go for the kill without pity? He knew the answer and refused to contemplate it.

And Qotan…

Have we lost the war before it has even begun?

"Mr. Savric?" Pear tugged on his robe sleeve. "Will you protect me from her and those like her?"

A hard, sick, twisted clarity washed over Savric. No matter how difficult the task, he served the will of Ʒäţūr. If that included facing the only woman he'd ever loved on the battlefield, he would do what must be done. People like Pear depended on him to be their defender.

Savric peered down at Pear. "As long as I have breath in my lungs, I will do everything in my power to protect you from all harm."

She smiled and took his hand. "Then I'm sticking with you."

Eshtak grabbed his other hand. "Eshtak too."

"Good." He took their hands and joined them together. "Now that we have settled that, I must speak to the people and encourage them to go back home."

Savric cleared his throat and held out his right hand, palm up. "*Əllíţ ʊb.*" An orb of yellow light formed above Savric's palm. With a simple gesture he pushed it into the air where it floated over him, Eshtak, and Pear, creating a dim circle of light that extended several meters around them.

He cleared his throat once more and then spoke as loud as he could. "Citizens of the Ancient Realm. Those of you who have ears to hear, gather around and listen to the words I speak and ponder them thoroughly." Dozens of people came out of the night and gathered around the outcropping.

Savric waited a few minutes and then continued, "As I am certain you have noticed, the people you love and care for will not be swayed into going back home. Hinder them, and they will take your life. It might not seem like it right now, but the best thing for you all to do is return home."

"We must know what's happening to them," said one woman. "Can't go home without knowing."

"I'm scared," said a young man. "Too afraid to stay but too afraid to go home. Home has nothing left for me."

"Me neither," said several others.

"We've nowhere else to go," said an older woman.

Savric held up a hand and waited for the chatter to die down. "I can only offer advice. If you refuse to go back home, then at least stay back from the horde of infected. Give them space and do not hinder them from reaching their destination."

"We can do that," several of them agreed. Others nodded their consent. No one spoke against his advice.

"Then we are of one accord. Thank you." Savric closed his palm and the orb of light fizzled out.

His stomach rumbled and hunger panged his side, but his thoughts remained on Zerenity.

There must be another way.

† † †

Calen had stumbled through the camp for a good hour, fatigued but desperate to find his aunt, when the fight broke out between several dozen men and an older woman deeper in the camp. That fight hadn't lasted long. The woman dispatched all of the men with green fireballs. He'd never seen anything like it, and it'd scared the wits from his mind.

But then he caught sight of a man in flowing robes standing atop an outcropping. A yellow orb of light floated over his head. The man stood with his back to Calen and held a walking staff in his left hand. At first, he'd thought for sure that it was Master Savric, but then he noticed the silhouettes of two children at the man's side.

Master Savric has no children.

Then the light had gone out.

Calen's heart sank, and his legs gave up the fight to go on. He fell face-first in the dead grass. The dry blades bit into his flesh, but he no longer cared. Aunt Tahmara would never be found.

I'm alone in this world.

Tears formed in his eyes as the pain of existence took hold of him. Why had he bothered coming so far? A hated, unwanted child, he had no reason to continue on. His father had always been right. Everything wrong in his life stemmed from him and his failures. He'd killed his mother, drove his father to jail, and his aunt into madness.

And I drove Master Savric away as well.

He figured he'd just lay there until death came to take him. It wouldn't be long. Death always found its target. He rolled over and stared up at the night sky. Once upon a time, he could see the vast sea of stars and it'd filled him with wonder, but the only thing he saw now was a blurred mess. He never wanted to wear spectacles, but he would've given anything in that moment to have seen the stars one last time.

He closed his eyes, and that's when he heard it. The familiar, unmistakable sound of Master Savric's chuckle. He'd know it anywhere. His heart raced in his chest and pushed the fatigue from his aching muscles.

Calen sat up and then stood. He called out to Master Savric, but his voice caught in his throat and failed to travel past his lips. With abandon, he bolted across the dry grass, dodging the infected and stumbling several times as he headed toward the outcropping where he'd seen Master Savric standing.

Wheezing and out of breath, Calen reached the top of the outcropping and fell to his knees before Master Savric. "Master. Savric," he managed between breaths.

Sparks of happiness lit Master Savric's eyes and his arms spread wide. "My dear boy!"

Savric leaned forward and embraced him. Nothing in the entire universe could've filled Calen with more joy than those three words and Savric's firm embrace. Fear fled from his mind, and the pain of loneliness withdrew from his heart. Three words filled his head and repeated incessantly.

I am home.

CHAPTER TWENTY-SIX

After spending several weeks at sea and out on the ocean, the sights of Trivers Lake and Vallah Harbor were much welcomed when they came into view. Morcinda jetted south, up the final leg of the Hotah River, and coasted into the harbor. Under normal circumstances, she would've felt a sense of relief pulling up to the pier and into her assigned dock position, but this day would be anything but normal.

She dropped anchor, exited her vessel, and moored it to the wooden piling that rose from the pier. Several men and women worked on various boats and ships along the pier, scrubbing or repairing various items. Every last man stopped what they were doing and watched her every move as she strode down the wooden-planked pier.

She'd grown used to the attention her blue hair and pale skin attracted, but she still didn't understand what they found so fascinating about her. She drew her hood over the top of her head and stuffed her hair into it. All but one of the men got the hint and went about their business, but that last one dogged her with greedy eyes.

There's always one rotten cabbage in the garden.

The lanky man, dressed in stained trousers and filthy rags that looked to have been neglected for years, stepped off his boat and blocked Morcinda's path just before she walked past. His bloodshot eyes were of different colors, one brown and the other yellow. She'd only seen mismatched eyes like his once before, but they'd belonged to a scroungy mutt.

Perhaps they're one and the same.

She doubted it though. Shifters were rare, plus the mutt had taken his last breath a dozen years back. She'd held him close and cried over him when it'd happened. She hadn't had a companion of any sort since.

The man held a bottle of ale in one hand and a maimed cigar in the other, his arms spread wide. "No need to go farther, lass. I've got all ya need right here." He smiled with parted lips, exposing a mouth with few enough teeth to be counted on a single hand, and his remaining teeth looked to be on the verge of vacating his dirty mouth as well.

Morcinda pushed his arm aside as she walked past, but it only emboldened the man. He grabbed the back of her cloak and yanked hard. She let the cloak slide off her arms, and then she spun into action. She whipped around to face the man, drawing her ivory-handled dagger from its sheath in the process. She held it with the blade facing down, ready to slash his throat if he breathed wrong.

"Feisty one, ain't ya?" His breath reeked of stale ale and rotted fish. "Reminds me of me ex-wife."

Morcinda's lip curled. "I'm certain she's your ex for good reason."

He lifted the right side of his shirt. A bloody bandage wrapped his middle. "Evil, black-eyed wench took a blade to me gut fer no reason. Slit 'er throat and dumped 'er in the lake."

"Walk away, or you'll find yourself joining her."

He lifted her cloak to his face and took a long whiff of it. His eyes turned wild. "Wife ne'er smelled so good."

The man whipped her cloak at her and managed to hook it around her wrist. The move surprised them both. She hadn't anticipated a fight. He yanked the cloak hard and spun her around backward, and then he tangled his arms around hers.

She kicked backward as hard as she could and connected with the man's groin, but he only grunted.

His hot breath crawled on her skin and his cigar scraped against her cheek with every word. "Me likes it rough, lass."

With a single thought, several tentacles of water rose out of the lake and wrapped around the man's legs and throat. Another tentacle fought its way into the man's mouth and snaked down his throat. He released her and reached for his throat, but two more tentacles rose up and restrained his arms as well.

Morcinda turned and faced the man. "Men like you never learn."

The man tried to speak but only spewed water.

Morcinda sheathed her dagger and retrieved her cloak off the pier. It'd need a thorough scrubbing after being touched by his filthy hands, but she didn't have the time to do so right then. She slid her arms back into its sleeves as she pulled it onto her shoulders.

"I warned you what would happen if you didn't walk away." She lifted the hood back over the top of her head and situated her hair. "Take him to be with his wife."

The man's eyes bulged from their sockets, and his mouth opened in a scream, but he only managed a gurgle. The water tentacles pulled the man off the pier and dragged him down into the depths of the lake where he'd never lay a finger on another woman again.

Morcinda looked around. Several people had stopped working to watch the spectacle, but none had made a move to help her. None ever did. They quickly moved on when her cold gaze met theirs.

Morcinda made her way across the pier and over to the massive, milky-white city gates. Each of the four ironwood gates stood twenty-five feet wide, thirty feet tall, four feet thick, and were reinforced with compounded steel. However, all four of them stood closed. Never had she seen the two gatehouses closed before. King Zaridus had established an open-gate policy the day he'd become king.

He must know of the threat already.

A small gate, just wide enough for a single person to squeeze through, stood open to the far left of the gatehouses. A dozen soldiers dressed in black boots, shirts, and helmets, white trousers, and teal leather armor bearing the king's coat of arms flanked the gate. Morcinda approached the gate, and the soldiers moved to block her path.

"Halt," said one of the soldiers. Morcinda obliged. "State your business in Vallah."

"I've come to see King Zaridus," she said.

"Then you've wasted your time," barked the soldier. "The king will not grant an audience with anyone. Go back home."

"I'm afraid you don't understand." Morcinda pulled back her hood. "He'll most certainly want to see me."

As with most of the king's soldiers, the young man knew of her and of her reputation. His wide eyes proved it. He turned and addressed his fellow soldiers, his voice a bit shaky. "Two of you fall out and escort this woman to the palace at once."

"Yes sir," said the two closest to the open gate. They turned and went through the gate.

The other soldiers moved out of Morcinda's way, and she entered the lower city. More soldiers roamed the city roads than she'd ever seen. Several of them were rounding up people and taking them to the underground prison.

"What's happening?" asked Morcinda.

"King's orders," said one of the soldiers escorting her. "Anyone who has been infected must be rounded up and put into the prison."

Such an order surprised her. Perhaps King Zaridus had grown wiser, but she doubted it. More likely, he'd become paranoid of contracting whatever illness or disease those with white skin and black eyes had. Either way, it served him well.

By the time they arrived at the fifth level of the city, where the King's Palace stood, the sun had begun to dip in the east. No matter how many times she stood in front of the palace, its beauty and majesty overwhelmed her.

Massive, fifty-foot-tall marble columns held up the front entrance of the King's Palace. Their white color, swirled with blues and grays, complemented the perfectly cut, four-foot-square granite tiles that created the walkway and the slabs of grey and tan flagstone that paved the road. From the walkway rose forty marble steps that led up to the palace entrance.

Morcinda thanked the two soldiers for escorting her and then made her way into the palace. She'd been there enough times over the centuries to have the layout memorized. The turquoise flags that bore the king's coat of arms—a black lion's head on a shield and crossed swords—hung throughout the palace.

She'd known many kings in her time, but none as kind yet pompous as King Zaridus. He had a way of connecting with his people like no other king she knew, but his policies on war and other such things like mezhik and prophecy were pathetic at best. Peace throughout the Ancient Realm for the last dozen decades had made the last few kings soft.

He will toughen up when he hears what I've got to say.

A dozen soldiers stood outside the doors to the Royal Court, pikes held tight in their left hands. Morcinda lowered her hood and needed no introduction.

"Lady Morcinda." Captain Bart greeted her with a curt nod. "The king isn't expecting you, is he?"

"No, but he will certainly want to hear what I have to tell him."

"He has retired to the Royal Bedchamber for an afternoon nap. Would you like me to escort you to his receiving room while you wait?"

Morcinda sighed. "What I have to say cannot wait. Is Prince Rictar or Princess Zelanora available for me to speak with?"

"Certainly. Prince Rictar is practicing archery on the rooftop."

"Then we shall start there."

† † †

Morcinda stood at a distance, admiring Prince Rictar's form as he nocked an arrow and drew back his bow string. The string thumped and the arrow whooshed through the air when he loosed it.

Sumph!

The arrow sank deep into the center of the wooden target.

Morcinda clapped her hands lightly. "A perfect shot, if I've ever seen one."

Prince Rictar turned quickly, another arrow nocked and ready and the string drawn back. The scowl he wore softened as recognition filled his eyes. He eased the tension on the string and lowered the bow.

"Lady Morcinda, to what do I owe this pleasure?" He shoved the arrow back into the quiver slung over his left shoulder.

She'd put up with the title of "Lady" from the palace guard and staff but never from the royal family. "Please, call me Morcinda. As I've told you and your father, I'm no lady."

Prince Rictar's blue-eyed gaze ogled her as he approached. "You oft say such things, but I know a lady when I see one."

His plain, white tunic, cinched at the waist with a silver belt, clung to him, enhancing his muscular features. Silver sandals hugged his feet. Their straps climbed up his chiseled calves and wrapped his muscular legs.

He'd always had a thing for her, even from a young age, and had continued to hold out hope that she'd eventually come around to appreciate the things he might offer her. But she never would. No man would ever hold her interest. No one would.

"I'm certain you're aware of the infection that has afflicted many of your kind?"

"Yes, of course. My father, the king, has assured me that everything is under control. He's taken certain measures to round them all up so that the disease doesn't spread further."

"Yes, I noticed that happening as I made my way up to the palace. However, such measures will only go so far." She folded her arms. "What else has he done?"

"We've tripled the number of royal guards in the palace. I assure you, we are quite safe from this infection." He smiled smugly.

Why are most humans so thoughtless and unaware?

"May I speak freely with you?" she asked.

"Yes, of course. I'd expect no less from you."

Morcinda searched for the right words that would convey her sentiment but not upset Prince Rictar. Such situations were often far more delicate than one might suspect.

She touched his arm, a gesture of kindness. "Your father is a kind and just ruler, but he doesn't always see things the way they truly are."

Prince Rictar stared at her hand on his arm. "How do you mean?"

She strolled away as she spoke. "Yes, there is a threat right here in Vallah, but its reaches far exceed the Three Kingdoms. The infected are spread all across the Ancient Realm, but they've begun to gather." She returned to face him. "All indications suggest they are converging in The Plains, some distance south of Elatos."

He rubbed his neck. She didn't know if he had an itch or if it was a nervous tick, but he'd done it several times. "And why do you think they've begun to gather?"

She could think of no better way to express her thoughts on the situation than to be candid with him. "War is coming, my prince. There is no mistaking it."

He shook his head and frowned. "I don't understand. What do these infected people have to do with war?"

"If prophecy holds true, a dark force controls them. How well do you know your history?"

He scowled as though offended she even asked the question, but he still answered her. "Well enough."

Even though they stood out in the open on the rooftop of the palace, she still felt a bit claustrophobic standing too close to him. She strode away again. "Then you know of the Great War and the mighty dragon named Cinolth?"

He chuckled. "Tales to scare young children, my father always said. I'd tend to agree."

She turned and glared daggers at him. "I assure you that those tales are as real as you and I." Her words came out with more anger than she'd hoped. She took a deep breath and calmed herself before continuing. "When *Ūrdär Dhef ʕäfn Dhä* defeated Cinolth and Magus, Cinolth cursed the world and swore he'd return one day to destroy the human race. When Cinolth died, his scales broke apart and spread throughout the Ancient Realm. Those scales are the cause of the current infection."

Prince Rictar laughed. "You never struck me as a madwoman, Lady Morcinda, but I stand corrected. You are as mad as the old wizard who came to us many weeks ago thinking he'd come with his brother. Utter lunacy."

Morcinda fought the urge to tear into Prince Rictar. She rarely stood by and took insults, but she needed to gain his confidence. Otherwise, there'd be no hope for the Three Kingdoms.

She opened her pack and withdrew the dragon scale she'd taken from the dryte named Rayah. She held it up so he could see it. "Here's your proof that what I'm saying is true." She offered it to him.

Prince Rictar took the black dragon scale and examined it for several minutes. "I've never seen anything like this." He looked up at her, his eyes full of wonder. "What is it?"

"That is one of those dragon scales I mentioned. As you can see, it is no fairy tale."

"But... what you're saying is impossible." He scratched his neck. "Curses don't exist and neither do dragons."

Trouble and confusion swirled in his eyes. She touched his arm to ground him. "Don't be like your father. See the truth for what it is. You're holding it, for ʕäʈūr's sake."

Prince Rictar moved over to a stone bench and sat down. He held the dragon scale in his hands and stared at it. "If what you say is true..."

She finished his thought, "Cinolth has risen from the dead and we're all in grave danger."

Princess Zelanora appeared at the top of the stairs that led down into the palace. Dark-brown bangs hung just above her thin eyebrows, framing the top of her heart-shaped face. One small braid with teal ribbon woven into it hugged the right side of her face, and the rest of her hair hung loose behind her back. The teal ribbon in her hair matched the colorful accents of her white, flowing dress and the sash around her waist.

"Morcinda!" Her face beamed as she rushed over and threw her arms around Morcinda.

Morcinda patted Princess Zelanora's back lightly. "It's good to see you, my princess."

Princess Zelanora stood back and inspected her. "You haven't aged a day. In fact, I think you might look younger than you did a few years back."

Heat rose in Morcinda's cheeks. "You're too kind. I'd say the same of you, but you've become quite the beautiful woman."

Princess Zelanora curtsied. "Thanks!" Her forehead wrinkled and her lips puckered. "Why are you here? I'm sure it's not a social call."

"War is coming," said Prince Rictar, his eyes still glued to the dragon scale in his hands.

"You're jok—" Princess Zelanora's face turned ghostly-white. She settled on the bench next to her brother, removed the glove on her right hand, and reached for the dragon scale. "Let me see that." Prince Rictar relinquished his hold on it.

Princess Zelanora's eyes rolled into the back of her head, leaving nothing visible but the whites of her eyes. After several moments, she blinked rapidly several times and then her eyes rolled forward once more. "I know what this is."

Morcinda and Prince Rictar said, "You do?"

"Yes..." Princess Zelanora rubbed the dragon scale with her fingers. "It's a dragon scale."

Prince Rictar frowned at his sister. "And how would you know that?"

"Because it told me so," she said.

Is it possible?

Morcinda eyed the young girl intently. A feeling in her gut told her that Princess Zelanora shared more than just looks with Queen Lanara, her late mother.

"That makes no sense," said Prince Rictar. "Inanimate objects don't speak."

Morcinda knelt in front of Princess Zelanora. "Do things often talk to you?"

Princess Zelanora glanced at Prince Rictar and then nodded. "For some time now."

"Since your sixteenth name day?" asked Morcinda. She already knew the answer.

Princess Zelanora nodded, and her gaze fell to her lap. She still wore a long, white glove on her left hand that rose to her elbow.

"May I see your left wrist?" asked Morcinda.

Fear flashed in her eyes, and her cheeks burst with hues of red. "I... it's not appropriate for a princess to remove her gloves. I shouldn't have removed the first one."

Prince Rictar snatched the dragon scale from Princess Zelanora's hand. "Don't be a foolish girl. Just do what she asks."

Tears swelled in Princess Zelanora's eyes. "If I do so, you and father will hate me forever."

Morcinda took Princess Zelanora's left hand in hers. "People only hate what they don't understand, but minds can be changed."

"I... I don't know." A tear ran down Princess Zelanora's cheek. "There will be no going back."

Morcinda looked at Princess Zelanora's gloved hand and then into her lavender eyes. She couldn't look more like Lanara without being her. "There will be no need to go back. May I remove it?"

Princess Zelanora nodded.

Morcinda slid the glove off the girl's hand. Her long, slender fingers trembled but not from the cool air.

"Turn your hand over," said Morcinda.

Prince Rictar slid from the bench and knelt next to Morcinda. He smiled at Princess Zelanora. "No matter what, I could never hate you."

She nodded and turned her hand over, exposing the inside of her wrist and the grayish mark upon it.

Prince Rictar gasped and fell back on his buttocks, dropping the dragon scale in the process. "I know what that is. I've seen it before. You're... you're... a sorceress."

"Indeed, she is." Morcinda held Princess Zelanora's hand and smiled. "As was your mother."

† † †

Morcinda sat on the plush couch in the receiving room outside King Zaridus's bedchamber, her mind focused not on how the king would react to the news of war but of his daughter's abilities. Prince Rictar paced back and forth in an apparent attempt to wear down one length of the teal-and-black rug he trampled. Princess Zelanora stood in the far corner, as close to the shadows as possible, and chewed on her fingernails. She spat them into the fire.

From the moment she'd arrived in Vallah Harbor that morning, events had twisted in ways Morcinda never would've contemplated. Growing up on the seas, she'd accustomed herself to handle unforeseen situations and circumstances. In fact, she'd thrived on them and relished the exhilaration of living in the moment without knowing what might happen or come next. Those who sailed with her had called her The Fearless One, and she'd lived up to her reputation, but something about the current situation set her on edge. Fear crept into the corners of her mind and spun webs of uncertainty.

How will Zaridus react?

She couldn't be sure, but Zelanora was his daughter, and he seemed to care deeply for her. However, after the strange circumstances and events surrounding Queen Lanara's death, she had to wonder if love alone would keep her safe.

Her left hand rested on her dagger's ivory handle. She had no plans of using it, especially against King Zaridus, but she'd do everything in her power to keep Princess Zelanora safe. It was the least she could do for Lanara after failing to save her so many years ago.

One day I will get to the truth of your death, Lanara.

The bedchamber doors creaked as they swung outward. Two handmaids backed away from the doorway, continually bowing to the man who stood just inside the two doors.

King Zaridus.

Princess Zelanora stuck to the shadows but ceased ravishing her fingernails. She slipped her gloves back on. Prince Rictar continued to pace, seemingly unaware of his father's presence.

Like Prince Rictar, King Zaridus wore a tunic as well, but his was teal instead of white. A similar silver belt cinched the tunic at his waist, and silver sandals hugged his feet. A turquoise-dyed fur cape rested on his broad shoulders, and turquoise, silver, and black necklaces hung from his thick neck. The man was well muscled but held a bit of extra weight around his waist and in his face. Silver locks, full of curls, draped his shoulders. A silver crown with many peaks sat atop his head, a bit off-kilter, and held his hair away from his clean-shaven face. Turquoise jewels lined the crown, each centered beneath a corresponding peak.

He held a silver scepter in his beefy left hand but didn't lean upon it for support as he walked into the receiving room. His deep-set, icy-blue gaze locked onto Morcinda, and a smile curled his lips.

"*Lady* Morcinda." His tone chilled her.

She rose to greet him as he crossed the room. He moved his scepter to his right hand and proffered his left. She took it and kissed the silver insignia ring on his middle finger. Her lips touched more skin than ring, and the lavender scent of his flesh appealed to her senses.

She straightened and looked him in the eye. "My king, it's been far too long."

"I'm certain you've not traveled all this way to exchange pleasantries." King Zaridus gestured toward the long couch with his hand. "Have a seat."

Morcinda took a seat on the left end of the couch, and King Zaridus took up residence on the far right. Four abled bodies could sit comfortably in the space between them.

King Zaridus scanned the room briefly, his eyes never taking an extra moment on any particular sight, including Princess Zelanora hiding in the corner. "I see you've riled up my children already. Your news must be of some grave importance. Tell it to me now so that I might be riled up as well."

Morcinda knew King Zaridus had little patience for circling a bush, so she dove right into the heart of the issue at hand. "Despite what you've heard and might believe to be true, an infection isn't what ails so many people in the Ancient Realm."

"I've not only heard it but have seen it first-hand." Condescension dripped from his words. "Are you implying that my eyes cannot be trusted? Are there not four of us in this room?"

Prince Rictar stopped pacing and knelt before his father. "Father, I urge you to listen to what Lady Morcinda has to say before making any sort of judgments."

King Zaridus slammed his scepter into the floor, but the rug muffled the sound. "Sit down and keep silent unless you've been addressed." Prince Rictar nodded and sat down on the couch next to King Zaridus.

"Your royal highness, I have direct knowledge that those who are infected are actually under the control of a..." She found it difficult to say the word "dragon" in his presence and looked for a better way to convey the same thing without setting him off. She thought she'd found the right description. "Dark presence."

"By the gods, what does that even mean? A dark presence," he scoffed. "Absurdity."

"She means they're controlled by a dragon." Princess Zelanora stepped out of the corner and came around the front of the couch.

King Zaridus's face blossomed in shades of red. He shot to his feet and shook his fist at Morcinda. "How dare you come into my palace spewing such blasphemy and corrupting the minds of my precious children!" Spittle peppered the air and drool ran from the corner of his mouth.

Morcinda withdrew the dragon scale from her pack and held it up. "Here's your proof, *my king*."

King Zaridus glared daggers at her. "You brought a black seashell as proof of the existence of a dragon? You're as mad as Lanara was!"

"Shut up, sit down, and listen!" screamed Princess Zelanora.

King Zaridus's scepter whipped around with lightning speed, and the crack of impact boomed like thunder in the large room. Morcinda leapt off the couch to catch Princess Zelanora's limp body, but she didn't fall. In fact, she still stood tall.

What just happened?

She stepped back and assessed the scene.

King Zaridus stood petrified, his mouth agape. Half a scepter remained in his clutched hand. The other half lay on the floor in pieces, and the crystal stone from its bulbous top shattered into dust.

An aura of light surrounded Princess Zelanora and slowly faded. She gasped for air as the last of it disappeared.

Prince Rictar sat on the couch, laughing without restraint. Tears streamed down his cheeks. "The look on your face," he exclaimed and laughed harder.

Princess Zelanora removed her gloves and threw them in King Zaridus's face. She held up her left arm and pointed to the mark on the inside of her wrist. "Look at this, Father! Do you see the mark? I am a sorceress, and there's nothing you can do to change it."

King Zaridus stumbled and collapsed back onto the couch, narrowly avoiding missing its edge. He grabbed at the left side of his chest and cried out, "Why have you afflicted me so, Ɂäṭūr?"

"Afflicted *you*? Listen to yourself." Morcinda fumed as her fingers tickled the handle of her dagger. One swift move and she could end him, but she wouldn't dare. She fought to preserve his rule, not end it. "You should be so lucky to have such a daughter." Venom laced her words.

Princess Zelanora knelt next to her father and touched his hand, but he snatched it away from her. "Can we set our differences aside for now and do what's right for the kingdom? Sometimes, I can see and hear things when I touch objects. I can assure you that 'seashell' as you call it spoke to me. As Morcinda said, it is truly a dragon scale. Never have I felt such unbridled evil and hatred than when I touched it. War is coming, whether you believe it or not." She stood, turned to Price Rictar, and kicked him square in the shin.

He yelped and rubbed it with the back of his other leg. "What was that for?"

"This isn't a game, Rictar. Get off your rump and raise the alarm. We must warn Borza and Elatos."

"Only Father has the authority to do such a thing."

King Zaridus stood and cinched his belt tighter. Some color had returned to his cheeks, but he still looked pale. "Do what your sister has requested of you." He walked back into his bedchamber and grabbed both doors.

"But she has no—"

"On my authority," thundered King Zaridus. He slammed the doors shut behind himself.

Prince Rictar stood, bade Morcinda farewell with a curt nod, and stormed out of the receiving room.

Princess Zelanora slumped on the couch next to Morcinda. "Now what will happen?"

Morcinda leaned back and put her arm around Princess Zelanora. "We will prepare for war."

She closed her eyes and let her mind carry her far into the past. To Vallah and the Great War.

Ɂäṭūr, don't let the past repeat itself.

CHAPTER TWENTY-SEVEN

Seven days had passed since Aria had backhanded him, but Alderan still felt the sting. Not physically, of course, but physical wounds always healed faster than the ones aimed at the heart. Somehow, the two of them had become so misaligned. The idea of such an occurrence would've been laughable less than a year ago. However, they'd exchanged less than a dozen words since she struck him, and not only because she worked incessantly on the large wall that had been erected north of Galondu Castle. The two of them simply had nothing to say to each other that hadn't already been said.

Alderan touched his cheek. *I still love you, sister.*

Despite living under the same roof again, a fissure the size of the universe lay between them. A divide seemingly impossible to cross. Now, Alderan lay on a bed inside a room deep within the cold castle, his left hand clinging to his mother's brass ring while his heart mourned the loss of his dead sister.

Ƨätür, he prayed, *to what end does this pain serve? I'm struggling to find a single answer. Point me in the right direction. Help me understand Your purpose in all of this. Show me how to mend my rended soul.*

A knock sounded at the door. Alderan shoved the necklace and ring back inside his shirt and wiped his eyes and cheeks with his shirtsleeve. He cleared his throat and swallowed down the phlegm it'd produced.

"Come in." His voice came out strained and stringy. Whoever stood on the other side of the door would know his secret.

The door creaked as it swung into the room. Wizard Wrik stood in the doorway with a candle holder in his left hand. The candle's flame multiplied and danced in his spectacles. "Aria and Cinolth have just about completed this side of the gateway. They will be leaving within the hour to go and build the other side. I thought you might want to know."

"Thank you." Alderan rose from the bed. His head ached and his eyes burned with fever, both issues likely caused from an hour's worth of crying.

"Are you headed down there?"

Wrik shook his head. "Hadn't planned on it. Unless you'd like the company."

Without Rayah around, Alderan desperately needed a friend. He opened his mouth to accept, but his lips betrayed him. "Appreciate the offer, but it's not necessary."

Not necessary? What is wrong with you, you big oaf?

"Very well." Wrik dipped his head. "I bade you good night." Wrik turned and walked away, casting Alderan back into the darkness.

Alderan stopped and turned back toward his bedchamber twice on the way down to the castle gates but forced himself to continue forward. He must see Aria off even if they didn't exchange any words. She needed to see that he still cared about her.

I won't give up on you.

† † †

Aria walked along the northern face of the thirteen-hundred-foot-long, forty-foot-tall, and ten-foot-thick wall that stood on the northern side of Galondu Castle, outside the castle walls. A large orb of light lit the wall and her path as she made her way from one end of it to the other. She examined the wall for two things: that the web of spells she'd conjured adhered to the wall and that the wall's structural integrity held fast. Both remained true across the entire wall, and it pleased her.

She walked back over to where Pravus, Cinolth, Mutius, and Bardaric stood. "Everything is in order."

"Excellent." Excitement strained Pravus's voice even though he'd tried to mask it.

Aria's words hadn't been aimed at Pravus, but she refused to let it bother her. Nothing would on this day. She'd accomplished something far greater than anything Pravus could ever hope to achieve.

Pravus continued, "By the time you've finished the northern side of the gateway, the entire army will be armed and ready for battle."

"Two weeks from now, the Three Kingdoms will fall." Cinolth's gravelly voice shook the world's foundation. At least that's what it felt like to Aria.

"And then the Ancient Realm," finished Aria.

Her skin prickled with gooseflesh. Two weeks, and she'd be a proper queen. Recognized by the entire realm.

Centauria will be mine.

Pravus steepled his fingers. "As we discussed before, and, as I promised, Karraar will meet you outside of Elatos. For what purpose I'm still uncertain."

Karraar.

She'd already accomplished what she'd wanted him to do, but she'd find another purpose for him easily enough. "Good. One can never have enough protection."

A six-foot cube of iron bars with a narrow, iron door stood to Cinolth's left. Aria pointed at it. "Mutius. Bardaric. Climb into the cage. We leave at once."

"But I thought—" Bardaric started to say.

"You're not here to think," said Aria. "You're here to work. Now, either get in the cage or prepare yourself for death. It's your choice, but make it quickly."

Bardaric and Mutius climbed into the cage without further protest. Pravus secured the door and handed Aria the key.

"You're certain you don't want me to come with you?" asked Pravus.

She knew his concern. He didn't trust Cinolth. But she didn't trust him.

She reached up and stroked his cheek. "As you've said before, you cannot be in two places at once. There are far too many things that need your attention here."

"Yes, I know." He sighed, but then his eyes brightened. "An hour's delay will be of little consequence. Accompany me to our bedchamber before you leave."

They hadn't lain together in a week and she missed his touch, but it'd have to wait. She needed to be at full strength to conjure the other side of the gateway. An hour in his arms would delay them at least a day. Perhaps two.

She rose on her tippy toes, kissed him deep, and then pushed him away. "I'm sorry, but that sort of conquest must wait."

She stepped into Cinolth's open hand, and he lifted her onto his back. She situated herself at the base of Cinolth's neck and grabbed hold of one of his spikes. "Be ready, husband."

"Be careful, my queen."

She looked around. Alderan hadn't shown up to see her off, and it stung a little, but what had she expected? For the time being, she wouldn't dwell on it. More important matters needed her attention.

He'll come around.

She almost believed herself.

During their training sessions, Cinolth had shown her how to clear her mind and focus only on the task at hand. With two calming breaths, she took every thought within her mind and shoved them inside a small metal box. Then, she took that box and placed it on a shelf. No thoughts within that box could escape as long as she kept watch over it. That was always the trick, but she improved every time she placed them there.

Satisfied and focused, Aria mindspoke to Cinolth. *"Ready when you are."*

Cinolth snorted smoke, grabbed the iron cage with one of his hind feet, and took to the sky in a flurry of beating wings. The ground below quickly shrank away as they climbed high into the night sky. She didn't envy Bardaric and Mutius's means of travel, but she imagined it still surpassed her experience in the clutches of that nítfinzh several weeks back. Even so, the thought brought a smile to her lips.

† † †

Pravus strolled back toward the castle. Another week, and their army would be within striking distance of the Three Kingdoms. The thought salivated his mouth. Nearly thirty years of work would soon pay off. He afforded himself a small smile, but the true celebration would have to wait a few more weeks.

He turned the corner and walked through the castle gates. Alderan met him just inside, his eyes red and bloodshot.

The boy's presence disturbed him, but Pravus would never allow it to show. He smiled wide. "To what do I owe this pleasure?"

Alderan glared at him. "Don't flatter yourself. I came down to see Aria off."

"Ah." Pravus steepled his fingers. "Then I'm afraid you've arrived too late." He pushed past Alderan and traversed the wide corridor.

With each step, he pushed Alderan further from his mind. Nothing would spoil his mood. Credan approached with a fervent gait, his complexion ghostly white.

"My lord." Credan turned and fell in beside Pravus.

"If you're about to deliver unfavorable news to my ears, I suggest you leave and resolve it yourself." Pravus marched on, not even giving Credan a sideways glance. "I'm in high spirits right now, and I don't need the likes of you dragging me down into your pit of squalor."

"In most circumstances, I would. However, there are several matters that can only be resolved by your presence and with your fortitude."

Pravus stopped and eyed Credan. "My fortitude? I'm already finding this conversation bothersome."

"Yes, yes. I know." Beads of sweat dotted Credan's brow. His gaze fell to the floor. "Three of the lords have withdrawn their support for your campaign."

"What?" Pravus seethed and ground his teeth. Mezhik rushed into his clenched fists and crackled. "Which three?" he demanded.

Credan shrank back. "Lord Jagesh Rubano, Lord Elder Baarth, and Lord Uli Edersheimer."

Those bastards dare cross me?

Pravus paced in the corridor. He needed the support of all the lords or more of them might pull out as well. He took a deep breath and rescinded the mezhik from his fingertips.

"Call for them at once. If any of them refuse, send Reubane."

"My lord?" Somehow, Credan's face managed to turn a shade paler.

"We're headed to war." Pravus waved Credan on. "Just do as I say."

"Yes, but Reubane?" His voice cracked. "You know he cannot be controlled."

Pravus turned to Credan with fire in his eyes. "And that's *exactly* what I'd be counting on."

Credan swallowed hard. "Yes, my lord. Consider it done." He turned and scurried down the corridor.

Pravus roared and stomped his foot.

"Trouble in paradise?"

Wrik.

Pravus glared daggers at the big man as he lumbered toward him. "Where the gods did you come from?"

Wrik smiled and pointed at an open door a little way down the corridor. "Just through there. Is there anything I can do to help?"

"You've *helped* far too much already." Pravus stormed down the corridor and yelled over his shoulder, "And stay out of my way!"

Damn this night already.

† † †

Wrik stood outside the small room occupied by Gnaud and verified that none of the wards had been tripped or manipulated in any fashion. Satisfied that everything was still in order and undisturbed, he teleported into the room.

Gnaud sat in a grey, cushioned chair next to a blazing fire. A hefty book sat upon his lap, but his head lolled, and his chin rested on his chest. Spectacles hung from his pink ears but didn't touch his gaunt, furry face.

A dwarf in a giant's chair. Wrik chuckled to himself.

Crimson seeped through Gnaud's bandages again. Every five or six hours, Wrik healed Gnaud's wounds, but they continued to split open and fester. To worsen matters, the frequency at which it happened seemed to be increasing as well. Nardus couldn't get back quick enough.

If the army marched before Nardus returned, Gnaud would be on his own, and that would put Wrik in quite the conundrum. Seeing prophecy fulfilled on the battlefield would be an exhilarating experience, but did it compare to Nasduron and the knowledge it held? He didn't know. How could he?

An impossible choice.

Wrik knelt next to Gnaud's chair and roused Gnaud. "Time to change your bandages."

Gnaud sat up and grimaced. "Oh my. Far sorer this time."

Wrik removed the soiled bandages from around Gnaud's torso. As expected, the wounds had opened up again. "They look worse as well."

Not only did Gnaud's wounds open at a quicker pace, but they also required an ever-increasing amount of mezhik to close them back up. Soon, Wrik would have to find an additional source of mezhik to supplement his own.

"Still got the stick?" asked Wrik.

Gnaud held an inch-thick stick up for a moment and then stuck it between his teeth and bit down on it.

"Good." Wrik pulled mezhik from within himself and poured it into Gnaud's wounds.

Gnaud groaned, seized in the chair, and his eyes rolled back in his head. Foam frothed around the stick and collected in the fur around his mouth.

"I'm sorry it's so painful, but there's nothing I can do. It's the bacteria in the wound that causes the pain."

Wrik worked for a good twenty minutes and got two of the three wounds closed up without issue, but the last one—the deepest of the three—wouldn't cooperate. By the time he moved from one end of it to the other, it began pulling apart at the start again.

An hour later, Wrik managed to seal the final wound and keep it closed. But it'd cost him most of his energy.

The stick fell from Gnaud's mouth. His eyes crossed and his head bobbed on his shoulders. "Thank you," he whispered and then passed out.

Wrik sat back and lay on the floor, too spent to get up. Tomorrow, he'd return with help.

And I know just who to bring.

With Aria gone and ᴢäbräᴢär around his neck, what better things did Alderan have to do anyway?

CHAPTER TWENTY-EIGHT

Nardus strolled through the caves deep beneath the Valley of Dragons as images and memories flooded his mind. All of them events from a past he'd all but forgotten. In his mind, he stood at the edge of Summitto Valley and faced Cinolth. Twelve hundred years ago.

The thought of it being one of his memories fractured his mind further than the rune spell Peorvem had cast on him five days earlier. In that instant, he realized that he didn't stand on that hill as a man named Nardus Remison. When he'd sought out Cyrus Nithik, he'd truly sought out himself.

But is that life this one as well?

He struggled to wrap his mind around everything. Had his life as Cyrus been a past life? Had Ɂäʈūr returned him to Centauria as Nardus Remison? In a world of mezhik, he knew anything was possible.

But he remembered details of his childhood as Nardus. The authenticity of them couldn't be matched. Yet, if what Tharos had told him was the truth, Nardus Remison never had a childhood because he never existed.

Nardus massaged his temples. How could he ever reconcile the two?

How can I be two people?

So many things filled his head that he could not explain away. He recalled everything from the Great War to the creation of the chambers to the vow Ūrdär Dhef Ɂäfn Dhä took to protect the world. The vow *he* took. All of it he could learn to accept, save one thing: Vitara.

My anchor and first love.

He remembered the first day he met her. He swam in the lake as she and her friends walked by. Never had his heart pounded so hard. It pounded just thinking about it.

But now I know the truth.

Sorrow welled within him and drove him to his knees.

Vitara doesn't exist. She never did.

But they'd had three kids together. That part must be real. Shanara proved it.

Through Cyrus's memories he'd discovered that Vitara, the woman he desperately loved or was tricked into thinking he loved, had been a woman he'd loathed as Cyrus. A sworn enemy of his family.

Ilia.

The two of them never saw eye-to-eye and were at odds about almost every topic ever discussed. The only reason they'd worked together during the Great War was because of their mutual enemies: Cinolth and Magus. At the time, saving the world mattered more than a bitter family rivalry.

So, how had it all happened? How had he lived two lives without knowing it? Even worse, how could he ever heal the damage he'd caused as the man named Nardus? In a single, failed swoop, he'd managed to destroy everything he'd worked so hard to prevent as Cyrus.

Cyrus took Cinolth's heart and locked it away in a place no one would ever be able to retrieve it from. Yet Nardus found a way. Everything currently wrong in the world stemmed from his reckless actions.

Everything is my fault.

Then again, had Cyrus done everything necessary to destroy Cinolth long ago, the world wouldn't be in its current situation.

Everything truly is my fault.

His mind returned to Vitara or Ilia. He didn't know what to call her anymore. Knowing what had happened troubled him so much. Even as one of the greatest mages to ever have lived, he never knew such mezhik existed that could cause two people at such odds to believe they loved each other. To make matters worse, he still loved her.

How could I not?

He'd never love another woman the way he'd loved Vitara ever again. And the children. Everything he did was for them. His mind clicked and everything made sense.

Somehow, Pravus planned this long ago.

Nardus clenched his jaws and balled his hands. Mezhik crackled across his knuckles.

He'll pay with his life.

Nothing would stop Nardus from killing the bastard.

Nardus rose. Theyn stood next to him, still stuck in her cat form. As promised, she'd stayed at his side through every step of the process. He loved her more than any words could ever express, but never in the way he'd loved Vitara.

"It's time we go heal Gnaud and then crush the life from Pravus."

"Lead the way," she said in his mind. *"I go where you go. Forever."*

They snaked their way back through the maze of caves until they came back to the pool where Peorvem rested. The old dragon had retreated deep beneath the waters again.

Nardus cleared his throat. "Peorvem The Ancient, we seek your council one last time."

The blue waters stirred, shifted, and then Peorvem rose out of the depths. "One last time?" Water dripped from the hairs on his chin.

Nardus knelt before Peorvem. "Thank you for everything you've done for me. I now remember every last detail of my life as Cyrus Nithik. I'm ready to face the consequences of my actions."

Peorvem stepped out of the water and eyed Nardus until Nardus's skin squirmed beneath his clothes. "I fear you are not ready. Mezhik derk still flows within you. You must stay and heal."

Nardus rose. He had business to take care of and a score to settle. "I'm sorry, but we're leaving now. Too much time has been lost already."

"Why do you seek my council if you wish not to heed my words?"

"My friend is dying." He thrust his arms in the air. "I don't have time to argue about it."

Peorvem sighed and water spewed from his nostrils. "If you leave, you may never be whole again."

"I'm willing to take the risk."

"Nardus, wait," said Theyn in his mind. *"Are you sure you're okay?"*

"Stay out of it," Nardus growled.

He closed his eyes and called upon his mezhik, something he never thought he'd do. His entire body shuddered and tingled. *"Sarai,"* he whispered.

But then it happened. Long, sharp fingernails pierced his temples and dug deep into his mind. He fought to keep control even as his memories of Cyrus faded from his mind once again. Perfect darkness pulled him into the depths as the tingle of mezhik faded.

† † †

Nardus sat up straight and exhaled water from his lungs. He spat and coughed up more water for several minutes before his chest and throat ceased to convulse. His eyes burned with fire, and he couldn't see anything but a bluish blur. When he rubbed them, they burned even more.

"Hello?" His voice echoed back.

"I'm still here," said Theyn in his mind.

Nardus reached out but his hand only found water. "What happened? Where am I?"

A booming voice filled the cavern. "You've been resting in my waters."

Memories slowly trickled back into Nardus's mind.

Tharos. The Valley of Dragons. Peorvem.

Nardus blinked several times as the cavern with the blue lake came back into focus. He sat in the water, several feet from the shoreline. Peorvem stood in the water before him and Theyn watched from the water's edge.

"You've cast the spell then?"

Peorvem gazed beyond Nardus. His face conveyed traces of concern, or at least that's what Nardus thought he saw. To be truthful, he had no idea how to read a dragon's emotions.

"Do you remember meeting Cyrus?"

Nardus closed his eyes and searched his memories but came up blank. "No. Was he here?"

Peorvem sighed. "This is what I warned you about, son of Ɂäţūr. You weren't ready. You may wish to thank Ɂäţūr that you hadn't already left."

Nardus pulled himself to his feet. His head throbbed and his legs wobbled beneath him. He turned toward Theyn. "What is he talking about? I wasn't ready for what?"

"To leave," she said in his mind.

"Leave? Why would I have wanted to leave when we arrived here just a few hours ago?"

"No, Nardus. We've been here five days."

Nardus stumbled forward but caught himself before he face-planted in the shallow water. Had they really been there five days already?

"What have I missed?"

Theyn hung her head. *"Everything."*

Nardus rubbed the back of his head as he walked toward the shore. "Now what?"

Peorvem followed him out of the water. "We start again, and this time you will not try to leave until I say you're ready."

"And what if I don't remember our conversation and I don't listen again?"

"Trust me," said Peorvem. "You won't have a choice. Now, sit down and don't move."

Nardus sat down on the hard rock floor and swallowed hard as the tingle of mezhik crept up from the ground and into his bones. The blue lights of the cavern shifted in his vision and began to blur.

"I don't remember feeling like this before. What's happening? Is something wrong?"

Theyn's voice entered his mind. *"Relax, my love. I'm sure Peorvem knows what he's doing."*

Darkness cradled Nardus as the mezhik continued to flow into him. Memories of himself began disintegrating into dust. Every last detail crushed and swept away until he no longer remembered his own name.

He struggled to hang on to something tangible but only the darkness remained. Fear drove the two questions that lingered in his mind.

Who am I? What if I don't return?

CHAPTER TWENTY-NINE

The Ruins of Nasda rose in the distance, little more than broken columns and mounds of rubble. The once mighty city reached up with despair even as it succumbed to the unforgiving sands of the Profugus Desert. Rayah understood its plight all too well. Every passing moment drew her and Urza closer to death.

Will we succeed or succumb to the sands as well?

She definitely hoped for the former. She still had a life worth living.

To everyone's surprise, she, Rakzar, Urza, and Normak arrived at the Ruins of Nasda without incident. It'd been the most boring four-day journey she'd endured in quite some time, and she thanked Ƨäțūr for it. However, seeing what lay in front of them sobered her mood.

Normak looked around, his hand held over his eyes to block the sun. "Where do we start lookin'?"

Rakzar and Urza turned and looked at Rayah.

She frowned. "What?"

"Figured this was kinda your thing," said Urza. "Dirt and all that."

"Find the entrance Torbrek spoke of," said Rakzar.

She had to admit that their logic made sense, but that didn't mean she had to like it. The task of digging down into unfamiliar sand, especially in the middle of a desert, would be dangerous. No telling what kinds of creatures or traps she might dig up or come across.

She took a long drink of water from her waterskin and then pulled the strap over her head. She shoved it and her pack of supplies at Rakzar. "Don't lose these."

"Wouldn't dream of it." Rakzar took them and tossed them over his shoulder.

Rayah gathered herself, took a deep breath, and sank into the hot, desert sand. About a foot down, the sand cooled to a reasonable temperature. She didn't really understand how her gift worked, but she could see through dirt and sand as though it wasn't there at all. Not only that, but her wings worked without hindrance as well.

She beat her wings as she sank deeper and drilled into the deep sand. About eight feet underneath the surface, she began to encounter structures long buried. Surprisingly, more of the city remained intact than she would've expected, given the surface view.

Torbrek was adamant about the details of where they'd find the dungeon entrance, but she couldn't see indefinitely through the sand. She only had a radius of about ten feet to work with, so finding a specific building and doorway would take some time.

As she searched the twenty-square-mile area of the ruins, she encountered nothing that remained alive. It concerned her. So much so that she began seeing things watching her and following her through the ruins.

Rayah began to surface, but then something long and skinny caught her eye. She turned, and it moved. Slithered. Away from her. She flew straight toward it and pushed herself hard to catch it, but the thing was fast. She reached out to snatch its tail, but by then it was too late.

She careened straight into a solid surface. The force crumpled her and knocked the air from her lungs. Her head pulsed with pain.

How stupid can you be, Rayah?

She pulled back and looked at what she'd slammed into. A set of large stone doors. Her pulse raced when she noticed the crescent moon symbol etched into each door.

These must be the doors!

But what had led her to them? And where had it gone? Underneath each crescent moon were several two-inch, round holes. All but one of them bottomed out.

That thing must've gone through the hole.

She turned to surface but couldn't seem to get traction. She looked back over her shoulder and panicked. Somehow, the two doors had swung inward and started swallowing the entire desert. No matter how hard she beat her wings she couldn't make headway. Eventually, she gave up and let the tide pull her down into the darkness.

✝ ✝ ✝

Rakzar pointed to the east. "Something's happening over there."

Normak shot across the desert, leaving a trail of dust in his wake. Several moments later, he returned. "I think Rayah might've found those doors we be lookin' for, but I didn' see 'er anywhere."

Damn.

Normak sped away again. Rakzar and Urza dropped on all fours and loped across the sand. Normak awaited them just beyond the edge of a massive sinkhole. A dark, square hole sat at the bottom of the sinkhole. From their vantage, Rakzar couldn't tell what had created the hole, but he knew nature didn't create things perfectly square. He also didn't know if Rayah had fallen in or if she was someplace else. Unfortunately, only one way existed for him to find out.

"I'm going to investigate," said Rakzar.

"We all will," Urza replied.

"No," growled Rakzar. "We don't know where it goes or if Rayah's even down there. Wait here."

"Fine, but be careful," said Urza.

"What she said," said Normak.

Rakzar made it halfway down the steep slope before the sand shifted and started funneling into the hole. He dug his claws into the sand to brace himself, but it didn't stop his momentum. The pull of the sand reminded him of the ocean current and drove fear into his heart. No recourse existed, so he went with the flow and prayed that he'd be able to grab onto the edge of the opening when he reached it.

The sifting sand made little noise, far less than would've been required to cover Urza's yelp. He didn't look up the slope and couldn't have if he'd wanted to. Urza would suffer the same fate as him.

The edge came faster than he'd hoped. His claws scraped and vibrated against the stone opening as he slid across its surface but found nothing to anchor him. His stomach rose into his throat as he slid into the pit of darkness.

Rakzar fell. And fell. And fell.

Is there no bottom to this pit?

The answer jarred his legs, contorted his back, and pushed the air from his lungs. A mountain of sand broke his fall. He tumbled at least a dozen times before coming to a rest face-down in the sand.

Rakzar rolled onto his back and spat sand from his mouth. Two loud grunts, one right after the other, sounded. Urza and Normak must've found the bottom of the pit as well.

A dim shaft of light hung impossibly high over his head, about an inch square from where he lay.

Even if we find the damned crystal how will we get back out of here?

The shroud of darkness slowly lifted as Rakzar's eyes began to adjust to the dark space. Normak and Urza lay in the sand twenty paces away, both on their backs.

Rakzar trotted over to them. "Either of you seen the *dryte*?"

Normak rubbed his eyes. "Nah. Lucky ta see anythin' with all the sand in me eyes."

"What's wrong with using Rayah's name?" asked Urza. "You use it and she becomes your responsibility? Is that it?"

"Shut up, *beast*," growled Rakzar.

Normak chuckled.

"You too, *dwarf*. Keep it up, and none of you will have names by the end of this journey."

"Living up to your name, bad thing?"

Rakzar nearly jumped out of his leather armor as he spun around. "Moves like that'll get you killed, *dryte*."

Rayah giggled and spun around in the air. "Never thought the day would come, but I finally got the jump on you!" Urza raised her hand and Rayah high-fived it. "I was sure he'd spot me or smell me long before I reached you all. He's not on his game today. Seems like that's been true for a while now."

"He's grown soft," said Urza. "Just look at that belly poking out underneath his breastplate."

"Don't you wish." Rakzar casually poked his stomach. He knew it wasn't really what Urza meant, but his stomach did have a little more give to it than he remembered.

Normak stood and looked around. "Where to?"

"It's great that the three of you can see in the dark, but I can't," said Rayah. "Did any of you happen to bring a torch?"

"I knew I shouldn't have let you come along," growled Rakzar. "You'll only slow us down."

"Oh really?" Rayah floated off the ground and matched Rakzar's height. She poked him in the chest with her finger. "You never would've found this place without my help."

"You think locating a sinkhole was difficult?"

"I found the doors Torbrek described and opened them!"

Rakzar scoffed, "By accident, I'm sure."

Rayah crossed her arms. "Ugh!"

Normak pointed at Rayah. "What's that thing on yer shoulder?"

Rayah reached up and stroked the creature's furry head. "I've decided to call him Chirpa. He's a sand rat. I chased him through the sand, and he led me straight—"

"To the doors." Rakzar snarled, "I knew it."

"So what?" said Urza. "We're here now. Let's find the crystal."

"Do you still have Eshtak's bag?" asked Rayah.

"Yeah." Rakzar reached behind his breastplate and pulled out a limp brown bag with drawstrings. He handed it to Rayah.

Rayah set the bag on the ground and spread its opening wide. A soft glow emanated from the bag. "I'll be right back." She dove into the bag.

Normak knelt next to the bag. "Now there be somethin' I ne'er seen before."

"Thought you dwarves had seen it all," said Rakzar.

Normak jumped back as Rayah zoomed out of the open bag with a lit torch in each hand. She handed one of them to Normak. "Now we can go find the crystal."

Rakzar scooped up the bag and stuffed it back behind his breastplate. "Now what?"

"Oh, wait. Do you still have my things?" asked Rayah.

"Yes." Rakzar handed her pack and waterskin to her. "We finally good to go?"

"I think we should split up," said Urza. "We could cover more ground that way."

"Or I could see what be 'round real quick," said Normak.

"Do it," said Rakzar.

Normak nodded and then shot across the sand, a streaking star with the torch he carried. Surprisingly, the torch stayed lit as he circled the entire area. A wave of sand engulfed Rakzar and Urza when he slid to a halt. Rayah had been smart enough to take to the air.

Rakzar spat sand from his mouth for the second time in fifteen minutes. "Do that again, and I'll leave you down here to rot."

"Sorry." Normak scratched the back of his neck. "Sometimes me feet move faster than me thinks. Plus it ain't no problem at 'ome in the rocky mountains. Very little dirt there."

"So, what did you see?" asked Urza.

"If legends be true, I know where we be." His voice lowered. "They called this place *Äränä Ballʊd.*"

"And that means what?" asked Rayah.

"Blood Arena." Normak looked around suspiciously. "Dangerous battles fought to the death here."

"Between men for sport?" asked Urza.

"Aye. More than that though. Battles between man and beast. Horrific creatures. Nightmares, they be."

"So how do we proceed?" asked Rakzar. "Did you find an exit?"

"Many large metal doors surround the arena. None be open."

"Then we're trapped..." said Urza.

Rayah looked around. "I can fly out of here and find another path. Just tell me which way to go."

"Nay. There be nets all around the arena. Impenetrable. Woven with mezhik they be."

Rakzar smacked his fist against his palm. "There must be some way out of here." He took a few steps, and the ground depressed several inches. He pulled his foot back and something clicked. "That can't be good."

The ground quaked violently, and the sound of chains pulling through gears filled the arena. Urza and Rakzar dropped on all fours, Rayah rose in the air, and Normak spread his legs wide.

Rakzar pointed at the mountain of sand they'd landed on. "Is it just me, or is that mountain shrinking?"

"It be shrinkin'," Normak confirmed.

A minute later, the mountain of sand no longer existed, and the quaking stopped.

Whoosh!

A ring of fire lit the upper edge of the arena, and then the fire climbed the arena net all the way to the ceiling a thousand feet above, bringing light to the entire room.

"That be helpful," said Normak.

Scrape!

Thunk-thunk-thunk! Thunk-thunk-thunk! Thunk-thunk-thunk!

"Sounds like a chain being pulled through gears," said Urza.

"Yeah, but for what?" asked Rayah.

The four of them huddled together, back-to-back and weapons drawn.

Boom! Boom! Boom! Boom!

Four of the steel doors dropped down into the arena floor, one in each direction. Snarls, howls, and growls filled the arena.

"Gods," said Normak. "If ya be seein' what me be seein', we be in trouble."

† † †

Rayah dropped her torch.

She didn't doubt what her eyes saw, but her brain still couldn't process it. Three beasts stalked toward her on all fours, each three or four feet tall and a good foot-and-a-half wide. Their shapes reminded her of dire wolves, but that's where the similarities stopped. She'd never seen anything quite like them.

Empty eye sockets stared her down. Nothing but black holes on the sides of skinless skulls. Greyish-white bones. No flesh. No tendons. No muscles. No organs.

Nothing but teeth, claws, and bones. Ɛäṭūr, save us!

"Reaper wolves!" shouted Normak. The name fit, but she'd never heard of them. "Filthy buggers."

Normak stood to Rayah's left and faced ninety degrees away from her. She assumed he had several of the beasts closing in on him as well but couldn't and wouldn't take her eyes off the ones headed straight for her.

Rakzar stood with his back to Rayah. "How do you kill them?"

"Can dead things be killed?" questioned Urza.

"Good question," said Normak. "All me knows is don' let 'em bite ya. Ya do and say goodbye to yer skin! Falls right off."

"Can't fight them this close together," said Urza. "We need to spread out."

"Agreed," said Rakzar. "If anyone figures out how to stop or kill these damned things, tell the rest of us."

The way the reaper wolves moved fascinated Rayah, but she didn't have time to appreciate or think about it. She drew her knives with a quick motion of her hands and zoomed into the air. With her mind and her hands, she directed her knives to slash and stab the reaper wolves, but the knives didn't seem to cause any damage. Then again, what had she expected?

After searching through the desert sand for more than an hour earlier, she knew she didn't have much energy left to stay in the air much longer. She looked around. The others fared no better than her. Normak had the advantage of speed, so he could attack and retreat easily enough, but even his war hammer couldn't kill the reaper wolves. No matter how hard he hit them, sometimes knocking their skulls from their bodies, they'd pick up the parts that got knocked off and reattach them as though nothing had happened. Both Rakzar and Urza were cornered but still maintained a fair distance from the reaper wolves.

I must do something!

The torch she'd dropped lay in the middle of the arena. So did Normak's. Had he discarded his in the same way she had, or had he tried to use it on the reaper wolves? She had no other ideas, so she flew toward the middle of the arena and swooped down to snatch up the torch.

Normak must've had the same idea.

Rayah collided with Normak, sending them both tumbling across the arena floor. Normak recovered quickly and sprinted away with his torch, but the reaper wolves chasing after Rayah closed in quickly. Too quick for her to recover and fly off.

The reaper wolf in the lead lunged for her, its claws poised to rip into her.

Rayah did the only thing she could. She sank deep into the sand floor, narrowly escaping the claws of the reaper wolf. But the reaper wolves started digging into the sand. She flew through the sand, giving herself some breathing room. The reaper wolves didn't seem to be able to track her. They continued to dig where she'd entered the sand. It gave her an idea.

Through the sand, Rayah snuck up underneath one of the reaper wolves and pulled it down into the sand by its hind legs. The reaper wolf struggled to free itself from the sand, so she did the same with the other three. Then she moved on to the ones that had Urza cornered. By the time she'd buried all twelve of them, the first reaper wolf had almost worked itself free from the sand.

"I can't keep doing this," Rayah said. "We need to figure out how to get out of here while we have a chance."

"Nay," said Normak. "Fights be to the death."

Rakzar wiped his snout with the back of his hand. "We'll be dead of exhaustion before we figure out how to kill them."

Urza walked up. She'd held up well, all things considered, but she panted far more than she should've.

Rayah placed her hand on Urza's wither. "Are you okay?"

"Me?" Urza turned her head to the side and her neck popped. "Never better. Are you? You're the one who's bleeding from the head."

Rayah reached up and found the tacky spot close to her left temple. "Must've happened when I ran into Normak." She wiped it with her hand, but it just made a mess on everything.

"Sorry, lass," said Normak.

"Incoming," growled Rakzar.

The first reaper wolf she'd buried had finally freed itself and headed straight for them. Four of the others were almost free as well. Rayah grabbed one of her knives and thrust it at the incoming reaper wolf. She guided the knife with her hand, and it struck the reaper wolf right between its eye sockets, lodging itself up to the hilt in its skull. The reaper wolf crashed to the ground and slid several feet in the sand.

Then, something unexpected happened.

Tendons, muscles, and flesh began covering the fallen reaper wolf.

Rayah's knife dislodged itself from the reaper wolf's skull. The reaper wolf stood and shook its head. Then it came at them again. Normak shot forward and swung his war hammer at the reaper wolf's head.

Rayah nearly felt the solid, thunderous crack when the war hammer connected.

A spray of blood peppered the air and painted the sand.

The reaper wolf flew off its feet, crashed to the ground, and lay in an expanding pool of blood.

Three more reaper wolves came at them. Rayah tried the same maneuver with a second knife, but it deflected harmlessly off the reaper wolf's skull. She didn't understand why it didn't work like it had the first time.

Urza, Rakzar, and Normak stepped forward and engaged the three reaper wolves. A fourth reaper wolf freed itself and charged her.

With her hands and mind, she called her knives back. They sailed through the air and back into her open palms. The reaper wolf lunged for her. She had no time to think as she threw her first knife—the one with her blood on it—at the reaper wolf. Again, she directed her knife straight at the center of the reaper wolf's eyes. Like the first time, it sank into the reaper wolf's skull all the way to the hilt. She sidestepped as the reaper wolf fell to the ground.

Rayah jumped on the reaper wolf's back just as it finished transforming and slit its throat with her second knife. The reaper wolf seized for a few moments and grew still as blood pooled around it.

That's when the solution hit her.

"Blood!" she screamed. "Use blood on your weapons and it will turn them. Then they can be killed."

The others cut themselves, smeared blood on their weapons, and made quick work of the last ten reaper wolves.

All four of them dropped to the ground, breathless and covered in blood and sweat. Thankfully, none of them had been scratched or bitten.

"Nice work, Rayah," said Urza.

"Yeah," said Normak. "Saved me butt fer sure."

Rakzar remained silent.

Rayah ribbed Rakzar. "Still wish you'd left me behind?"

Rakzar glared at her. "Dumb luck." Underneath that glare, she swore she saw something more. Something... tender.

She smiled and lay back in the sand.

Thunk-thunk-thunk! Thunk-thunk-thunk! Thunk-thunk-thunk!

"Not again," groaned Rayah.

She stood and watched for more of the steel doors to fall but none did. Instead, the floor opened up in the center of the arena.

Normak zoomed away and back in a few moments. "Looks like we 'ave ourselves a way out."

But what are we gonna have to face next?

† † †

Rakzar led the group down the stairway from the blood arena and into the water aquifers and sewers beneath the ancient city. Knee-deep water slowed their pace as they trudged forward. Every turn in the maze of tunnels looked the same, each intersection identical to the last. Rakzar stopped and looked back the way they'd come. They were lost, but he'd never admit to it.

Rayah looked back as well. "It seems like we've been walking in circles for the last hour."

"You think you can do better, *dryte*?" Rakzar stepped to the side. "Have at it."

Rayah huffed. "I never said that."

"Lemme do it," said Normak. "Mapping tunnels is what I do."

"And you're just now bringing that up?" questioned Urza.

Normak backed up with his arms raised. "Hey, not 'ere ta step on toes. Gimme a task an I'll do it."

"Fine," growled Rakzar. "Find us an exit."

"Gimme a few minutes." Normak left in a flash.

Urza leaned against the tunnel wall and panted. The reaper wolves had taken more out of her than Rakzar had first thought. It pained him seeing her that way.

The water rippled and then a black mark appeared on the wall.

"Did you see that?" asked Rakzar.

Rayah looked up. "See what?"

"Never mind."

Normak came back, out of breath. It was the first time Rakzar had seen him that way.

"Found an exit." Normak took a deep breath and held his chest. "Sixty paces up and to the left. Looks to be an iron door and a well of some sort. Should lead us to the surface."

"I didn't think you got out of breath with those shoes of yours," said Rakzar.

Normak grinned and took another deep breath. "We ain't alone down 'ere. Had ta double time it. Best we move."

Perfect.

Rakzar turned and sprinted in the direction Normak had pointed. When he reached the corner, he peered over his shoulder as he rounded it. Rayah and Normak were right behind him, but Urza wasn't.

He halted, and Rayah plowed right into his hip. She stuttered back a step, but the impact barely registered in his mind.

"What happened to Urza?" asked Rakzar.

Rayah and Normak looked back. The tunnel around the corner lay empty. Water swished about, recently disturbed.

"Told ya we ain't alone." Normak moved toward the iron door but Rakzar arm barred him.

"No one gets left behind, got it?" growled Rakzar.

"Might be too late," said Normak. "Them naga and nagi sirens don' mess around."

Rayah gasped. "What in Ɂäṭūr's name are naga and nagi sirens?"

"Naga be the boys. Nagi be the girls. Ya 'ear the singin'?" asked Normak.

"Yeah," said Rayah. "It's beautiful…" Her voice trailed off as her eyes glossed over. She turned back the way they'd come.

"Rayah!" yelled Rakzar, but Rayah kept going.

"Need some cotton or somethin' to put in 'er ears. Blocks their deadly singin'."

"No time for that!" Rakzar bolted after Rayah and tackled her in the water.

The water enhanced and amplified the song's volume. A dirge that would carry the dead into oblivion. Mournful, yet magnificent. It spoke to Rakzar. Comforted him.

Rakzar rose from the water and stared at the beautiful creature who stood forty paces away. No, she didn't stand because she had no legs. From the waist down, she had the body of a serpent. A thick tail with dark green scales. Above the waist, she had skin pure as porcelain and greenish-black hair that swayed back and forth with the song she sang. Her forked tongue flicked the air with each note, and a mouth full of razor-sharp teeth glistened with saliva or perhaps poison. Rakzar couldn't be sure, but it didn't matter. She sang for him, and that was the only thing that did matter.

Together, Rakzar and Rayah headed straight for the nagi siren.

† † †

Normak looked back at the iron door. So close to freedom. He sighed and shook his head.

Must I do everythin'?

Losing Urza wouldn't have kept them from finding the crystal and a way out of the ruins, but he couldn't do it all on his own. Not this time. He needed at least one of them.

He ran after Rayah and Rakzar and scooped up Rayah's pack on the way. She'd likely have something useful in it.

Thankfully, he'd mapped out the entire sewer system earlier, so he knew exactly where the nagi sirens had taken his companions. A quarter mile back, he'd found a medium-sized room off to the side of the tunnels with a large rock slab at its center. Because of his obsession with dark creatures, Normak understood the purpose of the tan slab.

According to legend, the naga and nagi sirens worshiped Äfäūm, the god of the desert. This god, like most, required blood sacrifices be made to it by its worshipers, so the stone slab served as a sacrificial table for the naga and nagi sirens to flay their victims upon.

Normak flew through the dark tunnels, spraying the walls with water as he went. The marks he'd left on the walls earlier would wash away, but saving his companions ranked a bit higher on his list. Not quite as high as the task his brother sent him to accomplish though.

Knowing the strict rituals of the naga and nagi sirens, he had a bit of time to spare before rescuing Rakzar, Rayah, and Urza. Both tasks were attainable. As he ran, he traced through his mental map of the sewers and located the place he'd likely find their nest: a small room with deeper water in the far reaches of the sewers. Thanks to his winged boots, it didn't take long to get there, and his hunch had been right.

At the bottom of the water lay several dozen brownish, leathery eggs. He closed his eyes and dove in. His fingers touched one of the eggs but then something rammed him square in the chest. The strong blow took him by surprise and drove the air from his lungs. Instinctively, he took a deep breath and filled his lungs with water.

A loud shriek filled the waters and pierced his ears.

Oy! The nagi siren queen.

How could he have forgotten about her? The prize had distracted him.

He struggled to find either the bottom or the surface, and his boots were practically useless. If anything, they weighed him down in the water.

The second blow came from behind, right in the small of his back. It drove him down, and his feet met something solid.

Gods, let it be the bottom.

Normak kicked off the solid object and surfaced just long enough to spit the water from his lungs before the nagi siren queen grabbed his feet and pulled him back under.

The water burned his eyes when he opened them, but that was the least of his problems. He desperately needed air and fought the urge to take another breath. But none of that would matter if he couldn't break free from the grasp of the nagi siren queen. Unlike the others, she didn't possess sharp claws or brandish knives. Her sole job was to lay eggs and nurture them.

She shrieked again.

Her shrieks wouldn't go unnoticed for long. More naga and nagi sirens would come to her rescue, assuming they weren't all huddled around the sacrificial table a half mile away. His luck had never been very good.

He slid his dagger from its sheath and stabbed at the hands latched onto his feet. The angle was off, and she kept twisting him around, but he finally connected with one strike. She shrieked and lost her grip on one of his feet. He kicked his heels together with everything he had and smashed her hand. She let go, and he managed to surface again.

Normak pulled himself up onto the edge of the sewer channel and coughed up water. She latched onto his feet again but didn't have the leverage to pull him back under. He took several breaths and dropped back into the water.

One of them would die, and Normak didn't plan on it being him.

She came at him full-force again and struck him in the gut with the crown of her head, but he'd been prepared that time. He grabbed her around the neck. She shrieked, squirmed, and turned around, and he drew his dagger across her neck.

Her shriek ended abruptly, and green liquid spread in the water. He shoved her away, quickly retrieved a half dozen eggs and stuffed them in his pack, and then got out of the water.

He huddled next to the wall and waited a minute to see if any of the other naga and nagi sirens would come for her, but none did. He took a deep breath and then headed back toward the room with the sacrificial table. Another perk to running fast was that it dried him and his clothes pretty fast.

Just outside the room, he rummaged through Rayah's pack and found a good-sized loaf of bread wrapped tight in a linen cloth. Water had soaked the bread and turned it into a soggy mess, but it made his job easier. He pulled off a small piece of the bread and rolled it between his fingers. Five more times he did that, sticking each piece in his pocket after he rolled it. He stuffed the rest of the bread and the cloth back into the pack and set the pack down.

Normak peered around the corner. Inside the room, thirteen naga and nagi sirens surrounded the large sacrificial table. Rakzar, Urza, and Rayah lay atop it, unmoving and in a deep trance. The naga and nagi sirens continued to sing their song, but they'd nearly reached the end of it. He knew because he'd heard it before. Thankfully, dwarves were far less susceptible to such enchantments.

With a quick breath and a prayer to the gods, he rushed into the room, his war hammer swinging. In one felled swoop, he struck two of the nagi sirens in the side of their heads, bashing them in. They dropped to the floor in a heap. Green liquid poured from their wounds and smoked and sizzled when it hit the floor. *Acid blood.* That was one fact of the naga and nagi sirens he'd forgotten about.

Keep it clean, Normak.

Normak leapt onto the table, dove over two sweeping daggers, and rolled over his shoulder and off the other side of the table. He swung his war hammer wildly as he dropped to the floor. Somehow, he caught one of the nagi sirens right in the gut. The thing doubled over and spewed green acid everywhere. Luckily, it missed both him and his companions lying on the table. Two of the other nagi sirens weren't so lucky. Their songs turned into screams as they dropped to the ground and writhed.

Eight more ta go.

Normak rolled to his feet and jumped back up on the table, narrowly escaping a strike from a naga siren. Unlike their female counterparts, the naga sirens didn't brandish weapons. Their eight-inch claws could cut right through bone in a single swipe.

He spun in a circle and whipped his war hammer around like a mace with one hand, driving the naga and nagi sirens back several steps. While doing so, he fished around in his pocket for one of the rolled-up pieces of bread. With several close calls already, he couldn't risk taking on the last eight alone.

Normak found two of the bread rolls. His feet were fast, but the shoes did nothing for his hands. As soon as he stopped spinning, the naga and nagi sirens would close in on him.

Let me hands be lightnin'.

He stopped spinning, bent down, and quickly worked a bread roll into Rakzar's left ear with trembling fingers. The second one fell out of his hand before he could get it into Rakzar's other ear.

A hiss filled Normak's left ear.

Jaws clamped down on his left shoulder.

Fangs sank into his flesh.

Pain blossomed and spread down his arm and into his chest.

He twisted and swung his war hammer.

The nagi held fast to his shoulder and plunged its knife into his side repeatedly.

Tightly woven, black chain mail cloth underneath his leather armor prevented the nagi's knife from doing major damage, but each blow knocked air from his lungs and bruised his ribs.

Crack!

His war hammer caught another naga underneath its jaw and ripped its head clean off.

Green acid splattered his chest.

Smoldering leather filled his nostrils.

The death clock ticked away.

Finally, he located the second bread roll and snatched it off the table.

Normak leaned into the nagi attached to his shoulder, found the edge of the table with his boot heels, and kicked off it as hard as he could.

The nagi hadn't anticipated such a move, and the two of them flew backward and into the adjacent wall.

The nagi released his shoulder.

Normak drove his elbow back and up as hard as he could, catching the nagi right in the nose.

He pushed off the wall, turned his head, and ducked just as a dagger swept past him.

Warm liquid ran down the side of his face.

The dagger must've connected, but he'd felt nothing.

He lunged forward, the bread roll still in his hand.

Something struck him in the back, right between the shoulder blades, but the blow only helped propel him forward.

The table edge caught him across the stomach. Drove the air from his lungs.

Darkness shrouded his vision. Threatened his consciousness. He fought it as he worked the bread roll into Rakzar's other ear.

More hissing.

"Bugger!"

Long claws raked the back of his gauntleted hand. But he'd managed to get the bread roll in.

Rakzar jolted upright on the table and shook his head.

"A little help would be good!" said Normak.

Rakzar grabbed his new double-edged battle axes off his back, leapt off the table, and tore into two naga sirens, chopping off their arms and then their heads. Acid sprayed everywhere and narrowly missed the side of Rayah's face.

"Nasty little bastards!" yelled Rakzar.

"Aye!" exclaimed Normak as he brought his war hammer straight down on the head of another nagi siren. A sick crack registered in his ears and green acid exploded from its crushed neck. He barely got his arm up in time to protect his face from the deadly spray.

Three remained. One naga siren and two nagi sirens. The nagi sirens stopped singing and hissed as they backed out of the room along with the naga siren.

"Yeah, that's right!" exclaimed Normak. "Yeh've lost the fight. Go slither away somewhere else and find victims who won' fight back."

Rakzar bolted out of the room after them.

Both Rayah and Urza sat up on the table and gasped for air. Rayah moved her hand and Normak yelled, "Don' touch the green stuff!"

It seemed that there were few places in the entire room that didn't have green acid eating away at something.

"Bloody little buggers!" said Normak. "Didn' think they'd put up such a fight."

Rakzar returned. "Well, you'd have been wrong if you'd bet on it."

"What happened?" asked Urza. She'd been under their trance longer than any of them.

"What happened is we saved your life," said Rakzar. "Those things were going to eat us all."

"Correction," said Normak. "They was gonna eat the three of ya. I be immune ta their singin'." He smiled but then grimaced and held his ear.

"What happened to your ear?" asked Rayah, looking at Normak's right ear.

"Dagger, I s'pose." Normak pulled a kerchief from one of his pockets and blotted his ear with it. Holding his hand up to his ear made his left shoulder ache. Blood saturated what was left of his leather breastplate. "One of those damned things bit me shoulder as well."

"This is one of those moments where it'd be good to have a wizard with us," replied Rayah.

"Ya don' say. Bad plannin' if ya ask me," said Normak. "A good raid be needin' a wizard."

"Wizard or not, we need to be more careful," said Urza.

"We need to move," said Rakzar. "I didn't manage to catch those last three things. They're fast in the water."

"And there could be more," said Rayah.

The four of them made their way back toward the iron gate and collected their belongings they'd dropped along the way.

Back at the gate, it took three good blows from Normak's war hammer to bust the iron lock that secured it. Beyond the gate was a circular space about twenty feet in diameter. The walls were lined with brown-and-gray-and-white river rocks and extended into the darkness above.

"Definitely looks ta be a well," said Normak.

"You gonna be able to climb with your shoulder?" asked Urza.

Normak smiled and winced. "These shoes be good for climbin' as well. A good runnin' start, and I be at the top in no time."

"Lead the way," said Rakzar. "And tell us what you find."

Normak nodded. "Aye." He raced around the bottom of the well several times and used his momentum to ascend the well walls, circling as he climbed ever higher. He ran right out of the well and crashed to the ground when he fell over its top lip.

He grunted and lay on the ground for a good minute while he caught his breath. Finally, he sat up and pulled himself to his feet. Sculpted sand and glass surrounded him. Buildings, statues, roads, benches. People. Everything was made of sand and glass. Even the fake trees and flowers.

Normak leaned over the edge of the well and called down to the others. "Think yer gonna want ta see this."

† † †

Utilizing her wings, the several-hundred-foot climb out of the well hadn't been so bad for Rayah. Urza, on the other hand, struggled. The curse continued to take its toll on her, and Rakzar had to help her climb the last fifty or so feet. Once they all stood on the glass road, Rayah took Eshtak's bag from Rakzar and retrieved another torch from it.

The torch burned brighter than it normally would have, or at least it seemed that way since the glass world around them reflected and amplified its light tenfold. Rayah circled, awestruck by the beauty of her surroundings. The four of them stood in the middle of a town square, but that square looked nothing like any other one Rayah had ever seen.

Detailed artwork surrounded them. Buildings carved straight out of the sandstone surrounded the square, each painted in a distinct shade of purple, red, blue, or green. No two buildings matched, not even in architecture. Sculptures of various kinds littered the square. Thousands of them. Plants, trees, benches, rocks, people, and various creatures. Like the buildings, none of them matched either.

Sculptures of people varied greatly. Several had freckles and dimples while others donned scars. Some were tall and hairy while others were short enough to be dwarves. Each had eyelashes and hair so authentic that Rayah could identify individual hairs. Pores, both large and small, pocked their skin. Had the sculptures not sported a glassy sheen she might've mistaken them for real people frozen in time.

"All this beauty hidden from the world." Rayah sighed. "Such a waste of talent."

Rakzar walked around sniffing the air and the statues. "Something's not right. I can smell these creatures and people."

Rayah frowned and then her eyes widened. "You're saying these are *real* people?"

"Rakzar's right." Urza stopped next to Rayah. "These aren't statues."

Normak gulped. "Then we be close to the crystal."

How long had they been that way? Rayah shuddered. "Are they still alive? If so, can we help them?" She said it as much to herself as to anyone else.

Rakzar dashed her hopes. "They might look well preserved on the outside, but death took them long ago."

The beauty of Nasda faded before Rayah's eyes. She didn't want to be there anymore. "Let's finish what we came here to do and get out of here."

"Aye," said Normak. "Where to?"

"Straight back, behind the square." Urza pointed to a towering red building. "See the double crescent moon on its roof? That's what we're looking for, right?"

Rayah fluttered several feet off the ground to get a better view. "And the stars… Yes, I believe so. It looks like the same symbol as the one on the doors we fell through in the desert."

"Then let's move," growled Rakzar. "We've wasted too much time already."

The four of them headed across the square and toward the red building. Rayah could only imagine what they might face within its walls.

With any luck, it'll be nothing.

She knew better.

CHAPTER THIRTY

The first room of the temple served as a worship area. Rakzar stalked through the rows of many individuals who knelt on the floor and faced into the building, toward the front wall. Each individual knelt in a unique position, each at a different point in their forward bow, immortalized forever.

A massive red curtain covered the front wall from ceiling to floor. Embroidered at its center with silver thread were the two crescent moons and stars.

Your god couldn't save you.

"But yours can," said Amicus.

"Not now," growled Rakzar under his breath. He walked over to the red curtain.

Amicus materialized in front of him. "The longer you wait, the harder it will be to reconcile."

"The damned can't be saved." Rakzar reached through Amicus and pulled the curtains apart.

"Perhaps not, but you're not damned yet, my friend." Amicus faded as Rakzar walked through him and into the second temple room.

Two grey, cylindrical columns rose to the ceiling and flanked a rectangular altar carved from a single stone. The altar had a red hue to it. Rakzar couldn't tell if the hue came from the stone itself or from the centuries of blood spilled upon it. Either way, blood sacrifices had been made. A small trough circled the altar, a channel to direct the blood into a holding chamber somewhere below the altar.

The room contained nothing else. No windows, doors, or any sort of decoration.

Frustrated, Rakzar punched one of the columns. "This can't be the right place."

"Perhaps there's a latch or trigger of some kind hidden in one of these rooms," said Rayah. "There's got to be something. The symbol on the roof can't be a mistake."

The four of them searched the temple for half an hour but found nothing. Each of them stood on a different side of the altar.

"Satisfied, *dryte*?" scoffed Rakzar.

"Enough, Rakzar." Urza stared intently at the altar. "Perhaps it takes a sacrifice."

"Whoa," said Normak, stepping back from the altar. "I like meself the way I be. *Alive*."

Click!

One of Urza's knives sprung into her right hand. "Don't be a fool. I'm not suggesting one of us needs to die."

"Then what?" asked Rakzar, eying the knife.

"Perhaps it only takes a small amount of blood to trigger something," said Urza.

Urza held her left hand over the altar and slid her knife across her palm. Blood pooled in the fresh wound. She turned her hand over and squeezed. Droplets of blood fell onto the altar. The blood sizzled and the altar quaked for several moments before stopping. Nothing else happened.

"I think she's right." Rayah set her torch on the floor, pulled off her left glove, and took one of the knives from her belt. She palmed the blade in her left hand and pulled it through her hand with a grimace. "Ouch!"

Blood dripped from Rayah's hand onto the altar, and the altar shook again, more violently this time. Rakzar and Normak joined in, each donating blood of their own. The ground trembled as the altar shook and turned crimson. Each of them squeezed their wound harder, adding more blood. The altar slid back six inches and then the front of it plunged into the ground, revealing a dark passage with sandstone steps.

"Nice work!" exclaimed Rayah. Then she glared at Rakzar. "Where would we be if we listened to you?"

Rakzar glared right back. "You'd still be at home." To Urza, he said, "Lead the way, *sister*."

† † †

As soon as the four of them entered the passage the altar rose back up and sealed the exit. Either they'd find a way out somewhere beneath the temple or they'd die in there. Urza preferred the first option.

Thirty-three steps led to the bottom of the passage and to a broad corridor. She knew that because she'd counted them. Something about mindless tasks always sent her brain into an obsessive frenzy. But she thought she hid her obsession well. Everyone thought she'd worn the string necklace to show the number of kills she'd made, but it had always been so much more for her. Counting the strings calmed her and kept her wit sharp. She missed the necklace but not what it represented. Like Rakzar, she'd chosen a different path. Death didn't hold all the answers and neither did killing for hire.

Twenty-seven paces along the corridor brought them to a massive room. Sandstone walls rose a good fifty feet on all four sides, and the ceiling rose from all four sides into a point in the center of the room. A pyramid structure about ten feet tall sat at the left center of the room. All four of its sides stepped up to a central platform no larger than a four foot square. Atop the pyramid stood a three-foot-tall pedestal. An orange, misshapen crystal protruded from the top of the pedestal, surrounded by glass.

Another pyramid with the same dimensions as the first sat at the right center of the room. Atop the second pyramid sat a large throne made of sandstone. The throne faced the first pyramid and some sort of helmet with horns sat on its seat.

About two hundred feet separated the two pyramids, and two enormous statues of a minotaur halved the distance on either side. Each statue stood at least a dozen feet tall, maybe more.

The hair on Urza's hackles rose. "I don't like the looks of this."

Rakzar and Normak pushed past Urza, and they both headed toward the pyramid with the pedestal.

Rayah stayed by Urza's side. "I've got a bad feeling about this as well."

Click-click!

Urza's knives fell into her waiting hands. The cold steel comforted her. She twirled the knives. "No matter what happens, I just wanted you to know you're one of the only friends I've ever had."

Rayah smiled but kept her gaze trained ahead. "Likewise." She held her hands close to her hips and the knives from her belt flew into them.

Normak took a step back from the pedestal and lifted his war hammer over his shoulder. "Stand back, and I'll git 'er outta the box."

Rakzar retreated several steps down the side of the pyramid. Normak grunted, cocked the war hammer way back over his shoulder, and gave a mighty roar as he swung it straight at the side of the pedestal encasement.

Crack!

Normak's war hammer fell from his hands and crashed down onto the pyramid. He shook his hands wildly and cried out. "Now that smarts."

Rakzar roared with laughter. "Told you the job was too big for a dwarf." He picked up Normak's war hammer and swung it at the encasement.

Crack!

Rakzar achieved the same result as Normak, and Normak howled with laughter. "Too big fer ya as well!"

Never send a man to do a woman's job.

Urza turned to Rayah. "Wait here."

Rayah nodded, her eyes little more than slits.

Urza sheathed her knives, dropped on all fours, and loped over to the pyramid with the pedestal. She examined the encasing. The two strikes from Normak's war hammer hadn't even left a scratch. Something must be required of them in order to retrieve the crystal, but what?

"Let's check out the other pyramid," said Rakzar.

Normak stood across the way atop the second pyramid in a few seconds flat. He held up what looked like the head of a minotaur. "Whoa, this be superb." He slid the head over his own.

"No!" shouted Urza.

Normak screamed and clawed at the minotaur head he wore.

Urza and Rakzar raced from one pyramid to the other, but Urza knew they'd arrived too late when Normak's screaming ceased.

Rakzar approached Normak and the throne. Urza came up behind Rakzar.

Normak dropped his war hammer.

Bones cracked.

Normak's body shook.

Arms and legs twisted. Cracked. Elongated. Bulked with muscle.

Boots split, revealing hoofed feet.

Eyes, wild with rage, grew into empty sockets.

Urza grabbed Rakzar's arm and pulled him back.

The ground quaked.

Urza and Rakzar retreated down the pyramid.

A guttural roar filled the room.

Boom!

A sandstone boulder the size of a cottage slammed down right behind Rayah, blocking the only exit.

"What do we do?" asked Urza, still clutching Rakzar's arm.

"Ready our weapons and prepare for death."

The Normak-minotaur hybrid sat down on the throne and clutched the armrests. He filled the entire throne.

A sound reminiscent of breaking pottery drew Urza's attention. "Gods…"

The two enormous minotaur statues cracked and exploded outward. Urza and Rakzar shielded their faces from the debris.

The dust settled.

Two minotaurs stood in their midst, each wielding an axe the size of Rayah.

The sound of hooves thundered in the room when they stomped the ground, but their twisted, maniacal roars are what drove Urza to action. "Run!" she screamed.

Rakzar went left and she went right. She didn't look back. Couldn't look back.

A whoosh at her back nearly toppled her. Must've been a swing from its axe.

As she ran, Urza searched desperately for Rayah, but couldn't locate her.

She screamed Rayah's name but the sound of all the chaos swallowed her voice.

A loud yelp drove a dagger through her heart.

Rakzar!

She chanced a glance to her right, where the yelp had come from. Rakzar lay on the ground, unmoving. The beast's ax arced downward, straight for him.

She couldn't watch. Couldn't look away.

Something wrapped around her waist as she ran and pulled her to the ground. Into the ground. The room disappeared. The ground shook all around her.

"Relax," said Rayah. "I've got you."

"Rakzar!" cried Urza.

"He's still alive."

A moment later they emerged from the ground on the opposite side of the room.

The minotaur who chased Urza still pounded the spot on the ground where she'd disappeared. Rakzar dodged and rolled from each attack, but Urza could see him slowing. They wouldn't be able to keep this up for long.

Urza drew her knives. "We need a plan."

"I think I know how we can end this," said Rayah.

The minotaur who'd chased Urza had spotted her again and started galloping toward her and Rayah. "I'm listening."

"We need to get them close so that they wind up attacking each other."

"Do you think they're that stupid?"

"No, but I'm certain that they can't see in the dark. Once you two get them close, I'll extinguish the torches around the room."

"And how will Rakzar know to do that?"

"The same way I told you. Watch yourself. I'll let you know when I'm ready."

"Okay."

Rayah dove into the dirt and disappeared. The minotaur had closed the distance and lunged forward, ax over its head.

Urza bolted.

Moments later, she spotted Rakzar talking with Rayah. He nodded. The plan had to work. Little time remained before one of them would make the wrong move or move too slow.

Rayah flew high. Rakzar ran toward her. "Round them up!" he screamed.

They circled. Dodged blow after blow.

The last one slammed right next to Urza's head. Her ears rang.

One by one, the torches blew out around the room until only one remained. Rakzar and Urza headed straight for each other. The two minotaurs closed on them fast. The final torch went out, casting the room into total darkness. Urza looked back as she veered to her left. She hoped Rakzar had veered left as well.

A thunderous crash shook the room, followed by two might roars. Then another crash. Urza looked back. The two minotaurs had embedded their axes in the sides of each other and struggled to dislodge them.

She turned back and headed straight for the one closest to her. At the last possible moment, she leapt in the air.

Click-click!

Her knives dropped into her hands.

The minotaur must've sensed danger. It looked right at her.

But she had the upper hand. It wouldn't react in time.

Another second and her knives would be buried in the minotaur's neck.

Driven by confidence and rage, she hadn't seen its hand moving to swat her from the air.

The blow caught her right in the ribs. She heard and felt several of them crack.

At that same moment, she'd let go of her knives and trusted them to find their mark.

The ground came hard. Knocked the wind from her. Cracked her ribs further.

Her vision blurred. Darkened. Then the room faded from her eyes.

† † †

Urza's body hit the ground hard. When she didn't move, Rayah panicked. Rayah flew out of the ground, but the room lay in darkness.

She couldn't remember where the pyramid with the throne sat, but a gut instinct told her that she needed to reach it. Somehow, the minotaur head Normak wore kept the other two minotaurs alive. Maybe she should've kept one of the torches handy, but it made little difference now.

Grunts and thuds and moans and roars bombarded her. Dust and fluids peppered the air.

She reached one of the pyramids but didn't know which one it was. She prayed it was the right one as she traversed the steps toward the top. Snorting and groaning clued her in to the fact that she'd found the correct one.

At the top, she found the throne.

But it sat empty.

Normak grabbed her by the throat. Choked her. She reached out, but he must've stood behind her.

Every breath tightened his grip further.

She couldn't breathe. Couldn't think.

Alderan's face flashed in her mind. She'd let him down.

Then, she remembered her knives. She needed nothing but her hands and mind to control them.

She relaxed and her knives flew into her hands. With her mind, she guided the blades up her body and across the length of Normak's minotaur arms. Around to the back of his neck.

With an upward thrust, she willed the knife to slice the back of the minotaur's head open. Once. Twice. Three times.

The hands fell from around her neck. She turned midair and zoomed forward. She reached around Normak's head, dug her fingers into the gash at the back of his head, and pulled as hard as she could.

The head wouldn't peel away. She bent her knees, placed her feet against Normak's chest, and shoved off as she pulled on the head. A sickening pop met her ears and then the head pulled away from Normak, sending her backward and onto the throne. She tossed the head away and shook her hands. Sinewy cords of mucus clung to her fingers and arms and smelled of wet fur and vomit.

She heard Normak's body drop to the ground and then the room fell silent.

No noise remained but her heavy breathing.

Then a pop and a crackle.

One of the torches on the outer wall of the room burst with flame. Then another. And another. Soon, the entire room filled with light once more.

Rayah wiped her hands on her trousers and climbed down from the throne. Normak lay face-down on blood-drenched steps. A deep gash on the back of his head bled and matted the hair around it. She reached down and touched the side of his neck. A faint pulse beat against her fingers.

Thank Ɛäţūr!

Rayah assessed the carnage spread throughout the room. The two big minotaurs lay in the sand, one with two knives embedded in its throat and the other with an axe through the top of its skull. Blood pooled in the sand around them. To her left, at the base of the pyramid she stood upon, lay the minotaur head she'd cut off Normak's head. The flesh and fur had disintegrated, leaving only the skull and the two large horns protruding from the top of it.

Urza still lay on the ground to Rayah's far right where she'd left her. Urza faced the opposite direction, but Rayah saw her ribcage slowly rise and fall.

Two still alive.

She looked around but couldn't locate Rakzar. Her pulse rose. "Rakzar!" she cried.

When he didn't answer, she zoomed around the room but didn't find him. Where could he have gone? Had he not made it? The thought sickened and overwhelmed her, and she thought she might retch. A deep breath only made the feeling worsen.

Rayah bent over and clutched her stomach. She needed to be strong for Urza and Normak. Their survival rested on her shoulders.

Unless we're already dead.

She shook the thought away as it served no purpose but to destroy her.

From the corner of her eye, Rayah thought she saw movement underneath the minotaur with the axe in its skull. Fear and hope tightened her chest and crushed her lungs. She held her breath and watched the sand for more than a minute, but all remained still. Hope dwindled within her once again.

Rayah closed her eyes and prayed. *Ɂäṭūr, save him.*

How far she'd come from that day on the beach. Thinking back on it, she hardly recognized the hateful, spiteful girl she'd been. She'd proclaimed herself a devout follower of Ɂäṭūr, the one true God, but she'd shown no love or mercy for Rakzar. She'd begged for his death and would've choked it out of him given the chance. Now, she thought of him as a friend, his loss devastating.

Shifting sand buried Rayah's feet. Her eyes sprang open. The two minotaurs had been reduced to a heaping pile of sand. Furthermore, a furry red paw rose out of the middle of the sandpile.

Rayah dove into the sandpile, located Rakzar, and pulled him to the surface. But he didn't breathe or respond. She turned him on his side and beat his back with her palm.

"Breathe, damn you!" she yelled, frantic.

Rakzar convulsed, coughed, and then spat sand from his mouth.

"Thank Ɂäṭūr you're alive!" She hugged his neck and kissed the side of his snout.

He tensed and growled deep in his throat. Rayah pulled back to give him some breathing room. That's when she noticed all the blood. It congealed around a large, circular puncture wound in his left shoulder and matted his fur down the side of his chest and down his arm to his elbow. One of the minotaurs must've skewered him at some point during the fight.

"Are you okay?" Fear crept into her voice and shook it.

Rakzar coughed and spat sand from his mouth several more times before sitting up. "I'm alive because of you."

"Gods, what happened?" Normak rolled over and sat up on the lower pyramid step. "Me head's throbbin' somethin' fierce." He reached behind his head and his fingers returned bloodied.

Urza stirred as well. She managed to rise on all fours and joined Rayah and Rakzar. "We should all be dead. What happened?"

Rakzar tried to move his left arm and winced. His eyes turned glassy with tears. "Rayah. She did what we couldn't."

Embarrassment rose in Rayah's cheeks. "No... this took effort from all of us."

"Don' remember doin' anythin'." Normak stood, stumbled a few steps toward the three of them, and bent over, his hands on his knees. "Kinda blacked out after puttin' on that minotaur 'ead."

"Someone had to do it," said Rayah. "I'm just glad it didn't kill you."

Normak nodded. "Aye."

The four of them looked toward the second pyramid and the pedestal. Even from two hundred yards away Rayah could see that the glass enclosure around the crystal had cracked. She stood.

Urza must've sensed what she was about to do and grabbed onto her leg. "We need to think this through."

Rayah looked back at Urza and frowned. "What's there to think through? We've defeated the minotaurs and now we can take the crystal."

"Look around, Rayah. We're still trapped inside this room." Urza groaned when Rayah shrugged. "I think we need a plan before we do anything else."

"You don't think an exit will present itself when we take the crystal?" asked Rakzar.

Urza paced. "I don't know, but what if it doesn't?"

"We've no choice," said Normak. He blurred from sight.

Glass shattered.

Normak returned, the crystal secured under his arm.

The room groaned and shook and then the two pyramids collapsed into piles of sand.

"What the gods—"

A thunderous boom cut Urza off. A large chunk of the ceiling broke away and crashed to the ground, bursting into sand upon impact.

Rakzar grabbed Normak with his good arm and lifted the dwarf off the ground. "You've damned us all, you little bastard!"

"The doorway!" yelled Urza.

The sandstone boulder blocking the exit had disintegrated. Rakzar dropped Normak, and the four of them raced toward it. Another chunk of the ceiling came crashing down, narrowly missing Rakzar and Urza. But it drove Rayah straight into the ground.

† † †

Rakzar tripped at the top of the stairs and landed on his bad shoulder. Pain blinded him as he skidded across the temple floor. Normak and Urza helped him to his feet.

The temple shook to its foundation.

The walls liquefied and began pouring onto the floor.

Sand rained from the ceiling.

Rakzar looked back. The altar disintegrated and fell into the collapsing stairway.

Panic ripped through him. "Where's Rayah?"

Urza and Normak looked back. "Gods..." they both said.

Rakzar pulled away from Urza's grip. "I'm going back!"

"Don't be a fool!" She grabbed his bad arm. Pain flared like never before. He knew she did it on purpose. "There's nothing to be done. We've got to go!"

"Rayah knew the risks," confirmed Normak. He stormed through the red curtains and they burst into sand.

Urza dragged him out of the temple just before the entire thing collapsed in on itself. A concussive wave knocked them off their feet. The glass road creaked and cracked underneath them like cubes of ice exposed to warm water. Sculptures all around collapsed into piles of dust. Buildings groaned, shook, and fell.

They were trapped in a collapsing city, but that was only the start of their problems. How long did they have before the entire desert crashed down on top of them and buried them alive? Suddenly, drowning sounded much better to Rakzar.

The entire city floor quaked and then dropped at least thirty feet in a matter of seconds, leaving Rakzar, Urza, and Normak airborne for several seconds. They had no time to react before meeting the ground once more. The impact jarred Rakzar and ripped the breath from his lungs. But that wasn't what scared the life out of him.

Far above, fissures developed in the roof of the cavern. Sand poured down from them like rain.

A beam of light shone through, turning the falling sand into a beautiful display of refracted light.

This is the end.

"What now?" asked Urza.

Rakzar reached over and took her hand. "We die together."

"Been an adventure," said Normak.

Sand began to pile up around them.

"Funny story," said Amicus. "I remember the day I met Eshtak."

"Let me die in peace," growled Rakzar.

"Fair enough," said Normak. "I be at peace with meself."

Amicus continued, "Down in the dungeons below Castle Portador Tempestade. Strangest little man I've ever met. Biggest heart too."

Rakzar slammed his fist into the ground. "What's your point?"

"Everything fit into that bag of his." Amicus chuckled. "Surprised me to no end. Thought it was mezhik, and it certainly was a form of it, but not like I'd thought. More like a gateway to a secret location."

Rakzar sat up. "Amicus, you're a genius. That's it!"

Normak cocked his head. "Who be Amicus?"

"What's it?" asked Urza.

Rakzar pulled Eshtak's bag from underneath his breastplate and held it up. "This."

"A bag?" questioned Normak. "What good be that?"

Rakzar ripped the top open and peered into it. "We go now." He looked at Normak. "You first."

"Aye—"

The entire ceiling caved in above them, creating an avalanche of sand. They had seconds before they'd be buried alive. Normak dove into the open bag.

"Go!" growled Rakzar when Urza just sat there.

She hesitated a second longer and then dove into the bag.

Rakzar got the bag pulled over his head just as the entire weight of the desert crushed and buried him. Pain drove all thoughts from his mind as it pulled him into the darkness.

† † †

Urza panicked when Rakzar didn't come all the way through the bag. The top half of Rakzar's body hung limp from the cave ceiling. Sand seeped into the cave from around him. Urza and Normak worked at pulling him the rest of the way into the bag but the weight of the sand on his legs proved too great for them to overcome.

Normak collapsed back against the cave wall and slid to the floor. "What now?"

"We wait until he comes around." Urza joined him on the floor. Every muscle in her body ached and she knew it wasn't just from fatigue. "I'm not sure how much more of this I can take."

Normak reached back and held the back of his head. "Did I miss somethin', or was 'e talkin' to 'imself?"

Urza had noticed the phenomenon several times over the last week. Rakzar excused it away each time, but something was definitely going on with him. "Not sure. He's... been under a lot of stress the last few weeks." She almost told Normak about the spell and curse but thought better of it. She had no idea how he might react to the fact that all of them were headed toward death.

But I'd want to know.

She decided to change the subject. "Maybe you should map out this cave. See where we're at and if there's a way out."

Normak sighed heavily. His lips vibrated and buzzed. "S'pose ya be right. Sittin' 'ere ain't gonna save us." He pulled himself to his feet and walked off.

Finally alone, Urza allowed herself to let go. Tears filled her eyes, and she wept for Rayah.

† † †

A loud squeak roused Rayah from death. She hadn't actually died, but the weight of the world still lay on her chest. Or at least the weight of the desert did. The piece of falling ceiling must've struck her in the head and knocked her out before she had a chance to sink all the way down into the dirt.

The densely packed sand proved hard to see through. She guesstimated she could see about ten feet in each direction, but it didn't help orient her one bit. For all she knew, she could be facing down. The thought terrified her. She only had so much strength, and just breathing in the sand sapped it pretty quick.

Ƨätür, where am I?

From where she sat or lay, she couldn't see any of her friends. She prayed they'd made it out of the temple before it collapsed.

If they didn't, then they're probably… No!

She refused to allow herself to even think about it, but her stomach grumbled with unease, nonetheless.

I must find them.

But where would she start? The wrong direction would spell her end. There must be a way to orient herself. She closed her eyes and cleared her mind. Which way had she drilled into the dirt? Did it even matter? The passage might've collapsed along with everything else.

Think, Rayah.

Something cold and wet tickled her ear. Nibbled on it but didn't bite down. She flinched back and reached for her knives as she turned her head. Beady, little, red eyes stared at her. Her little desert rat friend had returned.

"Chirpa," she squealed. "Am I glad to see you!" She knew he didn't understand a word she said but talking to someone other than herself calmed her nerves.

She reached out and stoked Chirpa's smooth head. He leaned into her touch and squeaked softly. A foolish thought crossed her mind. She needed to give it a voice before rationale kicked in.

Rayah looked into Chirpa's eyes. Words teetered on the tip of her tongue. Pressed against the backs of her teeth. Chirpa cocked his head when she continued to hesitate. She finally spit the words out. "I need to find my friends and make sure they're safe."

Chirpa craned his head around, and then he darted several yards through the sand before she lost sight of him.

Rayah sighed. *Well, that didn't work.*

But then Chirpa appeared at the far edge of her vision. He stared at her and waited. Excitement filled her chest.

He must want me to follow him!

Rayah shook the pain from her muscles and got herself turned around. Chirpa wiggled his nose at her, and then he darted through the sand again. She followed him through the sand, hoping he'd understood her and led her back toward her friends and safety.

They must've been quite some distance underneath the sand because the tremendous weight of it slowed her down. It took most of her strength just to keep her wings beating. Chirpa must've understood because he slowed when she did.

About twenty minutes passed as she followed Chirpa through the sand. Nothing looked familiar. Or rather everything looked the same. Sand, sand, and more sand. She didn't understand what'd happened to the city.

Just ahead, something large lay in the sand. Or part of something. She couldn't tell what she was looking at until they got right up on it. Fur-covered legs. *Red* fur.

Rakzar!

Had something chopped him in half? His body ended right about his ribcage. But she didn't see any blood.

Then she noticed the brown cloth bag. Eshtak's mezhik bag. Understanding and elation stole her breath. Rakzar must've gotten trapped in the sand before he could escape into the bag. Using the bag that way was a smart move, but did the bag actually lead somewhere?

It's better than being buried alive.

Rayah wrapped her arms around Rakzar's legs and worked to free them from the sand, but her strength faltered. Between fighting the minotaurs and digging her way through the sand, she'd just about spent all her energy. She tried to move the sand again, but it seemed to pack around them even tighter.

To make matters worse, the bag's opening wasn't wide enough for them both to pass through it at the same time. She scooched down and grabbed Rakzar's feet.

You can do this, Rayah. Save him.

She grunted and forced the sand away from Rakzar with everything she had left. At first, only a few grains of sand stirred. Then a few more. Then the entire area around them stirred. Shook. Quaked.

Rayah screamed. A concussive wave of energy rippled through the sand, pushing it back and turning it into glass.

Rakzar slid forward and disappeared into the bag.

Rayah lay there stunned. She'd never heard of a soil dryte turning sand into glass. She didn't even understand how it'd happened. But it had.

Heavy eyelids drooped. No strength left to hold them open. Darkness closed in around her, but she didn't care. She'd found a way to save Rakzar, and that was the only thing that mattered.

Chirpa nuzzled her hand. Squeaked several times. But she couldn't move. Didn't want to move.

A dim light shone through the darkness beyond her eyelids. In her mind, Rayah smiled.

Ɛät̪ūr, is that You?

CHAPTER THIRTY-ONE

Pravus stood over the table in the war room, studying the city diagrams of Elatos, Borza, and Vallah. In less than a week, his army would march the final sixty miles into Elatos. However, his dispute with Lords Jagesh Rubano, Elder Baarth, and Uli Edersheimer still remained unresolved. Their armies totaled an additional thirty-five thousand men and women. He needed their support.

Or at least their armies.

A knock sounded at the door. "Enter." He didn't look up from the table but knew Credan had entered the room based on the sounds of his footfall and labored breathing.

"My lord, I have very good news."

Pravus finally looked up. Credan stood on the other side of the table, beaming with pride, his eyes bright and sparkling behind wire-rimmed spectacles. "You're far cheerier than a few days ago. What is it?"

"Lords Jagesh Rubano and Elder Baarth have recommitted to the campaign and ready their forces as we speak."

A weight lifted from Pravus's shoulders. "Excellent. And what of the little swine in Cape Timor, Lord Uli Edersheimer."

Credan wiped his brow with a kerchief. "Progress has been made there as well, albeit an unexpected development."

"Unexpected?" Pravus leaned over the table on his palms. "Either he's recommitted, or you've released Reubane. Which is it?"

"Neither, actually." Credan swallowed hard, the sparkle lost in his eyes. "Turns out—"

Pravus slammed his fist down on the table. "You've disobeyed a direct order."

Credan visibly cringed. "My lord, if you'll just hear me out, you'll be pleased with the outcome."

"Then spit it out before I turn Reubane loose on you."

"Yes, of course." Credan gathered himself and continued, "Disgusted after finding out that his father had snubbed you, Tuan Edersheimer, Lord Uli Edersheimer's eldest son, took up arms against his father and captured him. Having gained control over Cape Timor, he's recommitted his forces to the campaign and has promised to deliver his father into your hands as well."

Pravus straightened and steepled his fingers. "Then all is well again."

"Yes, my lord."

Pravus sighed with relief. "Good. Is there anything else I should know about?"

Credan looked up to his left for a moment. "I don't believe so. Everything is in order for next week's march. The soldiers have readied siege weapons and towers and enough extra weapons and armor to supply an additional hundred thousand soldiers."

Two hundred thousand strong. Pravus smiled. *King Zaridus has no chance of winning this war.*

He nodded toward Credan. "Excellent news. You've done well, my old friend."

Credan bowed. "My lord." He turned and left the war room.

Pravus cracked his knuckles.

Soon, the realm will bow to a new god.

CHAPTER THIRTY-TWO

Aria stood in the middle of The Plains, sixty miles south of Elatos. Fingers of the Orbis Mountain Range reached toward the sky in the north, begging the gods for mercy. But none would be granted. They'd burn along with the Three Kingdoms.

A lone fire, bright against the dusk sky, burned atop Mt. Rashard, the southernmost peak of the range. Cinolth had informed her of its significance—a warning signal to the entire realm. Somehow, King Zaridus knew they were coming. Even so, it would make no difference. King Zaridus prepared for a war he believed would be several months away, but she and the army would be at his doorstep in less than two weeks.

They're squatting deer.

Justice, vengeance, timing, and righteousness favored them. King Zaridus wouldn't know what hit him until it was too late.

Already, her forces numbered more than she could count. Many of Cinolth's faithful arrived earlier that day, and more poured in by the hour. Along with them came scores of others. The zhebəllin of the Daltura Hills, the mountain ogres of the Sol Deus Mountains, and the giants of the southwestern Orbis Mountains. As instructed by Pravus and Cinolth, none of the many groups mingled. Doing so bred chaos, and it was the last thing they needed before attacking Elatos.

Mutius and Bardaric worked fast building the wall, having completed more than a third of it already. In three days, she'd conjure the second gateway. In five days, Pravus and the rest of her army would walk straight from Galondu Castle onto The Plains. Her skin prickled with excitement.

In two weeks, I will officially be queen of the Ancient Realm.

Nothing would stop her. Nothing could. Not even Alderan.

Aria still sensed Cinolth's presence even though he hunted dozens of miles northwest. The flight up from Galondu Castle had weakened him more than he let on. She sensed his fatigue through their bond. Sometimes, she discovered secrets hidden within his mind. Secrets that he'd likely kill her for if he found out she knew. She wondered what secrets he might know about her as well.

The thought of bonds set her mind on Alderan. She reached out with her mind but didn't sense him. Fear struck the core of her heart, but only for a moment as she recalled Pravus collaring him. Ƨäbräƨär suppressed not only mezhik but their bond and blinded them from each other.

Aria desperately wanted Alderan to understand what she and Pravus strove to accomplish, but he'd always been bullheadish. Getting through to him would prove difficult, but she'd done it many times before. However, they'd never been at such odds on anything so important before. She didn't know what she'd do if he never came around to her way of thinking.

He's a threat. All threats must be eliminated.

The thought astonished her. Sickened her. But had it been her own? After the control Cinolth had demonstrated over her outside Desolo Urbs she couldn't be sure.

She'd never do anything to harm Alderan. She couldn't possibly.

Why would it be any different than with Nardus?

Frustration curled her hands and drew mezhik into them. She punched downward. A blast of air cratered the ground beside her, compacting the dirt more than two feet in diameter and several feet deep.

Nardus is nothing more than a stranger from my past, but Alderan is my brother.

But how deep did the blood ties run? Would she sacrifice a kingdom for him? She refused to ponder the question.

He will come around.

† † †

Calen hadn't left Savric's side since they'd reunited several days back. How could he? Everything in his life had burned to ashes, and hope had all but died the day Aunt Tahmara had walked out of the house, but seeing master Savric standing atop the outcropping had changed everything. No event in his entire life prior to that moment had given him such joy and hope. Finding Aunt Tahmara might be the only thing that could ever top it.

Unlike the past, Master Savric no longer traveled alone. He had a strange little man in tow named Eshtak. Calen didn't know what to make of Eshtak at first. Strange tattoos covered his entire body. He'd never met anyone so different and unique.

Calen had never had a friend before, at least not one that served solely in that role. Master Savric had always been so much more than a friend. He served as both a father figure and a grandfather as well. So, when Eshtak called Calen his friend after an entire five minutes had passed since they'd met, he admittedly felt a bit shocked. But the feeling wasn't one-sided. Eshtak exuded sincerity, love, and loyalty—three things that demanded his friendship. Qualities Calen had only witnessed before in Master Savric.

Eshtak also had a way of bringing perspective into everything. He didn't even need to say anything. His presence and joyous outlook infected everyone around him. They'd become inseparable.

No matter the task, Eshtak rushed to do it with enthusiasm. He'd happily volunteered to help Calen find his aunt now that their group of infected had met up with a much larger group and settled down into what kind of resembled a camp.

Aunt Tahmara must be here somewhere.

After witnessing several violent events, Calen had no delusions of rescuing his aunt. Just finding her and knowing she still lived would satisfy him for the moment. He loved her like a mother.

Master Savric sat on a large boulder, his attention focused somewhere in the distance. Calen had begged him to join their quest for his aunt, but he'd simply declined. It wasn't good enough.

Calen stomped his foot. "I don't understand why you won't come with us." He knew such behavior was unbecoming of a boy his age, but he couldn't help it. He needed Master Savric at his side.

"Do not fret, my boy." Steam rose from a small bowl nestled between Master Savric's crossed legs. "We will see each other back here in a few hours' time. Now, there are things we both must do to achieve inner peace. With Eshtak's help, you must locate your aunt and assess her condition, and I must confront my goddaughter before the opportunity is lost."

Calen clutched Master Savric's shoulder. Tears brimmed in his eyes. "Promise me that you'll return, Master Savric. I can't lose you again."

Master Savric smiled his usual smile—the one that melted people's hearts with kindness and sincerity. "I assure you that at no point was I ever lost. Distracted and delayed for certain, but never lost." He patted the back of Calen's hand. "You never left my thoughts. Now, go find your aunt."

Calen eyed the ground and pushed a small rock in a circle with his foot. "You really think I can do this?"

"Of that, I have no doubt." Master Savric sipped some broth from his bowl. "Look at what you have already accomplished. You fought and escaped from the zhebəllin *and* rescued countless children in the process. Then you embarked on a journey beyond the walls of Daltura and into unknown and distant lands. You are so much stronger and braver than you give yourself credit."

Calen sighed. "How can I be brave when I'm scared?"

"We are all scared at times, and being so is nothing to be ashamed of. What you do when you are scared is what matters. Dwell on it, and it will control you. Act despite of it, and you will overcome it. Were you not scared when the zhebəllin captured you?"

Calen released Master Savric's shoulder and wiped his eyes. "Yeah."

"Yet you conquered your fears and your foe."

Master Savric is right. I was brave.

Calen took a deep breath and forced it back out through closed lips, vibrating them. "Thank you, Master Savric. You always have a way of helping me see things differently. One day, I hope I can see them for myself."

"Indeed." Master Savric downed the rest of his bone broth in one big gulp. He followed it up with a loud belch.

Eshtak laughed and danced in a circle. "Good good food!"

Calen proffered his hand, and Master Savric took it. "Good luck with your goddaughter."

"And you with your aunt." Master Savric released Calen's hand, winked, and then used his staff to get to his feet. "See you soon." He slammed the butt-end of his staff on the rock and disappeared in a whirlwind.

Calen's stomach lurched, and his pulse quickened. He took several deep breaths, but it didn't settle his nerve or his heart.

You can do this, Calen.

Eshtak grabbed Calen's hand and pulled on his arm. "Come! Come! Eshtak help friend find aunt."

Eshtak's touch evaporated his fear. He chuckled. "Okay, okay. Let's go."

An unending sea of infected lay before them. Finding Aunt Tahmara would be as likely as finding a booger on a sandy beach, but at least he and Eshtak had each other's company. They strolled down the side of the outcropping and into the throng, hand-in-hand.

Ƶäṭūr, guide us to Aunt Tahmara.

† † †

Savric moved through the camp, sticking to the shadows and displacing the light with mezhik as he went. He found it strange that Aria would be out there on her own without protection, but he didn't detect a threat as he approached her.

Ten paces away, Aria turned and faced him. A faint red glow illuminated her eyes as they narrowed. "There's no point in hiding. I can hear you breathing."

Savric released the light he'd trapped. "I dare say I am only here to talk."

"I have seen your face before, have I not?" Aria stalked forward. She held no weapon and conjured no mezhik that Savric could detect. Recollection lifted her eyebrows. "You're the one from Daltura."

"To be certain." Savric stroked his beard. "You have changed since last we met. Your hair. Your eyes. The way you carry yourself. Gone is the timid girl I once knew."

"I don't understand. Are you saying that you knew me before we met in Daltura?" She sighed and shook her head. "Yes, of course you must've. Why else would you have left me that note?"

"I prayed that you would understand its meaning."

"Those two words ruled my life for many days. Why did you not stay longer in Daltura?"

"I feared discovery. Alas, it would have made little difference if I knew then what I know now."

"Why are you here? What is it that you want? Better yet, who are you?"

"My name is Savric Naphor. I knew your mother, Gretchen."

"She wasn't my mother."

"Yes, of course. Not by birth at least. But I promise you that few could have loved you more than she did."

"She was no better than my father who abandoned me and my brother."

"I did not know your birth father, but I do know that he loved you very much. What happened was a tragedy."

"None of it matters. It's all in the past. Why are you here?"

Savric eyed the massive wall south of where they stood. "What purpose will this wall serve?"

Aria scowled at him. "That is no concern of yours."

"Very well. Perhaps you can inform me as to your dealings with that dragon. Surely you know he cannot be trusted."

"You know Cinolth as well?" Her left eyebrow rose, but the scowl on her face remained.

Even though Morcinda had told him of the curse and what the black scale must mean, hearing Aria confirm the dragon's name struck fear in Savric's heart. The prophecies had not been wrong.

Savric nodded. "Only of him. His brutal and contentious reputation has not been forgotten in more than a millennium."

Aria crossed her arms. "Then you know what he'll do to you when he finds you here."

"Perhaps." Savric looked around. "I am surprised that your brother is not here with you."

Crimson rose in Aria's neck and cheeks. He'd obviously struck a point of contention. "Alderan has yet to fully understand what we aim to accomplish, but he will soon enough."

"And what is it that you aim to accomplish? The Ancient Realm has been at peace for two decades. The only thing you will accomplish through war is death and suffering. That is not Ɂäʈūr's way. What righteous purpose could that possibly serve?"

"As a wizard, you must be aware of King Zaridus's views on mezhik. Or are you too blind to see it?" Vitriol laced her words and strained her voice. "In secret and through shadows he strives to eradicate our kind. A campaign such as his cannot and will not be tolerated."

The young, scared girl Savric had approached in Daltura no longer existed, and it pained him. Perhaps he should've done more than leave her a note that day, but he held no power to change the past. However, he held out hope that her mind could be changed.

He stroked his beard. "Aria, you have a choice in this. You must understand that what you are about to do is wretched and vile and goes against everything you were taught as a little girl. Slaughtering innocent people will do nothing but blacken your soul. Turn back now, Aria. It is not too late for you."

Aria's eyes burned brighter. "Don't you get it? There is no choice to be made. We do what must be done. This world is full of detestable people like

King Zaridus, and it must be purged." Mezhik crackled in her palm.

Savric stepped back and held his left hand up. "My dearest girl, I do not wish to fight you. That is not why I came here." He held Qotan's staff in his right hand. Mezhik warmed his palm.

"Yet you challenge me." Aria thrust her arm forward, aimed at Savric. An orange, red, and purple fireball flew from her palm. Savric conjured a light shield around himself just before the fireball slammed into him. A moment slower, and he would've been a human torch.

Two more fireballs slammed into his shield, driving him half a dozen steps backward. The fourth fireball shattered it.

"*Əllzíä!*" shouted Aria. Yellow vines with red leaves shot up from the ground all around Savric and ensnared him. The leaves, infused with fire, burned through his robes and scorched his skin.

Aria's strength and knowledge of mezhik astounded Savric. Her skill easily matched his, and he sensed she toyed with him. He needed to get away before it turned deadly—for him.

Aria approached, the red fringe around her irises glowing coal red. "The truth bleeds from your eyes. You're no better than King Zaridus." She spat at his feet. "You're a disgrace to our kind."

"No, Aria." He winced as pain burrowed deeper into his flesh. "The hatred you spew is not your own. I can see it in your eyes. The dragon controls you."

"No one controls me!" roared Aria. The ground shook as dozens of fist-sized rocks rose out of the earth. They circled Savric like a cyclone.

Savric opened his palm. "*Buallz əllítninzh.*" Lightning pulsed, crackled, and thundered, splitting the air, lighting the darkness, and shredding the vines that held him in place. The circling rocks exploded into dust clouds.

More rocks shot up from the ground.

Ten times the previous amount.

Aria yelled and slammed her hands together.

The rocks converged on Savric's position.

Savric slammed the butt-end of Qotan's staff into the ground and spun into the night, but not before one of the rocks cracked his jaw and bit into his cheek.

† † †

So many faces stared into the distance with black eyes and blank expressions. Calen wondered if they saw at all or if their world remained dark during the daylight hours as well. None of them reacted or cared about him shining torchlight on them.

Between traveling for more than a week in the dirt and mud and the infection turning their skin white and their veins black, the infected all looked similar. Any one of them could be his aunt. Well, at least any one of the women.

Calen and Eshtak searched for several hours without luck. He didn't know how many faces they'd checked, but it had to have been in the hundreds. Unfortunately, there were literally thousands of them. Tens of thousands. Maybe more.

Tears swelled in Calen's eyes. "What if we don't ever find her? What if she's not here or died along the way?"

Eshtak hugged Calen's waist. "Eshtak helps friend. Won't stop."

"I won't either." Calen turned around and ran right into the side of a large man. The man kept walking, unphased by the collision.

Calen started to move on but stopped abruptly. Recollection tickled his mind. He'd seen the man before in Daltura but didn't know his name.

"Come on, Eshtak!" Calen turned and followed the big man through the eastern part of the camp.

Finally, the man stopped and sat down in front of a blazing fire pit. Turning in a circle, Calen examined each of their faces. His heart thumped harder in his chest when he recognized several others, including Mr. Dougett.

"She must be here somewhere!" Excitement tightened his throat and squawked his voice.

He searched frantically, Eshtak close on his heels. Twice, he knew he'd found her, but they turned out to be someone else when the light reached their faces.

"Aunt Tahmara!" Calen screamed.

She wouldn't respond, but he couldn't help himself. He screamed her name again, tears streaking down his face. He swore they'd come close to finding her, but she just wasn't there. He dropped to his knees and sobbed.

Eshtak knelt next to him and took the torch from his hand. "Eshtak not give up. Friend not give up."

The torchlight flickered, twisting shadows and distorting faces. Calen gathered himself and wiped his face. Then, at the fringe of the torchlight, he noticed someone lying underneath a blanket, their face covered. He recognized the blanket from his aunt's bedroom. Yellow, brown, and orange yarn crocheted in chevron patterns. Many blankets consisted of the same colors, but he'd never seen another crocheted the same way.

He crawled over to the person, too nervous to stand on legs he knew couldn't support him. Eshtak followed with the torch. Calen touched the edge of the blanket. His fingers shook with nerves. The wool yarn, soft to the touch, slid between his fingers. He latched onto it. Held it.

What if it's not her?

Anyone could've found the blanket or stolen it from her. Had she even taken it with her? What if her blanket still lay on her bed at home?

Calen released the blanket and sat back on his heels. He didn't think he could handle it not being her. It would devastate him. Eshtak must've sensed his hesitation. Eshtak handed the torch back to Calen and knelt next to the person underneath the blanket.

Calen's heart thundered in his ears, and his pulse raced faster than he thought possible.

Eshtak took the edge of the blanket and lifted it up. Calen couldn't see. Didn't want to see. Shadows distorted the person's face.

"Look," said Eshtak.

Calen refused. How could it be her? He'd never find her again.

Eshtak snatched the torch back and held it over the person's head. "Friend's aunt?"

It's not her. It's not her.

Calen forced himself to look at the infected person. A woman. Fiery red hair dirtied with mud. Shoulder length. She did look like Aunt Tahmara, but it couldn't be her. Aunt Tahmara didn't have a gash on her cheek like that woman did. Aunt Tahmara's eyes were green, not black.

No, it couldn't be her.

But it was.

Nine days of searching, and he'd found her. Tears erupted from his eyes once again but this time with joy. Not only had he found Aunt Tahmara, but she still lived.

"Eshtak, it's her!" Calen shot to his feet, grabbed Eshtak, and hugged him. Shook him. Squeezed him like he wanted to squeeze his aunt.

Eshtak cried tears of joy with Calen as they jumped around in a circle together. Shadows beyond the torchlight danced with them as well. Somehow, Eshtak had managed to hold onto the torch.

"Friend finds aunt! Friend finds aunt!" cried Eshtak. His enthusiasm warmed Calen's heart.

They danced around for several minutes hooting and hollering, but not a soul looked their way. Calen didn't care. He looked to the heavens with tear blurred vision. "Ɂäṯūr, thank you for helping me find my aunt!" He smiled down at Eshtak. "And for giving me a friend."

Until that moment, Calen hadn't realized how much he'd longed to have a friend over the years. Never again would he have to wonder what it'd feel like to share moments like those with someone who cared about him. His cheeks ached from smiling so wide. That moment with Eshtak and Aunt Tahmara might've topped the one with Savric a few days back. Or at least equaled it. The two most important people in his life had abandoned him, neither by choice, but now he'd reunited with them once again.

And I have a friend.

Calen sucked tendrils of snot back into his nose and wiped the rest with the backs of his hands. "I love you, Aunt Tahmara."

She pulled the blanket back over her head, never giving him a moment's glance, but he didn't care. She was alive, and that's all that mattered. Master Savric would help him figure out how to save her. Of that, he was certain.

He rubbed Eshtak's bald head. "Let's go tell Master Savric that she's okay."

Eshtak nodded vigorously. "Yes! Yes! Old friend happy."

Calen couldn't help but laugh as he took the torch from Eshtak and started heading back the way they'd come.

Eshtak grabbed his arm and spun him back around. "Come! Eshtak knows way back."

Apparently, his sense of direction hadn't improved over the last week. He smiled.

That's what friends are for.

CHAPTER THIRTY-THREE

The aroma of roasted rabbit pulled Rayah up from the depths of a strange and fantastic dream, but she didn't want to be awake just yet. Another hour or so, and she'd be fully rested. She held her eyes closed and willed herself back into the dreamworld she'd left behind, but her stomach groaned with hunger pangs.

"Fine," she huffed. "I'll get up." Heavy eyelids fought her and the morning light, and, when she did manage to get them open, she struggled to see through the blur of colors and light.

What happened last night? Had she been drinking ale? She remembered nothing.

She yawned and lifted her arms to stretch them. Each arm must've weighed a hundred pounds. They flopped back down with a smack. A cold, leafy texture met her fingertips.

Rayah tried to lift her head up, but the task proved far harder than lifting her arms had been. "Hello? Is anyone there?"

Her feet dropped like two bags of sand when she swung them over the edge of whatever she laid upon. The abrupt shift in weight almost dragged her down.

"She's finally awake," said a rough but distinctly female voice.

"About damn time," growled a male.

"Aye," said another male with a thick accent.

Rayah recognized all three voices. They'd been in her dream, but the details had already skewed and faded like they always did after waking. However, her mind clung to the idea of a talking rat.

That's absurd. She snorted and laughed.

"Rayah?" said Urza.

Rayah reached up and touched her own lips. "Rayyyah. Rayahhh. Rayah." The word sounded silly and made her laugh harder.

"What the gods did they give her?" asked Rakzar.

"Whatever it be, might find meself some. Ya know, fer later."

"Don't even think about it, Normak," said Urza. "Give her a few minutes, and you'll understand."

Rayah's head swam on her shoulders when she sat up. A hand grabbed her arm and steadied her, but she hadn't been prepared for the nausea that swept through her gut. She bent forward and let the contents of her stomach fly.

"Oy!" yelled Normak. "That there ain't right. Nothin' comin' up should be squirmin' aboot."

"Wormroot," said Urza. "Pulls death from the blood and bones and helps restore a person's energy."

"And how do *you* know this?" demanded Rakzar.

"Observation. You should try it sometime. I've picked up many things over the years."

"And the vomitin' be normal?" asked Normak.

"The side effects are different for everyone. Some just get a bit of nausea while others experience full-blown episodes of delusion."

Rayah belched and felt much better. And then she didn't. More volume than she thought her stomach could hold came up the second time. The stench easily rivaled a bloated, day old corpse ripening in the summer heat. She leaned over again and spat the acidic taste from her mouth, but the back of her throat still burned.

"Swear, I don' like ya no more, lass." Normak stomped about. "Pray that washes outta me boots."

Rakzar scoffed, "I'll be praying that it doesn't."

The taste of death resided in Rayah's mouth, coating her tongue. She needed to expel it before she fell into a fit of dry heaves. "Can I get some water?" Someone shoved a waterskin into her hand. It took several swigs and a lot of swishing to lessen the taste.

A few minutes later, Rayah's surroundings began to come into focus. Urza sat next to her on what she could only describe as a suspended bed. Knitted, knotted, and woven vines stretched between two trees and held them several feet off the ground.

Rakzar leaned against a thick tree with red bark that nearly matched the color of his fur. Until that moment, she hadn't noticed how well his fur had grown in over the last week. Several of his scars now hid under tufts of fur.

Soon, they'd be fully covered and forgotten. Well, at least the physical ones.

Normak stood to the side, his brow scrunched and his jaw tight. She still had trouble reading the dwarf. Oft he looked to be in a fit of rage yet cracked jokes. Perhaps brooding was the only look he had.

Urza held fast to her arm as Rayah slid off the bed and onto shaky legs. She didn't look down to see if she'd stepped in her own filth. She didn't want to know.

When Rayah turned around, she saw that they stood at the edge of a small forest village. But she didn't recognize it. The handful of buildings—if one could call them that—stood between clusters of trees and consisted solely of roofs made from large branches and leaves. No walls. No privacy.

The village residents didn't resemble any other group of people she'd ever seen. They were humanoid shaped creatures, lanky yet muscular, and wore no clothing of any kind, but they didn't need to. Brown, black, and red feathers covered their bodies from the crown of their heads down to their ankles. Their large feet were reminiscent of a hawk's, three splayed appendages forward and one backward, each ending in a razor-sharp, hooked claw. Brown irises filled their eyes, leaving no whites to them, and their beak-like noses hooked down over small lower lips. No discernible ears protruded from the sides of their heads, nor did they seem to have necks. But that could've simply been an illusion created by their thick feathers. The males and females were distinguishable by their plumage. The males had dull, brown plumage whereas the females had bright, red-and-gold plumage.

Rayah sat back down. "Where are we?"

"Not sure," said Urza. "After entering Eshtak's bag, we found ourselves in the middle of miles of caves. Normak mapped them out for us and found an exit on the face of a cliff overlooking a body of water that stretched as far as the eye could see."

Rayah looked back over her shoulder. "And how did we get here?"

"Normak discovered a way to climb the cliff face and went for help because we were all in bad shape," said Urza. "One of the local healers came back with him and mended our wounds."

"Now that you're awake, we can find a way out of here," said Rakzar.

"Why not ask one of them where we are?" said Rayah.

"We're being tolerated, but the majority of them don't like us being here. Most of them don't speak our language either. Even if they told us where we are, their name for it might be different than ours, or we might not even know of it."

"I see." Rayah stood again. "How long have we been here?"

"Just over a day," said Rakzar. "We're wasting time."

Rayah turned to Normak. "And you haven't scouted this place?"

"What I could," said Normak. "Water to the west and north. South and east are more of an issue. Trees are too dense to run through. Figured yeh'd fly and see what there be."

"Or go underground," said Urza.

The succulent aroma of roasted rabbit wafted into Rayah's nostrils once again. Her purged stomach rumbled with hunger. "I'll do it, but I'm going to need some food first. Anyone else starving?"

Normak screwed up his face. "Was 'til ya ruined me boots *and* me appetite."

Rayah shrugged. "Guess that leaves more rabbit for me then."

Normak raised both hands. "Hold up, lass. Might not be starvin', but I still be hungry."

Twenty minutes later, the four of them stood at the southern edge of the village. Red spruce trees, tall and thick with spindly, crimson needles and yellow, teardrop-shaped cones, lined the forest edge. Bramble, vines, and bushes covered the forest floor and packed most of the space between trees. Now Rayah understood why Normak hadn't scouted the area.

With so much undergrowth, Rayah guessed the underground route wouldn't be viable. She sank into the ground for a quick check and confirmed it. Roots grew in a tangled mess everywhere because of the shallowness of the soil. At best, there might've been six feet of soil before hitting dense rock. It made perfect sense, given the cave system beneath them.

Rayah rose back out of the ground. "Flying it is." She fluttered off the ground. "I'll come back as soon as I can."

"Be careful," growled Rakzar.

Urza and Normak whipped their heads around and eyed Rakzar.

Rakzar glared at them. "What? I don't want to be stuck here."

"That be yer meanin', eh?" Normak winked at Rayah.

Urza smirked but made no comment. Rakzar growled and stormed off.

Rayah giggled, waved goodbye, and then zoomed up to the top of the forty-foot-high canopy. A crimson sea stretched for miles south, east, and west. Neither south nor east looked better, so she chose south and prayed she'd come across a place she might recognize.

Flying so high above the ground always terrified Rayah, but the thick canopy beneath her helped. She much preferred being down in the soil though. No way of falling there. Plus, it didn't make her head spin and her stomach queasy like flying did.

After flying for nearly an hour nonstop, Rayah noticed a change in the trees. The red spruces gave way to yellow aspen and other coniferous trees in hues of blue and green. To her left, far in the distance, mountains touched the sky and their peaks pierced the clouds. She thought she recognized them, so she adjusted her flightpath and headed straight for them.

Another twenty minutes and the mountain range still loomed far in the distance. Then she noticed a distinct break in the tree line. When she got a bit closer, she realized that the break in the trees spanned a much greater distance than she'd first thought—at least a good forty miles. To make matters worse, water spanned the distance, and the closer she got the more distinct the whitecaps became.

She reached the coastline and dropped down onto the narrow, rocky beach. Across the body of water, gleaming in the early morning sun, stood a lone wall atop a hill. Just north of that hill, nestled in the valley across the sea from her, she spotted the remnants of what used to be a pier.

Her heart soared. "We must be on Mortuus Vir Isle!" Of all the places Eshtak's bag could've led, she never would've guessed Mortuus Vir Isle would be it.

But how will we get back to the mainland?

A half mile down the coast she spotted two canoes pulled up onto the rocky shore.

Thank you, Ɛäṭūr!

She flew into the air and headed back toward Rakzar and the others. They'd be pleased with her success, but not with the route they must take. The journey through the forest would be long and arduous, but at least they'd have a way to get off the island once they reached the shore.

If we can reach it.

CHAPTER THIRTY-FOUR

The first rays of dawn painted the western skies in hues of blue, red, and purple, but it wasn't what roused Savric from the clutches of sleep. He'd awakened a solid hour before, his mind churning away as it searched for an answer as to the purpose of the monstrous wall that stretched a quarter mile from east to west.

For the last two days, he'd watched Aria from a distance as she worked her way back and forth along the wall, casting rune spells and weaving webs of mezhik he couldn't begin to comprehend. Layers upon layers of mezhik. Cinolth tracked her every move as well, never leaving her side as she worked day and night without rest.

Now, Aria rested in her royal tent set up in the middle of the camp. The tent's stark white fabric and its four black flags donning a red dragon's eye couldn't be missed. Savric had seen that coat of arms once before and knew its history stretched back millennia. Pugnus Rosai, the southern ruler decades ago, flew those same flags. He wondered if the man Aria accompanied in Daltura was related to Pugnus in some way. As far as he knew, Pugnus left no heirs alive, so it wasn't likely.

Unless Pugnus did not know about him.

As he walked along the wall, he studied the glowing rune spells hanging on its surface. Each stroke had purpose and every curve and line executed with perfection. But what goal did it serve being built dozens of miles from any city? And at such scale.

Savric pulled on his beard. "An entire army could walk—"

Understanding of the wall's purpose bloomed in his mind and shook him all the way down into his bones. Had he not been clutching Qotan's staff, he would've fallen to his knees. As it was, he struggled to keep his legs underneath himself.

"Dear Ɂäṭūr… she has built some sort of gateway."

But where did it lead? Or what led to it? He turned and faced the camp again. Its size grew daily, stretching a few miles in each direction, but what if it represented just a fraction of their entire army?

His heart thundered, and his knees weakened further. He slid down his staff and to his knees.

King Zaridus must be warned.

Savric laid the staff down and retrieved the small, leather-bound book with Ɂäəll Dhef Ɂäfn Dhä embossed on its cover from within the folds of his robes. "*In əllít Hiz.*" The clasp sealing the book clicked open. He took the fountain pen out of its pouch on the inside cover and turned to the first page.

He wrote to Morcinda with fevered urgency. "*Morcinda, the situation at hand has developed into something far more concerning than previously thought. At the camp sixty miles south of Elatos, Aria and Cinolth have built what I am certain is a gateway. I believe they plan to use it to bring up additional forces from another location. Warn King Zaridus. War is coming quicker than we thought possible. In əllít Hiz. -Savric*"

Savric tapped the page with the fountain pen and the words faded. Moments ticked by agonizingly slow while he awaited a response. But did a response matter? He'd sent the message. She'd get it soon.

The first rays of light shone from the west, exposing him to any number of potential threats while he knelt in the open. He returned the fountain pen to its pouch and the book to its place within his robes. With the aid of Qotan's staff, he rose to his feet.

The camp would soon awaken, but he needed to do more. The only question was what could be done? Sunlight glistened on the morning dew, sending pops of light dancing across the wall's surface. The effect distorted the runes and triggered a thought.

Perhaps I can modify a few of these rune spells without Aria noticing.

Savric had no understanding of how the rune spells worked, but a subtle change here and there might afford King Zaridus a little more time to prepare. Four times, he teleported to different spots along the wall and adjusted a line here and a curve there. He was about to teleport again to make a fifth change, but spotted Aria emerging from her tent. Her head rotated toward him just as he teleported back to the outcropping several miles to the west.

His heart ached in his chest, the pressure of the situation taxing. Even if she'd seen him, would she know what he'd done? To be honest, he wasn't sure if he'd altered the runes enough to disable the gateway when her and Cinolth activated it.

And what if the gateway blows up?

The loss of life, especially that of Aria's, would be devastating, but the casualties would still be far fewer than what would certainly be sustained with an all-out war. Still, it would crush him. He stood against foes like Cinolth to preserve life, not take it.

Ɛäṭūr, do not let their blood stain my hands.

† † †

Aria stood before the massive wall, her hands trembling at her sides. So much work went into building it and readying the gateway, and the pressure of its success weighed heavily on her shoulders. Failure would be devastating, even if it stemmed from some structural defect. She oversaw every aspect of it, the responsibility all her own.

Cinolth stood behind her, his eyes boring holes in the back of her head. His thunderous, gravelly voice filled her mind. *"It's time. Are you ready?"*

Aria nodded and closed her eyes. She'd checked the entire wall after she'd finished weaving the webs and casting the rune spells last night. Everything was in order.

"Remember your instruction," said Cinolth in her mind. *"Connect the two sides and build the gateway."*

She opened and closed her hands several times and wrung the nerves from them. With a deep breath, she pushed everything from her mind.

Just like we practiced.

Aria pictured the two walls in her mind. Parallel to each other, they stretched into the distance before her. Left to right, she strung a virtual rope between them.

A low thrum shook the ground and resonated in her chest. A blinding light erupted beyond her eyelids. With each rope, the light intensified, and the thrum grew louder.

One hundred layers of spells required one hundred virtual ropes. By the time she'd connected ninety-nine of them, the entire wall shook on its foundation and pulsed with energy. But it held.

Mutius and Bardaric had done their job as required, building each wall in five days. As promised, Cinolth had released them—into death. The stipulation of their release had been underscored with every conversation.

She doubted they'd understood it though. Even if they had, complying added two additional weeks to their lives.

Aria refocused on the two walls. One last connection, and the gateway would be complete. She strung the last rope between the two walls, connecting the last layer of each.

Opening her eyes and stepping back, Aria stared at the wall. Never had she seen such brilliant light, but it didn't sting her eyes or blind her. Instead, it grew with heat, turning the rock into magma. The wall shook so violently that she thought it might topple over, but it stood firm. The magma turned to black glass and solidified as the heat died out. Then, the wall's surface began to shimmer like that of sunlight on a lake. The shimmers intensified until the entire surface rocked and swirled.

Beneath the violent surface, a picture began to form. Pieces here and there came into view—an army dressed in black. Several minutes passed as the picture cleared and the surface stilled.

Through the gateway, Pravus stood, his robes and silver hair billowing in a wind she didn't feel standing in The Plains. Stoic as he stood, excitement burned in his eyes. He stepped toward the gateway and Aria's stomach leapt into her throat.

Her arm rose from her side, her palm straight forward. "Wait," she said, much louder and more forceful than she'd planned. "Do not be the first one through. I'm not ready to die even if you are."

Pravus scowled but nodded. "I brought a test subject for this very purpose." His voice came through the gateway like a distant echo, nearly a full second after his lips stopped moving. He turned and motioned two soldiers forward.

The soldiers dragged a man bound with manacles and chains between them right up to the gateway.

"Don't do this," begged the man. Blood seeped from a gash in his forehead and ran into his eyebrows, turning his silver hair crimson. He jerked his head around and pleaded with Pravus. "I've done everything you've asked."

Aria recognized the man from the stone ceremony at Galondu Castle. *Lord Uli Edersheimer.* As far as she knew, the man's fealty lay firmly with House Rosai. Had something changed in the last week? She looked over at Pravus and thought about asking him how Lord Edersheimer came to be bound in chains, but the look in Pravus's eyes held her tongue. They'd certainly discuss it later.

Pravus stepped up behind Lord Edersheimer and grabbed him by the back of his neck. The portly man's chains rattled and sweat poured from his brow, mixing with the blood from his wound. Sweat dampened his armpits and tears glistened in his eyes.

A man without backbone. How pathetic.

"Release him," Pravus commanded the two soldiers.

The soldiers complied and stepped back. Pravus leaned forward and whispered something in Lord Edersheimer's ear. The blood drained from his rosy, porkchop cheeks. A single shove, and Lord Edersheimer stumbled forward and through the gateway.

He dropped to his knees in front of Aria and kissed the ground. "Praise the god—" He gurgled and spit up blood. It ran down the corners of his mouth and hemorrhaged from his nostrils, ears, and eyes. He grabbed for his throat, but then his entire body convulsed and burst like a sack of wet flour. Blood and guts spilled across the ground. Lord Edersheimer crumpled and sank into a pile of skin and bones, his muscles, fat, tissue, and organs liquefied. Steam rose from the saturated ground, and a greenish-brown cloud rose from the remains; a putrid mix of methane, feces, and other unidentifiable smells.

Aria stepped back and dug her fingernails into her palms, willing her stomach to stay strong, but it would not comply. Bile erupted from her open mouth as she bent over, a geyser of bread, dried fish, and water mixed with stomach acid. She coughed and spat the taste from her mouth, but tendrils still hung from her parted lips. She wiped her mouth with her hand and shook the stringy substance from her fingers.

When she looked up, everyone stared at her. Thousands of eyes. Their queen a disgusting mess.

Pravus's scowl softened. "I don't think you need me to tell you that something is not right."

"You think?" Her nostrils flared and she spat again. "The gateway's been sabotaged."

Cinolth's voice entered her mind. *"You know who did this, don't you."* A statement, not a question.

Aria had no doubt as to where the blame lay. *"Savric Naphor,"* she replied through mindspeak.

Cinolth stomped the ground and shouted in her mind, *"Tell me what he looks like, and I will hunt him down and rip his soul from his body!"*

Aria turned and faced Cinolth. Craning her head, she peered into his eyes. Through mindspeak, she said, *"You can deal with him later. Right now, I need your strength to repair the gateway."*

Cinolth snorted smoke. *"Your recklessness will be the ruin of us all."*

The jab hurt, but she deserved it. Had she taken care of Savric when he confronted her a few days back, he wouldn't have been alive to sabotage anything. She had him in her clutches and could've killed him easily enough, but she'd hesitated. Their next encounter would be much different.

Aria moved farther east along the wall, mainly to get away from Lord Edersheimer—or at least what remained of him.

Pravus kept pace with her on the other side of the gateway. "Now what?"

She stopped and glared at him. "You wait. I'll have this repaired within the hour."

Pravus sighed heavily. "I'm sure you'll do just as you say. However, I'd like insurance that you get it right this next time."

Aria crossed her arms. "Meaning what?"

Pravus snarled, "Your brother will be the next one through." He turned and walked away.

Mezhik crackled at Aria's fingertips. *That bastard dares threaten my brother?*

"Don't let him goad you," said Cinolth. *"Now that your soul is bound to his, he'd never kill your brother because you share your brother's blood. Doing so would sever that bond, and then I'd kill him."*

Aria took a deep breath and released her hold on her mezhik. *"Do I need to sever the connections between the two sides of the gateway before I repair what's been damaged?"*

Cinolth growled, "Only the last one."

"Good. Let's begin."

Aria cleared her mind and visualized the two walls again. She carefully removed one of the virtual ropes connecting the two walls. As before, the entire wall shook and the air thrummed, but it only lasted a few seconds. The other side of the gateway tremored and then blinked out, leaving a solid wall with glowing runes once again.

Twice, Aria and Cinolth walked the entire wall as she examined every single layer of rune spells again. In three separate places, she found alterations to the runes she'd drawn. Subtle and sneaky, the changes lay underneath her own, nearly undetectable. She corrected them and examined them again.

She stood back and eyed the wall. "I think I've found them all."

"You think, or you know?" questioned Cinolth.

Aria shrugged. "How can I be certain without testing it?"

"There is another way, but it will require a sacrifice."

Sacrifice…

Two things crossed Aria's mind as she thought about that word. First, they headed toward war and a guaranteed loss of many lives. Second, what if Pravus wasn't bluffing? She couldn't risk Alderan's life, especially if another way of guaranteeing the gateway worked existed.

"Let's be certain then," said Aria.

Cinolth called over one of his followers, a young man with white hair. A green claw on the inside of his left wrist marked him as Fizärd Enämäəll. He wore dark-brown robes, cinched at the waist with a leather belt. A sheathed dagger hung from the belt on his right side.

"Take his dagger, say '*ʒä nʒän dhä*,' and then plunge it through his heart."

Aria reached over and unsheathed his dagger. A six-inch blade. Plenty of length to get it underneath his ribs and pierce his heart.

The young man pulled his robes open, exposing his abdomen and chest. More than that, but she dared not look. Thunderous drums pounded in her ears.

She froze. She'd taken several lives over the last year, but each had earned their death. This young man, controlled by Cinolth, had done nothing to her. In fact, he fought on her side.

Can I take his life?

In a blink, she held the dagger right underneath the young man's lower rib.

When had she moved her hand?

Sweat dampened her palms. Wet the dagger's bone handle.

She looked him in the eyes.

No life. Just inky black wells.

Her lips moved. *"Ƨä nƨän dhä."*

Mezhik welled within her. Intoxicated her. She breathed heavily. Panted.

A loud grunt sounded. Caught within her ear.

His or mine?

Sweat poured down her hand.

She looked. Crimson.

Sweating blood?

No, the dagger's hilt rested underneath the young man's lower rib.

His hands wrapped around hers.

Soft hands.

She looked him in the eye once more.

Black irises faded into piercing green.

Fear of death flashed in them.

His hands fell away from hers as his eyes glossed over.

A torrent of intoxicating mezhik flowed into her, reaching every point within her.

She arched her back and moaned.

The young man collapsed. Dead. Lifeless.

But he still remained within her. His mezhik essence.

"Turn around, Aria." Cinolth's voice in her head focused her attention.

She turned and stared at the wall. Each rune glowed a vibrant green, the same color as the young man's eyes in the end. Behind the runes, the wall glowed in patches of orange and red.

"What does it mean?" she asked through her mind.

"What you're seeing is the essence of the mezhik's caster. Each wizard displays a unique essence. Think of it like a signature. There should only be three of them. Yours, Mutius's, and Bardaric's. Touch each essence, and it will hide it from view so that you can find others."

Aria reached out and touched the vibrant green essence. Immediately, the rune spells disappeared in both directions as far as she could see. She then touched the orange and red ones, Mutius's and Bardaric's. The wall turned black.

"Okay, I don't see any more essences."

"Walk the wall. Be certain."

From west to east, they walked the wall once more. Nothing came up until they reached the far eastern edge. Three patches of yellow essence glowed. With Cinolth's help, Aria pulled the tainted portions from the wall.

Satisfied no other alterations remained, she and Cinolth returned to the center of the wall. Someone had cleaned up the mess formerly known as Lord Uli Edersheimer. A stain remained on the ground, and a slight stench still wrinkled her nose, but nothing like before.

Aria pictured the walls once more and reconnected the last virtual rope. As before, thrumming and shaking ensued. The wall melted, vibrated, shimmered, and transformed into glassy rock before the other side of the gateway came into view.

Pravus stood on the other side once again. His eyebrows angled down over his nose. "You're late." As before, the gateway delayed his voice.

"Did you not want me to be certain this time?" snarled Aria.

Pravus stepped to the side, revealing that Alderan stood behind him. Aria's gaze locked onto Alderan, but Alderan just stared at the ground.

Aria approached the gateway. Her nose nearly touched its filmy surface. "Are you okay?" Alderan didn't answer. Didn't look up. Didn't flinch.

Pravus snapped his fingers. Like before, two soldiers dragged some unlucky person wearing manacles up to the gateway. This time, the bound person didn't beg for their life. Aria didn't watch. Didn't glimpse the person who might've been sentenced to death. In that moment, the only thing that mattered to her was Alderan.

I love you, brother.

She stepped through the gateway.

† † †

"No!" yelled Pravus, but his words came out too late. Aria had already crossed through the gateway. He rushed to her side and pulled her into his arms. She struggled against him and managed to squirm out of his arms.

Aria backed away from him. Her glare could've melted steel. "Don't you dare touch me right now!"

Pravus took a deep breath. He needed to manage the situation before it spiraled out of control. An entire army stood at his back, and he would not be made to look weak in their presence. "Aria, remember yourself and where you stand at this moment."

"Trust me, I remember myself quite well. I also remember that you threatened my brother's life." She approached Pravus and spoke under her breath, "Touch me again without consent, and I'll show this army who is truly in control."

Rage chattered Pravus's teeth, but he held onto his words and swallowed them down. Dueling with Aria, especially in public, would likely tarnish his reputation. Cinolth had taught her much about mezhik, and she'd picked it up quickly.

It's the only thing that blasted dragon has done that's been worthwhile.

The thought of admitting Aria's mezhik abilities had surpassed his sickened him, but it was undeniable. Still, he'd never give voice to her achievements. Doing so would not only wound his pride, but it would also take him right out of the picture. He would never stand for that.

All this is because of my vision. The glory will be mine.

Pravus leaned down and whispered in Aria's ear, "I'm sorry about earlier, my love, but we need to present a united front right now. Please stand at my side while I address the generals, and then you can go do whatever it is you desire."

"You're lucky this means as much to me as it does you." She turned and faced the army, her gaze hardened.

Pravus turned his attention to the army as well. Nine generals stood at attention, awaiting his command. He paced a few steps, his arms folded behind his back. "Listen to me carefully. I expect the entire army to have cleared the gateway by nightfall. That includes siege equipment and weapons and armor for those under Cinolth's control. Am I clear?"

"Yes sir," eight of the generals said as one.

"Crystal, sir," said the ninth general.

Pravus recognized the burly man as General Rashard. His bald head and thick, yellow beard were hard to forget, especially with the four-inch-long scar that ran from his right temple to the crown of his head. From what Pravus had heard, the man took an axe to the head in a domestic squabble. He ripped that same axe from his own skull and used it to kill and dismember his adversary—a distant cousin aiming to make a move on his sister.

Pravus eyed General Rashard. He'd never heard a response like General Rashard's before but found it to be quite pleasing. He gave the man a curt nod.

Crystal clear.

He steepled his fingers. "Good. Also, make it clear to your men that any stragglers will be executed on the spot."

"Yes sir," they all said.

"Proceed," said Pravus.

All nine generals raised a fist to their left breast and then dismissed themselves.

Aria glared at him. "Satisfied?"

Pravus bowed. "Beyond measure, my queen."

Aria turned on her heel and walked over to Alderan. "Talk to me, Alderan."

Alderan looked up at her for only a moment, but in that moment Pravus glimpsed the disdain in his eyes. "You're covered in blood. I'm guessing it's not your own."

"Huh." Pravus hadn't noticed the blood. It covered Aria's arms and the front of her grey blouse. His eyes narrowed.

What happened while the gateway was down?

He'd certainly find out later, but for now the rift between Aria and Alderan held his interest. It'd grown far wider than Pravus had thought possible, and it delighted him to no end. Soon, given the proper nurturing, there'd be nothing left between them. Once that happened, he'd lock Alderan up for good and would never have to see him again.

Aria looked down at herself. "It's not, but it's not what you think, either."

Alderan pushed his fingers through his hair. "And you know what I'm thinking?"

"I... I tried to save a man, but his wounds were too great." No inflections in her voice belied the untruth pouring from her lips, but Pravus knew she lied.

Then he saw it. A fleeting look in her eyes. Just like the one he thought he had seen at the café in Daltura.

She does have a tell. Guilt.

Alderan shook his head slowly, his eyes full of hurt. "What happened to you, Aria? You never would've lied straight to my face in the past."

Aria hugged herself. "I swear, it's not a lie. I didn't want him to die." The sincerity in her voice almost fooled Pravus.

She's almost as good as I am.

"You're not helping yourself," said Alderan. "I've seen how powerful you've become. No one still breathing would die under your care."

Aria grabbed Alderan's hand.

"Auh!" Alderan pulled his hand away, his eyes wide with fear. He stared at Aria's hand as though it was tainted with poison. "His death clings to you like a sickness."

Aria reached for Alderan again, but he retreated farther. "Alderan, don't do this," she begged. "I still love you."

Alderan turned and walked away, his hands lodged in his armpits and tears in his eyes.

This could not be better.

† † †

Alderan walked through the gateway and into the sea of infected. He had no idea where he was heading and didn't care. He wanted to be alone.

Somehow, he'd witnessed the truth of Aria's actions, and it felt nothing like when he'd touched Rayah's pink scarf or Aria's bracelet. The vision hadn't manifested within his own mind but came from the blood of the man she slew. His stomach churned with grief.

Every step jarred him and pierced his heart, just like Aria's dagger had done to that man. He couldn't get the vision out of his mind. She'd killed that man so easily. A monster. No mercy in her eyes.

Alderan knew because he'd been that man. Stared into Aria's eyes as she drove the dagger underneath his ribs and into his heart. But he couldn't comprehend the overwhelming desire he'd felt for her to do it. He, as the man, practically begged her to spill his blood. Grabbed her hand and helped drive the blade into his heart. It sickened him. Confused him. Tortured him. How could he ever look Aria in the eye again without seeing the monster he knew she'd become?

He stopped and dropped to his knees, unable to process what he'd witnessed. Glancing skyward, he beat his chest and moaned with grief.

Ƨätūr, I beg of You, tell me I'm not too late. Tell me that she can still be saved. An afterlife without her would not be worth living. My God, bring her back to me.

† † †

The gateway, a quarter-mile-long expanse connecting two distant points, held Wrik's attention. He'd never seen anything so magnificent. Sure, the mirror portals held a special place in his heart, but they didn't come close to comparing to the gateway. Besides the obvious size advantage, the gateway also allowed the unzhiftäd to utilize it. That fact alone stoked the fires of his imagination.

Perhaps the mirrors could be altered to do the same.

Wrik wasn't sure what purpose or need such a modification would provide, but just being able to make a change like that would be an exhilarating experience. Combining mezhik and technology could have endless possibilities. His mind spun with ideas.

Pravus's voice snapped in his ear. "Wizard Wrik."

Wrik turned and faced him. "Ah, Lord Rosai. I was just admiring the gateway." He removed his spectacles and began cleaning them with one of the sleeves of his robes. "Can you imagine the power Aria must possess to conjure something so complex and grandiose?"

Pravus's left eye and cheek twitched. Wrik had hit a nerve, as he'd hoped. "I am fully aware of her power. I assure you that we are equally paired and made for one another." Daggers shot from his golden-eyed glare. "Such power carries into our bedroom as well."

Jab to the heart. Well played.

Wrik returned his spectacles to his face. "Yes, I'm sure you are. Was there something I can help you with?"

"Yes." Pravus cracked his knuckles. "You've been avoiding me and my wrath."

Wrik cocked his head. "Is there something I've done?"

Pravus's jaw tensed, and his eyes narrowed. "You lied to me about *2ţōn Dhef Dädh* and its purpose, you kept Alderan's presence at the castle from me, you've snuck away from the castle several times in the last few weeks, and you scheme to drive a wedge between Aria and me. If I didn't know better, I'd say you're working with that damned dragon as well." He glared at Wrik. "Tell me why I shouldn't kill you right now."

Wrik folded his arms over his chest. "I assure you that the stone was a surprise to me as well. As for Alderan, he came here right before the stone ceremony, and I didn't want to distract you with the news of him still being alive. I left the castle on several occasions to look after a dying friend, and I'd never dare cause a rift between you and Lady Aria. Cinolth does that well enough on his own. I serve you, as I always have."

Hatred boiled in Pravus's eyes. "You may have answers for everything, but it makes no difference. I know the truth. As of this moment, you will manage the daily affairs at the castle until Aria and I return."

Wrik frowned. "My lord? Isn't that Master Credan's job?"

Pravus sneered. "It is, but he will be at my side, advising me on matters of warfare."

"I had planned on being at the battlefield as well." Wrik crossed his arms. He wanted to crush Pravus's narrow skull. "As you know, my abilities extend far beyond prophecy and *daily affairs*."

Pravus's eyes narrowed. "I'm sure you had, but your… *abilities* will better serve the castle."

Wrik stood tall, towering over Pravus. "And what does Lady Aria think of this? Or does she not know?"

Pravus pointed between them. "*This* has *nothing* to do with her." Spittle peppered the air and foamed at the corners of his mouth. "And neither will you."

A single fist to the crown of Pravus's head would've settled matters for good, but his death would be Aria's as well, and Wrik couldn't live with that. Wrik tipped his head slightly. "As you say. Anything else?"

"No." Pravus turned around and walked through the gateway. Then over his shoulder he said, "By the way, we will be shutting the gateway down once the entire army has come through. Wouldn't want anyone attacking us from behind."

Gods forbid.

Pravus continued toward a massive white tent in the distance.

"Good riddance." Wrik unfolded his arms and headed toward the castle gates. "I've got matters to attend to. The castle can watch itself."

† † †

Savric stood atop the outcropping, his heart sinking farther as each hour passed. Soldiers and siege equipment had poured through the gateway throughout the afternoon and finally slowed to a trickle just before dusk. He'd never seen so many people and beasts gathered in one place. They covered the plains as far east and north as he could see.

Bugger bees.

He took out his small, leather-bound book and scribbled a quick note to Morcinda. "*Morcinda, the situation is far graver than I could have imagined. I cannot begin to count the numbers in Cinolth's army, but there must be more than two hundred thousand of them. Warn King Zaridus that time is running out. We are only about sixty miles south of Elatos. Given the distance, Elatos will most likely be attacked within the next seven days. I will let you know when the army heads north. Once they do, I must journey to where Ūrdär Dhef Ɂäfn Dhä rest and awaken them before all is lost. Please keep me informed of any developments on your end. In allíṭ Hiz. -Savric"*

Calen climbed up onto the outcropping and stood next to Savric. "Is everything okay, Master Savric."

Savric fussed with the fountain pen. The wretched thing wouldn't slide back into its pouch. "Yes, fine." His hands trembled profusely.

Calen touched Savric's wrist. "Let me do that for you." He took the book and fountain pen and slid the fountain pen into its pouch. Then, he closed the book and handed it back.

"Thank you, my boy." Savric took a deep breath as he stuffed the book back into the pocket within his robes.

"What are we going to do?" Calen's gaze focused far in the distance. "How can we stop this war from happening?"

"Some events are inevitable." He put his arm around Calen's shoulders. "I fear this is one of those."

"And Aunt Tahmara? What will happen to her?" Calen trembled.

Tears blurred Savric's vision. After seeing Zerenity use her mezhik to kill those men, he had no doubts as to what came next. He desperately wanted to protect Calen from all that went on, and lying to him would do just that, but it would only prolong the inevitable truth and sow seeds of mistrust between them. There was nothing he could do but tell him the truth, so he did.

"As with all the infected, she will fight against us. There is also a good chance that she will die."

Calen nodded as tears streamed down his face. "Thank you for being honest with me, Master Savric. I knew that would be the answer even though I've been praying that it wasn't."

Savric tousled Calen's hair. "Be strong, keep praying, and never lose faith. Ɂäṭūr has a plan for us all."

"Eshtak prays too."

Savric startled. He hadn't seen Eshtak standing next to Calen. "Very—"

The gateway flashed, thrummed, and shook the ground. Calen and Eshtak huddled closer to Savric.

"What's happening?" asked Calen.

The entire wall turned black, and the thrum died down. A minute later, the ground stopped shaking.

"I believe they have disabled the gateway so that no one can come through it and attack them from behind."

"Eshtak scared."

"Me too," said Calen.

As am I.

Savric knelt, laid Qotan's staff down, and pulled Calen and Eshtak to himself. "Ɂäʈūr will never abandon us."

He believed those words with all his heart but knew it didn't mean that they would all live through the war. Perhaps none of them would. Everything rested in Ɂäʈūr's hands.

Ɂäʈūr help us all.

CHAPTER THIRTY-FIVE

Nardus lay on the cavern floor, staring up at the underside of Peorvem's head. He didn't know how long he'd been laying there, but his entire backside ached from the hardness of the rocky floor. Especially his head. He would've shifted his weight a bit or moved into a different position, but the tingle of mezhik touched every part of him and prevented him from moving.

A low, mournful groan escaped from deep within Peorvem's throat and resonated throughout the cavern. The deep, guttural sound penetrated his chest and shook his bones. It reminded him of the sound a ram's horn made when blown.

Peorvem's eyes flitted underneath scaly eyelids for several moments before cracking open. "It is finished."

The tingle of mezhik dissipated, returning full mobility to Nardus once again. Sitting up made his head pulse with pain, but the effect didn't last long. However, one particular spot at the base of his skull smarted when he touched it. He must've been laying on a jagged rock.

Nardus stood, his legs a bit shaky. "And will it hold this time?"

"Then you remember?" asked Peorvem.

Memories of claws reaching into his mind and extracting sections of his life shook him to the core. "Yes." He shivered away the feeling. "I've been known to be stubborn at times."

"As Nardus or Cyrus?" Peorvem withdrew from the shore and entered the blue waters.

The question struck Nardus as odd. "Are we not one and the same?"

Peorvem lowered himself until only his head remained out of the water. "You're the only one who can answer that question."

Am I?

His two lives contradicted each other in many ways. Sorting out who he was and where he stood would take some time. As Nardus, he loathed mezhik and the use of it, so how could he, Cyrus, a powerful mage, rectify that? Who'd ever heard of a mage loathing mezhik? Yet the thought of using his powers still sickened him. Furthermore, everything bad that had happened stemmed from its usage. Then again, mezhik could've saved Vitara or prevented the entire event from ever happening.

How could I stop Cinolth without mezhik?

He didn't know the right answer and didn't need to figure it out right then. Far more pressing matters needed his attention. "How long should I wait to use my mezhik?"

"You'll know once you test yourself, but I suggest you refrain from doing so until you've left the valley. Many of the dragons here still remember Magus and resent humans that wield mezhik."

"Then I will wait." Nardus bowed low. "Thank you for helping me find myself again."

Peorvem blew water from his nostrils. "Think nothing of it. I merely showed you the path. You're the one who took the painful journey."

Nardus straightened and rubbed his left bicep. "Even so, I couldn't have done it on my own."

Tharos and Theyn entered the cavern together. Theyn's yellow-eyed gaze met Nardus's and stirred up love in his heart. As Vitara had been his first love, Theyn would be his last. The Cyrus side of himself didn't approve of either woman, for every woman presented a distraction from matters of importance. But Cyrus had never known love. Nardus smiled as much to himself as he did to Theyn.

Things will never be the same for either of us.

Tharos grinned, or at least that's how Nardus perceived his display of sharpened teeth. "Did you find the man you sought?"

Nardus grimaced. "Not what I expected at all, but yes, I've found Cyrus Nithik."

"Good." Smoke billowed from Tharos's nostrils. "It's good to have you back, my friend."

Theyn rubbed up against Nardus's leg. *"I've missed you,"* she said in his mind.

He bent down and rubbed Theyn's ears and scratched underneath her chin. "I've missed you as well."

Nardus's thoughts circled back to the mess he'd created. He peered up at Tharos. "How did all of this happen? How could I have been so naive to think that putting Cinolth's heart into a conjured world would keep us safe? And how could I have placed such a burden on your shoulders? I'm sorry you were stuck in *Räallm Kenzhärd Dhä* for so long."

"Men lie to themselves when they can't face the truth. Had you the weapon to destroy his heart, I'm certain you would've used it."

"That is true, but we should have searched harder for *Hemär Dhef Əllíṭ*."

"*What is* Hemär Dhef Əllíṭ?" asked Theyn.

"The Hammer of Light," said Nardus. "It's the only weapon that can destroy Cinolth's heart.

Tharos lowered his head to Nardus's level. "You knew and understood the words of the prophets, yet you chose your path. Perhaps you couldn't face the truth either."

"Obviously not." Nardus clenched his fist. "I'm such a fool. Cinolth has risen from the grave because of me. I've seen him with my own eyes."

Tharos nodded. "As I told you it would happen."

Nardus shot to his feet and shook his finger at Tharos. "You said nothing of it. You dragons speak so cryptically that I'm surprised anyone ever understands as to what you're referring or eluding to."

Tharos shot smoke from his nostrils. "Well, let me be perfectly clear this time. Don't make the same mistake again, my friend. Find *Hemär Dhef Əllíṭ* and destroy Cinolth's heart once and for all."

"Silence." Nardus and Tharos turned and faced Peorvem, who'd risen from the water again. "If what you say is true, son of Ʒäṭūr, we're all in danger." He looked at Tharos. "Quldrai must be warned. Eventually, Cinolth will return, so we must prepare for war."

Tharos snorted and puffs of smoke rose from his nostrils. "I've already tried to warn her, but she'll hear nothing of it. You and I are old enough to understand the threat that Cinolth poses to the entire world, but Quldrai was born after Cinolth's treacherous reign."

Peorvem slid back into the water and submerged himself until nothing but his head remained above the water. "Warn her again." His head vanished below the surface.

"As you wish, Ancient One," said Tharos.

Nardus peered down at Theyn. "We must leave at once. Gnaud needs my help."

"Do not narrow your focus so much," said Tharos. "The Ancient Realm needs your help, Cyrus."

Nardus gritted his teeth. "I've sacrificed *everything* for this realm. *Twice.* I will deal with Cinolth, but first I must do something for myself. Without Gnaud, Nasduron and its knowledge will be lost."

"You think I'm not familiar with sacrifice?" said Tharos.

"You know that's not what I implied. And don't call me Cyrus. He died long ago."

"Forgive me, Nardus. It's a force of habit, given our history." Tharos turned toward the cavern exit. "Follow me."

Tharos ushered them back up through the tunnel and into the main area with Quldrai. Nardus and Theyn bowed to Quldrai.

"Thank you for your kindness," said Nardus.

Venomous hatred flashed in Quldrai's eyes. "Be gone before I change my mind and eat the both of you."

Nardus, Theyn, and Tharos backed out of Quldrai's cavern without another word and made their way back to the surface and out of the upper cave. The valley teemed with activity, but none of it displayed an urgency or resembled preparations for war.

Nardus turned to Tharos. "How far can you take us from here?"

"No farther than Altus Pass. Beyond that there are humans."

"That will have to do. Can you take us there now?"

"As you wish." Tharos extended his hand and Nardus and Theyn climbed into it.

With a few beats of his massive wings, Tharos rose off the ground and flew them up out of the valley and to the south, toward Altus Pass. Within ten minutes, they'd arrived at the pass. Tharos dropped them off on a flat, narrow stretch between dueling peaks.

"Be careful, my friends," said Tharos. "Cinolth is a vile beast and not one to be taken lightly."

Nardus nodded. "I remember everything, including what you did for us all. Your sacrifice gave us hope for the future. I'm sorry I ruined that and brought the world to its knees once again, but I promise that I will make it right. Cinolth will not live through the summer."

"May Ɛätūr make it so." Tharos took to the sky and disappeared in the thick cloud cover.

"Where are we headed now?" asked Theyn in his mind.

"Back to Galondu Castle."

"That's going to be a long journey without the nítfinzh." Nardus detected a sigh somewhere in there. It was strange how he could pick up feelings and inflections through mindspeak.

He smiled. "If we were walking that'd be true, but there's no need for that now."

"Then what? A mirror or something?" she said in his mind.

"A special friend. You'll see."

"And why didn't we use this friend of yours when we traveled here?"

"I didn't remember how to call her before. Now I do. Just be happy knowing that we won't be walking all that way."

Theyn growled. *"Be happy I don't kill you."*

Nardus chuckled but then remembered how close she'd come on a few occasions. One day she might just be the death of him. If so, he'd take it in stride.

He cleared his mind and called for Sarai, the ṭrenᴢbūrṭ, using mindspeak.

A moment later, a pool of golden liquid appeared before them. Sarai rose from the pool in her glorious, golden form. "Master, it is a pleasure to serve you again. What is our destination?"

Theyn growled. *"Master?"* she mindspoke. Nardus thought he detected a hint of jealousy.

Nardus glanced down at Theyn and gave her a wink. "Galondu Castle. And make sure it's somewhere private. We're not exactly welcome there."

"Very good. I am ready when you are, master." Sarai melted back into the golden pool.

Nardus turned to Theyn. "Follow me, and don't forget to breathe her in. It's a fast but not instantaneous journey." He dove into Sarai.

† † †

Wrik sat on one of the benches in the atrium, enjoying the fresh air and the peace and quiet. Pravus and his pathetic army had left earlier that morning, virtually abandoning the castle. Only a handful of guards remained behind—basically enough to man the castle gates.

Many of the servants had traveled with the army as well. In fact, he hadn't seen a soul all day since they'd left, not including Gnaud. Unfortunately, Pravus took Alderan with him. Plus all of the captured wizards and sorceresses. Gnaud needed to be healed again within the hour, but he had no means of doing so on his own. Even with Alderan's help, he'd barely had enough energy to finish the job the last time.

The thought of losing Gnaud and all the knowledge of Nasduron frustrated him. The knowledge especially, but he'd bonded with Gnaud over the last two weeks as well. Kinda hard not to after spending so much time with the little gordak. As far as he could tell, he'd grown on Gnaud as well.

Wrik smiled. *He'd never admit it though.*

A small book bound with coiled tin sat next to Wrik on the bench. He ran his thumb down the coils. Each thrummed as it bounced back into place. It was a peculiar way to bind a book. He'd only seen one other bound in the same manner. That particular book held significance for two reasons, the first and perhaps most important one being its author, Reudeus Nithik. As far as Wrik knew, Reudeus had only ever written the one book. That in and of itself made little difference, but the fact that Reudeus was the uncle of Cyrus Nithik gave the book credence. The second reason it held significance was, of all things, the book's subject matter: shifters. Its title, *Shift Your View and Take Control*, spelled out what one would expect to find within its pages. The odds of such a find were astronomical given Theyn's current predicament.

Wrik picked up the book, tucked it into a large pocket within the folds of his robes, and headed down the gravel path toward the center of the atrium. From there, he'd take the north path. He needed to check on Gnaud, perhaps for the last time. A tear formed in the corner of his right eye. Then his left. He stopped, removed his spectacles, and wiped his eyes with the sleeve of his robes.

Events, whether sad or joyous, had always touched him and often moved him to tears. As a younger man, he'd hidden his emotions quite well both out of embarrassment and fear of ridicule. Now, he bore them with a sense of pride, and, given his size, few ever contested him over it.

Wrik placed his spectacles back on his face and started off again, but a subtle movement caught the corner of his left eye. Purple energy crackled at his fingertips as he turned and peered into the shadows created by the millennial pines. Nothing seemed amiss. He watched the shadows for a solid minute before shaking the unease from his shoulders.

He chided himself.

Sometimes the shadows are just that.

With a deep breath, he turned and sauntered on. The purple energy faded from his fingertips and returned from whence it had risen.

Ten paces ahead, a golden substance gurgled and bubbled up from the rocks, forming about a four-foot-diameter circle. Wrik stepped back, mezhik at his fingertips once again. Two figures rose from the depths of the golden pool, but the golden waters clung to them and masked their identities.

A purple fireball formed in Wrik's open palm. "Identify your—"

A bone-chilling snarl sounded right behind him.

Wrik turned, but moments too late.

A spiked club arced out of the shadows.

Straight at the side of Wrik's head.

A brilliant light flashed.

Split the air and chased the shadows back.

Left Wrik blinded.

Thunder cracked and boomed.

Rang in Wrik's ears.

Shook the ground.

A concussive wave followed the boom.

Took Wrik's feet right out from under him.

Slammed him to the ground.

Drove the breath from his lungs.

His heart knocked in his chest and drummed in his ears.

Thoughts scattered in his mind.

Chaos.

A voice called to him from the shadows. "Wrik."

Distant. Hollow.

Did he recognize it? He couldn't be sure.

The brilliant light faded, restoring his vision.

A beast stood over him.

Yellow fur and sharp fangs.

Wrik drew upon his mezhik again, certain for the second time in a matter of seconds that he couldn't defend himself.

But then he noticed the man who knelt next to the beast.

Brown eyes with yellow striations exuded wisdom. Hinted at kindness.

This man Wrik knew, but he'd certainly changed.

Nardus. Or is it Cyrus now?

Either way, the man had saved Wrik's life.

Wrik sat up and eyed the smoldering corpse lying on the ground. A hole the size of a giant's fist punched right through its middle. "What the gods was that?"

"Shadow troll assassin." Nardus nudged the corpse with his foot. "They usually only work at night. Must've been paid a high price."

Wrik looked around. Shadows surrounded them. Had it been just the one shadow troll, or were there more lurking about, biding their time to attack when he was alone again?

"You're safe for now," said Nardus. "They always work alone."

Wrik chided himself. Fear rarely possessed him, and when it did, he usually hid it well. "Good to know. And thank you for saving my life."

"I'm sure you'd have done the same." Nardus scanned the atrium and his eyes narrowed. "Is it me, or has this place been abandoned?"

Wrik's right ear—the one closest to the blast—still rang. He worked his jaw to try and get his ear to pop but had no luck. Twisting his finger into his ear didn't help either. Only time would.

"Pravus, Cinolth, and their collective armies are headed toward the Three Kingdoms. War will soon be upon the Ancient Realm."

"War?" Anger flashed in Nardus's eyes. "This is madness."

Wrik smiled within. *No, this is prophecy unfolding right in front of us.*

† † †

Nardus paced, driven by a torrent of emotions. He'd thought time favored him, but events progressed far too quickly. Facing Cinolth and Pravus would be difficult enough, especially with Aria involved, but how could he possibly save Aria, Gnaud, Theyn, Nasduron, and the entire world too? Foolish as he might be, he knew it'd be impossible to accomplish any of it on his own. Therefore, only one viable option came to mind.

I must revive the other members of Ūrdär Dhef Ƨäfn Dhä.

He didn't like the idea at all and knew the others wouldn't either, but what choice did he have? In truth, they'd placed Ūrdär Dhef Ƨäfn Dhä into a deep sleep for a single purpose: to prevent or thwart a cataclysmic event prophesied about long ago. Somehow, they'd reached that fork in the prophetic road.

War is coming…

Nardus rubbed the scars on either side of his left bicep. "And what about my daughter? Has she gone with them too?"

Wrik stood and dusted off his robes. "You're no fool, Nardus. You've witnessed Aria's state of mind firsthand. She leads them down that warpath. Her and that scaly beast."

"All this is Pravus's fault." Nardus spat. "He will pay with his life. However, you know that's not why I'm here."

"Of course not." Wrik started walking toward the north atrium doors. Nardus and Theyn followed. "I was on my way to check on Gnaud when you arrived. Your timing couldn't have been better."

The three of them stopped outside the door to Gnaud's room and Nardus unlocked it with the key Wrik had given him a few weeks back. As soon as the door cracked open Nardus caught a whiff of the sickness. Pungent, rank air gagged him.

Zätūr, don't let me be too late.

Gnaud lay on the couch wrapped in blood-soaked bandages. Not a hair on him moved nor a single muscle twitched. Sticky sweat glistened on his furry forehead, and his little hands were ice cubes.

Wrik checked for a pulse and held a mirror to Gnaud's mouth and nose. "He's gone."

"Just so, but it might not be too late to revive him." The poorly designed couch provided little room for him and Wrik to tend to Gnaud at the same time, so Nardus gripped the back of it and groaned. Mezhik tingled in his fingers as strength built up in his arms. With a grunt and then a loud crack of splitting wood, he broke and ripped the back off the couch and tossed it across the room.

"Revive him?" Wrik stared at Nardus, obviously puzzled at the notion. "His heart has given out."

"Yes, but if it hasn't been for long, we still have a chance to save him." Nardus knelt and placed a hand over Gnaud's chest. Mezhik tingled in his fingers once again, but this time miniature bolts of lightning arced between his fingers and crackled across his palm. He pressed down firmly on Gnaud's chest and released the lightning. Gnaud's body jolted and arched off the couch. Singed hair joined the pungent odor of sickness, creating the perfect combination to relieve one's stomach of its contents.

Wrik's face turned a shade of green, but he didn't back away from Gnaud. Nardus struggled to hang onto his stomach's contents and had to turn his head for several seconds but managed to compose himself. He wouldn't give up on Gnaud.

Lightning built in Nardus's hand again, and he thrust the lightning into Gnaud's heart once more, but the result didn't change. On the fourth attempt, everything happened just as before, but then Wrik's eyes grew wide.

"He's got a pulse!" exclaimed Wrik.

"Good." Nardus worked quickly to remove Gnaud's bandages and then placed both of his hands over Gnaud. He glanced up at Wrik. "I'm not sure how long this process will take, so be ready to seal the wounds when I say to."

Wrik nodded focused on Gnaud. "I'm ready."

Nardus closed his eyes, drew upon his mezhik once again, and began pouring it into Gnaud's three wounds. Like a cleansing process, he drew out the dark energy and sickness and replaced it with light energy. Within his mind, Nardus monitored Gnaud's aura. Minute by minute, it slowly transitioned from a dark, putrid brown to a lighter, pinkish-red. Nearly a half hour passed as he continued drawing and replacing Gnaud's energy.

Nearing the point of exhaustion and complete collapse, Nardus knew he had to pull his energy back soon, but he had just the one shot. He must finish the job, or the dark energy would return quicker and consume Gnaud. One more cycle and another scan of Gnaud's aura confirmed he'd removed the last of the dark energy.

"Close them," barked Nardus.

He slumped to the floor and convulsed.

† † †

Theyn howled, growled, and paced, but what could Wrik do about it? He worked feverishly healing Gnaud's wounds and couldn't tend to Nardus at the same time. "Relax, Theyn. He'll be fine. He's just exhausted from saving Gnaud's life."

Sharp pain stabbed Wrik right between the eyes and burrowed into his skull. Somehow, Theyn managed to penetrate the defenses of his mind and mindspoke to him. *"Brownish-black sludge is dripping from the corners of his mouth and pooling around his head."*

Her girlish voice threw him off. It didn't sound anything like what he would've expected, not that he'd actually contemplated it. Still strange coming from someone he only knew as a cat.

"I won't pretend to understand what it is that he did to Gnaud, but I believe that the sludge you're seeing is the physical manifestation of Gnaud's sickness." He wiped his brow with his sleeve as he worked on closing the third and final wound. "Turn him on his side so that he doesn't choke and so that the sludge can come out easier."

Theyn did. *"Now what?"* she asked in Wrik's mind.

"There's nothing else you can do but wait."

Gnaud's final wound began stitching itself together from the inside out. Muscles, tendons, fat layer, and finally the skin. The scars would remain. Nothing he could do about them. Strange how the wounds would scar, even when healed with mezhik, but the only thing mezhik really did was speed up the process. Pravus, being a Fizärd ləllūəzhän, had the ability to "hide" scars and other physical deformities, but no one could actually remove them. If mezhik could erase wounds, it'd be like reversing time. The wound would simply "unhappen."

Wrik sat back on the floor and propped himself up with his arms. Sweat poured from the crown of his head and ran down his face and the back of his head. Of all the mezhik spells, incantations, and webs a wizard could cast, healing took the most energy. Every time he healed someone, it gave him a deep sense of satisfaction and warmed his heart, but he didn't understand why. He wondered if it worked that way for all wizards or if it specifically tied to his oversensitivity. Either way, he was content with the outcome.

Gnaud's eyes flitted and slowly opened. He yawned and stretched and looked over at Wrik. "You're in a fit of cheer."

"Glad to have you back," said Wrik.

Gnaud cocked his head. "Was I gone?" He turned to his left and squealed like a mouse. He shot off the couch and hunkered behind Wrik. He peered over Wrik's shoulder and pointed toward the couch. "She's the one who attacked me," he whispered.

"Let him know how sorry I am about that," said Theyn in Wrik's mind.

"Yes, and she couldn't be sorrier," said Wrik.

"Dear Ɛäṭūr!" exclaimed Gnaud. "You speak to beasts? I didn't peg you as *Fizärd Enämäəll.*"

"That's because I'm not. Despite her current form, Theyn's no beast."

Gnaud drew a deep breath and his eyes nearly bulged from his head. "She's a shifter..."

"Yes, but she has no control of it right now and admittedly turns primal when she's separated from Nardus."

"Nardus is here?" Gnaud scanned the room and gasped. "Oh my! What's happened to him?"

"Saved your life." Wrik chuckled. "From what I understand, he owes you several of them."

Gnaud frowned. "I assure you that no score has been kept."

Wrik shrugged and cocked his head. "Maybe you're not keeping score, but Nardus is."

And so am I.

† † †

Many hours later, Nardus sat at a small table with Wrik and Gnaud. Theyn lay at his feet. With a full belly and a few hours of sleep, he felt surprisingly well. An earthy, moldy taste lingered in the back of his throat despite prescribing himself copious amounts of ale to wash it down with. Unfortunately, knowing what still lay ahead kept him sober. Morbidly so.

As the man named Nardus, he'd made so many mistakes. Most of them were minor, but a few were borderline catastrophic. One such major mistake involved the agreement he'd made with Wrik. Yes, saving Gnaud's life had been urgent, but not as urgent as keeping Nasduron's existence hidden from anyone who might use its knowledge for nefarious purposes.

As Cyrus, such an accord would never have been struck. In fact, Wrik would never have known Nasduron still existed. But he couldn't renege now. Wrik had held up his end of the agreement.

In short, Nardus didn't know if he could trust Wrik. The man seemed to be on level, but his association with Pravus tainted any goodwill he garnered by befriending Gnaud and Shanara. Then again, his own agreement with Pravus started the entire mess to begin with. Could he really judge the man for it?

Is Pravus holding something over Wrik's head? Or has he promised to do something for him like he did me?

Pravus manipulated and corrupted everything he touched. The probability of him controlling Wrik neared certainty. *Like he does Shanara.* The thought of Pravus's hands on his daughter drove Nardus toward madness.

How strange it felt knowing he'd never wanted a family and had abstained from any sort of relationship prior to his life as Nardus. Now, he couldn't imagine his life differently. Well, apart from regaining Shanara's love and trust. That battle might prove more difficult than defeating Pravus and Cinolth, but the reward for such a victory would surpass any treasure.

She will come around.

Wrik rose from the table. "I believe it's time we headed to Nasduron."

Gnaud eyed Nardus. "If anything remains of it." He might've winked a little.

Nardus understood what Gnaud eluded to and appreciated his concern, but Nardus could never live with such a lie. For better or worse, he'd bring Wrik into the fold. "Some parts of Nasduron might be damaged or lost, but I'm certain the majority of it remains. Your resilience is commendable, my furry little friend. Have faith in yourself."

Gnaud gasped and stood on his chair. "Oh my! My faith lies in Ƨäţūr, never in myself."

Nardus stretched and got to his feet. "Yes, of course. Simply a figure of speech. Now, let's all hold hands so that we can go to Nasduron."

Gnaud hopped off his chair and Theyn rose from the floor. Nardus and Wrik each took one of Gnaud's hands and then Nardus reached down and grabbed a handful of loose skin on the back of Theyn's neck.

"We'll all step forward on my word," said Nardus. "Understood?"

When everyone agreed, Nardus set his mind on Nasduron.

"Now," said Nardus.

The four of them stepped forward. As they did, the small room shifted, distorted, and phased out, and then the Great Library phased in. At least what was left of it.

Waist-high water greeted them. Theyn and Gnaud had to tread water to keep their heads afloat. Books, broken pieces of wood, and other debris bobbed on the water's surface. The damage far exceeded what he and Theyn had witnessed a few weeks back. To say the least, it disheartened him.

Wrik fished several pages from the water but they sloughed apart between his fingers. He turned in a circle, his face long with disappointment. "Did anything survive?"

Nardus drew upon his mezhik and pushed the water away from the four of them with a circular wall of air. He held it in place with his hand and his mind. The effort required a good deal of continuous energy, so he wouldn't be able to hold the water back for long.

"This will get better." He pointed with his free hand. "Look at the walls. You can see how far the water level had risen. The healing process has begun."

"But what about all the books? So much knowledge lost." Wrik groaned.

"And that's where you're wrong," said Nardus. "As Gnaud grows stronger, this place will repair itself. That includes the books."

Theyn shook the water from her fur. *"This place represents one of my darkest hours. I'm ready to leave when you are,"* she said in Nardus's mind.

Nardus mindspoke to Theyn, *"As soon as we can get Gnaud settled."*

At the least, Gnaud would need a table to sit on to stay out of the water. As Fizärd Brefä̧t, a Prophet Wizard, Wrik was of little use in reparations of any kind. Nardus would have to do everything on his own.

Still holding back the water with one hand, Nardus stooped down and collected a broken table leg with his other hand. He held the table leg upright on the floor, reached deep within himself, and poured mezhik näíţezhär into it. A variety of shards and splintered wood shot out of the water and rose off the floor. Each piece attached itself to the next, slowly assembling themselves back into a table. The entire process took less than a minute to complete, and the table looked brand new.

Wrik clapped. "Now that's impressive for a man who loathes mezhik and isn't a wizard."

Nardus released the table leg and took a deep breath. After expending so much energy healing Gnaud earlier, he didn't have the strength to do much else without more food and a good night's rest. The air wall dissolved, and the water came crashing back around them.

Gnaud jumped up on the table and sat down. He rubbed its smooth surface. "This will certainly do for now. Thank you..." He cocked his head. "Cyrus?"

Nardus rubbed his left bicep. The mental and physical scars from his past would remain with him beyond death. "I may have Cyrus's powers and memories, but I cannot be everything he was and stood for and still be the man I've become. For better or worse, Cyrus died with the past."

"Wise words," said Wrik. "Remind yourself of them often, especially when you're dealing with Aria. She's not the little girl you lost either."

As much as Nardus didn't like it, Wrik had a point. He lost and buried

Shanara long ago. Aria represented a new future in much the same way Theyn did. Perhaps thinking of it like that would allow him to move forward and accept Aria for who she was now.

Nardus and Wrik spent the next hour discussing the four rules of reaching Nasduron and how to go back and forth. Wrik caught on quickly and found loopholes of his own within the rules. Nardus prayed Wrik would be honorable in his usage of the knowledge he obtained from Nasduron.

Nothing's ever guaranteed.

Theyn lay on the table with Gnaud. Nardus stroked her back. "It's time Theyn and I left. We've many matters to attend and little time to accomplish them. Gnaud, I have faith that all your memories will be restored. When we return, I expect to see a full library once more."

"Oh my! That's a load of pressure, and I'm not so big." Gnaud pushed his spectacles back up his nose.

"Perhaps not in stature, but you've got the biggest heart and the greatest mind," said Nardus.

Theyn rose. *"I'm ready,"* she said in Nardus's mind.

"Wrik." Nardus proffered his hand.

Wrik grabbed Nardus and bear hugged him, pulling him right off the floor. "You've no idea what you've done for me."

Nardus groaned in Wrik's embrace. "I do, and if you don't use it wisely, I'll find you and kill you. Understood?"

Wrik nodded and released Nardus. "I do."

"Perfect. Now, there's something else I need you to do for me." Nardus looked at Gnaud. "Both of you."

Gnaud straightened his spectacles. "And what might that be?"

"I want you both to spend as much time as possible searching for anything that pertains to *Hemär Dhef əlliṭ.*"

"The Hammer of Light?" asked Wrik.

"That is correct," said Nardus. "We will need it if we have any hope of stopping Cinolth for good."

"We shall do our best, right Gnaud?" asked Wrik.

"Oh my, yes," Gnaud confirmed.

"There is one more thing..." Wrik fished through his robes. "Ah, here it is." He pulled out a small book with a coiled tin binding and handed it to Nardus. "I believe this will tell you everything you need to know about

Theyn."

Nardus read the title aloud, "*Shift Your View and Take Control.*" The author's name brought back memories of his childhood. "My uncle wrote this? As far as I can remember, he never mentioned knowing anything about shifters." He turned the book over in his hands several times and then eyed Wrik. "Where did you find this?"

Wrik waved him off. "It's of no significance. I just hope it helps."

"Speaking of help, I'd like my sword back. Do you know what Pravus did with it?"

"I do." Wrik grabbed a piece of blank parchment, drew a crude map on it, and handed it to Nardus. "This should be the place."

"Good."

Nardus stuffed the map and the book into his pack, grabbed Theyn by the scruff of her neck, and then the two of them stepped out of Nasduron and back into the small room in Galondu Castle. But they weren't alone when they arrived. A man the size of a mountain stepped out of the shadows.

"Thought I might find you here." His voice boomed.

† † †

Berggren knelt and hugged Theyn's neck. Her yellow fur tickled his nose. "Gods, it's good to see you."

Nardus clasped Berggren's forearm. "You're a sight for weary eyes. How did you find us?"

Berggren unsheathed the knife hanging from his belt and held it up. "My lucky charm."

"A knife?" questioned Nardus. "What does that have to do with finding us?"

"I told him a story about an old witch." Niesha stepped out of the shadows. She hadn't left Berggren's side since they'd met in East Hotah. "She could track individuals using an item they once possessed, even to their graves."

"Turns out the story was true." Berggren rubbed Niesha's head. "Knife belonged to Theyn. Led us right to this room."

"Some mezhik can be quite useful," said Nardus.

Berggren stood. "Thought you hated mezhik."

"It's complicated," said Nardus.

"Like you." Berggren crossed his arms. "Something's changed, hasn't it."

It wasn't a question but an observation. He'd been around Nardus enough to detect the subtle change in Nardus's eyes. The fire still remained, but there were many more layers than before. Berggren couldn't quite put his finger on the exact change. Wisdom perhaps.

In two weeks' time? What could cause such a change?

Nardus nodded. "How long have you been waiting for us?"

"Not long at all. Few hours, perhaps. Figured we'd wait until she showed back up."

"And Joriah? Has he recovered?" asked Nardus.

Berggren glared daggers at Nardus, not because Nardus angered him, but because Nardus reopened wounds that'd just begun to heal. "He's dead."

Nardus gasped, and Theyn moaned deep in her throat.

Memories of Joriah flashed in Berggren's mind, and his throat and chest tightened as he fought back tears of regret, but the battle over his emotions had caught him by surprise. He moved over to the couch and sat down. A torrent of tears rained down on his cheeks and streamed off his chin.

Sorry I couldn't save you, old friend.

Niesha joined Berggren on the couch and hugged his side. "Berggren carried Joriah for a good three miles before we realized he'd died."

"I don't understand." Nardus rounded the couch and faced Berggren and Niesha. "Didn't you feed him the concoction Sorsha gave you?"

Niesha tensed next to Berggren. "Of course we gave it to him, but it must've been too late."

Nardus lowered his head. "I truly am sorry for your loss. Joriah was a special man and will be missed."

"That he will," said Berggren.

Nardus stroked Theyn's head. Seemed so natural and yet odd to Berggren. "Theyn gives her condolences as well. Says he was like an uncle to her."

"Maybe not by blood, but family for certain." Berggren cleared his throat and stood. "So, what's the plan?"

† † †

The plan...

Nardus scratched the back of his head. Every step of the way the plan seemed to evolve. At least he'd managed to find himself and save Gnaud, but now there were many more pressing matters. The other members of Ūrdär Dhef Ɂäfn Dhä needed to be awakened, Theyn needed help returning to her human form, he hadn't slept in more days than he could remember, he needed to get his stuff back, especially his sword, and Cinolth's army marched to war. Oh, and his daughter hated him. There were most likely several other matters he couldn't recall at the moment as well.

Past experiences had taught him that sleep far outweighed most other issues because it helped clear the mind, rejuvenated the soul, and replenished energy stores. Without a clear head, he'd likely make rash decisions—more so than normal. Reluctantly, he decided that they'd stay the night before traveling to the Aether Mountains.

Nardus eyed Berggren. "Who knows you're here?"

"A handful of guards." Berggren frowned. "Why?"

Nardus massaged his left bicep. "Did you tell them why you came here?"

"Said it was for a job. Been here a few times, so no one should have suspicions." Wrinkles creased his brow. "You in trouble here as well?"

Nardus snorted. Seemed like he was in some sort of trouble everywhere he went. "Might say that. Pravus tried to kill me. Cinolth tried to kill me. Even my own daughter tried to kill me."

"Don't forget about me," said Theyn in Nardus's mind. He swore she snickered.

"Right. Theyn tried to kill me as well."

Berggren chuckled. "As did I."

"Anyway, I need to get my stuff back," said Nardus. "Pravus took everything from me when I arrived, including my sword. I have a map with its location."

"You asking me to get it all back?" asked Berggren.

Niesha rolled her eyes. "Of course he is." She took Berggren's hand. "He'll do it."

So much like Shanara.

"Thanks for offering. That'd save me some time." Nardus retrieved the crude map and the book on shifters from his pack, handed the map to Berggren, and plopped down on the couch. Theyn jumped up on the couch and settled next to him.

"Consider it done," said Niesha. She led Berggren out the door.

Theyn mindspoke to Nardus. *"I like that girl."* She licked his cheek and rubbed her head underneath his chin. *"As soon as I'm free of this form, you'd better be ready to be ravished."*

"I've got nearly 1250 name days under my belt. Are you sure you still want to be with me now that you know my age?"

"I've always liked older men."

Nardus skimmed through the book, garnering wisdom about the way shifters could control their ability and change form at will. According to the book, shifters used mental images to transform their body between forms. It reminded him of a rune spell in a way, the image a pattern for the mezhik to follow.

Akin to wizards and sorceresses possessing a single type of mezhik, shifters dealt with a single type of animal transformation. However, in extremely rare cases, some shifters had the ability to morph into a multitude of animals and creatures, like a mage with mezhik types. The author called that type of shifter a multi-shifter.

As far as Nardus knew, Theyn could only shift from human form to cat form. Then again, she had no control over it and had only transformed a few times in her life.

Could she become something larger like a dragon?

With mezhik, many things were impossibly possible. He didn't know where the additional matter would come from to make such a shift, but his mind refused to discount the notion.

As he read further, he learned that once a shifter mastered shifting, they would no longer lose themselves to their base instincts while in their altered form. However, the book contained several safety warnings throughout as well. The most important of those being full control of the ability would take time, and the shifter could still slip back into their base instincts without warning until they fully mastered it.

Another interesting fact dealt with clothing. Once mastered, a shifter had the ability to shift their clothing as well. It made sense, given the way shifting worked. The book contained several other noteworthy items, too. Like a familiar, a shifter could bond with someone and stay connected to their higher self when around that person, preventing them from reverting to their base instincts, but the chances of one establishing such a bond were almost non-existent.

But Uncle Reudeus didn't know Theyn. She's beyond rare.

Nardus smiled and set the book on a side table next to the couch. "I think I understand how this shifting business works. Would you like me to talk you through it?"

Theyn growled at him. She mindspoke, *"I've been stuck this way for the last month. What do you think?"*

"Alright." Nardus turned on the couch, faced her, and began mindspeaking with her. *"Close your eyes and concentrate on my voice."*

Theyn closed her eyes. *"Okay. Now what?"*

"No more responding to me unless I ask you a question. Just listen. Block everything else from your mind and do exactly what I tell you."

Nardus reached out with his mind and connected with Theyn on a deeper level, the connection reminiscent of the one he'd shared with her on the boat the day they'd met. *"Picture yourself in your human form. I'll guide you along in case you've forgotten."*

Nardus recalled his own memory of her when she took the burlap sack off his head on the boat. *"Let's start with your face. Slender and beautiful with high cheekbones and a sloped forehead. Caramel skin stretched smooth and taut. Yellow eyes, frayed on the outer edges and lined in black. Light-pink lips and pearly-white teeth. Fangs on upper and lower sets. A dimple in your left cheek. White strands of hair tucked behind pointed ears hang at your shoulders. A yellow orchid pushed through your hair over your left ear. Its coloring accentuates your eyes."*

Beauty perfected.

Theyn's furry face rippled like a pond's surface after skipping a rock. For a moment, Nardus saw her beautiful human features return, but then they reverted just as quickly. *"Good. Very good. While you're picturing yourself as a human, start taking your cat-like features and placing them into a box or closet in your mind. Humans have no whiskers or fur or a tail. Remove the fur like you would a coat. Unzip it and slip it off if that helps. The tail could be an extension of the coat. Perhaps the fur and whiskers on your face are a mask you've worn to a masquerade ball. Take it off too."*

With each effort, Theyn became more human. First the fur, then the face, and then the arms, legs, and tail. The last thing to finally transform were her elongated bones. After a solid hour of stepped progress, she managed to return herself fully to human form and then back into a cat.

"Again," urged Nardus through mindspeak. *"Four more times, and you*

can have your way with me."

By the last shift, Theyn transitioned effortlessly from cat to human. Her shoulders widened as they protruded from her narrowed torso. Hips widened from her slender cat pelvis, her torso and legs shortened while her arms lengthened, and her tail retracted back into her tailbone. Her hocks returned to heels, and her paws reverted to hands and the fronts of her feet. Her box-like snout contracted back into her face, and her fur thinned and retracted underneath her skin. The entire shift took less than ten seconds. With practice, she'd be able to shift almost instantaneously.

"Satisfied?" Theyn's voice, still that of a young girl's, rang in his ears for the first time in weeks. Chills swept through him from head to toe.

Nardus eyed her. Every. Single. Inch. He licked his lips and sighed. "Yes. You're even more beautiful than I remember."

Theyn pounced on top of him and made quick work of removing his shirt. She tossed it on the floor, kissed him deep, and panted. "You'd better bar the door. It's going to be a long night."

A knock sounded at the door. "We're back," called Niesha.

Nardus winced. *Damn their timing.*

He reached out and his shirt flew into his hand. Pulling it on, he yelled, "It's open."

Niesha and Berggren entered the room, and Berggren shut the door. His face lit up and tears rolled down his cheeks when he noticed Theyn sitting on the couch.

"My girl is back!" Berggren dropped everything he held, including Nardus's sword, and rushed the couch. He lifted Theyn off the couch and pulled her into his arms.

Niesha walked around the other side of the couch and stood next to Nardus. "She's more beautiful than I'd imagined."

Nardus's chest swelled, and a lump rose in his throat. "That she is."

Theyn kissed Berggren's cheek. "I've really missed hugging you, boss."

"Back to 'boss' now, are we?" asked Berggren.

Theyn kissed his other cheek. "Didn't think you liked me calling you father."

Berggren shrugged. "Didn't think I liked Nardus, either. Yet here we are."

Theyn pulled away and glanced back at Nardus. "Told you he'd come around. Sometimes he's just a bit thickheaded and slow."

Niesha walked back over to Berggren's side. "It's not just sometimes." She smiled big.

"The two of you are really funny." Berggren shook his head and eyed Nardus. "So, what's the plan now?"

Nardus rose from the couch. "First, we sleep." He glanced down at Niesha. "Preferably in separate rooms."

Berggren tousled Niesha's hair. "Agreed. And then?"

Nardus rubbed the back of his neck. "There's somewhere Theyn and I must go in the morning. You and Niesha can do whatever you want."

"No," growled Berggren. "From now on, we stick together."

"Where we're headed is a place unfit for—" He glanced at Niesha out of the corner of his eye. "—children."

Niesha glared up at Nardus. "Well, it's good that there aren't any *children* here."

"You've only had six name days," said Nardus.

"And yet I possess half the smarts in the room from the sound of it!" Niesha crossed her arms and plopped down on the couch with a snort.

I really like this girl.

The room erupted with Berggren's boisterous laughter. Soon, Theyn and Nardus joined him.

Niesha smiled. "Then it's settled. In the morning we're all going to this secret, not-for-children location. I can't wait!" She rose from the couch and corralled Berggren. "Let's go, big man."

Berggren looked back over his shoulder at Nardus as Niesha escorted him to the door. "You leave without us, and I'll kill you when we meet again, understood?"

Nardus didn't like the idea of everyone going to Ūrdär Dhef Ꝛäfn Dhä, but he could use Berggren's size and might soon enough. He nodded. "We will go together."

Berggren and Niesha exited the room. By the time the door latched closed, Theyn was tackling him back onto the couch.

Nardus chuckled as she wrangled his trousers down his legs. "Easy, Theyn. We've got all night."

She looked up at him with passion in her eyes. "And I plan on using every second of it."

CHAPTER THIRTY-SIX

Two canoes sat on the rocky shore, but one of them had several holes in its hull. Rayah hadn't scouted them like she should've. Then again, she was a dryte and not accustomed to doing scouting of any kind. To her credit, she'd found them a way off the island. At least that's how she saw it. The others didn't seem nearly as enthusiastic about their prospects.

"You expect us to paddle our way across the Discidium Sea?" Rakzar scoffed. "Look at the whitecaps. We wouldn't survive twenty yards before capsizing."

Urza stood at the water's edge, twirling her knives in her hands. She glanced back at Rakzar. "And *you've* got a better plan?"

Rakzar snorted and plopped down on a large rock. "The plan is that I'm not going to drown again. The first time cured me of needing to do it again."

Normak stood next to Rayah. Perhaps a bit too close. "Two options we be havin'. Either we be sailin' 'cross the sea or we be stuck here 'til we die." He nudged Rayah. "Me thinks the first sounds better than the latter."

"I agree." Urza faced them and eyed Normak's boots. "Think you could run across the water with those?"

Normak reached down and rubbed one of his boots. "Aye. For a short distance."

A brilliant idea popped into Rayah's head. Perhaps it matched the target Urza aimed for with her question, but it didn't matter.

"What if you held onto the back of the canoe?" asked Rayah. "Could you push it across the sea?"

Urza winked at Rayah, and Rayah smiled back.

Female minds must think the same way.

Normak stroked his chin as he surveyed the choppy waters. "Believe so. Worth a try." He leaned close to Rayah, who stood next to him. "There be a shortcut into Tectus from the sea as well," he whispered. Ale soured his breath.

Urza must've heard Normak's poor attempt at a whisper. "A shortcut? How much of one?"

Normak rubbed the back of his head. The healer back at the village had done a good job of cleaning the wound and sealing it up. "Cross the sea, and we be in Tectus by nightfall." He walked over to the water's edge, knelt, and plunged two fingers into the water. His shoulders shook. "Them be cold waters though. Doesn' work, and we be good as ice cubes."

"I don't like it," growled Rakzar.

Rayah glared at Rakzar over her shoulder. "You don't like anything. Besides, you won't be happy with any solution we come up with unless it's one you thought of."

"That's not true," Rakzar huffed. "I've gone along with several plans today alone."

"Name one," said Urza, flatly.

Rakzar raised his arms. "Fine. You want to risk dying, then go for it. I'll just wait right here."

"We stay here, and we'll be dead. Remember?" Rayah's wings fluttered. Sometimes it happened when she became angry. Rakzar had a way of getting under her skin.

A parasite.

She snorted.

"Dead?" Normak's face contorted. "Why ya think that?"

"It's the—"

Rakzar cut Rayah off. "Let *me* fill him in."

Rayah rolled her eyes. "Suit yourself."

Rakzar continued, "Rayah and Urza were cursed by an evil sorceress who never stays solid long enough to be killed. That's why we need the weapon. If we don't kill the sorceress soon, Rayah and Urza will die."

Surprisingly, it wasn't far from the truth, but she would've told Normak everything. He had the right to know his life hung in the balance as well, along with everyone they'd encountered in Tectus, including Torbrek.

And that's why he stopped me.

Urza walked over to the good canoe and slid it into the water. "Let's go, Rayah." She hopped inside and the canoe sank several inches but stayed afloat.

"No leaks?" asked Normak.

Urza shrugged. "So far, so good."

Rayah flew over and settled in the front of the canoe. There wouldn't be enough room for Rakzar as well, so they'd have to make two trips. "Looks like you'll get your wish after all, Rakzar. We'll have to come back for you."

Rakzar leaned forward on the rock. "Don't expect to be rescued."

Normak grabbed the back of the canoe and started running. The canoe jolted forward so fast that it nearly threw Rayah overboard. Luckily, Urza had grabbed her and steadied her.

Halfway across the sea, Normak began slowing down as the canoe gradually tipped farther backward. The front of the canoe rose so high that Rayah couldn't see where they were headed.

"Any last words, lassies? 'Bout ta be fish food out 'ere."

An idea sprang into Rayah's mind. A brilliant idea. She wished she'd thought of it from the start.

"I'll hold onto the front of the canoe and fly. That should lighten the load and give us the boost we need."

"And I'll lean forward," said Urza.

Once Rayah started pushing the canoe forward, the sailing went smooth, well except for the rough whitecaps. They reached the hidden cave entrance soon after. The cave stretched for a solid mile before the floor began to rise out of the water.

Urza hopped out of the canoe, found a dry spot, and laid down. She looked like a beaten rug. "Guess I'll wait here while you go get Rakzar." Her lantern, yellow eyes winked out.

Zätūr, please help her hang on. We only need a few more days.

"Be careful, lass," said Normak to Urza. "Sometimes there be cave dwellers."

Rayah didn't know what that meant and didn't want to. She and Normak turned the boat around and journeyed back to the island. About two hours later, the four of them were back on dry land. Urza moved slower than usual and attributed it to lack of sleep when probed, but she and Rakzar knew it was more than that. Unfortunately, there was nothing they could do but push forward and get the job done.

Normak led them through several miles of the lower cave system. Intentionally devised as an unending maze, they would've been lost at the first turn had he not been there to guide them. At three different points, he led them up through hidden passages. Even as they came right up to them Rayah didn't detect a single one.

The last hidden passage brought them up through a sarcophagus on the seventh level of Tectus, the lowest level. Chiseled into the lid of the sarcophagus were three runes. The first was an 'o' shape with a tail on the bottom: 9. The second rune looked like an upside-down 'v': ^. The last rune reminded Rayah of a backward '3': ε. She ran her fingers across them.

"What do these mean?" she asked Normak.

"It be a runnin' joke with me clan. Meanin' be 'exit only' in the dwarven language."

"Clever," said Urza.

Rakzar snorted. "Enough resting. Let's get the crystal to your brother so he can make us a weapon."

Normak laughed heartily. "Me brother ain't be an expert in forgin' or cuttin'. Ya best do it yerself if ya be relyin' on 'im."

"Whatever," growled Rakzar. "We're running out of time. Let's move."

† † †

After dropping Rakzar, Urza, and Rayah off with Verdik Shardshaper, their master crystologist, Normak headed down to the armory. Inside the armory, he headed toward the back where he knew his brother would be. Always predictable, Torbrek leaned against a large table with his back to Normak, talking with a younger female dwarf named Ridan Strongblade. Normak chuckled to himself.

Sly devil.

If nothing else distinguished them as brothers, he and Torbrek had a way with women, and not just those of their own race. Humans, elves, halflings, giants, hamadryads, and faeries to name a few. On one occasion, he had to fake his own death and hide out down in the catacombs for almost two weeks to avoid the advances of an overzealous orc named Brulach. He shuddered thinking about the burly female and her natural odor.

As he thought back on it, Rayah had been the only female he could remember that didn't fawn over him. She hadn't fawned over Torbrek either. Alas, the beautiful dryte intrigued him, and her indifference made him want to pursue her.

What makes 'er different?

That question needed answered, and he'd do everything possible to figure it out. Given time, she'd come around. Perhaps he'd join them on their next quest so that he could continue to work his charm on her. In a fortnight, she'd be begging to lie with him.

It be settled. I be goin' where she do.

Torbrek would understand. He'd do the same if duty didn't bind him to the armory.

Ridan's gaze met his as he strode toward her, and color rose into her cheeks. She'd spent many a night snuggled up next to him. He figured she'd spent several nights with Torbrek as well but didn't care to ask. He had no claim on her, nor did he want one, but that wouldn't stop him from teasing her.

Normak pulled Ridan into an embrace when he reached her and buried his tongue in her mouth. Her tongue tasted of ale and cloves. Not only did she not resist his advance, but she also wrapped her hands around his buttocks and squeezed him tighter for several seconds *after* he tried to pull back.

"I didn't think I'd see ya again," she said, her eyes glistening in the torchlight.

Torbrek clasped Normak's shoulder, a smirk on his face. "Then you don't know my brother. Not even Nasda could take him down."

Normak turned and faced Torbrek, a grin on his face. "Aye, but she tried 'er damnedest."

Torbrek leaned back against the table again and crossed his arms. "Well?"

Normak frowned and motioned toward Ridan with his head and eyes. "Now?"

"What we're trying to accomplish is no secret—" Torbrek winked at Ridan. "—especially among close friends."

Normak shrugged. "So be it." He unslung his pack from his shoulder, sat it on the table, and slid it over to Torbrek. "'Ave yerself a gander."

Torbrek took the pack and dumped its contents onto the table. His eyes grew wide when the cluster of nagi siren eggs plopped down. He glanced up at Normak.

Normak grinned. "Pretty, ain't they?"

Ridan gasped. "Are those…"

"Nagi siren eggs," Normak finished. "Would 'ave grabbed more but time be short."

"Six is good." Torbrek pulled one of the eggs from the cluster with a grunt. Tendrils of sticky green slime roped between it and the others. He held it up to the torchlight. A shadow moved within the translucent egg and coiled against the side closest to the torch. "Still alive…"

"Can I hold one?" asked Ridan.

Torbrek severed the sticky tendrils with a dagger and handed the egg to Ridan. "Be careful with it. The bite from a naga or nagi siren baby can be fatal."

Ridan held the egg in her palms and stroked it with her thumbs. "Feels so strange. Soft as silk yet tough as leather. Wet and dry simultaneously."

Normak dug his finger in his ear, certain he hadn't heard his brother right. "What ya say? Little buggers be venomous?"

Torbrek nodded. "Yes, but only until they're old enough to defend themselves. The glands that produce their venom eventually dry up."

"Geesh." Normak rubbed his chin. "Would 'ave been good ta know before riskin' me life gettin' 'em."

"Those books of yours didn't say anything about it?" asked Torbrek.

Normak shook his head. "Nay a damned word aboot it."

Ridan handed the egg back to Torbrek. "So, what's the plan with those? Breed them and sell them on the dark market?" She chuckled nervously.

Torbrek guffawed. "Not a chance. We'll study the makeup of the eggshell and find a way to create armor in a similar fashion."

Ridan scrunched up her face. "I'm not following you. What do the eggs have to do with armor?"

"Everythin'." Normak took Torbrek's dagger and stabbed the egg with it, but the blade harmlessly glanced off the egg's side. Then he tried to saw through the egg with the dagger, but it couldn't penetrate the eggshell. He held up the egg. "See? Nothin' amiss."

"There is that, but far more as well," said Torbrek. "Not only is the eggshell light and virtually indestructible, but it is resistant to the elements as well. Watch." He grabbed the torch from the sconce on the wall and held it next to the egg. The flames scorched the tabletop but didn't leave a mark on the egg.

"That's remarkable," said Ridan. "Armor like that could change warfare completely."

Torbrek placed the torch back in its sconce. "Yes, it would, and its resistance to elements include those conjured and manipulated by mezhik."

Ridan ran her hand back through her long blond hair as she stared at the egg with wonder. "Damn…"

"Aye," said Normak, his eyes focused on Ridan's curved form. She'd share his bed later.

"Did you bring back anything else?" Torbrek looked right at Normak with expectancy.

"Risked me life fer those," grumbled Normak. "Be happy I even got 'em."

Torbrek slapped Normak on the back. "Ease up, brother. You've done well. *Very* well."

No matter how much time Normak spent with his brother, he could never read Torbrek. It frustrated him without end. One day, he'd find a way to return the favor.

He pulled Torbrek into a headlock and kissed the top of his head. "This call fer a celebration?"

Torbrek broke away from the hold. "Perhaps a small one at the pub, but nothing more. Understood?"

Normak brooded. "Aye."

"Cheer up, brother." He patted Normak's shoulder. "Once we've unlocked the secrets of the naga and nagi siren eggs we'll notify the king. You will be honored as a hero."

Normak shrugged. "If I be 'ere."

"Meaning what?" demanded Torbrek.

Normak avoided his brother's gaze. "Thinkin' aboot goin' with Urza and the others. Got me a bug fer adventure."

"You're a damned fool." Torbrek sighed. "These eggs were the only reason I sent you to Nasda. There's no need to go risking your life again, especially when you've not been invited to do so."

Normak huffed, "Thought Urza be yer friend."

"What does she have to do with this?"

"She and Rayah are dyin'. That's why they be needin' the weapon."

"Oh, I see." Torbrek blew air from his nostrils and shook his head. "Rayah's got your head turned, hasn't she?"

Normak glanced at Ridan and swallowed hard. "Nay. Me intentions be noble and such."

Ridan laughed. "I don't think ya have a noble bone to your name. Ya chase tail faster than a hound after a rabbit."

"Oy! That be unfair," groaned Normak.

"It can't be unfair if it's accurate," retorted Torbrek.

Ridan returned to his side and grabbed his right buttock. "Don't worry. It changes nothing between us. I'll just have to try harder to keep your attention focused on me." She squeezed his buttocks harder. "I do love a challenge."

Normak grabbed his face and pulled on his beard. "Both of yeh be vipers." He shoved everything back into his pack, sans the eggs, and slung it over his shoulder. "I'll round up the others an' meet ya both at the pub."

"Can't wait to meet this Rayah," said Ridan. "She must be a looker."

"That she is," said Torbrek. "Wings and all."

Ridan cocked her head, her eyebrows raised. "Wings?"

Normak shook his head and walked away.

Them wings be mezhik.

† † †

Rakzar slammed his fist down on the pub table the six of them sat around. Ale sloshed from several of the wooden tankards, spotting the table with puddles of golden liquid. "How long does it take to cut a crystal and mount it to a weapon?"

"Relax," said Torbrek. He sat across from Rakzar, a tankard clutched between his small hands. "Verdik is the best at what he does, but crystals are quite delicate and take lots of care when being cut. I assure you that it'll be ready when it's ready, my friend."

Rakzar glared at Torbrek. He'd eaten animals larger than the dwarf. "We're not friends. Nor are we acquaintances."

Torbrek held up his hand. "Fair enough. Perhaps one day we will be."

"Don't count on it," Rakzar growled.

Amicus sat at the end of the table, next to Rakzar. A smile plastered his face as he eyed Rakzar's tankard. "I don't think it'd hurt for you to be nice every once in a while."

Rakzar shook his fist at Amicus. "You just don't get it, do you? I don't need or want you around."

"Yet here I am." Amicus's smile widened. "Look around. You're surrounded by friends and people who love and care about you. Can't you be content with that for a few hours?"

Rakzar sighed. "How can I be when I know they're all headed to their graves?"

"Open your eyes, my friend." Amicus laid his hand on Rakzar's forearm. "They're the ones dying, not you. Yet they're the ones enjoying themselves. Is it just me, or is that ironic?"

Rakzar didn't understand how he could feel the touch of a man long dead, yet he did. Moreover, that touch gave him a sense of comfort. His mind couldn't wrap itself around such absurdity.

"I'm sorry, Torbrek." The words tasted bitter on Rakzar's tongue, especially the "sorry" one.

Torbrek lifted his tankard. "Think nothing of it. I certainly won't be after a few more of these." He pitched his head back, drained what remained of his ale, and slammed the tankard back down.

Rakzar nursed his ale. He planned on leaving Tectus the moment Verdik finished the weapon and didn't want to do so drunk. Given his size, he could knock back several rounds without blinking, but dwarven ale tended to be a dozen times more potent than that of other races. One would suffice.

Urza sat to his left. She looked a bit livelier than she had earlier, but he still worried about her. How much longer did she have before the curse ran its course?

I must kill Käíeɀ. Sooner than later.

Rayah sat on the opposite side of the table, sandwiched between Torbrek and Normak. Several times in the past hour, she'd moved Normak's hand away from hers. The man seemed oblivious to Rayah's rejections of his advances. Rakzar would have to keep an eye on the situation. Ale always makes men—and women for that matter—lose their inhibitions and causes them to do things they normally wouldn't. Rayah's heart belonged to the White Knight, and he'd defend her honor to the death if need be.

But it won't come down to that.

From what he gathered, Ridan sought Normak for herself. She sat on the same side of the table as him, on the other side of Urza. The young dwarf seemed to have a good head on her shoulders, notwithstanding her infatuation with Normak. Her eyes never wavered from watching him.

Normak jumped to his feet and climbed onto the table. The other four grabbed their mugs and held them close. Rakzar left his where it sat. He could care less if it got knocked over.

"Everyone, get off yer tuchuses and put yer hands ta'gether!" shouted

Normak. "It be time fer a bit 'o song 'n dance."

The entire pub clapped and roared with laughter as Normak danced and sang his song:

> *A tankard of ale is all it takes*
> *Ta set yer spirit free*
> *Rightin' the wrong of past mistakes*
> *It's good enough fer me*
> *Aye! Aye! Aye!*
>
> *A nibble, a touch, a little kiss*
> *Can set yer heart afire*
> *Just don' get caught by yer miss*
> *Or ye be on the pyre*
> *Aye! Aye! Aye!*

The song seemed to go on for days with more stanzas than one ought ever remember. After listening to the first few, Rakzar tuned it all out. He set his mind on the upcoming task. Even with a weapon that could kill her, Käíez would still be difficult to defeat. He prayed that Murtag and the orcs hadn't moved on from the valley yet. If they had, he'd have to track her down.

A bald dwarf with a goatee and spectacles entered the pub and headed straight for their table. The dwarf bowed slightly toward Torbrek and then proceeded to whisper something in his ear. At least it seemed that way, but he could've just as easily shouted given the noise level. The man turned and walked back out of the pub.

Torbrek motioned Rakzar to follow him and headed out of the pub. Rakzar fell in right behind Torbrek, easily keeping pace with the man's quick but short strides. Urza and the others pursued from behind but quickly caught up as they headed down into the fifth level of Tectus. Rakzar assumed they were heading back to the armory and they did just that.

Verdik Shardshaper stood just inside and held a large object wrapped in a black cloth. Rakzar resisted the urge to snatch it from the man's tiny hands.

Once the six of them piled into the armory, Verdik unfolded the black cloth, revealing an ornate dagger with a translucent orange blade. The blade extended about five inches from the golden crossguard, and the black handle reminded Rakzar of a large claw, hooked at the end. He'd never seen anything quite like it.

Rakzar reached for the dagger but Urza knocked his arm down.

"Don't be so impatient," she whispered through gritted teeth. "You don't know how it works or how to handle it."

"It's a dagger," he growled. "How complicated can it be?"

Verdik cleared his throat. "Let me give you a brief demonstration."

Torbrek glanced at Rakzar. "Yes, please do."

Behind Verdik sat an elongated table. Several containers spread down its length. Verdik moved around to the other side of the table and stood behind the first container. He laid the dagger and black cloth down on the table and picked up the container.

"I've filled this container with water." He tilted it and a small amount of water splashed onto the table. Then he took the knife in his other hand and held it over the table. "Watch." His eyes sparkled behind thick spectacles. He began pouring water onto the table and then plunged the knife into the steady stream. At once, every drop of water turned into solid ice, from the container all the way down to what had pooled on the table surface.

"Whoa," said Normak.

The rest of them kept quiet.

Verdik pulled the blade from the ice, and the ice immediately turned back into water. He demonstrated the dagger's power several more times with sand and other various liquids and powders. The effect was truly mesmerizing.

"Those demonstrations are great," said Rakzar, "but what about other things like smoke and steam?"

Verdik smiled and pulled a piece of parchment out of one of his pockets. "Ridan, would you be so kind as to assist me with this?"

Ridan nearly squealed, "Yes!" She rounded the table and stood next to Verdik. "What do ya want me to do?"

"Grab one of the torches." He crumpled the parchment and tossed it on the table while she retrieved a torch. 'Now, light the paper on fire."

She did, and red smoke rose from the paper in a plume reminiscent of a thunderhead. Verdik stabbed the dagger into the smoke, and it solidified into a smoky-red glass. Verdik peered over the top of his spectacles. "Satisfied?"

"To no end," said Urza.

Rakzar grinned. *Käïeʐ is dead.*

Verdik pulled the blade from the smoky glass, and the smoke began rising again. He wrapped it in the black cloth and presented it to Rakzar. "Be very careful with this. A single nick from its blade could cause someone's blood to turn to tar."

Rakzar nodded. "Thank you for doing this. You've saved countless lives."

"It's always a pleasure working with new and rare materials." Verdik moved around the table and exited the armory.

Rakzar placed the dagger underneath his breastplate. "I must leave at once."

Torbrek stood in his path. "There are a few matters to discuss before you leave. First, take this. It will make transportation of the blade easier." He presented Rakzar with a sheath. "That sheath is made from elven earthsteel and skinned in leather. It will keep the blade safe during your travel."

Rakzar pulled the dagger back out from behind his breastplate and unwrapped it. The dagger, hefty for its size yet perfectly balanced, slid into the sheath with ease and fit snugly. He strung the sheath onto his belt. "Thank you."

Torbrek nodded. "Now, based on everything you've told me about the situation you're facing, I insist that my brother accompanies you once again. He's fast on his feet and a cunning warrior."

Rakzar knew a demand like that would come, but he didn't care who came along. If they couldn't keep up, they'd be left, plain and simple. That included Urza and Rayah. "He's proven his worth. Anything else?"

"I'm coming, too," said Ridan.

Everyone in the room turned and looked at her.

"There be no need," said Normak, concern creasing his brow.

Ridan folded her arms and scowled at Normak. "I insist."

"You'll never keep up," said Urza.

"With Bakkan, I'm almost as fast as Normak."

"Who's Bakkan?" asked Rayah.

"He's a black-and-silver mastiff familiar." Ridan smiled wide. "He runs like the wind, even with me upon his back."

"Devil dog if ya ask me," gruffed Normak.

"No one's asking you."

"Your circle of friends keeps growing," said Amicus. "It makes my heart sing."

"Don't you dare start singing," growled Rakzar.

"Where'd that come from?" asked Normak, a hint of hurt in his voice.

"Never mind." Rakzar eyed Torbrek again. "We good, or is there more?"

Torbrek licked his lips and smacked his tongue on the backs of his teeth. His stare intensified, any hint of humor gone. "This may sound a bit strange, but I want the body returned here. Käíez you said, correct?"

"Ugh. What the gods do you want with her body?" asked Urza.

"As you know, threats of many kinds rise up as the years pass. As craftsmen of some of the finest weapons and armor in the realm, we strive to innovate." Torbrek folded his arms in front of himself and paced. "Having her body, we can study how she manipulates herself to become a fluid-like mist. Understanding physical attributes like those would allow us to create weapons that penetrate any substance and armor that can absorb a weapon's force by displacing the impact. Imagine all the possibilities."

"Once she's dead, I don't give a damn what happens to her body." Rakzar crossed his arms. "But that's all on your brother."

Torbrek nodded. "Agreed." He held up a finger. "However, there is one last thing. We'll need that dagger back once you're finished with it."

"Fine." Rakzar eyed each of the people in the growing group, including Amicus. "Gather your belongings and any provisions you might need and meet me on the first level of Tectus. We leave within the hour." He turned and walked out of the armory.

Your time has come, Käíez.

CHAPTER THIRTY-SEVEN

Dawn painted the sky in shades of pink, red, yellow, and orange, oblivious to the trouble it brought with its passing, but Savric knew. He sat atop the outcropping and watched the camp rouse from sleep. Had he the power, he'd turn back time and alter key events, namely those surrounding Alderan and Aria. But he didn't. No one did. At least no human did.

Savric sent a quick note to Morcinda informing her that the army would begin their march north within the hour, and then he woke up Calen and Eshtak who both somehow managed to stay asleep despite the growing ruckus. Twenty minutes later, the three of them stood on the outcropping and watched the army pack up the camp.

Calen rubbed his stomach. "Can we eat before leaving?"

Savric's stomach rumbled in agreement. "I dare say, we must take a few moments to re-energize ourselves."

"Eshtak hungry too." He bounced back and forth on his toes and twirled a few times.

"Good." Calen found a stone worthy of sitting upon and took a seat. "What do we have left to eat? Anything besides fish? I'm a little tired of fish. But I'll eat fish if that's all we have."

"Eshtak loves fish." He plopped down next to Calen.

"How about some dates, honey, and a bit of bread? Would that satisfy you more than a few fish?" asked Savric.

Calen's eyes brightened. "We've got dates? Why didn't you say so?"

Savric smiled. He'd missed Calen so much over the weeks prior to this last one. He'd never been away for such a long time. On top of it, he'd missed Calen's fourteenth name day. He'd never forgive himself for that.

He sat down on the other side of Calen, and the three of them ate in silence after he doled out the food. He'd been to Ūrdär Dhef Ɂäfn Dhä a few times during his early years to check on them, but he'd neglected to do so for the last few decades. With everything that had happened with Qotan and Zerenity, he'd lost his fire. Why events had happened the way they did would likely never be revealed to him, but he'd give anything to go back four decades and make different choices. Had he realized what'd happened to Qotan back then, they wouldn't be in the mess they were in now.

All the blame rested solely on his shoulders. Zerenity held no blame in any of it. She didn't know. *"You're an old fool, Savvy."* That's what she'd say to him.

Savric hadn't told Calen of the change in plans and worried how he might react, but there was no point in avoiding it any longer. He exhaled the nervous energy he'd stored all night and blurted it out. "My boy, you have a decision to make, and it will be a tough one, but I cannot and will not make it for you."

Calen looked up at him and cocked his head. "What decision is that?"

"I know how much you want to stay with your aunt, and I will not prevent you from doing so, no matter how dangerous it will certainly be. However, I cannot continue to follow the army now that we know their full plans. Instead, I must travel far and awaken those of *Ūrdär Dhef 2äfn Dhä*. I fear they are the only hope we have left."

Calen chewed on his lower lip for several seconds. "I guess I'll go with you. As you said, there's nothing that can be done for Aunt Tahmara right now. I love her like a mother, but following her into a war could get me killed, and I don't really want to die."

Savric smiled at Calen. The boy never failed to make him proud. "Very good."

"Master Savric, what are we going to do once we get there?"

"Simple, my boy. We will wake Cyrus Nithik. He will know how to kill Cinolth."

"But how is it that he's still alive after 1200 years? I didn't think wizards lived that long."

"Under normal circumstances, we do not. However, the place where we are headed is special. There are things there that I cannot even begin to explain to you. You will just have to see for yourself to understand."

Calen moped. "I guess I can wait."

"Indeed." Savric wiped his mouth with his sleeve. "Now, you and Eshtak go gather up your belongings. We will leave when the army does."

Eshtak twirled around. "Eshtak ready now."

"Then you can help me get ready," said Calen. He grabbed Eshtak's arm and pulled him along. "Come on."

In the distance, Cinolth stood next to a large white tent. Smoke rose from his nostrils and plumed in the cool morning air. From where he stood, Savric couldn't make out the person who mounted Cinolth, but he had no doubt as to their identity.

Aria.

Cinolth took to the sky, circled, and headed right toward Savric. Aria leaned over the side of Cinolth's neck. They seemed to be looking for something. His pulse rose as realization sank in.

They are looking for me.

Savric held out his hand, and Qotan's staff flew into it. He jumped off the outcropping and landed hard on his feet. His knees buckled underneath him. It'd only been about a four-foot drop, but he couldn't remember why he'd thought it to be a good idea to jump down. He crouched down, drew his hood over the top of his head, and prayed they wouldn't spot him.

Thump-thump. Whoosh!

The sound of beating wings filled his ears and grew louder. He dared not look up for fear Aria would spot him at the exact moment. Such large wings cracked like thunder as they caught wind on the down stroke. He hunkered lower. Hugged the rocks. Pulled himself into the shadows as he pushed the light away.

Thump-thump. Whoosh!

So close now, he could feel the air vibrate. Wind sucking and pushing underneath Cinolth's mighty wings.

Thump-thump. Whoosh!

His cloak pulled around himself and billowed as they passed by.

"Master Savric?" called Calen, his voice frantic. The boy stood three feet in front of him but didn't see him hiding in the shadows.

"Eshtak sees." The little man pointed right at Savric.

Savric put a finger to his lips.

Eshtak nodded and turned away. "Old friend not gone," he said to Calen. "Eshtak sits and waits with friend."

Thump-thump. Whoosh!

Beating wings grew louder once again. They must've circled back around.

Thump-thump. Whoosh!

Savric grabbed Calen and Eshtak and pulled them into the shadows with him.

Fire roared, and the air crackled with heat.

Sulfuric fumes, smoke, singed grass, and burning flesh blossomed.

Screams erupted, barely audible over the roaring fire and thunderous wings.

The shadow of the outcropping stretched far against the bright flames to the west.

Then the flames rolled over the edge, licked the air, and blackened the rock.

Savric's cloak smoked from the heat of the flames as they came within inches of consuming him, Calen, and Eshtak.

Through the smoke and haze, people scattered in all directions. A scene of chaos.

Savric fought back tears as he held Calen and Eshtak against his chest, shielding them from the madness.

Then, just as fast as it had begun, the roar died out and the *thump-thump whoosh* of beating wings faded into the distance.

With a ragged breath, Savric let the light back in. "Wait here," he whispered, his voice weighed down with exhaustion and sorrow.

He released Calen and Eshtak and stood on wobbly legs. Leaning hard on Qotan's staff for support, he climbed back up onto the scorched outcropping and surveyed the damage.

Charred remains littered the field of trampled grass, most unrecognizable as human. More than a hundred from what he could see. It didn't matter that most of these people would've died soon enough. What did matter was the reason they had. He'd brought the wrath of Cinolth and Aria upon them, and their deaths would rest on his shoulders until the day he died.

All this bloodshed for an hour's delay.

Grief stricken, Savric fell to his knees and wept.

Ɛ̓äṭūr, forgive me.

✝ ✝ ✝

An hour earlier, Nardus awoke on a couch in the arms of a beautiful woman. Theyn lay next to him, her heartbeat in rhythm with his own. It was the most peaceful he'd felt in quite some time, but that moment didn't last. Niesha and Berggren came knocking early. With Sarai's assistance, the four of them traveled from Galondu Castle to the base of the Aether Mountains in less than five minutes.

Now, Theyn stood at his side, not on all fours as she had for the last several weeks but on her own two feet. Berggren and Niesha stood behind them, and rocky crags and steep terrain lay ahead. The path to Ūrdär Dhef Ƨäfn Dhä was made difficult on purpose so that no one would happen upon them by chance. The possibility of that happening was slim at best anyway.

Several wards protected the cave nestled deep in the heart of the mountains, and a mezhik barrier around the mountains prevented anyone from using mezhik to enter them. Very few would ever venture so far into the mountains without good cause. Nightmares of many kinds lurked about underneath the canopy of trees, waiting for victims to fall into their deadly traps.

Nardus knew the mountains and forest well, but even with his knowledge he treaded lightly, especially with Berggren and Niesha in tow. "We must get to the top of this cliff and then ascend another before we can make our way down into the hidden valley and to the cave where the other members of *Ūrdär Dhef Ƨäfn Dhä* sleep."

"Lead the way," barked Berggren.

The four of them made their way to the top of both cliffs and descended into the hidden valley. Nothing looked the same as he'd remembered. The earth lay cracked and blistered with dryness and most of the grass and vegetation had died. Several dry springs in a row could've caused the damage. Most of the Ancient Realm had seen less rain and snow over the last few years. Either way, the sight disheartened him.

Surprisingly, Niesha hadn't complained at all on the trek. The same couldn't be said of Berggren. The man moved like a glacier and left a trail of blood in several spots after losing his footing.

At the other end of the valley they climbed again into thick underbrush and tall conifer trees. Two familiar rock formations rose from the ground, and he knew they were close. A few turns and a bend around another hill and they came up to a rock face that rose more than a thousand feet high. He moved close and put his hand against the rock. When he did, he should've felt the tingle of mezhik. Instead, he felt nothing but cold, hard rock. His skin prickled and the hairs stood on his arms and his nape.

Theyn cocked her head. "Something's wrong, isn't it?"

Nardus grimaced. "Yeah. Someone's been here and didn't reset the wards that protect this place." He stepped forward, right through the face of the rock wall, and into the start of an extensive cave system.

Niesha gasped with wonder, and it made Nardus smile a little. He called to her, "Come on in, Niesha. You can step right on through."

Niesha emerged from the rock wall. "Whoa! I can't believe I just did that!"

Nardus winked at her. "You're well on your way to becoming a great sorceress."

Niesha scoffed, "I know how things work. My father and mother most definitely didn't exhibit any sort of *special* abilities."

"You're quite perceptive given your age." Theyn tousled Niesha's hair.

Niesha shrugged. "My mother called me a handful."

"Can attest to that," said Berggren.

"*Əllít ʊb.*" An orb lit over Nardus's open palm and then flew ahead of them, lighting up a good section of the caves as they headed through several corridors. The place was purposely setup like a maze. So many paths led back to the beginning, each twisted with mezhik. Nardus knew the correct path and could've led them through the maze without incident, but he didn't need to. Someone had drawn arrows on the walls, marking the way.

This isn't good.

Ahead lay a door. Steel and black. No handle protruded from it. Nardus drew several runes in the air with his finger but nothing happened. The door should've unlocked. He pushed on it and it creaked as it swung inward several inches.

After finding his true self in the Valley of Dragons, he'd known someone had awakened him and Ilia, but he hadn't allowed himself to think about it further. Now, he feared what he might find inside the room that stood before him. Thunder crashed in his chest with each heartbeat.

Nardus peered over his shoulder. "The three of you stay here. I'm uncertain of what I might find inside and don't want to risk any of you getting hurt. Do you understand?"

Theyn and Berggren nodded.

Niesha groaned and hung her head. "Yes, sir."

"Good."

Nardus pushed the door open farther and stepped inside, leaving the floating orb of light with the others. He wouldn't need it inside the room. Fluorescent tubes lined the ceiling and buzzed with life as they filled with energy and lit the room. Many things occupied the giant room, but he only cared about the seven metal chambers sitting in a circle at the center of the room. Each chamber sat at a slight incline, the head end higher than the foot end.

Derrik Spencer, a man from a place they called the Shadow World, had referred to the chambers as cryogenic chambers—a technology that would preserve an individual by lowering their core temperature and basically freezing them. Mezhik from the Shadow World. Each of the seven chambers accommodated a single member of Ūrdär Dhef Ɂäfn Dhä. Two of them had preserved him and Ilia for nearly 1200 years.

The lights buzzed and flickered overhead, casting shadows throughout the room and distorting his vision. From his angle, he could only see the fronts of two of the chambers. Both lay open, as he knew they would. The other five looked like they were still sealed.

He moved toward the center of the room, each step harder to take than the previous. His gut twisted with angst and the arteries in his neck jerked with every heartbeat.

Glass crunched underfoot as he approached the first chamber.

The sense of death crawled across his skin.

Every indication of trouble along the way heightened his fear, and he'd expected the worst, but he still hadn't prepared himself mentally for what he found. His gaze settled on cracked glass and a puncture hole through the chamber lid.

Only a skeleton and clothes remained inside the chamber.

A single hole right through the center of the skull.

Pharius. I'm sorry, my old friend.

The four remaining chambers each had a similar hole through cracked glass and the remains of one of the other members of Ūrdär Dhef Ɂäfn Dhä.

Anger and sorrow raged within him. He didn't know how it'd happened, but he could think of only one man who might be responsible.

Pravus.

Nardus spat on the floor. He headed toward the exit and met the others at the door. "There's something else I must do, so it's going to be a while longer."

"Can we come inside now?" asked Niesha.

"I'm not sure that's the best idea," said Nardus.

"I might be young, but I know how adults think," said Niesha. "Something happened in there, didn't it? Something horrible. I can see it in your face."

Nardus rubbed his bicep. "You are perceptive. All my friends have been killed, and I'm the last member of *Ūrdär Dhef 2äfn Dhä* still alive."

"I'm so sorry." Theyn took his hand and kissed it. "What can I do to help?"

Berggren nodded and took Niesha's hand. "We'll wait out here. Do what you need to."

"I've seen dead bodies before." Niesha looked up at Berggren. "Helped my mother dispose of one once. The man's heart must've given out during the night." She eyed Nardus, her eyes pleading. "I promise it won't shock me."

"Fine. Come inside, but do *not* touch anything," said Nardus.

Niesha hugged Nardus's waist. "Thank you!" She pushed passed him and stopped. "Wow! Where did all this come from?"

"Another world." Nardus walked past Niesha and toward another part of the room. "I'll tell you all about it sometime, but right now I must summon *Fee2härz Dhä* and get to the bottom of what happened."

"The Watchers?" asked Theyn.

"Yes." Nardus stopped in an area cleared of furniture and everything else. Five white circles, about three feet in diameter, were drawn on the floor in a circular pattern. Those circles surrounded a central yellow circle of about the same size. Nardus stepped into the yellow circle. Theyn, Berggren, and Niesha had followed him.

"Stand back beyond the white circles," said Nardus. The three of them moved back.

Berggren fished something out of his pack. Nardus recognized its silver shine immediately.

2äbrä2är.

"What are you doing with that?" growled Nardus.

Berggren clutched the collar tight. "Safety precaution. I've learned to expect anything when it comes to mezhik."

In truth, Nardus didn't blame him. But those collars represented slavery. They'd certainly have a talk about it sometime in the future.

Nardus called upon his mezhik and brought it to his fingertips. His brain sent mixed signals as the tingle of it intensified. Cyrus relished it, but Nardus loathed it. It would forever be a matter of contention. He cleared his mind and began drawing a rune spell in the air. First, he drew an oval shape and then two nearly parallel lines from its narrow points. Then, he connected the ends of the two lines, forming what looked like a spyglass. Underneath the spyglass he drew four lines, forming a "W" shape. The rune glowed yellow.

The mark of Feezhärz Dhä.

Satisfied with his work, he called upon them. "*Feezhärz Dhä, ɛʊmn Í zíū.*"

The rune shattered into a thousand beams of light. The floor quaked and thunder rumbled the air. The light fizzled and disappeared.

Niesha frowned. "That's it? A bit disappointing if you ask me."

"It might take a few minutes," said Nardus. "Be patient."

"Not my strongest attribute," admitted Niesha.

† † †

Savric, Calen, and Eshtak waited in the shadows of the outcropping as the rest of the army began heading north toward Elatos. The small camp of uninfected moved as well, keeping back a good quarter mile from the army. Leaving Qotan and Zerenity made Savric feel sick to his stomach but nothing could be done. At least not until he awakened Ūrdär Dhef Ɂäfn Dhä.

After the last few stragglers moved on, Savric released his hold on the light, and the shadows dissipated. He stood and stretched his legs. Calen and Eshtak followed his lead.

Calen looked about nervously. "Are we safe?"

"For now." Savric reached out and Qotan's staff jumped into his hand. "We have a long journey ahead of us."

"Eshtak ready." He bounced from foot to foot.

Suddenly, Savric felt very strange. Warmth engulfed him, and then his hands and feet began falling apart like ashes.

"Master Savric!" yelled Calen, his eyes bulging from their sockets. "What's happening?"

"I am uncertain, my boy." Panic crushed his chest. "I have never experienced anything like this." He closed his eyes for a moment and collected his thoughts. "You and Eshtak need to head east, toward the Hotah River, and wait for me there. If for some reason I am unable to meet you, I will send Morcinda to fetch you."

Calen cried, "Don't leave!"

Another moment, and Savric disappeared into a world of darkness.

† † †

It only took a few minutes for Feɀhärz Dhä to begin materializing within the five white circles surrounding Nardus, but only two of them came. A male and a female, both older. Immediately, Nardus recognized that the female Feɀhärz Dhä was one of the infected he'd heard about. She had black veins, pale skin, and black eyes.

Even before the woman finished materializing, mezhik rose into her fingertips. She hissed like a serpent as a green fireball flew from her open palm. Nardus dropped and rolled, narrowly escaping its fiery trajectory. She attacked the older man who had come with her as well, but he'd been better prepared and produced a light shield to block her attack.

Nardus yelled at Theyn, Berggren, and Niesha. "Take cover!" He didn't have time to see if they had as another fireball whizzed past his head.

"Whatever you do, do not hurt her," yelled the old man. "She is not in control of herself."

Damn.

Nardus scrambled to his feet, blocked another fireball with a rock shield he'd conjured, and pressed forward. Using his mezhik, he commanded the rock to hold the woman in place. Two pillars of rock rose out of the floor and snared the woman's feet.

It didn't faze her even a little.

The floor fissured as vines grew up from it and attacked Nardus and the old man simultaneously.

Nardus unsheathed his sword, Brinzhär Dädh, and hacked at the vines, but there were so many of them.

The old man lost ground and then the vines took him down.

Nardus caught a flash of light out of the corner of his eye, but not soon enough.

The fireball hit him in the chest and sent him flying backward. He hit the floor hard and skidded several feet before hitting the wall. Had Brinzhär Dädh not been between him and the fireball he'd be dead.

The woman occupied herself with the rock shoes, firing several fireballs into the rock to try and melt it.

Nardus pulled himself to his feet and dusted himself off.

With a flick of his wrist, Nardus freed the old man from the vines that bound him.

Nardus stalked forward, determined to end the skirmish. A red, yellow, and blue fireball rose out of his palm.

The woman's black-eyed gaze met Nardus's. She snarled and conjured a fireball of her own.

"Feathers!" yelled the old man.

A flash of silver arced across the room.

The woman's upper body lurched forward. She coughed and grabbed for her throat.

The fireball fizzled out in her palm.

Nardus pulled his mezhik back, fizzling his fireball as well.

The woman struggled to free herself from both the rock restraints and *ƨäbräƨär*, but she didn't have the strength for either. She writhed and screamed and hissed. "My master will punish—"

"*Ƨalläb*," snarled Nardus.

The woman crumpled backward and would've hit the floor hard if Theyn hadn't caught her.

Nardus commanded the rock around the woman's ankles to release her and then turned his glare upon the old man. "What is wrong with you people?"

The old man slowly pulled himself to his feet and brushed off his robes. He pulled on the end of his beard as he looked around. "I know this place. I was just about to come here." He scratched his head and looked at Nardus. "But how did I get here?"

Nardus pointed a finger at the old man. "I summoned you here to answer for what's happened."

"Summoned me? And who might you be?" asked the old man.

Nardus stalked forward. "My name is Cyrus Nithik. Who in *Ef Demd Dhä* are you?"

The old man's face turned sheet white. He half-bowed/curtsied/nodded. "My name is Savric Naphor, and I am also known as Savric the Wise. I am honored to make your acquaintance."

Nardus curled his hand into a fist. "Enough with the pleasantries. Where are the other *Feezhärz Dhä*?"

Savric glanced toward the old woman. "She and I are the only two who remain." He frowned. "How did you come to be awakened?"

Nardus poked Savric in the chest with his finger. "An excellent question, wizard. Perhaps you should've asked it twenty years ago."

"I misunderstand your meaning. Are you implying that you have been awake that long?"

"There is no implication." Spittle peppered the air. "It is a fact."

Savric gazed toward the seven chambers. "Are you the only member who has been awakened?"

Anger drove Nardus to get in Savric's face. "The dead cannot be awakened. You were supposed to keep watch over us. What happened to the others, and why weren't more chosen?"

Savric pulled on his beard. "Someone found out about *Feezhärz Dhä* and started hunting us. We went into hiding, but not before the other three of us were killed. They did not get a chance to name successors."

Nardus pointed at the woman. "And what is wrong with her?"

"In a single word, Cinolth."

Nardus stepped back and brooded. "Cinolth... What does her condition have to do with him?"

"Do you remember the curse he put on the world when you killed him?" asked Savric.

Nardus rubbed his left bicep. "I do, but that was so long ago."

"Indeed, but when Cinolth died, his scales spread across the Ancient Realm and buried themselves deep in the earth. When his heart was brought back into the world, those scales grew into venomous vines that infected humans and turned them into these walking shells."

Nardus retreated farther, his hands on his head. "My God... Is that really what happened?"

"I am afraid so," said Savric.

Everything truly is my fault.

His stomach wrestled to keep its contents contained as his head swam through the murk of his past.

Is there nothing in this world that I didn't cause?

"How long will this woman remain asleep?" asked Theyn.

"Could be seconds or hours." Nardus took a deep breath.

One problem at a time.

"Berggren, help Theyn get the woman onto that metal table over there. I think I have an idea."

"Got it," said Berggren.

Nardus went over to one of the cryogenic chambers and reached up into a hidden compartment. His fingers found the flexible, metal bracelet inside. He pulled it out and shoved it over his hand.

"What's that for?" asked Niesha.

Nardus nearly jumped out of his skin. "Am I going to need to put a bell around your neck so that I know where you are?"

Niesha shrugged. "Quiet feet are necessary when sneaking around a single-room home."

Nardus eyed the bracelet as he walked over to the table that Berggren and Theyn had lain the woman down on. "This bracelet's been storing mezhik energy for the last 1200 years."

"So you can use it?" Niesha asked, right on his heels.

Six years old?

Nardus shook his head and chuckled. "Precisely."

He placed his hands on the table. "Stand back. I'm going to try and see what's wrong with her and if there's a way to cure her of the sickness she's suffering from." The others stepped back several feet.

Nardus poured a small amount of mezhik into the table. The metal bubbled and stretched over the woman's arms and ankles, restraining her. Now it wouldn't matter if she woke up.

He closed his eyes, reached deep within himself, drew upon his mezhik, and began pouring it into the woman. Through eyes of mezhik, he saw into her. Down through her skin and muscles.

Darkness as black as tar wrapped around her organs, stretched up into her brain, and pumped through her veins. He'd never seen anything like it before. To worsen matters, the darkness seemed to be conscious and sensed his presence within her. At first, the darkness retreated from the places he probed with his mezhik, but then it started fighting back.

Sick, sadistic, disgusting images and thoughts flooded Nardus's mind. He fought through them easily enough, but the darkness proved far more powerful than anything he'd ever experienced before. He dug deeper within himself and poured light into the woman. More and more, he pumped it into her, but the darkness resisted. It pushed back against him and forced itself into his stream of mezhik and ascended toward him.

I'm losing ground.

The darkness reached his hands. Touched his fingers. Crawled onto his skin.

"No!" he shouted.

Nardus groaned as he fought harder to regain control. He accessed the mezhik stored in the bracelet and pushed with everything he had, forcing the darkness out of his body and back into the woman. Harder he pushed, draining the energy from the bracelet as he filled the woman with pure light, dispelling the darkness until none remained within her.

"Feathers!" exclaimed Savric. "I can see the darkness pouring from her pores. I daresay whatever you are doing is working."

A dozen minutes passed as the last of the darkness finally left the woman's body.

"Is it finished?" asked Savric.

"I believe so." Nardus dropped to his knees and then collapsed on the floor. "I've never fought anything so powerful before. The darkness within her was alive. Conscious. It fought me for control and tried to take control of me. I've never felt such evil before."

Theyn and Berggren helped Nardus back to his feet and stabilized him.

The woman on the table coughed and moaned.

† † †

Savric rushed to the table and leaned over the woman. He took her hand in his. "Reni? Can you hear my voice?" His hand trembled more than hers did.

The woman blinked rapidly, coughed again, and then she opened her eyes. They were no longer black. The black veins had receded as well, and her skin had gained some of its color back.

She squinted at him. "Savvy? What happened?"

"Dear Ƨäṭūr, you have returned to us!" exclaimed Savric.

"Returned from where? The last thing I remember is collapsing on the floor of my kitchen." She tried to sit up but the restraints on her arms held her down. "Why am I restrained?"

"Allow me." Nardus reached out and touched the table and Zerenity's restraints melted away.

"Thank you." Zerenity sat up and looked around. Her brow wrinkled. "And, where are we? This place looks familiar."

Savric patted the back of her hand. "We have returned to the location of *Ūrdär Dhef 2äfn Dhä.*"

"But why are we here? What have you done?"

"Bugger bees, woman. I assure you that I am absolved of any wrongdoing in reference to the open chambers."

Zerenity's eyes grew wide as she processed his words. "You've opened the chambers?"

Savric pulled on his beard as he eyed the room. "The state of this room has not been altered since our arrival a half hour past. The two chambers were already opened when we arrived. Cyrus is the only one left alive."

"Barely," Nardus said.

Zerenity's gaze shot over to Nardus. "Cyrus Nithik…"

Savric gestured toward Nardus. "Cyrus saved you and brought you back to me."

"Save me from what?" Zerenity reached up and felt her neck. "Why am I wearing a collar?"

Savric grimaced. "Cinolth possessed you."

"Cinolth The Dark? How is that possible? He's been dead a long time." She rubbed her head. "Why don't I remember anything?"

"I promise you that Cinolth is alive. I have witnessed his presence with my own eyes. He controlled you, just as he controls Qotan and tens of thousands of others."

"He controlled me?" She frowned. "Does this have something to do with the vines?"

"Precisely," Savric confirmed.

Zerenity's eyes narrowed. "What are you not telling me, Savvy? Have I done something terrible?"

Savric eyed the floor and didn't answer.

"Please, Savvy, tell me." She grabbed his arm. "I must know."

Savric sighed and looked her in the eye. "You are responsible for the deaths of many people."

"I am?" her voice quavered. "Why? What happened?"

Tears welled in Savric's eyes. "They were trying to save their families."

"Dear Ʒätūr!" She leaned over the side of the table and retched.

"I am sorry, Reni. I could do nothing to stop you short of killing you, and I would never do that. I would die before being driven to such lengths."

She wiped strings of vomit from her mouth. "You should've killed me."

"The situation is far worse. An army marches on the Three Kingdoms as we speak, and Cinolth leads that army. Also…" Savric's voice trailed off.

"Also what?" demanded Zerenity.

"It is Aria. Our girl is in league with the dragon." Tears spilled from Savric's eyes. "She has killed so many…"

"Aria?" Zerenity gasped and placed her hand over her mouth.

Nardus straightened. "Aria has killed people?"

"It cannot be her doing," said Savric. "Cinolth controls her. I am certain of it."

"That bastard is going to pay!" Nardus slammed his fist on the table.

Savric nodded, a grave look in his eyes. "If we do nothing to stop them, the entire realm will pay."

"Can you remove this collar?" asked Zerenity.

Nardus reached out and the collar flew off Zerenity's neck.

She rubbed her neck. "Thank you, darling."

"You're welcome." Nardus leaned on the table. "Now, tell me who you are and why you didn't prevent this disaster from happening."

"My name is Zerenity Salton." She took a long, deep breath before continuing. "To be honest, it all fell apart several years before the twins were born."

Nardus leaned forward and prodded, "What twins?"

"Aria and Alderan."

Nardus tensed. "Alderan?" His throat nearly closed. "Are you saying my son is alive?" he whispered. Tears rushed to the corners of his eyes and spilled onto his cheeks.

"Your son?" Zerenity cocked her head. "Now that you've said it, I can see the resemblance."

Savric frowned. "How is it possible? The prophecy states that the twins would be born to *ʊnzhiftäd*."

Niesha stepped up to the table. "What does *ʊnzhiftäd* mean?"

"Ungifted," answered Theyn. "Without mezhik."

Niesha nodded. "Like me."

"Vitara and I both thought we were." Nardus rubbed his left bicep. "I didn't even know who I was until yesterday."

"Mezhik derk," said Savric. Chills shrugged his shoulders.

Nardus wiped his cheeks. "Exactly. Now, back to… Alderan, you called him?"

"Yes," said Zerenity. "He is quite the handsome young man."

Nardus smiled. "And Shanara… err Aria looks just like her mother."

"Who is their mother, if you don't mind me asking," said Zerenity.

"Vitara, but you might know of her as Ilia Klae."

"Ilia of the Seven?" asked Savric.

Nardus nodded. "She must've been awakened at the same time as me. Our memories and identities were altered so that we thought we were in love with each other."

"My God…" Zerenity's eyes lit with wonder. "It makes so much sense now. Aria and Alderan are the children of Cyrus Nithik and Ilia Klae."

"Two mage parents…" Savric stroked his beard.

"For certain," said Nardus.

"I'm so sorry this happened to you," said Zerenity. "After going into hiding and then seeing the prophecy being fulfilled by the twins being born, we fell short of our duties to watch and protect *Ūrdär Dhef Ɂäfn Dhä*."

Nardus raked his head with his fingers. "I'd gladly put all the blame on the shoulders of you two, but it's actually mine. Every last bit of it. The order should've sacrificed their lives instead of preserving them. Because of that mistake, we are here in this moment. Furthermore, I'm the one who retrieved Cinolth's heart from *Räällm Kenzhärd Dhä*. I'm responsible for everything." He shook his head. "I don't know how I can live with the guilt, but I must. I will rectify this if it's the last thing I do."

"Do you know who is behind all of this?" asked Zerenity.

"I'm quite certain that it's Pravus Rosai. He orchestrated everything but must've had help from several other wizards. What makes matters worse is that he married my daughter."

"Dear Ɂäṭūr," exclaimed Zerenity. "That must be difficult to swallow."

"It is." Nardus squeezed his eyes shut for a moment. "Enough of this. We can catch up on everything else after we've stopped Cinolth and Pravus."

"Agreed," said Savric. "What would you have us do?"

"I will send you back from where you came." He looked between Savric and Zerenity. "Do not delay in heading to the Three Kingdoms. Protect King

Zaridus with your lives if that's what it takes. I will meet you there as soon as I can."

Zerenity hung her legs over the table edge and dropped onto the floor. "We are ready."

"Good. And do you know where I can find others?" asked Nardus.

"Other wizards?" Savric sighed when Nardus nodded. "I fear most of them have disappeared or have been hunted and killed. My brother, Qotan, is under Cinolth's control, otherwise he would be honored to fight by your side. However, there is an aquatic elf named Morcinda who is sympathetic to our cause. She meets with King Zaridus as we speak. Other than her, I know of none who would fight for our cause. Not including your son, of course."

"And where will I find my son?" asked Nardus.

"With your daughter and Pravus."

Nardus smacked the table. "Damn."

"We'll find him," said Theyn.

"And make Pravus pay," Berggren added.

"Of course we will." Nardus retrieved the rest of the bracelets from underneath each of the cryogenic chambers and handed two to Savric and one to Zerenity. "These will help you defend the Three Kingdoms. The extra one is in case you meet up with another wizard or sorceress who is willing to fight." They both nodded and shoved the bracelets over their hands.

Nardus discarded the spent bracelet, shoved another one over his own hand, and pocketed the last two. He looked at them both. "Ready?"

Savric eyed Zerenity but knowing what she did made it difficult for him to maintain eye contact with her. He looked away and fondled one of the bracelets on his wrist. "Meet me back at the gateway wall. We will travel from there."

"Agreed," said Zerenity.

"We are ready," said Savric and Zerenity.

Nardus drew the rune spell for Feʒzhärz Dhä in the air with his finger. "*Feʒzhärz Dhä, diʒmiʒʈ zíū er.*"

Savric's hands and feet warmed as he and Zerenity transformed into pure energy and evaporated.

CHAPTER THIRTY-EIGHT

Pravus stared at the maps spread across the table but didn't study them. Credan and several of the generals huddled around the table as well, discussing strategy for their impending attack on Elatos. No matter how hard he concentrated on Credan's voice, thoughts of Aria plagued his mind and stole his attention.

They'd spoken little if any since the incident at the wall. Had he known the repercussions of using Alderan as a pawn to motivate her, he might've reconsidered. Still, he enjoyed the rift it had created between Aria and Alderan. The boy could still ruin everything, so Pravus begged the gods to sever the bond the two of them shared for good.

"My lord, what do you think?" asked Credan.

Pravus blinked several times, his mind unfocused. Credan stared at him, concern wrinkling his brow. "Do you plan on saying something, or are you content with your gaze fixated upon me like a fool?"

Credan's gaze shifted away from Pravus as he addressed the generals. "Gentleman, I believe we've had enough discussion for this evening. We will resume planning when we setup camp again tomorrow night."

The generals gladly packed up and exited the tent. Credan gathered up his things as well.

"I will take my leave now, my lord." Credan bowed slightly.

"Yes, of course." Pravus squeezed his eyes shut for a moment. "Before you turn in for the night, make sure you find Aria and insist that she returns to me at once."

"As you wish." Credan exited the tent.

Pravus moved from the table to the bed and sat down on the end of it. The tent opening parted, and Aria stepped inside. His eyes met hers for the briefest of moments before she looked away.

"Where have you been?" he asked.

"Enjoying the night." She stripped bare, crawled into the bed, and turned her back to him.

Pravus grabbed her arm. "Look at me."

She rolled onto her back and looked at him, or rather through him, her glare burning holes right through his head. "What do you want?"

"I'm concerned about you, my love." He smiled faintly. Genuine concern twisted his stomach. "I understood when you vomited after what happened to Lord Uli Edersheimer, but then you did so again this morning. Have you come down with some sort of sickness?"

Aria shook her head and snapped, "I'm not sick, you fool. I'm carrying your child."

My child…

Pravus's entire body went rigid. He couldn't have forced a breath into his lungs if he'd tried.

"This is why I didn't tell you. You're too weak to handle anything." She rolled back onto her side.

Pravus finally exhaled. He no longer cared how much she insulted him. She carried his baby. An heir to the throne they would claim within the next week.

Excitement and fear collided in his chest. "Call Cinolth. You must leave at once."

"Leave?" She turned and faced him again. "And where exactly would I be leaving to?"

"You shall return to the castle at once. I can't have you out here risking your life when my son lies in your belly."

"I will do no such thing," she snarled. "And for your information, I'm having a girl."

A girl?

The word tripped him up. He'd never contemplated having a girl. In his mind, his heir had always been a son. What the gods would he do with a daughter? The prospect strangled him. He couldn't control Aria. A smaller version of her would surely be insufferable.

He groaned and severed all thoughts on the matter.

The baby's gender doesn't matter.

His focus must be on Aria and her safety.

I must insist she leaves at once.

"This matter isn't up for discussion. You must return to Galondu Castle tonight. Ask your scaly beast. I'm certain he'd agree with me on this."

"When are you going to learn that you have no control over me or what I do?" She stormed out of the tent.

"Aria, wait!" He followed her out, but she pushed him aside as she marched back into the tent.

She grabbed her clothes and pulled them back on. "Just do your part in the war while I kill the king." Contempt radiated from her gaze when she looked up at him. "And stay out of my way."

Pravus rubbed his head. "Aria, you're not being rational."

He followed her out of the tent again. Thunderous wings moved the air as Cinolth approached.

Thump-thump. Whoosh!

Several soldiers dove out of the way as Cinolth dropped to the ground with a loud thud. Cinolth roared and his neck glowed red-hot, poised to spew fire. Pravus backed away.

"Aria!" yelled Pravus. "Where are you going?"

Cinolth lifted Aria onto his neck and then took to the air. The draught from his wings knocked Pravus back several steps and rattled the tent poles. The thick canvas snapped taut, cracking the air like a whip.

Pravus shook his fist at the dark skies.

Damn that scaly beast.

† † †

Sarai dropped Nardus and the others off in the middle of The Plains, about fifty miles south of Elatos. It wouldn't take a tracker to follow the trail of destruction left behind by the army. A strip of land more than a mile wide and trampled into dirt stretched north.

"The three of you must wait here while I go confront Pravus," said Nardus.

"And miss my opportunity to smash that bastard in the mouth?" grumbled Berggren. "Don't think so. He's the reason Shaul's dead."

"I get that, Iceberg, but you must stay here and protect Niesha and Theyn."

"You're not leaving me," growled Theyn. "Ever again."

"I'm sorry, but I can't risk it. If any of you come along, I'll be worrying about you and not paying attention to what's happening."

"I'm going with you," demanded Theyn. "I'll stay out of sight."

Nardus rubbed his head. He knew there was little point in arguing with her. Aside from knocking her out, he wouldn't be able to stop her from following him. "Alright, but you must stay out of sight. No heroics no matter what."

"Agreed, but there is one more thing that I insist on. I need to see our future first."

"We don't have time." He emphasized each word with his hand.

"Then make time." She stared him down hard. "It's not a request."

Nardus sighed. "We already know what happens. You're killed by a dragon."

"I've thought about that experience a lot, and I don't believe any of it is true."

"And why is that?" asked Nardus.

"When the stone—Cinolth's heart—was inside your chest, it influenced that first vision we shared. I believe he didn't want you finding out who you really were and tried to deter us from ever going to the Valley of Dragons."

Theyn's logic was sound. It explained a lot, just like the dragon telling him that he only had so many days to give the stone to his daughter. All of it had been lies, and he'd played the part of the fool perfectly. Now, he didn't want to know what might happen, but nothing would deter Theyn from hounding him to the ends of the world until she had her answer.

"Fine. That makes sense, but you said before that we only see a potential future. What good will that do us?"

Theyn's grim expression didn't suit her beautiful face. "We'll know if one of us is meant to die this very night."

Nardus knelt before Theyn. "Then hurry." He still didn't want anything to do with it.

Theyn pierced the pads of her thumbs with her upper fangs and placed them on Nardus's temples. Mezhik tingled against his skin as Theyn's mind joined his.

She mindspoke to him. *"Are you ready?"*

For this to be over.

"As I'll ever be," Nardus replied through their link.

As with the first time on the boat, Nardus felt himself slip down into what felt like a dream.

† † †

Theyn stood alone on top of a barren hill, the last of her enemies vanquished. Plumes of smoke rose in every direction as far as the eye could see, the destruction beyond anything she'd ever witnessed. Corpses strewn everywhere, fodder for carrion birds and scavengers of every kind.

The sight of so much carnage brought with it a sense of deep satisfaction. She raised her head skyward and roared. Never had she felt so free.

Blood dripped from her jowls, its coppery taste still fresh on her tongue. A corpse lay beneath her bloody front paw, its chest shredded, and its throat ripped out. She'd hated the bastard, and his death satiated her blood lust. At least for the time.

Nardus slowly climbed the hill before her and met her gaze as he ascended. Shallow breaths came from his lips in ragged succession. Blood covered him from head to toe. She couldn't distinguish between his blood and that of their enemies.

"It is done." Each word wheezed from Nardus's mouth as though he had a hole punched through his throat. He fell on his knees two-thirds of the way up the hill.

Theyn met him where he'd dropped to his knees and licked the blood from his face. The right side of his face bled anew, the white of his cheekbone visible through a gaping hole stretching from his earlobe to the underside of his right nostril.

"And we're still alive."

Shick!

Nardus jerked forward and drooped against Theyn.

"No!" she growled.

He fell on his side. A quad-tipped, blacksteel spear protruded from the left side of his chest. The rest of the five-foot spear hung from the entry point in his back. Blood seeped from the wound and pooled around him at an alarming rate.

Theyn shifted back into her human form and pulled Nardus into her arms. His eyes rolled back in his head, and his body went limp.

Tears blurred her vision, and her heart ached more than she thought possible.

"Don't die on me now," she whispered.

But he already had.

† † †

The entire world crashed down on top of Nardus when Theyn withdrew her thumbs from his temples. He grabbed his chest and swallowed back pain he knew didn't exist. Theyn held her chest as well, her face contorted with agony. After several deep breaths, the pain subsided, but its memory didn't fade.

Nardus pulled Theyn close and held her as she cried. Neither of them said a word about it. What words could be said? She'd felt the pain, same as him. Tasted the blood. Smelled death. Nothing would change the experience.

Theyn trembled in his arms as tears continued to streak her face. She looked into his eyes. Hers were full of sorrow and despair. He imagined his mirrored hers.

Drawing a deep breath, he swallowed his emotions. "At least the vision had nothing to do with facing Pravus." He stood and grabbed her hand.

Theyn looked into his eyes. "What are you doing?" Fear quavered her voice.

"Getting us closer." Nardus kissed her forehead and then her lips.

"Then call Sarai."

"It's far too dangerous. I'll manage."

"Are you mad? You could kill us both!" Theyn tried to pull her hand away but Nardus held firm.

"Trust me, my love. And yes, I've always been a bit mad." He smiled deviously.

With a single step, Nardus teleported the two of them northward and into the darkness of the unknown.

† † †

Pravus didn't need to turn around to verify a hostile gaze pierced the back of his skull. Based on experience, he knew the gaze didn't belong to Aria either. He pretended not to notice the presence while he gathered mezhik into the palm of his hand.

With a grunt, Pravus spun around and thrust a reddish-white fireball in the direction of his visitor. But the fireball hung in the air, suspended over his palm. It didn't undulate, spark, or crackle. Notwithstanding it's shape and color, it could just as easily have been an ice ball.

The tent canvas no longer billowed and snapped as it had moments ago, and the wind had lost its howl. No papers rustled on the table. His robes did not sway. All motion in the tent had ceased, including his own.

But the shadows moved.

Stalked him.

Circled him.

Pravus lost track of them as they passed beyond his field of vision. He tried to speak, but his mouth failed to open, and his tongue refused to move.

His heart still beat. Harder and harder.

Air wheezed from his lungs as he exhaled and sounded ragged and raw as he drew another breath in.

Then, the shadows drew back.

Physically unchanged, the man who stood before Pravus was no longer Nardus.

"Pravus Rosai." Lightning flashed in Cyrus's eyes. "Know that I have come here to kill you, but first you will answer for your crimes."

Pravus's tongue loosened, and defiance wet his lips. "Ah, the infamous Cyrus Nithik. I see you've finally found yourself. Your manipulation of time is quite impressive, but not impressive enough to turn it backward. How does it feel knowing your life for the past twenty years has been a lie?"

"Every sentence that leaves your mouth is twisted with deceit." He grabbed Pravus by the throat and squeezed. "By the time I've finished with you, you'll be begging for death."

Pravus choked. He could do nothing else. Cyrus released him, and he sucked in a deep breath. "Before you decide to torture me further, you might want to consider the fact that my soul is bound with Aria's. Any pain you inflict upon me will also be inflicted upon her."

Cyrus's eyes narrowed. "You're a liar. Why should I believe a word of what you say?"

"If you don't, then proceed as planned, but know that her death will be on your hands."

Cyrus hesitated.

Now I've got the upper hand.

"Release me, and I will confess everything, including the way I manipulated you and Ilia into having relations."

"You had no right!" Cyrus swept his arm across his body.

Pravus flew backward and crashed into a chair before hitting the ground. Pain shot through his lower back and down the backs of his legs. He lay there and caught his breath as the pain subsided. The only fight he'd win that night would be one of words, and he planned on bleeding Cyrus to death.

Cyrus stood over him in a flash. "As twisted as it is, I understand why you did what you did to Ilia and me. You wanted power and knew how to breed a mage, but why did you kill the other five? Why not leave them in stasis?"

"And risk someone waking them and ruining everything?" Pravus shook his head. "I had no choice."

Cyrus rubbed his left bicep. "Vitara and Savannah then. Why kill them?"

"Don't pretend that you don't understand," snarled Pravus. "I needed you to be motivated. You're the only one who could've retrieved *Ꝣtōn Dhef Dädh*. Everything in my plan to resurrect my father's kingdom hinged on you. Without you and Ilia, Aria and Alderan would've never been born, and Ilia's prophecy about *Fädinzh dhä Ballek* would never have come to pass."

Rage burned in Cyrus's eyes. "How did you find out about the resting place of *Ūrdär Dhef Ꝣäfn Dhä*?" With a flick of his wrist, Pravus sat up.

"I have eyes and ears everywhere," said Pravus. "Finding one of the *FeꝢzhärz Dhä* and persuading them to help me took little effort. Family is all most people have, and they will do just about anything to save them. Like you, Omerus, the one who helped me, was no different. He helped me locate you, and I rewarded him with a quick and mostly painless death.

"The hardest part of the plan was suppressing yours and Ilia's memories and implanting false ones. That took more time than I would've liked, but it had to be perfect and infallible. Do you realize how much detail had to go into that process? So many things could've gone wrong. False memories were planted into the minds of everyone you ever encountered. Bradwr, rest his wretched soul, claimed to be your best friend, but he sold you out without hesitation to save his own skin and that of his wife and daughter. Had he known they were already dead, he might've failed to finish the task. Then again, I'm certain he would've blamed you for their deaths."

"You're a bastard." Cyrus spat in his face.

Pravus chuckled as he wiped the spit from his cheek on his shoulder. "I am, but so are your children. Speaking of them and what they represent, have you contemplated the intricacies of prophecy? It's a funny thing. As written, the prophecy about twin wizards born to *unzhiftäd* parents sounds impossible and quite literally is based on the laws of mezhik, but it's the details of the prophecies that matter.

"The prophecy about your children never specified that the parents must physically be *ʊnzhifṭäd*. For all intents and purposes, you and your Vitara were *ʊnzhifṭäd*. Planting the idea in your head that you hated mezhik was a personal favorite of mine, and watching you struggle with it still, even knowing who you truly are, is priceless."

Cyrus glared at him. "You think you've got it all figured out, don't you?"

"Yes, I orchestrated everything that happened, right down to rescuing and marrying your daughter. Now, my seed grows inside her belly."

Cyrus's eyes widened for only a moment, but Pravus caught it.

That's right, you smug, righteous bastard.

Pravus continued, "She'll never be yours again. Everything has gone according to my plan, and there's nothing you can do to stop me. The Three Kingdoms will fall, and I will rule the Ancient Realm."

Cyrus grabbed Pravus by the collar of his robes and lifted him clear off the ground. "Baby or not, Shanara will return to me." Spittle peppered the air and Pravus's face.

"She was never yours," snarled Pravus.

Cyrus head-butted Pravus right in the nose. The crack rang in Pravus's ears, and the pain consumed him for several seconds. Blood gushed from his nostrils.

Cyrus threw him to the ground. "Where's my son?"

"Your son? He's just like his father. Quite useless. The only thing he knows how to do is sit around and sulk over his sister. Pathetic."

Cyrus stalked forward. "And where is… Alderan?" He groaned, and his hands trembled.

A gentle breeze tugged on the tent flaps and rustled the maps and diagrams on the table.

Cyrus is growing weak.

Pravus broke away from Cyrus's mezhik hold and cracked his knuckles. "Looks like your time has ran out, old man." He drew upon his mezhik, healed his bleeding nose, and wiped it with the back of his hand. "I'll be certain to tell Aria that you're the one who broke her nose." He rose to his feet and wiped the blood off his hand with his robes.

Alderan walked through the tent flaps. "Where's my sister?"

Cyrus turned and Pravus had the opening he needed. Within the folds of his robes, he withdrew *ᴢäbräᴢär* and thrust it at Cyrus. The forward edge of the collar slipped right through Cyrus's neck and wrapped it. Then, with mind and mezhik, Pravus began shaping the world around them.

The ground quaked as four steel walls rose and surrounded the three of them.

A steel roof unrolled and stretched over the top of the walls.

The ground cracked open with a thunderous groan as gallows burst forth from it.

Thick ropes snared Cyrus. Tightened around his neck. Bound his hands and feet. Pulled him into the air and onto the gallows platform.

The rope around Cyrus's neck wrapped itself around the top of the gallows and tied itself off, leaving a foot of slack. Sufficient to snap Cyrus's neck when he dropped through the platform.

A single light focused on Cyrus. Shone in his face. He squinted to see through it.

Pravus walked up the platform stairs and faced Cyrus.

With a twist of Pravus's wrist, Alderan flew up from the ground and landed on the platform next to the gallows lever. Alderan's hand wrapped around the lever and rope bound them together.

"What's going on?" demanded Alderan, his attention split between Pravus and Cyrus.

Pravus steepled his fingers and grinned at Alderan. "Your timing couldn't have been better, Alderan. Or should I call you Shardan?"

Alderan frowned. "And why would you call me Shardan?"

Cyrus struggled against his restraints. "Is it really you? You're Shan—Aria's brother?"

Alderan glanced at Cyrus and then back to Pravus. "Do I know this man? He looks familiar."

Pravus laughed. "Your own son doesn't even know your face!"

"F-father?" Alderan's eyes widened. "Aria told me about you."

"Excellent. Then you know whom it is that you'll kill."

Alderan's head jerked down to his hand on the lever. "No! Don't make me do this." Tears welled in his eyes when he looked back up at Pravus. "Please, Pravus. I'll do anything you ask, but not this."

Cyrus smiled. "It's okay, son."

"I'm not asking," sneered Pravus.

"None of this is real," said Cyrus. "Look at me, son."

Confusion warped Alderan's face. "I don't understand."

"None of this is real," mocked Pravus. His smile widened. "Trust me, Alderan. Nothing could be further from the truth."

Pravus thrust his arm down. Alderan's arm mimicked the motion and threw the gallows lever.

Alderan cried out as the platform door dropped out from underneath Cyrus's feet.

But Cyrus didn't fall. His neck didn't snap. The rope hadn't broken.

Cyrus floated over the opening. "Enough of your mind games, Pravus."

The illusion Pravus had created began to unravel, starting with the rope around Cyrus's neck.

The gallows sank back into the ground, leaving the three of them standing firmly on the ground.

The steel walls and roof disintegrated.

Cyrus pulled ƨäbräƨär off his own neck, and it turned to ash.

"Your powers are weak." With a flick of Cyrus's wrist, ƨäbräƨär slipped off Alderan's neck and wrapped itself around Pravus's.

Pravus dug at his neck and yanked on the collar, but it wouldn't come off. "You can't do this to me."

"I already have." Cyrus sneered. "Imagine how weak you'll look in Aria's eyes when she finds you subdued this way."

Gods, she can't find me this way!

Alderan rubbed his neck. "Thank you."

Pravus pleaded with Cyrus. "Tell me what you want, and it's yours. Anything."

"What I want is for you to suffer the way I did, but I know that's not possible. For now, your humiliation will suffice."

Vines grew up from the ground and ensnared Pravus.

Cyrus scoffed, "It's no wonder you sought Aria's mezhik for yourself. As with the stone, you failed to read all the words as they pertained to the soul binding you performed with Aria. The only power of hers you received was what had already awakened. Had you not been so hasty to seal the deed you could've been tenfold stronger. A hundredfold perhaps."

Pravus swallowed hard. He didn't want Cyrus's words to be true, but he'd already known. His powers had barely increased after binding his soul to hers, and he'd tried to blame the poor results on the bond she shared with

Cinolth.

Gods, what have I done?

Cyrus turned to Alderan and proffered his hand. "Come with me, son. We have much to discuss."

Alderan glanced over at Pravus and took Cyrus's hand. "I'm certain we do."

"This is far from over!" shouted Pravus as Cyrus and Alderan teleported out of the tent.

Pravus roared with rage. "Guards!"

Two men dressed in battle armor rushed in through the tent flap and halted upon seeing Pravus bound with vines. They just stood there, mouths agape.

Ɔäbräɔär glowed red around Pravus's neck and enraged him further. "Remove these vines at once, and find me a wizard!"

One soldier turned and left the tent while the other approached Pravus with caution, drawing his dagger as he neared. "Do not move, my lord."

The soldier gasped, and his dagger dropped from his hand. In a flash, the soldier sat next to Pravus, the two of them bound together.

Pravus seethed.

That bastard's dead when I see him again.

CHAPTER THIRTY-NINE

The Plains, scarred and devoid of vegetation for miles on end, tore at Zerenity's heart. As a child, she'd longed to build a home there and live among its vast sea of golden grasses. As she walked alongside Savric, she imbued the ground with mezhik. Tufts of grass sprang up with new life everywhere her foot landed. Had there been no pending war, she would've drained her energy into the ground and revitalized the entire area. It still tempted her, but her small contributions would have to do for the moment.

Savric hadn't uttered more than ten words since they'd met back up at the gateway wall. Deep lines creased his brow, and the corners of his mouth drooped unnaturally—at least for him. She needn't ask what spoiled his mood. Between worrying about Qotan and finding his godson, Calen, he had a lot occupying his thoughts. But she knew that wasn't the real issue.

Despite not being in control of her own actions and unable to recall what she'd done to several innocent people a few days back—or anything else that had happened over the last few weeks for that matter—, Savric still brooded over the incident. Even so, if the tables were turned, she might've been a tad bit upset with him as well, so she placed no blame on his weary shoulders. She'd apologized several times in the last few hours, and now she needed to move forward.

Zerenity set her eyes on the plains ahead and her mind on the impending war. Many more lives would be lost in the days and weeks ahead, and the thought of it sickened her. Blood would flow in the streets and turn the ground crimson.

And my Aria fights against us.

Had she the ability, she would've turned back time and raised Aria and Alderan as her own. She laid no blame at the feet of Redante and Gretchen. They'd done as good of a job raising the twins as could be expected, but if she'd been there for Aria and Alderan perhaps things would've turned out a bit different. Maybe she could've fought harder and hid them better.

But this is Ɂäṭūr's plan, not mine.

Zerenity glanced over at Savric. His scowl had deepened. She thought some light conversation might help ease the tension between them. "How far are we from the Hotah River?"

Savric continued to stare into the distance. His lips pursed awkwardly. She wondered if they'd forgotten how to form words. "Another mile, perhaps." His voice sounded flat and dry.

She offered Savric a drink from her waterskin, but he refused it, albeit graciously. She decided to give him more time to reconcile what he'd witnessed her do with the fact that it wasn't actually her that did it. Yes, she physically murdered those people, but she likened it to calling an axe a murderer after burying it in someone's skull. No remorse weighed her down, but she did feel sympathy for their loved ones.

Soon, she noticed the moonlight glinting off a large body of water ahead. The Hotah River, the largest in the Ancient Realm, spanned nearly a mile across along several portions of its length and sank nearly a hundred feet at its deepest. Its breadth and width allowed vessels of all shapes and sizes to utilize it for travel between Aberporth in the north and West and East Hotah in the south. Fifteen minutes later, they stood on its western bank.

Zerenity looked around. No boats sailed the flowing waters, and as far as she could tell, they were alone. "Now what?"

"We wait," grumbled Savric.

† † †

Savric stood on the riverbank, clutching Qotan's staff. "*Ɂllíṭ ʋb.*" The crystal orb atop Qotan's staff came to life with glowing, yellow light, illuminating the surrounding area. Zerenity stood next to him, her silver hair bathed in the light. It made her look a decade younger, and he would've told her as much, but he still stewed over the people she'd killed.

Rationally, he knew she hadn't done it, but his mind kept tripping over the look she'd had in her black eyes when she unleashed her mezhik on them. That sadistic, venomous look haunted him and would do so for the rest of his life.

Savric turned and headed north, along the muddy riverbank. "We need to keep moving and pray that we find Calen and Eshtak before Morcinda arrives."

Zerenity followed close behind. "I still don't understand. If you contacted this Morcinda person an hour ago and she's in Vallah, it could take a good ten hours for her to reach us even with her traveling downriver."

Savric hadn't explained Morcinda's ancestry or unique capabilities to Zerenity and didn't plan to. She'd see for herself soon enough.

Mud slopped underfoot and suctioned Savric's feet to the ground with each step, slowing him down and tiring his weary legs further. "I assure you that we have twenty minutes or less before she arrives."

Zerenity seemed to have less difficulty with the saturated ground than he did, perhaps because her feet were significantly smaller and her step lighter. No matter what the reason, it soured his mood further. He pulled and twisted his beard in his fingers as he walked.

"There." Zerenity pointed at the ground five paces ahead.

Savric, his eyes not what they used to be, didn't see anything. "What am I supposed to be seeing?"

"Two pairs of tracks. One set of boot prints and one set of bare feet." She stepped around Savric and crouched close to the ground. "It must be them. I'd recognize Eshtak's barefoot prints anywhere."

"Calen!" Savric's throat, parched, protested from the strain.

I should have taken her up on the offer of water.

Zerenity rose and placed her hands around her mouth. "Eshtak!" Her method of amplifying her voice proved far superior to his vocal cord shredding one. Even so, the roar of the river decimated both their cries.

Far in the distance, a vessel approached on the river. Its unnatural speed could only be achieved by one person.

Morcinda.

Savric held Qotan's staff as far above his head as he could and waved it in the air. The swaying motion of the light it cast rocked the world underneath Savric's feet. He stumbled forward and right off the riverbank.

† † †

Just as Morcinda spotted it, the light signal from the western riverbank snuffed out. Moments later, she pulled her vessel up next to the riverbank. A silver-haired woman ran south along the riverbank, her arms flailing and green light emanating from her hands.

Morcinda closed her eyes, connected her mind with the river water, and sought out any sort of disturbance. Images flashed in her mind. Mud. A staff. Brown robes. Silver beard.

Savric.

Through her hands and mind, she commanded the waters to pull Savric and Savric's staff up from its depths as she directed her vessel forward. Savric and the staff shot in the air atop two waterspouts and crashed down onto the deck of the boat as it sailed underneath them.

Morcinda commanded the water to hold the boat in place and rushed down from the upper deck, but the silver-haired woman had already boarded the boat and knelt next to Savric. He didn't move, nor did his chest. The woman turned Savric onto his side. Green light flowed from the woman's hands and into Savric's body.

Morcinda halted at the bottom of the stairs and waited. She controlled water better than anyone, even a seasoned Fizärd Fūţär, but she didn't possess mezhik, especially not the kind that could save a person.

"Master Savric!"

The call drew Morcinda's attention toward the riverbank. A young man stood bent over with his hands on his knees, yelling Savric's name. Another person—a strange little fellow with pale skin—hopped and danced from toe to toe, seemingly needing to urinate.

Peculiar.

Back on the lower deck, Savric spasmed for several seconds and then coughed up water. He spat more out and took a deep breath. The silver-haired woman's hands stopped glowing green, and she bent down and wrapped her arms around Savric. The woman obviously loved him.

For Morcinda, love meant nothing. She'd never been in love and had no intention of seeking it out. The only thing it ever did was make people vulnerable. She didn't need that, especially not in her line of business.

She walked over to the pair and knelt next to them. "There are better ways to board a vessel, Savric Naphor."

Savric rubbed his fire-red eyes. Morcinda assumed he'd had them open while in the river. "Feathers," he muttered. "It would have served me better had you mentioned that before I tossed myself into the river."

Morcinda smiled slightly. "Those two are with you as well?" She nodded toward the western riverbank.

Zerenity rose to her feet and peered toward the riverbank. "I believe so."

"I will retrieve them." Morcinda leapt over the side of the boat. Spouts of water rose to meet her feet and carried her over to the riverbank.

The young man's eyes nearly bulged from his head. "Whoa! I've never seen anything like that before."

"Eshtak can't believe!" The odd little man danced around and pulled down on his face.

Morcinda held out her hand to the young man. "Come with me." The young man took it, but his feet didn't move.

"I... I..." His hand trembled.

"There's nothing to fear." She tugged his hand, but his feet stayed planted on the riverbank. "I promise you that it's as safe as walking on land."

"Eshtak goes!"

The odd little man reached for Morcinda's other hand. She proffered it, and he latched onto it. He stepped right off the riverbank without hesitation. She commanded the water to hold him up, and it obeyed. Seemingly emboldened by his friend, the young man took a reluctant step off the riverbank. Water rose to meet his foot.

Morcinda smiled. "See, not so scary." She led the two of them over to the boat, and the three of them climbed over the railing and onto the deck.

Savric stood next to the silver-haired woman and favored his staff. "My dear boy, I am pleased to see you."

The young man rushed over to Savric and threw his arms around him. "Where did you go?"

"Pretty lady! Pretty lady!" The odd little man wrapped his arms around the silver-haired woman's legs.

Morcinda walked over to Savric. "Is this the entire party?"

Savric groaned. "Afraid so."

"Good." She commanded the water to sail them back to Vallah and then they all made introductions.

During the two-hour-long journey, Savric filled her in on everything he'd seen, including meeting Cyrus, the last of Ūrdär Dhef Ɛäfn Dhä. Between an army of humans, zhebəllin, giants, orcs, gnolls, a dragon, and who knew what else, she didn't see how they'd survive the war.

God help us...

CHAPTER FORTY

Alderan leaned over the three-and-a-half-foot-tall, hand-sculpted railing that sectioned off the King's Palace from the city of Vallah below it. At any other point in his life, he would've drunk in the majestic view of the surrounding Orbis Mountain Range and the sparkling blue waters of Trivers Lake far below. But the day weighed heavily on him. Crushing, brutal weight he didn't think he could bear.

Aria…

How could he save the world from his own sister? That exact scenario crossed his mind several times over the last several months, but he never gave it much thought. His sister pitted against him. Bent on destroying the world. How absurd that'd seemed, yet there he stood facing the biggest dilemma of his entire life. How could he possibly choose the world over his own flesh and blood? A twin sister he shared a bond with that superseded everything. Then again, how could he sacrifice the world to save one life? Would life be worth living at that point?

Am I living now?

Alderan raked his fingers through his hair and pulled on it. There had to be a solution. Somehow, he must find a way to break the bond between Aria and Pravus. The bond she shared with Cinolth would be severed once they killed the scaly beast. But that task seemed insurmountable as well. How could he slay the dragon if the seven greatest mages and wizards in the world couldn't accomplish such a feat 1200 years ago?

And I am only one.

Alderan stared at his calloused hands. He knew hard work and hunting, but mezhik and war were as foreign to him as the man standing beside him. Nardus had muscles and strength for days, and confidence exuded from his pores. Alderan didn't understand how he could be the offspring of such a great man.

Zätūr, I am nothing. Why put everything into my hands? Why place such a burden upon my shoulders?

Growing up, his mother, Gretchen, had often read passages to him and Aria from a book called *Ƨäṭūr's Holy Scriptures*. One such passage came to mind. *"Fear not what your hands and mind cannot do, for I make the impossible possible sayeth Ƨäṭūr."*

Then take it all from me.

Nardus leaned over the railing next to Alderan. "It's hard realizing that you're not the person you thought you were. Gaining that knowledge can devastate you if you allow it to. Two days ago, I learned who I truly am. Until that moment, I didn't have the slightest notion that my entire life—at least what I remembered of it—was a lie planted in my mind by the fiend who stole your sister.

"The things I learned devastated and enraged me. How could someone be so vile and dastardly? He wrecked my entire life and set our world on a course destined for destruction. At the same time, his heinous acts gave you and Shanara to me, two of the best things in the world. It sickens me to think about what could have been, but there are consequences and conciliations with every decision."

Nardus sighed and continued, "What I'm trying to say is that I wouldn't change any of those moments for anything. They're what brought us here and into *this* moment. I'd love to get to know you and earn the right to call you my son again."

Alderan and Nardus spent the next two hours talking about the past, the present, and the unknown future. The more they spoke, the closer Alderan felt to him. Buried memories of his early childhood began surfacing. This man had truly been his father. Aria shared the same memories, so she should've arrived at the same conclusion, but she hadn't. The fact that she'd tried to have Nardus killed pained him.

Is there anything left of the sister I once knew?

The answer wouldn't come easily, but he'd have to figure it out if he wanted to save her and the world. Another thought that niggled in the back of his mind was why Pravus hadn't killed him sometime during the last few weeks when he'd had the chance. After all, Pravus was the man behind the gnolls attacking him and his village and had ordered Alderan's death. Alderan had been running for his life right up until that point. Something didn't make sense, and he didn't think it had anything to do with Aria being there.

Something must've changed, but what?

Nardus clasped Alderan's forearm. "Are you ready to head inside? We've got a war to finish preparing for."

Alderan peered into the man's yellowish-brown eyes and thought he saw himself in them. He nodded and smiled, "I am, Father."

† † †

The entire trek through the King's Palace blurred in Nardus's mind. He focused on a single word uttered from the lips of his son, and it lifted his head to the clouds. His chest rose high and his steps became direct and crisp.

Father.

He marveled at the power of words. The same words could build a person up or tear them down, given the context and person who utters them. Aria had used the word "father" to drive a dagger through his heart, but he continued to cling onto the hope of her coming around. He sent a quick prayer to Ɂäʈūr asking for as much. Finding himself in the Procerus Mountains altered his mindset and brought him closer to the God he once knew, but there were still issues that needed to be worked out between them. Nothing but time would restore his faith completely. However, getting half of his family members back certainly helped.

I do thank You for that, Ɂäʈūr.

Nardus followed Alderan through a set of double doors and into a small hall. A single table, narrow and long, ran the length of the sparse room. A turquoise runner split the table lengthwise, and twenty-two chairs surrounded it, ten on each of its long sides and one at each of its ends. Several maps of the Three Kingdoms area lay on the table. Conversation filled the room but died down once the room's occupants caught notice of his and Alderan's presence.

King Zaridus sat at the far end of the table, a scowl drawn on his face. His ice-blue eyes shot daggers at Nardus. Prince Rictar and Princess Zelanora flanked King Zaridus, and an empty chair sat next to each of them. Nardus headed toward the seat next to Prince Rictar and directed Alderan to sit in the one next to Princess Zelanora. To Nardus's right sat Theyn, then Morcinda, Zerenity, and four others Nardus didn't recognize—two men and two women dressed in black and teal armor.

Across the table and to Alderan's left sat Berggren, Savric, and four additional men and women dressed in black and teal armor. A squat man with a bald head and a long mustache curled at the ends sat at the opposite end of the table. He wore dark-blue robes and a lighter blue cloak. From what Nardus recalled, Zerenity had called the man Druden. Calen, Niesha, and Eshtak were off exploring the King's Palace.

King Zaridus rose from his chair and tapped the end of his scepter on the table. "I'm certain I need not explain why you're all gathered here." All the heads in the room shook in unison. "Good. I will make this as brief as possible." He swept his scepter across the table. "I hereby charge each of you with the task of defending Vallah and its citizens."

Murmurs broke out around the table but none loud enough to reach Nardus's ears. Given his initial thoughts, he guessed as to what they discussed. Despite an unremarkable rule of decades of peace, everyone knew King Zaridus to be frightfully rigid when it came to saving his own skin. If all of them set their sights on defending Vallah, Elatos and Borza would certainly fall.

King Zaridus continued, "Anyone leaving the city from this point forward will be charged with treason and executed on the spot. Is that clear?"

Nardus frowned. "Are you saying that you do not wish to evacuate the cities to preserve life?"

King Zaridus leaned over the table and glared at Nardus. "I believe my last statement stands without question, *wizard*." He snarled the last word.

Nardus glanced at Prince Rictar. The man's face, stoic as it was, belied the tremor in his hand. His jaws slowly worked together as well, the tension clearly building. No one spoke a word.

Rage flashed in King Zaridus's eyes and a dark, purplish-red hue crept up the front of his neck and colored his cheeks. "Have I made myself clear?" he said through clenched teeth.

Everyone at the table gave a solemn nod, none brave enough to defy the wishes of their king.

King Zaridus grunted. "Then I'll leave you all to discuss the details. I am not to be disturbed except in an emergency." He shoved his chair back with his foot and strode out of the small hall.

Prince Rictar stood and moved to the head of the table. "You heard my father, the king. Let's figure out how to best defend Vallah." He and Nardus shared a glance.

Princess Zelanora scowled at Prince Rictar. "Brother, you do realize how cowardly this plan is?"

Nardus liked her already.

"Silence, sister." Prince Rictar took in the whole room, eying each person individually for several moments before moving to the next in line. When his steel gaze reached Nardus, his glower faltered. "Master Nardus." His head dipped forward ever so slightly. Perhaps nothing more than a shift of his neck, but Nardus thought otherwise.

"My prince." Nardus returned the nod. "Please refrain from calling me 'master'. I am in control of no one."

The right edge of Prince Rictar's mouth curled upward. "As you wish. Nardus will guide us through all the final preparations of war."

I will?

Nardus raised his eyebrows. He hadn't expected to be handed the reins right from the get-go, but he'd planned on taking them. Prince Rictar simplified his job. "I am more than happy to do so, but might I ask why?"

"In truth, you are the only one here with actual war experience. My father might not value such expertise, given your nature, but he and I do not share all of the same values and views." He sat down and winked at Princess Zelanora. "Tell us how we can defend all three cities."

Nardus stood and paced behind his chair. It gave him the room to think. As words came to mind, he stilled and addressed Prince Rictar. "Your father, the king, did get one thing right. The people are what matter, and defending them should be our first priority."

"Agreed," said Prince Rictar.

Nardus continued, "First of all, we know the enemy marches toward Elatos as we speak. Our first order of business should be to evacuate anyone unable or unwilling to defend the city. Are there strongholds in the mountains?"

"Yes," said Princess Zelanora. "Each city has underground tunnels that lead to one centralized stronghold in the western Orbis Mountains." She pointed to the location on one of the maps spread across the table. "There's a hidden entrance located here for anyone who cannot escape through the tunnels."

"Good." Nardus clasped his hands together. "We will begin evacuating Vallah at once and will send word to Elatos and Borza to do the same."

Princess Zelanora bit the side of her lower lip and frowned. "As simple as it may seem, sending word will not help. Most if not all of the people have forgotten where those entrances lie."

"Then we'll send them into the mountains," said Nardus.

Princess Zelanora's eyes widened, and she shook her head. "That's not an option. As beautiful as they are, the Orbis Range can be cruel and deadly. Winter may be ending, but its frigid effects last here well into spring."

Nardus held up his hands. "Evacuation is not optional. There must be another way."

Prince Rictar fidgeted with the ring on his middle finger. "There is. In the treasure vault are ancient maps of the three cities and the tunnels beneath them. With those maps, we can lead the people to safety."

"Perfect—"

Prince Rictar cut Nardus off. "Only my father has a key to the vault. He'll never go along with it no matter how much sense it makes."

Princess Zelanora leaned forward and whispered, "I have a way inside." Neither Nardus nor Prince Rictar asked for details.

Nardus turned back to the others around the table. He pointed to two of the soldiers on the opposite side of the table. "You two will be in charge of evacuating Borza." They nodded. He then looked at Berggren. "As will you."

Berggren sighed. "Guess I'm going to Borza."

Nardus pointed at two soldiers on his side of the table. "You two will be in charge of evacuating Elatos. Calen and Eshtak can help you." The soldiers nodded.

"And I'll lead the evacuation here," Princess Zelanora piped up.

"Good. We've got one thing settled. Now, if any of you have unique skills, this is the time to disclose them."

Morcinda, the aquatic elf, spoke up first. "I can control the flow of water."

Nardus exhaled and rubbed his left bicep. "How good are your skills? Can you control the flow of water across a great expanse?"

"I believe so. You have something specific in mind?"

"Elatos is built next to the river and nestles the surrounding mountains. Could you use the rivers to create a massive wall of water to protect the city and block the enemy from advancing?"

Morcinda nodded. Nardus thought she might've even smiled a little. "I can, but not indefinitely."

"Of course not. When the time comes to erect the wall, I will let you know."

The man at the end of the table spoke up next. "I am a skilled water wizard."

"Druden, correct?" The man nodded at Nardus. "I have the perfect plan for you. Ever heard of a water titan?"

Druden's eyes narrowed. "Yes, and I'm certain I could conjure one, but I wouldn't have the strength to hold it together for more than twenty or thirty minutes."

Nardus slipped one of the bracelets out of his pocket that he'd taken from Ūrdär Dhef Ɂäfn Dhä and tossed it down the center of the table. The weak throw only got the bracelet about two-thirds of the way to the man, but the others at the table passed it down to him.

"That's got 1200 years of energy stored in it. How long can you maintain a water titan with that?"

Druden slipped the bracelet over his right hand. The ends of his mustache touched the sides of his nose when he smiled. "Long enough to do some damage."

"I believe I can help with the water titan," said Zerenity.

Druden scoffed. "In what manner?"

Zerenity crossed her arms and pursed her lips. "Seaweed is prevalent at the bottom of Trivers Lake. I can help strengthen the water titan using it."

"Excellent idea," said Theyn. She looked up at Nardus. "My job is to protect you. I won't leave your side."

Nardus shook his head. "I've little doubt of that." He turned and addressed Zerenity and Druden. "Your main focus with that water titan will be to separate Aria from Cinolth. Do whatever it takes, but try to keep Aria alive."

Zerenity grimaced and nodded.

Druden shrugged. "Sure, but no guarantees."

"Noted," said Nardus.

Savric rose and walked around the table. "And I will create a light shield over Vallah so that Cinolth cannot attack or land." He fished inside his robes, pulled out a small, leather-bound book, and offered it to Nardus. "I am sure you remember this."

Nardus took the book and examined it. How long had it been since he and the others had created them? He smiled. "And its twin?"

"I have it," said Morcinda.

"Good. This will certainly come in handy." Nardus turned toward Prince Rictar. "You will send your army to Elatos."

Prince Rictar rose from his chair and dipped his head. "As you say. My army and I will set sail for Elatos at first light."

"Very good. Now, everyone knows where the stronghold is located if this war goes south, correct?" He pointed at the location on the map, and everyone at the table nodded. "Good. We will use it to regroup if needed." He clapped his hands together. "I believe that shores everything up."

Prince Rictar looked to the eight soldiers and pointed at seven of them. "Gather your troops." To the last soldier he said, "Defend the city and our king at all costs."

All eight soldiers rose from the table, smacked their left breast with their right fist, and exited the room. Prince Rictar followed them out.

Princess Zelanora rose from her chair and addressed Nardus. "I will return within the hour with those maps and deliver them to you." She nodded curtly and walked away.

Alderan stood and rounded the table. "And what am I supposed to do?"

"You'll be with Theyn and me." Nardus rubbed his left bicep as flashes of the past flew through his mind. "Our job will be to take down Cinolth. That bow of yours will be the key."

Alderan frowned. "My bow?"

"No other bow like it exists in this world. It's the same one that was used to kill Cinolth the first time. You'll have to tell me the story of how it came into your possession when this is all over."

Alderan nodded, but then fear rose in his eyes. "What about Pravus and Aria?"

Theyn touched Alderan's shoulder. "We must focus on Cinolth. He will be the greatest threat."

Nardus couldn't bring himself to think about their truly biggest threat. Aria would be a force to be reckoned with and trying to subdue her without injuring or killing her would be difficult if not impossible.

Ɛätūr help us all.

CHAPTER FORTY-ONE

Rayah crouched on the edge of the canyon rim just north of the Orbis Mountain Range, staring down at nothing. Rakzar, Urza, Normak, and Ridan flanked her. Bakkan, Ridan's black-and-silver mastiff, hung back in the shadows, apparently afraid of heights. The orc army still hid in the canyon below, cloaked beneath a veil of mezhik.

If Rayah hadn't flown down below the rim and seen the army for herself, she wouldn't have believed the army was even there. She'd never seen such powerful mezhik that could mask not only things from view but their sounds and smells as well. A wizard wielding such powerful mezhik left her bones aching with chills.

"I'm tired of waiting around while the four of you squabble about the next move we should make," growled Rakzar. He stood and swatted the air. "She'd already be dead if I'd come alone."

Rayah couldn't believe her ears. Every time she thought Rakzar had started to become a bit friendlier and began to rely on those around him, he'd go and say or do something completely asinine. She'd grown tired of the circular ride and wanted off.

She flew into the air and got right in Rakzar's face. "Look, if you think you can march right into the orc camp and face Käíez without anyone stopping you along the way, then go right ahead. Just remember who you'd be killing in the process."

Rakzar snorted and glared at her. "Doing nothing will get you killed just as quickly."

"Rayah's right." Ridan rose to her feet. "Even under the cover of night, you'd be hard-pressed to find this Käíez. If you're determined to walk right into the camp like a fool, you still need a way to locate her first."

The more time she spent with Ridan, the more Rayah liked her. The girl had a solid head on her shoulders and a knack for getting straight to the point. At first, there'd been a bit of strife between the two of them over

Normak. Ridan fancied Normak, and Normak fancied Rayah, but Rayah's heart forever belonged to Alderan. Once she explained the bond she shared with Alderan and the fact that it could never be broken, everything cleared right up. Well, it didn't keep Normak from ogling her and making passes, but it had satisfied Ridan.

Even though she didn't like it, Rayah had a solution. At least to the first part of the problem. "I'll do it." Her words came out with confidence and authority. It surprised even her, especially given the moths in her stomach and the tremors in her hands.

Rakzar squared his shoulders to her. "Do what?"

All four of them stared at her with blank expressions. Had she not explained the plan?

"Oh… right." She settled back on the ground, wrapped one of her curls around her finger, and twirled it. "Given that winter is finally losing its hold, I think I can travel through the dirt. It's the perfect way to locate Käíez without being detected."

Rakzar eyed her for several moments and then nodded. "I'm pretty sure I know where she'll be, but a confirmation would prove beneficial."

"Then it be settled," said Normak.

Rayah faced Rakzar. "So where do you think I'll find her?"

"There are some caves on the far east side of the camp. They've built a shrine there to some worthless god. It's where…" Rakzar didn't continue but looked toward the canyon. Rayah thought she saw tears in his eyes. The others must've too because none of them asked him to continue.

The answer hit her like a gut punch.

It's where Amicus died.

She took a deep breath and forced back tears of her own. "I'll be back as soon as I can." A loud sigh escaped through her nose as she stepped toward the canyon rim.

Fear skittered beneath her skin, both from the height she stood above the canyon floor and from the risk of getting caught, no matter how slim it might've been. With one last breath, she leapt off the canyon rim and dove beneath the veil of mezhik before she had a chance to talk herself out of it.

The ground rushed toward her even as the air fought to slow her down. She beat her wings with fury and almost closed her eyes right before impact with the canyon floor.

Give me courage, Ʒäṭūr.

† † †

Crossing the entire camp took longer than Rayah had expected. The orcs had spread far and wide, nearly a dozen miles. She wasn't exactly sure what Käíeʑ looked like, but she had a general idea. Flowing red robes would likely stick out among the orc army.

She sighted the guarded cave entrance before she reached the eastern edge of the camp, but there was a problem. The soft canyon floor began to transition to sandstone as she got closer. Unfortunately, sandstone proved extremely difficult to travel through. She could do it, but the displacement of the sandstone didn't work the same way as dirt and sand. She'd basically have to tunnel through it, and that would take a good amount of time and effort, neither of which she had.

Rayah stopped and gathered herself. Each breath came with more effort than she'd have liked, and her energy seemed much lower than it should've been. At first, she didn't understand what her problem was, but then it hit her.

The curse.

She should've thought of that before she set out on her reconnaissance mission. Several deep breaths slowed her pulse and calmed her mind.

New plan. Verify Käíeʑ isn't anywhere else in the camp.

Rayah set to work. She created a grid of the camp in her mind and began searching it section by section. Almost two hours later, she'd searched all but three sections and hadn't seen her anywhere. Granted, there were a lot of tents, but all of them only had sides and a roof, even the massive tent she assumed was Murtag's.

The third to last section was quite sparse, housing a single small tent and only two small fires with a handful of orcs and humans around them. Oddly, the five-foot-square tent had a bottom. She'd just passed underneath it when a name caught her ear. She raced back and rose to the surface beneath the tent so she could hear the conversation.

"I thought the plan was to attack Vallah." The female voice sounded strange. Foreign. Almost like it'd come from two different mouths.

A harsh, slurred, male voice responded, "The plan is to do whatever Lord Rosai commands. You know what will happen if you cross him. You will leave for Elatos at once."

"We fear nothing," said the female.

We?

From everything that Rakzar had told Rayah about Käíeᴢ, this had to be her. Or them. Whatever the thing was. Two halves of a whole. The thought made her squirm. The squirm sent dust flying in her small pocket of air. Rayah grabbed her nose, but the tickle remained. Intensified. Became unbearable. She squeezed her eyes tight and held her nose, but it made little difference. Her head jerked back as she sneezed, and her foot kicked the underside of the tent floor.

A bright light flashed overhead.

Rayah sank deep underground as fast as she could.

An intense heat burned the earth as a blackish-purple light rocketed toward her.

The ground quaked and split open.

Rayah turned and flew as fast as she could through the dirt.

Ȥäṭūr, let me escape.

† † †

Rakzar stood at the cliff's edge, anticipating Rayah's return. She'd been gone for several hours and he worried himself sick over it. His mind raced with scenarios of what might've transpired, each one more gruesome and tragic than the last.

Amicus stood at his side, and for once Rakzar welcomed his companionship. "Rayah is a smart and tough girl. Have faith that she'll be along soon."

Rakzar scowled at the far edge of the canyon. "You're the one with a god and faith, Shadowman, not me."

Amicus rubbed his bare chin. "Are you certain about that?"

"Certain of what? That you have a god and faith or that I don't?" Rakzar's scowl deepened.

"You know the answer to the first. Ȥäṭūr *is* the one true God. Now, as to the last, I think you have more faith than you let on about." Amicus reached up and clasped Rakzar's shoulder. "In fact, there are many things you try to hide. The real question is why. Do you think the others will think less of you if you show compassion or seem to actually give a damn about something other than yourself?"

"I knew your being here wouldn't be a good thing for long." Rakzar shrugged Amicus's hand from his shoulder. "Buzz off—"

The air crackled, and the veil that lay over the canyon faltered and disappeared. Rakzar crouched down and the others joined him.

"That be good or bad?" asked Normak.

"Not sure." Rakzar leaned forward and peered over the edge. "Is it just me, or is the ground moving?"

Urza leaned over the edge. "Not just you. Rayah's coming in hot."

"Gods, what did she do?" asked Ridan.

Smoke rose in the distance from a small tent. Rakzar pointed at it. "I don't know, but that can't be good."

Normak grabbed his battle axe. "Me thinks yer right."

A trail of dust followed Rayah right up the canyon wall. She shot right past the four of them, a good fifteen feet in the air, before arcing back toward the canyon. As she came down, Rakzar noticed she no longer flapped her wings. He reached out and snatched her from the air without thinking. His left foot slid over the rim, and he teetered on the canyon's edge, but the only thing on his mind was saving Rayah's life. Nothing else mattered. Pushing off of the rim and twisting in the air, he shoved Rayah toward Urza and Ridan. The two of them caught Rayah together, but Rakzar dropped from the sky.

As he fell, a calming peace swept through him. His eyes snapped shut, but he didn't brace for the impact. It would come soon enough. Then, something grabbed hold of his middle, and he felt himself slowing down. The sensation didn't make sense until he opened his eyes.

Normak held Rakzar around the waist. The dwarf's feet moved in a blur as he worked at slowing them down by running up the canyon wall, working against the gravity that pulled them toward the canyon floor. By the time they hit the ground, the impact jarred Rakzar little more than falling a few feet would've. Normak grunted and moaned, but Rakzar knew it wasn't from the fall. He lay on top of Normak. Several hundred pounds of flesh, bone, and muscle.

Rakzar rolled to the side and got to his feet.

Normak groaned and held his chest. "Ya tryin' ta kill me?"

Rakzar growled with laughter. "You're the one who came after me, not the other way around."

He scowled and sat up. "Didn' think ya'd squish the life from me lungs."

"Thank him for saving your ugly hide." Amicus stood next to Rakzar, his arms crossed.

Rakzar said "thanks" under his breath and then headed west along the canyon wall. A switchback trail a mile back would get them back to the top of the canyon. Normak trailed him, but not by much. The others walked along the top, but he didn't see Rayah with them. His heart thundered.

Why would they have left her behind?

He took a deep breath and sighed with relief when he caught a glimpse of Rayah sprawled on Bakkan's back. The thought of losing her pained his heart almost as much as losing Urza. It sickened him a little as well. He had grown soft. He pushed those thoughts aside and focused ahead.

The little dryte better have some good news.

✝ ✝ ✝

Rayah's eyelids fluttered as she fought the urge to drift down into sleep. She'd expended so much energy escaping from Murtag and Käíeƨ that she didn't think she could hold out much longer. Food and a good nap would do her well and fix her right up.

But we don't have time.

Snap! Snap! Snap!

Rayah dragged her eyelids open. Ridan squatted over her, fingers poised to snap again. She held her hand up. "I'm awake already."

Ridan smirked. "That's what ya said the other four times too."

Rayah sat up and shook the sleep from her head. "How long have I been out?"

"About twenty minutes." Ridan straightened. "Rakzar's about to lose his mind and has threatened to go down there himself. What happened?"

"Found Käíeƨ. A man named Lord Rosai summoned her... or them to join him in Elatos."

Lord Rosai.

Rakzar had never met Lord Rosai but knew him to be the one responsible for creating the blood bond between orcs and gnolls. He'd give anything to sink his teeth into him as well.

"When?" growled Rakzar.

"Immediately." Rayah rose to her feet and the world spun around her. Ridan grabbed hold of her arm and steadied her.

Rakzar dropped on all fours. "The quickest way there will be the western shore of Trivers Lake. Let's move!"

"Leave me," said Rayah. "I'll slow you down."

"Fine." Rakzar took off.

Normak sped away too.

Urza stood there. "I'll stay here too."

"Go, Urza," said Ridan. "Rakzar will need your help as well." She helped Rayah over to Bakkan. "We'll catch up."

"You're certain about this?" asked Urza.

Rayah looked back at Urza. "It's okay. Go."

Urza nodded and took off after Rakzar and Normak.

"Please, Ridan. Leave me here." Rayah leaned against Bakkan's neck. His soft fur tickled the inside of her ear. "You really don't need to do this. I'll figure something else out."

"There's nothing to figure out." Ridan handed Rayah something wrapped in a small piece of parchment. "Eat that. It tastes like gnoll feces but will get you going again in about ten minutes."

Rayah unwrapped the parchment. It held a brownish-green cube, about an inch in size. It squished a little when she picked it up, and the smell it put off could've choked a dragon. She looked at Ridan, and the dwarf nodded encouragement. Rayah popped it into her mouth and immediately gagged. Every sense told her to spit it out, but she bit down on it instead. A sour liquid squirted out of the foul morsel and rained fire down the back of her throat as she forced herself to swallow it down. Chills raced across her flesh and shook her to the core.

"Ugh!" Rayah raked her tongue on the backs of her teeth. "I'm not sure what gnoll feces tastes like, but that'd be a good first guess."

Just her throat tingled at first, but then the sensation began spreading across Rayah's chest and into her back. "Something's happening."

"Good." Bakkan knelt, and Ridan slipped her leg over his back. She patted the leather saddle in front of her. "Get on."

Rayah climbed into the saddle and Ridan wrapped her arms around Rayah's waist. Bakkan stood tall and lurched forward. Soon, they were flying across the rim of the canyon.

Ridan shouted, "Let me know when the tingling wears off."

Rayah nodded and leaned forward in the saddle. The sensation was sort of like flying, but without all the effort. She could get used to traveling that way.

† † †

Once past the canyon, Rakzar headed straight for the Hotah River. Only one crossing existed between where they were and before reaching Vallah, and he knew she wouldn't go through the city. When he reached the dock, only a single barge remained.

A seedy man with a devious grin greeted him and Normak. "Headin' west?" He spat black sludge from between his missing front teeth.

Rakzar didn't have time for pleasantries. He grabbed the man by the front of his shirt and pulled him close. "Anyone cross here recently?"

The man nodded. "Strange woman. Stranger beast."

"Then let's move." Rakzar shoved the man back and released his shirt.

"Ain't free."

Rakzar reached for his battle axe but Normak offered the man a single gold coin. "Fast as ya can."

The man snatched the coin and squished it between his back teeth. "Good. Hop aboard."

They shoved off and headed across the half-mile-wide river.

A minute into the journey someone yelled, "Wait."

The three of them looked back. Rayah, Ridan, and Bakkan halted at the river's edge.

The man looked at Rakzar. "Friends?"

"Go back, but make it quick," he growled.

"Cost—"

Normak handed the guy an additional silver coin. "We square?"

The man nodded and reversed direction.

Twenty minutes later, they hopped off the barge on the western bank of the Hotah River and headed south. It didn't take long for Rakzar to locate Käíeƶ's trail as the grasslands transitioned into dirt and rock as they neared the mouth of Trivers Lake.

Around the third bend of the river, Urza spotted Käíeƶ. The fiend rode a black steed with a single horn. An unnatural creature from what Rakzar could tell.

"She's only a few minutes ahead." Rakzar pushed himself harder. Didn't care if the others could keep up.

She won't get away.

† † †

"Käíez!" yelled Rakzar. She rode twenty paces ahead of him. His lungs burned with fire and his legs jellied with fatigue, but he knew what he must do.

Käíez slowed her steed and brought it around to face Rakzar. In a flash, she'd dismounted and stood on the bedrock and sand that made up the lake's shoreline. Then, she separated into two forms, each cloaked in red. Rakzar didn't need to see their faces to know each of them only had half a face, but they both removed their hoods.

"We remember you," they said. "Come to find death?"

Rakzar advanced. "I've come to kill you."

"Then you'll be disappointed." Their silver faces merged and frowned and then separated again. "We can't be killed."

"Were you born into this world?" He crept closer, his right hand on the hilt of the dagger that would end her life.

"Yessss," they hissed.

Rakzar stopped ten paces in front of Käíez. "Then you can die."

Ridan came up next to Rakzar, sitting tall in her saddle and her spear raised. Normak flashed across the sand and slid to a stop on Käíez's left, sending a spray of sand high in the air. He brandished his war hammer and a formidable glower. Rayah flew over Käíez and landed behind them, gloves on and knives poised for battle. Urza came up on Käíez's right but didn't look well at all. She hadn't drawn her knives.

Käíez continuously merged and separated as she turned in a tight circle, her shadowy forms never staying solid. "I see you've brought friends. Do they know they're already dead?" She laughed. "Ah, the dwarves are clueless. What a surprise."

Normak yelled some sort of battle cry and lunged forward with a mighty swing. His war hammer arced around and back up, right toward the underside of Käíez's chin, but it passed right through her. His momentum threw him off balance, but his quick feet helped him recover without falling.

Käíez's two forms moved like a blur, one stepping into the same space as Normak and the other into Rayah's space. Rayah arched back and released a bloodcurdling scream just before launching an assault against Urza. Normak hunkered over, his body contorted unnaturally. With a growl, he shot forward and attacked Ridan.

Rakzar stood back, his eyes darting between the two battles. Two problems presented themselves. He only had one dagger and didn't know if killing one part of Käíeƨ would kill the other or not. He also couldn't remember which part of her was in Rayah and which part was in Normak. If he had to kill both parts of her, she'd need to be together, otherwise she'd never let him get close again after the first one died.

"You know what to do, my friend." Amicus stood next to him, his eyes focused on the battle between Rayah and Urza. "In her current condition, Urza won't last much longer. You need to take Rayah out."

"I can't kill her!"

Amicus turned and shook his head. "I never suggested that and never would. Find a way to knock her out so Käíeƨ can't control her."

Rakzar dropped on all fours and galloped toward Rayah. Three paces away, he launched himself at her. She whipped around and turned her knives on him, but not in time. His fist caught the side of her head and drove right through her with a sickening crunch. She twisted and weaved in the air, and then she dropped to the ground in a heap and didn't move. Her knives fell out of the air and clanged on the rocks.

Urza collapsed. Blood matted the fur along her arms, legs, and torso. She still breathed, but he didn't know for how much longer.

Käíeƨ pulled herself out of Rayah and shot over and into Ridan. Bakkan backed away from Ridan and growled.

Ridan and Normak turned on Rakzar and advanced.

The only way this would end was for him to draw Käíeƨ out. He grabbed his double-edged battle axes off his back and waited.

Normak flashed past him and attacked from behind, but Rakzar had anticipated the move and easily dodged Normak's wide swing. With a reverse twist and a low yet powerful swing, the flat side of Rakzar's axe caught Normak square in the jaw. Normak stumbled back several steps, dropped to his knees, and then face-planted in the sand.

Blinding pain erupted in Rakzar's left thigh and numbed his leg down to his toes. He turned just in time to see Ridan yank her spear from his leg. Blood dripped from its tip. He pushed the pain down, but his leg was practically useless. It wouldn't bear his weight.

Käíeƨ pulled away from Normak and entered Ridan. Both halves of her were inside Ridan now. He needed to get closer in order to take Ridan down, but her spear had great range. A dark and twisted thought entered his mind.

Maybe I can stab Ridan with the dagger and kill Käíez.

He shook his head. *It might kill them both or just Ridan.*

If he somehow damaged the blade trying such a move, he'd never forgive himself. He decided it wasn't worth the risk. Right now, he needed a way to disarm Ridan before she wound up killing him, but the pain clouded his mind.

Ridan moved in for another strike. Rakzar blocked her jab with his axe, but just so. The next blow glanced off his breastplate. In his state, he couldn't match her speed. Every other strike hit home.

He dropped to his knees as she pulled back for a final assault. He lifted one of his battle axes, but his arm shook with fatigue and blood loss. He knew he didn't stand a chance.

Ridan lunged forward. Her spear came right for Rakzar's face. But then her arm jerked back, and her body slammed to the ground. Bakkan held her arm in his teeth and pinned her down.

Rakzar took a breath, but then Käíez emerged from within Ridan.

She stalked forward, her two halves undulating and joining. "Had enough yet?"

Rakzar dropped his battle axes on the ground and gathered his strength. Somehow, he forced himself back to his feet. Dizziness spun his head, and his vision sparkled and darkened around the edges. Standing wouldn't be an option for much longer.

He spat blood and snarled, "I'm just getting started." The hilt of the crystal dagger soothed his aching hand when he grasped it.

Käíez eyed Rakzar's hand for a moment and laughed. "You just won't give up, will you?"

She shot forward and right up to Rakzar's face, hovering a few feet off the ground. Her form cycled between a blur and solidity. Pulsing.

Her silver face contorted with malice. "You'll be finished soon enough."

Rakzar plunged the blade upward into her shadowy chest but nothing happened.

"No blade can harm me," she hissed.

Then, her form solidified, burying the knife within her.

Käíez shrieked. The sound pierced Rakzar's ears.

She dropped to the ground with a thud but stayed on her feet. Her hands ripped at her chest.

Rakzar's leg wobbled, and he collapsed.

"What have you done to us!" she screamed.

Something moved behind Käíeƨ.

Urza.

Somehow, Urza had found the strength to rise again.

"This is the end of you, bitch." Urza roared as she plunged both of her knives into Käíeƨ's sides, right underneath her ribs.

Käíeƨ shrieked louder still as blood ran from her wounds. She turned and Urza flew backward after a crimson flash.

Ridan scrambled to her feet and launched her spear at Käíeƨ. It flew true and buried itself right through the center of Käíeƨ's throat. Its tip exploded through the back of Käíeƨ's neck.

Käíeƨ dropped to her knees.

Ridan lay on the ground. Rakzar missed what felled her. Smoke rose from her chest. Bakkan nudged her with his nose but she didn't respond.

A flash and guttural cry drew Rakzar's attention. Normak's war hammer connected with the side of Käíeƨ's head. A sick, wet thump followed by crunching bones. She toppled over. Blood and brains spilled from her cracked and concaved skull.

Normak leaned on his war hammer, the only one left standing. His chest heaved, and his eyes swam in their sockets. He said something, but Rakzar couldn't hear anything but buzzing. Normak bent over and vomited blood.

Black smoke poured from Käíeƨ's nose and mouth. No, it wasn't smoke but a shade from the lower world. Its screech filled the air.

Rakzar covered his ears but the sound still pierced them.

The demon shadow circled the shoreline several times and then swept right through Normak. Normak's mouth opened wide. He must've been screaming, his face contorted with agony. A blurred orange aura pulled away from Normak like rain streaks in the sky, and then the aura and the shade faded into nothing. Normak fell over, his mouth still agape and his eyes bulging, but there was no life left in them.

Rakzar pulled his hands away from his ears. Blood wet his fingers, and a high-pitched buzz filled his head. He held on to consciousness for a few more moments, but the unrelenting pain sank its teeth into his mind and dragged him into the darkness.

† † †

Rayah reached into her pack and grabbed the brass-handled mirror. "I need to warn Master Savric about the orcs."

Ridan shook her head. "Don't think that'll be doing anything for you."

Several cracks fissured the mirror's glass. "No, ʕäṭūr!" Rayah tried to contact Master Savric but the mirror didn't respond.

CHAPTER FORTY-TWO

Wrik skulked about the corridors of Galondu Castle, his head on a swivel. After the incident with the shadow troll in the atrium four days prior, every shadow represented a potential threat. For all he knew, Pravus had sent an army of them to kill him.

He didn't actually have proof that Pravus orchestrated the assassination attempt, but who else could have done it? Keeping his nose buried in books of prophecy, he'd made few enemies. And, as far as he could tell, Aria liked him well enough. However, she did have the dragon influencing her as well. But Cinolth didn't seem to have a personal vendetta against him. Cinolth just hated mankind as a whole.

Pravus must be the one.

Wrik returned to his bedchamber and gathered the handful of items that belonged to him: three books of prophecy, an extra pair of spectacles, a second set of silver robes identical to the ones he wore, a brass toe ring with a black dragon's head spewing fire, a coin purse with thirty-seven gold coins and twenty-two silver ones, a leather necklace with a hollowed-out magnet, and a vial of serum hidden inside the wall behind his bed. The serum wasn't his own.

He slipped the necklace over his head and tucked it into his robes. It'd always brought him good luck in the past. Perhaps it would again in the future.

From his room he teleported into the corridor that ran perpendicular to the one with his secret room. Using half a dozen orbs of light, he verified the shadows were nothing more than just shadows. Satisfied, he traversed the corridor to the intersection point and used the same technique to check the shadows again.

To his left, the shadows shrank back against the probing orbs of light as they should. To his right, a hundred paces away, the torches began snuffing themselves out. The darkness moved toward him at an alarming pace. He sent the orbs of light flying toward the darkness, but they fizzled out as well.

Damn!

Back to his left, the torches began snuffing themselves out as well. He turned back toward the corridor he'd come from, but the darkness closed in on him from that direction too.

Wrik abandoned the notion of retrieving anything from his secret room. With determination, he set his mind on Nasduron and stepped forward.

Nothing happened. Nothing changed.

The darkness drew near. Fifty paces away.

His heart drummed in his ears.

Again, he stepped forward to no avail.

Twenty-five paces.

Moths fluttered in the pit of his stomach. A flurry of wings.

Ten paces.

Then it hit him. Not the darkness, but the second rule of Nasduron. Gnaud's voice filled his head: *"You cannot come here to escape death."*

Five paces.

In a flash, Wrik teleported out of the corridor and atop the southern ramparts. The distance jarred him and sapped more energy than he would've liked, but he'd had no other choice. His heart knocked against his ribcage as his hands fumbled with the brass toe ring.

East and west, the darkness poured out of the stairwells.

Wrik dropped the toe ring, and it rolled toward the parapet and the large crack that ate into the rampart. "No!" He dropped to his knees and dove forward, but his large fingers only hastened the toe ring's pace toward the crack. He crawled forward and swiped with his hand just as the toe ring dropped into the crack and out of sight.

The darkness edged closer, but the open air seemed to slow it down a bit. He'd gladly take as much time as he could get. He leaned over the crack to see how far the toe ring had fallen, and it shot back out of the crack. He peered down and saw it hanging from his necklace with the magnet.

Still my lucky charm.

The darkness seemed to move quicker as though it sensed its prey might escape. Forty paces and closing fast.

Wrik slid the brass toe ring onto the second-smallest toe on his left foot. It'd been a long time since he'd worn the ring, and it seemed a bit snugger than he remembered, but it wouldn't be for long.

Thirty paces.

Fire seared Wrik's flesh.

Twenty paces.

No matter how many times Wrik used the ring, he never got used to its flaming touch.

Ten paces.

Bones cracked. Elongated.

Feet became talons.

Hands clawed and splayed.

Robes morphed into scales and leathery wings.

Five paces.

Spikes grew out of his spine. Edged his jaws.

Horns sprouted from his temples and swept back over the top of his bald head.

Four paces.

Ears melded into the sides of his head.

Spectacles sank into his face, their lenses covering his serpentine eyes.

Three paces.

A tail sprouted from his tailbone. Long, spiked, and pointed at the end.

Two paces.

Nose, cheeks, and jaws moved forward. Elongated. Became a snout.

Teeth multiplied. Sharpened like razors.

One pace.

Wrik jumped up on top of the parapet, spread his wings, and dove into the darkness of the night.

CHAPTER FORTY-THREE

Pravus gazed ahead as his massive army marched north and into the Arian Valley. A great wall made of wooden logs, sixty feet high at its tallest points, rose in the distance and spanned much of the wide gap between the Orbis Mountain's southwestern and southeastern ranges. Only the Hotah River separated the two halves. Elatos, a sprawling city with more than three hundred thousand citizens, spanned both sides of the river and hunkered down behind the wall.

Pravus gripped his reins tighter and stood tall in his stirrups as excitement stirred in his chest. Victory would undoubtedly be his. He looked skyward.

We will not be stopped, Father.

A dust cloud rose in the distance, and the thunder of hooves rode on the wind. Aria and Cinolth swooped down from the clouds and circled over Pravus and the army.

Aria mindspoke to Pravus. *"The enemy dares to meet us on the battlefield."*

"And they will be crushed," he replied.

"It looks like they've sent four representatives ahead of their forces."

"Then let's go meet them." Pravus raised a fist in the air, and the army slowed to a halt.

"Where's my brother?" she asked.

"Opposing us." He severed the link with Aria, whipped his horse, and galloped ahead.

By the time Pravus reached the spot where Cinolth had touched down, Aria had dismounted and stood at Cinolth's side. Simultaneously, the four riders from Elatos pulled up twenty yards away, their horses snorting and eyes wild with fear, clearly spooked by Cinolth's presence. The riders, all clad in green armor, dismounted and approached, swords drawn but held toward the ground. Three men and one woman. By her gait, the woman looked to be in charge.

Five yards away they halted, and then the woman took three additional steps forward. She removed her black helmet and held it under her arm. Snow-white hair bellowed behind her. Although she had to have been middle-aged, her dark skin showed few signs of wrinkles. Her brown-eyed stare pierced like a hawk's.

Aria and Pravus approached the woman together, but the woman spoke first. "I am Ursula Picking, commander of the Elatos City Guard. I command you to disband your army and return to your homes. Failure to comply will be met with force."

Pravus stood tall, his hands behind his back. Mezhik crackled at his fingertips. "You have no authority to command me to do anything. My name is Pravus Rosai, Lord of Galondu Castle and rightful king of the Ancient Realm. Command your army to surrender, or you will be decimated. If you choose to engage us in combat, there will be no quarter."

Commander Picking's mouth opened, but Aria cut her off. "My husband has spoken. Surrender now or die this day."

"We shall never surrender!" cried Commander Picking.

"Perhaps this will persuade you." Three orangish-blue fireballs flew from Aria's palms and incinerated the three men who stood behind Commander Picking.

Commander Picking gasped. "You've violated the conventions of war set forth by millennia of rulers!"

Aria moved forward and circled the woman. A lioness stalking its prey. "The only rule that matters is mine. Return to your army and let them know that death comes for them this day. Send word to your city ruler that his reign has ended. As it did in the Great War, Elatos will burn to the ground before the sun sets." She spat at the woman's feet and walked back toward Cinolth.

Pravus smiled. *Gods, she is ruthless.*

He backed away from Commander Picking and mounted his horse. Turning his horse around, he signaled the army to advance. War cries filled the air, and the army surged forward with the thunder of more than two hundred thousand pairs of boots, hooves, feet, and paws. Drums pounded away, quaking the ground and shaking the air. Nothing could've sounded sweeter to his ears.

Commander Picking ran back to her mount and took off back toward Elatos and her army. Aria mounted Cinolth without another word, and Cinolth took to the sky, beating the air with his mighty wings and raising a cloud of dust from the parched plains.

Pravus mindspoke to Aria. *"Head for Vallah and leave the army of Elatos to me."*

"It is in your hands," she replied. *"If possible, don't let yourself be injured again. I can't afford to sustain a broken nose or something worse while engaged in battle. And try not to get tied up with vines."* Her laughter echoed in his mind.

The jab infuriated Pravus, but he took a breath and let it slide as he severed the connection with her. This was his day for glory, and nothing would spoil it, not even his wife.

Pravus drew upon his mezhik and hid himself and his mount from view. Then, using his mind, he reached out to Karraar, the designated leader of the gnolls. *"Disengage and head east."*

"My lord, I've promised them bloodshed," replied Karraar.

Pravus grinned to himself. *"And bloodshed they shall have. Move swiftly through the Orbis Mountains and attack Borza. Kill them all."*

"Consider it done, my lord."

Pravus severed the connection. His pure black mount stomped its foot and snorted. A war horse from birth.

He leaned forward and patted the horse's neck. "Sorry, but you won't be seeing combat anytime soon."

Pravus urged the horse forward and headed south, through the middle of his surging army, until he reached a point just outside the range of the Elatos archers. Reaching into his satchel that hung from the saddle, he retrieved his diary and a fountain pen. He opened the diary to the first page, a blank one, and wrote a single sentence. *"The time has come to lay siege on Vallah. -Lord Rosai"*

The words faded when he lifted the fountain pen from the page, his message sent. He closed the diary and placed it and the fountain pen back in his satchel, not needing or expecting a response.

Pravus steepled his fingers as he watched his army march ahead.

The Three Kingdoms will fall into chaos by nightfall.

Satisfied everything progressed as planned, he set to work weaving his mezhik and creating an illusion the enemy would never forget.

✝ ✝ ✝

Arrows peppered the sky from the north, forcing Aria and Cinolth to fly higher. Such weapons couldn't penetrate Cinolth's scales, but she didn't have the luxury of armored skin, and wearing any sort of mail didn't suit her. It didn't take much effort to destroy or deflect the arrows that came close using her mezhik, but their mission would certainly require them both to be at full strength. Take out the king, and the people's hope would falter.

Hundreds of her forces already lay dead on the battlefield, arrows buried in their flesh. But it didn't matter. King Zaridus couldn't muster an army the size of hers if he had ten years to do so.

Arrows continued to rain down on both sides of the field even as the armies met in the middle of the battlefield with a thunderous clash of metal and guttural cries of war. In a strange way, she longed to be down there. Killing the zhebəllin back in the Daltura Hills and the nōmed in the Inferus Wastelands had been an exhilarating experience. Now, with her mezhik, she feared nothing.

Just as they were about to leave the battle behind, Cinolth banked hard to his left. She hadn't expected the sudden change in direction and nearly slid off his neck.

"What are you doing?" she demanded through mindspeak. The only response she received from their connection was one of blinding rage. She scoured the battlefield but found no threat worthy of a response.

She was about to ask Cinolth what he was doing again, but then she spotted the target of his wrath. Nardus, her father, stood in the middle of the battlefield, directing soldiers on every front and taking out droves of zhebəllin with a variety of mezhik attacks.

"I thought my father wasn't a threat."

"He wasn't until he found himself," replied Cinolth in her mind.

Aria leaned forward. "What does that mean?"

"Your father is Cyrus, my prior captor and sworn enemy." Hatred dripped from his words. *"He didn't remember that until recently."*

Understanding washed over Aria.

No wonder Pravus told me he was dangerous and to keep away from him.

"Why didn't Pravus or Wrik tell me the truth?" she asked.

"When will you finally learn that they have both manipulated you from the start?"

Heat rose in Cinolth's neck, and his scales took on a red, ember-like glow. Aria quickly pulled moisture from the air and layered the insides of her legs with ice.

"Leave him!" she shouted. "Vallah is our target."

Cinolth dove toward Nardus and let loose a pillar of fire.

Nardus moved his hands in a circle and everyone around him flew backward.

The fiery blast engulfed Nardus, the fire so bright that Aria had to shield her eyes.

Cinolth circled back around.

A scorch mark ten feet wide and fifty feet long scarred the earth, but Nardus stood in the middle of it unharmed.

He must've shielded himself with ice or something else.

Lightning flashed and struck Cinolth's left wing. Another bolt struck his right wing. The air rumbled, and Cinolth jerked back and forth.

A six-inch hole pierced each of his wings where the lightning hit. Cinolth roared with fury and banked back toward Nardus.

Aria entered Cinolth's mind and spoke to him, her voice spry with urgency. *"We don't have time for this! Remember our mission."*

"He must die," Cinolth roared in her mind.

"And he will," said Aria. *"I swear it on my life. But now is not the time."*

Cinolth turned back toward Elatos and gained altitude. His scales cooled and returned to their normal black color. Aria sighed with relief and looked ahead.

We're coming for you, King Zaridus.

✝ ✝ ✝

Nardus watched Cinolth head toward Elatos. The sight of Shanara riding that foul beast sickened Nardus. Every moment she spent upon his back and in his presence corrupted her mind further. He'd witnessed it happen once before with Magus Carac. A lifetime ago. He'd fight to his last breath to save her from Cinolth.

He returned his attention back to the battlefield and the onslaught of enemy forces he and the Elatos City Guard faced. He tried to preserve the lives of those under the influence of Cinolth when he could, but the chaos of battle limited his ability to do so. No matter how many zhebəllin, giants, ogres, and soldiers he took out, another wave replaced them. Their numbers seemed endless. Nardus estimated that they faced close to a million foes, including a dozen wizards and sorceresses.

A sight far in the distance to the south grabbed Nardus's attention and chilled his blood. Three massive dragons, bound in chains and led by giants, marched toward the battlefield. Chunks of flesh and scaly skin hung from whitish-beige bones of one of the dragons. Another looked to be covered with bluish-white ice crystals. The third dragon, greenish-black in color, seemed to have no physical structure whatsoever.

A bone dragon, an ice dragon, and a mist dragon. Where in Centauria did Pravus find them?

Cinolth presented a huge threat by himself, but with four dragons, Pravus's army would prove all but impossible to defeat. Everywhere Nardus looked, the Elatos City Guard were being overrun. They needed to retreat before it was too late.

Nardus gathered the few men around him and told them to spread the word to fall back. As it was, they were already backed up dangerously close to the great wall. Seeing their position, realization set in that falling back was no longer an option for most if not all of them.

Theyn stood next to him, a bloody sword clutched in her hands. She fared well with the weapon but would've done better had she shifted into a cat. Fear of losing herself again kept her on two feet.

"Are we falling back?" she asked.

An ogre lumbered toward them. Theyn's speed outmatched its size and strength, and she dispatched the beast with three quick swings of her sword, one to the back of each of the ogre's knees and one to its throat. Alderan took out another with an arrow right through the center of its eyes. Once it hit the ground, Alderan stepped on its neck and pulled the arrow back out.

"Yes, but I need to send a message to Morcinda." Nardus pulled the leather bag over his head and grabbed the book out of it. "You two watch my back."

Nardus knelt and jotted a quick note to Morcinda on the first page. *"The Elatos City Guard is being overrun. It's time to raise the water wall. -Nardus"*

He snapped the book shut before the words finished fading and shoved it back in his bag. "Let's move!" He slung the bag back over his head as they ran toward Elatos and the great wall.

† † †

Even as Alderan ran toward Elatos he knew the city guard wouldn't make it back in time. Water from the Hotah River had already begun to rise and overflow its banks. At the rate the water built up, they only had a few minutes before crossing it would no longer be an option.

Alderan yelled at Nardus who ran ahead of him. "Can we create some sort of tunnel through the water for the soldiers to escape through?"

Nardus slowed and allowed Alderan to catch up. "Yes, but that would require a massive amount of energy and would only save a handful of lives."

Alderan halted. Anger rose in his gut. "Preserving life is why we fight. Or at least why *I* fight."

Nardus turned back and faced Alderan. "Yes, son, but you must also consider what will happen *after* this moment. Those soldiers swore an oath to defend Elatos and holding the enemy back a little bit longer will allow the rest of us to regroup and double our efforts to thwart that same enemy. If we stay here and help them live a few moments longer, we will be sacrificing lives on the other side of the wall."

Alderan couldn't argue with Nardus's logic, but it didn't settle his anger or ease his conscience. "Then we should stand with them and fight to the end."

"I admire your bravery, but that would serve no purpose. We must stop Cinolth and your sister or all will be lost. Do you not understand that?"

"What about Sarai? How many people can she transport?" asked Theyn.

"Twelve perhaps, but no more," said Nardus.

Dozens of fireballs whizzed over their heads. A few hissed as they careened into the growing wall of water, but most of them reached their target, the great wall.

A chilling roar shook the air and grabbed Alderan's attention. The three dragons had been loosed. The ice dragon stormed forward, crushing everything in its path. Shards of ice shot from its mouth with deadly accuracy, impaling friend and foe without discrimination. The bone dragon raged too, screeching and shooting shards of bone from itself like porcupine quills. Unlike the other two, the mist dragon moved across the battlefield in silence, engulfing soldiers and leaving a trail of bloated bodies in its wake.

Alderan swallowed hard, fear wringing his neck. *How can we win?*

Hundreds of soldiers in black armor with a red dragon head sigil on their chests rushed toward them, swords, pikes, maces, and battle axes drawn and ready. A few city guardsmen intercepted them but were dispatched quickly and without mercy. Alderan raised his bow, nocked an arrow, and took aim as he drew the string back. A single shot would do him little good with so many approaching.

Nardus reached out and touched the end of the arrow. The arrow began to glow with a blue hue. "Aim for the closest one. We retreat after this."

Alderan locked in on one of the soldiers. The brutish man screamed obscenities as he ran toward them, somehow audible over the growing frenzy surrounding them. Alderan loosed the arrow and it sailed true, plunging right through the man's open mouth. Blue light flashed, and a concussive arc of icy wind shot out from behind the man. Dozens of soldiers froze solid and crashed to the ground, their bodies shattering upon impact.

The ground fell out beneath Alderan's feet, dropping him into a pool of golden liquid. Nardus must've called Sarai after imbuing the arrow with an ice bomb. Alderan breathed in the golden liquid as the battle scene above disappeared from view.

† † †

Nardus met Prince Rictar atop the great wall. "Glad to see you've made it."

"Just so." Prince Rictar gazed at the water wall below. "It worries me that the dragon didn't attack our ships."

"That's because the bigger prize is taking down Vallah. He'll conserve as much energy as possible to do so."

"And we're down here now." Prince Rictar shook his head. "Perhaps my father was right. Look at the size of the army we face. There is no end to their numbers, and they have three more dragons as well."

Nardus grimaced. "I won't pretend that things are looking up, but your army arriving has given hope and strength to the city guard. Sometimes, that's all it takes to turn the tides of war."

"Eshtak not see dragons." He hopped from one foot to the other.

"Perhaps your vision isn't that good," said Nardus.

"Eshtak sees fine!"

"Wait..." said Alderan. "Amicus told me that Eshtak is immune to mezhik. Could the dragons be an illusion? Something Pravus is conjuring perhaps, like he did with the gallows."

"Gah." How foolish could Nardus have been? Pravus would be doing everything possible to make the odds seem insurmountable. "Let's see if I can break the illusion."

Nardus closed his eyes and focused his mezhik on the three dragons.

† † †

Alderan stared in awe as Nardus held his arms in the air and gathered light from the sun. Nardus's hands and face began glowing so bright that Alderan had to shield his eyes. Nardus lowered his arms and took aim with his hands at the battlefield below.

"Dissipate!" yelled Nardus.

Alderan turned and watched as light shot from Nardus's hands and streaked across the battlefield, dispelling all shadows in its path.

The intense light reached the three dragons and caused them to shimmer. In fact, a sizable portion of the enemy army shimmered as well. Then, the mist dragon and several patches of Pravus's soldiers shattered like mirrors of light and disappeared from the battlefield. Then more of Pravus's army met the same fate. A few minutes more and the bone and ice dragons shattered into shards of light and disappeared as well, along with four fifths of Pravus's forces. Despite the victory, their numbers were still staggering, but it still warranted celebration.

"You've done it, Father!" The word father sounded strange from his lips but calling him Nardus or Cyrus seemed even stranger.

Nardus leaned against the top of the wall and took a deep breath. "Pravus must have some source of energy, otherwise he'd never be able to conjure such an elaborate illusion."

Cheers erupted across the top of the wall.

"Good job, Nardus," said Prince Rictar. "You've given our forces more hope."

"Agreed," said Alderan. "We have a reprieve for the moment, but Morcinda won't be able to control the water for much longer." He sighed deep. "When the water wall falls, Elatos will surely go with it."

"True." Prince Rictar turned to one of his soldiers. "Aren, you, Eshtak, and Calen need to start the evacuation of Elatos at once."

"Yes, my prince." Aren gathered Calen and Eshtak and escorted them down from the wall.

Alderan surveyed the battlefield beyond the water wall. "Now what—"

Rayah's voice entered Alderan's head and interrupted him. *"Alderan… help us."* Her voice came through weak and distraught. Flashes of blood and knives bombarded his mind for a few seconds and then everything faded, including her presence.

Alderan grabbed the sides of his head and pulled on his hair. "Rayah!"

"What's happening?" Concern lined Nardus's brow.

Tears blurred Alderan's vision. "She can't die. I won't let her." His body tingled with mezhik. Nardus reached for him, but then he no longer stood atop the great wall.

CHAPTER FORTY-FOUR

A brilliant white light roused Rayah. She tried to sit up, but every muscle and bone in her body ached, especially the right side of her face. As she became more alert, she realized she couldn't see out of her right eye at all.

"Relax, my love."

Rayah knew that voice but couldn't place it. In fact, she couldn't place herself either. The last thing she remembered was a barge ride across the river.

Blonde locks draped over Rayah's face, and light shocks twinged the right side of her face. "What's happening?"

"I'm healing you. Keep still."

It'd been a while since she'd felt the touch of mezhik and had forgotten the way it shocked her skin with tiny static charges. The ache in her jaw lessened, and light began to reach her right eye. A few minutes later, she could see again, and the handsome young man leaning over her overjoyed her.

"Alderan!"

"The one and only." His brow furrowed further as he concentrated on Rayah's neck. "Ah, there we go."

The shocking sensation ceased and Alderan rose to his feet. Rayah sat up and worked her jaw and neck. No physical pain lingered, but her memories of the fight with Käíeꝫ flooded her mind and brought her to tears.

Alderan made quick work healing Rakzar, Urza, and Ridan but made no move to heal Normak.

Rayah got to her feet and wiped her face. "You still need to heal Normak. What are you waiting for?"

The others stood around Normak but said nothing. She stormed over to the circle and was about to demand answers, but Normak's gaping mouth and dead-eyed stare stole her breath.

"Dear Ꝫätur!" Rayah fell on her knees and touched Normak's cheek. His cold skin sent waves of grief through her. Despite his inappropriate advances and lewd comments, she'd grown fond of him. He'd saved her life more than once.

Rayah stood back up and embraced Ridan. She repeated "I'm sorry" over and over, but the young dwarf showed no emotion. Instead, she shoved Rayah away and knelt at Normak's feet.

It took Rayah a moment to realize that Ridan was removing Normak's boots. It made sense. She probably would've done the same had it been Alderan.

Once Ridan finished removing the boots she looked up at Rayah. "Will you bury him?"

Rayah nodded solemnly. "Absolutely, but shouldn't his body be taken back to Tectus?"

"Once I've settled the score with those orcs, I'll come back for him," said Ridan.

"What score?" asked Urza.

Ridan glanced toward Rakzar. "You said that the orc leader, Murtag, commanded Käíeʒ to curse you, right?"

"Yeah." Rakzar physically tensed.

"Then it's him I'm going after." Ridan took the boots and stuffed them into a large, leather saddlebag on Bakkan's back. "I won't rest until he's dead."

"Fair enough," said Urza.

Rakzar dragged Normak's body away from the shoreline and to a spot with more sand than rock. Rayah sank into the sand and pulled Normak's body down with her as far as she could. Despite his small stature, Normak weighed a ton. Satisfied she'd done what she could, she rose back out of the sand. Ridan marked the grave with two grayish-white stones.

Godspeed, Normak, and may Ʒäṭūr's light shine upon you.

"Thank you." Ridan looked north. "Now, those bastards will pay." She mounted Bakkan, dug her heels into his ribs, and they took off up the shoreline.

"I'm going with her." Rakzar dropped on all fours and took off after Ridan.

Urza reached down and squeezed Rayah's shoulder. "I can't let my brother fight alone."

Rayah nodded. "I understand."

"Be safe, my friend." She lunged forward and onto all fours and soon disappeared into the distance.

Rayah wrapped her arms around Alderan's waist. "I don't know how you found us, but I thank ʕäʈūr that you did."

Alderan shrugged. "You called for me and somehow I wound up here."

"You must've teleported here, and then you healed us all." She hugged him harder. "Have you finally learned how to use your mezhik?"

"No, I just knew I couldn't let you all die. It's all I thought about. The mezhik just flowed from my hands." He kissed the top of her head.

Rayah gasped and pulled away. "I almost forgot that the orcs are headed to attack Vallah. I must warn them!"

"Drat!" Alderan pulled on his hair. "Most of their forces have gone down to Elatos. They're not prepared for a ground attack."

Rayah grabbed his hand. "Then we'd better get back and warn them."

"You go, Rayah. You're much faster than I am." He shook her hand away. "I'll be right behind you."

"Can you teleport over there?" she asked.

Alderan shrugged. "How?"

"I don't know. Maybe you could just think about being at the city gates and take a step toward them."

Alderan faced Vallah. His eyes narrowed, and the left side of his face rose as he sneered. He took a step forward but remained on the beach. He grumbled, "This isn't working, and we're wasting time. Just go!"

The last thing Rayah wanted was to separate herself from him again, but she knew he was right. Vallah must be warned as soon as possible.

She fluttered off the ground and kissed Alderan on the lips. "I love you!"

"Love you, too." His tone sounded dejected.

Rayah wanted to stay and lift his spirits but didn't have the time. Instead, she turned and flew toward Vallah.

ʕäʈūr, let me get there before the orcs do.

CHAPTER FORTY-FIVE

Savric and Zerenity stood atop the King's Palace. Smoke rose far to the south, and the sight of it disheartened him. It wouldn't be long before Elatos itself burned.

Ɂäṭūr, watch over Calen and Eshtak. Keep them safe for me.

Zerenity moved close and rested her hand over his on the railing. He fought the urge to flick it away. His mind still warred with his heart over her actions while under Cinolth's influence. The thought of what Qotan might be doing in Cinolth's name weighed heavy on him as well.

"Look at me, Savvy." Her voice trembled.

He turned toward her with reluctance and a deep sigh. "What is it I am supposed to see?"

Zerenity squeezed his hand. "Tell me I'm not the love of your life. Tell me you no longer love me. I need closure before we head into battle. This might be the end for one or both of us. Have you not thought of that?"

So many years later, wrinkles and all, her beauty still took his breath away. Given their history and the way he'd accused her of mistreating Qotan for so long, he had no self-righteous ground to stand upon. Her smile and the tears glistening in her eyes broke down the walls he'd erected around his heart. His anger toward her dissipated, and urgency tugged at his heart.

"Reni..." His voice shook almost as much as his hands. "...nothing and no one will ever take your place in my heart. As usual, I have been a fool. I know your heart, and I know you. The actions you took while entranced by Cinolth were ones I know you would never make on your own. Please forgive this old fool."

Zerenity rose on her tippy-toes and kissed Savric. "There is nothing to forgive, darling. Knowing you are fighting at my side strengthens me." She glanced to her right, and her eyes bulged. "Cinolth's nearly here!" She pulled Savric's arm with such force that it nearly took him to the ground.

"Feathers, woman," grumbled Savric. He rubbed his arm. "I still have eyes and need of my arm."

"Then what are you waiting for?" she asked.

Savric ignored her and drew upon his mezhik and that which was stored in the bracelet Nardus gave him. With all his strength, he slammed the butt-end of Qotan's staff down onto the palace roof and shouted, *"Ɂzhäälld əllíţ!"*

A brilliant, yellow light shot up from the staff's orb, about fifty feet in the air, and began spreading outward in an ever-expanding circle. Cinolth roared and spewed a column of fire toward the lowest section of Vallah, but Savric's light shield managed to reach that point just before the fire did. The shield held and absorbed the fire, but Savric felt the effects of the attack all the way down to his toes. With the bracelet, he'd be able to keep the shield active for a solid week, but every blast of fire would eat into that time. Barring a miracle, Vallah would eventually fall.

Ɂäţūr, we are counting on You to save us.

† † †

Zerenity found Druden in front of the palace watching the sky. She walked up next to him. "It's time."

Druden twisted his long mustache between his fingers and thumbs. "So it is."

"How close do you need to be to the water?" she asked.

"With this?" He thumbed the bracelet Nardus had given him. It barely fit on his thick wrist. "Here's good. Any closer, and we'd be vulnerable. Not to mention that it'd be harder to track Cinolth."

"Agreed. Have you ever combined your mezhik with someone else's before?"

Druden shook his head. "Nope. Never crossed my mind to do such a thing."

"Then I will guide us." She closed her eyes for a moment and took a long breath.

He pulled the sleeves of his robes up to his elbows. "What do you want me to do?"

"Start conjuring the water titan, and I will intertwine my mezhik with yours and strengthen the water titan with vines of seaweed."

Druden cleared his throat, pointed his hands toward Trivers Lake, and began drawing runes in the air with his fingers.

The calm surface of Trivers Lake began churning. Waves formed and crashed, and then two columns of water began to rise from it.

Zerenity moved closer, placed one hand on Druden's shoulder, and began drawing runes of her own. The warmth of mezhik filled her, and she began pushing it through Druden's shoulder and into the runes he continued to draw. A dark mass moved beneath the columns of water and started twisting and climbing up through the middle of them.

As her own energy waned, she began drawing upon the energy stored in her bracelet.

Ɂäṭūr, guide our hands.

† † †

From the corner of his eye, Rakzar glimpsed something rising out of the lake but didn't have time to see what it was. Losing even a second of focus would guarantee his failure to catch Ridan.

"Ridan, wait!" yelled Rakzar. He wasn't sure she'd hear him over the increasing roar of water.

The dwarf girl's stubbornness nearly matched his. She looked back but didn't slow as she reached the mouth of the Hotah River. He pushed himself harder and gained ground on Bakkan, but the mastiff seemed to have boundless energy. If he didn't catch them soon, he never would.

Urza bolted past him, and it spurred his anger. How could she outrun him after being so sick and sluggish of late? The answer hit him and nearly tumbled him to the ground.

Killing Käíeɀ must've worked!

Relief washed over him, and the burden he'd carried for weeks fell away. Suddenly, he didn't feel so tired and worn out. He lowered his head and ran faster, overtaking Urza and closing the distance to Bakkan and Ridan. Five more strides, and he'd catch them. Lunging forward, he caught Bakkan's hind legs. The three of them crashed to the ground and tumbled a good ten feet before coming to a stop.

Ridan moved quick, jumping to her feet and wielding her spear. She had it pointed at Rakzar's face before he had a chance to get to his feet. "I will kill ya if ya try and stop me."

Rakzar held up his hand. "Listen to me, Ridan. I want Murtag dead more than you can imagine, but storming into a horde of orcs will do nothing but get you killed."

"Ya think I care about death?" She spat on the ground. "That thing back there took away the only person I've ever loved. I've nothing left to live for except vengeance."

"And what about Torbrek? I saw the way you looked at him."

Urza caught up and slid to a stop, her eyes wide. "Look across the river! The orcs are storming Vallah as we speak."

Ridan and Rakzar both turned toward the east. The orcs had fashioned crude ladders and used rope and grappling hooks to scale the tall, white walls. What looked like only a few dozen soldiers fought to fend them off.

Rayah came zooming up to the three of them. "We're too late!"

Rakzar peered down the shore. Rayah had come alone. "Where's the White Knight?"

"On his way, but he's much slower than we are."

"Maybe he should've taken the boots," said Urza.

"Over my dead body." Ridan glared at the three of them. "The orcs attacking Vallah changes nothing. I'm still going after them and will kill as many as I can." She mounted Bakkan.

"We're all going," said Rayah. "Let's get back to the barge and get across the river."

Rakzar had little hope of Ridan and Rayah surviving for long, but he and Urza couldn't be killed by the orcs because of the blood bond Pravus created between gnolls and orcs, so at least there was that.

But I can't let them die.

Ridan dug her heels into Bakkan's sides, and they took off again. Urza and Rayah followed her.

Rakzar waited a few moments to see if Amicus would make an appearance, but he never did.

"Figures." Rakzar took off after Bakkan and the three girls.

† † †

Aria shot two fireballs into the light shield as she mindspoke with Cinolth, *"There's no way that old wizard will be able to keep that light shield up for long. Keep attacking it."*

Cinolth banked back around. *"We've got a bigger problem."*

A watery fist slammed into his underbelly. They plummeted several dozen feet before Cinolth recovered. Aria turned and focused her mezhik on the massive water beast standing in the lake. It must've been a hundred feet tall.

Aria's eyes bulged. *"What in Centauria is that?"*

"A water titan, but there's something different about it. That watery punch was far stronger than it should've been."

"What kind of mezhik should I use against it?"

Cinolth circled the beast and avoided several swipes from its massive fists before answering. *"Perhaps we can boil the water below its knees with my fire and your fireballs—"*

"—and literally sever its legs." Aria finished.

"Yes."

Cinolth dove toward the water titan's feet, and Aria readied several fireballs.

CHAPTER FORTY-SIX

Pravus still raged over Cyrus. Everything he did to bolster their numbers and strike fear in the hearts of their enemies had been thwarted far too quickly. Not only that, but it'd cost him most of his energy. Thankfully, he knew the secret to replenish it quickly. It was the only thing he'd learned from Cinolth.

He called two soldiers over and drained the life from them with nothing more than a simple touch. The soldiers fell to the ground in a heap, nothing more than husks of human skin and bone encased in armor. His strength restored, Pravus mounted his horse and rode toward the wall of water.

Cinolth's legion of infected drove right into the wall of water that separated them from the great wall of Elatos, driven by the madness of their master. Many of them drown within the first fifteen feet, their bodies ejected from the water wall. He assumed that some of them made it through, but they'd certainly be picked off on the other side. Not having any control over them frustrated him.

Mindless sacks of flesh.

A few of the wizards engineered tunnels through the water wall using earth, air, and ice, but each of them collapsed within a few minutes of being built. They'd have to wait out whatever force kept the water wall suspended. It wouldn't be long. The amount of energy a feat like the water wall would take left him wondering who had that kind of power aside from Cyrus.

Have we underestimated our enemy?

Minutes later, the water wall came crashing down with a thunderous roar, taking a thousand soldiers and creatures with it as it dispersed back into the Hotah River. The army surged forward through the receding waters and reached the great wall within minutes. Arrows rained down on them, but dozens of strategic strikes with fireballs scorched the defenders and set the wall ablaze. A fairly dry winter had left the great wall parched and ripe for fire.

Credan rode up next to Pravus. The older man looked ridiculous atop a horse. "Everything is progressing according to plan, my lord. I've ordered the men to ditch most of the siege equipment since it seems we won't be needing it."

"Good."

With the raging fire weakening the wall and eight giants using a massive, felled tree as a battering ram, the large gates stood no chance of holding. A loud crack of wood confirmed it. The gates shuddered with each strike and finally buckled. Two more blows busted them open. Steel met steel once again, and the sounds of war rose to match that of the raging fire.

Pravus cracked his knuckles. "Elatos will burn to the ground within the hour, and the Three Kingdoms will become the Two Kingdoms."

"Yes, my lord," confirmed Credan. "Victory is all but guaranteed."

Pravus flexed his hand and made a fist.

I am becoming a god.

† † †

When the water wall came down, the hope of saving Elatos fell with it. Nardus stood on the harbor with Theyn and Prince Rictar, his focus directed across the lake. With the water titan risen and the light shield erected over Vallah, Cinolth and Aria had their hands full. Soon, they'd have him to contend with as well.

Thanks to Aren, Calen, and Eshtak, the evacuation of Elatos was well underway.

"What do we do now?" asked Theyn.

"I must go face Cinolth." Nardus touched her face and stroked her cheek.

Theyn leaned into his hand and kissed it. A smile curled her lips. "You mean 'we.'"

He shook his head. "No, I must go alone."

Her smile faded. "And what am I supposed to do?"

"You can stay here and fight or you can head to Borza and make sure Berggren and Niesha are evacuating the people there." He could tell she didn't like his answer, and he knew why. "Look, Theyn. You must learn to trust yourself when you're away from me. And you also need to practice your shifting. Now is as good of a time to do that as any."

Theyn growled deep in her throat. "If I lose myself again, I'm going to take it out on you when you find me."

"Deal." Nardus kissed her.

She turned to Prince Rictar. "What's the quickest route to Borza?"

"Cross the bridge to the other side of Elatos and follow the road along the shoreline. It leads straight there."

"Thanks." Theyn took Nardus's hands and kissed him goodbye. "Don't go getting yourself killed while I'm gone."

Nardus touched his forehead to hers. "Not possible. You've seen the future."

Their fingers lingered together for several seconds, and then Theyn headed toward the bridge. Using his mezhik, Nardus called forth a mighty griffin that lived in the western Orbis Mountains. A few minutes later, the majestic creature swooped down from the sky and landed before him. Half lion and half eagle, the beast would've scared most people. Prince Rictar didn't back away.

"My word, that's a beautiful creature," exclaimed Prince Rictar.

"To be certain. I must go and do what I can to stop Cinolth. I fear Elatos will fall soon. Fall back as soon as it's evident."

Prince Rictar clasped Nardus's arm. "We will. Be careful."

Nardus nodded and set his sights on the griffin. Through his mind, he connected with the creature and learned its name through a series of images.

Nardus patted the griffin's feathery neck. "Streak it is."

He hopped on Streak's back, and Streak took to the sky in effortless fashion. Using his mind, he directed Streak toward the north end of the lake where Cinolth and Aria battled the water titan. The fearless creature darted north.

I'm coming for you, you scaly bastard.

† † †

Calen thought the time he'd been captured by the zheballin was the scariest of his life, but it paled in comparison to his current situation. Fire burned the great wall and blackened the sky with plumes of smoke. The citizens of Elatos ran around in a panic, none of them knowing what to do or where to go. Trying to direct tens of thousands of them toward the temple on the west side of Elatos proved extremely difficult.

"There's an underground tunnel that leads to the stronghold," shouted Calen. Aren, the soldier Prince Rictar sent with him and Eshtak, shouted and directed people as well, but their efforts seemed futile.

A thunderous explosion shook the ground and rocked the city. Everyone around stopped where they were, shocked by the sound. The great wall had fallen. Calen shook his head to snap himself out of the shock and started directing people toward the temple again. This time, the people listened. Word of the plan spread throughout Elatos like wildfire and soon droves of them entered the temple and the tunnel below it.

"Go with them," shouted Aren. "They will need someone strong to keep them calm."

Calen blinked. Had Aren just called him strong? As absurd as it sounded in his head, the compliment steeled his heart and swelled his chest. "What about you?" he asked Aren.

"I will stay here and continue to direct people to the temple until the enemy is upon us. Then, and only then, I will enter the tunnel and trigger the mechanism that will destroy the temple and bury the tunnel entrance."

"And what if you're killed before you can get to the tunnel?" asked Calen.

"If it comes down to that, gods help us all." Aren put his right fist over his heart. "Now go, soldier."

Calen returned the salute, and then he and Eshtak joined the throng down in the tunnel. Yellow stones lined the walls and filled the tunnel with their ambient light. Torches would've created toxic smoke and fumes in such a confined space, so the stones made perfect sense.

As scared as he was, Calen found his mind wandering toward their destination. He had no idea what to expect of an underground stronghold. In fact, he'd never heard of one before. With so many people heading there without the time to gather their belongings, he prayed that someone had stocked the stronghold with food, blankets, and other provisions.

And weapons.

CHAPTER FORTY-SEVEN

Vallah should've been burning by now, but the water titan proved a formidable foe. Aria held on tight as Cinolth continued to evade its attacks. Nothing they tried seemed to work against the beast. With the lake being such a vast resource, she and Cinolth didn't have the combined strength to boil away enough water to even make a dent in a single leg, let alone two.

She also couldn't figure out how the beast hadn't even begun to fall apart. The energy it had to take to conjure and maintain such a beast seemed impossible. To the south, she saw that more than half of Elatos burned. The thought of Pravus relishing such a victory sickened her.

"We need to do something different," she mindspoke to Cinolth.

"Agreed."

An ice ball the size of a large boulder slammed into Cinolth's side. The surprise strike sent him careening right into the water titan's arcing fist.

Thwack!

Tendrils of seaweed shot out from the water titan's fist, ensnared Aria, and ripped her from Cinolth's back.

Dazed by the two strikes, Cinolth plummeted straight into the lake.

Aria summoned fire and burned the seaweed that held her, and then she called upon the wind to catch her and suspend her in the air. She looked for the source of the ice ball and found Nardus riding on a griffin. They circled around the spot where Cinolth had plunged into the water.

Cinolth mindspoke to Aria, *"Leave Cyrus to me. Go find the wizard conjuring the water titan and kill them."*

"They will not live for long."

Aria flew toward the northern shore and the white walls of Vallah.

† † †

The light shield still held, but the attacks from Cinolth and Aria had drained more energy from the bracelet than Savric had wanted. Apparently, dragon's fire was quite strong. So was Aria's mezhik for that matter. Druden and Zerenity did well defending Vallah from Cinolth and managed to separate Aria from him just as Nardus had wanted, but it seemed like that was the only thing going well.

"What in the high heavens is happening?"

Savric turned to see King Zaridus approaching. "My king."

"Where are my son and daughter? I've searched the entire palace and haven't found them." His glare burned with fire.

"Prince Rictar is in Elatos, and Princes Zelanora is helping evacuate Vallah."

King Zaridus's face turned several shades redder and fringed upon a purplish hue. "Was I not clear last night? Did I somehow misspeak? I said no one was to leave Vallah."

Savric nodded. "Your words were quite clear. Everyone at that table understood that you cared only for your own hide." King Zaridus looked like he might explode, but Savric continued, "However, your son and daughter do not share your self-preservation. They made their own decisions."

"Everything I do is for their sake, not mine!" The man shook with rage, and saliva dripped from his lips. "All of you will hang for this!"

"I understand your rage, but you brought this upon yourself. I warned you long ago about an impending war, and you laughed at me and kicked me out of your palace. Had you heeded my warning, much of this could have been avoided. As it is, I am the only thing standing between you and certain death. Have some dignity and show me some respect. Be the king that the people need, not some coward afraid of his own shadow."

King Zaridus marched over to the balcony railing and gasped. "Elatos is nearly gone! What of my son? What of Prince Rictar?" He fell to his knees.

Savric held his tongue. No words would change what had been done.

† † †

Smoke rose from far below and drew Zerenity's attention. The light shield continued to hold, and they'd succeeded in knocking Aria from Cinolth, so what had caused the fires below? She withdrew her mezhik and released Druden's shoulder.

"Something's happening at the lowest level of the city. I'm going to go check it out."

Druden nodded, his eyes never leaving the water titan. "I can handle the dragon, especially with the help of Nardus."

"Good. I'll be back as soon as I can." Zerenity spun around and teleported down to the main street on the first level of Vallah.

Fires burned in several shops and homes, and hay wagons blazed. Soldiers wearing the king's sigil lay everywhere, their blood spilled upon the road. As far as she could tell, none of them were citizens. Princess Zelanora must've done a good job evacuating them. A stench she couldn't quite identify hung in the air.

Zerenity teleported up to the city's second level. Someone called her name as soon as she appeared. She turned around and saw Rayah flying toward her. Urza and another gnoll came running up the road as well, followed by a dwarf riding a large dog.

"The orcs are here!" cried Rayah.

"Orcs?" It explained the stench she couldn't identify.

"They came from the north," said Urza.

"We must defend Druden and keep them from reaching the King's Palace," said Zerenity.

Zerenity stumbled forward, and pain erupted in her right shoulder. "Auh!" A crude arrowhead punctured her robes and blood flowed from the wound it'd caused.

"Take cover!" yelled Rakzar.

† † †

The water titan held Cinolth underneath the water, but its strength weakened significantly when the seaweed died off. Nardus gathered sand and rock from the lake bottom and piled it on top of Cinolth but knew it wouldn't hold the beast down for long. He circled and waited and readied another assault.

The water titan stumbled backward, and Cinolth shot out of the water, right for Nardus and Streak.

Nardus loosed fireballs and struck the beast with bolts of lightning but hadn't anticipated the counterattack.

Cinolth flew dangerously close and hurled a large boulder at Streak. Streak didn't have time to dodge it and took the blow square in the head.

Nardus hovered in place using air mezhik as Streak fell from the sky and splashed into the water below.

Enraged, he pummeled Cinolth with ice shards, but they didn't slow the dragon down.

Cinolth roared and shot a column of fire at Nardus. The flames didn't touch him, but they disrupted the air Nardus stood upon. He crashed into the water and Cinolth dove after him, but the water titan batted Cinolth away.

Nardus rose to the water's surface. Cinolth stood on the western shore and shook off the strike from the water titan. Nardus loosed hundreds of massive icicles at Cinolth, but the beast melted them with fire and took to the sky just before the water titan stomped on him.

Nardus felt his energy getting low. He didn't know how much longer he could battle Cinolth. The beast proved far stronger than he remembered.

It must be because of the bond he shares with Shanara.

Given Cinolth's strength, he would never be able to defeat the dragon in such a battle. However, all he needed to do for now was distract Cinolth long enough to save as many people as possible.

Cinolth came hard and fast, wings back and head narrowed. Nardus stood his ground atop the water and braced for impact. At the last possible moment, Nardus turned the water's surface into a thick layer of ice and teleported a hundred yards back.

Cinolth had no chance of pulling up or blasting the ice with fire and hit it with a sick thud. The water titan followed up with a fist to Cinolth's head. The ice cracked, split open, and swallowed Cinolth.

Nardus poured his mezhik into the lake, freezing a sizable portion of it solid. It would hold Cinolth for a little while.

† † †

A loud clanging of metal drew Alderan's attention to Vallah's city gates. Mangled and ripped from their hinges, they laid on the road in a heap. He didn't need a closer look to see that the woman who caused the damage was Aria. With bare hands, she tore soldiers apart. The sight sickened him, and anger swelled in his chest.

"Aria!" he screamed, knowing she'd never hear him from across the lake or with the deafening roar of the water generated by the water titan.

Aria entered the city, and he needed to act. In a single step, Alderan moved from the western shoreline of Trivers Lake to a blood-stained road inside Vallah's city gates. Aria climbed the steep road ahead of him.

"Stop!" yelled Alderan. The road in front of Aria cracked and groaned and rose to form a wall.

She turned and faced him, mezhik crackling and arcing between her fingers. "Stay out of this, brother." Her words slurred with rage; the usual green of her eyes glowed a menacing red.

He took a step toward her, his arms spread wide. "This isn't you."

"Stay out of my way." A concussive pulse of air shot from Aria's hand. The blast hit him in the chest, took him from his feet, and drove him into the road. His head snapped back and cracked against the hard stone. A groan slipped through his lips, and his vision doubled. When he tried to sit up his head pulsed with pain. Aria's menacing face faded as the darkness pulled him into its clutches.

CHAPTER FORTY-EIGHT

Berggren thanked Zhedäz Zun that Borza was significantly smaller than Vallah and Elatos. Only about forty-five thousand people lived within its paper-thin walls. However, he hadn't expected to find the escape tunnel that led to the stronghold completely filled in and inaccessible. From the looks of it, someone had collapsed it recently. A few minutes time gave him the answer to the mystery. The city magistrate and her council were gone.

The unforeseen circumstance left them with three equally bad options. They could stay and help the measly Borza City Guard defend the city, they could flee up into the Reis'Duron Grasslands, or they could scatter into the Orbis Mountains. As an outsider, he had no say in what the people should do, so he gave them their options.

None of the people elected to hang back and help the city guard. That didn't surprise Berggren in the least. The majority of the people decided to head for the mountains. Some would cross the Tamda River and head into the northern Orbis Mountains while the others would go south and into the southeastern Orbis Mountains. The handful left would also cross the Tamda River and head northeast, toward the Reis'Duron Grasslands.

Berggren took Niesha's hand and peered down at her. "Given the choice, what would you do?"

She gritted her teeth and raised a small fist. "I say we stay and fight!"

Berggren snorted. "Figured you'd say that. That's why you're not in charge."

"Nothing scares me." She chewed on her lower lip.

"Shh," said Berggren.

Geographically speaking, Borza was an anomaly. The bowl-shaped city rose on a slight plateau around its edge and plummeted a good fifteen feet at its center. From Berggren's vantage on the western end of the city, he witnessed the beginning of what he knew would be a slaughter on its east end. It didn't take long for the cries of terror, screams of death, clashes of steel, and guttural, bone-chilling howls to reach them.

A thousand gnolls descended on the people.

Niesha stood on her tippy toes and craned her neck. "What's happening, big man?"

Berggren swept Niesha into his arms and over his shoulder. "Gnolls." He lumbered toward the docks.

"What are gnolls?" Her voice vibrated.

"Massive, wolf-like creatures that can walk on their hind legs and talk."

"Not gonna lie. That sounds interesting."

Berggren shook his head. "Except that they have no regard for life."

She patted his back. "What are we going to do about it?"

"Run. It's the only thing that might save our lives."

Berggren skidded to a halt. Smoke and flames rose from the docks ahead. The roads crawled with gnolls every direction he looked.

"Damn," growled Berggren. He and Niesha had no choice but to hole up somewhere and defend themselves. The only question that remained was where.

She squirmed in his arms. "What now?"

"Be still, Niesha. I need to think."

"We both know I'm the brains of this operation." She managed to squirt out of his arms and landed hard on her feet. "That's better."

Berggren wiped beads of sweat from the top of his head. "We need somewhere to hide."

Niesha grabbed his hand and yanked but Berggren didn't budge. "Follow me!"

Berggren looked around. "Where to?"

"The temple." She yanked on his arm harder. "I've never been in one that didn't have catacombs. We can hide in one of those dead person things."

"Sarcophagus."

She smiled. "Yeah! Kinda surprised you know such a big word."

"Funny." He picked her up and headed toward the beige, three-story temple that stood right in the middle of the city.

† † †

Flames engulfed a good portion of Borza by the time Theyn reached the city's edge. Howls and screams filled the air and prickled her skin. With caution, she approached what remained of the western gates. Beyond them, ungodly beasts chased people down and ripped them to shreds. She imagined that's what it had looked like when she'd been the ungodly beast in West Hotah. The thought terrified and sickened her.

Seeing the carnage, she knew she stood no chance of going in as a human. As a large cat, they might leave her alone. Her hands trembled with fear as the thought of losing herself again weighed on her mind. If she did nothing and Berggren hadn't escaped through the tunnel, she'd never forgive herself.

Just do it, Theyn. Like Nardus showed you.

With a deep breath, she reached within herself and released the beast from within its tiny box in her mind. The shift took only seconds. She prayed to Zhedäꝛ Ɔʊn that she'd find Berggren in time and that her form would keep the beasts from attacking her.

She entered the city and started searching for Berggren's scent. She knew it well. It didn't take long for her to pick up on it, and she followed it into the heart of the city.

Take care of that girl, Father. I'm coming for you both.

CHAPTER FORTY-NINE

King Zaridus's forces had come to Elatos in thirty massive ships but Pravus watched them sail away in just one with a hundred men at most. Prince Rictar was among those who retreated, but it wouldn't be long before Vallah fell as well. Two facts perplexed Pravus: the water titan still protected Vallah, and the light shield remained over the city.

Looks like I must do everything.

The thought aroused his pride. He relished watching Cinolth struggle. Thinking of Cinolth made him wonder what had happened to Käíeƨ. Had she disobeyed his order to come to Elatos, or did she get delayed somewhere? He didn't doubt her loyalty, so it had to be the latter.

Elatos still burned at his back, and little of the city remained. By the time he and his army reached the north shore of the lake, the city would be nothing but ashes. Already, the majority of his army marched along the western shoreline.

In his haste, Prince Rictar had failed to torch all the ships he left behind. Two remained untouched and would set sail in a few minutes. Pravus would be on one of them.

Cinolth's minions butchered everyone who opposed them, but Pravus had made clear to his army to take prisoners when possible. After all, what good would it do to rule the realm without subjects? Even so, he had little faith that the orcs and gnolls would exercise such restraint in Borza and Vallah.

Not counting the fallen soldiers on both sides of the skirmish, fewer than twenty thousand had died or been captured in Elatos. Given its population, that number seemed quite low. The city must've evacuated somewhere while the water wall held him and his army back. It made little difference though. Once King Zaridus and his two children hung from Vallah's walls, the people would fall upon their knees and worship him.

I am the god they've always sought.

Credan approached and bowed low. "We are ready to sail, my lord."

"Excellent."

From his vantage, Pravus couldn't quite tell if smoke rose to the northeast, where Borza stood. If not, it soon would. He turned his gaze toward the water titan. Confidence swelled in his chest as he envisioned himself taking it down.

If it still stands when we arrive on the other side, I will take care of it myself.

He followed Credan to the lead ship and boarded it. "Set sail," he commanded.

In his mind, Pravus altered the small fleet of ships, making them invisible. Tapping into his mezhik, he brought the illusion to life. Still, a chance remained of the titan sensing them or crushing them as it continued to battle Cinolth and Aria.

If he were not a god himself, he might've prayed to one for safe passage.

CHAPTER FIFTY

Zerenity hunkered down in the side alley along with Rakzar, Urza, Ridan, Bakkan, and Rayah. The orcs had them surrounded. Rakzar had removed the arrow from her shoulder, but the wound continued to bleed no matter how much mezhik she poured into it. To worsen matters, the wound affected her abilities as well. She tried to conjure a fireball, but it fizzled out in her palm almost as quickly as it had burst with life.

Orcs were known to use poisons and mezhik derk on their arrows and weapons so that even a minor flesh wound could kill an enemy target if not treated. Either could also disrupt one's mezhik, as it had hers. Given her knowledge as Fizärd Näíţ₂zhär, she just needed to find the right herb. Easier said than done in their current predicament though.

"Come on out, little dog," called Murtag. "I promise your death will be quick once Lord Rosai arrives."

The one saving grace afforded them was the deep-rooted hate Murtag had for Rakzar. His presence alone kept the entire orc army occupied and the king safe for a while longer. Murtag wouldn't leave without capturing him.

Ridan clutched her spear. "I'm tired of standing here twiddling my thumbs when I could be sending more of those filthy pigs to *Ef Demd Dhä*."

The young dwarf was a firecracker. She reminded Zerenity of herself when she'd been as young. "Kill one or two of them now and face your own death, or show restraint now and live to see them all die later. The choice is yours, darling."

"What difference does it make? We're all dead if we just stay here."

"I've got a plan," said Urza, "but no one's going to like it."

"Does it involve getting killed?" growled Rakzar.

Urza shrugged. "All depends on the blood bond."

"Let's have it then," said Ridan.

† † †

Rakzar had to admit that Urza's plan could work. The two of them just needed to distract the horde long enough for Rayah to fly up the road to the herb shop and find the items Zerenity needed. Once healed, Zerenity could teleport them one at a time to safety. Assuming she had enough power left in her bracelet. If not, it could kill her and whoever she tried to teleport with.

He and Urza walked to the end of the alley and faced the horde of orcs. Murtag's worthless mug stared them both down. Rakzar returned the glare.

"Imagine my surprise to find you here, dog." Snot dripped from Murtag's porcine nose. "I knew you were heartless but cursing an entire city with your presence rivals my own ruthlessness."

"We're nothing alike," said Rakzar. "Käíeż lies in a pool of her own blood on the western shore of Trivers Lake, and her curse died with her."

"Die, pig!" Ridan's spear flew at Murtag's face.

Damn you, Ridan!

Murtag easily sidestepped the attack and caught the spear. Ridan charged ahead, but Urza caught her by the hood of her cloak and pulled her back.

One of the larger orcs grunted and shot an arrow right at Ridan's chest. Rakzar had a single instant to contemplate whether or not the blood bond actually worked and thought about just letting the arrow kill Ridan, but Amicus's memory wouldn't allow it. He wouldn't allow it.

Rakzar dove in front of Ridan. The arrow pierced his left temple and hammered the inside of his skull. He dropped to the ground in a heap, the pain unbearable. When he looked up, Amicus stood over him with a smile.

"What?" Rakzar growled.

"Now you know what you would've done for me, given the chance. You've done well, my friend. Very well." A bright light overtook Amicus. "You don't need me anymore!"

"Wait, Shadowman!" The light faded, and with it the pain. Urza stood over him.

The orc who shot the arrow dropped dead, his own arrow buried in his skull.

Rakzar got back to his feet and glared at Murtag. "Need I remind you filthy pigs that hurting one of us only hurts yourselves?"

"Noted." He motioned several of the orcs forward. "Keep them occupied. We've got more city to ransack and women to rape."

"Master," said one of the orcs.

Murtag turned. "What now?"

The orc handed Murtag a book. "A message from Lord Rosai."

Murtag's expression hardened as he read the message. Finished, he handed the book back to the orc. He glared at Rakzar. "Today's your lucky day, dog. Soon, your lucky days will run out." Murtag turned to his horde. "Move out."

"That's right. Run when your master calls," mocked Rakzar.

Urza grabbed his arm. "This is our only chance to escape. Let's not squander it."

They returned to the alleyway, and Rakzar helped Zerenity to her feet. "Time to get you healed."

† † †

Savric plead with the king for a good twenty minutes to evacuate the palace, but the man was beyond stubborn. King Zaridus reminded him of Zerenity in that regard.

He threw his arm up with exasperation. "Look out there. Elatos and Borza have already fallen. I assure you that Vallah will not be far behind."

King Zaridus shook a meaty finger in Savric's face. "My son is still out there fighting, and my daughter is nowhere to be found. I am not leaving, and that is final."

"I'm here, Father."

King Zaridus swung around. "Zelanora!" The surprise on his face turned to anger in a flash. "Why are you still here?"

She folded her arms and scowled. "You ordered that no one be evacuated, and now you question my presence?"

He waved her off. "I don't claim to be of sound mind all the time." When she got closer, he embraced her. "I love you more than this world. You must evacuate at once."

She kissed his cheek. "That's not possible. The tunnel has been sealed."

"You… I… What? Why would you do that?" he stammered.

"We're under attack, Father. Orcs have invaded the lower city. There was no time left. As you know, someone had to seal the tunnel from this side, and I refused to sacrifice even one person for my own sake."

"Give me the name of the soldier who allowed this!" demanded King Zaridus.

Princess Zelanora crossed her arms. "You shall have no names, father. I assured the man that I would enlist the help of a wizard to teleport myself into the stronghold as soon as I made sure you were safe."

Savric smiled. *Thank Ɛäṭūr she is nothing like her father.*

King Zaridus sighed. "You're almost as stubborn as I am."

Thunder shook Vallah and the mountain.

"Dear Ɛäṭūr!" exclaimed Savric.

King Zaridus and Princess Zelanora rushed over to the railing.

"The water titan has fallen back into the lake," confirmed King Zaridus.

"Druden!" exclaimed Princess Zelanora.

"What has happened to him?" asked Savric.

"His body lies in a pool of blood on the stone pathway, and his head is missing." Princess Zelanora backed away from the railing, her face ashen. "A woman with blonde hair streaked with red holds a bloody sword made of ice in her hand."

"Feathers." Savric's heart sank. "Then it is too late." He let the light shield drop and sighed. Facing Aria would buy Nardus a little more time, albeit likely very little, but he had no other options.

King Zaridus knelt at Savric's feet. "Wizard Naphor, I beg you to take my daughter and hide her."

"Stand on your feet, you fool," snapped Savric. He stepped back several steps. "Look around. Where is it that you think she will be safe?"

King Zaridus rose and approached Savric. He leaned down and whispered in Savric's ear, "Take her to the Shattered Realm. No one must know where you're heading. Find a woman there who goes by the name of Korin."

Savric grimaced. "If I leave, you will die this day, and your kingdom will fall."

King Zaridus's icy blue eyes widened as he looked past Savric. "My kingdom has fallen, and I'm already dead."

Savric didn't need to look back. He felt Aria's menacing presence. Instinct told him to shield himself, and he did just in time. The force of Aria's fireballs drove him to the ground. He rolled onto his back and stared into the red eyes of death.

Aria stood over him. "The next shot will go right through your light shield and into your heart." Lightning arced between her fingers and crackled.

The flash scorched the shadows and burst right through Savric's light shield. Thunder rumbled, but the shot stopped short of hitting Savric. Aria stepped back, her eyes wide.

Savric shot a bolt of his own toward Aria, cracking the air, but she'd already been moving and narrowly escaped its deadly strike.

Savric rose to his feet and dusted off his robes. "Has your master taught you nothing?"

The floor quaked, rattling the debris atop it, and the stones began to crack. Savric didn't know what was coming but knew his demise was forthcoming if he just stood there. Princess Zelanora stood to his left and trembled as she reached for her father's arm.

Savric grabbed Princess Zelanora's hand and teleported her and himself away from the King's Palace.

† † †

Prince Rictar's ship had reached the Vallah Harbor moments before the water titan fell. With Morcinda's help, Nardus knew they'd survived the tsunami created by the sudden downpour of water. Then the light shield had faded. Those two events alone didn't bode well for King Zaridus. And then Cinolth burst from Trivers Lake, his scales red-hot. Steam plumed from his body as the remaining ice Nardus had encased him in melted off.

Unleashing his wrath, Cinolth spewed a dozen columns of fire at the lower three levels of Vallah. From where he stood, Nardus felt the heat and witnessed the city walls melting before his eyes. Never had he seen such raw power, and it terrified him.

Nardus teleported over to the Vallah Harbor just in time to see Prince Rictar bid his sister farewell. Morcinda prepped her boat for sailing as Savric and Princess Zelanora climbed aboard. Prince Rictar and what remained of his army raced toward Vallah's city gates. Nothing he could've said would've stopped the man from doing so.

Nardus turned his wrath on Savric. "Where do you think you're headed?"

"I am sorry, Nardus, but our destination cannot be known to anyone. Just know that Princess Zelanora must survive."

This is King Zaridus's doing.

He shook his head and walked away. Moments later, the ship pulled out of the harbor and headed north. Cinolth circled and spewed fire at Nardus and the ship. Morcinda's ship outran Cinolth's fire, and Cinolth gave chase to them. Nardus had no doubt that Cinolth's speed couldn't match that of the aquatic elf.

Using his mind, Nardus called out to Theyn but received no response. His heart panicked even as his mind told him Borza lay fifty miles away, a distance too great even for him. He reached into his pocket and retrieved the last bracelet. With it slipped over his wrist, he turned back just in time to see a massive fireball streaking right at him. Pravus had arrived from Elatos.

Nardus stepped forward and teleported away from Vallah an instant before the fireball struck.

† † †

Pravus fumed. A second or two sooner, and Cyrus would've been dead. Instead, the fireball skidded harmlessly across the sand and died out.

"How many lives does that man possess?" In need of energy once again, Pravus grabbed the nearest soldier and stole the woman's essence. Her energy rushed into his veins and restored him once again.

The rest of the army still marched across the western shoreline of Trivers Lake. It'd be several days before they arrived in Vallah, well after the war ended. All three cities burned. The only thing left to do was kill King Zaridus and his spawn.

Pravus and his men followed Prince Rictar through Vallah's city gates and right into the man's trap. Or so Prince Rictar had thought. In reality, Prince Rictar had been the one who walked into a trap. On his way across the lake, Pravus had contacted Murtag and directed him to set up an ambush for the prince. It'd worked perfectly.

Pravus strolled through the felled gates and right up to Prince Rictar who knelt in front of Murtag. The rest of his men had been executed. To their credit, nearly six dozen orcs lay dead as well. Blood saturated the road and ran down its steep incline.

He looked around. "Where the gods is Käíeƨ?"

"Dead," said Murtag.

Pravus took a deep breath to calm his fury. "Dead? I don't understand. I thought she couldn't be killed."

"Anything living can be killed. She was ambushed by two gnolls and several others on her way to Elatos. That's all I know."

Now how will I kill the dragon?

Pravus gathered himself and bent down in front of Prince Rictar. "Did you really think you'd get the upper hand on me?"

Blood oozed from Prince Rictar's split lower lip and a bruise had already begun to form around his left eye, the tender flesh puffy. He spat blood at Pravus's feet. "Conquering a peaceful people and taking the throne by force doesn't make you a king. You're nothing but a spineless tyrant. Mark my words—the people will rise up."

Pravus backhanded the man. The rage within begged for his blood. But an example must be made. Prince Rictar would hang from the King's Palace rooftop next to his father.

Pravus grabbed the back of Prince Rictar's head and shoved him to the ground. "You will bow when in the presence of a god." He rose and addressed Murtag. "Take him to the King's Palace."

Murtag dipped his head. "Yes, my lord. What would you like us to do with the other one?"

Pravus frowned, duly perplexed. "What other one?"

"Bring him," shouted Murtag. Two orcs dragged a young man forward by his armpits.

Alderan…

Every fiber of his being urged him to take the boy's life or order it done, but doing so would serve no purpose but ensure his own demise. Instead, he retrieved a *ɀäbräɀär* from within the folds of his robes and tossed it to Murtag. "Bring him as well."

Murtag shoved the collar around Alderan's neck and nodded. Several orcs grabbed Prince Rictar and hauled him to his feet.

Pravus took a deep breath and steepled his fingers.

Despite the death of Käíeɀ, this day could hardly get better. Save Cyrus's and Cinolth's deaths.

† † †

Aria paced the King's Palace rooftop. Sixteen men and women lay dead. Each had tried to end her life. Had they known who she was, they would've thought better of such fateful moves.

King Zaridus stood at the railing and watched the Three Kingdoms burn. "Why are you doing this? What have I or any of the people you killed done to you?" He turned and faced her. Blood crusted over the two gashes across his cheeks.

Aria stopped pacing and glared at him. "Do you think the Ancient Realm is unaware of your treatment of the *zhifţäd*? Every year you've reigned over the realm has brought my kind farther down. We will not be oppressed any longer."

King Zaridus stared at his hands for several moments. "I admit that *your* kind—those who possess mezhik that is—have not been welcome in my kingdom for quite some time. But I have good reason for it."

Aria flicked her finger downward and the king yelped. The back of his right ear fell off. Fresh blood ran down his neck and colored his silver hair brown. "There is no excuse for your actions. Furthermore, you utter another word, and I will remove your tongue. Understood?" The old man nodded. He'd aged ten years in the last fifteen minutes.

Aria returned to pacing and reached out to Cinolth with her mind. *"The king is in my possession. Come back at once."*

"I am pursuing his daughter. No heir shall be left alive."

Aria stomped her foot. *"She means nothing and holds no power over the people. Return at once so we can hang Zaridus from his own palace."*

"You forget your place, young one. You serve me, not the other way around."

Aria sighed through her nose. *"I remember. We will await your return."*

Cinolth severed the connection.

Aria moved over to the railing and peered down at the burning city. A procession of soldiers and orcs climbed the steep road far below. Pravus had arrived. Nothing he did could compare to what she'd accomplished on her own. She'd gloat when he joined her on the rooftop.

Who's the god now?

CHAPTER FIFTY-ONE

The *tick-tick-tick* of claws on stone frayed Berggren's nerves. Had he been alone, he would've fought his way out of the temple and Borza, but it wasn't only his life in his hands. Niesha had become a second daughter to him. As with Theyn, he'd give his life to save Niesha's.

The catacombs underneath the temple had been a great place to hide right up until three gnolls entered the large space. Poorly lit, Berggren couldn't see anything going on through the cracked lid of the sarcophagus he lay in. Because of his size, he had to put Niesha in a sarcophagus of her own. It was the last thing he wanted to do, but he'd had no choice. Thankfully, she lay in one fifteen feet above the catacomb floor. The gnolls would have to climb to get to her, and he'd be ready to spring from his sarcophagus at a moment's notice.

Every noise sent his pulse racing faster, and with it came beads of perspiration. Even if the gnolls didn't hear him breathing heavy, they'd surely smell his sweat.

Stone slid on stone. A jarring, scraping noise.

A man whimpered, "Please, no. I am a priest of Zin."

"Then you shouldn't fear death," said a gruff and gravelly voice. Berggren couldn't tell if it belonged to a male or female.

The man screamed, but it lasted only moments.

Thwack!

The sick, wet sound rattled Berggren. The walls of the sarcophagus closed in on him, and each breath became more ragged. Somehow, they'd sucked the air from his confined space. His lungs burned. He needed to get out, the consequences be damned.

Through the crack, he saw an opening. One of the gnolls stood close. He could crush the beast's head with the sarcophagus lid. Not knowing where the other two gnolls stood, his plan could backfire quickly, but if he waited much longer his opportunity might be lost. Weighing the odds, and verging on a claustrophobic attack, he made his decision.

Palms against the underside of the lid, Berggren started to lift it away from the vessel. But the damned thing seemed to be stuck on something. He grunted, and the gnoll reacted, but not to him. Someone else had entered the catacombs.

† † †

Theyn's plan had worked flawlessly right up to the moment she'd entered the catacombs beneath the temple. With so much chaos in the city above, none of the gnolls had given her a second glance. To them, she was just a large cat on the prowl looking for its next meal.

Now, she faced three gnolls who worked their way through the catacombs to surround her. Why they hadn't ignored her like the others left her a bit confused. She stalked forward, hoping her boldness would give them pause.

Berggren's scent permeated the air. She hoped she hadn't arrived too late. The largest of the gnolls stepped in front of her, blocking her path. She halted but didn't back away. Given that the other two gnolls were behind her, it would've done her little good anyway.

The gnoll before her, the obvious leader of the pack, rose on his hind legs and towered over Theyn. He cocked his head and sniffed the air. "My, my, my. You're not what you seem, are you?"

Theyn growled deep in her chest and hunkered down like she might attack.

"You're fooling no one with that act." He knelt and smiled at her, or at least that's what she assumed he attempted to do. The only thing it really accomplished was baring his sharp, yellowed teeth. "The name's Karraar. What's yours?"

She knew there was little point in hiding her identity, but she still hadn't figured out how to talk while in her cat form. She reached within herself and opened the black box in her mind. It took great effort to shed her fur and stuff the beast back into the box, but she managed to do so.

Theyn stood, arched her back, and shook out her hair. "I'm Theyn."

Karraar rose again, towering over her by several feet. "I've heard tales of shifters, but I admit you're the first I've ever met."

Theyn crossed her arms. "What gave me away?"

"Your scent." Karraar leaned down and sniffed her again. "Not quite human, but definitely not a beast."

"I wanna spill her blood and see what she tastes like," said one of the other gnolls. His voice sounded far more twisted and stranger than Karraar's.

"Theyn, where are you?" Nardus's voice in her head startled her.

"Beneath the temple," she replied through mindspeak. *"Hurry."*

Karraar stepped back and grinned deviously. "I think you underestimate this shifter, Qordak, but I'm willing to let you have a go with her."

Theyn heard Qordak's claws dig into the stone floor. She quickly dove and rolled to her left. The beast narrowly missed taking off her head with his claws.

She drew her sword from its scabbard. The ring of steel echoed through the catacombs. Qordak came at her again, this time with a battle axe drawn. She blocked his blow with her sword, but his strength and weight took her to her knees. His devilish yellow eyes churned with hate as he leaned close. The smell of rancid meat on his breath warmed her face and almost gagged her.

Theyn needed more strength to have a chance against Qordak. She rolled away and called upon the beast within as she did so. She gained traction and lunged forward, claws extended. Qordak had only been half prepared for her attack and swung his axe wide. Its handle cracked her right in the ribs but didn't knock her away. She dug her claws into his sides and went for his throat. His other fist hammered the side of her head but not before her teeth gained purchase of his throat. She bit down with all her strength and tore out his throat even as her head whipped to the side.

Qordak fell backward, and she went with him. Her vision teetered on darkness but giving in to it would be her death. She spat the chunk of fur and flesh from her mouth and tried to shake off the blow, but the catacombs spun around her.

Crack!

Theyn and Karraar both turned toward the third gnoll. A female, given her shape and enlarged breasts. She dropped to her knees as stone crumbled and crashed around her. Her neck bulged. Blood poured from her mouth as she fell face-first onto the floor. Berggren stood in her wake, half a sarcophagus lid still clutched in his hands.

Karraar roared and lunged at Theyn, his weapon high over his head.

† † †

Borza had two temples, one at the center of the city and the other to the south, close to the Orbis Mountains. Nardus went to the one to the south first but found no passage that led beneath it. However, he did find a pack of gnolls stalking the temple followers who'd sought refuge within its walls. By the time he left, the temple walls glistened with crimson streaks. Not a single gnoll still stood.

Moments after he'd entered the second temple, a loud crash sounded behind the altar curtain. Nardus streaked through the temple like a wraith and shot down the circular stairwell in a blur. Each moment ticked away in slow motion, but Nardus still moved at full speed.

Ahead and to the right, Berggren held some large stone in his hands, a yell still bellowing from his gaping mouth. A giant gnoll flew through the air to the left, his battle axe raised and poised for a killing blow. Nardus didn't see Theyn but knew she must be the target of the gnoll's strike. Two blasts of air shot from Nardus's extended arms, rippling the surrounding air as they crossed the catacombs. Both met their mark.

Time sped back up as the gnoll flew across the catacombs and crashed into a wall of sarcophagi. Nardus rushed over and grabbed Theyn and teleported her into the middle of the southwestern Orbis Mountains. He laid her down and went back for Berggren. The big man hardly had time to react before they stood in the middle of the forest.

Berggren looked around. "Where's Niesha?"

Nardus had forgotten about the girl and didn't remember seeing her in the catacombs. "You tell me."

"She was hiding in one of the sarcophagi," he barked. "Any harm comes to her, and it's on your head."

Nardus readied his mezhik and teleported back into the catacombs. He hadn't expected to arrive in the dark, but someone had snuffed out all the torches.

A sinister laugh sounded from behind him. Nardus turned and saw two yellow eyes glowing in the darkness.

"*Əllíṭ ʋb!*" Three small orbs of light sprang from Nardus's palm and pushed back the darkness, but not nearly enough.

The glowing eyes were gone, but the tell-tale click of claws alerted him that the gnoll had circled back behind him. Nardus turned, fire in his palm.

"Not so fast, wizard," snarled the gnoll. He clutched Niesha in his clawed hands.

Niesha struggled against him. "You've got bad breath. It's no wonder you're so angry."

"What do you want?" asked Nardus.

"I've heard about you," said the gnoll. "You're the father of my queen."

He knows Shanara?

"What of it?"

"Surrender, and I'll let this sack of bones go."

"Don't do it, Nardus. He's a liar, and a bad one at that," said Niesha.

Nardus took a step forward. "I have a better idea. You let her go, and I won't kill you."

"You may have mezhik, but I've got the upper hand," he snarled. "One little squeeze, and she bursts."

Another step. "Is death your final decision?"

"Three…" replied the gnoll.

Nardus shook his head. "Don't say I didn't warn you."

"Two…"

"One!" shouted Nardus.

He released a fireball straight at the gnoll's chest. Then, with a single thought, he brought time to a stop in the catacombs. Sidestepping the fireball, he retrieved Niesha from the gnoll's arms. Retreating into the darkness, he released his hold on time. The gnoll's howl echoed in his ears even as he and Niesha teleported out of the temple and into the forest where he'd dropped off Theyn and Berggren.

Niesha hugged Nardus's neck and then squirmed out of his arms. She looked up at him, her eyes as big as the moon and her smile stretched to the edges of her face. "That. Was. The. Most. Unbelievable. Thing. I've. Ever. Seen!" She thrust her fist in the air and jumped a foot off the ground.

Berggren scowled at Nardus. He returned the look with a shrug. Theyn had shifted back to her human form while he was gone. A massive bruise colored the right side of her face. She winced when he touched it.

With a bit of mezhik, he healed her face. "That's more like it." He bent down and kissed her.

Every time he used his mezhik, the loathing of it faded more and more. It made him wonder if he'd begun to lose the man he thought he was. If so, would his feelings for Theyn die as well? And what of Shanara and Shardan? Would his love for them become lost too?

I'll worry about it once Pravus and Cinolth are dealt with.

He glanced at Berggren and then nodded at Theyn. "Let's get to the stronghold before nightfall."

CHAPTER FIFTY-TWO

When Pravus arrived on the rooftop of the King's Palace in Vallah, Aria stood at the far end with her back to him. King Zaridus sat on the floor next to Aria, his silver crown turned upside-down and smashed down on his head. Blood covered his face and soiled his white tunic. Never had Pravus seen a man more dejected.

"Hello, my queen." Pravus strolled across the rooftop, his head held high.

Aria turned and faced him as he approached. Every last bit of green was gone from her eyes, replaced with a glowing red. "You march in here as though you've accomplished something. Have you already forgotten the fact that it was I who built the gateway, and I who took down the water titan? How about the light shield and the wretched king himself?"

Every insulting, venomous word that came out of her mouth came from the mind of Cinolth and the hate he bred within her. Prior to getting her hands on Ɂṭōn Dhef Dädh, she'd been so appreciative of everything he'd done for her. Soon, he'd find a way to rid himself of Cinolth once and for all and take back his wife's heart.

Pravus steeled his nerves and brushed her words from his shoulders. "I've said nothing of the sort. You have done very well, indeed." He bent down and kissed her cheek. "However, I've made some accomplishments as well. Elatos, Borza, and Vallah burn this day because of me. Not only have these accomplishments been mine, but I've also captured Prince Rictar and brought your brother to you. What do you say of that?"

"The victory over Elatos was not yours alone, dear husband. And anyone could've taken Borza. Nevertheless, I am thrilled you've brought my brother here." She walked over to Alderan and lifted his chin. "Do you finally understand whose side is that of righteousness, or have your delusions not been broken yet?"

Alderan didn't look Aria in the eye. "The only thing you serve is evil.

You're not my sister, but I believe she's still inside there somewhere."

"You're such a fool, Alderan. You've always been." She let go of his chin. "Evil is in the eye of the beholder. You say our cause is evil, but I assure you that everything King Zaridus stood for served evil purposes. You will witness him hang from the palace walls, along with his traitorous son."

Pravus turned and motioned to Murtag. "Bring Prince Rictar and the rope."

Two orcs dragged Prince Rictar over to where King Zaridus sat and shoved him to the floor. They bound them both with rope and tied nooses around their necks. Then they tied the other end of the ropes to the rooftop railing.

Pravus walked over to Prince Rictar and King Zaridus. Aria joined him.

Pravus addressed King Zaridus. "Because of your arrogance, you will watch your son hang and hear his neck snap as the rope stretches to its full length."

"Any last words, Prince Rictar?" asked Aria.

"This is not the end!" yelled Prince Rictar. "The people will revolt. Your reign will be among the shortest ever recorded if anyone bothers to record it at all."

Aria backhanded Prince Rictar. His face reddened where she struck it. Pravus nodded to Murtag and stepped back. Murtag hauled Prince Rictar to his feet and lifted him onto the railing. Tears streaked down King Zaridus's face, but he held his tongue.

"Fear not, Father!" Aria shoved Prince Rictar over the railing. "We will see each other again soo—"

The rope pulled taut, and Prince Rictar's neck snapped.

"No!" cried Alderan. He fell to his knees. "Stop what you're doing, Aria. I beg of you in the name of Ɂätūr."

"Your god has no power in this world," snarled Pravus. "We are the only ones worthy of bowing down to."

Murtag bent down and pulled King Zaridus to his feet.

Pravus looked King Zaridus in the eye. "Any last words, you pathetic, old man?"

"Perhaps I deserve such a death, but my son did not." He glared at Pravus with contempt. "You'll both burn in *Ef Demd Dhä* for what you've done."

Enraged, Pravus shoved King Zaridus over the railing. The rope snapped tight and jerked back. The rooftop railing groaned, and the pylon they'd attached the rope to cracked up its side, but it held.

Pravus leaned over the railing. The two bodies dangled at the ends of their rope, neither of them fighting for life. He turned and eyed Aria. "And what of the princess?"

"She's gone," Aria growled. "Cinolth chased them all the way to the Gelu Ocean before losing them."

Pravus smacked the railing. "Damn!"

Aria folded her arms across her stomach. "It makes no difference. Once we return to Galondu Castle and establish our rule over the Ancient Realm, we will scour the world for her. There is nowhere she can hide."

Pravus took a deep breath. *She's right.*

He pushed Princess Zelanora from his thoughts and focused on the more important matter. "We've not yet discussed it, but there's the matter of Cyrus."

"Yes, and I have a plan to kill the bastard." Aria faced Alderan and smiled. "I believe you'll be useful to us yet."

Pravus scowled. "How so?"

"Cyrus cares about the people and will do almost anything to save as many as he can."

"I agree, but what does this have to do with Alderan?" Pravus raised a hand dismissively. "We can't threaten his life."

"Of course not, you fool." Aria paced along the railing. "We'll use Alderan to deliver a message to Nardus. If Nardus doesn't come to Arian Valley by sunrise three mornings from now and surrender his life to us, we will continue our assault on every city and village until none remain."

Alderan glared at Aria. "Even if I do what you ask and Nardus agrees, that's not enough time."

"Would you rather I make it *tomorrow* morning instead?" Aria seethed. "The fates of the Duos Flumen citizens lie in your hands."

Alderan shook his head, and Pravus groaned.

If Cinolth gets his way, there will be no one left to rule.

But the plan would draw Cyrus out. He saw no other option, so he acquiesced. "Very well."

Aria moved over to Alderan once again. "Go to our father and give him our terms." She kissed his cheek. "If you don't, or Nardus hasn't surrendered in three days, I will hunt you down using our bond, personally take the life of your little girlfriend, and then Duos Flumen will burn!"

Alderan stood there, his eyes wide and jaw slackened.

"Tick-tock," said Pravus.

Alderan turned and walked away.

"Should we follow him, my lord," asked Murtag.

"No." Pravus cracked his knuckles. "Once Cyrus is dead, the others will have nothing left to fight for."

Murtag sent the orders down to let Alderan leave the city unopposed.

"Gather the troops. We will head back down to Arian Valley at once." He turned to Aria. "Tell the beast to send his followers back to Arian Valley. Cyrus will soon be crushed."

Pravus turned and faced Trivers Lake. The beauty of the surrounding mountains wasn't lost on him. Given different circumstances, Vallah would've made a tremendous location to rule from.

But I'm taking your place at Galondu Castle, Father.

† † †

Once Rayah had located and retrieved the proper supplies to counteract the poison, she, Rakzar, Urza, Ridan, Bakkan, and Zerenity had hidden inside someone's vacated home while Pravus and his army of orcs trekked up to the King's Palace. It took a team effort to talk Ridan out of chasing down the orcs and facing them alone. The girl seemed to have a screw loose, but Rayah couldn't imagine what she'd do if Alderan were killed. She hoped she'd never find out.

After some reconnaissance, Rakzar confirmed that the entire orc army had gone with Pravus. Zerenity still hadn't recovered from the poison, so they'd have to take the long route to the stronghold. Rayah prayed that they wouldn't run into the rest of Pravus's and Cinolth's armies that headed up the western shoreline of Trivers Lake.

By the time they reached the lowest level of Vallah the sun had begun its descent in the east. Smoke from the fires in Borza turned the sky red, orange, and purple. It would've been a beautiful sight had she not know the source. To the south, flames still licked the sky. A city like Elatos where basically every structure erected had been made of wood could burn for days.

"Rayah!"

Rayah's heart fluttered in her chest. She turned around and flew into Alderan's arms. She'd been too afraid to even wonder where he was.

They held each other for a solid minute before either of them said a word. When Rayah pulled back, she saw the pain and sorrow in his eyes. Tears streaked his face. She wanted to fix whatever ailed him.

"What's happened?" she asked.

He shook his head as tears began to flow faster. She held him again, her heart aching for him.

She hugged him tighter and whispered in his ear, "It's your sister, isn't it?"

Violent sobs wracked him, the answer obvious. Hatred boiled in Rayah's veins, and she purposed in her heart to strike Aria down if the bitch ever hurt Alderan again.

CHAPTER FIFTY-THREE

Like a plague, the darkness followed Wrik everywhere he went. Fear of it had driven him across the Ancient Realm. From East Hotah to Cuspis to Flumenpars. Then on to Daltura and Galaportus. Instinct, likely driven by the toe ring he wore, told him to head into the Procerus Mountains.

Although he'd never seen the home of the dragons, he knew it existed, long before Nardus had gone there and returned with wild stories.

Across Altus Pass and into the high mountains he soared. The thin air burned his lungs and tired him much faster than the lower hills, valleys, and plains had, but he couldn't stop. Doing so would be his death.

The darkness rolled behind him like thunder clouds, never more than half a mile behind him. During the day, he could keep an eye on the darkness and stop and rest for a few minutes and hunt for food, but at night he had nowhere to escape from it.

The moist, frigid air formed ice crystals on his wings and weighed him down but he couldn't give up. The peaks before him rose into the clouds. He knew somewhere above that cloud line lay the Valley of Dragons nestled between the peaks.

Every muscle in his body ached as he soared upward and into the thick layer of clouds. Just when he thought he could go no farther, he burst through the tops of the fluffy clouds and caught sight of a narrow passage between two of the peaks. He darted forward, aware of the darkness closing in. He didn't look back. Didn't need to. It nipped at his heels.

Through the passage he flew, a long stretch draped in darkness. It pulled at him. Clawed at his wings. The last of his strength gave out just as he cleared the passage. He plummeted down the inside slope of the peak and crashed into the valley floor, tumbling head over heels a dozen times before coming to a rest in the tall grass.

The darkness pounced on him and tore at his soul.

† † †

A faint blue light penetrated Wrik's closed eyelids. His ears rang, and his neck and back ached like they'd been trampled. When he forced his eyes open, he'd expected to find himself on the other side of death, but instead he stared into the icy blue eyes of a water dragon. He hadn't seen one before, but the water dripping from its scaly hide made it obvious.

The valley floor tumbled inside his head, a reminder of the spill he'd taken. But what of the darkness that had chased him? As far as he could tell, he retained his limbs, body, and soul.

Wrik sat up. Blood drained from his skull, causing his head to throb. Massaging his head with one hand, he propped himself up with his other. After his crash landing, his mind held no more memories before waking a minute ago. "Gods... what happened?"

"You brought death into our peaceful valley." The dragon's voice echoed through the vibrant cave and shook Wrik's heart right through his chest.

Guilt tore at Wrik's heart. "Someone died?"

The dragon nodded. Water dripped from his hairy chin and splashed in the pool of water in which he stood. "Certainly, but I was able to revive you."

Wrik craned his serpent-like neck toward the elder dragon. "Are you saying that *I* died?"

"Indeed."

As both a scholar and a prophet, he'd read books on almost every subject in existence, save one. Unlike many people he knew, the afterlife never fascinated him the way prophecy and history did. So much could be gained from studying history, and prophecy foretold of potential future events, but the afterlife didn't matter unless you were dead. He'd assumed there'd be a bright light and a familiar presence drawing him into it upon death, but he'd felt nothing. Didn't know he'd died. Not even a vague sense of lost time niggled recollection.

So where did I go? Fear slithered underneath his skin. *Is there nothing after death?*

The dragon rose from the water's depths. "Allowing you to die was the only way to rescue you from the shade."

A shade?

It explained a lot, but also conjured dozens of questions and thoughts in his mind. Unless summoned, a shade would never leave the lower world.

Pravus is too weak to summon such a demon to hunt me, so who could have done it?

Wrik focused his mind back on Aria, but what reason would she have to kill him? He strove to get on Aria's good side and thought he had, so he just couldn't get behind the idea of her being involved. And, as far as he knew, dragons didn't have the ability to summon shades.

Someone else has it out for me, but who?

He reached far into the recesses of his mind and pulled up memories of his past but couldn't put a finger on whom or what event could've triggered such a vendetta. One thing he knew for certain though: Pravus had hired the shadow troll to kill him, but that incident had nothing to do with the shade. As a prophet and student of prophecy, he understood the odds of two such events happening within days of each other and not being linked, but facts were still facts.

Perhaps the old dragon knows more.

Wrik stood on clawed feet with splayed toes. After four days, it still felt awkward. "Do shades not wait to capture the soul of the one they've sifted?"

"Sifted. An interesting word choice for the act of reaping." The old dragon spread his wings and stretched. "The sole purpose of summoning a shade is to bring about death, not to capture and control souls. Had it been a spectre at your heels, we would not be having this conversation."

"Ah, yes." Heat rose in Wrik's cheeks, and the sensation made him wonder if his embarrassment was noticeable while in his dragon form. He dared not ask. "Pardon my confusion. It's been awhile since I've studied ancient spirits and creatures."

"And dragon culture for that matter." The old dragon moved closer. "You're not one of us."

Wrik's pulse quickened. He'd heard tales of the way the dragons dealt with outsiders, especially ones not of their kind. "Yes, of course, I'm not from the Valley of Dragons."

"Don't be coy." Water sprayed from the old dragon's nostrils. Two geysers. "You are no dragon."

Wrik looked around, but they were alone. "Do the others know?"

"If they did, the shade would've been the least of your problems."

Wrik glanced down at his own dragon form. "How did you figure it out?"

"I know all dragons. Past, present, and future. You are none of them, and my memory is infallible." The old dragon grinned. "The brass toe ring is a good indication as well. I knew its maker."

Wrik leaned forward, his voice little more than a whisper. "And my secret is safe with you?"

The old dragon sank back into the water, all the way to his shoulders. "For now. However, I may have need of your services in the future."

"Then you're holding me hostage?" asked Wrik.

"In a manner of speaking, yes. Events soon to unfold will devastate many. In that time, I will look to you for help and sanctuary."

Wrik dipped his head toward the old dragon. "In such a capacity, I will be honored."

"Very good. Now, tell me your name, wizard."

"Oh, yes. I've lost a bit of my wits over the last few days running from that shade. My name is Wizard Wrik Isler, *Fizärd Brefäţ*. You may simply call me Wrik."

"Ah, yes. A prophet. Much to my liking. Wrik, I am Peorvem The Ancient. Your acquaintance is an honor and a privilege."

Wrik bowed. "Likewise."

Rising, he took in the enormity of the cavern. The blue lake filled most of its space, leaving only a small area of rocky beach where he stood. Two paths led away from the cavern, one ascending and the other descending. It seemed like a good jumping point to Nasduron.

Wrik spread his arms wide and pointed toward the two paths. "Where do these paths lead?"

Peorvem raised an arm. "Ascend to the valley." He smacked his hand on the water's surface. "Descend into oblivion."

"And how often do you get visitors down here?"

"If you'd asked me three weeks ago, my answer would've been never. However, you are not the first as of late, nor will you be the last."

Wrik reached for his spectacles and then remembered they'd become part of him when he'd transformed into his current dragon form. "So, you're the one who helped Nardus find himself."

"I am. Is he a friend of yours?"

"Acquaintance, though we are on friendly terms."

"And why do you ask if I have visitors?"

"So that I'd know if I should leave soon."

"As long as you do not ascend, you are free to remove the toe ring that holds your form. You will be safe enough." Peorvem descended into the waters, leaving only his head exposed.

"Very good," said Wrik. "I really do appreciate you saving my life and for your hospitality. However, I still have several questions that you might be able to help with."

Peorvem drew closer. Water manifested and trickled down his scales like sweat. "I will answer any questions you have to the best of my ability."

"The shade that attacked me... Do you know who or what may have summoned it?"

"Given the fact that it chased you across the entire realm for several days, the summoner must have possessed great power. However, there is no way to determine the actual summoner unless you recognize their essence. As I'm certain you're aware, every spell leaves a distinct aura of color and smell, even those used to summon a shade."

Wrik looked to the cavern ceiling and sighed. "Given my state of mind at the time, I lacked the capacity and energy to take note of any such detail."

Peorvem rose out of the water and walked over to the water's edge. "But you do have the skill?"

"Yes."

Peorvem reached out and pressed his middle claw into Wrik's forehead. "Then perhaps this will help you."

A bright light filled Wrik's vision, blinding him. Then, as it faded, the Valley of Dragons came into view. He and several other dragons gathered around a shape darker than the night. Red eyes, full of rage and hate, shone from that darkness. The shade sucked the life from the small dragon it stood over. As the dragon slipped into death, a faint light, full of the colors of a rainbow, surrounded the shade. The essence of its caster. In a blink, the light faded.

Wrik stumbled back a step as the valley faded and the cavern returned. His heart thumped in his chest. The aura he knew better than any other. He'd witnessed it and studied it several times over the last month. "It can't be..."

Peorvem withdrew into the water. "Ah, you've been betrayed by a friend. I am deeply sorry."

Wrik found no words adequate to describe his fury and sorrow. The dagger of betrayal twisted in his heart and rended his soul in two. Bound by prophecy and duty, he'd never interfered with events before, but how could he not do so now? How could he stand by and not retaliate? The answer stared him down and taunted him.

I must act.

He took a long, deep breath, gathered himself, and faced Peorvem. "I sincerely thank you for your help, Ancient One. Now, I must go."

"Of course, but don't forget about our agreement." Water dripped from Peorvem's beard.

Wrik nodded. "I will not, but I do have one last question. How will you summon me when the need arises?"

"The toe ring will glow." Peorvem's voice faded as he disappeared beneath the water's surface.

Wrik peered down at the brass ring wrapped around his toe.

Interesting.

With that, Wrik flapped his wings and took off toward the path of ascension. Rage and destiny pushed him toward the Three Kingdoms.

You'll pay with your life, Aria.

CHAPTER FIFTY-FOUR

Nardus, Theyn, Berggren, and Niesha were the first to arrive at the stronghold the night before last, and it worried Nardus until he thought about the distance those from Vallah and Elatos would have to travel through the tunnel systems to reach it. Either city lay a good thirty miles from the stronghold. Perhaps farther traveling underground, especially considering how deep the tunnels must run beneath the Hotah River.

That morning, a few began trickling in, each worn and wearier than the last. Every last one of them knew they'd lost everything they'd ever had, including family members and friends for most of them. Nardus kept watch of the tunnels both from the cities and from the surface. Alderan and the others would likely come from the surface entrance.

Noon rolled around, and Alderan still hadn't arrived. Nardus paced between the tunnels and would've worn the ground out had it not been made of solid rock. Finally, his patience wore out.

It took him about ten minutes to locate Theyn in the growing crowd. When he did, her face said it all.

She cupped his face in her soft hand. "Don't worry. Alderan *will* show up."

"You don't know that. It's been two days."

Several shrieks sounded above the murmur.

"The enemy has found us!" shouted a woman.

"Run!" yelled a man.

Panic swept through the stronghold like wildfire and created a stampede.

Nardus fought his way through the throng. When he finally caught a glimpse of the surface tunnel entrance, he saw what had caused the commotion. Two gnolls, battle worn and covered in dried blood stood at the tunnel entrance. He teleported closer and targeted the threats, fireballs ready in his palms.

"Stop!" yelled someone from behind the gnolls.

Zerenity appeared in front of the two gnolls in a whirlwind of fury, kicking up ages of settled dust. She raised her hands. "There's no need for alarm. Rakzar and Urza are with me."

The fireballs sputtered in his hands and fizzled out.

"And me." Alderan appeared from within the tunnel, his arm around a young girl.

"Shardan!" Nardus approached his son.

Berggren's deep voice boomed over the cacophony of mass hysteria. "Enough!" His voice echoed throughout the stronghold and brought the chaos to a halt. "No threat lies within these walls other than your own fears. Gather your wits and think rationally before you act, or you may become the threat you fear."

Nardus smiled to himself. Berggren, in spite of his many flaws, would make a great leader.

Nardus turned his attention back to Alderan and his strange band of friends. All of them, including the female dwarf who entered the stronghold riding a mastiff, looked browbeaten. Bloodstains covered their clothing and armor. A fair amount of it looked to be theirs and from recent wounds.

Alderan's gaze held far more pain and sorrow than it had the day before. Nardus longed to unburden him and take it all away but knew all too well that nothing could. He rubbed the scars on his left bicep, a reminder of his own agony.

He looked Alderan over. "What happened? Do you have any wounds that need healed?"

Alderan peered down at himself and shrugged. "I don't think so. Zerenity is good at what she does." He took hold of the hand of the girl standing next to him. "Father, I'd like you to meet the love of my life, Rayah."

Rayah stepped forward and tilted her head. Nardus hadn't noticed her wings until that moment. They glimmered in the ambient lighting of the stronghold.

How long has it been since I've seen a dryte?

Her striking beauty filled him with pride for his son. Alderan had done well for himself.

"It's an honor to meet you, sir," she said.

Nardus took her other hand and bent down and kissed her knuckles.

"The honor is most definitely mine. Your radiance and beauty fill the entire stronghold." Her cheeks blossomed with a reddish hue as she withdrew her hand.

"You're far too—"

Zerenity interrupted Rayah. "Where's Savric?" Concern strained her voice.

Nardus glowered at her, but then his features softened as he remembered they all suffered. He took her arm and pulled her close. His mouth next to her ear, he said, "Savric sent me a message yesterday. King Zaridus tasked him with keeping Princess Zelanora safe."

"Auh!" Zerenity swallowed then said, "I didn't realize she'd escaped. Aria hung King Zaridus and Prince Rictar from the palace rooftop. Alderan was forced to watch her do it."

Nardus cringed. Cinolth's hold over her ran far deeper than he'd hoped. Evil and power seduced the best-intentioned individuals, but with driving forces like Pravus and Cinolth in her life she stood little chance of recovering without intervention. He released Zerenity and stepped back as his hands curled into fists. Eying his hands, he offered up a prayer.

Zätür, guide these hands. Allow them to choke the life from my enemies and free my daughter from bondage.

Zerenity tapped her chin. "Then there's still hope."

Nardus brooded. "Hope remains as long as we have breath in our lungs."

"Speaking of hope, we need to go somewhere quiet so we can talk," said Alderan.

"Back outside," said Nardus. "I could use a bit of fresh air."

"I'll round up Berggren, Calen, and the others," said Theyn, "and meet you up there."

Alderan nodded. "Okay, but bring only those you trust." He looked at Rayah. "I'll meet you *all* in an hour. I need some time to myself."

Rayah kissed Alderan's cheek. "An hour. No longer."

† † †

Alderan stood atop Silex Peak at the edge of an overlook, a stoic statue amidst the chaos below. In front of him, the evening sun began to dip below the eastern slope of the Orbis Mountains. Its rays still warmed his face, but the chill in his bones remained.

He gazed down at Arian Valley, his heart wrenched, and his stomach twisted with sorrow. No semblance of the silvered grass meadows remained. Charred remnants of man, beast, and vegetation spread beyond his vision. Fires dotted the landscape and screams of agony rode on the winds as the enemy's celebration of victory began. Bright flashes of color burst in the air and lit the cloudless sky, an illusionary display no doubt conjured by Pravus.

Across the valley, only a handful of battle flags remained that bore the coat of arms of House Zaridus—a field of turquoise donning a black lion's head on a silver shield and two iron swords crossed under it—, but the battle flags of House Rosai—a red dragon's eye against a solid black field—couldn't be counted.

Alderan exhaled. *Master Savric warned them.* Would it have made a difference if they'd listened and prepared for battle? *Days, maybe. A week at most.* King Zaridus's delusional complacency blinded him from the truth and crippled his army. They never stood a chance against a mezhik wielding army, let alone the resurrected Cinolth and his army of infected.

Somewhere amongst the horde below, Qotan did Cinolth's bidding—not because he chose to do so, but because of the poisonous plant he'd been infected by. Master Savric would've been wrought with sorrow if he'd been there to witness the hundreds of bodies smashed and half-buried by mounds of earth and rock. Alderan had no doubt most of that carnage came at the hand of Qotan.

Prophecy had warned of this day, but how could anyone have known the way it would unfold?

Alderan looked skyward. *You did, Ƶäţūr.* He breathed deep. *That's why I'm here.*

A strong gust of wind whipped Alderan's cloak, ruffled his hair, and carried with it a deathly stench. His eyes stung and teared up, but the tears had little to do with the wind.

Alderan lowered his head and gazed at the valley again. *I know this isn't your doing, Aria. I know your heart. Cinolth and Pravus will pay for what they've done to you.*

He thought about Nardus, his father, and how difficult everything must be for him. How could anyone live a lie for several decades without being jaded and calloused? The strength Nardus displayed despite everything he'd suffered at the hands of Pravus filled Alderan with pride and bravery.

I will try to be strong and brave like you, Father.

His mind focused on prophecy, death, and what awaited beyond.

The afterlife… Alderan's heart ached, and he trembled. *Ƶäṭūr, I'm not ready.*

Alderan wiped his eyes and shook his head slowly. "I'll never be prepared for what must be done…" His voice quavered, and he took a deep breath to calm himself. "But there is no other way. I must save Aria."

With a deep sigh, he turned back and headed toward the stronghold.

Ƶäṭūr, help me. The morning comes too quick, and death awaits.

✝ ✝ ✝

Alderan stared at the dozen—eleven not counting Bakkan—members representing the last hope of the Ancient Realm. They all sat in a circle in the middle of the woods, not far from the hidden entrance that led down to the stronghold. Tension hung thick in the air. Every one of them, including Eshtak, held their tongue and awaited the news he'd brought with him from the King's Palace.

Every which way he thought of twisting the words wouldn't change the message they conveyed, so he just blurted out the ultimatum. "Father, I am to deliver you into the hands of Pravus and Aria tomorrow morning, and you will be executed. Doing so will end the war and save countless lives."

Gasps and murmurs came from every direction.

Theyn shot to her feet. "No," she growled. "If I've learned anything, it's that Pravus cannot be trusted."

"Agreed," said Berggren. "The slippery bastard killed my son."

Nardus stood and raised his hand. Theyn huffed and sat back down, and the others quieted. "Hold on, friends." He squared his shoulders with Alderan. Concern trenched his brow. "And what is the consequence if we don't comply with their demand?"

Alderan sighed and raked his head with his fingers. "They will destroy every city in the Ancient Realm, starting with Duos Flumen, and will take no prisoners." He purposely left out the part about Aria's threat on Rayah's life. Rayah needed no more fuel to hate Aria with.

"It sounds like they've left us with little choice," said Zerenity. "However, I don't see how acquiescing to their demand could possibly help our cause. If we allow them to eliminate Nardus, what would stop them from destroying all the cities anyway?" She stared hard at Alderan. "I don't want to speak ill of anyone, but I don't think Alderan has the ability to save the world no matter what the prophecies say."

Rayah flew from her seat and got right in Zerenity's face. "Maybe if you'd spent more time teaching him, we wouldn't be in this mess."

Alderan grabbed Rayah around the waist and pulled her away from Zerenity. "Stop it, Rayah. This isn't her fault."

"Then whose fault is it?" demanded Ridan. "Yours?"

Alderan shrugged. "As much as anyone's."

"Gods, people. Stop your bickering," said Urza. "We're not here to lay blame at anyone's feet. We need to find a solution, or we'll all be dead sooner or later."

"Look," said Rakzar, "giving up the old man solves nothing and puts us into a far worse situation. As I understand it, killing Pravus will also kill Aria, and that will kill Cinolth as well. Is that not the best solution? Three birds with one arrow so to speak?"

Nardus fumed. "Don't you dare threaten my daughter's life!"

"Then give us another solution," said Calen. "We've all lost people in this. Can you not see the benefit of sacrificing one to save many?"

Eshtak shook his head violently. "Eshtak hates idea."

"So do I," said Calen. "A sacrifice should be willing, not chosen. But what else can we do?"

"There must be a way to sever the bond between Pravus and Aria," said Theyn.

"It's unbreakable," Nardus countered.

"Everyone, please sit down." Alderan waited for compliance and continued, "I've been thinking about the situation for a long time. First, the solution to kill Pravus and or Aria and remove all three of them from the picture sounds good on the surface, but you must also consider the fact that every last person under Cinolth's control will be killed as well."

"Is that true?" asked Zerenity. She looked to Nardus for an answer.

"Where did you hear that?" asked Theyn.

"Wizard Wrik. According to him, it's some sort of failsafe trigger Cinolth built into the curse."

"Gods," said Theyn. "That's far too many people to sacrifice."

"Still better than the entire realm," Ridan retorted.

"My aunt is one of those... if she's still alive." Calen's lower lip quivered but he didn't cry.

"And Qotan," said Zerenity.

"And my mother." Niesha scrunched up her face. "But I've got Iceberg now." She looked up at him. "You care about me more than my mother ever did. Not that it's saying much," she added.

"Yes," said Alderan. "Everyone knows someone under Cinolth's influence."

"I don't," Ridan argued. "Fact is I don't care."

"Thought I'd be the one to say that," said Rakzar.

Alderan saw the change in Rakzar's eyes. The beast cared more than he'd ever let on. Why else would he be there?

"We're getting off track." Alderan stood and walked the inner circle. "Let me get to the heart of what I'm trying to say without further arguments. Agreed?" The others nodded. "Good. Now, despite what any of you may think, the bond between Aria and Pravus *can* be broken without killing either of them. While a *guest* at Galondu Castle, I read the prophecy about the soul binding Pravus cast on Aria and himself."

"That's great news, darling," said Zerenity. "What must we do to break this bond?"

"It requires self-sacrifice." Alderan glanced at Rayah but couldn't stand to look her in the eye knowing the next words that would fall from his lips. He closed his eyes for a moment and took a deep breath.

I am the savior of the world.

Somehow, Rayah sensed his fear and hesitation. She flew over to him. "Don't say it, Alderan!" Her eyes were wide with fear.

"I'm sorry, my love, but we're out of options." He pulled her close and kissed her cheek.

To the others, Alderan said, "I must be the sacrifice."

"Absolutely not!" growled Nardus. "That would solve nothing."

Rayah cried on his shoulder. "You can't do this to me."

Rakzar stood. "So, what then? We kill you and everything goes back to normal?"

"If it were that simple, I'd let you kill me now." He carried Rayah over to Urza who took her from his arms. "Look, the last thing I want is to die, but it's the only way to free Aria from Pravus."

Nardus crossed his arms. "Explain yourself, son. Even if I were open to such an idea, which I am *not*, how would killing you break their bond?"

"Aria and I are twins. Nearly identical other than being opposite sexes. We share a bond and the same blood. Why do you think Pravus sent Rakzar to kill me and then, ever since he married Aria and bonded his soul with hers, has gone out of his way to keep me alive? If he kills me now, even through a third party, then the bond between him and Aria would break."

"Given the fact that if either of them kills each other then they both die, wouldn't that apply to them killing you as well?" asked Theyn.

Alderan really liked Theyn. She had a sharp mind. "No, because that's not quite how it works. The prophecy spells it all out."

"Which prophecy?" asked Nardus.

"It was called *Fädinzh dhä Bɘllek,*" said Alderan.

"The Black Wedding," confirmed Nardus. "That prophecy has been fulfilled. I attended the abomination of a wedding."

"Yes, between Aria and Pravus," said Alderan.

Nardus grimaced. "Don't remind me."

"The wedding is only part of the prophecy, but it also speaks of how it can be broken." Alderan paced. "I don't remember the exact wording, but basically the person who shares the same blood as either Pravus or Aria can break the union through self-sacrifice. It must be Aria and me that share the blood."

"Or me," said Nardus.

Alderan shook his head. "Not true. You only share part of Aria's blood. Besides, if the prophecy were true for you as well then Pravus and Aria wouldn't be trying to kill you."

"I don't get it." Ridan stood and approached Alderan. "Why would they be scared of killing you if the prophecy speaks of self-sacrifice?"

Nardus snorted. "Pravus interpreted it wrong, just as he does everything else."

"That makes sense," said Zerenity. She tapped her nose. "Let's pretend we agree to go through with a plan to make you the sacrifice. How would it be possible to get either of them to kill you?"

"In truth, it's simple. I've been thinking about it for several days." He looked to Nardus. "My father and I will switch places."

"I don't understand," said Urza. "How can you switch places?"

Nardus sighed. "We create an illusion."

"Exactly," Alderan agreed. "We will switch places, and that's how Pravus will kill me. I will serve as the self-sacrifice required in the prophecy." Hearing the words out loud twisted his stomach into knots.

Ridan nodded and paced. "It would allow Pravus to be killed. Once he's dead, the blood bond between the orcs and gnolls will be severed."

"And then we'd kill Murtag," Rakzar finished.

Ridan smiled. "Exactly."

Alderan continued, "Yes, but that's only part of the solution." He sat back down. "Figuring out how to kill Cinolth and save those he controls will be up to the rest of you."

Alderan swallowed hard. Somehow, he'd managed to get everything out without breaking down. But he still couldn't look Rayah in the eye. Instead, he stared at his hands. Calloused and worn from hunting and chores. Bruised and scabbed by war. His middle finger, where he'd wear a wedding band, would never bear the honor.

Forgive me, Rayah.

Rayah pushed out of Urza's embrace and flew to the middle of the circle. "Are you all mad?" She spun around, eying each of them in turn. "This asinine plan does nothing but kill Alderan! Not only that, but it will likely send Aria into a rage that can't be stopped. She'll destroy Duos Flumen and every other city in the realm. Can't you see it?"

Nardus groaned. "I hate this." He knelt in the middle of the circle and lifted his head skyward. "Lose one child to save another. How cruel can You be, Ɂäʈūr?"

"No!" shouted Rayah. "This plan won't work. You'll end up killing Aria in the end anyway."

"Agreed." Nardus's face visibly relaxed. "We must find another way."

"We only have two choices, and one of them is flawed," said Zerenity. "We must kill Pravus."

Alderan's heart crashed in his chest and tears flooded his eyes.

Aria... How can I save the world if it means you're no longer in it?

† † †

Nardus stared into the flames of a flickering torch while his mind searched deep into the past. So much planning and preparation went into setting a trap for Cinolth the first time he defeated him, but he hadn't acted alone. It took him, the other members of Ūrdär Dhef Ɂäfn Dhä, and a multitude of other wizards and allies to take down Cinolth and Magus. Even so, they'd almost failed.

Now, the threat they faced seemed insurmountable. Magus Carac had wit and unsurpassed knowledge but didn't possess Aria's raw power. Combined with Aria's growing power, Cinolth would prove a far stronger adversary than before.

Alderan nudged his shoulder. "Father?"

Nardus pulled himself back into the present. As he looked around the circle, he noticed the eyes of the entire group lay upon him. "I am here."

Alderan knelt before him, his eyes glistening with tears. "Tell me you've figured out another way. Tell me Aria can be saved."

"I've figured out another way, son. We will save your sister." With a wink, he rose to his feet and gestured toward the stump he vacated. "Have a seat, son." Alderan took his place on the stump.

Nardus slowly walked the inside perimeter of the small circle as he talked. "As you all know, my name is Cyrus Nithik, First Mage of *Ūrdär Dhef 2äfn Dhä*. You also know that I faced Cinolth once before and ripped his heart from his chest. Trust me when I tell you that we do not possess the strength or numbers as when I faced him before. However, that does not mean I am without hope. On the contrary, I have more hope now than I ever did that day, even more so than in that moment when the glow in Cinolth's eyes faded."

The entire group sat still, captivated by his every word. Only a breeze through the trees disrupted the perfect silence. He continued, "We can win, and we will."

"How?" asked Zerenity.

Nardus turned and faced her. Despite his age, she'd experienced far more years than he had. Her silver locks and wrinkled skin proved it, yet her bright-blue eyes still held onto a youthfulness he envied. He held out his hand. "Give me the bracelet."

Zerenity slipped the metal bracelet off her wrist and handed it to him. "I'm not sure how much energy is left in it."

Nardus held the bracelet against the matching one on his own wrist. Light arced between the two for a split second as the energy from Zerenity's bracelet transferred to his. The deed done, he stuffed the spent bracelet into his pocket.

He glanced skyward. *2äṭūr, let that be enough for what must be done.*

"Thank you." He paced again as he laid out the plan. "Zerenity, Alderan, Theyn, and I will face Pravus in the Arian Valley tomorrow morning. The rest of you will wait here and keep the citizens of Elatos and Vallah calm and safe."

"I'm going too," said Rayah. "My duty is to protect Alderan, and nothing you say will hinder me from doing it."

Nardus sighed. "Very well."

Alderan leaned over and whispered something to Rakzar, but Nardus wasn't close enough to hear what he said.

"Count me in," growled Rakzar.

"I go where he goes," added Urza.

Ridan stood. "Since we're not killing Pravus, I will retrieve Normak's body in the morning and return home." She left the circle and headed toward the tunnel.

Berggren stood. "Don't think you can have all the fun without me."

Nardus whipped around. "No, Iceberg." His voice boomed. "I saw how the people in the stronghold responded to you and followed your command. They're in desperate need of a good leader. They need you."

Berggren crossed his arms. Muscles bulged like boulders. "Theyn does too. And I've yet to avenge Shaul's death."

Theyn stood and joined Nardus in the middle of the circle. She wove her fingers into his. "Nardus is right, Father. You must stay back and protect the people. Protect Niesha. They are the ones who still live. They matter more than risking your life for vengeance. Besides, you know killing Pravus will kill Aria as well. It's not an option."

Nardus held tight to Theyn's hand. She'd become the physical anchor Vitara could no longer be, and her presence strengthened him. "If you won't listen to me, then listen to your daughter, Iceberg. She is far wiser than either of us."

Berggren grumbled and mumbled something under his breath as he sat back down.

Nardus looked around. "Shall I continue?" No one said another word. "Good." He released Theyn's hand and began pacing once more. Theyn sat back down.

"Look, the plan is quite simple." He pointed at his wrist. "With the energy left in this bracelet, I'll be able to stop time."

Several around the circle gasped. Eshtak bounced up and down and clapped. Niesha's eyes grew almost as big as her smile.

Nardus continued, "Holding time requires a lot of energy to begin with but holding it against another mage *and* a dragon will be far more taxing. Once invoked, I'll only be able to hold them for about ten seconds."

He turned toward Alderan. "This is where you come in. The bow you carry is far more special than you might know. Combined with its strength, the metal arrows you possess can be used to penetrate Cinolth's scales. A perfect shot will pierce his heart. I've seen you in action, son. There's no better shot than you."

Nardus locked eyes with Zerenity. "The arrow tips are made to splay out and grab hold of whatever they've pierced. Once that arrow is loosed and meets its mark, you will rip it back out of Cinolth's chest."

Zerenity shook her head and scowled. "You cannot ask that of me. I refuse to be the cause of tens of thousands of innocent deaths."

"And you won't be," said Nardus.

"Earlier, you said they'd all die if we killed Cinolth," said Calen.

"I know, but I hadn't had time to think it through. Now I have, and I believe everyone would still be safe."

"Why?" asked Rayah. "What's changed?"

"I lived with Cinolth's heart lodged in my chest for weeks. During that time, he spoke to me and influenced my thoughts and actions. I thought I was mad at first, but his spirit lived on through his heart. Because of this, I am certain that his failsafe will not be triggered unless his heart is destroyed."

Zerenity cocked her head and tapped her chin with her finger. "I can see the logic in that." She nodded slowly. "I'll do what you've asked of me but know that there will be retribution if what you've said turns out to be wrong."

Nardus smiled. "And I won't stop you from doing so."

He approached Rakzar and Urza. "Since you insist on coming along, your jobs will be to distract Aria and Pravus long enough for me and Alderan to get positioned. Remember that anything you do to Pravus happens to Aria too. Use that to your advantage but *do not kill* either of them. Understood?"

Click-click!

Urza's knives dropped into her hands. "Trust me, we're quite good at causing distractions." She twirled the knives a few times and sheathed them.

"Neither of them will be a problem," Rakzar confirmed.

"Shardan—Alderan—son." Nardus shook his head. "Forgive me. There are two important factors you must remember when taking the shot. A dragon's heart is on the left side of their body, not the right. In addition to that, even with your arrows, you cannot shoot Cinolth straight on. His scales are positioned in a way that will twist and bend the arrow as it penetrates. A shot like that will be worthless. You must shoot him right through the armpit. It's the only chance we have."

"Then we'll need to make sure his arm is raised before you stop time," said Alderan.

Nardus smiled. "Precisely."

"And what happens once we have his heart?" asked Theyn.

"We will take it to the one place Aria and Pravus can't go," Nardus replied.

"*Räällm Kenzhärd Dhä?*" asked Zerenity.

"No," said Nardus. "The Conjured Realm no longer exists. Removing Cinolth's heart from *Ţämbəll Dhef Däd Dhä* destroyed it."

"Then where?" demanded Zerenity.

Something in the air made Nardus's flesh crawl. He peered into the shadows surrounding the group but saw nothing. Still, he couldn't shake the feeling that they were being watched. "This is no place to discuss such a matter. Rest assured that everything will fall into place as needed." He clapped his hands together. "Now, let's get back inside and get some rest. The morning will be here soon."

Nardus grabbed Alderan's arm as he walked by. "Wait, son. There's one more thing."

Alderan stopped and turned around. "What is it?"

"Cinolth knows he can't use his fire to kill me, but he won't hesitate to use it on you."

Alderan frowned. "Aria wouldn't allow it."

"Do not be deceived, son. She has no control over that beast." Nardus removed his necklace with the dragon amulet and offered it to Alderan. "Put this on. It will protect you from his fiery breath."

Alderan backed away, his hands raised in front of himself. "No. I can't take that from you. Your life is far more valuable than mine."

Nardus gritted his teeth to stave off a torrent of tears. "You couldn't be further from the truth. I would die a thousand deaths for you. *You* are the savior of the world, Shardan, *not* me. Ilia, your birth mother, prophesied it." He grabbed Alderan's hand and shoved the amulet into it. "Wear the damned thing."

Alderan sighed. "Yes, Father." He pulled the necklace over his head and tucked it beneath his shirt.

Nardus clasped Alderan's arm and pulled him into an embrace. "Tomorrow, everything will happen as it should. Remember that."

"I will."

† † †

Wrik waited patiently for the last member of Nardus's group to descend into the hidden tunnel before he flew down from the tree he'd perched in. He'd heard every word of their plan and began formulating one of his own. They would provide the perfect distraction for him to take Aria's life. She'd never know what hit her.

CHAPTER FIFTY-FIVE

Gooseflesh prickled Rayah's arms as weeping, howling, and wails of agony and ecstasy filled the early morning. A symphony concocted of wretched and vile acts. She tried to block it out by singing a hymn in her head, but it surrounded her.

A full moon hung overhead, spotlighting the chaos that engulfed the Arian Valley. Groups of both man and beast tortured and raped women, children, and men alike, laughing, fighting, and drinking until they vomited or passed out.

Rayah shuddered and tightened her grip on Alderan's hand. *Ɂäṭūr, how can You allow such evil to exist? Come down from Your perch and lay waste to them before it's too late.*

Rayah breathed through her mouth to counter the pungent odor that stung her nostrils and burned her throat, but it didn't prevent the taste of the air from roiling her stomach. She kept her focus straight ahead as she, Alderan, Nardus, Theyn, Rakzar, Urza, and Zerenity walked through the middle of the scorched valley. She didn't look for them but knew Ridan and Bakkan watched from the overlook atop Silex Peak. Berggren and the others stayed back at the stronghold. The people there would need his leadership in the coming months.

Severed heads lined the path they followed, dipped in tar and set ablaze atop long pikes driven into the ground. Death flies swarmed around the pikes and nipped at Rayah's arms and legs, some drawing blood. She swatted at them with her free hand, but it didn't deter them.

The dead surround us, and you choose to feast on me?

After enduring the myriad trials over the last several weeks, she imagined that she smelled of death.

About a quarter mile ahead, two dozen giants began pounding drums six feet tall and at least as many feet in diameter. Their rhythm supplanted the beat of her heart and left her numb. She looked up at Alderan, but his gaze focused straight ahead. She followed his gaze with her eyes.

In the distance, a hill rose to meet a wide plateau, and at its brow sat two white thrones—undoubtedly fashioned from recently acquired bones. Torches lined the sides and backs of the thrones, shrouding the faces of the figures sitting on them in darkness, but enhancing the enormity of the obsidian dragon that squatted behind them.

Cinolth.

Rayah's throat dried in an instant. Beads of sweat formed on her brow and ran down her nape and the center of her back. She swallowed hard, but it left a lump in the back of her throat.

She didn't need to see the faces of the two people sitting on the thrones to know who they were. Fear rose in her gut and manifested as side-splitting pain. It nearly doubled her over. She set her jaw and clenched her free hand.

You will not rule me, Aria Rosai. Nor will you, Lord Rosai. I'd rather die.

Her chest convulsed with the thought, and she choked back tears. Alderan didn't look at her but shook her hand forcefully. Distraught, she hadn't noticed that she'd been squeezing it as hard as she could.

She loosened her death grip and reached out to Alderan with her mind. *"I'm sorry."*

Several moments passed, and Alderan didn't respond or even glance down at her. His gaze never left Aria. She seethed with hatred and glowered at the woman.

The giants' relentless drumming thrummed in her ears, and the ground shook as their small procession passed through the middle of them. Rayah and the others stopped at the bottom of the hill, and the drumming ceased. Lord Rosai rose from his throne and raised his fist in the air. Within a handful of seconds, the entire horde quieted, save one large orc who continued to rape a bound and gagged human woman.

Rayah's cheeks burned, and she gagged, but she couldn't look away.

How can they be so disgusting and evil? Have they no shame?

Moments later, an arrow whooshed through the early morning and buried itself in the side of the orc's head. His head lolled and drooped. He grunted and collapsed.

Rayah gasped and looked away, but not before witnessing Nardus flinch. She'd caught pieces of the story of how Nardus's wife and youngest child had died, and his reaction to the arrow through the orc's head pained her.

I'm sorry, Nardus.

She couldn't imagine how much pain he'd endured losing those so close to him, and she feared she'd know soon enough.

Alderan…

Tears welled in her eyes as she turned to the side and dry-heaved.

"Rayah, calm yourself," said Alderan. "I am the savior of the world, and Ӡäṭūr is on our side. You've nothing to fear." His voice exuded a confidence she'd never known him capable of, and it settled her nerves.

Rayah took a deep breath and regretted it immediately. The air, permeated with death, smoke, and every other foul odor in existence, stung her throat and nostrils and left the taste of burned flesh and feces in her mouth and on her tongue. She spat on the ground, but the taste remained with her.

† † †

Pravus cracked his knuckles and glared at Cyrus, the festering thorn in his side.

You'll die by my hand this very morning.

He rose from his throne fashioned from the bones of his enemies and sauntered down the hill, stopping a dozen paces from Cyrus. Pravus counted Cyrus and the others with his finger. *Seven.*

He chuckled. "Is it a coincidence that there are seven of you, or is this your pathetic attempt to reform *Ūrdär Dhef Ӡäfn Dhä?*"

Cyrus didn't respond but glanced over at Alderan and nodded.

Alderan released the hand of the dryte who stood next to him and stepped forward. "As per our agreement, I've delivered my father into your hands. Take his life and end this damned war."

Pravus cocked his head. Something seemed amiss, but he couldn't place its source. He had little doubt Cyrus would show his face, but was the man truly so righteous that he'd freely give his life to save a world full of pathetic and unworthy people? Surely he knew his death wouldn't end the killing.

So, what is his angle? Has he come here to fight me?

No, he knows anything he does to me will be done to Aria as well.

Pravus brooded. *Then what?*

Cyrus glanced down at himself and smiled. "I'm not dead yet. Have you had a change of heart?" he mocked. "No, that would require having a heart to begin with."

You know nothing of how truly heartless I am.

Pravus reached within and called upon his mezhik. It crackled at his fingertips, begging to be released. "For the longest time, I thought this day would never come." A red fireball rose into his outstretched palm. He sneered, "I hope you burn in *Ef Demd Dhä*, you bastard."

Suddenly, there were a dozen copies of Cyrus. The other six with him drew weapons and called upon their mezhik as they spread out.

Pravus targeted the original Cyrus and thrust his fireball. The Cyrus copy shattered like glass upon impact. His eyes narrowed as he conjured another fireball. For a split second, he swore he glimpsed Cyrus's true location.

You cannot lie to the master of lies. Your illusion skills are pathetic compared to mine.

He sneered and loosed the fireball.

† † †

Nardus conjured a thick wall of ice between him and Pravus, easily blocking Pravus's fireball. The wall wouldn't hold for long, but he didn't need it to. Rakzar, Urza, and Rayah would engage Pravus and keep him busy.

"Time to find—" The ground quaked as Cinolth dropped to the ground between him and Alderan, joining the fray. "Never mind."

Flames burst from Cinolth's open maw and engulfed Alderan and Rayah. He thanked Ʒäṭūr not only for having the foresight to give Alderan the amulet but also for the fact that Rayah had been touching Alderan's arm. That single fact had saved her life. She likely wouldn't be lucky twice.

The ice wall exploded toward Nardus with a thunderous crack, but the icy shards melted before they reached him.

Aria approached, arms at her sides and the left side of her lip curled into a snarl. Mezhik arced and crackled across her splayed fingers.

Ʒäṭūr, don't make me hurt her.

Nardus turned to defend himself, but thick vines lashed out, wrapped Aria's waist, and hurled her backward. Zerenity gave him a nod and then headed in the direction she'd thrown Aria.

A giant rumbled toward him from the right. Brinzhär Dädh sang as he unsheathed it. A somersault and three quick moves brought the giant down, but several zheballin and a couple of ogres headed his direction.

Theyn's voice entered his mind as she lunged forward and shifted into her cat form. *"Concentrate on getting Cinolth into position and leave everything else to me."*

"Be careful."

Her laughter filled his mind. *"This isn't where I die."*

Ʒäṭūr, let that be true.

He turned his attention back to Cinolth and stalked forward with Brinzhär Dädh at the ready.

✝ ✝ ✝

Facing Cinolth would do nothing but get her killed, so Rayah shadowed Alderan, uncertain of what she should do. To her left, Rakzar hurled one of his double-edged battle axes at Pravus and rushed forward. Urza followed Rakzar, her knives in her hands and ready for action. Pravus deflected Rakzar's thrown axe with a pair of glowing red glaives. Rayah's mind couldn't process where they'd come from. In one moment Pravus's hands were empty and in the next he held the glaives.

It didn't matter. The move had given Rakzar and Urza time to close the distance. Rakzar swung his second axe, but Pravus easily blocked the blow and countered with a strike of his own, sending Rakzar reeling backward.

Urza slashed at Pravus with her knives and Rakzar joined back in with his battle axe swinging, but neither of them landed a single blow. Somehow, Pravus sensed their attacks before they happened and fought with inhuman speed.

Pravus landed a blow that sliced right through Rakzar's leather breastplate. Crimson trickled from the gash.

Alderan yelled at her. "Don't just stand there, Rayah! Go help them subdue Pravus."

Subdue him? How?

The dirt was soft underfoot. She could take him out for good.

Along with Aria.

Rayah dove into the ground and flew through the dirt toward Pravus. She had but one thought as she approached Pravus from underground.

Whatever I do to him will affect Aria.

By the time she reached the spot where Pravus stood, Urza and Rakzar had yet to land a single blow against Pravus, and each of them had sustained several deep gashes. From her vantage, none of their wounds looked to be life-threatening, but it was only a matter of time before that changed.

Unless I do something.

Rayah reached up, grabbed Pravus's ankles, and pulled him down into the dirt.

† † †

Aria dodged the old woman's attack and turned just in time to see Pravus get swallowed by the ground. She hurled another fireball at the old woman and then two more at the gnolls who'd been attacking Pravus. Her shots missed the targets, but Murtag and Karraar had stepped in and engaged the two gnolls.

She teleported to the spot where Pravus had disappeared and doubled over. Her lungs burned with fire, and she couldn't seem to catch her breath. Her first thought was of her baby. Perhaps being pregnant had weakened her. But then the truth hit her.

Pravus is suffocating!

So was she, and she needed to act quick. Although she hadn't seen it with her own eyes, she knew Alderan's wretched girlfriend was responsible for pulling Pravus down into the dirt. The miserable little dryte still hid underground somewhere.

Maybe she's holding Pravus down.

Alderan would be furious if he knew the little wretch had tried to kill her, and she'd be certain to let him know once the dust settled.

If she survives.

Aria bent down and placed her hands on the ground. Drawing upon her mezhik, she conjured roots that dug deep into the dirt and wrapped around Pravus's arms and legs. The ground trembled as she commanded the roots to pull Pravus back up. The ground erupted like a volcano, spewing dirt skyward. Pravus gasped for air when his head broke through the surface. Aria shared his need for air and gulped it down.

Assisted by the roots, Pravus crawled out of the hole and lay flat on the ground on his back. The dryte still hadn't surfaced, and Aria knew of a way to make it more difficult.

Letting the roots die off, Aria pumped more mezhik into the ground and turned the top layer of dirt into stone. The effect spread a good hundred yards in every direction.

† † †

Nardus had no time to assess the battlefield and prayed everyone would be ready to do their part when the moment arrived. Brinzhär Dädh sang as he whipped it through the air, slashing at Cinolth arms, legs, and wings and blocking Cinolth's deadly claws and teeth with an accuracy he'd never attain wielding another sword.

Diving to the side, Nardus narrowly escaped Cinolth's fist as it quaked the ground in his wake. The call was close, but Nardus had anticipated it and the opening he knew it would present. He hadn't been wrong.

Cinolth raised his right arm to strike again.

Nardus drew all the energy from the metal bracelet on his wrist and called upon his mezhik.

The air crackled and popped as a concussive wave of energy rippled across the valley.

Cinolth stood before him, frozen in time with his maw twisted with rage. His right arm hung in the air, positioned perfectly for Alderan.

Every last enemy within two hundred yards had become living statues too.

"Now!" yelled Nardus.

Time ticked away too quickly, his energy draining at an alarming rate.

No more than a handful of seconds remained.

Alderan grunted as he drew his bow string and took aim.

Nardus's vision shook from the strain of holding back time.

Take the shot, son.

† † †

Wrik streaked across the valley, his eyes focused on his target. Cinolth and the others hadn't moved in nearly ten seconds. He pushed himself harder. Faster.

Alderan saw him coming, but it didn't matter. The boy could do nothing even if he wanted to.

Wrik closed in on Aria. With his hands held beneath his chin, he hurled three consecutive fireballs at her back from fifty feet away. The quick releases created the desired illusion. The fireballs looked like a column of fire spewed from a dragon's mouth. No one would ever know the difference or suspect otherwise.

No time remained for him to see the strikes hit their mark if he wanted a chance to escape. He banked hard and headed south, his revenge for her sending the shade complete.

† † †

Alderan's eyes grew wide. "No!" he screamed.

Thunder rumbled in his ears. Slow. Methodical. A heartbeat. *His* heartbeat.

Aria stood right in the path of the flames. She didn't move. Couldn't move.

Save Aria. Save Aria.

Alderan could think of nothing else. Couldn't piece together where the little dragon had come from or why it attacked Aria. It didn't make sense. Didn't matter.

Save Aria.

The feel of his recurve bow in his hand and the texture of the bowstring against his fingers faded.

Save Aria.

The world shifted beneath his feet.

In a flash, he stood with his back to Aria. Felt her presence. Stared right at the dragon's fire. Had no time to do anything else.

At least I have the amulet.

The strength of the blast surprised him. Three successive punches right to the center of his chest. He'd expected it to pass around him like Cinolth's fire had minutes before, but it didn't.

The blast sent him reeling backward several steps, knocking him into Aria. His breath caught in his throat, and his lungs seized up. He staggered forward, dazed, and dropped to his knees. He looked down at his chest; cauterized flesh surrounded a gaping hole about eight inches in diameter that nearly went straight through him. The fringes around the hole continued to burn and blacken.

Damn that hurt.

Pain scorched his flesh like brushfire, but it didn't last long. Tears bled from his eyes and blurred his vision. His arms fell limp at his sides and twitched unnaturally.

Did I at least save Aria?

Alderan turned his head, or rather willed it to turn, but it didn't respond. All his pain, both physical and mental, subsided, and an inner calm settled his mind. He imagined himself sitting in front of a warm fire on a blustery day.

He sent his thoughts to Rayah. *"I'm sorry, my love. Forgive me. You were always my only love."*

Alderan collapsed face-first on the ground. He knew Rayah had screamed his name, but the sound of her voice came to him in a whisper.

Rayah's voiced crashed into his mind, an ocean wave on a rocky shore. *"Don't you leave me, Alderan Somneri!"*

Alderan lost all feeling in his body, and the remaining light faded from his vision. He gave in to the darkness, and it pulled him down into death where he knew the pain could not follow.

"Goodbye..."

CHAPTER FIFTY-SIX

Rayah flew through the dirt until she located a soft spot and shot up out of the ground and into the air. She spun around and faced the direction where Alderan lay face-down on the ground.

"Alderan!" she screamed.

Pain ripped through her chest. Tore her heart apart. She cried out, the bond she shared with Alderan severed.

The ground smacked her hard. Jarred her. She tried to move. Tried to crawl toward Alderan but couldn't.

Had she been shot with something? Or had she just fallen from the sky? She didn't know. Couldn't think.

The darkness pulled her into its arms and devoured her.

† † †

Aria staggered forward and dropped to a knee. The fresh stench of singed hair and burnt flesh livened the air. She couldn't recall what'd set her off balance, but Nardus yelled for Shardan even as he engaged with Cinolth.

Something felt different. Strange. Wrong. She couldn't place its source. She pulled herself to her feet and turned around. A body lay face-down a few feet in front of her.

She recognized the hair. The clothes. Her heart knocked so hard in her chest she stumbled forward.

"It can't be him," she whispered.

She wouldn't allow it. Couldn't stomach the thought. But she must be certain.

Gingerly, she wedged her foot underneath the body.

Her pulse soared.

Deafened her.

She hesitated. Didn't want to know anymore.

Turned the body over anyway.

Alderan stared up at her.

Dead eyes.

Lifeless.

Nausea overwhelmed her. She turned to the side and retched but nothing came forth.

A hole the size of the world split her heart in two. Rended her soul.

Pravus stood next to her. Consoled her. She tried to push him away, but he pointed at the sky.

"Little dragon," he said.

What in Ɂäʈūr's name did that even mean?

She didn't know. Didn't care.

Hadn't prepared herself for his death.

How could she have? In what scenario would such an outcome have ever occurred?

Pravus stalked away, fireballs flying from his palms.

Little dragon.

She forced her gaze skyward.

† † †

Pravus's hands blistered with heat by the time he stopped conjuring fireballs. His chest heaved, and his legs fought to hold his weight. Only one shot had met its target, and just so as the little dragon continued to flap its wings as it flew away.

Out of breath, Pravus located Karraar with his mind and spoke through the link. *"Stop what you're doing and capture that damned dragon!"* Karraar didn't respond, but he saw Karraar and several other gnolls take off toward the south.

Alderan's death had taken him by surprise. Not because he hadn't expected it, and not because of the way it happened, but because of the way it affected him. He cared nothing for the boy and would've relished Alderan's demise, but it had come with a surprising twist. A blow to the gut. Severed his bond with Aria.

But it didn't make sense. He had nothing to do with Alderan's death, so why had it severed the bond? Words of the prophecy turned in his mind.

...cannot be broken except by one who shares the same blood...

As Aria's twin, Alderan shared her blood. As he interpreted it, killing Alderan would sever the bond.

...bound together for eternity...unless the one who shares the same blood

breaks the union through self-sacrifice.

He couldn't see the flaw. Didn't understand it. Alderan hadn't saved Aria from him. The attack against her had nothing to with him at all.

Then why?

He bent over and held his knees. He needed more energy and a source for it. Cyrus would be the perfect target, but he'd never get close enough to drain the man's life. Not only that, but Cyrus also wouldn't give it freely. However, several orcs were within earshot. He called one of them over and pulled the life from her bones.

† † †

Zerenity couldn't believe her eyes. Aria stood over Alderan, seemingly dazed. Alderan didn't move.

Panic drove her forward, but it didn't slow her wit. She called upon her mezhik and cast a spell as she ran toward Aria.

Aria turned toward Zerenity, hands still at her sides. She never saw the tree spring up behind her. Didn't even flinch until it had already snared her arms and legs. Her head cocked to the side, and she looked down at herself.

Zerenity had ʒäbräʒär in her hand and flung it at Aria. The collar spun through the air. Plunged into Aria's neck and jerked her head back.

Rakzar raced past just as Zerenity reached Alderan. "Going to save Rayah," he barked.

She nodded and knelt next to Alderan, but nothing could be done for him. Fire continued to consume him. It wouldn't stop until nothing remained to burn.

She didn't understand. Where was ʒäṭūr in all this? How could the world be saved without a savior?

She shook with rage but didn't know where to direct it. It ate her up inside. Consumed her.

The son she always wanted and never had lay dead before her.

She glanced back over her shoulder.

Met Nardus's gaze. Strong. Intense.

Shook her head as tears streaked her face.

His face contorted with agony and rage, and an inhuman cry belted from his lips.

Chilled her to the core.

She echoed his cry with one of her own.

† † †

Nardus clenched his jaw. Sickness swirled in his gut, and rage filled his heart. His mind reeled back to the day Bradwr and the others had attacked him and his family. Rage had consumed him that day as well. He'd given in to it, and it had nearly destroyed his life.

This day will be different.

He roared again, raised Brinzhär Dädh above his head, and charged toward Pravus. "You're gonna pay for Shardan's death, you bastard!"

Pravus turned, his gaze steeled. Yet Nardus detected fear in his eyes. Understood its source.

His bond with Shanara has been severed.

That realization drove Nardus harder. Faster. He had no fear of ending her life when he took Pravus's.

Nardus lunged forward, swinging Brinzhär Dädh with all his might, but his blade met glowing red steel and deflected away from Pravus. The unexpected counter caught Nardus off-guard, and his momentum caused him to stumble and skid to the ground. Pravus hadn't held a weapon an instant before the strike.

An illusion.

Nardus rolled forward and back to his feet in a single move and turned to face Pravus once again.

A swirling, red fireball danced atop Pravus's open palm. "I'm going to pay for it? No. I've dedicated my entire life to rebuilding my father's kingdom, and it's finally within my grasp, but now you threaten to take it away from me. I should've killed you the day you came back."

Nardus spat on the ground. "And I should've listened to the dragon and killed you when I had the chance. I guess that makes us both fools."

To Nardus's right, Theyn had shifted back into her human form. She fended off three zhebəllin with a rusted blade. They worked together and surrounded her, but they were no match for her speed.

Cinolth's roar shook the air, and his shadow flitted between Nardus and Pravus and grew rapidly. Nardus dove sideways, and Cinolth quaked the ground as he landed where Nardus had stood a moment before.

Pravus backed away, and the fireball he held faded into nothing. He looked to Cinolth and snarled, "Cyrus is all yours, my friend."

"You're no friend of mine," roared Cinolth.

Cinolth whipped his tail around and spewed a column of fire. Nardus shielded himself from the flames with a light shield, but Cinolth's tail smacked Pravus square in the back of the head with one of its spikes. The spike drove right through Pravus's head, its tip exiting through the middle of his forehead. Blood poured from the wound, covering Pravus's face and saturating his robes. His body went limp and hung from Cinolth's tail.

Nardus scrambled to his feet and backed away from Cinolth.

Cinolth reached back, jerked Pravus free from his tail spike with his clawed fingers, and bit Pravus clean in half. Then, he tossed Pravus's bloodied, half-eaten body aside and snaked his head down toward Nardus. "Surrender now—" Blood and saliva dripped from his spiked chin, and a length of bone hung between two of his lower teeth. "—and I'll make your death quick and painless."

A bloodcurdling scream echoed through the valley, drawing Nardus's and Cinolth's attention.

The tree binding Aria burst into flames as molten silver dripped from her neck. She stalked forward, her gaze locked on Nardus.

The hairs on Nardus's arms stood on end just before a bolt of lightning ripped down through his right shoulder and exited out through his right foot. The strike lifted him off his feet and threw him back fifteen paces. Smoke rose from the hole in his blackened shirt, and the smell of charred flesh filled his nostrils. He should've expected the strike but didn't.

Aria screamed again, her hands stretched toward the sky. Fire and ice rained down from the heavens. Pummeled the ground and struck those that didn't run for cover or shield themselves.

The ground quaked. Split open as shards of rock jutted up.

The wrath of a mage unleashed, Nardus knew there was nothing he could do or say to temper her rage.

Cinolth stalked toward Nardus and unleashed a column of fire.

Nardus shielded himself again with an air shield and called for Sarai, the ţrenᴢbūrţ, with his mind.

Moments later, Sarai replied in Nardus's mind. *"I am ready."*

"Round up the others, and then get Zerenity and Theyn," said Nardus.

"Yes, master."

At some point, Ridan and Bakkan had joined the fight. They and Urza warred against a large orc. Ridan tossed a spear at the orc and then disappeared into the ground, along with Bakkan. The spear met its mark and took the orc to its knees. Urza moved in for the kill but fell away from view inches away from striking.

Rakzar and Rayah were nowhere to be found, but he didn't have time to worry about it. He cocked his head and looked passed Cinolth. "Grab Alderan's bow and get over to Zerenity!" He yelled to Theyn.

Cinolth whipped his head around, launching boomerangs of saliva and blood from his chin spikes. Theyn reached for Alderan's bow, but Cinolth reacted faster. He grabbed it in his claws and smashed it to bits. Theyn rolled away and shifted in stride, dropping on all fours. She galloped toward Zerenity, who still knelt over Alderan's dead body sobbing and convulsing.

Cinolth dropped his lower jaw, and his chest expanded and glowed bright red.

Nardus pulled himself to his feet. "I'm right here, you scaly bastard. Am I not the one you want dead?"

Cinolth paused for a moment, but then released several bursts of flames toward Zerenity. Her eyes fixated on Nardus, Aria stepped right into the path of Cinolth's fire.

Nardus swept his hand to the side. A mighty wind ripped across the valley and tossed Aria to the side like a ragdoll. She hit the ground hard and lay still.

Theyn leapt, shifted in mid-air, wrapped Zerenity in her arms and legs, and skidded across the charred grass just ahead of Cinolth's flames. A moment later, she and Zerenity disappeared into the ground.

"They are with me," said Sarai in Nardus's mind.

Nardus glanced back at the pool of molten gold that swirled on the ground behind him. *"And what of my son?"*

"I am sorry, master. I cannot transport the dead. Doing so would kill us all."

Nardus huffed and nodded.

Cinolth stomped the ground, whipped his head around, and spewed a column of fire at Nardus. Flames surrounded Nardus, whipped his hair back, and ruffled his trousers and shirt, but they didn't harm him or his clothing. The air shield he'd conjured did its job.

Nardus sneered at Cinolth. "Haven't you realized by now that your fire cannot touch me? You'll have to do better than that."

Cinolth roared and charged Nardus, but Nardus threw himself backward and into the golden pool—into Sarai.

"You coward!" roared Cinolth. "You cannot hide from me. No rock will be left unturned until I've found you!"

"I'm betting on it," said Nardus, directly into Cinolth's mind.

"You're a dead man, Cyrus!"

I've heard that several times before.

Cinolth spewed a column of fire into Sarai, and Sarai groaned.

Nardus closed his eyes and breathed Sarai into his lungs. *"Go, Sarai."*

† † †

Aria roused. Her neck ached, but not nearly as much as her heart. She rose to her feet and looked around as she massaged her neck. Her father and the others were gone.

Pravus's remains lay in a pool of blood and saliva. Only his legs and lower torso remained intact. A few yards away, she found his hand. Knew it was his because of the ring. She picked it up and held it to her cheek. Already, his flesh felt cold against her skin. She begged to feel his intoxicating touch one last time but knew it would never come. She kissed his fingers, kissed the top of his hand, and then dropped it on the ground next to his other remains.

Aria drew mezhik into her hands. Its intoxicating touch did nothing to silence the sorrow and rage storming within her. Nothing would. A fireball formed on her upturned palm. It undulated with flames of red, yellow, green, blue, purple, and orange.

Goodbye, husband.

The fireball rolled off the ends of her fingers and landed on top of Pravus's remains. The intense heat cremated Pravus in a flash and left nothing behind but scorched earth. The deed done, she turned her attention back on Cinolth.

Cinolth stood at a distance. Smoke bellowed from his nostrils as he examined his wings. Several holes punctured the leathery membrane connecting bone and muscle. Many of those wounds came from the fire and ice she'd rained down on the valley, and it gave her a small measure of satisfaction.

Malice rose in her heart. Cinolth must've sensed it because he looked right at her with a hate-filled glare.

"Your rage is misguided," said Cinolth in her mind.

"You ate half my husband!" Mezhik crackled at her fingertips.

"*I did what was necessary. What you wanted to do but couldn't. Think of all the things he did to you. How he manipulated you. Killed your family. Killed your friends. Enslaved you for his purposes. I've set you free.*"

"Set me free? I'll never be free as long as you're alive!" She balled her hand and pulled it down to her side. A bolt of lightning shot down from the sky and struck Cinolth between the shoulder blades. The strike didn't faze him.

Cinolth spoke, and fire spewed from his lips. "Strike me again, and you'll see just how short your leash is."

Aria turned away. *Hate him if you want, but he's all you have left.*

She gathered herself and returned to Alderan's side. The dragon's fire continued to consume Alderan, his flesh and bones little more than charcoal.

"I'm here, brother." She touched his grayed cheek, and his form collapsed into a pile of smoldering ash.

She lifted her head skyward and screamed.

Everything she'd ever loved lay dead on a charred field in a land she'd grown to loathe. Tears of blood fell from her eyes, and her heart grew cold. Invoking the name of Diẓäfär, she vowed to soak the earth with the blood of her true enemy.

You're dead, Father.

Blood streaked the backs of her hands when she wiped her eyes. She stood and gazed southward. Nothing of beauty remained in the world.

She placed a hand on her stomach. *But beauty will be reborn.*

She turned and faced the mighty dragon. "Come, Cinolth. We've got a little dragon to hunt and a man to kill."

CHAPTER FIFTY-SEVEN

"*Where am I headed?*" asked Sarai in Nardus's mind. Her voice sounded hollow and weak.

"*Nasduron,*" replied Nardus.

"*Nasduron? It still exists?*"

"*Yes. I will show you the way,*" said Nardus.

"*Yes, master,*" said Sarai in Nardus's mind.

Nardus set his thoughts toward the sunken city and opened his mind to Sarai. "*Do you see it?*"

"*I do. I will get you there, but it shall be the last time we travel together.*"

"*What do you mean?*" asked Nardus.

"*My strength is fading. This journey will consume what little I have left, and I will soon be no more.*"

"*Then stop wherever we are and let us out. I'll take everyone there myself.*"

"*Stopping now will make little difference,*" said Sarai. "*I will not survive long no matter what path you choose. Cinolth's fire has critically damaged me.*"

Nardus clenched his fists. *Damn you, Cinolth. Must you take everything from me?*

"*This is my fault,*" said Nardus. "*I shouldn't have asked you to do this.*"

"*No, master, it's exactly what you created me to do,*" countered Sarai. "*Allow me to serve you this last time.*"

"*Very well, Sarai. Nasduron it is.*"

"*We will be there by sunset.*"

"*Good.*" Nardus set his mind on the Great Library in hopes that thinking of Gnaud and the numerous trips there would keep him from dwelling on Shardan's self-sacrifice saving Shanara's life, but the plan didn't work. Instead, his mind obsessed over the single anomaly of the event.

Why didn't the amulet protect Shardan?

Had its power simply run out, or was there more to it? Had something far more sinister and devious occurred? He couldn't put his finger on an answer, but his mind would never stop mulling it over. In time, he'd figure it out.

For now, he must focus on finding a way to save Shanara and the world from Cinolth's clutches. Even as the darkness surrounded them and threatened to snuff out the light for good, one last ray of hope remained. A single ray. It focused him and drove him to press on.

I hope you're ready, Gnaud.

CHAPTER FIFTY-EIGHT

Dozens of books piled high across five tables, many of them opened or bookmarked for further reading. Most of the books dealt with accounts of historical significance, but a handful of them pertained to prophecy, both fulfilled and unfulfilled. Wrik sat at the third table, his nose buried in one particular history book titled *The Banishment of Light*.

A certain passage caught Wrik's attention. He looked up from the book and adjusted his spectacles. "I think I might've found something."

Gnaud sat atop the first table, scouring through several books of his own. He glanced up for only a moment. "Either you have, or you haven't. There is nothing outside of those two choices."

Wrik had previously spent several weeks with the little gordak and had grown quite fond of his company. He knew Gnaud felt the same about him but didn't think Gnaud would ever admit to it. At least not after being so adamant about keeping Wrik away from Nasduron.

Wrik rose from his chair and carried the book over to the first table. He set the book down in front of Gnaud. "Take a look for yourself."

Gnaud's eyes grew ever wider as he read several paragraphs to himself. "Oh, my!" He shot to his feet and danced around the table, knocking several books to the floor. "That is most certainly of significance!"

"As I thought. Now, we must—"

A rush of wind rustled the pages of Wrik's book as a gold-and-black swirling vortex materialized in the middle of the floor of the Great Library. Wrik jumped to his feet and readied a fireball. Nardus, Theyn, and several others Wrik didn't recognize rose out of the vortex, and then the vortex disappeared with a loud sizzle and a puff of smoke.

Wrik's fireball fizzled out as he exhaled a breath he didn't realize he'd held. He pulled a chair from underneath the table and sank into it. "Gods, what happened to you?"

Nardus stood, his face streaked with dirt, ash, and tears. "We did everything we could, but the Three Kingdoms fell."

Based on all the prophecies he'd read, Wrik had guessed the outcome of the war long before it had begun. His fingers wrapped around the ring in his pocket. "And your son? Where is he?"

Nardus stared at him without emotion. "Shardan is dead."

"Dear Ɂäʈūr," said Gnaud. "How did it happen?"

"He sacrificed himself to save Aria from dragon's fire," said a young woman. Her wings shimmered in the light.

"And did it work?" asked Wrik. Sweat began beading on his brow.

"Yes," replied the young woman. She started sobbing.

Guilt ate Wrik from within. *Gods… He wasn't supposed to die.*

Wrik clasped Nardus's shoulder. "I'm sorry for your loss." Nardus only nodded.

"His sacrifice served another purpose," said Theyn. "It severed the bond between Aria and Pravus. Then Cinolth killed Pravus."

Pravus is dead…

Wrik had hoped for such an outcome but hadn't been optimistic about it. Giddiness swirled in the pit of his stomach. "And what's become of Aria?"

"She's still controlled by that wretched dragon." Nardus slammed his fist on the table. "Cinolth must be stopped by any means necessary."

"Yes, but not until we figure out how to free all those under his control," said an older woman with silver hair. "The cost would be far too great."

"Don't you dare talk to me about cost," snarled Nardus. "I don't give a damn how many lives it takes to kill that beast. Shardan won't have died for nothing."

"Agreed." Wrik leaned forward in his chair and rested his elbows on his knees. "For what it's worth, I have some good news."

Nardus glared at Wrik but said nothing, so Wrik continued, "I believe I've located *Hemär Dhef Əllíʈ.*"

TO BE CONTINUED ...

The story concludes in *True Heir*, Book #4 of *The Dark Heart Chronicles*. Visit **danielkuhnley.com** for more information.

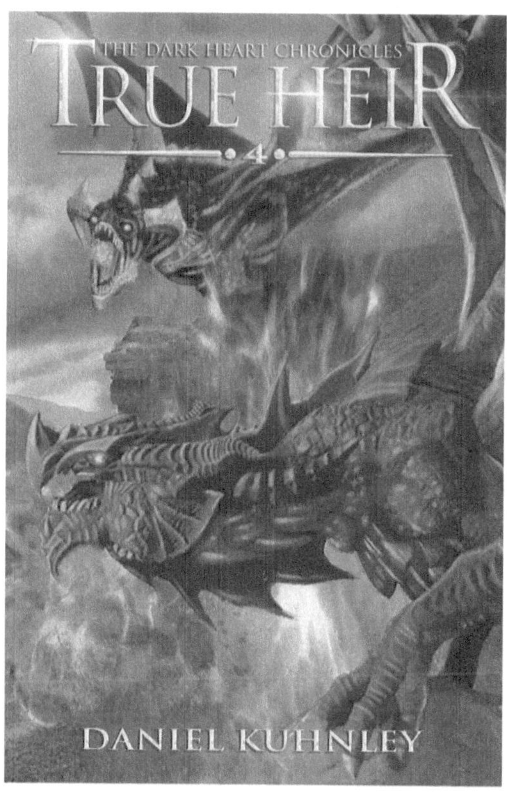

PLEASE TELL OTHERS WHAT YOU THOUGHT

Thank you for taking this journey with me. If you'd like to show your support for my work, please leave a review wherever you purchased this book. It's free to do so, and it'll only take you a minute to write a quick sentence expressing your thoughts about the book.

Your review is especially important to independent, self-published authors like me. Internet and online bookstore algorithms favor books with reviews. They display in search results and at the top of search results more often than books without reviews.

Did you know that there's a minimum number of reviews needed to purchase certain advertising? It's true. Help me reach that threshold by leaving a review. Doing so will help more people find this book and will in turn help me sell more books, which means I can keep authoring more books for you.

Go to danielkuhnley.com/reviews if you need a link to where you can leave a review.

Thank you!

READ *SCOURGE* FOR FREE

Do Eshtak's tattoos hold the key to the between?

danielkuhnley.com/become-a-conqueror

Sign up and read *Scourge*, A World Of Centauria Novella. Be the **FIRST** to get sneak peeks at my upcoming novels and the chance to win **FREE** stuff, like signed books.

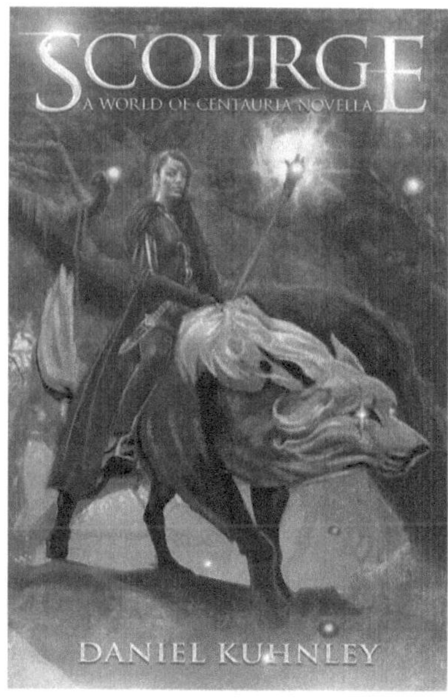

Never use persuasion magic on a powerful wizard.

That was Emorith's hardest lesson to learn. Right from that fateful moment, Magus forced her to use her manipulative sorcery to further his evil purposes. She regretted everything he put her through with one exception: their son Illian. Him, she loved with all her heart.

Magus demanded she cast an apocalyptic curse and destroy an unsuspecting city. She steeled herself to refuse him... but then he threatened the life of her beloved child.

With Illian's life on the line, what choice did she have? She wanted to protect the city and its citizens, but her son would always come first. No, there must be another way. Will she be able to thwart Magus and save them all in time? Or is their fate already sealed?

Scourge is a prequel novella to *The Dragon's Stone*, the first book in *The Dark Heart Chronicles* epic dragon fantasy series. If you like thrilling adventures and terrifying magic, then you'll love Daniel Kuhnley's enthralling tale.

ABOUT THE AUTHOR

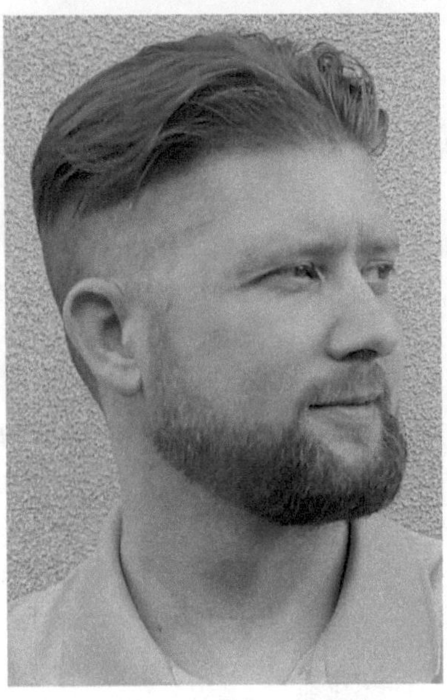

Daniel Kuhnley is an American author of Epic Dragon Fantasy, Supernatural Serial Killer, and Christian YA Sci-Fi/Fantasy stories. Some of his novels include *Reborn*, *The Braille Killer*, and *Kiara Kole And The Key Of Truth*. He enjoys watching movies, reading novels, and programming. He lives in Albuquerque, NM with his wife who also writes.

CONNECT WITH DANIEL

danielkuhnley.com/connect

www.ingramcontent.com/pod-product-compliance
Lightning Source LLC
Chambersburg PA
CBHW032153180726
48284CB00001B/29